May 23–25, 2018
Rome, Italy

Association for
Computing Machinery

Advancing Computing as a Science & Profession

SIGSIM-PADS'18

Proceedings of the 2018 ACM SIGSIM Conference on

Principles of Advanced Discrete Simulation

Sponsored by:

ACM SIGSIM

Supported by:

Sapienza Università Di Roma and Lockless

**Association for
Computing Machinery**

Advancing Computing as a Science & Profession

The Association for Computing Machinery
2 Penn Plaza, Suite 701
New York, New York 10121-0701

Copyright © 2018 by the Association for Computing Machinery, Inc. (ACM). Permission to make digital or hard copies of portions of this work for personal or classroom use is granted without fee provided that copies are not made or distributed for profit or commercial advantage and that copies bear this notice and the full citation on the first page. Copyright for components of this work owned by others than ACM must be honored. Abstracting with credit is permitted. To copy otherwise, to republish, to post on servers or to redistribute to lists, requires prior specific permission and/or a fee. Request permission to republish from: permissions@acm.org or Fax +1 (212) 869-0481.

For other copying of articles that carry a code at the bottom of the first or last page, copying is permitted provided that the per-copy fee indicated in the code is paid through www.copyright.com.

ISBN: 978-1-4503-5092-1 (Digital)

ISBN: 978-1-4503-6163-7 (Print)

Additional copies may be ordered prepaid from:

ACM Order Department
PO Box 30777
New York, NY 10087-0777, USA

Phone: 1-800-342-6626 (USA and Canada)
+1-212-626-0500 (Global)
Fax: +1-212-944-1318
E-mail: acmhelp@acm.org
Hours of Operation: 8:30 am – 4:30 pm ET

Message from General Co-Chairs

Dear friends, Dear colleagues, Dear participants,

it is a great pleasure to welcome you at the 2018 edition of the ACM SIGSIM Conference on Principles of Advanced Discrete Simulation (PADS). With a very long tradition, ACM SIGSIM PADS has become a successful series of conferences that serves as a large international forum for presenting and sharing recent research results and technological developments in the fields of advanced simulation.

This edition of ACM SIGSIM PADS features a lively, interesting, and stimulating program with a lot of opportunities for discussing new results, on-going projects, and the future trend in our field. Moreover, this edition brings many novelties, in the continuous strive to increase the quality of the conference.

For the first time, and as the first simulation conference, PADS has joined the ACM initiative to improve the likelihood that computational research results can be independently replicated and reproduced by establishing an additional reviewing process. All authors had the opportunity to submit their computational results for being replicated and any artifacts that accompany their paper for being evaluated. As a result, all papers that took part in the initiative (50% of the accepted papers) have received various combinations of the ACM badges, which show that results published in this year PADS' Proceedings have been successfully replicated, and that accompanying artifacts have been found to be available, functional, and reusable. We sincerely thank Prof. Adelinde Uhrmacher for giving us the opportunity to join this initiative, and for leading the Reproducibility Committee, which has made an excellent job in a very tight time.

For the first time, the "TOMACS to PADS" initiative is taking place, which allows authors of original papers accepted in ACM TOMACS to present their results to the PADS audience. This year's conference opening will feature the ever first presentation stemming from this initiative. We think this is an important opportunity to further disseminate consolidated research results within the PADS community.

The Technical Program Committee, consisting of 48 distinguished experts, made the papers' selection during a lively annual meeting which lasted close to 5 hours. We thank from our hearts our Program Chair Prof. Georgios Theodoropoulos for leading the review process, the Technical Program Committee, and the 8 external reviewers who helped in the review process for their invaluable effort in this process, which made possible this year's excellent program. A special thanks goes to Prof. Richard Fujimoto for his continuous support to PADS and for taking care of setting up all the facilities that served for hosting the Program Committee lively meeting.

As in the previous editions, the conference is organized in thematic sessions that reflect the diversity of topics. This year, we received a total of 46 submissions, and accepted 15 as full papers, which is a selective rate of acceptance of less than 33%. Additionally, 8 contributions have been accepted as short papers, to allow for a more dynamic and interactive event.

We are also thankful to Prof. Kevin Jin, who has organized an interesting and lively PhD Colloquium. ACM SIGSIM PADS continues its tradition to push on young researchers and to give them the opportunity to pave their way into the research community. They are the future of our research field, and we warmly welcome them to the Conference.

We are also pleased to host two keynote speeches from Prof. Michela Taufer and Prof. Mateo Valero. They will bring us their perspective on innovative aspects which can definitely benefit the simulation community. We are sure they will interest everyone attending the conference.

The topics of this year's edition are well reflecting the needs of simulation. Some of them include energy efficiency and power saving, new simulation paradigms, and significant steps ahead for known paradigms and techniques. We hope that this edition of ACM SIGSIM PADS will allow all participants to come back home refreshed and with new ideas to continue their research efforts.

The success of a conference is mainly on the side of the participants, we therefore warmly thank all the contributors and participants. The team of chair persons did a huge work which finally led to a very attractive program. We wish you a successful conference, and a pleasant stay in the beautiful Rome!

Francesco Quaglia
SIGSIM-PADS'18 General Co-Chair
University of Rome "Tor Vergata", Italy

Alessandro Pellegrini
SIGSIM-PADS'18 General Co-Chair
Sapienza University of Rome, Italy

Message from Program Chair

An enthusiastic welcome to the 2018 ACM SIGSIM Conference on Principles of Advanced Discrete Simulation (PADS 2018), the 32nd for the PADS series, which this year is held in Rome.

Building on its long successful history, this year the conference attracted high quality submissions on a range of topics on modelling and simulation. In total, forty six (46) submissions were submitted, thirty three (33) as regular papers and thirteen (13) as short papers. Following the rigorous double blind reviewing tradition of PADS, every paper received at least three (3) reviews. All papers and their reviews were then discussed extensively at a Programme Committee meeting that took place on the 2nd of March, 2018. Based on the deliberations of the Programme Committee, fifteen (15) papers were finally accepted as regular papers and eight (8) as short papers. Three (3) regular papers were conditionally accepted and were assigned to three shepherds respectively, who supervised their revision to a successful outcome.

PADS has a long tradition of embracing the work of early career researchers as well as new ideas and cutting edge research which is in progress. A PhD Colloquium and a Poster session will showcase these exciting ideas.

A significant recent development is the participation of PADS in the ACM Reproducibility Initiative. Evaluation of artifact and results replication was handled by a separate Reproducibility Committee. From the originally submitted papers, sixteen (16) regular and five (5) short papers opted for reproducibility evaluation, which is a very encouraging sign and suggests that our community is embracing this important initiative. From the finally accepted papers, five (5) regular and five (5) short have been further evaluated for reproducibility.

Four (4) papers that ranked most highly by the reviewers were nominated for the Best Paper Award and were further considered by a panel to select the best paper for PADS 2018. The nominees, in no particular order, are:

- "Fast-Forwarding Agent States to Accelerate Microscopic Traffic Simulations", by Philipp Andelfinger, Yadong Xu, Wentong Cai, David Eckhoff and Alois Knoll

- "Comparing Dead Reckoning Algorithms for Distributed Car Simulations", by Youfu Chen and Elvis S. Liu

- "Porting Event & Cross-State Synchronization to the Cloud", by Matteo Principe, Tommaso Tocci, Alessandro Pellegrini and Francesco Quaglia

- "Simulation Study to Identify the Characteristics of Markov Chain Properties", by Atiqur Rahman and Peter Kemper

The winner of the award will be announced during the Conference Banquet. Keeping up with ACM SIGSIM PADS traditions, we will also announce the winner of the PhD Colloquium Award, assigned to the student who distinguished most for their research and their presentation – we thank the judges who carefully assessed all the proposals and the presentations to assign this award.

We are delighted to have as our two keynote speakers this year Professor Michela Taufer from University of Delaware and Professor Mateo Valero from Barcelona Supercomputing Center.

It was a true privilege to work with such a fantastic organisation committee. Francesco Quaglia and Alessandro Pellegrini, as the General Chairs of PADS 2018, have done a superb job organising the workshop and dealt with every detail in such a dedicated and effective manner. I am immensely grateful to all the program committee members and the additional reviewers for delivering such high quality reviews within a tight schedule. A special thank you to the shepherds for their invaluable input and to Richard Fujimoto for all his support and for graciously hosting the Programme Committee meeting on his webex facilities!

High-quality submissions are at the very core of any successful symposium. I extend my strong appreciation and thanks to all authors for choosing PADS to submit their work.

I hope you enjoy the program and the workshop as much as I enjoyed being part of organising it and I wish you all a wonderful time in timeless Rome!

Georgios Theodoropoulos
SIGSIM-PADS'18 Program Chair
Southern University of Science and Technology, China

Table of Contents

Session: Agent-Based Simulation and Virtual Environments

Session: Hybrid Simulation and Co-simulation

Session: Model Execution (ii)

Author Index

2018 ACM SIGSIM Conference on Principles of Advanced Discrete Simulation Organization

General Co-Chairs: Francesco Quaglia *(University of Rome "Tor Vergata", Italy)*
Alessandro Pellegrini *(Sapienza University of Rome, Italy)*

Program Chair: Georgios K. Theodoropoulos *(Southern University of Science & Technology, China)*

Reproducibility Committee Chair: Adelinde M. Uhrmacher *(University of Rostock, Germany)*

Ph.D. Colloquium Chair: Dong (Kevin) Jin *(Illinois Institute of Technology, Illinois, USA)*

Financial and Registration Chair: Davide Cingolani *(Sapienza University of Rome, Italy)*

Publicity Chair: Cristina Montañola Sales *(Barcelona Supercomputing Center, Spain)*

Steering Committee: Osman Balci *(Virginia Tech, Virginia, USA)*
Paul Fishwick *(University of Texas at Dallas, Texas, USA)*
Richard M. Fujimoto *(Georgia Institute of Technology, Georgia, USA)*
John A. (Drew) Hamilton, Jr. *(Mississippi State University, Mississippi, USA)*
Jason Liu *(Florida International University, Florida, USA)*
David M. Nicol *(University of Illinois at Urbana-Champaign, Illinois, USA)*
George F. Riley *(Georgia Institute of Technology, Georgia, USA)*
Adelinde M. Uhrmacher *(University of Rostock, Germany)*

Program Committee: Nael Abu-Ghazaleh *(University of California at Riverside, California, USA)*
Anastasia Anagnostous *(Brunell University, UK)*
Peter Barnes *(Lawrence Livermore National Laboratory, California, USA)*
Fernando J. Barros *(University of Coimbra, Portugal)*
Wentong Cai *(Nanyang University, Singapore)*
Laurent Capocchi *(University of Corsica, France)*
Christopher D. Carothers *(Rensselaer Polytechnic Institute, New York, USA)*
Andrea D'Ambrogio *(University of Rome "Tor Vergata", Italy)*
David Eckhoff *(TUM CREATE, Singapore)*
Paul Fishwick *(University Texas at Dallas, Texas, USA)*
Richard Fujimoto *(Georgia Institute of Technology, Georgia, USA)*
Philippe J. Giabbanelli *(University of Cambridge, UK)*
John A. (Drew) Hamilton, Jr. *(Mississippi State University, Mississippi, USA)*
Maâmar El-Amine Hamri *(Aix-Marseille University, France)*
Dong (Kevin) Jin *(Illinois Institute of Technology, Illinois, USA)*
Yun-Bae Kim *(Sungkyunkwan University, South Korea)*
Elvis S. Liu *(Nanyang Technological University, Singapore)*
Jason Liu *(Florida International University, Florida, USA)*
Margaret Loper *(Georgia Tech Research Institute, Georgia, USA)*

Program Committee (continued):

Madhav Marathe *(Virginia Tech, Virginia, USA)*
Yahaya Md. Sam *(Universiti Teknologi Malaysia, Malaysia)*
Teo Yong Meng *(National University of Singapore, Singapore)*
Misbah Mubarak *(Argonne National Laboratory, Illinois, USA)*
Navonil Mustafee *(University of Exeter, UK)*
David M. Nicol *(University of Illinois at Urbana-Champaign, Illinois, USA)*
Ernest Page *(MITRE Corporation, Virginia, USA)*
Alessandro Pellegrini *(Sapienza University of Rome, Italy)*
Kalyan Perumalla *(Oak Ridge National Laboratory, Tennessee, USA)*
Francesco Quaglia *(University of Rome "Tor Vergata", Italy)*
George F. Riley *(Georgia Institute of Technology, Georgia, USA)*
Hessam S. Sarjoughian *(Arizona State University, Arizona, USA)*
Steffen Strassburger *(Technical University of Ilmenau, Germany)*
Claudia Szabo *(University of Adelaide, Australia)*
Wenjie Tang *(National University of Defense Technology, China)*
Satoshi Tanaka *(Ritsumeikan University, Japan)*
Simon Taylor *(Brunel University, UK)*
Andreas Tolk *(Old Dominion University, Virginia, USA)*
Stephen Turner *(King Mongkut's University of Technology Thonburi, Thailand)*
Adelinde M. Uhrmacher *(University of Rostock, Germany)*
Anthony Ventresque *(UCD Dublin, Ireland)*
Gabriel A. Wainer *(Carleton University, Canada)*
Philip A. Wilsey *(University of Cincinnati, Ohio, USA)*
Levent Yilmaz *(Auburn University, Alabama, USA)*
Lin Zhang *(Beihang University, China)*
Yuhao Zheng *(Data Visor, California, USA)*

Reproducibility Committee:

Philipp Andelfinger *(Karlsruhe Institute of Technology, Germany)*
Lachlan Birdsey *(Unviersity of Adelaide, Australia)*
Sounak Gupta *(University of Cincinnati, Ohio, USA)*
Amine Hamri *(CNRS, France)*
Mauro Ianni *(Sapienza University of Rome, Italy)*
Till Köester *(University of Rostock, Germany)*
Romolo Marotta *(Sapienza University of Rome, Italy)*
Alessandro Pellegrini *(Sapienza University of Rome, Italy)*
Andreas Ruscheinski *(University of Rostock, Germany)*
Anthony Ventresque *(UCD Dublin, Ireland)*

Additional Reviewers:

Sören Bergmann	Mark Jackson
Aradhya Biswas	Till Köster
Davide Cingolani	Philip Pecher
Niclas Feldkamp	Steven Smith
Soroosh Gholami	Jae-Seung Yeom
Tobias Helms	Yadong Xu

x

ACM SIGSIM PADS 2018 Sponsors & Supporters

Sponsor:

Supporters:

Modeling the Next-Generation
High Performance Schedulers
(Keynote Talk)

Michela Taufer

J.P. Morgan Case Scholar

Professor in Computer and Information Sciences

University of Delaware

ABSTRACT:

High performance computing (HPC) resources and workloads are undergoing tumultuous changes. HPC resources are growing more diverse with the adoption of accelerators; HPC workloads have increased in size by orders of magnitude. Despite these changes, when assigning workload jobs to resources, HPC schedulers still rely on users to accurately anticipate their applications' resource usage and remain stuck with the decades-old centralized scheduling model.

In this talk we will discuss these ongoing changes and propose alternative models for HPC scheduling based on resource-awareness and fully hierarchical models. A key role in our models' evaluation is played by an emulator of a real open-source, next-generation resource management system. We will discuss the challenges of realistically mimicking the system's scheduling behavior. Our evaluation shows how our models improve scheduling scalability on a diverse set of synthetic and real-world workloads.

This is joint work with Stephen Herbein and Michael Wyatt at the University of Delaware, and Tapasya Patki, Dong H. Ahn, Don Lipari, Thomas R.W. Scogland, Marc Stearman, Mark Grondona, Jim Garlick, Tamara Dahlgren, David Domyancic, and Becky Springmeyer at the Lawrence Livermore National Laboratory.

Short vita:

Michela Taufer is a Professor in Computer and Information Sciences and a J.P. Morgan Case Scholar at the University of Delaware; she has a joint appointment in the Biomedical Department and the Bioinformatics Program at the same university. She earned her undergraduate degrees in Computer Engineering from the University of Padova (Italy) and her doctoral degree in Computer Science from the Swiss Federal Institute of Technology or ETH (Switzerland). From 2003 to 2004 she was a La Jolla Interfaces in Science Training Program (LJIS) Postdoctoral Fellow at the University of California San Diego (UCSD) and The Scripps Research Institute (TSRI), where she worked on interdisciplinary projects in computer systems and computational chemistry.

Taufer's research interests in high performance computing include scientific applications, scheduling and reproducibility challenges, and big data analytics. She has nearly 100 publications and delivered nearly 80 talks at various conferences and research institutes. She is currently serving on the NSF Advisory Committee for Cyberinfrastructures (ACCI). She is a professional member of the IEEE and a Distinguished Scientist of the ACM.

Permission to make digital or hard copies of part or all of this work for personal or classroom use is granted without fee provided that copies are not made or distributed for profit or commercial advantage and that copies bear this notice and the full citation on the first page. Copyrights for third-party components of this work must be honored. For all other uses, contact the Owner/Author.

SIGSIM-PADS '18, May 23–25, 2018, Rome, Italy

© 2018 Copyright is held by the owner/author(s).

ACM ISBN 978-1-4503-5092-1/18/05.

https://doi.org/10.1145/3200921.3204478

Runtime Aware Architectures

(Keynote Talk)

Mateo Valero Cortes

Director of the Barcelona Supercomputing Center

Professor, University of Catalonia (UPC)

Barcelona, Spain

ABSTRACT:

In the last years the traditional ways to keep the increase of hardware performance to the rate predicted by the Moore's Law vanished. When uni-cores were the norm, hardware design was decoupled from the software stack thanks to a well defined Instruction Set Architecture (ISA). This simple interface allowed developing applications without worrying too much about the underlying hardware, while computer architects proposed techniques to aggressively exploit Instruction-Level Parallelism (ILP) in superscalar processors. Current multi-cores are designed as simple symmetric multiprocessors on a chip. While these designs are able to compensate the clock frequency stagnation, they face multiple problems in terms of power consumption, programmability, resilience or memory. The solution is to give more responsibility to the runtime system and to let it tightly collaborate with the hardware. The runtime has to drive the design of future multi-cores architectures.

In this talk, we introduce an approach towards a Runtime-Aware Architecture (RAA), a massively parallel architecture designed from the runtime's perspective. RAA aims at supporting the activity the parallel runtime system in three ways: First, to enable fine-grain tasking and support the opportunities it offers; second, to improve the performance of the memory subsystem by exposing hybrid hierarchies to the runtime system and, third, to improve performance by using vector units. During the talk, we will give a general overview of the problems RAA aims to solve and provide some examples of hardware components supporting the activity of the runtime system in the context of multi-core chips.

Permission to make digital or hard copies of part or all of this work for personal or classroom use is granted without fee provided that copies are not made or distributed for profit or commercial advantage and that copies bear this notice and the full citation on the first page. Copyrights for third-party components of this work must be honored. For all other uses, contact the Owner/Author.

SIGSIM-PADS '18, May 23–25, 2018, Rome, Italy

© 2018 Copyright is held by the owner/author(s).

ACM ISBN 978-1-4503-5092-1/18/05.

https://doi.org/10.1145/3200921.3204479

Short vita:

Mateo Valero obtained his Telecommunication Engineering Degree from the Technical University of Madrid (UPM) in 1974 and his Ph.D. in Telecommunications from the Technical University of Catalonia (UPC) in 1980. He is a professor in the Computer Architecture Department at UPC, in Barcelona. His research interests focuses on high performance architectures. He has published approximately 700 papers, has served in the organization of more than 300 International Conferences and he has given more than 500 invited talks. He is the director of the Barcelona Supercomputing Centre, the National Centre of Supercomputing in Spain.

Dr. Valero has been honoured with several awards. Among them, the Eckert-Mauchly Award 2007 by the IEEE and ACM; Seymour Cray Award 2015 by IEEE; Charles Babbage 2017 by IEEE; Harry Goode Award 2009 by IEEE: ACM Distinguished Service Award 2012; Euro-Par Achievement Award 2015; the Spanish National Julio Rey Pastor award, in recognition of research in Mathematics; the Spanish National Award "Leonardo Torres Quevedo" that recognizes research in engineering; the "King Jaime I" in basic research given by Generalitat Valenciana; the Research Award by the Catalan Foundation for Research and Innovation and the "Aragón Award" 2008 given by the Government of Aragón. He has been named Honorary Doctor by the University of Chalmers, by the University of Belgrade, by the Universities of Las Palmas de Gran Canaria, Zaragoza, Complutense de Madrid, Cantabria and Granada in Spain, by the University of Veracruz and CINVESTAV in Mexico. "Hall of the Fame" member of the ICT European Program (selected as one of the 25 most influents European researchers in IT during the period 1983-2008. Lyon,November 2008); Honoured with

Creu de Sant Jordi 2016 by Generalitat de Catalunya. It is the highest recognition granted by the Government.

In December 1994, Professor Valero became a founding member of the Royal Spanish Academy of Engineering. In 2005 he was elected Correspondant Academic of the Spanish Royal Academy of Science, in 2006 member of the Royal Spanish Academy of Doctors, in 2008 member of the Academia Europaea and in 2012 Correspondant Academic of the Mexican Academy of Sciences. He is a Fellow of the IEEE, Fellow of the ACM and an Intel Distinguished Research Fellow.

In 1998 he won a "Favourite Son" Award of his home town, Alfamén (Zaragoza) and in 2006, his native town of Alfamén named their Public College after him.

Simulation Study to Identify the Characteristics of Markov Chain Properties

Atiqur Rahman
Department of Computer Science
William & Mary
Williamsburg, VA, USA
mrahman@email.wm.edu

Peter Kemper
Department of Computer Science
William & Mary
Williamsburg, VA, USA
kemper@cs.wm.edu

ABSTRACT

Markov models have a long tradition in modeling and simulation of dynamic systems. In this paper, we look at certain properties of a discrete time Markov chain including entropy, trace and 2nd largest eigenvalue to better understand their role for time series analysis. We simulate a number of possible input signals, fit a discrete time Markov chain and explore properties with the help of Sobol indices. This research is motivated by recent results in the analysis of cell development for Xenopus laevis in cell biology that relied on the considered entropy measure to distinguish development stages from time series data of Calcium levels in cells.

CCS CONCEPTS

• **Computing methodologies** → **Model development and analysis**;

KEYWORDS

Monte Carlo Simulation; Discrete Time Markov Chain (DTMC); Sensitivity Analysis; Partial correlation coefficients (PCC); Sobol indices; Entropy; Trace; Eigenvalue

ACM Reference Format:
Atiqur Rahman and Peter Kemper. 2018. Simulation Study to Identify the Characteristics of Markov Chain Properties. In *SIGSIM-PADS '18 : 2018 SIGSIM Principles of Advanced Discrete Simulation, May 23–25, 2018, Rome, Italy*. ACM, New York, NY, USA, 12 pages. https://doi.org/10.1145/3200921.3200934

1 INTRODUCTION

Time series analysis is a topic that is present in many domains to describe, understand, and interpret the behavior of a dynamic system. In the field of Modelling and Simulation, a simulator essentially creates a synthetic time series during a simulation run that is then usually aggregated on-the-fly to estimate values of interest such as throughput or queue length. Markov models have been successfully applied in the analysis of time series for a number of different purposes, most prominently in the form of Hidden Markov Models

Permission to make digital or hard copies of all or part of this work for personal or classroom use is granted without fee provided that copies are not made or distributed for profit or commercial advantage and that copies bear this notice and the full citation on the first page. Copyrights for components of this work owned by others than the author(s) must be honored. Abstracting with credit is permitted. To copy otherwise, or republish, to post on servers or to redistribute to lists, requires prior specific permission and/or a fee. Request permissions from permissions@acm.org.
SIGSIM-PADS '18 , May 23–25, 2018, Rome, Italy
© 2018 Copyright held by the owner/author(s). Publication rights licensed to the Association for Computing Machinery.
ACM ISBN 978-1-4503-5092-1/18/05. . . $15.00
https://doi.org/10.1145/3200921.3200934

to recognize temporal patterns in speech, but also in handwriting and gestures recognition. Markovian arrival processes or MAPs are used to capture autocorrelation or long-range dependencies in time series. And in its most simple version, a Discrete Time Markov Chain (DTMC) captures the notion of state and state-dependent transition probabilities from one state to another.

In a recent study in cell biology Marken et al. [12] attempt to capture the characteristics of observed Calcium levels over time in developing Xenopus laevis cells by a DTMC. The key point is to derive a compact representation of a time series of Calcium levels that can be used to recognize similarities among cells at a particular development stage and to separate them from cells at a different development stage. Source entropy of a DTMC is recognized as a useful property to make this distinction. While the procedure to calculate the entropy is straightforward and there is a general understanding of what entropy measures, it remains less clear which aspects of the time series are specifically measured this way and which ones are not. For instance, Marken et al. [12] report that their findings are robust against the presence or absence of a trend and the use of certain trend removal techniques.

This leads to the questions that we want to address in this paper. Which properties of a time series influence entropy and other related measures and which ones do not? Specifically, we will look at the role of a trend (a long term change in the mean) and the role of a seasonal pattern (modeled with sinusoidal signal and parameters frequency, phase, and amplitude). What is the role of noise and the role of the signal to noise ratio? To what extent does the sampling rate, the time resolution, matter for the outcome measure?

In this context, we also recognized that two other measures, namely the trace and the 2nd largest eigenvalue of a DTMC are related to its entropy, in particular for the case of a DTMC with few states and a band structure. So we perform a case study based on Monte Carlo simulation to evaluate how sensitive entropy, trace, and 2nd largest eigenvalue of a DTMC are to changes in the characteristics of the time series that the DTMC is derived from. The paper is structured as follows. Section 3 recalls fundamental definitions, Section 4 describes the derivation of a DTMC from a time series of values. Section 3 starts with a description of partial correlation coefficients (PCC) and Sobol indices that we will use to recognize if entropy, trace, or 2nd largest eigenvalue are responding to a variation in parameter settings for the stochastic input model to generate time series data. For the rest of the section, we describe the outcome of a series of experiments to identify time series characteristics that are measurable with entropy, trace or 2nd largest eigenvalue. Section 6 contains a discussion of our findings and we conclude in Section 7.

2 RELATED WORK

Many techniques have been proposed to conduct a sensitivity analysis. One simple approach is to measure the effect on an outcome variable if one changes one input factor at a time. Murphy et al. [13] use this approach to model uncertainty in regional climate change. This method cannot detect the interaction of input variables as it does not fully explore the input space. Another approach to measure sensitivity is based on the partial derivative of the output with respect to an input factor. Automated Differentiation [4] is an example of this approach. This approach is not able to quantify interactions between several input variables as it does not fully explore the input space either. Regression analysis has also been used to estimate sensitivity but it is not well suited for nonlinear models. Variance-based methods overcome these issues. M. Sobol [11] has proposed a widely used variance based sensitivity analysis named Sobol method or Sobol indices. It computes two indices, the first order and the total index. The first order index only measures the contribution of an individual input variable to the output variable. The total index also takes possible interactions among input variables into account. Calculation of Sobol indices is challenging and there is a lineage of related work. Iman and Hora [6] and later Homma and Saltelli [5] proposed methods that are capable of computing the first order index. In [17], Schaibly and Shuler proposed a frequency based method, which can compute both the first order and the total index, which takes the interaction of all parameters into consideration. Saltelli's approach [15] computes the Sobol indices for both the first order and total indices at the same time. In [8], Janon et al. measure Sobol sensitivity indices using certified metamodels. The lineage of work for the calculation of Sobol indices further includes [7], an estimation of the Sobol sensitivity indices using asymptotically efficient formulas, and [10], a kriging-based global sensitivity analysis that takes both the meta-model and the Monte-Carlo errors into account. Jansen's simultaneous estimation of the Sobol indices for the first-order and the total indices is good for large first-order indices and for both large and small total indices [9].

3 DEFINITIONS

We briefly recall some common terminology and establish some formal notation.

Definition 3.1. A Discrete Time Markov Chain (DTMC) is a discrete time stochastic process $\{X_n : n \geq 0\}$ with discrete state space S that satisfies the Markov property,

$$P(X_{n+1} = j | X_n = i_n, X_{n-1} = i_{n-1}, ..., X_0 = i_0)$$
$$= P(X_{n+1} = j | X_n = i_n)$$

where i_k is a state of the process for any $k = 0, 1, ..., n$.

In a DTMC, the future evolution of the system depends only on the current state, any other previous state does not have any impact. $P(X_{n+1} = j | X_n = i_n)$ denotes the transition probability from state i_n to j.

In this context, we will focus on a DTMC where S is finite such that the transition probabilities can be represented by a finite real-valued matrix P of dimension $S \times S$. For simplicity of notation,

we refer to states i and j by their index value for matrix P, i.e., $i, j \in \{1, 2, ..., |S|\}$. Each row of P has a row sum of 1 and describes the conditional probability distribution to go from the state i to any other state $j \in \{1, 2, ..., |S|\}$. As each row describes a probability distribution, we can calculate its entropy. The information entropy of a probability distribution takes units of Bits and is a measure of uncertainty in the distribution. A high Bits value suggests that the probability distribution describes a system with less predictable dynamics, and a low Bits value suggests a system with more predictable dynamics [3]. The information entropy E is calculated using Shannon's formula [18]

$$E = -\sum_{i=1}^{n} p_i log_2(p_i)$$

where each p_i is the probability of some event i. If we apply this to a DTMC, we obtain a conditional entropy

$$E_i = -\sum_{j=1}^{|S|} p_{ij} log_2(p_{ij})$$

that gives the entropy given that the system is in state i.

$$E = -\sum_{i=1}^{|S|} \pi_i \sum_{j=1}^{|S|} p_{ij} log_2(p_{ij})$$

gives the entropy for the DTMC, where π_i is the steady state probability of state i. This single value can be interpreted as an indication for the number of paths that are statistically typical for this Markov chain. A higher value implies a larger number of typical or common paths. It is sometimes denoted as source entropy. In [12], the entropy for a DTMC is defined as the average of E_i over all rows of the DTMC. These two definitions coincide if the steady state distribution π is uniform. In [12], the DTMC is derived from a time series in such a way that all states are equiprobable such that at least the observed frequencies are that of a uniform distribution.

For a DTMC, E is higher if state transitions are equiprobable. On the contrary, for a matrix that is diagonally dominant and has a band structure on its main diagonal, transitions are more predictable and thus its entropy is lower. This type of matrix is known to describe a random walk model but it will also naturally result from a discrete time series whose values are sampled from a continuous function over time at a high enough sampling rate.

If a DTMC is diagonally dominant, it will have its largest values per row on its diagonal element which will create an imbalance for the probability distribution per row that in turn influences the entropy measure. The diagonal elements also impact the trace of a matrix, which is why we consider the trace as a related property to entropy in this context.

To allow for a comparison across different settings of $|S|$, we divide the sum of row entropy values by $|S|log_2(|S|)$, such that the entropy value E is scaled to a range of 0 to 1.

Definition 3.2. The trace of a matrix is the sum of its elements on the main diagonal.

For a DTMC, the trace of P is

$$Trace = \sum_{i=1}^{|S|} p_{ii}$$

As for trace, we divide the trace value for a DTMC by $|S|$ to scale it to a range of 0 to 1 such that we can compare trace values across DTMCs that result from different settings for $|S|$. Obviously, if the DTMC is diagonally dominant, this implies a higher trace value than for one that is not. The trace in turn relates to the eigenvalues of a matrix.

Definition 3.3. For a square matrix A and a column vector v if $A \cdot v = \lambda v$ then λ is an eigenvalue of A and v is called the eigenvector.

Here, A scaled the eigenvector v by eigenvalue λ. If A has k eigenvalues and $(\lambda_1 > \lambda_2 > .... > \lambda_k)$ then λ_1 is called the first eigenvalue, λ_2 is the second. For any transition probability matrix, the first eigenvalue is always 1, which implies that the second can carry information on A. Also, the trace of A equals its sum of eigenvalues. So, the 2nd largest eigenvalue influences the trace value (and vice versa), which is why we include λ_2 in our analysis.

Similar to the trace, the 2nd largest eigenvalue shows a high value if the DTMC is diagonally dominant and a low value when state transitions in the DTMC are more equiprobable.

4 MARKOV MODELS OF TIME SERIES DATA

In the following, we consider a single continuous variable whose values evolve over time and observing these values at particular points in time leads to the time series that we want to analyze. We partition the range of observed values into intervals (bins) that are labeled by an index or symbol. We index the partitions from low to high with $1, 2, \ldots, |S|$ and thus associate each bin with one state of the DTMC. We transform the original time series into a time series of index values and calculate frequencies f_{ij} by counting the number of bigrams ij in the sequence of symbols for each pair $i, j \in 1, 2, \ldots, |S|$. Normalizing f_{ij} by $\sum_j f_{ij}$ gives us values p_{ij} for the DTMC. The estimation of p_{ij} from a given sequence of discrete symbols is common practice to fit a DTMC, for an example in [1].

4.1 Impact of discretization

Time series discretization is the process of transforming a time series to a sequence of symbols where each symbol represents a bin with a specific range of values. Since the differences between values in the same bin are not represented in a sequence of symbols, binning has the effect of filtering certain high frequency noise, which is one important benefit of discretization. Moreover, it can reduce non-linearity, speedup the processing, and may improve the accuracy of a predictive model because of the noise reduction.

Despite these benefits, discretization carries the risk of creating artifacts and one needs to choose the binning procedure and its parameter settings carefully. For instance, the equidistant partitioning of the range of values, which is one of the most common unsupervised methods for discretization, is prone to be affected by artifacts as an outlier with extremely high or low value can affect the whole data range and consequently change the discretization thresholds severely. On the other hand, the equiprobable partitioning of the range of values is not affected by a small number of outliers as the range of values is partitioned such that each bin contains approximately the same number of values. Regardless of how the bins are determined, by its very nature, discretization only represents changes across discretization thresholds and ignores all

other changes. This can create artifacts in that it overemphasizes minuscule changes, when a value slightly less than a discretization threshold falls into a different bin than a subsequent value that is slightly higher than the threshold, which is a drawback of discretization.

The number of states (bins) has significant impact on the accuracy of a predictive model based on discretization. The discretization may overly simplify the data and loose most of the changes in data if the number of states is too low. On the contrary, too many states are able to capture changes at a very detailed level but will also retain high frequency noise that is present in the data.

4.2 Impact of sampling rate

The sampling rate (or resolution) can severely affect certain properties of the DTMC. If we observe a continuous function, partition the range of values into intervals that are indexed from low to high values, then state transitions p_{ij} will be between adjacent intervals i and j. If the sampling rate is high enough, we will only see transitions p_{ij} where $j \in \{i - 1, i, i + 1\}$. This will lead to a transition matrix with zero values outside of the main band and p_{ii} being the largest value in row i. As the trace is the sum of the diagonal element of the matrix, a diagonally dominant matrix will increase the trace. As the trace also equals the sum of the eigenvalues and the first eigenvalue is always 1, the second eigenvalue is expected to increase along with the trace. On the other hand, entropy is expected to be much lower because there is less uncertainty in estimating the transition to the next state.

If the sampling rate is too low, existing autocorrelation will be missed in the sampled time series and samples will appear as if generated from an independent and identically distributed (iid) source. A low resolution will allow for transitions between arbitrary bins i and j and the transition matrix will be less sparse and less diagonally dominant, transition of states will be rather equiprobable and as a consequence trace and eigenvalue will be lower. However, equiprobable state transitions will maximize the entropy.

Therefore, we expect that a high sampling rate is positively correlated with the trace and 2nd largest eigenvalue, and negatively correlated with entropy. We will conduct a sensitivity analysis with partial correlation coefficients (PCC) to see the direction of the correlation between sampling rate and the three properties of a DTMC we are interested in.

In addition, the Nyquist-Shannon sampling theorem confirms that for a given sampling rate f_s, a perfect reconstruction of the signal is possible for a bandlimit $< f_s/2$. This could lead us to a resolution test, if interpolation on low resolution leads to the same result than twice the resolution then the resolution is fine enough.

5 ANALYSIS RESULTS

We briefly recall the calculation of partial correlation coefficients and Sobol indices before we discuss the outcome of our simulation experiments.

5.1 Partial correlation coefficients

A partial correlation coefficient (PCC) characterizes the linear relationship of one input parameter with the output after the elimination of linear effects of other parameters. The PCC is the correlation coefficient (CC) between the two residuals $(x_i - \hat{x}_i)$ and $(y - \hat{y})$ for the input parameter x_i with the output y, where $\hat{x}_i$ and $\hat{y}$ are computed by the following linear regression models:

$$\hat{x}_i = c_0 + \sum_{p=1, p \neq i}^{k} c_p x_p$$

$$\hat{y} = b_0 + \sum_{p=1, p \neq i}^{k} b_p x_p.$$

One attractive feature of PCC is, it can inform us whether the input parameter is positively or negatively correlated with the output. But PCC does not account for interactions among input parameters, it does not fully explore the input space, and it only considers linear relationships, which are major limitations of this method.

5.2 Sobol indices

Sobol indices capture the impact or variability in model output created by each of the input parameters. One can calculate Sobol indices for the main effect or first order sensitivity index along with the total sensitivity index. The first order sensitivity index measures the contribution to the output variance of a parameter alone, whereas the total sensitivity index includes all variance caused by interactions of a parameter with any other input variables.

Sobol's method is based on a decomposition of the model output variance into summands of variances of the input parameters in increasing dimensionality as shown in (1), for details see [2].

$$f(x_1, x_2, \ldots, x_n)$$

$$= f_0 + \sum_{i=1}^{n} f_i(x_i) + \sum_{i=1}^{n} \sum_{j=i+1}^{n} f_{ij}(x_i, x_j) + \ldots$$

$$.. + f_{1,2,3\ldots,n}(x_1, x_2, \ldots, x_n) \quad (1)$$

$$where, \int_0^1 f_{i_1, \ldots i_n}(x_{i_1}\ldots x i_n) dx_{i_k} = 0, \text{ if } 1 \le k \le s$$

$$and \int_{K^n} f_{i_1, \ldots i_n} f_{j_1, \ldots, j_l} dx = 0, \text{ for } (i_1, \ldots i_n) \neq (j_1, \ldots, j_l)$$

The total variance is defined as, $D = \int_{K^n} f^2(x) dx - f_0^2$,

where $f_0 = \int_{K^n} f(x) dx$, and K^n is the input space.

Partial variance is

$$D_{i_1, \ldots i_n} = \int_0^1 \therefore \int_0^1 f_{i_1, \ldots i_n}^2 (x_1 \ldots x_s) dx_{i_1} \therefore dx_{i_n}$$

Sensitivity $S(i_1, \therefore, i_n)$ relates input parameter contribution to model output variance and is defined as,

$$S(i_1, \therefore, i_n) = \frac{D_{i_1, \therefore, i_n}}{D}$$

The integrals to compute total variance and partial variance are computed with a Monte Carlo integral [2].

Monte Carlo estimation of $\hat{f}_0$, D and $\hat{D}_i$,

$$\hat{f}_0 = \frac{1}{N} \sum_{m=1}^{N} f(x_m)$$

$$\hat{D} = \frac{1}{N} \sum_{m=1}^{N} f(x_m) - f_0^2$$

$$\hat{D}_i = \frac{1}{N} \sum_{m=1}^{N} f(\mathbf{x}_{\sim im}^{(1)}, x_{im}) f(\mathbf{x}_{\sim im}^{(2)}, x_{im}^{(1)}) - f_0^2$$

This requires us to compute too many (2^n) Monte Carlo integrals, such that Homma and Saltelli [5] proposed to compute the total influence of an individual parameter x_i as

$$ST(i) = S(i) + S(i, \sim i) = 1 - S(\sim i)$$

Sobol sensitivity analysis has a number of advantages over PCC analysis. The latter assumes a linear relationship between input parameter and model output. Sobol analysis is not restricted in this way. PCC analysis only considers the influence of each parameter to the model output on its own, whereas Sobol analysis considers also the variance caused by any interactions among parameters.

5.3 Experimental setting

We perform a number of experiments where we calculate Sobol indices and partial correlation coefficients (PCC) values for entropy, trace, and 2nd largest eigenvalue for the DTMCs that result from sampling from a range of possible parameter settings. Table 1 lists the ranges that are used in all of our experiments. For all experiments, we consider a time series of 2 hours worth of data and vary the number of data points across experiments with the help of the sampling rate parameter. The sample rate interval given in Table 1 translates into time series with at least 72 and at most 14400 data points.

Time series data is sampled from a generating equation, e.g., a sinusoidal function whose parameters are set by the Sobol or PCC procedure. So one source of variability for the outcome is the randomized setting of parameter values due to Sobol or PCC, a second source is the use of random variables for noise in the otherwise deterministic generating equation. From the generated time series data, we compute a DTMC (again, parameters are set by the Sobol or PCC procedure) for an equiprobable partition of the data set. From the DTMC, we compute a property of interest, namely entropy, trace, or the 2nd largest eigenvalue, whose variability in response to parameter variability is then the final outcome of the Sobol or PCC analysis.

For the computation of PCC values and Sobol indices, we use the 'pcc' and 'soboljansen' [9, 16] functions of the sensitivity package [14] of R [19], a software environment for statistical computing. The author of [14] suggests that some of the sensitivity estimators of the package suffer from a conditioning problem but this does not apply to 'soboljansen'. In addition, the Sobol and Jansen [9, 16] method has the advantage of computing both the first-order and the total indices at the same time and is also good for both large and small total indices.

As the amount of sampling data for a fixed 2h time frame grows with the sampling rate (f_s), we expect that with a growing sampling rate (f_s) and all other parameters fixed, the individual estimates for

Table 1: Ranges of values for parameters in different experimental settings.

Parameter	Range	Comment
Additive constant (c_0)	-100 to 100	
Slope (c_1)	-15 to 15	about a -87 to 87 degree slope
Coefficient (c_2)	-15 to 15	
Amplitude (A_1, A_2)	-100 to 100	
Frequency (ω_1, ω_2)	0 to 10	Number of cycles per second
Phase (ϕ_1, ϕ_2)	0 to $2 * \pi$	
Sampling rate (f_s)	0.01 to 2	Number of samples per second
Signal to noise ratio (SNR)	0.1 to 100	
Number of states (n)	2 to 8	Number of symbols for discretization

matrix entries p_{ij} become more stable and eventually converge to some fixed value. The number of states n determines the number n^2 values that need to be estimated for the DTMC, such that increasing values of n should result into higher variability of outcomes as the p_{ij} sample estimates of the DTMC rely on less data. If the underlying signal is from a continuous function and noise is not dominating the numerical outcome (the signal to noise ratio is high enough) and the sampling rate is high enough, we expect the matrix to show a band structure along the main diagonal and be diagonally dominant. The band structure implies that the number of entries to estimate goes down from n^2 to $3n - 2$. With these general expectations in mind, we conduct a number of experiments.

5.4 Analyzing a time series with a linear trend or a low-degree polynomial

It is common practice to detrend data in a preprocessing step as many analysis techniques assume absence of a trend. However, in [12], it was observed that results of entropy analysis of DTMCs for cell data did not benefit from trend removal. So we conduct an experiment with a time series

$$Y = c_1 * t + c_0 + e * \epsilon$$

with parameters c_1, c_0, ϵ as well as sampling rate, signal to noise ratio (SNR) and the number of states n in the DTMC. SNR is defined as $SNR = \sigma_f^2 / \sigma_{e\epsilon}^2$ with σ_f^2 being the variance of the signal, here $f = c_1 * t + c_0$ and $\sigma_{e\epsilon}^2$ is the variance of noise $e * \epsilon$. Any fixed value for SNR is maintained by setting $e = \sqrt{\frac{\sigma_f^2}{SNR * \sigma_\epsilon^2}}$ which follows directly from the definition and the fact that $Var(cX) = c^2 Var(X)$.

In the time series, the linear trend will contribute values that pass through the n states over time in only one direction depending on the sign of c_1 and at most stay in the current state but not return to a previous state. Since n is much smaller than the number of samples, the linear trend will contribute to a diagonally dominant DTMC and a single transition from one state to the next. Only the noise part will add some random transitions and thus contribute to random DTMC transitions to other states. The parameter that

directly impacts the effect of noise is SNR. n does so indirectly, the larger n the more fine-grained the discretization and the less its noise-filtering effect.

The Sobol indices and PCC value calculation use ranges for parameter selections as given in Table 1. For the entropy value, the Sobol indices for c_1, c_0 and f_s have no influence as shown in Fig 1a. As expected, SNR influences the entropy most. n influences entropy as well but less than SNR. The PCC result (Table 2) confirms this and shows that SNR is strongly negatively (-0.84), and n is positively (0.44) correlated with the resulting entropy value.

The trace measure shows a similar behavior as shown in Fig. 1a, but the impact of n is much stronger on trace than entropy. Similar to entropy c_1, c_0 and f_s have no influence on trace. PCC values (Table 2) however show that SNR is strongly positively correlated (0.81) with the outcome for trace but negatively correlated (-0.81) with n.

The 2nd largest eigenvalue is almost entirely influenced by SNR according to its first order Sobol index. n has almost negligible and c_1, c_0 and f_s have no influence at all. According to the PCC analysis (Table 2), SNR is positively correlated (0.57) and n is very lightly positively correlated (0.28) with 2nd largest eigenvalue.

For this simple time series model, we see that none of the properties are influenced by parameters c_1 and c_0 for the linear trend. To validate, we simulate the linear model without any noise and with fixed n and f_s. The result shows entropy, trace and 2nd largest eigenvalue remain constant for different c_1 and c_0. As the signal part does contribute to the properties of interest, it is plausible that f_s has no impact as well. For measuring properties of the i.i.d. noise values, the sampling rate is not crucial if the total number of data points is sufficient.

If we extend this scenario slightly to a time series that includes a polynomial

$$Y = c_2 * t^2 + c_1 * t + c_0 + e * \epsilon$$

and conduct the Sobol and PCC analysis, we see consistent and very similar results as shown in Figs. 2a, 2b, and 2c. Note that t only has a non-negative range of values, such that t^2 only implies a non-linear increase in values over time. Again, SNR and f_s have significant influence on the properties of interest. But, on the contrary to the linear model, coefficients c_1 and c_0 along with c_2 show negligible impact on the properties. To compare the influence of these coefficients, we removed the noise from the polynomial model and simulate with fixed n and f_s. As shown in 2d, 2e, and 2f, c_2 and c_1 both have significant influence on the properties of interest without the presence of noise and with sufficient f_s though c_0 does not have any influence on the properties.

The analysis of the linear and polynomial model suggest that a trend does have influence on entropy, trace and 2nd largest eigenvalue if there is a nonlinear trend in the time series, data is noise free and sampled with sufficient sampling rate.

5.5 Analyzing a time series with a trigonometric function as signal

Representing a function as a summation of trigonometric functions is the key concept for Fourier analysis. We want to see how entropy, trace and 2nd largest eigenvalue respond to periodicity in a signal.

Table 2: PCC value for entropy, trace and 2nd largest eigenvalue.

	c_0	c_1	c_2	A_1	A_2	ω_1	ω_2	ϕ_1	ϕ_2	f_s	SNR	n
						Entropy						
Linear	0.00	0.00	-	-	-	-	-	-	-	0.01	-0.84	0.44
Poly	0.02	0.01	0.01	-	-	-	-	-	-	-0.01	-0.84	0.52
Sine	0.00	-	-	0.01	-	0.64	-	-0.02	-	-0.47	-0.50	0.09
Linear+Sine	0.00	0.00	-	0.00	-	0.21	-	0.01	-	-0.26	-0.61	0.26
Poly+Sine	0.00	-0.01	0.00	0.00	-	0.00	-	0.01	-	-0.02	-0.85	0.55
Sine+Cosine	-0.01	-	-	0.00	0.00	0.44	0.43	-0.01	0.00	-0.66	-0.36	0.12
Linear+Sine+Cosine	0.01	0.00	-	0.00	0.00	0.14	0.15	0.00	0.00	-0.34	-0.55	0.25
Poly+Sine+Cosine	0.02	-0.01	0.00	0.00	-0.01	0.00	0.00	0.00	-0.02	-0.02	-0.84	0.52
						Trace						
Linear	0.00	0.01	-	-	-	-	-	-	-	0.00	0.81	-0.81
Poly	-0.02	-0.01	0.00	-	-	-	-	-	-	0.02	0.83	-0.88
Sine	0.02	-	-	0.00	-	-0.75	-	0.00	-	0.72	0.12	-0.75
Linear+Sine	0.00	0.00	-	0.00	-	-0.21	-	-0.01	-	0.27	0.50	-0.63
Poly+Sine	0.00	0.01	0.00	0.00	-	0.00	-	-0.01	-	0.04	0.83	-0.89
Sine+Cosine	0.01	-	-	0.01	0.01	-0.45	-0.44	0.02	0.00	0.75	0.15	-0.72
Linear+Sine+Cosine	-0.02	0.00	-	0.00	-0.01	-0.14	-0.14	0.00	-0.01	0.35	0.47	-0.66
Poly+Sine+Cosine	-0.02	0.01	-0.01	0.00	0.01	0.00	-0.01	0.00	0.01	0.03	0.82	-0.88
					2nd	largest eigenvalue						
Linear	0.00	0.00	-	-	-	-	-	-	-	-0.01	0.57	0.28
Poly	0.00	-0.02	0.00	-	-	-	-	-	-	0.01	0.56	0.28
Sine	0.00	-	-	-0.01	-	-0.54	-	0.01	-	0.50	0.32	0.37
Linear+Sine	0.00	0.00	-	0.00	-	-0.13	-	-0.01	-	0.20	0.40	0.22
Poly+Sine	-0.01	0.01	0.00	-0.01	-	0.00	-	-0.01	-	0.01	0.57	0.30
Sine+Cosine	0.00	-	-	0.00	0.00	-0.31	-0.31	0.00	0.00	0.63	0.22	0.26
Linear+Sine+Cosine	0.00	0.00	-	0.00	0.00	-0.09	-0.10	0.00	0.01	0.27	0.36	0.20
Poly+Sine+Cosine	-0.02	0.02	0.01	0.00	0.00	0.00	0.01	0.00	0.01	0.02	0.55	0.27

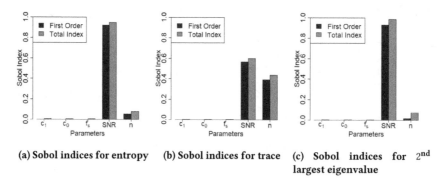

(a) Sobol indices for entropy (b) Sobol indices for trace (c) Sobol indices for 2nd largest eigenvalue

Figure 1: Entropy, trace and 2nd largest eigenvalue of linear model

We start with the simplest possible series

$$Y = A_1 sin(2\pi\omega_1 t + \phi_1) + c_0 + e * \epsilon$$

and have parameters amplitude A_1, frequency ω_1, phase ϕ_1, an additive constant c_0, noise ϵ scaled with e to achieve a given SNR as before, the sampling rate f_s, and the number of states n.

The Sobol indices and PCC value calculation use ranges for parameter selections as in Table 1. An unanimous outcome for entropy,

trace, and 2nd largest eigenvalue for both Sobol and PCC values is that parameters A_1, ϕ_1, and c_0 do not influence the outcome.

For entropy, we see from Fig. 3a that ω_1 achieves the most significant first order and total index. SNR and f_s show significant total index values as well. However, the first order index for n is near zero, which indicates that n itself does not have any influence on entropy but due to interactions with the remaining parameters of the model. The PCC value (Table 2) for n also shows near zero correlation which supports the outcome of the Sobol sensitivity

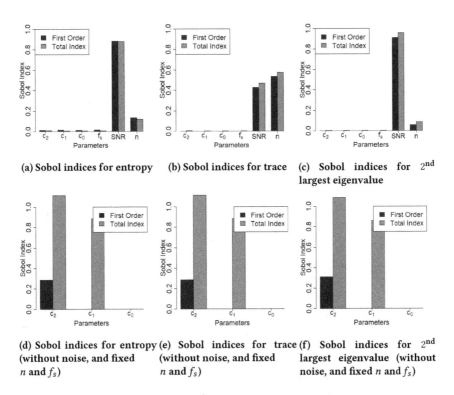

(a) Sobol indices for entropy

(b) Sobol indices for trace

(c) Sobol indices for 2nd largest eigenvalue

(d) Sobol indices for entropy (without noise, and fixed n and f_s)

(e) Sobol indices for trace (without noise, and fixed n and f_s)

(f) Sobol indices for 2nd largest eigenvalue (without noise, and fixed n and f_s)

Figure 2: Entropy, trace and 2nd largest eigenvalue of polynomial model

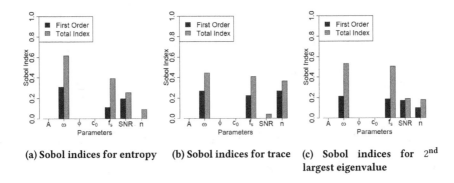

(a) Sobol indices for entropy

(b) Sobol indices for trace

(c) Sobol indices for 2nd largest eigenvalue

Figure 3: Entropy, trace and 2nd largest eigenvalue of sinusoidal model

analysis. For the remaining parameters, the PCC value (Table 2) for ω_1 is positive and well above 0.5. f_s and SNR have negative PCC values and around -0.5.

As shown in Fig. 3b, like the polynomial model, Sobol sensitivity analysis for trace shows n has bigger impact than SNR. PCC analysis also supports that n has much higher impact than SNR on the trace. However, similar to entropy, ω_1 achieves the most significant first order and total index for trace. PCC values (Table 2) indicate that unlike entropy, ω_1 is strongly negatively correlated (-0.75) and f_s is strongly positively correlated (0.72) with trace .

Fig. 3c illustrates that the 2nd largest eigenvalue is moderately influenced by ω_1, f_s, SNR, and n, in decreasing order of their first order Sobol index, with ω_1 having the highest index of 0.2. Similar

to entropy and trace, the total index for ω_1 and f_s show significant influence on 2nd largest eigenvalue. From PCC analysis (Table 2), we see that ω_1 is negatively correlated (-0.54), while f_s, SNR, and n are positively correlated.

Analysis of a slightly more complex series with the summation of sine and cosine functions

$$Y = A_1 sin(2\pi\omega_1 t + \phi_1) + A_2 cos(2\pi\omega_2 t + \phi_2) + c_0 + e * \epsilon$$

shows that at least for PCC values (Table 2) amplitude (A_1,A_2), phase (ϕ_1,ϕ_2) and additive constant (c_0) are not recognized. However, for Sobol indices, all properties at least to some small extent react to changes in any of the parameters.

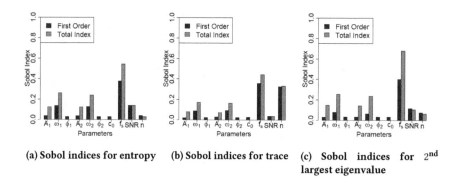

(a) Sobol indices for entropy   (b) Sobol indices for trace   (c) Sobol indices for 2nd largest eigenvalue

Figure 4: Entropy, trace and 2nd largest eigenvalue of the summation of sinusoidal and cosine functions

As illustrated in Fig. 4 and similar to the sinusoidal model, frequency (ω_1, ω_2), sampling rate f_s, SNR, and the number of states (n) show influence on the properties of interest. Again, f_s has the most influence on the properties. n has more influence on the trace than SNR which we have seen for the polynomial and sinusoidal model before. Adding the cosine function introduced one notable difference: the total index for amplitudes (A_1, A_2) becomes significantly important though the first order index is near zero. It suggests the fact that, both cosine and sinusoidal contribute to the resulting time series proportional to their amplitudes and thus changing the amplitudes can change the pattern of the time series and eventually the properties significantly. On the other hand, as the first order index suggested, amplitude on its own does not have any influence on the properties if other parameters of the model are fixed.

From the analysis, we can conclude that periodicity in time series has significant impact on entropy, trace, and 2nd largest eigenvalue. In addition, based on the PCC analysis, increased values for trace and 2nd largest eigenvalue indicate a low frequency signal and on the contrary an increased entropy indicates the presence of a high frequency signal.

5.6 Analyzing a time series with a combination of polynomial and trigonometric functions as a signal

In addition, we evaluate combinations of previous cases which include a) linear and sinusoidal, b) polynomial and sinusoidal, c) linear, sinusoidal and cosine, and d) polynomial, sinusoidal and cosine model. As before, we use ranges for parameter selections given in Table 1. We begin with

$$Y = c_1 * t + A_1 sin(2\pi\omega_1 t + \phi_1) + c_0 + e * \epsilon$$

Interestingly, Fig. 5 shows that slope (c_1) has significant impact on entropy, trace, and 2nd largest eigenvalue. In Section 5.4, we see that the linear trend does not have influence on any of these properties. But, in this additive model the linear trend becomes significant in the presence of the sinusoidal model. For the remaining parameters, the model shows similar behavior as the sinusoidal model except for amplitude (A_1). A_1 becomes significant in the presence of trend and we see that c_1 and A_1 essentially act as weights in a weighted

summation to scale the influence of the linear summand or the sine term for the overall outcome.

Fig. 6 shows the results for

$$Y = c_1 * t + A_1 sin(2\pi\omega_1 t + \phi_1) + A_2 cos(2\pi\omega_2 t + \phi_2) + c_0 + e * \epsilon$$

that have similar sensitivity indices for the parameters as the model of the summation of the linear and sinusoidal model. This model also reveals a high influence of the linear trend on entropy, trace, and 2nd largest eigenvalue.

Analysis of the summation of polynomial and sine function,

$$Y = c_2 * t^2 + c_1 * t + A_1 sin(2\pi\omega_1 t + \phi_1) + c_0 + e * \epsilon$$

and analysis of the summation of polynomial, sinusoidal and cosine function,

$$Y = c_2 * t^2 + c_1 * t + A_1 sin(2\pi\omega_1 t + \phi_1)$$
$$+ A_2 cos(2\pi\omega_2 t + \phi_2) + c_0 + e * \epsilon$$

show (Fig. 7a-7c and Fig. 8a-8c) significant influence of SNR and n on the properties of interest. The remaining parameters have near zero impact. To analyze this in further detail, we also simulated a noise free model with fixed n and f_s. From Fig. 7d-7f and Fig. 8d-8f, we see that c_2 and c_1 have significant influence on entropy, trace and 2nd largest eigenvalue. This again confirms that a trend and seasonal effects have a large impact on entropy, trace and 2nd largest eigenvalue.

5.7 Convergence of entropy, trace and 2nd largest eigenvalue

As mentioned earlier, Marken et al. [12] recognized entropy of a DTMC as a useful property to separate cells of different development stage of developing Xenopus laevis cells. Our study finds that trace and 2nd largest eigenvalue would serve the same purpose. As these properties can vary with the sampling rate (f_s), the number of states (n), and the presence of noise, we evaluate which property is more stable and converges faster. For this analysis, we focus on f_s, n, and SNR and vary one parameter at a time for all of the additive models that we analyzed so far. Table 3 illustrates the result.

From Table 3, we see that for sampling rate (f_s), the 2nd largest eigenvalue varies less than the trace and entropy. Trace also varies less than entropy except for the summation of sinusoidal and cosine

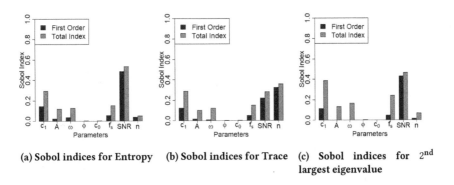

(a) Sobol indices for Entropy   (b) Sobol indices for Trace   (c) Sobol indices for 2nd largest eigenvalue

Figure 5: Entropy, trace and 2nd largest eigenvalue of the summation of sinusoidal and linear function

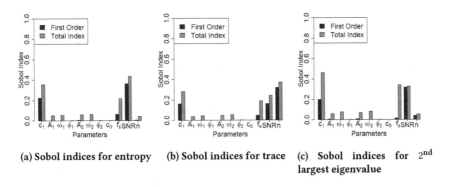

(a) Sobol indices for entropy   (b) Sobol indices for trace   (c) Sobol indices for 2nd largest eigenvalue

Figure 6: Entropy, trace and 2nd largest eigenvalue of the summation of sinusoidal, cosine and linear function

model. The 2nd largest eigenvalue converges faster than the other two properties.

For the number of states (n), the trace varies significantly more than the other two properties. Especially, in the presence of a periodic function, the trace does not converge and is not stable. In previous sections, we saw that n influences the trace a lot. With a higher number of states, the probability of switching states increases, which in turn decrease the trace value. Among entropy and 2nd largest eigenvalue, the latter again shows more stability.

In the presence of noise, the 2nd largest eigenvalue varies most while entropy and trace almost performs equally in terms of convergence and stability.

In summary, we can conclude that the 2nd largest eigenvalue is preferable to entropy and trace if the data is not dominated by noise as it is less sensitive to particular parameter settings.

6 DISCUSSION

From the analysis, we see that periodicity in time series has significant influence on entropy, trace, and 2nd largest eigenvalue. One interesting aspect is that the trace decreases in the presence of periodicity in the time series while entropy and 2nd largest eigenvalue increase. It gives us useful insight that these properties and especially the trace can be a useful metric to identify the periodicity in a time series. The phenomenon is plausible according to the definition of trace and entropy. If the times series shows less

of a periodic pattern, it increases the probability of being in the same state again and thus increases the value of trace. On the other hand, if a time series shows a high frequency periodicity (that is not filtered out by the discretization), the probability of switching from one state to another increases and contributes to an increased entropy.

Beside periodicity, our analysis shows that a trend has an impact on the properties of interest. In the presence of a linear trend, trace becomes higher but entropy becomes lower. A second order polynomial has a greater impact than a linear trend on these properties. Though Marken et al. [12] suggest that a trend does not affect the robustness of their findings, our study suggests that detrending the data is helpful if entropy, trace or 2nd largest eigenvalue are considered and the time series includes a trend and seasonality.

In the analysis, we see that for most of the models the properties are severely affected by the SNR, the number of states (n) and sampling rate (f_s). It confirms the necessity of testing if the sampling rate is sufficient before performing an analysis based on trace, entropy, or 2nd largest eigenvalue. The impact of the number of states (n) also needs to be tested to get robust findings.

In the comparison of stability and convergence of entropy, trend, and 2nd largest eigenvalue, our finding is that the 2nd largest eigenvalue is more stable than entropy and trace.

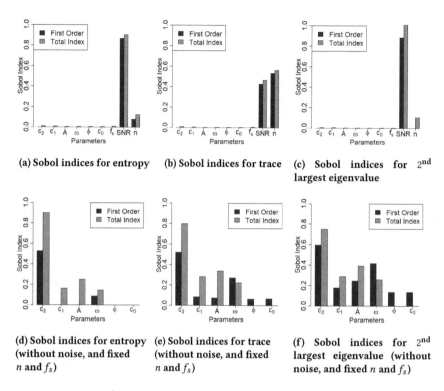

(a) Sobol indices for entropy

(b) Sobol indices for trace

(c) Sobol indices for 2nd largest eigenvalue

(d) Sobol indices for entropy (without noise, and fixed n and f_s)

(e) Sobol indices for trace (without noise, and fixed n and f_s)

(f) Sobol indices for 2nd largest eigenvalue (without noise, and fixed n and f_s)

Figure 7: Entropy, trace and 2nd largest eigenvalue of summation of sinusoidal and polynomial function

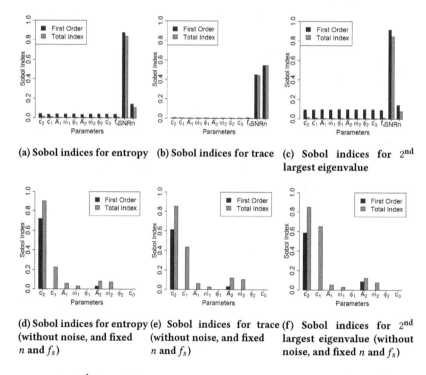

(a) Sobol indices for entropy

(b) Sobol indices for trace

(c) Sobol indices for 2nd largest eigenvalue

(d) Sobol indices for entropy (without noise, and fixed n and f_s)

(e) Sobol indices for trace (without noise, and fixed n and f_s)

(f) Sobol indices for 2nd largest eigenvalue (without noise, and fixed n and f_s)

Figure 8: Entropy, trace and 2nd largest eigenvalue of summation of sinusoidal, cosine and polynomial function

Table 3: Convergence and stability of entropy, trace and 2nd largest eigenvalue.

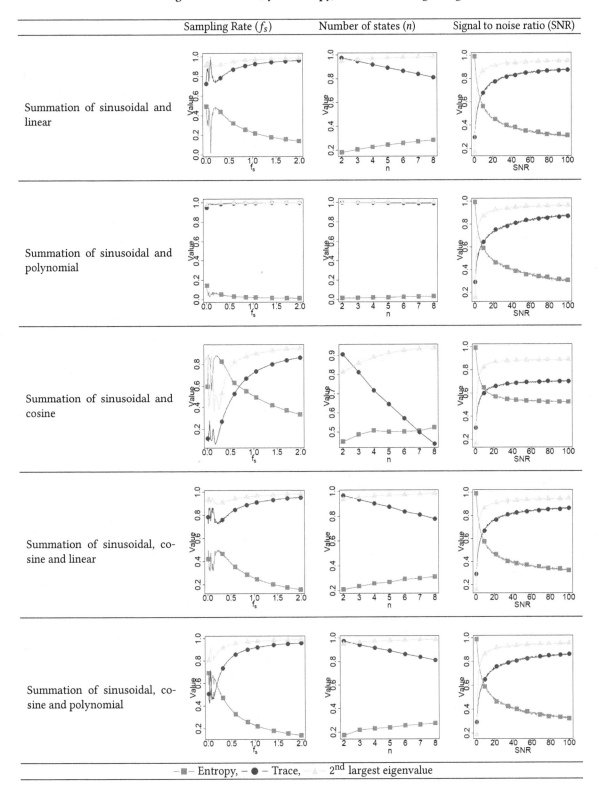

7 CONCLUSION AND FUTURE WORK

In this paper, we conduct a simulation study to better understand which characteristics of a time series influence the entropy, trace, and 2nd largest eigenvalue of a discrete time Markov chain that results from a discretization of time series data. We use Monte Carlo simulation to estimate Sobol indices and partial correlation coefficient (PCC) values. Sobol indices and PCC values inform us about the sensitivity of the considered DTMC properties to changes in the time series characteristics. Our study finds that these properties can effectively recognize the extent of periodicity or seasonality in a time series. We also observed that the sensitivity increases with the complexity of the model that we used to generate the time series data. In a complex model, all the model parameters tend to show some influence on the properties of interest. In contrast to a case study on a specific data set [12] but consistent with a common recommendation in time series analysis, our study suggests that a trend does have an impact on the properties and thus it is recommended to remove a trend to obtain more robust results. We have also recognized that the 2nd largest eigenvalue is more robust for different settings of sampling rate, signal to noise ratio and the number of states for the DTMC discretization than trace and entropy.

In this study, we only explore linear, low-degree polynomial and trigonometric models to generate data for computing a Discrete Time Markov Chain. In the future, we would like to extend our findings to Markov chains with history variables, i.e, a Markov chain where the future state depends on one or more past states. We would also like to explore more complex models for the generation of data including but not limited to various linear and non linear models such as Autoregressive Integrated Moving Average (ARIMA), Seasonal Autoregressive Integrated Moving Average (SARIMA), Exponential Smoothing State Space Model (ETS), Autoregressive Conditional Heteroskedasticity (ARCH), Generalized ARCH (GARCH), Exponential Generalized ARCH (EGARCH), Threshold Autoregressive (TAR), Non-linear Autoregressive (NAR), and Nonlinear Moving Average (NMA) models. Exploring these models will give us a better understanding of how the properties of interest react in the presence of autocorrelation, long range dependencies, and non linearity in time series data.

REFERENCES

[1] Frank Bickenbach and Eckhardt Bode. 2003. Evaluating the Markov Property in Studies of Economic Convergence. *International Regional Science Review* 26, 3 (2003), 363–392. https://doi.org/10.1177/0160017603253789 arXiv:https://doi.org/10.1177/0160017603253789

[2] Karen Chan, Andrea Saltelli, and Stefano Tarantola. 1997. Sensitivity analysis of model output: variance-based methods make the difference. In *Proceedings of the 29th conference on Winter simulation*. IEEE Computer Society, Atlanta, GA, USA, 261–268.

[3] Thomas M Cover and Joy A Thomas. 2012. *Elements of information theory*. John Wiley & Sons.

[4] Andreas Griewank. 2000. *Evaluating Derivatives: Principles and Techniques of Algorithmic Differentiation*. Society for Industrial and Applied Mathematics, Philadelphia, PA, USA.

[5] Toshimitsu Homma and Andrea Saltelli. 1996. Importance measures in global sensitivity analysis of nonlinear models. *Reliability Engineering & System Safety* 52, 1 (1996), 1 – 17.

[6] Ronald L Iman and Stephen C Hora. 1990. A robust measure of uncertainty importance for use in fault tree system analysis. *Risk analysis* 10, 3 (1990), 401–406.

[7] Alexandre Janon, Thierry Klein, Agnes Lagnoux, Maëlle Nodet, and Clémentine Prieur. 2014. Asymptotic normality and efficiency of two sobol index estimators. *ESAIM: Probability and Statistics* 18 (2014), 342–364.

[8] Alexandre Janon, Maëlle Nodet, and Clémentine Prieur. 2012. Certified metamodels for sensitivity indices estimation. In *ESAIM: Proceedings*, Vol. 35. EDP Sciences, 234–238.

[9] Michiel J.W. Jansen. 1999. Analysis of variance designs for model output. *Computer Physics Communications* 117, 1 (1999), 35 – 43.

[10] Loic Le Gratiet, Claire Cannamela, and Bertrand Iooss. 2014. A Bayesian approach for global sensitivity analysis of (multifidelity) computer codes. *SIAM/ASA Journal on Uncertainty Quantification* 2, 1 (2014), 336–363.

[11] I M. Sobol. 1990. Sensitivity Estimates for Nonlinear Mathematical Models. *Matematicheskoe Modelirovanie* 2 (01 1990).

[12] John P. Marken, Andrew D. Halleran, Atiqur Rahman, Laura Odorizzi, Michael C. LeFew, Caroline A. Golino, Peter Kemper, and Margaret S. Saha. 2016. A Markovian Entropy Measure for the Analysis of Calcium Activity Time Series. *PLOS ONE* 11, 12 (12 2016), 1–20. https://doi.org/10.1371/journal.pone.0168342

[13] James M. Murphy, David M. H. Sexton, David N. Barnett, Gareth S. Jones, Matthew Collins Mark J. Webb, and David A. Stainforth. 2004. *Quantification of modelling uncertainties in a large ensemble of climate change simulations*. Nature. https://doi.org/10.1038/nature02771

[14] Gilles Pujol, Bertrand Iooss, Alexandre Janon with contributions from Khalid Boumhaout, Sebastien Da Veiga, Thibault Delage, Jana Fruth, Laurent Gilquin, Joseph Guillaume, Loic Le Gratiet, Paul Lemaitre, Barry L. Nelson, Filippo Monari, Roelof Oomen, Bernardo Ramos, Olivier Roustant, Eunhye Song, Jeremy Staum, Taieb Touati, and Frank Weber. 2017. *sensitivity: Global Sensitivity Analysis of Model Outputs*. https://CRAN.R-project.org/package=sensitivity R package version 1.15.0.

[15] Andrea Saltelli. 2002. Making best use of model evaluations to compute sensitivity indices. *Computer Physics Communications* 145, 2 (2002), 280–297.

[16] Andrea Saltelli, Paola Annoni, Ivano Azzini, Francesca Campolongo, Marco Ratto, and Stefano Tarantola. 2010. Variance based sensitivity analysis of model output. Design and estimator for the total sensitivity index. *Computer Physics Communications* 181, 2 (2010), 259 – 270. https://doi.org/10.1016/j.cpc.2009.09.018

[17] John H Schaibly and Kurt E Shuler. 1973. Study of the sensitivity of coupled reaction systems to uncertainties in rate coefficients. II Applications. *The Journal of Chemical Physics* 59, 8 (1973), 3879–3888.

[18] Claude Elwood Shannon. 2001. A mathematical theory of communication. *ACM SIGMOBILE Mobile Computing and Communications Review* 5, 1 (2001), 3–55.

[19] R Core Team. 2017. *R: A Language and Environment for Statistical Computing*. R Foundation for Statistical Computing, Vienna, Austria. https://www.R-project.org/

Sampling Simulation Model Profile Data for Analysis

Patrick Crawford
University of Cincinnati
Cincinnati, Ohio
crawfopw@mail.uc.edu

Peter D. Barnes Jr.
Lawrence Livermore National Laboratory
Livermore, California
barnes26@llnl.gov

Stephan J. Eidenbenz
Los Alamos National Laboratory
Los Alamos, New Mexico
eidenben@lanl.gov

Philip A. Wilsey
University of Cincinnati
Cincinnati, Ohio
wilseypa@gmail.com

ABSTRACT

The capture of data about the events executed by a discrete event simulation can easily lead to very large trace data files. While disk space is relatively inexpensive and mostly capable of storing these large trace files, the manipulation and analysis of these large trace files can prove difficult. Furthermore, some types of analysis must be performed in-core and they cannot be performed with the trace data exceeds the size of the physical RAM where the analysis is performed. Because of these limits, it is often necessary to strictly limit the simulation run time to satisfy the analysis time memory limits. Experience with the DESMetrics tool suite (a collection of tools to analyze event trace files), demonstrates that our in-memory analysis tools are limited to trace files on the order of 10GB (on a machine with 24GB of RAM). Furthermore, even when it is possible to analyze large trace files, the run time costs of performing this analysis can take several days to complete. While high performance analysis of traces data is not strictly necessary, the results should be available within some reasonably bounded time frame. This paper explores techniques to overcome the limits of analyzing very large event trace files. While explorations for out-out-core analysis have been examined as part of this work, the run time costs for out-of-core processing can increase processing time 10-fold. As a result, the work reported here will focus on an approach to capture and analyze small samples from the event trace file. The work reported in this paper will examine how closely the analysis from sampling matches the analysis from a full trace file. Two techniques for comparison are presented. First a visual comparison of analysis results between the full trace and a trace sample are presented. Second, numerical quantification of the different analysis results (between the full trace and trace sample) will be reported using the Wasserstein, Directed Hausdorff, and Kolmogorov-Smirnov distance metrics. Finally, the ability to process trace samples from a very large trace file of 80GB is demonstrated.

Permission to make digital or hard copies of all or part of this work for personal or classroom use is granted without fee provided that copies are not made or distributed for profit or commercial advantage and that copies bear this notice and the full citation on the first page. Copyrights for components of this work owned by others than ACM must be honored. Abstracting with credit is permitted. To copy otherwise, or republish, to post on servers or to redistribute to lists, requires prior specific permission and/or a fee. Request permissions from permissions@acm.org.

SIGSIM-PADS '18 , May 23–25, 2018, Rome, Italy
© 2018 Association for Computing Machinery.
ACM ISBN 978-1-4503-5092-1/18/05...$15.00
https://doi.org/10.1145/3200921.3200944

CCS CONCEPTS

• **Computing methodologies** → **Modeling and simulation**; **Discrete-event simulation**; **Simulation tools**;

KEYWORDS

Profiling simulation models; Sampling; Discrete event simulation; Parallel discrete event simulation

ACM Reference Format:
Patrick Crawford, Peter D. Barnes Jr., Stephan J. Eidenbenz, and Philip A. Wilsey. 2018. Sampling Simulation Model Profile Data for Analysis. In *SIGSIM-PADS '18 : 2018 SIGSIM Principles of Advanced Discrete Simulation, May 23–25, 2018, Rome, Italy*. ACM, New York, NY, USA, 12 pages. https://doi.org/10.1145/3200921.3200944

1 INTRODUCTION

The capture and analysis of event trace data from discrete event simulators has been used to develop optimization and configuration techniques for parallel simulation [1, 12]. These studies have demonstrated the effective use of profile data to develop new algorithms and data structures for improved parallel simulation performance. In addition, the profile results have shown utility in the partitioning of the parallel components of the simulation model for higher performance execution. In general the profile data is captured from a simulation run where each event generated/processed in the simulation is recorded into a trace file. Unfortunately recording all of this event trace data can easily generate sizable data file sizes (on the order of 10s to 100s of GB).

One project to perform analysis of Discrete-Event Simulation (DES) models is called the DESMetrics project [22]. The public webpages for the DESMetrics project are available at github.com/wilseypa/desMetrics. In the past, the DESMetrics project has collected and reported data by instrumenting simulation kernels and directly obtaining simulation model profile data. This approach permits control over the simulator run time parameters and, consequently, the size of the trace files can be regulated. Recently the project has received trace files for analysis that were captured by others. Two of the trace files delivered were quite large (80GB and 442GB). These files exceeded the processing capabilities of the DESMetrics tool suite. Therefore new techniques to process such large trace files have become necessary.

This paper explores the problem of analyzing very large event trace files. Our initial efforts to solve this problem was to build out-of-core analysis solutions. Unfortunately, the resulting solution had excessive run time costs for the analysis that generally resulted an a 10-fold slowdown from the in-core solution. In particular, in-core analysis on a relatively modest 7G trace file would complete in 15 hours; the out-of-core solution took more than 150 hours to complete. Thus, we turned to an approach to extract samples of sub-traces from the full event trace file to analyze. To evaluate this approach, profile analysis is performed on both the full traces and on the sub-trace samples. The analysis results are then compared to evaluate how closely the sub-trace analysis results track those from the full trace analysis. Comparison of results is achieved using two approaches, namely: (i) producing graphs that summarize and overlay analysis results between the full trace and the subtraces; and (ii) by computing different distance metrics between the full trace and the sample traces. As a result, this paper focuses primarily on moderate sized trace files where it is still possible to perform an analysis on the full trace. That said, one study with a large 80GB trace file is reported.

While this paper focuses on the comparison of analysis results from sub-trace samples to analysis results with the full trace, it is important to consider that production of the same results may not always be desirable. If particular, the expectation that results match closely among the different (sub-)trace analyses is correct only when the simulation models have static run time characteristics throughout the simulation lifetime. In fact, some of the analysis results shown in this paper expose some variations that might help provide illuminating results on the run time properties of different simulation models.

The remainder of this paper is organized as follows. Section 2 contains some background information and discusses related work. Section 3 provides a high level overview of the sampling process followed in this work. Section 4 presents the simulation models studied and reported herein. Section 5 presents the basic comparative analysis performed on two of the studied simulation models. Section 6 examines the impact of sizes on the simulation traces and shows how it impacts the accuracy of the analysis of the sampled traces to the full trace. Section 7 illustrates the use sampling of a large event trace and the subsequent analysis of only the samples. Section 8 briefly examines mathematical comparisons between analyses from the full trace to analyses from the sample traces. Finally, Section 9 contains some concluding remarks.

2 BACKGROUND & RELATED WORK

Capturing profile data to optimize architecture design trade offs for performance optimization is a well established practice in the computer architecture community [13]. Some of the earliest work with DES model analysis was directed to the analysis of potential parallelism and lookahead [4, 14–16]. Recent work with the DESMetrics project has attempted to incorporate profile data from Discrete-Event Simulation (DES) models to improve the performance of parallel simulation [1, 12, 22]. Likewise, profile data can help capture model configuration errors [12] as well as help set configuration parameters for synthetic simulation model generators [2, 8, 10, 18]. Finally, profile guided partitioning can be used to setup and deploy more efficient configurations of simulation models for high-performance parallel simulation [1, 20].

DESMetrics is a project that has been developed to capture, analyze, and visualize various properties of discrete event simulation models [22]. The project captures event trace data and examines several features of the simulation model behaviors. Some examples of the analysis and visualization results include: (i) the potential parallelism among the available events, (ii) the percentage of the total events executed that each LP has performed [22], (iii) the amount of lookahead and events available for group scheduling [12], and (iv) the coupling of events exchanged between the LPs of the simulation model [7]. In addition to the papers in the literature, the DESMetrics project has made all of the source code freely available from github.com/wilseypa/desMetrics for others to use.

3 SAMPLING

A challenge to the profiling DES models is that often the simulation trace files can quickly grow to difficult to manage sizes (10s to 100s of GB). Sampling may hold the answer to this problem. From the traditional sampling literature, some of the popular sampling methods are:

Simple Random Sampling (SRS): This method is the most naive, and straightforward approach, where the probability to choose any portion is equal for all portions, by choosing random portions from the population up to a desired sample size. This method is vulnerable to error since the randomness of the selection may not reflect the entire population accurately. The other methods attempt to overcome this problem by "using information about the population" to make a selection. SRS may also be cumbersome and tedious when sampling for unusually large populations.

Systematic Sampling (Interval): This method involves first ordering the population and then selecting every k^{th} element from a random starting point. This method can be fairly efficient and is easy to implement. However, it is vulnerable to periodicities and in some populations may result in being less accurate than SRS.

Cluster Sampling: This method forms clusters in the population and chooses random clusters to sample from. This method can be relatively inexpensive, and good for large data sets. In addition, it generally increases the variability of sample estimates compared to SRS. Cluster sampling is usually implemented as multistage sampling, where in the first stage constructs the cluster, and the later stages take a random sampling from each cluster. This effectively takes random sub samples from preceding samples. The downside to this method is that it may be difficult to cluster samples representing the entire population.

Stratified Sampling: Involves dividing the population based on some characteristic, known as the stratifying variable, into groups, known as strata. Then, another sampling method, such as SRS, is applied to each strata. One important thing to note is that this method has to be mutually exclusive and collectively exhaustive. This method tends to give more accurate information than clustered sampling, but is more difficult to implement in larger populations. The major difficulty with this method is selecting a stratifying variable to form the strata.

Post-stratified Sampling: This method is a different ordering of the process in stratified sampling. In post-stratified sampling, another sampling method can be used on the population, such as SRS. Then, stratified sampling is performed on the sample. This method is typically used when there is a lack of prior knowledge of the population before sampling, or when the researcher lacks sufficient information to create a stratifying variable. Post-stratification can increase precision of the chosen samples.

Unfortunately, the analysis of DES models requires that a *sample contains a collection of temporally related events* so that a meaningful representation of the execution behavior emerges from the sample. Furthermore, we believe that it is likely that for some simulation models, observations will ultimately show that behaviors emerge in time. More specifically we suspect that simulation models of evolving physical systems such as wildfires [21] or objects drifting on ocean currents [9, 11] will also exhibit dynamic behaviors in event executions and LP interactions. Therefore, the method explored in this paper will be structured following a method similar to Systematic Sampling described above. The remainder of this section is organized into two brief subsections. The first subsection describes the sampling strategy that is explored. The second describes the tooling that has been developed and used.

3.1 Extracting Samples

For purposes of this study, the particular selection of which regions of the original trace file the samples are extracted is not significant. More specifically, at this time, we are mostly interested in discovering if analysis results using the samples provide results similar to that seen from the original full trace. Finally, since much of the analysis is performed on the relationship between LPs and events at the time that the event is executed, all samples extracted for this paper will be *blocks* (or *chunks*) of adjacent events that are ordered by their scheduled (simulation) time for execution.

The sampling strategy that is followed in this study is configurable to the simulation model and permits the extracting of a variable number of uniformly distributed samples of a specified length. Due to simulation startup/teardown issues that were observed in previous work [22], the sampling method also supports a skipping of events at the head and tail of the original trace. This will be called the *skip distance*. Each extracted sample is a block of adjacent events that are ordered by their scheduled (simulation) time for execution. In order to extract a sample size that is meaningful to the overall size of the simulation model, the sample sizes are specified as a multiple of d events per LP. The extract process does not ensure that each LP has processed d events in the trace, instead the extract process simply captures $d \times ||LP||$ events from each interval extracted. Thus, the process of extraction is to ignore the "skip distance" events at the head/tail and extract n samples each containing $d \times ||LP||$ events. The midpoint event of each sample is centered at the n locations uniformly spaced through the sample (within the skip distance bounds). This method of sampling provides a collection of sample blocks of events distributed throughout the simulation trace that can be analyzed. If the simulation model runtime behaviors are fairly constant throughout the entire simulation, the analysis results for all of the traces should appear similar. If the simulation model behaviors are more dynamic, we expect to see more variances in the analysis results computed from the different samples.

Figure 1: The Selection of Samples from the Full Event Trace.

An illustration of the event samples (shown in red) extracted from a full trace is show in Figure 1. In this figure, the lines represent the stream of events in the file. Note the skip distance at the head/tail and the Sample i intervals (shown in red). The sample intervals do not necessarily begin/end with the end/head of the skip distances as they actually come from the region around the n midpoints of the (skip distance bounded) sample.

3.2 Tooling to Extract Samples

For the purposes of sampling, the DESMetrics tool suite has been extended with two new elements. The first, called desSampler.go, is a go program that makes two passes over the full trace file. The first pass counts the number of events and LPs. On the second pass, it uses these values and a set of input parameters defining the size and shape of the samples to be extracted. The second element, called sampleMeasures.py, processes a set of samples to produce graphical presentations that depict how well the samples correlate to one another. This tool also computes the *Wasserstein*, *Directed Hausdorff*, and *Kolmogorov-Smirnov* distances using the first sample (or full trace) as the base case. Thus, if the full trace is included in the input set, the distances are computed against it; otherwise the distances are computed relative to the first extracted sample. From these tools, the process is to: (i) use desSampler.go to extract samples, (ii) use (the already existing DESMetrics tool [22]) desAnalysis.go to analyze each sample (including the original trace if desired), and (iii) use sampleMeasures.py to prepare and output graphs and distance measures from the analysis results. An illustration of this process is given in Figure 2. A more detailed explanation of the output results from the sampleMeasures.py program are described below. All of these tools are available from the project webpages at github.com/wilseypa/desMetrics. All of the tools in the DESMetrics project are open sourced and freely available for use.

4 DES MODELS STUDIED

In this study, results with three DES models are presented. The studied models are:

NeMo: A simulation model of a neumorphic computing model [19]. This model comes from the ROSS parallel simulation engine [6]. This model has a total of 65,664 LPs and the trace file contains a record of 121,372,541 events.

Epidemic: A simulation model that simulates an epidemic outbreak phenomena following the description found in [3]. This model comes from the WARPED2 parallel simulation engine [20]. This model has a total of 10,000 LPs and the trace file contains a record of 253,926,992 events.

Bitcoin: A simulation model of the Bitcoin network at a full scale of 6,000 nodes [17]. This is a custom model developed specifically for modeling Bitcoin networks. This model has a total of 17,707 LPs and the trace file contains a record of 1,964,005,745 events.

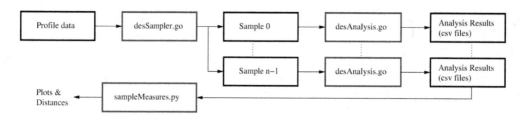

Figure 2: The DESMetrics tool flow.

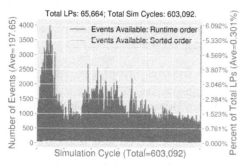

Full Trace of NeMo DES Model

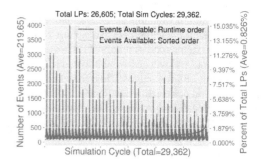

Sample Trace of NeMo DES Model

Figure 3: Direct Comparison of `desAnalysis.go` Results from the NeMo Simulation Model.

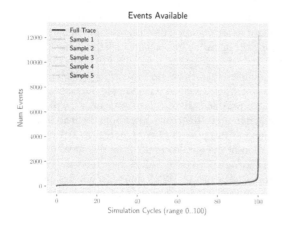

Figure 4: Events Available from the NeMo Simulation Traces (full and samples).

Data for the first two DES models were captured locally by the paper authors. The trace data for the Bitcoin model was captured by the authors of the paper by Neudecker *et al* [17] and sent to the DESMetrics investigators. The original trace data from the first two models are, respectively, 6.4GB and 7.3GB; the original trace data file size from the Bitcoin model is 80GB. Full trace analysis is possible only on the first two models.

5 EXPERIMENTS WITH SAMPLING

When comparing the analysis results from the full trace and samples, we will focus on four specific analysis areas, namely: (i) the total events available for execution (on a cycle-by-cycle basis), (ii) the

number of events executed by each LP (as a percentage of the total events executed in the sample), (iii) the event chains by LP (as described in [12, 22]), and (iv) the connectivity of the LPs (in this case defined by their modularity [7]).

In the experiments performed and reported in this section, all samples were taken as follows: (i) the first and last 1% of events in the original trace file are skipped, (ii) 5 samples were extracted, and (iii) the sample width multiplier was set at 100 (which means that each sample will contain information on $100 \times ||LPs||$ events (where $||LPs||$ denotes the total number of LPs in the simulation). The evaluation of the multiplier for sample size extraction is explored more fully in Section 6.

5.1 Events Available

The events available analysis results considers a synthetic simulation engine that assumes all events execute in unit time and that a complete history of events for each LP is available to examine at each simulation cycle [22]. The process considers a conservative execution where an event (at each LP) is considered available at each time stamp only if: (i) it was generated prior to the current time step and (ii) it is at the head of the LP's event list.

Comparing the output results between full traces and samples is not very instructive. An example of this problem is illustrated in Figure 3. This figure shows the cycle-by-cycle "events available for execution" (as described in [22]) graphic for one sample and the full trace of the NeMo simulation model. The scale of the different traces is completely different and fails to deliver a meaningful graphic for comparison. As a result, another process for comparing output results must be developed.

To provide a better graphic for a comparative analysis between the full trace and the sample traces, a new graphic is produced that

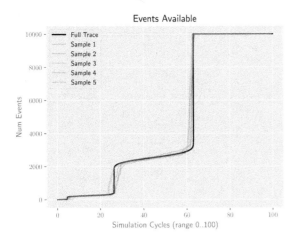

Figure 5: Events Available from the Epidemic Simulation Traces (full and samples).

takes the number of events available data, sorts it, and then plots the analysis results points from each sample (including the full trace) on a fixed scale. The sorting is necessary as the cycle-by-cycle results oscillate and pollute the graphic (*cf* Figure 3). By sorting the counts of events available in each cycle, we gain better insights as to how the various samples track the original trace. Furthermore, since there are significantly more simulation cycles to be considered in the full trace, the events available points are placed in a common fixed scale. In this case, we used a fixed scale of 0-100, although any scale will be sufficient. In all graphs plotted in this paper, the graphic colors will use black for the base case comparison sample (full or otherwise) and different colors for each sample.

The results of this analysis with the ROSS NeMo simulation model are shown in Figure 4. In this plot the original trace and all 5 samples are plotted on the same 0-100 scale. Interestingly enough, this graphic shows that the events available by simulation cycle are quite close to one another between the full trace and the samples.

The events available graphic of the sampled data from the WARPED2 epidemic model are shown in Figure 5. In this case, there are some minor discrepancies between the sample data and the full trace data. However, the overall curve and changes to the curve appear in similar locations in the distribution of simulation cycles (coinciding with the x-axis). Based on these two figures, it appears that the sampling method preserves the events available analysis result.

5.2 Events Processed by the LPs

In this part of the results comparison, we examine the number of events processed by each LP as a percentage of the total events executed in the sample interval (again full or sampled). This provides a sense of how well distributed the event executions are among the pool of LPs. Due to the large variances among the LPs event processing percentages, the y-axis is plotted on a log scale. In these samples, not all LPs are represented in the trace. As a result, zeros are added to the samples to complete the results for all LPs in the sample. The results of the events available comparison is shown in Figure 6. Interestingly, unlike the events available results, the NeMo sampling results show notable variance from the full trace

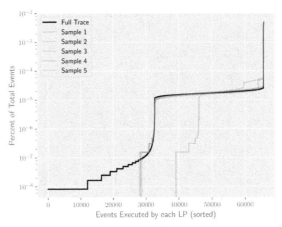

(a) From the NeMo Model

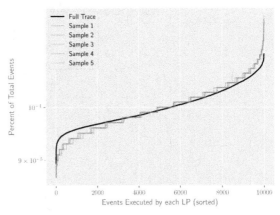

(b) From The Epidemic Model

Figure 6: Events by LP (full and samples).

results and the Epidemic model model results closely follow the full trace results.

5.3 Event Chains

Event chains are the number of events in the sorted LP input event list that are all generated from times earlier than the first event of the chain [22]. Basically these event chains attempt to identify the links of events that can be bulk scheduled [12] from the LP's input event set. In the original work with event chains, three classes of event chains are identified, namely: *local*, *linked*, and *global*. Local chains are collections of events that were all self generated. Any remote event (and event generated by some other LP) or any event not generated before the execution timestamp of the lowest member of the chain will break the chain. Global chains are similar to local chains except that an event from a remote LP does not break the chain. Finally, linked chains can include additional events that are generated by the executing LP anytime during the active processing of events from the chain. Event chains are organized by length (1, 2, 3, 4, and >= 5). In this study, the percentages of event chains by class (*i.e.*, the percent of all local chains of length n=1, 2, 3, 4, and >= 5) are plotted. The results are plotted in Figure 7 (note

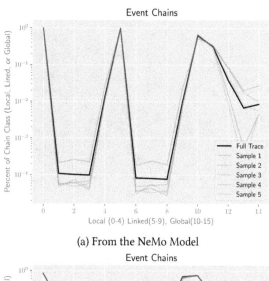

(a) From the NeMo Model

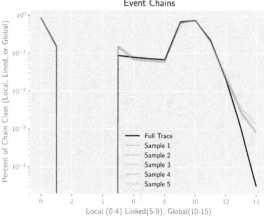

(b) From The Epidemic Model

Figure 7: Events Chains (full and samples).

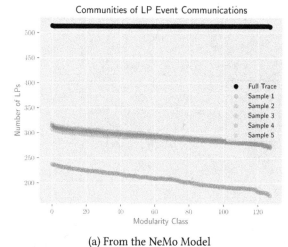

(a) From the NeMo Model

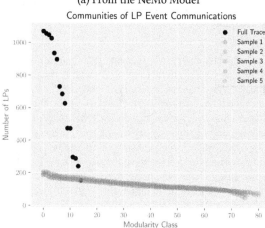

(b) From The Epidemic Model

Figure 8: Modularity (full and samples).

that the y-axis is on a log scale). The local, linked, and global chain percentages are plotted consecutively at x-axis points 0-14 (0-4 are the local chain results, 5-9 are the linked chain results, and 10-14 are the global chain results). As can be observed from the figure, the event chains from the sampled traces follow closely the full trace results for both simulation models studied.

5.4 Modularity

Modularity characterizes the structure of communicating networks and measures how well sub-networks (*communities*) a large network are organized [5]. In the context of simulation networks, communities describe sets of highly inter-connected LPs [7]. A simulation model with a high modularity has dense connections within the LP communities and sparse connections among different LP communities. Thus, LPs within a community have more frequent exchanges of event information whereas those in different communities tend to have less interactions of event exchanges. Modularity, and specifically, the identified communities of LPs can readily be formed into partitions for parallelization [1, 7]. DES models with

numerous communities containing a non-trivial number of LPs are each good candidates for partitioning and parallel execution; those with few communities or with limited LP membership in each community may prove challenging for partitioning and parallel execution.

With respect to sampling, the modularity results are somewhat perplexing. While the other analysis results with samples tend to return results that are often fairly close to the full trace results, the same cannot be said for the community results. Figure 8 shows some results with modularity analysis. In both models, the communities produced with samples are significantly different than those produced from the full trace. As we will see in Section 6 below, this is difference persists even with larger and larger sized samples. However, while the results are different than those from the full trace, it is not clear (at least to the authors) that this is a significant problem for the application of modularity to partitioning. More precisely, in both DES models, the number of LPs in the communities are non-trivial and there are a significant number of communities. While the number of LPs and communities are

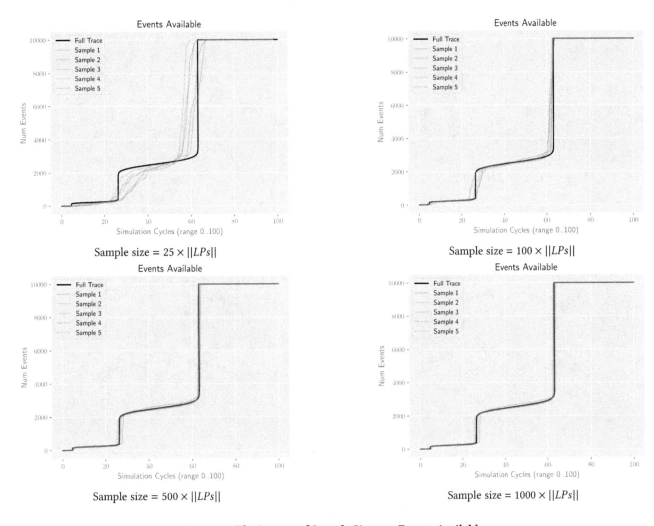

Figure 9: The Impact of Sample Sizes on Events Available

mostly similar among the different traces, it is not clear that the communities are formed in the different traces by the same LPs. This is a complex issue and requires significant additional study that is beyond the scope of this paper.

6 IMPLICATIONS OF SAMPLE SIZES

The results shown in the previous section are all performed with samples of the same size, specifically each sample contains the number of events equal to 100 times the number of LPs ($100 \times ||LPs||$). This section explores the question of sizing the samples. Is the 100 multiplier sufficient? Is 25, or does an accurate representation require larger sample sizes? In this part of the work, sample size multipliers of 25, 100, 250, 500, 1000, 1500, 2000, and 2500 were collected for the Epidemic model. Of the models studied, the Epidemic model was selected for representation in this part of the study due to the fact that it provides interesting results where the smaller sample sizes begin to depart from the full trace model results. Some of the models studied maintained fairly close representations even with sample size multipliers as low as 25.

Due to space considerations all of the results from these studies are not shown. However, for all results except modularity, the results generally converge to the full trace results. As a result, we will briefly examine each of the first three classes of analysis results from Epidemic together and then examine modularity separately.

The comparison results with sample size multipliers of 25, 100, 400, and 1000 are shown in Figure 9 (for events available), Figure 10 (for events executed by LP), and Figure 11 (for event chains). From these graphs there appear to be meaningful variances in the analysis results from samples taken with size multipliers of 25 and 100. Once the size multiplier reaches 500, the results of these parts of the analysis (events available, events executed per LP, and event chains) tend to follow the full trace sample results fairly closely.

The modularity results for various sample size multipliers is shown in Figure 12. Due to the fact that there is a significantly larger variance between the samples and the full trace results, the number of multipliers has been expanded to include 25, 100, 400, 1000, 1500, and 2500. With the larger multipliers, the communities produced show some evidence of trending toward the full trace

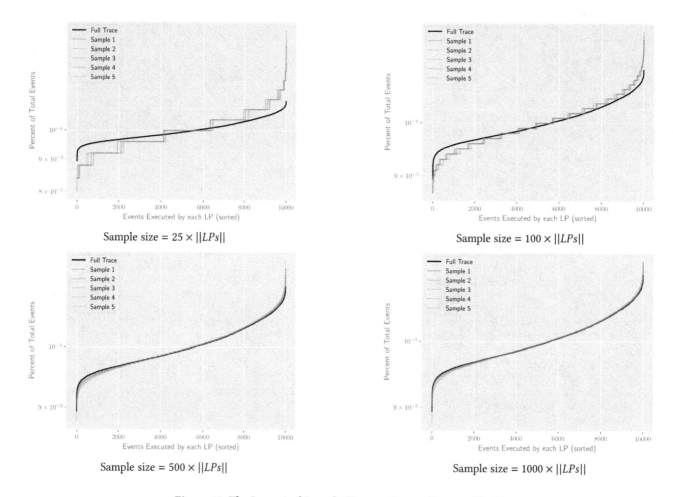

Figure 10: The Impact of Sample Sizes on Events Executed by LP

results. However, the variation is still quite large even with the largest multiplier. As stated in the previous section discussions with modularity, this deviation from the full trace results may not necessarily be a concerning result. The implications of these results will require additional study that is beyond the scope of this paper.

Finally, the above size multiplier results are captured using only one DES model data point and it is possible (likely) that some DES models will not track a full trace very closely no mater the size multiplier. In fact, we suspect that there are likely to be classes of DES models with evolving behaviors. Ideally, such models might be best suited to analysis with a sampling methodology. The samples might well show trends in model behaviors that could aid tool builders in the construction of solutions that respond more readily to a range of dynamic DES model behaviors.

7 ANALYZING LARGE TRACE FILES

The original motivation to consider sampling of event trace files was triggered by the delivery of two very large event trace files from a research group in Germany. The two models were 80GB (Bitcoin) and 442GB (Bittorrent) in size. One of these models (Bitcoin) contained approximately 2 billion event records and the other

(Bittorrent) contained approximately 13.4 trillion event records. We were unable to analyze either file with the in-core tools that were available to us at that time. The first solution we attempted to enable analysis of these large files was to converted the analysis tools to operate out-of-core. However, the run time costs of the out-of-core solution was at least an order of magnitude slower than the in-core solution and, as a result, deemed infeasible. This challenge lead us to explore the sampling methods outlined in this paper.

This section contains the results of comparisons among the sample traces extracted from the Bitcoin trace. The samples were taken as follows: (i) the first and last 1% of events in the original trace file are skipped, (ii) 9 samples were extracted, and (iii) the multiplier was set at 25 (which means that each sample will contain information on $25 \times ||LPs||$ events. The results are shown in the four plots of Figure 13.

These results show that the samples are similar in the events available, events executed per LP, and the event chains analysis. There is some variability among the samples in these analyses, but the general trends are shared by all of the samples. The modularity results are, however, quite interesting. The first sample (shown in black) is significantly different from the other samples. That said,

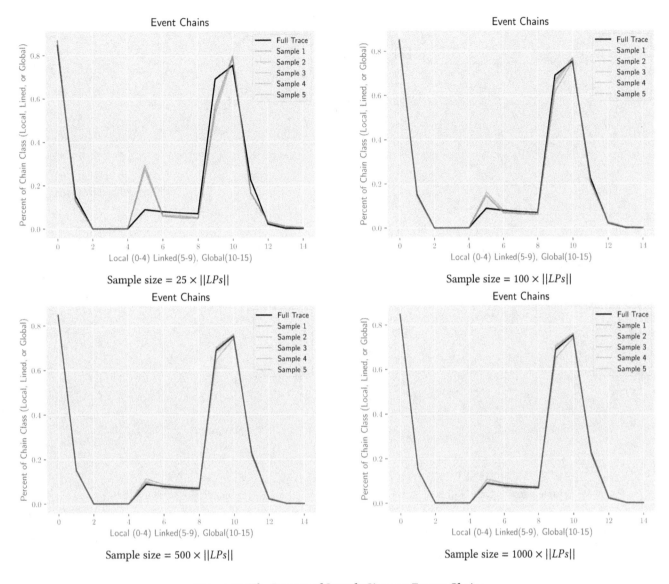

Figure 11: The Impact of Sample Sizes on Events Chains

there is also significant variations in the modularity results from all of the samples.

8 DISTANCE METRICS

In the previous sections, the comparison results are presented as visual depictions. While this is convenient and easy for the human examiner to evaluate, there may be times when it would be desirable to consider these results within a computer program. This might occur for example, if one is exploring the use of samples to configure a very large simulation for a weeks or months long execution run and concerns for partitioning drives a need for accurate results. This means that some other numerical based comparison result might be desirable. As a result, in addition to constructing the visual comparisons of the samples, the `sampleMeasures.py` tool was also

configured to capture three different distance metrics between the samples. The distance metrics captured are:

Wasserstein Distance: Informally this distance metric compares two different distributions (samples) and computes the minimum amount of "work" (or dirt) that would be necessary to turn one of the samples into the other. This metric is also known as the *earth mover's distance.*

Directed Hausdorff: This distance measures how far two samples are from each other. Essentially this metric takes the worst case difference between the two samples.

Kolmogorov-Smirnov: This tests the continuous equality of two samples through a one-dimensional probability distribution.

While there are many possible metrics that could be used for this comparison, these metrics are reported here because: (i) they represent three of the more common distinct types of measures that can

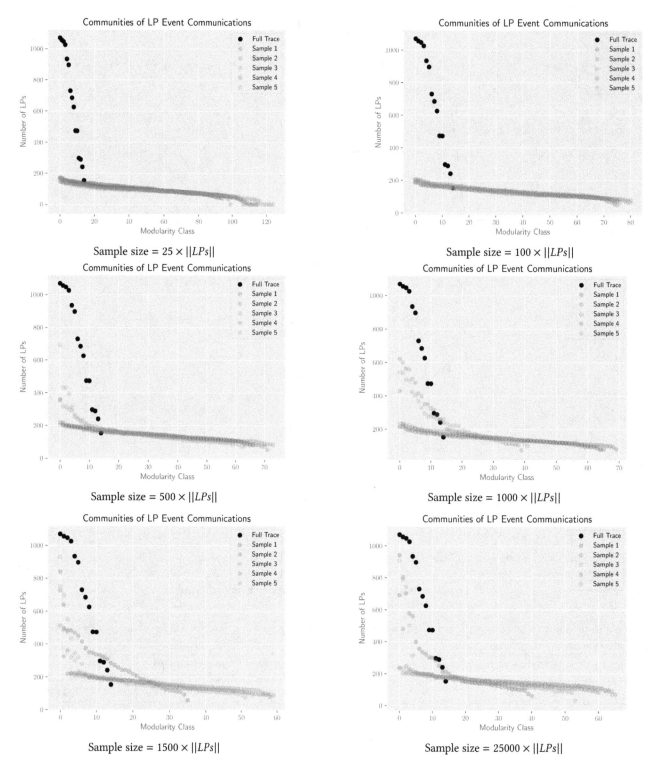

Figure 12: The Impact of Sample Sizes on Modularity

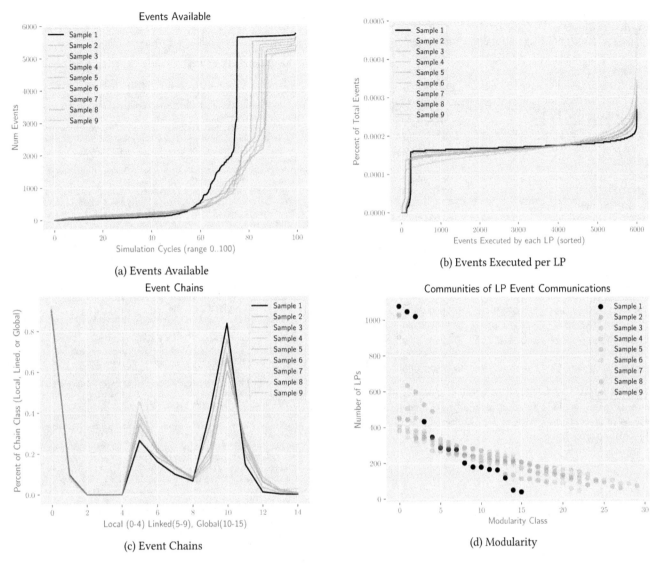

(a) Events Available

(b) Events Executed per LP

(c) Event Chains

(d) Modularity

Figure 13: Comparison of Bitcoin Simulation Traces (samples only).

be made between two samples, and (ii) there are well documented and easy to use libraries to compute these different metrics within the publicly available python ecosystem

A summary of the distance metrics results is presented in Table 1. Most of these results are computed on the resulting analysis vectors even when they were mismatched in size (*e.g.,* modularity). However, for the first analysis result (Events Available) some alignment is necessary. That is, for example, the number of points in the NeMo events available measure is 603,092 points whereas the sample trace contained only 29,362 points (see the number of simulation cycles on the x-axis of the graphs in Figure 3. With this large of a mismatch, the numeric distance measures would report excessively large results. As a result, for the events available metric, we simply picked equally distributed values from the full trace to match the number of measures in the sample trace.

In summary, the specific values for the distance metrics are not especially significant. What matters is their relative comparison to one another. Treated as relative values, one can (in a mechanized manner) observe the trend of change between samples. That should be sufficient in many situations for algorithmic decision making. For other situations, perhaps a significant value range for these or other metrics would be more desirable.

9 CONCLUSIONS

This paper explores the sampling of event trace data to profile various properties of Discrete-Event Simulation (DES) models. Studies were performed with two simulation trace files that were small enough that the entire trace could be analyzed but also large enough that 5 samples of varying sizes could be extracted from them for analysis. The analysis results from the full trace and samples were

Range of Events	W	DH	KS
Events Available			
26924114-27924114	108.40191388	270.11849252	0.06220096
76693804-77693804	95.48325359	31.14482300	0.06220096
126463494-127463494	94.75119617	50.24937811	0.03827751
176233184-177233184	105.00956938	133.01503674	0.07655502
226002874-227002874	116.36363636	292.04280508	0.05741627
Events Executed by LP			
26924114-27924114	0.00000099	0.00000889	0.13370000
76693804-77693804	0.00000084	0.00000689	0.12450000
126463494-127463494	0.00000080	0.00000783	0.11910000
176233184-177233184	0.00000076	0.00000783	0.12080000
226002874-227002874	0.00000075	0.00000683	0.11730000
Event Chains			
26924114-27924114	0.01117240	0.07425611	0.13333333
76693804-77693804	0.01046904	0.06146053	0.13333333
126463494-127463494	0.00999761	0.05587406	0.13333333
176233184-177233184	0.01073756	0.05778216	0.20000000
226002874-227002874	0.01037989	0.05461808	0.20000000
Modularity			
26924114-27924114	535.08771930	883.00000000	0.93333333
76693804-77693804	543.23456790	863.00000000	0.93333333
126463494-127463494	543.22222222	878.00000000	0.93333333
176233184-177233184	535.11403509	869.00000000	0.93333333
226002874-227002874	536.86147186	883.00000000	0.93333333

Table 1: Distance Metrics for the Epidemic model with sample multiplier = 100. The column heading abbreviations denote: W: Wasserstein Distance, DH: Directed Hausdorff, and KS: Kolmogorov-Smirnov.

compared to evaluate how closely the samples matched the full trace results. With respect to events executed, events executed by LP, and event chains, the results with sample sizes above 100 times the number of LPs matched the full trace results fairly well. However, the results of modularity were significantly different in all cases. That said, the communities produced from the modularity studies of the traces might well provide adequate results to replace (at least for partitioning purposes) the different results produced by the full trace file.

Originally the approach of sampling the full trace file was deemed necessary to enable the analysis of very large event trace files. While sampling does enable this capability, it also became clear that performing analysis on limited regions of the simulation trace could enable the discovery of emerging and dynamic properties that some DES models may exhibit.

ACKNOWLEDGMENTS

This material is based upon work supported by the AFOSR under award No FA9550-15-1-0384. The authors would also like to thank Philipp Andelfinger and his colleagues at the Karlsruhe Institute of Technology for their generous collection and contribution of DES trace file to this project.

REFERENCES

[1] A. J. Alt and P. A. Wilsey. 2014. Profile Driven Partitioning of Parallel Simulation Models. In *Proceedings of the 2014 Winter Simulation Conference*, A. Tolk, S. Y. Diallo, I. O. Ryzhov, L. Yilmaz, S. Buckley, and J. A. Miller (Eds.). Institute of Electrical and Electronics Engineers, Inc., Piscataway, New Jersey, USA, 2750–2761.

[2] V. Balakrishnan, R. Radhakrishnan, D. M. Rao, N. B. Abu-Ghazaleh, and P. A. Wilsey. 2001. A Performance and Scalability Analysis Framework for Parallel Discrete Event Simulators. *Simulation Practice and Theory* 8 (2001), 529–553.

[3] Christopher L. Barrett, Keith R. Bisset, Stephen G. Eubank, Xizhou Feng, and Madhav V. Marathe. 2008. EpiSimdemics: An Efficient Algorithm for Simulating the Spread of Infectious Disease over Large Realistic Social Networks. In *Proceedings of the 2008 ACM/IEEE conference on Supercomputing (SC '08)*. IEEE Press, Piscataway, New Jersey, USA.

[4] O. Berry and D. Jefferson. 1985. Critical Path Analysis of Distributed Simulation. In *Distributed Simulation*. SCS, SCS, San Diego, CA, 57–60.

[5] V. D. Blondel, J.-L. Guillaume, R. Lambiotte, and E. Lefebvre. 2008. Fast Unfolding of Communities in Large Networks. *Journal of Statistical Mechanics: Theory and Experiment* 10 (2008), 10008.

[6] Christopher D. Carothers, David Bauer, and Shawn Pearce. 2000. ROSS: A High-performance, Low Memory, Modular Time Warp System. In *Proceedings of the Fourteenth Workshop on Parallel and Distributed Simulation (PADS '00)*. IEEE Computer Society, Washington, DC, USA, 53–60. http://dl.acm.org/citation.cfm?id=336146.336157

[7] Patrick Crawford, Stephan J. Eidenbenz, Peter D. Barnes Jr., and Philip A. Wilsey. 2017. Some Properties of Communication Behaviors in Discrete-Event Simulation Models. In *2017 Winter Simulation Conference (WSC)*. 1025–1036. https://doi.org/10.1109/WSC.2017.8247852

[8] A Ferscha and J Johnson. 1996. A Testbed for Parallel Simulation Performance Predictions. In *1996 Winter Simulation Conference Proceedings*, J. M. Charnes andd D. J. Morrice, D. T. Brunner, and J. J. Swain (Eds.). Institute of Electrical and Electronics Engineers, Inc., Piscataway, New Jersey, USA, 637–644.

[9] Jean-Baptiste Filippi, Teruhisa Komatsu, and Kyushu Tanaka. 2010. Simulation of drifting seaweeds in East China Sea. *Ecological Informatics* 5, 1 (2010), 67–72.

[10] R. Fujimoto. 1990. Performance of Time Warp under Synthetic Workloads. In *Proceedings of the SCS Multiconference on Distributed Simulation*, David Nicol (Ed.), Vol. 22. SCS, San Diego, CA, 23–28.

[11] R. GarcÃa-MartÃnez and H. Flores-Tovar. 1999. Computer modeling of oil spill trajectories with a high accuracy method. *Spill Science and Technology Bulletin* 5, 5–6 (1999), 323–330.

[12] Sounak Gupta and Philip A. Wilsey. 2017. Quantitative Driven Optimization of a Time Warp Kernel. In *Proceedings of the 2017 ACM SIGSIM Conference on Principles of Advanced Discrete Simulation (PADS 17)*. ACM, New York, NY, USA.

[13] John L. Hennessy and David A. Patterson. 2012. *Computer Architecture: A Quantitative Approach* (5th ed.). Morgan Kaufmann Publishers Inc., San Francisco, CA, USA.

[14] D. Jefferson and P. L. Reiher. 1991. Supercritical Speedup. In *Proceedings of the 24th Annual Simulation Symposium*, A. H. Rutan (Ed.). IEEE Computer Society Press, 159–168.

[15] Y-B. Lin. 1992. Parallelism Analyzer for Parallel Discrete Event Simulation. *ACM Transactions on Modeling and Computer Simulation* 2, 3 (July 1992), 239–264.

[16] M. Livny. 1985. A Study of Parallelism in Distributed Simulation. In *Proceedings 1985 SCS Multiconference on Distributed Simulation*. SCS, San Diego, CA, 94–98.

[17] T. Neudecker, P. Andelfinger, and H. Hartenstein. 2015. A simulation model for analysis of attacks on the Bitcoin peer-to-peer network. In *2015 IFIP/IEEE International Symposium on Integrated Network Management (IM)*. 1327–1332. https://doi.org/10.1109/INM.2015.7140490

[18] Eun Jung Park, Stephan Eidenbenz, Nandakishore Santhi, Guillaume Chapuis, and Bradley Settlemyer. 2015. Parameterized Benchmarking of Parallel Discrete Event Simulation Systems: Communication, Computation, and Memory. In *Proceedings of the 2015 Winter Simulation Conference*, L. Yilmaz, W. K. V. Chan, I. Moon, T. M. K. Roeder, C. Macal, and M. D. Rossetti (Eds.). Institute of Electrical and Electronics Engineers, Inc., Piscataway, New Jersey, USA, 2836–2847.

[19] Mark Plagge, Christopher D. Carothers, and Elsa Gonsiorowski. 2016. NeMo: A Massively Parallel Discrete-Event Simulation Model for Neuromorphic Architectures. In *Proceedings of the 2016 ACM SIGSIM Conference on Principles of Advanced Discrete Simulation (SIGSIM-PADS '16)*. ACM, New York, NY, USA, 233–244. https://doi.org/10.1145/2901378.2901392

[20] Doug Weber. 2016. *Time Warp Simulation on Multi-core Processors and Clusters*. Master's thesis. University of Cincinnati, Cincinnati, OH.

[21] RO. Weber. 1991. Toward a comprehensive wildfire spread model. *International Journal of Wildland Fire* 1 (1991), 245–253.

[22] P. A. Wilsey. 2016. Some Properties of Events Executed in Discrete-Event Simulation Models. In *Workshop on Parallel and Distributed Simulation (PADS 16)*. ACM, New York, NY, USA.

An SDN-inspired Model for Faster Network Experimentation

Eder L. Fernandes
Queen Mary, University of London
e.leao@qmul.ac.uk

Gianni Antichi
University of Cambridge
gianni.antichi@cl.cam.ac.uk

Ignacio Castro
Queen Mary, University of London
i.castro@qmul.ac.uk

Steve Uhlig
Queen Mary, University of London
steve.uhlig@qmul.ac.uk

ABSTRACT

Assessing the impact of changes in a production network (e.g., new routing protocols or topologies) requires simulation or emulation tools capable of providing results as close as possible to those from a real-world experiment. Large traffic loads and complex control-data plane interactions constitute significant challenges to these tools. To meet these challenges we propose a model for the fast and convenient evaluation of SDN as well as legacy networks. Our approach emulates the network's control plane and simulates the data plane, to achieve high fidelity necessary for control plane behavior, while being capable of handling large traffic loads. We design and implement a proof of concept from the proposed model. The initial results of the prototype, compared to a state-of-the-art solution, shows it can increase the speed of network experiments by nearly 95% in the largest tested network scenario.

CCS CONCEPTS

• **Networks** → **Network simulations**; *Programmable networks*; • **Computing methodologies** → *Discrete-event simulation*;

KEYWORDS

Discrete Event Simulation, Network Emulation, Software Defined Networking

ACM Reference Format:
Eder L. Fernandes, Gianni Antichi, Ignacio Castro, and Steve Uhlig. 2018. An SDN-inspired Model for Faster Network Experimentation. In *Proceedings of SIGSIM Principles of Advanced Discrete Simulation (SIGSIM-PADS'18)*. ACM, New York, NY, USA, 4 pages. https://doi.org/10.1145/3200921.3200942

1 INTRODUCTION

Computer networks have become incredibly and unexpectedly large infrastructures, frequently underpinning a wide range of critical activities. While experimentation and innovation in these infrastructures is rather desirable, innovation (e.g., new routing protocols) or even simple alterations (e.g., changes in the topology or its configuration) result in often hard to predict behaviors. Experimenting on a real production network is problematic, and the sheer size of some of these networks can be overwhelming.

While physical testbeds are one obvious solution, they can be too costly, complex, and may suffer from tighter space constraints than the typically geographically distributed network under study. This makes the use of testbeds limited to very small-scale scenarios.

Network simulators and emulators have been extensively adopted as simpler and more accessible option for complex topologies. However, choosing the best approach between simulation or emulation is far from easy. Indeed, they both come with their own benefits and drawbacks. **Simulators** rely on mathematical and discrete-event models of reality, to reproduce the behavior of the network. Typically, network simulators achieve high reproducibility thanks to the underlying mathematical models, e.g., finite state machines. In contrast, the intricacy of configuration is a challenge to obtain solid results, given the large state-space they aim to reproduce.

On the other hand, **emulators** provide real network stacks and thus can be used to test for real behaviors. Although they can provide more realistic results than simulations, they are resource-consuming (as much as the emulated network), effectively restricting the emulated network size, especially when run on a single machine. While distributed versions of emulators increase scalability, it increases the cost of the deployment and its complexity, by for instance, requiring coordination among multiple machines.

Table 1 shows the main available options for simulating or emulating both legacy and Software Defined Networks (SDN) [6]. *Discrete Event Simulation (DES)* tools such as NS2 [4] and NS3 [9] are a good solution to foster reproducibility of network experiments. Unfortunately, the complexity to create experiments and the time required to run large scale simulations limits its potential. Fs-sdn [2] improves simulation speed, but its scope is limited to SDN environments. In contrast, emulators like Mininet [3] bring flexibility in terms of network creation, as well as for the real applications that can be used. Sadly, resource constraints make large scale experiments practically infeasible. Mininet-VT [11] and Selena [8] improve the emulation accuracy with virtual time scheduling approaches. Unfortunately, they slow down execution and require changes the Operating System kernel. Finally, S3Fnet [5] proposes an interesting mix of *Parallel DES* and emulation, to support larger scale experiments. However it also requires kernel changes and its speed suffers under high data plane loads.

This paper proposes a combination of DES and emulation but with a completely different spirit to S3fnet. While the latter emulates the TCP/IP networking stack for any traffic, we opted for

Permission to make digital or hard copies of all or part of this work for personal or classroom use is granted without fee provided that copies are not made or distributed for profit or commercial advantage and that copies bear this notice and the full citation on the first page. Copyrights for components of this work owned by others than the author(s) must be honored. Abstracting with credit is permitted. To copy otherwise, or republish, to post on servers or to redistribute to lists, requires prior specific permission and/or a fee. Request permissions from permissions@acm.org.
SIGSIM-PADS'18, May 23–25, 2018, Rome, Italy
© 2018 Copyright held by the owner/author(s). Publication rights licensed to Association for Computing Machinery.
ACM ISBN 978-1-4503-5092-1/18/05...$15.00
https://doi.org/10.1145/3200921.3200942

Table 1: Advantages and drawbacks of Network Emulators and DES

Tool	Type	Advantages	Drawbacks
NS2/NS3	DES	High reproducibility	Slower as scale increases, complex configuration
Mininet	Emulator	Flexible, real network stacks	Scale limited by machine resources
Mininet-VT/ Selena	Virtual Time Emulator	Increases emulation accuracy	Changes to kernel/hypervisor, slower execution
fs-sdn	DES	Fast and lightweight	SDN only, controller coupled to simulation
S3Fnet	PDES/Emulator	Large scale	Changes to kernel, slows down under high load

a solution that emulates only the control plane of the network, i.e., routing and SDN control protocols. Its rationale comes from two main insights related to control plane traffic: (1) it is the only one that can alter network behavior, hence to guarantee fidelity in an experiment it is important be close to its real counterpart, (2) there are way fewer control plane messages compared to dataplane traffic, so approximating/aggregating the dataplane is sufficient. Our solution is inspired by the SDN approach of decoupling control from data plane. In a nutshell, we propose a novel approach that emulates the network control plane and simulates the data plane. Our design speeds up simulation while keeping control plane fidelity. Additionally, our approach can be used to perform experiments on both legacy and SDN networks. We present a prototype and show how it succeeds in achieving rather low execution times that barely grow in a test with increasing network sizes.

2 A MODEL FOR CO-EXISTENCE OF SIMULATION AND EMULATION

Inspired by the original goal of SDN, our approach decouples control and dataplane, by emulating the former and simulating the latter. Such a separation introduces a key challenge: designing a solution that allows the simulation and emulation layers to co-exist. In our solution, both abstractions use different traffic granularities and concept of time. Whereas the former uses coarse granularity abstractions, e.g., flow models, and adopt a pure DES approach, the latter works in a per-packet manner and relies on a *Fixed Time Increment (FTI)* mechanic, to reproduce a continuous time environment. The platform thus runs DES when there is no interaction with the emulated control plane, and the FTI mode when control messages events are executed. The resulting model is scalable, as the amount of control traffic, i.e., routing protocol packets, SDN control messages, in networks is much lower than the data traffic. The two modes operate as follows:

Pure DES. In traditional DES, the simulation clock advances to the time of the most recent event. Algorithm 1 shows that the events are executed in DES mode until an event from the control plane happens. After such event, the simulator switches to the FTI mode to execute in real-time. The event with the highest timestamp possible in the system (e.g., in a 64 bits system the value is an unsigned 64 bits integer) signals the end of the simulation.

Fixed Time Increment. When triggered, the clock advances in equal time intervals, and all the events scheduled before the current time are executed (Algorithm 2). A user-defined parameter (**controller idle interval**) defines the interval required to switch back to the DES approach, when the interaction between the simulated and emulated planes is considered done. It is important to define an appropriate interval due to possible inconsistencies in

---

Algorithm 1 Discrete Event Simulation mode

1: **while** not $fixed\_mode$ **do**
2:     $event \leftarrow scheduler\_retrieve(scheduler)$
3:     $sim\_clock \leftarrow event.time$
4:     $handle\_event(event)$
5:     **if** $event.type = CTRL\_MSG$ **then**
6:         $fixed\_mode \leftarrow$ **true**
7:         Switch to FTI mode
8:     **else**
9:         **if** $event.type = END$ **then**
10:             Finish the Simulation
11:         **end if**
12:     **end if**
13: **end while**

---

the simulation. If the controller idle timeout is lower than the time required for the control plane to react to a control plane event, the simulation will switch to DES and execute the next event that might be ahead of a control plane reply. On the other hand, a too large value will slow down the execution, as the duration of the FTI mode will last longer than necessary.

Algorithm 2 Fixed Time Increment mode

1: **while** $fixed\_mode$ **do**
2:     $sim\_clock \leftarrow sim\_clock + 100$
3:     $event \leftarrow scheduler\_retrieve(scheduler)$
4:     **while** $event.type \neq END$ and $event.time \leq sim\_clock$ **do**
5:         $handle\_event(event)$
6:         **if** $event.type = CTRL\_MSG$ **then**
7:             $last\_ctrl \leftarrow event.time$
8:         **end if**
9:         $event \leftarrow scheduler\_retrieve(scheduler)$
10:     **end while**
11:     **if** $(sim\_time - last\_ctrl) \geq idle\_interval$ **then**
12:         $fixed\_mode \leftarrow$ **false**
13:         Switch to DES mode
14:     **end if**
15: **end while**

2.1 Dataplane Traffic Model

To be able to experiment with large topologies, we use a flow-level representation of network traffic, consisting of packets aggregated by common headers, but potentially differing in size (similarly to fs-sdn [2]). To account for traffic loss, we split flows' arrival and departure into two different events. Congestion occurs when the aggregated size of concurrent flows and same (output-port) destination arrive simultaneously to a node with insufficient output-port capacity. Currently, the system cannot compute the packet loss referred to a specific flow, so it randomly distributes the excess of traffic that will be dropped among all the competing flows.

3 A DESIGN FOR PAST AND FUTURE CONTROL PLANES

In this section we present the design of a simulator that uses the proposed model. Figure 1 pictures the general architecture of the solution. The top part represents the emulated network control plane. It supports future proof approaches such as the those based on a logically centralized SDN control or legacy protocols such as the *Border Gateway Protocol (BGP)*. The Connection Manager (CM) sits in-between the control and data plane, and delegates messages generated by events from the simulation to the emulation and vice versa. To avoid possible loss of performance caused by frequent changes from DES to FTI, some control plane traffic, like the connection of an SDN controller with switches and common *keep alive* messages are handled by the CM and never reach the simulation side. The bottom part of the figure depicts the simulated data plane. The Scheduler is responsible for adding and retrieving events from the Event Queue in the correct order. At the Event Handler, five events are processed: start of applications, arrival and departure of flows, control messages from and to the control plane. The last two trigger the mode change from DES to FTI. The Topology block contains the simulated logic of network nodes such as hosts, routers and SDN switches. Statistics from the simulation are stored in a file or an independent database, so it can be accessed by the control plane.

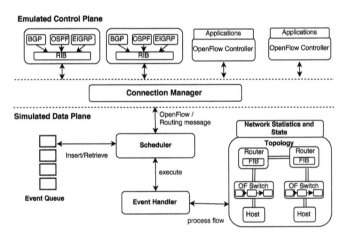

Figure 1: General Architecture of the Simulator

In the following, we show how our approach can work with both SDN solutions or legacy control plane protocols.

SDN. This is the most natural candidate, as our model is inspired in the control-data plane decoupling. In our design, the switches are nodes implementing OpenFlow [7], the most widespread SDN realization. Controllers are part of the control plane, thus can be real and independent software instances. Consequently, when interactions between SDN controllers and the network are needed,

the operation mode changes from DES to FTI. This change enables the controller to interact with the simulator in near real-time. Furthermore, new events from the controller are inserted in the event queue, ahead of data plane events with the same timestamp. This ensures the timely occurrence of control plane events preventing data plane disruptions (e.g., traffic loss). We now illustrate this with the example of a controller reacting to an event from the data plane:

- The simulator starts in the DES mode and executes an event where a host sends a flow to a switch connected to it.
- The switch does not have an OpenFlow rule to handle the flow. Following the default no-match action, a message must be sent to the controller.
- When the message is executed, the system changes to FTI operation. The controller handles the message and sends a reply message which is added to the event queue.
- The reply from the controller is then executed, and the controller does not interact with the platform until the controller's idle timeout. The system switches then back to DES.

BGP. Applying a legacy control plane to our architecture can be done by enabling as many controllers as the data plane routers in the topology. Indeed, the logical difference between a logically centralized solution such as SDN and a distributed one, such as BGP, is that the former presents a mapping of one or more controllers for one to many switches, while in the latter case, each router has its own embedded controller. In this scenario, the emulated part runs lightweight BGP speakers (e.g., ExaBGP [1]) that allow real BGP sessions in the control plane to generate the *Routing Information Base (RIB)*. From the RIB, the *Forwarding Information Base (FIB)* can be derived and installed in the data plane.

In the BGP design, announcements are sent to the control plane from the simulation side, triggering the FTI mode. The CM will instruct the emulated BGP speaker to create a real announcement to its destination. The receiving BGP peer will then store the reachability information and build the local RIB. Finally, a FIB can be derived and installed in the respective simulated router as an event coming from the control plane. Upon BGP convergence, the system is expected to resume to the pure DES mode.

4 PROOF OF CONCEPT AND EVALUATION

In this section we present and evaluate a prototype of our approach, which is publicly available [2]. The prototype is implemented in C with Python bindings for the *Application Programming Interface (API)*, to enable simpler creation and configuration of network scenarios. We abstract the connection of real controllers to the simulated data plane using an OpenFlow driver [10] in the CM. The CM runs in an independent thread with access to the Scheduler, so the messages received from the controller can be added to the Event Queue. Each operation mode (i.e., DES and FTI) has its own thread that implements Algorithms 1 and 2, respectively. The thread of the FTI runs periodically every 100 milliseconds, although the time between two executions may vary slightly due to the system scheduling. For this reason, time increases in FTI as the difference between the system clock and the last execution of the thread.

[1]https://github.com/Exa-Networks/exabgp
[2]Repository: https://github.com/ederlf/paper-sigsim-pads-18

We compared our solution with Mininet, as it is the de-facto tool for SDN experimentation. Specifically, we assessed our solution in terms of speed and reproducibility[3]. Our experiment runs a traffic pattern five times in a k-ary Fat-Tree: a common topology for data centers. Each host sends 1Mbps of UDP traffic to a single destination over a 60 seconds period. The expected aggregated bandwidth per second, for the whole experiment, is equal to the number of hosts. The topology is rather appropriate for large-scale networks: it is composed of three layers of switches (edge, aggregation and core) connecting hosts in a number of pods equal to a variable k. The number of hosts increases exponentially with k, while the number of switches nearly doubles. The network consists of SDN switches controlled by one SDN controller that runs *Equal-Cost Multipath (ECMP)* to load-balance traffic among the links. All the links have enough bandwidth to avoid congestion, so the total aggregate traffic can be observed. To demonstrate that our solution runs fine in modest hardware, the experiments are performed in a computer with two physical cores at 2.9 GHz of speed and 8GB of RAM.

Our solution clearly achieves its goal of low execution times. Table 2 shows how our the execution times (in seconds) are almost constant as the network grows. Moreover, it takes just about 5% of the time it takes for Mininet to reproduce the largest scenario ($k = 8$).

Table 2: Comparison of the total execution time for 5 trials of experiments in a Fat Tree topology controlled by ECMP implemented as an SDN application.

k/switches/hosts	Our Approach	Mininet
4/20/16	57s	416s
6/44/54	58s	562s
8/80/128	60s	1141s

For reproducibility, we compare the average aggregated bandwidth in the 5 trials. The expected value for a test where k equals 6 and 8 is 54Mbps and 128Mbps, respectively. Figure 2 shows that our implementation reproduces the expected amount of traffic in both cases. On the other hand, Mininet struggles as the topology grows, because it requires much more computing resources, showing less traffic than expected in half of the experiment when $k = 8$.

Note that we also checked other tools from table 1. We experimented with an OpenFlow module for NS3 [1] but did not execute five trials per network size because a single run with with $k = 8$ took more than 50 minutes to finish. As for the other tools, the configuration overhead to implement the tests made them too time-consuming to obtain results in time for this paper. We hope to perform a thorough comparison in our future work.

5 CONCLUSION

In this paper, we presented a platform for fast and accurate reproduction of network experiments. Our architecture, inspired by the SDN approach of decoupling control and data planes, is based on an emulation layer for the control plane traffic, and a simulation layer for the dataplane traffic. We discussed how the proposed solution can be used to perform experiments on both legacy and

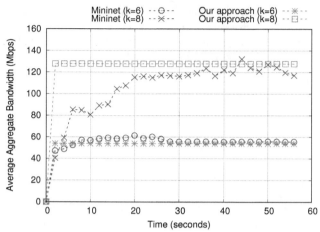

Figure 2: Comparison of the average aggregated bandwidth after 5 test trials using our approach and Mininet. The expected average value, during the whole experiment, for k=6 is 54Mbps and for k=8 is 128Mbps.

SDN-enabled networks. We implemented a proof of concept and assessed its potential by comparing speed and reproducibility capabilities, against state-of-the-art solutions such as Mininet. We found that our platform provides control plane fidelity, while delivering results nearly 95% faster than the most commonly used solution.

ACKNOWLEDGMENTS

This research is supported by the UK's Engineering and Physical Sciences Research Council (EPSRC) under the EARL: sdn EnAbled MeasuRement for alL project (Project Reference EP/P025374/1).

REFERENCES

[1] Luciano Jerez Chaves, Islene Calciolari Garcia, and Edmundo Roberto Mauro Madeira. 2016. OFSwitch13: Enhancing Ns-3 with OpenFlow 1.3 Support. In *Proceedings of the Workshop on Ns-3*. ACM, New York, NY, USA.
[2] Mukta Gupta, Joel Sommers, and Paul Barford. 2013. Fast, Accurate Simulation for SDN Prototyping. In *Hot Topics in Software Defined Networking (HotSDN)*. ACM.
[3] Nikhil Handigol, Brandon Heller, Vimalkumar Jeyakumar, Bob Lantz, and Nick McKeown. 2012. Reproducible Network Experiments Using Container-based Emulation. In *Conference on Emerging Networking Experiments and Technologies (CoNEXT)*. ACM.
[4] Teerawat Issariyakul and Ekram Hossain. 2010. Introduction to Network Simulator NS2. Springer Publishing Company, Incorporated.
[5] Dong Jin and David M. Nicol. 2013. Parallel Simulation of Software Defined Networks. In *Principles of Advanced Discrete Simulation (PADS)*. ACM.
[6] D. Kreutz, F. M. V. Ramos, P. E. Veríssimo, C. E. Rothenberg, S. Azodolmolky, and S. Uhlig. 2015. Software-Defined Networking: A Comprehensive Survey. (2015).
[7] Nick McKeown, Tom Anderson, Hari Balakrishnan, Guru Parulkar, Larry Peterson, Jennifer Rexford, Scott Shenker, and Jonathan Turner. 2008. OpenFlow: Enabling Innovation in Campus Networks. In *Computer Communication Review, Volume: 38, Number: 2*. ACM.
[8] Dimosthenis Pediaditakis, Charalampos Rotsos, and Andrew William Moore. 2014. Faithful Reproduction of Network Experiments. In *Architectures for Networking and Communications Systems (ANCS)*. ACM.
[9] George F. Riley and Thomas R Henderson. 2010. The ns-3 Network Simulator. In *Modeling and Tools for Network Simulation*. Springer Berlin Heidelberg.
[10] Allan Vidal, Christian Esteve Rothenberg, and Fábio Luciano Verdi. 2014. The libfluid OpenFlow Driver Implementation. In *32nd Brazilian Symposium on Computer Networks (SBRC)*. SBC, 8.
[11] Jiaqi Yan and Dong Jin. 2015. VT-Mininet: Virtual-time-enabled Mininet for Scalable and Accurate Software-Define Network Emulation. In *Symposium on Software Defined Networking Research (SOSR)*. ACM.

---

[3]This aspect is even more important than speed. With this test we look into the ability of a tool to reproduce results given same inputs.

ML-Aided Simulation: A Conceptual Framework for Integrating Simulation Models with Machine Learning

Mahmoud Elbattah
National University of Ireland Galway
Ireland
m.elbattah1@nuigalway.ie

Owen Molloy
National University of Ireland Galway
Ireland
owen.molloy@nuigalway.ie

ABSTRACT

Recent trends towards data-driven methods may require a substantial rethinking regarding the practice of Modelling & Simulation (M&S). Machine Learning (ML) is now becoming an instrumental artefact for developing new insights, or improving already established knowledge. Reflecting this broad scope, the paper presents a conceptual framework to guide the integration of simulation models with ML. At its core, our approach is based on the premise that system knowledge can be (partially) captured and learned from data in an automated manner, aided by ML. We believe that the approach can help realise adaptive simulation models that learn to change their behaviour in response to behavioural changes in the actual system of interest. Broadly, the study is conceived to foster new ideas and possible directions in integrating the practice of M&S with data-driven knowledge learned by ML.

KEYWORDS

Modelling & Simulation; Machine Learning.

ACM Reference Format:
Mahmoud Elbattah and Owen Molloy 2018. ML-Aided Simulation: A Conceptual Framework for Integrating Simulation Models with Machine Learning. In SIGSIM-PADS '18: SIGSIM Principles of Advanced Discrete Simulation, May 23–25, 2018, Rome, Italy. ACM, NY, NY, USA, 4 pages. https://doi.org/10.1145/3200921.3200933

1. Introduction

The ever-rising complexity of real-world problems and the abundance of information call for further utilisation of machine intelligence to assist the practice of Modelling & Simulation (M&S). In this respect, the M&S community has been reconsidering the emerging opportunities and challenges to the field in such an era marked by data-driven knowledge. For example, the 2017 edition of Winter Simulation Conference witnessed the inclusion of a new track named as 'Simulation & Analytics'. The new track is expected to develop as a stand-alone application of hybrid simulations. It is worth mentioning that earlier years also included similar tracks such as 'Data Analytics & Simulation Synergy' in 2015. This translates into the increasing trend towards integrating simulation methods

Permission to make digital or hard copies of all or part of this work for personal or classroom use is granted without fee provided that copies are not made or distributed for profit or commercial advantage and that copies bear this notice and the full citation on the first page. Copyrights for components of this work owned by others than ACM must be honored. Abstracting with credit is permitted. To copy otherwise, or republish, to post on servers or to redistribute to lists, requires prior specific permission and/or a fee. Request permissions from Permissions@acm.org.
SIGSIM-PADS '18, May 23–25, 2018, Rome, Italy
© 2018 Association for Computing Machinery.
ACM. ISBN 978-1-4503-5092-1/18/05...$15.00
DOI: https://doi.org/10.1145/3200921.3200933

with techniques from the data analytics sphere, such as Machine Learning (ML) for example.

Several studies also draw attention to the benefits of and needs for such integration. For example, a thought-provoking study [20] envisioned that the next generation of simulation models would be integrated with ML, and Deep Learning in particular. The study argued that bringing M&S, Big Data, and Deep Learning all together could create a synergy that can significantly improve services to other sciences. Another study [18] introduced the *Big Simulation* term to describe a set of grand challenges in this regard. Big Simulation addressed issues of scale for Big Data input, very large sets of coupled simulation models, and the analysis of Big Data output from these simulations, all running on a highly distributed computing platform. Similar studies (e.g. [16, 17]) discussed the potential of integrating System Dynamics (SD) models with Big Data, or other disciplines related to Data Science.

In this context, the study follows on the path of integrating simulation models with ML. The initial goal was towards realising adaptive simulations that can adjust their behaviour with minimal human input, if any. To achieve this, ML is implemented to continuously learn and predict the behaviour of the system of interest. With a hybrid approach, simulation experiments are guided by ML models trained to make predictions on the system behaviour.

2. Motivation: Modelling Dynamic Behaviour of Systems Aided by Machine Learning

Jay Forrester [1] described a model as a theory of behaviour, which represents the way in which some parts of the real system works. Simulation models are developed to replicate such behaviour with some level of realism based on knowledge from experts and/or empirical data, or other sources.

However, systems inherently exhibit dynamic, goal-seeking, self-preserving, and sometimes evolutionary behaviour, making a system more than simply the sum of its parts, as Meadows [4] emphasised. With such dynamic behaviour, a simulation model may become an inadequate representation of reality over time. This is what is described as the *Concept Drift* [5]. The Concept Drift refers to modelling a non-stationary problem over time, where a changing context can lead to a mismatch between models and actual problems.

In this respect, we pose the following question: what if simulation models can become aware of new information or knowledge in an automated manner? In other words, what if a simulation model can adapt to new situations without being explicitly informed by a modeller or simulation expert?

In fact, that hypothetical question represented the key impetus for the study. Our initial view was to avail of ML to realise a self-adapting behaviour in simulations. To focus the study's objectives, the questions below were formulated:

1. How can simulation models learn about changes in the actual system's behaviour or conditions with minimal human input?
2. Is it possible to integrate simulation models with ML models in a way that enables that learning process to happen in an automated manner? If so, how?
3. Can the integration with ML lead to a higher level of confidence in simulations, given by a more measurable accuracy of ML models?

3. Related Work

The work presented could be viewed from different contexts in literature. However, it is believed that the development of hybrid simulations could be more relevant.

As suggested by [14], a hybrid M&S study refers to the application of methods and techniques from disciplines like Operations Research, Systems Engineering and Computer Science to one or more stages of a simulation study. Likewise, this study aimed to integrate simulation models with a method from the Computer Science discipline (i.e. ML). Viewed this way, we aimed to review hybrid studies that attempted to integrate simulation methods with ML. To focus the search, two main sources were selected for review over the past 10 years including: i) Winter Simulation Conference, and ii) SIGSIM PADS. It is acknowledged that other relevant studies could have been published in other conferences or journals, but we believe that the selected venues provided excellent, if not the best, representative studies.

A good example is the study [13] that applied hybrid modelling, where simulation and ML were used altogether for a use case related to modelling the Panama Canal operations. A set of simulation models, including DES and SD, were used to generate information about the future expansion of the canal. This information was further used to develop ML models (e.g. neural networks) to help with the analysis of the simulation results. Another study [12] embraced a relatively similar approach with application to healthcare. They developed a hybrid approach that integrated a DES model with ML for discharge planning of patients. The study claimed that the use of ML could improve the credibility of simulation results.

Other recent studies (e.g. [9, 10]) tended to avail of ML techniques within the conceptual modelling phase. For instance, study [26] utilised data clustering in a healthcare problem. The discovered patient clusters represented stocks in the SD model. Interestingly, pertinent issues were recently featured in an industry workshop from PwC in the Winter Simulation Conference 2017 [15]. The workshop discussed the integration of simulations with AI techniques. For example, they demonstrated an agent-based model aided with reinforcement learning for autonomous fleet coordination.

The limitations of space unavoidably thwarted referring to more contributions. We view all those efforts as important and interesting endeavours that opened new frontiers for integrating simulations and ML. However, our critique is that most attempts can be largely described as ad hoc pursuits with no clear methodology. There is quite limited guidance of why, when, and how to integrate ML at different stages of M&S. Literature obviously lacked pragmatic studies that can practically address these issues, to the best of our knowledge. We believe that the M&S community needs further studies that formulate generalisable methodologies, and a collection of examples that help encourage and popularise that integration.

4. The Framework

The framework presented in this paper focuses on integrating simulation models with ML at the experimentation phase to realise adaptive behaviour. Our intention was to develop a conceptual framework that can serve as a guide to help this integration to develop in a consolidated manner. The following sections provide the key ideas embraced to develop the framework approach.

Key Idea I: Learning to Predict the System Behaviour

Starting with a basic outlook on the components underpinning a system. As viewed by Zeigler [3], a system is composed of a set of i) Structural description, and ii) Behaviour description. A typical simulation model is constructed based on the combination of both descriptions, as shown in Figure 1.

The initial view of our approach extends that structure by adding another component for ML integration. Generally, it is aimed to avail of ML to predict the behaviour of the system under study. It is assumed that the actual system produces sufficient amounts of data that can be used for ML training.

With this combination, a simulation experiment is intended to be guided by ML models trained to make predictions on the system behaviour. The predictions would reflect the behaviour of the system's actors, and how they would have likely reacted in the actual environment setting.

Key Idea II: Identify Predictable Influential Variables

It was briefly discussed how a simulation model could be augmented with ML. However, it may not seem reasonable to train ML models to predict all variables in a simulation model for many reasons. First, a typical simulation model can include a plethora of variables, so it would not be feasible to train hundreds or even tens of ML models. This can significantly overburden the process of building simulation models.

In addition, further issues have to be considered pertaining to the suitability of ML for the problem itself. As recognised in ML literature (e.g. [2]), a pattern has to exist within data in order to consider ML as a valid path for building predictive models. Therefore, ML would not be useful in case that the system behaviour largely occurs in a random manner.

To address these issues, our approach follows a simple process for screening variables ahead of building ML models. The screening process is particularly concerned with filtering system variables in terms of: i) Significance with regard to the system behaviour, and ii) Predictability. In other words, we seek variables that have a considerable influence within the problem context, and can be predicted. We refer to those variables as *Influential Variables*.

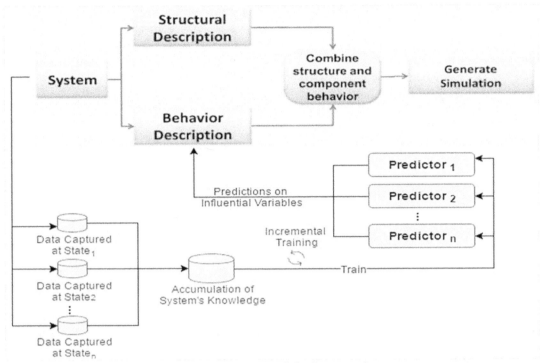

Figure 1: Overview of the framework.

Figure 2 outlines the screening process as a flowchart. The initial step is to identify variables that can have a significant influence on the system under study with respect to the question(s) of interest. Afterwards, two conditions have to be met. First, there should be enough empirical data for ML. Second, the initially screened variables should be presumably predictable. Means of data visualisation can be useful in this regard. Different types of plots can reveal promising patterns. If any of the two conditions are not met, then ML is not appropriate in that case. Subsequently, ML models can be trained/tested using data available. Eventually, trained models can be integrated with the simulation model.

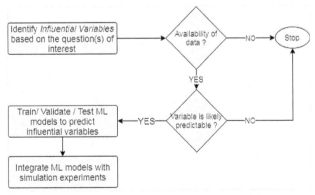

Figure 2: The process of screening variables.

Key Idea III: Incremental Learning = Adaptive Behaviour

The primary goal of our approach is to realise an adaptive simulation model that can adjust its behaviour with minimal human input. The behavioural adjustment would correspond to changes or new conditions in the actual system. This can only be realised if the ML training is an incremental process, rather than one-off. As such, ML models can play the proposed role of making the simulation model aware of new information or knowledge updates.

The idea of incremental learning is based on the premise that new system states are being continuously captured in timely snapshots of data, and added up to an accumulated repository representing the system knowledge. In this manner, ML models can be iteratively trained in order to learn about possible changes in system behaviour. Figure 1 visually concludes the framework along with the three key ideas presented.

The idea of incremental learning can be linked to one of the common concepts in systems modelling, which is the feedback loop. As viewed by Forrester [6], the feedback loop is a closed path connecting in sequence a decision that controls action, state of the system, and information about that state returning to the decision-making point. In this context, the central idea is to consider new data generated by the source system as a form of feedback. With such data-driven feedback, ML models can be continuously trained to reflect the system behaviour. The incremental training of ML models can therefore capture knowledge updates. In turn, changes in the system behaviour can be inferred through ML predictions. Figure 3 illustrates the rationale of our approach in a feedback loop-based fashion.

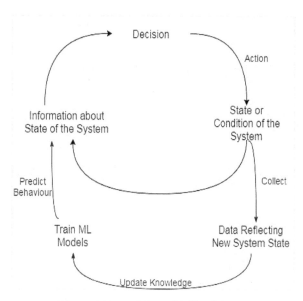

Figure3: Data-driven feedback loop.

5. Limitations

It is acknowledged that there would be other technical issues pertaining to the implementation of ML-guided simulation experiments. For example, what are the simulation software available that allow for a rapid injection of new states or transitions into a simulation model? More efforts are needed in this regard to prove wider applicability of the proposed framework and its practicality.

6. Conclusions & Future Directions

Augmenting ML capabilities into simulation models can be an enabler to realise an adaptive behaviour with minimal human input. This can forge a distinctive path for modelling dynamic systems that essentially exist in rapidly changing environments. Table 1 concludes the study's view with reflections on common definitions of ML.

We believe that the future holds further interesting possibilities for integrating the practice of Modelling & Simulation with ML. For example, more sophisticated ML techniques such as Deep Learning can be used in order to distil the knowledge underlying further complex systems or scenarios. In a broader sense, the need for constructing a high-fidelity representation of real-world problems shall bring up new practical aspects for taking advantage of ML potential.

Table 1: ML-aided simulation models.

Definitions of ML	ML-Aided Simulations (Simulation + ML)
The subfield of computer science that gives computers the ability to learn without being explicitly programmed [19].	Simulation models given the ability to adapt to new system knowledge without being explicitly informed by modellers.
Things learn when they change their behaviour in a way that makes them perform better in the future [7].	Simulation models learn when they change their behaviour in a way that makes them represent the system of interest better in the future.

REFERENCES

[1] Forrester, J.W., 1994. System Dynamics, Systems Thinking, and Soft OR. System Dynamics Review, 10(2-3), pp.245-256.

[2] Abu-Mostafa, Y.S., Magdon-Ismail, M. and Lin, H.T., 2012. Learning from data (Vol. 4). Singapore: AMLBook.

[3] Zeigler, B.P. and Sarjoughian, H.S., 2012. Guide to Modeling and simulation of systems of systems. Springer Science & Business Media.

[4] Meadows, D.H. and Wright, D., 2008. Thinking in Systems: A Primer. Chelsea Green Publishing.

[5] Schlimmer, J. C., and Granger, R. H. 1986. Incremental Learning from Noisy Data. Machine Learning, 1(3), 317-354.

[6] Forrester, J.W. 1968. Principles of Systems. MIT Press, Cambridge, MA.

[7] Witten, I.H. and Frank, E., 2005. Data Mining: Practical Machine Learning Tools and Techniques. Morgan Kaufmann.

[8] Forrester, J.W., 1961. Industrial Dynamics. MIT Press, Cambridge, MA.

[9] Abohamad, W., Ramy, A., Arisha, A., 2017, December. A Hybrid Process-Mining Approach for Simulation Modeling. In Proceedings of the 2017 Winter Simulation Conference (pp. 1527-1538). IEEE Press.

[10] Elbattah, M. and Molloy, O., 2017, December. Learning about Systems Using Machine Learning: Towards More Data-Driven Feedback Loops. In Proceedings of the 2017 Winter Simulation Conference (pp. 1539-1550). IEEE Press.

[11] Abu-Mostafa, Y.S., Magdon-Ismail, M. and Lin, H.T., 2012. Learning from Data (Vol. 4). New York, NY, USA: AMLBook.

[12] Elbattah, M. and Molloy, O., 2016, May. Coupling Simulation with Machine Learning: A Hybrid Approach for Elderly Discharge Planning. In Proceedings of the 2016 ACM SIGSIM Conference on Principles of Advanced Discrete Simulation (pp. 47-56). ACM.

[13] Rabelo, L., Cruz, L., Bhide, S., Joledo, O., Pastrana, J. and Xanthopoulos, P., 2014, December. Analysis of the Expansion of the Panama Canal Using Simulation Modeling and Artificial Intelligence. In Proceedings of the 2014 Winter Simulation Conference (pp. 910-921). IEEE Press.

[14] Powell, J. and Mustafee, N., 2014, December. Soft OR Approaches in Problem Formulation Stage of a Hybrid M&S Study. In Proceedings of the 2014 Winter Simulation Conference (pp. 1664-1675). IEEE Press.

[15] Wallis, L. and Paich M., 2017, December. Integrating Artificial Intelligence with AnyLogic Simulation. In Proceedings of the 2017 Winter Simulation Conference (pp. 4449-4449). IEEE Press.

[16] Pruyt, E., 2016. Integrating Systems Modelling and Data Science: The Joint Future of Simulation and 'Big Data'Science. International Journal of System Dynamics Applications (IJSDA), 5(1), pp.1-16.

[17] Pruyt, E., Cunningham, S., Kwakkel, J.H. and De Bruijn, J.A., 2014. From Data-Poor to Data-Rich: System Dynamics in the Era of Big Data. In Proceedings of the 32nd International Conference of the System Dynamics Society, Delft, Netherlands. The System Dynamics Society.

[18] Taylor, S.J., Khan, A., Morse, K.L., Tolk, A., Yilmaz, L. and Zander, J., 2013, April. Grand Challenges on the Theory of Modeling and Simulation. In Proceedings of the Symposium on Theory of Modeling & Simulation-DEVS Integrative M&S Symposium (p. 34). Society for Computer Simulation International.

[19] Samuel, A.L., 1959. Some Studies in Machine Learning Using the Game of Checkers. IBM Journal of Research and Development, 3(3), pp.210-229.

[20] Tolk, A., 2015, July. The Next Generation of Modeling & Simulation: Integrating Big Data and Deep Learning. In Proceedings of the Conference on Summer Computer Simulation (pp. 1-8). Society for Computer Simulation International.

Performance comparison of Cross Memory Attach capable MPI vs. Multithreaded Optimistic Parallel Simulations

Dhananjai M. Rao
Miami University
Oxford, Ohio
raodm@miamiOH.edu

ABSTRACT

The growth in many-core CPUs has motivated development of shared-memory, multithreaded solutions to minimize communication and synchronization overheads in Parallel Discrete Event Simulations (PDES). Analogous capabilities, such as Cross Memory Attach (CMA) based approaches have been added to Message Passing Interface (MPI) libraries. CMA permits MPI-processes to directly read/write data from/to a different process's virtual memory space to exchange messages. This paper compares the performance of CMA capable, MPI-based version to our fine-tuned multithreaded version. The paper also discusses implementation and optimization of the multithreaded infrastructure to elucidate the design alternatives being compared and assessed. Our experiments conducted using 2–28 threads and a fine-grained (time per event 0.7 μs) version of PHOLD benchmark shows that message-passing outperforms multithreading (by 10%–20%) in many scenarios but underperforms in others. The complex performance landscape inferred from our experiments suggest that more in-depth analysis of model characteristics is needed to decide between shared-memory multithreading versus message-passing approaches.

CCS CONCEPTS

• **Theory of computation** → **Data structures design and analysis**; • **Computing methodologies** → **Discrete-event simulation**; **Distributed simulation**;

KEYWORDS

Discrete Event Simulation (DES); Optimistic Parallel Simulation; Time Warp; Multithreading; Cross Memory Attach; NUMA; Ladder Queue (ladderQ); Three Tier Heap (3tHeap)

ACM Reference Format:
Dhananjai M. Rao. 2018. Performance comparison of Cross Memory Attach capable MPI vs. Multithreaded Optimistic Parallel Simulations. In *SIGSIM-PADS '18 : SIGSIM-PADS '18: SIGSIM Principles of Advanced Discrete Simulation CD-ROM, May 23–25, 2018, Rome, Italy.* ACM, New York, NY, USA, 12 pages. https://doi.org/10.1145/3200921.3200935

Permission to make digital or hard copies of all or part of this work for personal or classroom use is granted without fee provided that copies are not made or distributed for profit or commercial advantage and that copies bear this notice and the full citation on the first page. Copyrights for components of this work owned by others than ACM must be honored. Abstracting with credit is permitted. To copy otherwise, or republish, to post on servers or to redistribute to lists, requires prior specific permission and/or a fee. Request permissions from permissions@acm.org.
SIGSIM-PADS '18 , May 23–25, 2018, Rome, Italy
© 2018 Association for Computing Machinery.
ACM ISBN 978-1-4503-5092-1/18/05...$15.00
https://doi.org/10.1145/3200921.3200935

1 INTRODUCTION

Modern computational platforms are continuing to trend towards high density architectures with compute nodes having 2 or more, many-core CPUs. In these architectures, the main memory is shared between CPUs. Accordingly, shared-memory approaches for Parallel Discrete Event Simulation (PDES), often accomplished via multithreading, are gaining momentum [1, 3, 5, 11]. The primary advantage of shared-memory design stems from eliminating overheads of message-passing for *intra*-node communication by directly sharing events between threads. Prior investigators have reported good performance improvements using shared-memory multithreading approaches over message-passing designs [2, 10, 11]. Analogous optimizations have also been incorporated into the infrastructure of message-passing libraries. For example, Cross Memory Attach (CMA) capabilities, discussed in Section 1.1, have been added to the Linux kernel and Message Passing Interface (MPI) libraries to further reduce message-passing overheads.

Recently, in our cluster (details in Section 2) the number of CPU-cores per node more than doubled from 8 to 28 cores (with hyperthreading disabled). Consequently, we have significantly revised our MPI-based, optimistically synchronized PDES framework (discussed in Section 3) to operate in multithreaded mode. The overarching objective of multithreaded PDES is to realize better performance when compared to our message-passing design. Our multithreaded design, detailed in Section 4, uses decentralized pending event set design due to its advantages [1, 2] – *i.e.*, each thread has its own pending event queue and scheduler. Furthermore, we have explored several design alternatives to maximize multithreading performance, including: ❶ sharing-events between threads vs. exchanging copies, ❷ NUMA-aware memory allocation for events, and ❸ Lock-based vs. lock-free inter-thread queues. Section 5 compares and contrasts our designs to those proposed by other investigators. The objective is to identify and use the most performant design solution from the aforementioned alternatives.

Literature survey supported our hypothesis that multithreaded PDES would yield performance improvement over MPI-based implementations [1, 2, 11], particularly in fine-grained applications. However, experiments using fine-grained (time-per-event < 0.7 μsec), PHOLD benchmark revealed a more complex performance landscape, with MPI version (with CMA-capability) conspicuously outperforming multithreaded simulations and vice versa. The experiments discussed in Section 6 highlight the complex landscape with no clear winner. The results lead us to conclude that a comprehensive analysis of application characteristics (future work) is needed in order to choose between message-passing and multithreading designs.

1.1 CMA & Open MPI's vader BTL

Cross Memory Attach (CMA) is a mechanism to directly transfer data between the virtual memory space of two processes running on the same compute node – *i.e.,* intra-node Inter-Process Communication (IPC). CMA enables data transfer without passing through kernel space. CMA has been added to the Linux-kernel starting with version 3.2 (Jan 2012 release). In Linux, CMA is accomplished via two system calls, namely process_vm_readv and process_vm_- writev. CMA enables processes to accomplish "zero copy" intra-node data transfers. Note that in Linux parlance "zero copy" implies using a single copy of data (or messages) and avoiding overheads of requiring extra copies.

Starting with Open MPI version 1.8.4 (early 2015), the CMA capabilities of Linux have been used to develop a Byte Transfer Layer (BTL) subsystem called vader [9]. The vader BTL improves small message latency via "zero copy" transfers, typically via the process_vm_readv CMA system call [9]. The BTL has also shown to have substantially better throughput than traditional shared memory BTL, in multi-CPU nodes [9]. An experimental comparison of CMA-based vader BTL versus conventional shared memory BTL is discussed in Section 3

2 EXPERIMENTAL PLATFORM

The experiments reported in this paper have been conducted using shared-memory compute nodes with two (dual socket) Intel Xeon® CPUs (E5-2680 v4) with hyperthreading disabled. Each CPU has 14 cores and 35 MiB of shared L3 cache between the cores. Each core has 64 KiB L1 (*i.e.,* 32 KiB instruction + 32 KiB data split cache) and 256 KiB of L2 cache. The 128 GB of DDR4 RAM (64 GB per CPU) in Non-Uniform Memory Access (NUMA) configuration as detailed in Figure 1. The cores on the two CPUs are logically interleaved. Memory access time or distances is 10 units between cores on the same CPU but more than doubles to 21 units for cross-CPU memory access. The compute node runs Red Hat Enterprise Linux (kernel version 3.10.0-514) that supports Cross Memory Allocation (CMA). The simulation software and benchmarks were compiled using Intel C++ Compiler (ICC) version 16.0 at -03 optimization level. Open MPI version 2.1.2 with vader BTL that utilizes CMA capabilities (also compiled using ICC 16.0) has been used for inter-process communication.

```
$ numactl -H
available: 2 nodes (0-1)
node 0 cpus: 0 2 4 6 8 10 12 14 16 18 20 22 24 26
node 0 size: 130850 MB
node 0 free: 128020 MB
node 1 cpus: 1 3 5 7 9 11 13 15 17 19 21 23 25 27
node 1 size: 131072 MB
node 1 free: 122325 MB
node distances:
node 0 1
  0: 10 21
  1: 21 10
```

Figure 1: NUMA configuration on compute node

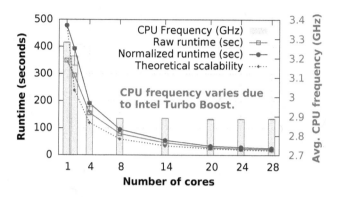

Figure 2: CPU frequency changes due to Intel® Turbo Boost & runtime normalization

2.1 Normalization due to turbo boost

The nodes used for experiments have Intel® Turbo Boost Technology 2.0 enabled. Consequently, the core frequency significantly varies, from base frequency of 2.4 GHz, depending on temperature and utilization of the node as shown in Figure 2. In our experiments the CPU-core frequency varied by about 12%. Furthermore, variations in CPU-core frequencies was also observed between successive runs, when the same number of cores were used – *e.g.,* with 2 cores a ±5% variation was observed. These variations in CPU clock frequency causes runtimes to vary resulting in inconsistent comparisons. Unfortunately, the compute cluster is a shared, state-wide resource which makes modifications to hardware or BIOS settings a cumbersome process.

Consequently, we have normalized all observed runtimes to a common CPU-core frequency of 2.4 GHz using the following equation:

$$t_{norm} = \frac{Cycles_{cpu}}{Utilization_{cpu} \times 2.4 \times 10^9} \quad (1)$$

where t_{norm} is normalized runtime, $Cycles_{cpu}$ is number of CPU cycles used, and $Utilization_{cpu}$ is CPU utilization averaged over the entire run of the program. Given c cores for a run, CPU utilization can be in the range $0 < Utilization_{cpu} \leq c$. The statistics for normalization is obtained by running all of the simulations via Linux perf and recording necessary CPU counters.

3 MPI-BASED DESIGN & OPTIMIZATION

The implementation and assessment of multithreading vs. CMA-enabled MPI has been conducted using a Parallel Discrete Event Simulation (PDES) framework called MUSE. It has been developed in C++ using object-oriented approaches and the Message Passing Interface (MPI). MUSE uses Time Warp and standard state saving approach to accomplish optimistic synchronization of the LPs. A conceptual overview of a parallel, MPI-based simulation is shown in Figure 3. The simulation is organized as a set of processes that communicate via MPI. Each process has one thread and manages a set of Logical Processes (LPs) assigned to it. Each process uses a centralized Least Timestamp First (LTSF) priority queue for managing pending events and scheduling event processing for all local LPs. LPs are permitted to generate events only into the future – *i.e.,*

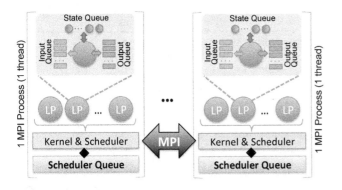

Figure 3: Overview of MPI-based PDES

the timestamp on events must be greater than their Local Virtual Time (LVT). Consequently, with the centralized LTSF scheduler, event exchanges between local LPs cannot cause rollbacks. Only events received via MPI can cause rollbacks.

The Logical Processes (LPs) in a simulation are developed by overriding necessary methods in an Agent base class. The input, output, and state queues used for rollback operations in Time Warp are managed by the Agent base class in coordination with the simulation-kernel. Similarly, the MUSE provides an Event base class that can be extended to implement custom events for use by the model. The simulation-kernel implements core functionality associated with LP registration, event processing, state saving, synchronization, and Global Virtual Time (GVT) based garbage collection.

3.1 PHOLD benchmark

Experimental analysis of design alternatives has been conducted using different configurations of the PHOLD benchmark. The PHOLD benchmark has been used by several investigators [2, 8, 11] for experimental analysis because it has shown to effectively emulate the steady-state phase of a typical simulation. Our PHOLD implementation provides a number of configuration settings to alter its behavior thereby streamlining design of experiments. In our experiments, we have used a PHOLD model with 10,000 LPs organized in a 100 ×100 torroidal grid. The simulation commences with 20 events (40 bytes per event) per LP, resulting in a pending event set of 200,000 events. The timestamps on the events is determined using an exponential distribution (λ=10). The destination LP for each event is computed using two different approaches as detailed in the following subsections. Additional details on our PHOLD benchmark is included in supplementary materials.

3.1.1 Config #1: Fixed Inter-LP interactions (strong scaling). This configuration reflects a typical parallel simulation experiment in which the properties of the model do not change based on number of processes/threads. In this mode of operation, the range of LPs to which events are scheduled is bounded by a value specified via the recvr-distrib command-line argument to PHOLD. Specifically, given an LP with ID k and a recvr-distrib value of x, a destination LP d is uniformly chosen from the range $k - \frac{x}{2} < d < k + \frac{x}{2}$, with wrap around due to toroidal space. The choice of destination LPs is determined by value of x and does not change with partitioning. In other words, the behavior of the model is independent

of the number parallel processes used, reflecting a strong scaling configuration. However, it must be noted that, as the number of partitions (or parallel threads/processes) are increased, the probability of Inter-Process Communication (IPC) increases, resulting in increased synchronization overheads. In our benchmarks we have used the following values for the recvr-distrib (*i.e., x*) – 10, 100, 1000, and 10000. Note that larger values result in increased probability of IPC.

3.1.2 Config #2: Fixed fraction of remote events (weak scaling). Events exchanged between pairs of processes or threads are called *remote* events. In our design, only remote events can trigger rollbacks, which play an influential role on the performance of optimistic PDES. In other words, communication characteristics strongly influence probability of rollbacks, with increased remote events resulting in increased *probability* of rollbacks [7, 11]. Accordingly, this configuration is designed to fix the number of remote events to assess its impact in a controlled manner. Specifically, each LP chooses a destination such that the fraction of *remote* events remains fixed. The fraction of remote events (in the range 0.0 to 1.0) is specified via a remote-events command-line argument to the benchmark. Since remote events between any pair of threads is fixed, the communication and synchronization overheads are also bounded, immaterial of number of process/threads used. This setting is analogous to weak scaling configurations that are often used for performance assessments [11]. It must be noted that in Time Warp synchronized parallel simulations, the net number of inter-process messages may vary due to exchange of anti-messages. In our benchmarks we have used the following fraction of remote events, *i.e.,* value for remote-events parameter: 0.1, 0.25, 0.5, 0.75, and 0.9.

3.2 Selection of scheduler queue

The Least Timestamp First (LTSF) priority queue associated with each process (or thread) plays a conspicuous role in realizing efficient and performant parallel simulation. In this study, we have used the Three-tier Heap (3tHeap) proposed by Higiro *et al* [4] as the scheduler queue rather than the Ladder Queue (ladderQ). The 3tHeap was chosen because it yielded better performance in several configurations, particularly in simulations with large number of events with small differences in virtual timestamps. Comparison of scheduler queues was performed using single process simulations in which state saving, rollbacks, GVT, etc. are automatically turned-off in the simulation-kernel. Single process simulations have used for comparisons for the following reasons: ① the ladderQ has been primary designed for use in sequential simulations. The 1 process simulation is analogous to a sequential simulation, thereby enabling consistent/fair comparisons; ② eliminating synchronization protocol overheads enables effectively isolating impact of scheduler queues; and ③ assess the fine-grained nature of the benchmarks used for further analysis.

The chart in Figure 4(a) illustrates a comparison between our ladderQ and 3tHeap implementations. The experiments were performed on the hardware platform discussed in Section 2 using the configuration of PHOLD benchmark discussed in Section 3.1. The total number of committed events in the simulation (the independent axis in Figure 4(a)) was varied by increasing the simulation end

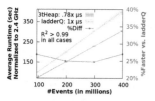

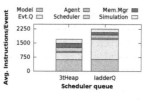

(a) Time & linear regression (b) Instruction use per event

Figure 4: ladderQ vs. 3tHeap: comparison of runtimes and instructions/event in a single process simulation

times. The chart plots the average runtime from 10 independent replications at each data point along with linear regression fits. The regression fits were very strong with $R^2 > 0.99$ in all cases.

Linear runtimes for ladderQ with amortized $O(1)$ runtimes is expected, as per its design discussed by Tang *et al* [8]. The average time for processing an event with ladderQ varied between 0.96–1.06 μs (normalized to 2.4 GHz as discussed in Section 2.1), based on 95% CI for the regression fit. The chart in Figure 4(b) shows the distribution of average instructions per event in the model. Each event requires about 2,374 instructions, of which 1,058 instructions (44%) are used by ladderQ operations. The PHOLD model uses 635 instructions to process an event, of which 50% is used by random number generation to determine future timestamps and destination LPs for scheduling new events.

Interestingly, the 3tHeap also exhibits a linear runtime profile for the PHOLD benchmark, as shown in Figure 4(a). We attribute this characteristic to the constant number of events (but with different virtual timestamps) in the simulation. Furthermore, the event processing time decreased to 0.77–0.79 μs (also normalized to 2.4 GHz), with the 3tHeap, as it requires only 619 instruction/event (instead of the 1,058 instructions for ladderQ). The 58% reduction in event count enables the 3tHeap to consistently outperform the ladderQ, but only by about 25%–27% (blue curve in Figure 4(a)) in our benchmarks. The discrepancy in speed is attributed to the following observations – ① some operations (such as, checking if queue is empty) requires a few additional instructions in the case of 3tHeap which slightly increases instruction counts within the simulation-kernel as illustrated by Figure 4(b); ② the CPU's instructions-per-cycle decreased slightly from 1.05 (*i.e.*, over 1 instruction/cycle on a superscalar core) for ladderQ to 0.95 (*i.e.*, a 10% decrease) with the 3tHeap. However, the CPU-cache hits per instruction was comparable for both queues indicating that caching was not a significant factor in performance difference. Overall, the 3tHeap provided performance improvement (when compared to Ladder Queue) for the benchmarks reported in this paper. Consequently, we have used it for all empirical analyses in this paper.

3.3 GVT-based Adaptive Time Window (ATW)

The first phase of this investigation focused on identifying effective configuration for MPI-based simulations. We have explored the effectiveness of both standard shared-memory Byte Transfer Layer (BTL) and CMA-based vader BTL in Open MPI. In our initial experiments, we observed that aggressive optimism was causing significant number of rollbacks, degrading performance. Therefore,

---

Algorithm 1: Adaptive Time Window algorithm

1 **begin rollback**(*agent*, *event*, *GVT*)
2   rbDist = e→recvTime - gvt;
3   adaptTW = avg(adaptTW, Δt);
4   **if** *adaptTW.samples > 100* **then**
5   timeWindow = adaptTW.mean;
6   **end if**
7 **end adaptRollback**
8 **begin scheduleEvent**(*agent*, *event*, *GVT*)
9   **if** *timeWindow == 0* **then**
           // time window not yet set
10   return **true**
11   **end if**
12   Δt = event→recvTime - GVT
13   **if** *Δt ≤ timeWindow* **then**
14   return **true**
15   **else**
16   adaptTW = avg(adaptTW, Δt)
17   timeWindow = adaptTW
18   **end if**
19 **end scheduleEvent**

---

we have implemented a GVT-based, Adaptive Time Window (ATW) algorithm summarized in Algorithm 1. It uses average rollback distance with respect to GVT to determine a "safe" time window in which events can be optimistically scheduled. Shorter rollbacks result in decreasing the time window restricting optimism. The event scheduler (*cf.*, scheduleEvent in Algorithm 1) uses the adaptive time window and GVT to schedule events. If an event's timestamp is within the time window then it is scheduled for processing. Otherwise, the difference between GVT and the event's timestamp is used to grow the time window. The ATW is a fully distributed algorithm in that it uses only locally available information. Moreover, the averaging approach using by ATW enables the algorithm to be immune to transient fluctuations in steady-state models. On the other hand, the shortcoming of averaging is that it it hinders quickly adaptation to non-transient changes in model characteristics. However, in this paper we have focused on steady-state benchmarks. Consequently, as discussed in Section 3.3.1 this algorithm proved to be effective in managing optimism.

3.3.1 Assessment of ATW for MPI-based PDES. Communication patterns influence rollback characteristics which strongly influences the behavior of the Adaptive Time Window (ATW) algorithm summarized in Algorithm 1. Consequently, have used Config #2 discussed in Section 3.1.2, with fixed fraction of remote events for assessing impact of the ATW. The charts in Figure 5 compare runtime (average and 95% CI from 10 replications) of the benchmark, with different fractions of remote events, with both CMA-enabled vader and shared memory (shown as Shr. Mem in charts) Byte Transfer Layers (BTLs) in Open MPI. The inset charts show raw percentage difference in runtime with respect to CMA/vader+ATW (—×—) setting, which outperformed all other configurations. As illustrated by the charts,, with shared memory BTL, the ATW (curve —•—)

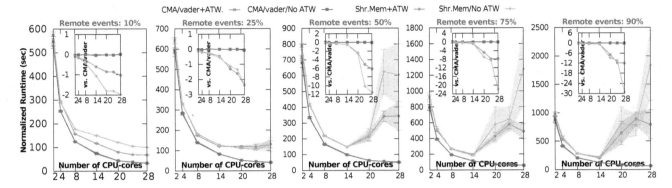

Figure 5: Performance comparison of PHOLD (Config #2 in Section 3.1.2) runtimes with different settings. In inset charts, data points below the zero-axis correspond to results in which CMA/vader+ATW performed better.

consistently outperforms the setting without ATW (curve —+—) and improves performance up to 200×, particularly in configuration with a large fraction of remote events. However, with vader BTL, the performance improvement with ATW (curve —■—) was statistically negligible (< ±2%) as illustrated by Figure 5. We attribute the lack of significant performance improvement to the low latency communication enabled by CMA-capable vader BTL. However, in some runs of Config #1 (see Section 3.1.1) the ATW yielded 10% performance improvement. Consequently, we have consistently used vader BTL with ATW in our subsequent experiments. We have also used ATW with our multithreaded configurations (cf., Section 6.1), because it provided more conspicuous improvements in several cases.

4   MULTITHREADING DESIGN & TUNING

In conjunction with this paper, we have extended our simulation framework to enable multithreaded PDES. The multithreading capabilities reuse our existing Application Program Interface (API). Consequently, existing models and benchmark can be readily reused. Figure 6 presents an overview of our multithreaded PDES infrastructure. The design of our multithreaded infrastructure mirrors several key elements from the MPI-based design discussed in Section 3. A multithreaded PDES is organized as a collection of interacting threads. Each thread is synonymous to an MPI-process (see Figure 3). Each thread manages lifecycle activities of LPs partitioned to it, including: scheduling events, state saving, rollback recovery, and GVT-based garbage collection. We have retained the API, design, and model-specific characteristics from our MPI-based design. Consistency in API and design enables effective reuse of existing models by isolating it from the underlying framework's operational modes. Moreover, it enables consistent comparison of performance of different framework features and optimizations.

The design of event scheduling and pending event management also similar to our prior MPI-based design. Each thread uses an independent local scheduler queue (e.g., a 3tHeap) for managing pending events. The internal framework design is identical to the MPI-design thereby enabling reuse of existing priority queue implementations. In this study, we have used the Three-tier Heap data structure proposed by Higiro et al as discussed in Section 3.2.

As illustrated by Figure 6, the multithreaded design uses decentralized scheduler queues – i.e., one scheduler queue per thread to manage pending events. Each thread has its own GVT manager (reused from our MPI-based implementation) that uses Mattern's GVT algorithm. Currently, the scheduler queues operations do not involve any locking or lock-free instructions; i.e., they are not designed to be thread-safe. On the other hand, implementation, optimization, and validation of the queues is relatively straightforward when compared to their concurrent counterparts. Most of the design is similar to our MPI-based implementation making them comparable. However, certain key aspects differ and are discussed in detail in the following subsections.

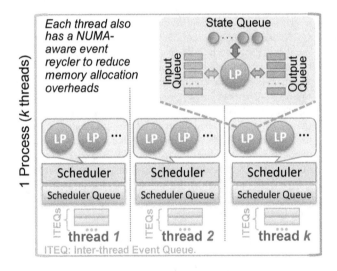

Figure 6: Overview of multithreaded PDES

4.1   Inter-thread Event Queues (ITEQs)

In our framework, all inter-thread communication is accomplished via exchange of *conventional pointers* (we currently do not use std::shared_ptr, std::unique_ptr etc.) through one or more Inter-thread Event Queues (ITEQs). In our design, the ITEQs of one thread are accessible by any other thread. Given k ITEQs per thread, when an event e (or kernel message) is to be sent from thread t_a to t_b, an ITEQ $iteq_i (0 \le i < k)$ in the destination thread t_b is chosen via bit-wise-AND (&) operation – *i.e.*, $iteq_i = recvr(e)$ & $ITEQ_{mask}$, where $ITEQ_{mask} = 2^{\lfloor log_2 k \rfloor} - 1$ and $recvr(e)$ is the destination LP's unique ID (an integer value). In other words, $ITEQ_{mask}$ is the nearest, lower power of 2 minus 1 so that all of its least-significant-bits set to 1. The mask covers the full set of ITEQs when k is an integral power of 2, but a smaller subset in other cases. We use bit-wise-AND over modulo to ensure maximum performance. Note that, in our design, the selection of ITEQ is based on the destination (or receiving) LP's ID because it generally varies the most between consecutive events exchanged between pairs of threads. The variation helps to distribute events between different ITEQs to further minimize thread contention.

Since ITEQs are the only source of contention between threads, we have assessed the following two different types of ITEQs to ensure a performant implementation:

❶ Lock-based ITEQ: As the name suggested, lock-based ITEQ use standard `std::mutex` (from C++11) to serialize concurrent operations on it. Each ITEQ is just a standard `std::vector` which contains a list of conventional pointers to the queued events. Locking/unlocking of the mutex is performed at individual ITEQ level to ensure finer-grained locking. Events are always appended to the queue and involve locking/unlocking the mutex. However, dequeue operations are performed in bulk – *i.e.*, all queued events are removed as a batch to reduce mutex overheads. The dequeue events are moved into a temporary list that is used for further thread-local processing.

❷ Lock-free ITEQ: Lock free data structures take advantage of special atomic instructions to enable concurrent, thread-safe operations without any direct interaction with the operating system. Lock-free operations are guaranteed to finish in a finite number of steps, with some operations taking longer depending on contention. We have used `boost::lockfree::queue` from the BOOST C++ library for implementing lock-free ITEQ. In order to fully realize its efficiency, we have used a fixed size queue. In BOOST, fixed size queues are implemented using arrays rather than linked lists thereby improving cache performance. We have used a fixed size of 2048 entries. This value is a balance between memory use (as number of ITEQs grow) versus cost of retries if queue is full. In our experiments, this limit was seldom reached. Unlike bulk operation in the lock-based version, in lock-free ITEQs entries are dequeued one at a time as necessitated by its lock-free implementation.

4.1.1 ITEQ processing periodicity. Each thread periodically processes events in its ITEQs at the end of processing a batch of events for each LP, similar to our MPI-based implementation. In our experiments, varying the periodicity did not have a statistically significant impact on simulation performance. Consequently, we have used a periodicity of 1 in our experiments – *i.e.*, poll for incoming events after each LP completes processing events at a given virtual time.

4.1.2 Choice and number of ITEQs. The number of ITEQs per thread (*i.e.*, k) is a balance between thread contention and overheads of processing each ITEQ. Fewer ITEQs increase contention but reduce iterations required to process each queue. This subsection

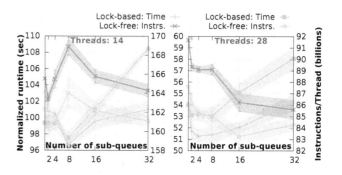

Figure 7: Comparison of lock-based vs. lock-free Inter-thread Event Queues (ITEQs)

discusses experiments conducted to identify effective choice of ITEQs and the value for k, *i.e.*, the number of ITEQs per thread. The experiments have been conducted using `Config #2` (weak scaling mode) of PHOLD, discussed in Section 3.1.2, with 50% of the events being exchanged between threads. Full set of charts is included in supplements.

The charts in Figure 7 provide a comparison of normalized runtime for different simulation configurations with lock-based and lock-free ITEQs (additional charts in supplements). The 14 thread runs used only one CPU (14 cores/CPU) while 28 thread runs used two CPUs. The charts in Figure 7 show that the lock-based queues generally outperform their lock-free counterparts. In all cases, the net number of events (including anti-messages) exchanged between threads was comparable. The net number of events slightly increased by about 6% with increase in threadsdue to 10% increase in rollbacks (charts in supplements). Nevertheless, the poor performance of lock-free queues was counter-intuitive to the putative understanding of lock-free implementation in the scientific community. Consequently, we conducted more detailed analysis using Linux `perf` profiler.

The charts in Figure 7 also provide a comparison of the total number of instructions executed by each thread in the different configurations. Perplexingly, the lock-free implementation generally executes fewer instructions than its lock-based counterpart and is yet slower. The lower number of instructions is expected because lock-free operations are accomplished in user-space using special instructions. In contrast, lock-based operations require interaction with the operating system, thereby generally requiring more instructions. Further analysis of the profiler data showed that the root cause in degraded performance of lock-free queues arises from from two key factors summarized in Figure 8 – ① the number of committed Instructions per CPU-clock cycle (Instr./cycle) is degraded for lock-free queues – *i.e.*, 0.7 ± 0.16 (lock-based) vs. $0.0.65 \pm 0.18$ (lock-free) or 7.7% degradation. This degradation is attributed to the atomic instructions which require additional coordination between CPU cores. The degradation in Instr./cycle is most pronounced with 28 threads at 11% (*cf.*, Figure 8). ② A small but consistent degradation was observed in Last Level Cache (LLC) hits reported by Linux `perf` as shown in Figure 8. The slight increase in cache misses is expected with atomic instructions as CPU has to maintain cache coherence across the cores. However, the cache miss rate is small

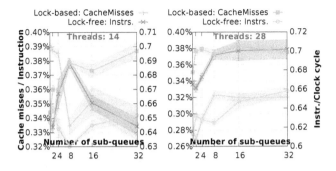

Figure 8: Lock-based vs. lock-free ITEQs: Instrctions/CPU-cycle & cache misses

and does not have a significant impact as illustrated by the 8 and 14 thread configuration in which cache miss rates were comparable and yet the runtimes are slower due to degradation in Instr./cycle.

In summary, these experimental analysis enabled us to identify the following settings for Inter-thread Event Queues (ITEQs) for further empirical analysis: ❶ the lock-based ITEQs are a better design alternative as they provide consistently better performance than the lock-free queues in a broad range of settings; and ❷ Lowest runtimes were generally observed when the number of ITEQs (k) was half the number of threads – i.e., $k = \frac{n}{2}$, where n is number of threads.

4.2 Shared vs. non-shared events

Our multithreaded infrastructure supports two different strategies for exchanging events (as conventional pointers) between threads – ① non-shared mode where copies are exchanged for all inter-thread events, and ② shared mode in which a single copy of an event is shared by two threads. These two modes are primarily a tradeoff between overheads of an extra copy versus the overheads of releasing the event during event cancellation or garbage collection. Freed events are recycled to minimize memory management overheads as discussed in Section 4.3. Furthermore, these two approaches also impact CPU-cache performance.

Non-shared events incur copy overheads but releasing the event for recycling is straightforward and is accomplished using a simple reference counter (a byte) in each event. A simple reference counter is necessary and sufficient because because an event is stored locally on a thread. Consequently, only one thread ever modifies the reference counter streamlining recycling of events.

On the other hand, shared events do not have copy overheads but incur some garbage collection overheads. In the case of shared events, two separate reference counters are maintained per event, one for the sending thread and another one for the receiving thread. The dual-counter design eliminates concerns of race conditions and thread-safe operations. However, when one thread releases an event, it cannot be immediately recycled because another thread may still be holding the pointer. Consequently, with shared-events, GVT-based garbage collection requires two phases. First, when the reference counter for the sending process reaches zero, the events are not immediately recycled but stored in a temporary list. This list is processed in subsequent garbage collection cycles and only

events where both counters are zero are recycled. The intermediate list can be large (millions of event pointers) depending on number of inter-thread events. Therefore, processing this list adds garbage collection overheads that are absent in the non-shared mode.

4.3 NUMA-aware Memory Management

Non-Uniform Memory Access (NUMA) is the most commonly architecture for high density compute nodes. The compute nodes used for experiments in this paper also have a NUMA configuration as summarized in Figure 1. NUMA-aware Memory Management (NMM) has shown to improve performance in several multithreaded simulation studies [5, 11]. Consequently, we have included NMM for events in our multithreaded simulation framework. The NMM layer can be enabled or disabled at runtime and can be used with both shared or non-shared event modes (cf., Section 4.2). Our NMM is designed as a static object with thread local storage – i.e., each thread gets its own unique, global instance of the NMM. Consequently, thread contention or synchronization is not an issue. Operations of this layer is transparent to the model. The NMM layer provides two key functionalities. It enables NUMA-aware recycling of events to minimize memory management overheads. In addition, it also acts as a lower-level memory management layer as discussed in the following subsections.

4.3.1 NUMA-aware memory recycling. When NMM is enabled, memory for events is allocated on the NUMA-node associated with the destination thread where the brunt of event processing occurs. Each event allocation is routed to the NMM layer which first attempts to recycle previously freed events allocated on the destination NUMA-node. The event recycling infrastructure is relatively straightforward. For each NUMA-node, a hash map called `RecycleMemMap` of free events is maintained. The key into the `RecycleMemMap` is the size (in bytes) requested and each entry contains a list (implemented using `std::stack`) of memory chunks that can be reused. A stack is used here to increase probability of effective cache use. If a given size entry is found in the `RecycleMemMap` it is popped from the stack and returned. Otherwise, a request for memory is dispatched to the lower-level NUMA-memory layer. In order to enable correct recycling upon deallocation, the recycler reserves the first 4 bytes to store the NUMA-node number (an `int`). Then a memory aligned (alignment of events and messages is at 8 byte boundary) pointer is returned. Conversely, deallocation results in the freed chunk being pushed onto the appropriate stack in the `RecycleMemMap`, using the NUMA-node number stored just before the event. Note that all memory management operations occur using conventional pointers and C++'s in-place new operator.

4.3.2 Lower level NUMA memory management. The lower-level memory management operation is analogous to custom memory management accomplished by `operator new` in C++ – the memory manager allocates large, fixed-size blocks from which it allocates smaller chunks of varying sizes. The memory manager allocates large, fixed-size blocks of memory via call to `numa_alloc_onnode` library call. The block size is currently set to 64 KiB, but configurable at compile time. The memory manager tracks the blocks on various NUMA nodes to eventually free the memory blocks at the end of simulation (via calls to `numa_free`). Upon receiving a request from the event recycling layer, it returns the next chunk of memory. If sufficient memory is unavailable, then a new block of NUMA memory is allocated and returned.

4.3.3 Rebalancing of recycled memory chunks. With our NUMA-aware memory recycling strategy we observed significant imbalances in recycler performance based on simulation scenario. In several cases, the recycler hit rate (*i.e.,* ratio of successful reuse of events) would degrade from the desirable 90% or higher hit rate down to about 50%. The imbalance also causes memory growth which in long running simulations would eventually result in memory exhaustion. The source of the imbalance arises primarily from event interaction patterns and such imbalances have also been reported by prior investigations [11].

Accordingly, our NMM checks and redistributes recycled memory chunks to rebalance memory usage across the threads. Redistribution is triggered at end of GVT-based garbage collection and only when the unused recycled memory is 2× times greater than the memory actually allocated by that thread. The extra unused chunks are evenly redistributed to all of the other threads. Redistribution of events is a necessary aspect of NMM without which long running simulations would experience memory exhaustion [11]. As a side effect, it also enables to maintain high recycler hit rates and thereby reducing overall NMM overheads.

5 RELATED WORK

A key aspect of this paper relates to design and assessment of shared-memory multithreaded approaches for optimistic, Parallel Discrete Event Simulation (PDES). The use of shared-memory approaches for PDES have a rich and long running history, for both optimistic and conservative PDES, since early 1990s. Nevertheless, due to space constraints, this section focuses on more recent, closely related optimistic PDES investigations, while referring readers to references therein.

Chen *et al* [1] propose a global schedule mechanism based on distributed event queues to improve performance of shared-memory, multithreaded Time Warp PDES. Our multithreading design also uses distributed event queues, *i.e.,* one per thread. However, we do not use a global schedule mechanism and also account for NUMA in our memory management design. Dickman *et al* [2] explore the effectiveness of single versus multiple scheduler queues for multithreaded optimistic PDES. Their single vs. multiple Least-TimeStamp-First (LTSF) queues is comparable in design to the Inter-Thread Event Queues (ITEQ) used for exchanging events. However, in our design each thread has a single thread-local scheduler queue – *i.e.,* the ITEQs are not the scheduler queues. Even so, consistent with our experimental results, Dickman *et al* also conclude that using multiple queues improve performance. In a follow-up work to Dickman *et al*, Gupta *et al* [3] explore the use of lock-free queues for bottom of the Ladder Queue used for managing pending events. They report about 20%–30% performance improvement. Gupta *et al*'s use of lock-free queues for ITEQs is similar to our lock-free ITEQ implementation.

Wang *et al* [11] explore issues of enabling effective, multithreaded PDES and show performance improvements of 3× on Core *i7*, 1.4× on AMD Mangy-Cours (4 CPUs, 12 cores/CPU) , and 2.8× on the Tilera Tile64. Similar to their work, this paper also explores single

and multiple CPU configurations, explores NUMA-aware memory management, and effectiveness of multiple inter-thread queues. They compare against MPI-based ROSS simulator that uses a custom shared-memory inter-process message queue. In contrast, we compare against a more recent Cross Memory Attach (CMA) capable MPI implementation, albeit on one hardware platform. In addition, we also explore the effectiveness of lock-free implementation for ITEQs.

Vitali *et al* [10] explore the effectiveness of dynamically reassigning CPU-cores to different simulation-kernel threads to maximize performance. They propose a split design with the top-half focusing on per-LP operation while bottom-half managing inter-LP operations. Our design is monolithic with tight coupling between LP and the simulation-kernel. Pellegrini *et al* [5] propose a Linux-based NUMA-allocator that allows management of per-LP memory consisting of disjoint sets of pages while supporting both static and dynamic bindings. In contrast, our NUMA-aware Memory Management (NMM) layer operates purely in user-space. Recently, Pellegrini *et al* [6] propose fine-grained preemption and dynamic scheduling of high priority tasks to improve performance of multithreaded PDES. In our design LP operations are not preempted and currently we uses polling to process incoming messages. However, in our experiments we found that 90% of the time we had incoming messages to process, due to the low latency of both CMA-capable MPI and multithreaded ITEQs.

Importantly, it would be remiss not to stress that, similar to this research, every one of the aforementioned investigations also used PHOLD for assessments.

6 EXPERIMENTS & DISCUSSIONS

The experiments in this study focus on comparing the performance of CMA-capable MPI versus comparable multithreading solutions. The objective is to identify better of the two approaches, in terms of performance, so as to inform design choices for optimistic parallel simulations from a more generic context. In our analyses, the runtime characteristics of the CMA-capable MPI implementation has been used as the reference. Our multithreaded framework involves two major design alternatives, namely: use of shared events discussed in Section 4.2 and use of NUMA-aware Memory Management (NMM) discussed in Section 4.3. Accordingly, comparisons with multithreaded simulations has been conducted using the following four configurations: ❶ Shr.Evt+NUMA: Shared Events with NUMA-aware Memory Management (NMM), ❷ Shr.Evt/No NUMA: Shared Events without NMM, ❸ No Shr.Evt/NUMA: Shared events are not used and copies of events are exchanged between threads. However, this mode uses NMM, and ❹ No Shr.Evt/No NUMA: In this mode the use of shared events and the NMM are disabled.

All of the experiments in this section have the following common settings to minimize variables and streamline further analyses:

- Each configuration was run on a dedicated node, even if it did not utilize all of the resources. For example, a 2-thread run was conducted on a compute node with all 28 cores reserved. The ten replications for each configuration were run on the same node (one after another and not simultaneously). This setup was used to enable full utilization of caches and to minimize issues with turbo boost side effects.

- Runs with 14 or fewer cores/threads were conducted on a single CPU. Threads were pinned to the CPUs using Linux's `numactl` tool. Similarly process affinity was enforced for MPI-processes using `--cpu-set` feature available in Open MPI.
- All of the configurations were run with Linux `perf` to record CPU usage characteristics (account for Turbo Boost as discussed in Section 2.1) and CPU-cache performance.
- The MPI runs used event recycling and Adaptive Time Window (ATW) as discussed in Section 3.
- All of the multithreading runs used event recycling (immaterial of NUMA-awareness) and Adaptive Time Window (ATW). The number of Inter-Thread Event Queues (ITEQs) was set of half the number of threads, based on the calibration results discussed in Section 4.1.2.

The experiments have been conducted using PHOLD benchmark with 10,000 LPs, each generating 20 (pending event set of 200,000 events) with exponential distribution (λ=10) of time stamps values. As elaborated in Section 3.1, two different communication configurations has been used, namely: ① Config #1: Fixed Inter-LP interactions (strong scaling) and ② Config #2: Fixed fraction of inter-process events (weak scaling). Results from the experiments for these two configurations are discussed in the following subsections.

6.1 Effect of Adaptive Time Window (ATW) with Multithreading

First, we have assessed the effect of using our GVT-based ATW algorithm, discussed in Section 3.3, using the experimental procedure discussed in Section 3.3.1. The charts in Figure 9 provide a comparison of runtimes of the 4 multithreading configurations with and without ATW. For example, the purple curve (—•—) shows percentage difference between simulations with ATW versus without ATW, when using shared events and NUMA-aware Memory Management (NMM). Data points below the zero-axis correspond to results in which ATW performed better. With multithreading, overall the ATW provided performance improvements of up to 10%. In some cases it was a 2% slower which we conjecture was due to throttling of optimism. Nevertheless, since the ATW overall improved performance, we have consistently used ATW in our subsequent experiments, in an identical manner to our MPI-based simulations.

6.2 Config #1: Fixed Inter-LP interactions

The charts in Figure 10 illustrate a comparison of the observed runtime for CMA-capable MPI version versus the 4 different multi-threaded configurations. The charts show mean and 95% CI from 10 replications. The inset charts show raw percentage difference in runtime with respect to the MPI version. In the inset charts, data points above the zero-axis correspond to configurations in which the given multithreaded configuration outperformed the MPI version. As illustrated by the charts in the figure, among the 4 multithreaded configurations, the No Shr.Evt/No NUMA configuration (—•—) is generally the slowest. This is to be expected because of additional event copies as well as NUMA overheads. As expected, the NUMA-aware Memory Manager (NMM) layer reduces the overhead (cf., —•—), particularly when more than one CPU is used.

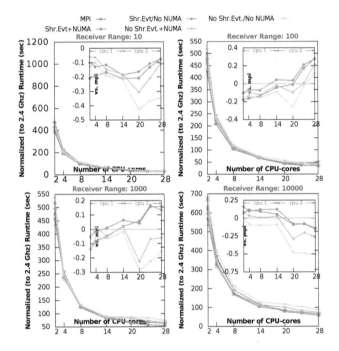

Figure 10: Config #1: Comparison of normalized runtimes. Inset charts show percentage difference versus MPI, with positive values indicating speed-up

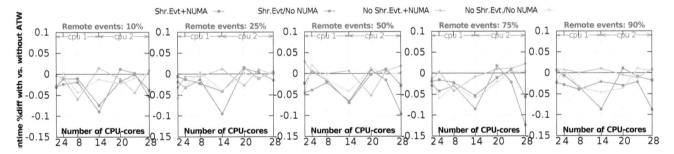

Figure 9: Multithreaded performance comparison of PHOLD runtimes (Config #2 in Section 3.1.2). Data points below the zero-axis correspond to results in which ATW performed better.

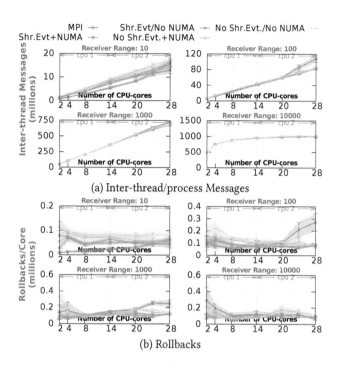

Figure 11: Config #1: Messages & Rollbacks.

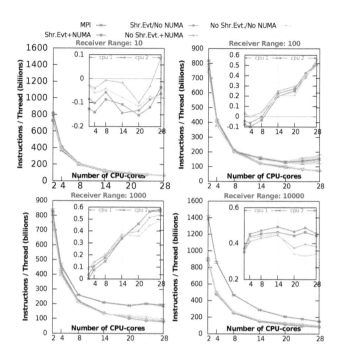

Figure 12: Config #1: Instructions executed. Inset charts shows percentage difference versus MPI, with larger positive values corresponding to fewer instructions.

The shared-events configurations, Shr.Evt+NUMA (——) and Shr.Evt/No NUMA (——) outperform the non-shared versions. This is expected because sharing events eliminates overheads of creating an extra copy of the events. However, the Shr.Evt+NUMA configuration with NUMA-awareness slightly under-performs the Shr.Evt/No NUMA configuration, particularly in single CPU settings by about 5%. The performance degradation is proportional to the slightly increased increased number of rollbacks experienced with Shr.Evt+NUMA as shown in Figure 11. However, the slight increase in rollbacks causes the net number of instructions (due to rollback recovery operations) to increase as illustrated by Figure 12. The inset charts in Figure 12 show raw percentage difference in number of instructions for crossvalidation. In these simulations, rebalancing operations used by NMM to redistribute unused memory (discussed in Section 4.3.3) that could impact performance, did not occur.

The runtime performance of CMA-capable MPI based runs (——) are competitive with the multithreaded version in many instances as illustrated in Figure 12. The "zero copy" capabilities of CMA-based MPI generally outperforms the No Shr.Evt. configuration as it eliminates the need to copy messages. In the lowest Inter-Process Communication (IPC) communication scenario with receiver range set to 10, the MPI-version experiences fewer rollbacks than the threaded version (cf., Figure 11(b)) and consequently outperforms all of the threaded runs. However, with the receiver range setting of 100, the MPI version experienced a conspicuous increase in number of rollbacks as shown in Figure 11(b) which degraded overall performance. Interestingly, in these high rollback scenarios, the superscalar capabilities of the CPUs were effectively utilized as illustrated by Figure 13. The number of instructions retired per CPU-clock cycle more than doubled from about 0.6 to

about 1.4 instructions/cycle. We conjecture that this improvement occurs because rollback recovery operates on consecutive events in batches, which improves speculative execution. Full set of charts are included in supplementary materials.

6.3 Config #2: Fixed fraction of remote events

Recollect that in this configuration the fraction of inter-process / inter-thread events called *remote* events is fixed as discussed in Section 3.1.2. The total number of remote events at remote event settings of 10%, 25%, 50%, 75%, and 90% settings were on average about 100.6 million, 251.7 million, 507.1 million, 762.8 million, and 917 million respectively (charts in supplements). These averages also include additional anti-messages exchanged during rollback recovery and show a slightly increasing trend, because probability of rollbacks increases with increased communication.

The charts in Figure 14 illustrate a comparison of the observed runtime for CMA-capable MPI version versus the 4 different multithreaded configurations. The inset charts show raw percentage difference in runtime with respect to the CMA-capable MPI version (——). In the inset charts, data points above the zero-axis correspond to configurations in which the given multithreaded configuration outperformed the MPI version. The charts in Figure 15 shows the corresponding number of rollbacks. All plots curves show mean and 95% CI from 10 replications for each data point.

As illustrated by the charts in the figure, the performance landscape is similar to those from Config #1. The shared event configurations perform better because extra copies of events are not created. However, between Shr.Evt+NUMA (——) and Shr.Evt/No

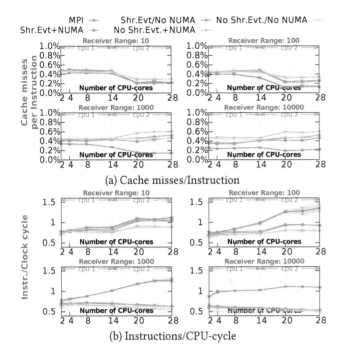

Figure 13: Config #1: Cache miss & instructions per cycle

NUMA (—■—), the NUMA-aware Memory Management (NMM) configuration has slightly lower performance. The performance gap arises due to two reasons. First, the NMM has one additional look-up overhead – *i.e.,* the NMM has to look-up the NUMA node ID corresponding to the receiving LP's ID in a hash map. The NMM also has a minor overhead when recycling events as it has to track the NUMA ID. These operations add 90 instructions/event on average, which is a 5% increase. Second source of performance degradation is attributed to the slightly higher number of rollbacks experienced by Shr.Evt+ NUMA (—■—) as illustrated by Figure 15. However, the performance gap between Shr.Evt+NUMA (—■—) and Shr.Evt/No NUMA (—■—) diminishes when cores on the second CPU are used – *i.e.,* core >14 in Figure 14 and Figure 15. In these configurations, the advantages of NMM outweigh its overheads.

Similar to Config #1 results (see Figure 10), the charts in Figure 14 also highlight the complex performance landscape when compared with CMA-capable MPI-based runs. In many cases, the MPI-based runs outperformed the corresponding fastest multithreaded runs by up to 20%. The performance trends are comparable to the trends in number of rollbacks shown in Figure 15. Interestingly, with 75% and 90% remote events, where number of rollbacks are comparable, MPI-based runs performed better with increasing number of cores. Profiler data showed that CPU-cache performances of MPI and the 2 shared-event configurations were comparable (charts in supplements).

However, the number Instructions per CPU-clock cycle (Instr./cycle) was much higher for MPI-based runs than for the multithreading runs, similar to Figure 13(b). We conjecture that the reduced Instr./cycle for multithreading arises from synchronization overheads. Recollect that threads synchronize only to add/remove events from the several shared Inter-Thread Event Queues (ITEQs). Even though having several ITEQs decreases contention, even the short synchronizations negatively impact speculative execution, decreasing Instr./cycle and thereby degrading performance. Nevertheless, overall the complex performance landscape poses a challenge in identifying a clear winning configuration. The results suggest that further analysis on model characteristics and model behaviors would be needed to choose between these alternatives.

7 CONCLUSIONS

The recent, steady trend towards increased CPU-core densities in compute nodes has stimulated investigations in using shared-memory, multithreaded approach over message-passing alternatives for Parallel Discrete Event Simulations (PDES). One of the primary advantages of of shared-memory approaches is that they provide opportunities to reduce communication and synchronization overheads. Motivated by the current research trends, we have significantly redesigned our MPI-based simulation framework to operate using multiple threads. This paper discussed details of our multithreaded framework, its decentralized design, implementation, and assessment.

In our decentralized scheduler design, inter-thread interactions were accomplished using one or more Inter-Thread Event Queues (ITEQs). Two alternative implementations for ITEQs was proposed and evaluated, namely: lock-based versus lock-free. Experimental results showed that despite its novelty, the lock-free implementation underperformed the lock-based implementation. Profiler data showed a key source of 7% performance degradation was due to reduction in instructions per CPU-clock cycle (Instr./cycle) for the lock-free implementation. The observation indicates that maintaining a higher Instr./cycle is more beneficial, suggesting that a spin-lock is a viable candidate for future assessments. The experimental data showed that given k threads, $\frac{k}{2}$ ITEQs yielded a good performance with lock-based ITEQs. This setting provides a good balance between thread contention versus overheads of processing multiple queues.

This paper also discussed and assessed two key design alternatives used in our multithreaded implementation, namely: shared vs. non-shared events and NUMA vs. non-NUMA memory management. Combinations of these alternatives were assessed using a wide range of strong-scaling and weak-scaling configuration of PHOLD benchmark. The simulations were fine grained (time-per-event as < 0.7 μsec), thereby emphasizing communication latencies. Results from our experiments show that overall shared-events setting in which events are shared between threads consistently perform better than the non-shared mode. Shared-events mode performs better because it eliminates the need to make copies of events. The NUMA versus non-NUMA modes had a mixed result based on configuration. When just a single CPU was used, shared-event with non-NUMA memory management performed better. On the other hand, NUMA-aware Memory Management (NMM) performed slightly better with 2 CPUs. However, there is room for fine tuning our NMM – the current implementation of our NMM includes one hash map look-up to determine the NUMA node, given an LP's ID. Reducing overheads of this look-up can further improve effectiveness of our NMM.

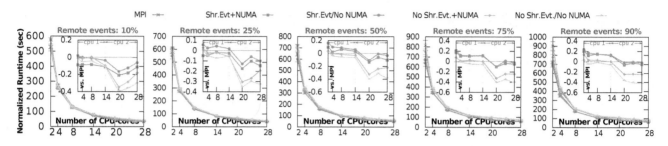

Figure 14: Config #2: Comparison of normalized runtimes. Inset charts show percentage difference versus MPI, with positive values indicating speed-up

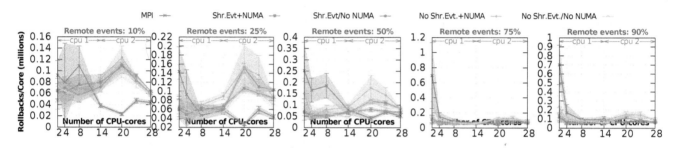

Figure 15: Config #2: Comparison of rollbacks corresponding to runs in Figure 14.

The performance of our multithreaded PDES framework was compared against our existing MPI-based, distributed memory alternative. However, a key aspect taken into account is the Cross Memory Attach (CMA) based capability introduced in the Linux kernel and Open MPI. CMA permits MPI-processes to directly read/write data to a different process's virtual memory space, thereby lowering the latency for exchanging messages. Our experimental analysis revealed a complex performance landscape with no clear winner – *i.e.*, the multithreaded, shared-memory approach performed better only in some cases when compared to the message-passing approach. With our weak-scaling benchmarks, the MPI-based version consistently outperformed the multithreaded version when 2 CPUs were used.

The complex performance landscape suggests that a split design could be beneficial – *i.e.*, multiple threads on a single CPU and message-passing for inter-CPU interactions. Of course, we plan to explore this design in our future work. More importantly, the complex performance landscape suggests that a careful assessment of "influential" model characteristics needs to considered to choose between multithreading versus contemporary CMA-capable message-passing solutions. This requires identification and ranking of model characteristics to determine the most influential ones, which also has considerable potential for future research.

Supplementary Material

Source code for MUSE and supplementary material available online at http://pc2lab.cec.miamiOH.edu/muse/

Acknowledgments

Support for this work was provided in part by the Ohio Supercomputer Center (Grant: PMIU0110-2).

REFERENCES

[1] L. Chen, Y. Lu, Y. Yao, S. Peng, and L. Wu. A well-balanced time warp system on multi-core environments. In *Proceedings of the 2011 IEEE Workshop on Principles of Advanced and Distributed Simulation*, PADS '11, pages 1–9, Washington, DC, USA, 2011. IEEE Computer Society.

[2] T. Dickman, S. Gupta, and P. A. Wilsey. Event pool structures for pdes on many-core beowulf clusters. In *Proceedings of ACM SIGSIM PADS*, pages 103–114, New York, NY, USA, 2013. ACM.

[3] S. Gupta and P. A. Wilsey. Lock-free pending event set management in time warp. In *Proceedings of the ACM SIGSIM PADS*, pages 15–26, New York, NY, USA, 2014. ACM.

[4] J. Higiro, M. Gebre, and D. M. Rao. Multi-tier priority queues and 2-tier ladder queue for managing pending events in sequential and optimistic parallel simulations. In *Proceedings of the 2017 ACM SIGSIM Conference on Principles of Advanced Discrete Simulation*, SIGSIM-PADS '17, pages 3–14, New York, NY, USA, 2017. ACM.

[5] A. Pellegrini and F. Quaglia. Numa time warp. In *Proceedings of the 3rd ACM SIGSIM Conference on Principles of Advanced Discrete Simulation*, SIGSIM PADS '15, pages 59–70, New York, NY, USA, 2015. ACM.

[6] A. Pellegrini and F. Quaglia. A fine-grain time-sharing time warp system. *ACM Trans. Model. Comput. Simul.*, 27(2):10:1–10:25, May 2017.

[7] D. M. Rao. Efficient parallel simulation of spatially-explicit agent-based epidemiological models. *Journal of Parallel and Distributed Computing*, 93-94:102–119, 2016.

[8] W. T. Tang, R. S. M. Goh, and I. L.-J. Thng. Ladder queue: An O(1) priority queue structure for large-scale discrete event simulation. *ACM Trans. Model. Comput. Simul.*, 15(3):175–204, July 2005.

[9] J. Vienne. Benefits of cross memory attach for mpi libraries on hpc clusters. In *Proceedings of the 2014 Annual Conference on Extreme Science and Engineering Discovery Environment*, XSEDE '14, pages 33:1–33:6, New York, NY, USA, 2014. ACM.

[10] R. Vitali, A. Pellegrini, and F. Quaglia. Towards symmetric multi-threaded optimistic simulation kernels. In *Proceedings of the 2012 ACM/IEEE/SCS 26th Workshop on Principles of Advanced and Distributed Simulation*, PADS '12, pages 211–220, Washington, DC, USA, 2012. IEEE Computer Society.

[11] J. Wang, D. Jagtap, N. Abu-Ghazaleh, and D. Ponomarev. Parallel discrete event simulation for multi-core systems: Analysis and optimization. *IEEE Transactions on Parallel and Distributed Systems*, 25(6):1574–1584, June 2014.

Parallel Application Performance Prediction Using Analysis Based Models and HPC Simulations

Mohammad Abu Obaida
Florida International University
Miami, FL
mobai001@fiu.edu

Jason Liu
Florida International University
Miami, FL
liux@cis.fiu.edu

Gopinath Chennupati
Los Alamos National Laboratory
Los Alamos, NM
gchennupati@lanl.gov

Nandakishore Santhi
Los Alamos National Laboratory
Los Alamos, NM
nsanthi@lanl.gov

Stephan Eidenbenz
Los Alamos National Laboratory
Los Alamos, NM
eidenben@lanl.gov

ABSTRACT

Parallel application performance models provide valuable insight about the performance in real systems. Capable tools providing fast, accurate, and comprehensive prediction and evaluation of high-performance computing (HPC) applications and system architectures have important value. This paper presents *PyPassT*, an analysis based modeling framework built on static program analysis and integrated simulation of target HPC architectures. More specifically, the framework analyzes application source code written in C with OpenACC directives and transforms it into an application model describing its computation and communication behavior (including CPU and GPU workloads, memory accesses, and message-passing transactions). The application model is then executed on a simulated HPC architecture for performance analysis. Preliminary experiments demonstrate that the proposed framework can represent the runtime behavior of benchmark applications with good accuracy.

CCS CONCEPTS

• **Computer systems organization** → **Parallel architectures**;
• **Computing methodologies** → **Modeling methodologies**; •
Software and its engineering → **Automated static analysis**;

KEYWORDS

Program analysis, high-performance computing, performance prediction, performance modeling, simulation

ACM Reference Format:
Mohammad Abu Obaida, Jason Liu, Gopinath Chennupati, Nandakishore Santhi, and Stephan Eidenbenz. 2018. Parallel Application Performance Prediction Using Analysis Based Models and HPC Simulations. In *SIGSIM-PADS '18 : 2018 SIGSIM Principles of Advanced Discrete Simulation, May 23–25, 2018, Rome, Italy*. ACM, New York, NY, USA, 11 pages. https://doi.org/10.1145/3200921.3200937

ACM acknowledges that this contribution was authored or co-authored by an employee, contractor, or affiliate of the United States government. As such, the United States government retains a nonexclusive, royalty-free right to publish or reproduce this article, or to allow others to do so, for government purposes only.
SIGSIM-PADS '18 , May 23–25, 2018, Rome, Italy
© 2018 Association for Computing Machinery.
ACM ISBN 978-1-4503-5092-1/18/05...$15.00
https://doi.org/10.1145/3200921.3200937

1 INTRODUCTION

High Performance Computing (HPC) is advancing towards exascale at a rapid pace; however, challenges of building such complex systems are manifold. First, hurdles exist in having system architectures to realistically scale to exascale in terms of cost, performance, and energy consumption. Second, one must ensure applications can also scale with the massive processing capability. Third, one needs to overcome difficulties in supporting workloads with unknown computation and communication patterns. Understanding and developing efficient parallel applications remains to be a challenging task in the context of fast-changing architectures.

Analytical models, simulation, hardware prototyping, and hybrid techniques are key methods to gain insight into application and system performance. Important challenges of such techniques, include quantifying computation and communication demands, identifying energy requirements, understanding scalability, and so on. Modeling methods including simulation, analytical and hybrid techniques heavily rely on models of application and architecture. The prediction accuracy, performance, scalability, and flexibility afforded by the models varies greatly.

Some of the compelling reasons for the prediction variation lie in the level of detail and granularity captured by different prediction methods. Analytical models [1–3] generally run fast, are flexible, and offer great scalability. However, high-level models lack accuracy. Detailed models of specific components do exist. Simulations, either functional or cycle-accurate, can offer better accuracy than analytical models. However, they can be time consuming to run and are oftentimes difficult to examine large applications.

These limitations prohibit rapid prototyping and reliable application co-design. Performance predictions for rapid prototyping has to be accurate while capturing necessary details of computation and communication. Moreover, such predictions has to be generated easily and quickly. Detailed simulations, such as Structural Simulation Toolkit (SST) [4, 5], GEMS [6], run more slowly and can generally model systems on a smaller scale. Distributed-memory "skeleton" application models, such as SST/macro [7], can offer faster to solution at a coarse grained level compared to previous techniques; however, the lack of modeling details may also preclude accurate results. For example, the communication models used by SST/macro inherit the inaccuracy of LogP [1] and LogGP [2] models, which cannot capture the necessary runtime effects from potential congestions in the interconnection network.

A number of modeling approaches build application models based on partial or complete real runs. For instance, ScalaExtrap [8] attempts to reduce the trace size of parallel communication by identifying and grouping similar message-passing patterns to extrapolate application communication for scalability studies. Acurdion [9] proposes some clustering techniques to reduce the trace size. FACT [10] is a communication simulator that extracts the parallel messages from application's source code. The above techniques are used to extrapolate and reproduce high-level application communication behavior. However, they do not include sufficiently detailed computation models to examine the time complexity of applications. In addition, unstructured communication may also lead to unrealistic representation.

To maintain accuracy and improve performance, flexibility, and scalability so as to allow studies of large-scale applications on HPC systems, we propose a parallel application performance prediction framework that combines analysis based models and HPC simulations. Important considerations have been given to balancing between performance and accuracy of the predictive framework. Four important aspects in combination set our framework apart from existing approaches.

First, our framework uses program analysis to capture application runtime behavior. Analysis based modeling makes predictions about the application by applying program analysis to application source code. There are prominent tools in this category, including ROSE [11], Cetus [12], and COMPASS [13]. Sophisticated analysis based performance models include ExaSAT [14] and PE-MOGEN [15], which are either limited to specific performance metrics, or apply to only certain types of applications or architectures. Program analysis can capture important dynamics of the application behavior, such as the shift of execution phases during runtime between computation-intensive and communication-intensive regions. Our proposed framework currently builds on analytical models using static program analysis.

Second, our framework uses abstract memory models in order to identify the data availability and data dependency. For that, we employ and extend the cache hierarchy models, PPT-AMM, by Chennupati et al. [16]. These memory models use static analysis using the intermediate representation (IR) of application source code. We represent the application source code as a probabilistic state graph where each node of the graph represents a basic block of an IR. Each of these basic blocks executes with a certain probability depending on the input of the program. We calculate the reuse distance [17] for each basic block. Combining all of them gives the memory reuse profile of a program, which is used further to estimate the cache hit-rate. We extend PPT-AMM to predict the resource usage such as number of floating-point operations, as well the load and store operations (in bytes). We use PPT-AMM to predict the runtime of the applications when executed on single-core CPUs.

Third, our framework incorporates workload models for accelerators. Most of the supercomputers today are featuring accelerators, such as Graphics Processing Units (GPU) and Xeon Phi, to improve data parallel applications and achieve higher flop counts. However, writing legacy applications for new architectures can be difficult. OpenACC [18] emerged as a standardization effort, which defines a set of directives that compilers can make use of to generate architecture dependent parallel code by transforming parallel kernels specific to accelerators or streaming processors. Modeling these accelerators is crucial in the performance prediction of modern HPC applications. Additionally, GPU code is optimized to support specific configurations. A detailed replication of the GPU execution by cycle accurate simulators would not be able to capture the application behavior on a wide range of accelerator platforms (including future architectures). To cope with this problem, our framework incorporates relatively high-level accelerator models to support performance prediction of application parallel kernels.

Last, our framework captures detailed communication behaviors of applications. It is often the case that communication is the bottleneck of HPC applications. For example, in [19, 20], the authors show that large variation in application performance can be attributed to changes in architecture and runtime conditions. In some cases, the performance penalty caused by runtime conditions, such as network state and improper task mapping, can increase application runtime significantly (e.g., over 200% for an application performing point-point communications among even-odd ranks). Our model represents detailed communication among the processors by preserving the message count and message size, as well as the spatial and temporal properties of the network transactions. In doing so, we can accurately capture the data movement of the applications over the HPC interconnection network.

The rest of the paper is organized as follows. In Section 2, we discuss related work. In Section 3, we first present an overview of the proposed framework, and then dive into the specific details about each component. In Section 4, we present experiments and show results that validate the proposed framework. Finally in Section 5, we summarize our findings and outline future work.

2 RELATED WORK

Recent advancements in model-based predictions include Aspen [21] and Palm [22]. Palm requires application developers to write an abstract model based on a good understanding of the application. Aspen is a domain specific language that bridges the gap between analytical modeling and application simulation. It defines both abstract application and machine models. While Aspen is shown to be able to capture the application performance with decent accuracy, it can still be difficult and time-consuming to build large-scale application models for exascale systems. This is a process that requires heavy developer involvement.

To automate application model building, Lee et al. proposed COMPASS [13] for Aspen. COMPASS is built on the Cetus compiler infrastructure [12] and the Open Accelerator Research Compiler (OpenARC) source transformation framework. Cetus is a Java-based C compiler that allows source-to-source transformation and passes for code optimization. It specializes in optimizing parallel programs. OpenARC is a complete implementation of OpenACC standard 1.0 built on Cetus. COMPASS takes application source code in C and transforms into an abstract Aspen model by using static analysis of the source. COMPASS has been shown to be able to capture application dynamics with several micro-benchmark applications, as well as some HPC applications, such as LULESH. Models generated by COMPASS do not include necessary communication and computation features. The model abstraction for Aspen does not include detailed communication and computation modeling.

Recently, Carothers et al. proposed Durango [23], an application performance modeling and simulation framework. Durango enables performance prediction using either synthetic workload generation or execution of Aspen application models generated using COMPASS. The execution engine of Durango is comprised of CODES [24] and Bigsim [25]. The former is a parallel workload simulator build on the parallel simulator ROSS [26]. Durango also supports trace-driven simulation. Durango models collective operations for the message-passing interface (MPI) in parallel applications fairly well. However, the point-to-point communications cannot be rendered accurately in Durango with necessary spatial features. In addition, the accuracy of computation model can be questionable for large application models. There is also no accelerator models in Durango.

Our work aims at improving the level of detail of parallel application performance prediction (especially for future architectures) and easing the burden of model development. Our system, *PyPassT*, is developed on the basis of static analysis and simulation modeling: a Python application model is generated using the Cetus compiler in multiple Passes and is then used by the Performance Prediction Toolkit (PPT) for performance prediction. In a nutshell, PyPassT combines the analytical model building capabilities from COMPASS [13] and PPT-AMM [16], and rapid HPC performance prediction simulation using PPT [27].

We use PPT [27], which is a rapid application and system prototyping framework and can predict the performance of large-scale applications on HPC architectures with good accuracy. PPT has been validated for different computational physics kernels [16, 28–30]. We chose PPT as the execution environment because of its rapid prototyping capabilities. PPT has detailed communication models and high-level compute models of processors, memory [16], accelerators [31] and application workloads [19]. PPT is built on Simian [32], a parallel discrete-event simulator implemented using just-in-time compilation for interpreted languages, such as Python, Lua and JavaScript.

3 OVERALL DESIGN

The proposed parallel application performance prediction framework consists of three core components: static analysis, model generation, and application execution. Fig. 1 sketches the architecture of the *PyPassT* prediction framework. First, the static analysis module takes the application source code and builds an abstract model by analyzing the sources statically. The model generation module, which is called PPT Transform, identifies CPU, accelerator, and communication kernels and builds an application executable model. The execution model is output in Python. Finally, prediction framework takes application model and launches it on Performance Prediction Toolkit (PPT) with desired model parameters. During the program execution in the simulation framework, performance counters can be collected which may be used for profiling and further analysis. In the following subsections we discuss the details of these modules.

3.1 Static Analysis

The goal of static analysis is building a model of the original application by analyzing source code independent of the deployment

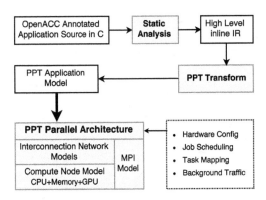

Figure 1: An overview of PyPassT prediction framework.

architecture. This stage takes parallel application source code written in C, annotated with OpenACC directives for parallelization by the accelerators, and outputs inline High Level Intermediate Representation (HLIR). It identifies communications, computations, memory, and GPU operations in the source code and converts to integers, flops, and MPI messages, stores and loads in between CPU/GPU. The proposed framework supports the OpenACC directives which builds the accelerated GPU model of the application sources.

3.1.1 Building Intermediate Representation (IR). IR builder takes the application source code and parses the statements to generate intermediate representation. The IR builder is built on *COMPASS*, a program analysis and model generation framework. COMPASS is originally intended for generating Aspen application models from OpenACC annotated C sources. It is built on OpenARC [33], which is an OpenACC annotated accelerator source compiler. It parses the input program and preprocessor directives and performs general optimizations. It provides traversable IR objects with iterators that can be used in breadth-first, depth-first, flat fashion, and so on. The IR can be seen as an Abstract Syntax Tree (AST) like syntactic view of the application source which can be further analyzed, summarized or optimized in different compiler passes.

In our implementation, COMPASS [13] is further extended to extract and abstract additional information about communication and computations from the statements in application source. Such information allows improved transformation and captures greater details about the messages and computations. As a result, volume, spatial, and topological properties of communication are preserved. Similarly, this enables computations to be modeled in a more realistic way. In the following sections we dive into the specific details of extraction and abstraction. For ease of making distinction, the modified static analysis framework, which abstracts application at a higher granularity, will be called *COMPASS++* in the rest of the paper.

Abstracting Computation: In COMPASS, Aspen execute blocks are the initial abstraction of computation happening in basic clocks. An expression analyzer analyzes the statements to find the computation, memory usage and attaches different attributes and traits to the control block. These attributes can be *flops*, representing computation, or *loads*, *stores*, *allocates*, *resizes*, and *frees*,

```
1  #pragma aspen control label(block_main38) loop((-2+n))
2  for(j=1; j<(n-1); j ++ ){
3
4  #pragma aspen control label(block_main40) loop((-2+m))
5    for (i=1; i<(m-1); i ++ ){
6
7  #pragma aspen control execute label(block_main41)
       flops(((((4*(-2+m))*(-2+n))):traits(dp, simd))
8  loads((((((4*aspen_param_sizeof_double)*(-2+m))*(-2+n))
       )):from(A):traits(stride(1))) stores(((((1*
       aspen_param_sizeof_double)*(-2+m))*(-2+n))):to(
       Anew):traits(stride(1)))
       Anew[j][i]=(0.25*(((A[j][(i+1)]+A[j][(i-1)]) +
9                        A[(j-1)][i]+A[(j+1)][i])));
10    }
11
12 }
```

Figure 2: COMPASS produces inline HLIR of CPU kernel.

```
1  #pragma acc  kernels loop gang(16) worker(16) copy(m,
       n) present(A[0:4096][0:4096], Anew
       [0:4096][0:4096]) private(i_0, j_0)
2  #pragma aspen  control label(block_main50) loop((-2+n)
       ) parallelism((-2+n))
3  for (j_0=0; j_0<=(-3+n); j_0 ++ ){
4  #pragma acc  loop gang(16) worker(16)
5  #pragma aspen  control label(block_main51) loop((-2+m)
       ) parallelism((-2+m))
6    for (i_0=0; i_0<=(-3+m); i_0 ++ ){
7  #pragma aspen  control execute label(block_main52)
       loads((1*aspen_param_sizeof_double):from(Anew):
       traits(stride(1))) stores((1*
       aspen_param_sizeof_double):to(A):traits(stride(1))
       )
8    A[(1+j_0)][(1+i_0)]=Anew[(1+j_0)][(1+i_0)];
9    }
10 }
```

Figure 3: COMPASS produces inline HLIR of GPU kernel.

```
1  #control statement
2  if (my_rank==0) {
3      execute  "block_stencil1d59" {
4          #mpi send/recv
5          messages [MAX_STRING] to (my_rank+1) as send
6          messages [MAX_STRING] from (my_rank+1) as recv
7      }
8  }
9  #mpi collective operation
10 execute "block_stencil1d66" {
11     messages [MPI_COMM_WORLD] as barrier
12 }
```

Figure 4: COMPASS++ produces communication kernel.

representing memory operations, or *intra-node* and *internode*, representing in-node or out-of-node transfers. Fig. 2 shows a COMPASS generated HLIR snippet of a compute kernel. The execute blocks are the basic compute and communication instruction sets, transformed from the original source code including inline abstractions. Fig. 3 shows the HLIR snippet of a GPU kernel, which identifies necessary block and grid sizes of the accelerator kernels.

Communication Extraction: The *PyPaasT* framework abstracts and reconstructs communication calls among the participating ranks. In the abstraction process, all such calls are preserved along with the supplied parameters except for the data or buffer used. In this way, we can guarantee that the spatial and temporal property of the communication is preserved during the abstraction. Detailed communication will allow modeling of application performance in various runtime conditions. Extraction has been previously explored to model parallel applications. Similar to the messaging abstraction used in the proposed framework, in an early effort Adve et.al [34] used compiler-optimized techniques to extract useful information about performance critical MPI calls, which was then used to drive large-scale simulation. Their work focuses mainly on modeling the communications at a detailed level while the consecutive task-list items are collapsed. In contrast, our work builds an abstract memory model that captures detailed memory

access patterns based on [16, 30] and simulates computation with a model of the target architecture.

Static analysis abstracts MPI calls as *messages*. COMPASS++ parses these library calls and collects necessary attributes sufficient for rebuilding MPI calls used in simulation, which include all parameters supplied to the MPI calls except the data. For point-to-point communication, it records {MPI_Call, sender, receiver, transfer size, domain} in the IR. For collective operations, {MPI_Call, root, size, *operation*, domain} parameters are kept. Figure 4 shows a sample representation of an MPI communication kernel generated by the COMPASS++ analysis and transformation.

3.2 Model Building: PPT Transform

At this stage, we build a representative execution model of the application source code by transforming the HLIR to the application model. The application model is generic and built on the positives of analytical modeling. Therefore, it can be transformed to any target framework. We configure the model builder to output the results in Python, which can then be simulated using the Performance Prediction Toolkit (PPT) [27]. The application model consists of kernels, which can be broadly classified as either computation kernels or communication kernels. A computation kernel is targeted for a CPU or an accelerator. We represent the COMPASS++ computation kernels in a format called *tasklist*, which represents different types of CPU/accelerator operations for PPT. The next step is to find the execution time of the *tasklist* on a target processor or accelerator. Once the compute time is known, the simulator invokes *sleep*, which suspends the simulation process representing the MPI rank for the exact duration. In sec. 3.2.1 and sec. 3.2.2, we discuss the details of building the computational models.

PPT features a packet based communication model with a detailed simulation implementation of the messaging passing interface (MPI) on interconnection network models. COMPASS++ generated communication kernels are formed of MPI point-to-point and communication calls, which provide sufficient details to reconstruct the operations in PPT. In the subsequent sub-sections, we discuss these models in greater detail.

3.2.1 Computation Model: Assume a program is parsed into a set of basic blocks that can be evaluated in a target architecture to obtain the computation time. For any basic block B_j we can

Table 1: Transformation Mapping

Declarations and Definitions	
scalar variable	scalar variable (Aspen param)
pointer variable	MEM_ALLOC (Aspen data)
global array	MEM_ALLOC (Aspen data)
function	function
Control-flow structures	
function call	function call (Aspen Kernel calls)
if statement	if statement (Aspen IfBlock)
for-loop	for-loop (Aspen IterateBlock)
for-loop	for-loop as gpu-kernel (Aspen MapBLock)
compound stament	compound statement (Aspen CompoundBlock)
expression statement	tasklist or communication calls (Aspen ExecuteBlock)

formulate the time spent in computation $T(B_j)$ as follows:

$$T(B_j) = T_{cpu}(B_j) + \Delta_{mem}(B_j) \tag{1}$$

where $T_{cpu}(B_j)$ is the fixed time required to execute instructions in B_j, and $\Delta_{mem}(B_j)$ is the time required to access main memory, which is dependent of the data availability:

$$\Delta_{mem}(B_j) = \delta_{loads}(B_j) + \delta_{stores}(B_j) \tag{2}$$

where $\delta_{loads}(B_j)$ is the time required to make the data available to CPU, and $\delta_{stores}(B_j)$ is the time required to write the results out to memory. If the data is already available before executing the instructions, $\delta_{loads}(B_j)$ will be 0. The framework statically analyzes an application to retrieve the values of Δ_{mem}. The application is compiled to generate the memory traces, which is then used to obtain the re-use profiles of memory references.

To generate the PPT application model the program HLIR is traversed in *depth-first* order and desired computation kernels are transformed into execution model. Table 1 shows the mapping of HLIR to PPT output.

In PPT, the simulation processes that represent individual MPI ranks model computation by sleeping for the time required to execute a set of instructions. PPT supports different kinds of operations, such as integer/float ALU operations. Table 2 lists the instructions currently supported by the PPT processor model.

Currently, Aspen supports only floating point operations called *flops* with single precision (*sp*), double precision (*dp*), and single instruction multiple data (*simd*) if it has *simd*-ized) traits. In the transformation phase these instructions are treated as fALU operations. In the future, we plan to extract more information from the static analysis so that the transformation can be more accurate and take advantage of all operations available in PPT. An example kernel is shown in fig. 5 where the *tasklist* is evaluated by a *core* (processor) model to determine the execution *time*.

Note that PPT supports clusters built with various processor models; therefore, the proposed framework can be used to model such architectures. In addition to predicting the computation time, PPT provides statistics relating to

Table 2: Processor Tasklist Operations

MEM_ACCESS	cycles to move data through memory and cache
HITRATES	direct input of cache level hitrates
L1	direct input of L1 accesses
L2	direct input of L1 accesses
L3,L4,L5, RAM,mem	direct input of higher cache and memory accesses
CPU ops	CPU operations
iALU	integer operations
fALU	floating point operations (add/multiply)
fDIV	floating point divisions
INTVEC	Integer vector operations
VECTOR	Integer vector operations
intranode	transfers within node (as memory access)

```
1  # select the right hardware
2  host = mpi_ext_host(mpi_comm_world)
3  core = host.cores[core_id]
4
5  # tasklist = {instructions}
6  tasklist = [["ALU", 5*ops], ["fALU", ops],
7    ["HITRATES",0.9,0.9,0.9,1,ops,1,1,2*ops,False]]
8
9  # evaluate with hardware model
10 (time, stats) = core.time_compute(tasklist, True)
11
12 # sleep for the duration
13 mpi_ext_sleep(time)
```

Figure 5: An example of a PPT compute kernel

Table 3: Accelerator Related Tasklist Items

alloc	[host] memory alloc. in # of bytes
unalloc	[host] memory de-allocate
DEVICE_ALLOC	device allocations
DEVICE_TRANSFER	device transfers
KERNEL_CALL	call a GPU kernel with block/grid

ALU and memory usage. Memory related statistics are reported as L1_float_hits, L2_float_hits, L1_int_hits, L2_int_hits, L1_int_misses, L2_int_misses, L1_float_misses, L2_float_misses, RAM accesses, L1 cycles, L2 cycles, and RAM cycles. CPU statistics are reported in the form of CPU cycles, iALU cycles, fALU cycles, fDIV cycles, INTVEC ops, INTVEC cycles, VECTOR ops, VECTOR cycles, internode comm time, intranode, and comm time.

A processor equipped with an accelerator supports an additional set of tasks. This set of instructions is required to issue transfers of data between host and device memory, invoking accelerator kernels and memory allocations. Table 3 shows a list of operations required to model an accelerator.

3.2.2 Analytical Memory Model: Analytical memory model (AMM) [16, 30] is a scalable performance model that relies on reuse distance [17] analysis. AMM employs compiler-driven static analysis, where the source code is transformed into an intermediate representation (IR) using LLVM. The AMM IR of a program consists

```
1  int main ()    {
2   int sum = 1, i;
3   for(i=0;i<N;i++)
4       sum+=i*2;
5  }
```

```
1  B0: (main, entry)
2  B1: (main, for.cond)
3  B2: (main, for.body)
4  B3: (main, for.inc)
5  B4: (main, for.end)
```

Figure 6: Program   **Figure 7: Basic Blocks**

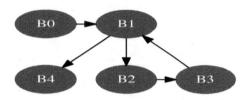

Figure 8: Probabilistic state graph

Table 4: Accelerator Tasklist Items

`GLOB_MEM_ACCESS`	access GPU on-chip global memory
`iALU`	integer operations
`diALU`	double precision integer operations
`fALU`	floating point operations(flops)
`dfALU`	double precision flop
`SFU`	special function calls
`L1_ACCESS`	direct GPU L1 accesses
`L2_ACCESS`	direct GPU L1 accesses
`DEVICE_SYNC`	synchronize GPU threads
`THREAD_SYNC`	synchronize GPU threads w/ CPU

of basic blocks; the program is represented as a probabilistic state graph. Each node of the graph is a basic block while the edges represent the control (execution) flow of the program.

Figure 6 shows an example program, Figure 7 presents the corresponding basic blocks, and Figure 8 is the corresponding probabilistic state graph. From the graph, Chennupati et al., [16] formulated the probability of executing a basic block, $P(B_i)$, as follows:

$$P(B_j) = \frac{N_j}{\sum_{i=0}^{n(B)} N_i} \quad (3)$$

where $n(B)$ is the number of basic blocks in a program, N_i and N_j are the number of times basic blocks B_i and B_j are executed. N_j relies on the number of times that particular basic block being called from its predecessor basic blocks:

$$N_j = \sum_{i \in Pred(j)} \pi_{ij} \times N_i \quad (4)$$

where π_{ij} is the transition probability from basic block B_i to basic block B_j, which can be measured using the LLVM coverage analysis. Here, N_j is a system of homogeneous linear equations with many solutions. Since most of the source code executes the starting basic block only once (i.e., $N_1 = 1$), we will have a finite set of linear equations whose cardinality is equal to the number of basic blocks of a program.

With $P(B_i)$, the reuse profile $Pr(D)$ of the program can be evaluated using the Gaussian mixture models:

$$Pr(D) = \sum_{i=0}^{n(B)} P(B_i) \times P(D|B_i) \quad (5)$$

where $P(D|B_i)$ is the conditional reuse profile of basic block B_i. We measure the conditional reuse profile using the basic block labeled memory traces. These traces are produced using the architecture independent application characterization tool, Byfl [35]. In order to guarantee scalability of our approach, we only sample (1%) the memory traces, similar to [36]. Moreover, we collect traces at a few smaller input sizes of a program, and use them to extrapolate the reuse profiles of larger inputs, similar to [30]. Using the reuse profiles of a program (Eq. 5) we measure the cache hit-rates, and

thereby predict the runtime of the program at any given input (as shown in Eq. 1).

Along with the runtime prediction, AMM can accurately measure the number of loads, stores, and floating-point operations of a program. With AMM IR, we access the memory references and floating-point operations, and employ the homogeneous system of linear equations (Eq. 4) in order to model resource specific operations.

3.2.3 Accelerator Model: PPT transformer identifies whether a compute kernel is intended for a CPU or an accelerator such as GPU. For a GPU kernel, the instructions belonging to it need to be transformed into a PPT accelerator kernel call with computations and memory transfers. In the proposed model, an HLIR with `#pragma acc` (OpenACC directive) and all other basic blocks that are rooted at it are treated as parts of the GPU kernel.

Intra-node communications (*intracomm*) are modeled as data transfer requests within a node in PPT. Additionally, *copyin* and *copyout* are translated as DEVICE_TRANSFER, which are data transfers between CPU's main memory and GPU's global memory.

In the model generation we retrieve *block* and *grid* sizes along with instructions that will ultimately be grouped as a *WARP*. WARPs are sequence of operations to be carried out by the accelerator cores. WARPs belonging to the same block and grid usually executes same set of instructions supplied as PPT GPU*tasklist*. Table 4 shows the available instructions in the PPT accelerator model.

In the current PyPaasT model, a WARP *tasklist* can be formed of *flops*, *loads*, and *stores* and is orchestrated in random sequence or some specific order as in the HLIR. One can define the chain dependency among the WARP instructions. Such as a floating point operation `fALU` may depend on a previous operations. This dependency can be imposed on the succeeding instruction by suppling the indexes of the previous operations. For example, the tasklist entry `['fALU', 2, 3]` implies `fALU` appearing at index 2 and 3 must be executed first before executing current instruction. Loop iterators will not be a part of WARP *tasklist* as those will be adjusted with grid and block sizes accordingly.

An alternative implementation of the COMPASS++ reported computations is building the WARPs from PTX [37] of CUDA kernels generated by OpenARC. The PTX model can be used to model detailed data availability. Fig. 9, shows an example GPU kernel which is evaluated with the processor (core) and accelerator model to determine the runtime and retrieve necessary hardware counters.

```
1  # accelerator warp instructions
2  GPU_WARP = [['GLOB_MEM_ACCESS'],
3      ['GLOB_MEM_ACCESS'], ['L1_ACCESS'],
4      ['fALU'], ['GLOB_MEM_ACCESS'],
5      ['GLOB_MEM_ACCESS'], ['L1_ACCESS'], ['dfALU']]
6
7  # calling the ward with block size and grid size
8  CPU_tasklist = [['KERNEL_CALL', 0, GPU_KERNEL,
9      blocksize, gridsize,regcount],['DEVICE_SYNC', 0]]
10
11 # evaluate with hardware model and collect statistics
12 now = mpi_wtime(mpi_comm_world)
13 (time, stats) = core.time_compute(CPU_tasklist,
14                                   now, True)
15 # sleep for the duration
16 mpi_ext_sleep(time)
```

Figure 9: An example *kernel* call in PPT

3.2.4 Communication Model. PPT supports similar constructs for messages as in the MPI standard implementation. Communication in the simulation is carried out as packet based transfers that are queued at router and host interfaces. This method enables modeling of congestion and runtime effects on application performance. We extended the existing COMPASS framework to abstract standard MPI communications and operations so that all the required parameters are extracted. Communication model in the PPT transform converts the MPI communication HLIR to equivalent PPT point-to-point and collective calls in the PPT transform.

A list of supported MPI operations include the following calls: MPI_Send, MPI_Recv, MPI_Sendrecv, MPI_Isend, MPI_Irecv, MPI_Wait, MPI_Waitall, MPI_Reduce, MPI_Allreduce, MPI_Bcast, MPI_Barrier, MPI_Gather, MPI_Allgather, MPI_Scatter, MPI_Alltoall, and MPI_Alltoallv. Once the application model is ready, it is evaluated using HPC simulation.

3.3 Execution Model

At this stage we execute the final application model in the PPT parallel simulator. The application model is launched in the simulation of the target HPC architecture. The application model is run in the presence of runtime conditions from job scheduling, task mapping, and network behavior. The existing options for runtime behavior model include:

- *Job Scheduling and Task Mapping:* PPT allows workload scheduling and task mapping among the available cores on the HPC architecture [19].
- *Background Traffic Model:* One can model the interference from other applications (we call background traffic). The interconnection network may experience congestion by implementing rate limiting on the queues or by introducing traffic flows (such as point-to-point communications) on the specific links shared by the application.
- *Interconnection and MPI* One can configure the interconnection network with various network topologies (such as *torus, dragonfly, fat-tree,* and *omni-path*) and set desired MPI parameters.

The simulator is designed for rapid prototyping. An execution model can be configured to collect certain hardware counters or traces. Once simulation is complete, results are reported in terms of time spent in computation, bandwidth of the memory used, and other hardware counters. In the following section, we discuss experiments to validate PyPassT performance prediction framework and report our findings.

4 EXPERIMENTS

In this section we discuss the experiments designed to validate the proposed framework, PyPassT. Our validations are performed in three different sets of experiments in order to assess the prediction accuracy. They are: i) computation model intertwined with analytical memory model (AMM), ii) accelerator model, and iii) communication model. The predictions in all three models are performed using PPT.

4.1 Computation Model with AMM

The first validation step of PyPassT, computation model intertwined with AMM (CAMM) follows the first principles, especially due to the static analysis on IR (see section 3.2.2). We show that the results of these models are valid when compared with the source code. Our validation of CAMM is two-fold: 1) we validate the resource utilization, and 2) we validate the predicted runtime.

We validate PyPassT-CAMM on compute intensive *Laplace2D* benchmark at four different mesh sizes, {64x64, 128x128, 256x256, 512x512}. *Laplace2D* occupies most of the processor cycles because of a large number of floating point operations in its compute kernel. The target machine used in the experiments contain two *Intel Xeon E5645* processors with a clock frequency of *2.4 Ghz* and *48 GB* of shared memory. The PPT-AMM model is configured with the same clock frequency and the respective cache sizes of *E5645*: $L_1 = 32K$, $L_2 = 256K$, $L_3 = 12288K$.

4.1.1 Resource Utilization. We validate resource usage in terms of the number of floating-point operations (FLOPS), memory loads and stores in bytes. We first generate the *ground truth* (the actual number of FLOPS, loads and stores) values of Laplace2D at four different input sizes. In order to generate the ground truth we compile the source code using *Byfl* [35][1], both with and without optimizations while vectorization is disabled. We measure FLOPS, loads and stores using the Byfl compilation flags -bf-types and -bf-inst-mix.

Figure 10 shows the resource utilization results (predicted versus measured) of Laplace2D when compiled with and without optimizations at four different experimental inputs. For the number of FLOPS, Byfl reported no difference in the measured values with and without optimizations, while there is a clear difference in the case of loads and stores. From the results, it is evident that the probabilistic state graph approach of AMM exactly predicts with respect to the ground truth. Another interesting observation is that, AMM prediction works for both with and without optimizations as opposed to the COMPASS prediction [13] of optimized resource utilization. In both the cases, we observe an accurate prediction when compared with that of COMPASS. Moreover, AMM promises a scalable prediction where the prediction results will remain consistent even when the input size increases, similar to COMPASS. In order to validate scalability, we experimented with three more mesh sizes

---

[1]an architecture independent application characterization tool, similar to PAPI

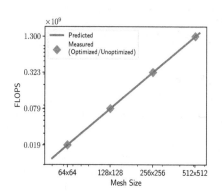
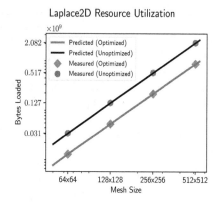
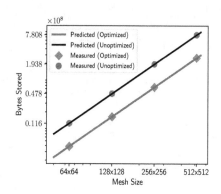

Figure 10: Predicted versus measured (with and with compiler optimizations enabled) resource usage of Laplace2D. Resource utilization is validated in terms of flops (left), loads (middle) and stores (right) in bytes. The validation results indicate an exact prediction for both with and without optimizations.

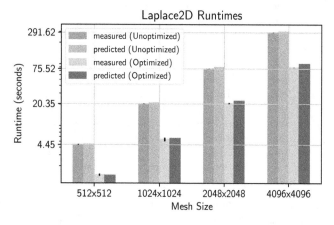

Figure 11: PyPassT-CAMM measured versus predicted runtimes (with and without optimizations) of Laplace2D benchmark at four different mesh sizes.

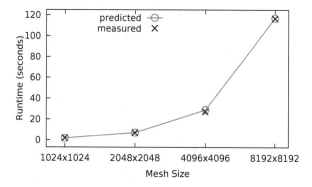

Figure 12: Accelerator runtime prediction

{1042x1024, 2048x2048, 4096x4096} of Laplace2D, in all the three cases, we observe an accurate prediction.

4.1.2 Runtime prediction. In validating the PyPassT-CAMM runtime, we run the C executable on a single core of *E5645* processor. We bind the the execution to a single core through `taskset` utility. This utility assigns the affinity of a process to the specified core. Thus, we guarantee similar execution environment for the application and the simulated model.

Figure 11 compares the measured and predicted runtime of Laplace2D on four different mesh sizes ({512x512, 1042x1024, 2048x2048, 4096x4096}) with and without compiler optimizations. The measured runtime takes the mean of five executions; the standard deviation is too small to be shown distinctively in the figure. We observe that the predicted runtime both with and without optimizations align closely with that of the measured runtime. On average, the error rate over the four mesh sizes with (*O3* flag) and without (*O0* flag) optimizations are 7.08% and 3.12% respectively.

These accurate predictions result from the use of reuse profiles and designing the program as a probabilistic state graph. Especially, with the help of reuse profiles, we calculate the cache hit-rates instead of explicitly assigning a random value (a common practice in modeling the performance of applications). From the results, it is evident that the analytical memory model combined with computation model achieves decent computation accuracy on CPUs and these models are reliable to predict the performance of CPU intense applications.

4.2 Accelerator Model

The purpose of this experiment is to determine accuracy of the static analysis and the GPU kernel transformation. We model Jacobi iterative method with OpenACC annotations with the proposed framework. We compare predicted runtime of the application with measurements collected from real hardware runs.

In the application source, the main computation loops were configured with `16x1x1` block dimensions and `32x1x1` grid dimensions using OpenACC annotations `#pragma acc parallel num_gangs(16) num_workers(32)`. The secondary data transfer loops of Jacobi method were configured with `16x16x1` block dimensions and `16x16x1` grid dimensions. The automatically generated PyPaasT execution model will have the exact parameters.

The experiment starts with 1024x1024 mesh size and doubles the dimensions until 8192x8192. The target system was configured with two Xeon E5645 processors running at at 2.4 GHz clock frequency with 48 GB of shared memory. For actual runs we use NVIDIA GM 204, which is a Maxwell architecture GPU running at 1050 MHz clock frequency with 4GB of GDDR5 memory.

We use the open-source OpenACC compiler, OpenARC [33] to generate the target hardware specific accelerator code (CUDA kernels). We evaluate the PyPassT generated accelerator model in PPT. We collect the runtime for both set of experiments.

Results of the real and simulation runs are presented in Figure 12. The X-axis is the *mesh size* and the Y-axis is the *runtime* measured in seconds. From the figure, it is evident that the accelerator makes good predictions of the program's runtime.

For 8192x8192 matrix mesh sizes error in runtime prediction is 0.16%. Error for 4096x4096 is 6.3%, 0.892% for 2048x2048 and 13.8% for 1024x1024 mesh sizes. The higher errors for smaller kernels were originated from code startup in real hardware as compared to simulator where the startup time is simply a constant. For large kernels the differences are mostly negligible as the startup cost becomes less significant and is amortized over the larger amount of data processed in the accelerator.

The front-end and back-end of the OpenARC [33] framework were configured with optimizations which improves the performance of the runtime libraries and the accelerator module, some of which are absent in our static analysis framework, which may introduce some errors in the prediction. Another possibility is the code optimizations performed by the CUDA resulting from CUDA toolkit updates; these optimizations are not included in the model as well. We plan to improve the accelerator module to capture these optimizations or differences and exploit data availability and caching techniques to better match the runtime predictions.

The accelerator model in PyPassT features a mid-level accelerator model which is expected to generate fast runtime predictions. In the proposed framework, the actual time for predicting runtime of 1024x1024 matrix multiplication using NVIDIA GM 204 accelerator model takes only 1.877 milliseconds. For 8192x8192 matrices, the runtime is only 2.234 milliseconds. We expect the accelerator model is highly scalable.

4.3 Communication Model

This experiment is designed to measure accuracy of the modeling framework in predicting the communication cost. Specifically, we measure the reproduction of spatial and volumetric properties of the message passing functions. The target application is a parallel implementation of Jacobi iterative method, which is a numerical algorithm for determining the solution of linear equations for a diagonally dominant system. This application performs 1000 iterations of the Jacobi Method on 2048x2048 matrices. The target application was run on an HPC system and compared with the PyPassT produced model simulated with PPT. Point-to-point and collective communications were reported during the tracing and we compare the total bytes and number of packets transferred among the MPI ranks for point-to-point and collective operations.

The real run was conducted on *Grizzly*[2], which is a 53, 352 cores cluster located at the Los Alamos National Laboratory. The machine has a peak performance of 1, 792.63 TFlop/s and features an Omnipath communication architecture. We used 1024 ranks on Grizzly for this experiment. Maximum message size on the cluster was set to be 8192 bytes. We used Intel MPI for the experiment which allows easy trace collection and analysis. The PyPassT generated analysis model was used for driving simulation. We set the PPT system model in accordance with the Grizzly configuration. The simulated run was deployed on 1024 simulated ranks as well. The simulation traces were collected at MPI processes.

We intercept each of the MPI calls as a transfer is requested. We compare the number of bytes received by participating ranks between the real experiment and simulation. Fig. 13 shows spatial and volumetric properties of the communication models. Sender rank is plotted on the X-axis and receiver rank along the Y-axis. The palette shows total bytes received. Fig. 14 shows the number of packets received by the participating MPI processes.

In the upper-left panel of Fig. 13 we show approximately 8.2 MB of point-to-point data has been transferred among the neighboring ranks along the main diagonal of the source-destination plot. An equal amount of transfers are issued for each of the 1000 iterations performed over the matrix. The total number of packets is seen on the upper-left panel of Fig. 14. These results were observed in the actual execution of the application (in the upper-right of Fig. 13 and in the upper-right panel of Fig. 14). We see that the simulator can preserve the volumetric and spatial properties of the MPI point-to-point communications.

In the lower-left panel of Fig. 13 we show that approximately 4.00 kB of MPI collective data has been received at each of the participating ranks in the actual run. They are from the MPI_Allreduce calls, invoked after each iteration of computation on the data at each rank. The collective calls were used to retrieve *min* error after each iteration. An equal amount of transfer is issued for each of the 1000 iterations performed over the matrix. Total number of packets is seen on the lower-left panel of Fig. 14. The lower-right panel of Fig. 13 represents total number of bytes, which matches well for the actual run. Similarly, an equal number of packets has been transferred in the simulator (lower-right panel of Fig. 14) among the participating ranks. The results show that the communication calls match perfectly between simulation and the actual run.

5 CONCLUSIONS

In this paper, we present static analysis based parallel application framework *PyPassT*. The framework predicts application performance based on a computation model using analytical memory models, accelerator model and detailed communication model. The accelerator model offers good performance prediction without compromising the simulation speed. The communication module preserves the spatiality of the messages transferred and thus allows more accurate representation of the runtime conditions such as network congestion, task mapping, and so on. Modeling an application at this level of detail using completely automatic analysis

---

[2]https://www.top500.org/system/178972

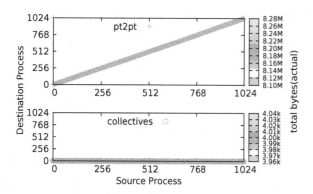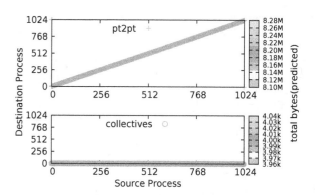

Figure 13: Actual communication bytes measured versus predicted for parallel implementation of the Jacobi iterative method. We report point-to-point bytes received at real process (top-left), actual collective bytes received (bottom-left), predicted point-to-point bytes received at a process (top-right), and predicted collective bytes received (bottom-right). The validation results indicate an exact prediction for both point-to-point and collective communications.

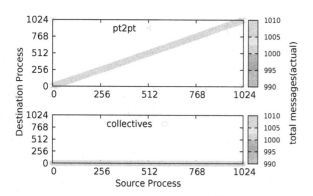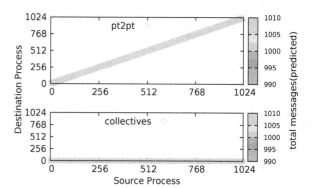

Figure 14: Validating spatial and volume property of the communication model. Plots show packet counts for participating sender-receiver pairs: point-to-point messages received at real process (top-left), measured collective messages received (bottom-left), predicted point-to-point messages received at a process (top-right), and predicted collective messages received (bottom-right). The validation results indicate an exact prediction for both point-to-point and collective communications.

based models eases burdens of model building for simulation and analytical approaches.

One limitation of our proposed framework is the inability to capture runtime decisions that are dependent on data delivered by communication. For example, the number of iterations of a loop or a branching probability can be determined by a memory reference dependent on communication or computation. One can predict these branching probabilities [38]. The proposed tool is incapable of predicting such runtime dependent conditions as those details are lost during abstraction. The loss of details can be the greatest difference between modeling the applications and performing the actual runs.

In future we plan to evaluate the accuracy of PyPaasT models in large, complicated and full-fledged application models. The accelerator model accuracy can be improved further by incorporating optimizations, more details on data availability and caching mechanisms. The communication module largely depends on the parallel performance of the simulator. We hope to improve the communication modeling capability to run massive models, made faster

by using predictive and learning models for communication and runtime data dependency.

6 ACKNOWLEDGMENTS

This research is supported in part by the NSF grant CNS-1563883 and a USF/FC2 SEED grant. We thank anonymous reviewers for their constructive comments. We would also like to thank the authors of OpenARC, specially Dr. Seyong Lee at the Oak Ridge National Laboratory, for generously sharing their work.

REFERENCES

[1] David Culler, Richard Karp, David Patterson, Abhijit Sahay, Klaus Erik Schauser, Eunice Santos, Ramesh Subramonian, and Thorsten Von Eicken. *LogP: Towards a realistic model of parallel computation*, volume 28. ACM, 1993.

[2] Albert Alexandrov, Mihai F Ionescu, Klaus E Schauser, and Chris Scheiman. Loggp: incorporating long messages into the logp modelâĂŤone step closer towards a realistic model for parallel computation. In *Proceedings of the seventh annual ACM symposium on Parallel algorithms and architectures*, pages 95–105. ACM, 1995.

[3] Torsten Hoefler, Timo Schneider, and Andrew Lumsdaine. Loggopsim: simulating large-scale applications in the loggops model. In *Proceedings of the 19th ACM*

International Symposium on High Performance Distributed Computing, pages 597–604. ACM, 2010.

[4] A. F. Rodrigues, K. S. Hemmert, B. W. Barrett, C. Kersey, R. Oldfield, M. Weston, R. Risen, J. Cook, P. Rosenfeld, E. CooperBalls, and B. Jacob. The structural simulation toolkit. *SIGMETRICS Perform. Eval. Rev.*, 38(4):37–42, 2011.

[5] Arun Rodrigues, Elliot Cooper-Balis, Keren Bergman, Kurt Ferreira, David Bunde, and K. Scott Hemmert. Improvements to the structural simulation toolkit. In *Proceedings of the 5th International ICST Conference on Simulation Tools and Techniques (SIMUTools)*, pages 190–195, 2012.

[6] Milo M. K. Martin, Daniel J. Sorin, Bradford M. Beckmann, Michael R. Marty, Min Xu, Alaa R. Alameldeen, Kevin E. Moore, Mark D. Hill, and David A. Wood. Multifacet's general execution-driven multiprocessor simulator (gems) toolset. *SIGARCH Comput. Archit. News*, 33(4):92–99, November 2005.

[7] Curtis L Janssen, Helgi Adalsteinsson, Scott Cranford, Joseph P Kenny, Ali Pinar, David A Evensky, and Jackson Mayo. A simulator for large-scale parallel computer architectures. *Technology Integration Advancements in Distributed Systems and Computing*, 179:57–73, 2012.

[8] Xing Wu and Frank Mueller. Scalaextrap: Trace-based communication extrapolation for spmd programs. In *Proceedings of the 16th ACM Symposium on Principles and Practice of Parallel Programming*, PPoPP '11, pages 113–122, New York, NY, USA, 2011. ACM.

[9] Amir Bahmani and Frank Mueller. Scalable communication event tracing via clustering. *Journal of Parallel and Distributed Computing*, 109:230–244, 2017.

[10] Jidong Zhai, Tianwei Sheng, Jiangzhou He, Wenguang Chen, and Weimin Zheng. Fact: Fast communication trace collection for parallel applications through program slicing. In *Proceedings of the Conference on High Performance Computing Networking, Storage and Analysis*, SC '09, pages 27:1–27:12, New York, NY, USA, 2009. ACM.

[11] Dan Quinlan. Rose: Compiler support for object-oriented frameworks. *Parallel Processing Letters*, 10(02n03):215–226, 2000.

[12] C. Dave, H. Bae, S. J. Min, S. Lee, R. Eigenmann, and S. Midkiff. Cetus: A source-to-source compiler infrastructure for multicores. *Computer*, 42(12):36–42, Dec 2009.

[13] Seyong Lee, Jeremy S. Meredith, and Jeffrey S. Vetter. Compass: A framework for automated performance modeling and prediction. In *Proceedings of the 29th ACM on International Conference on Supercomputing*, ICS '15, pages 405–414, New York, NY, USA, 2015. ACM.

[14] Cy Chan, Didem Unat, Michael Lijewski, Weiqun Zhang, John Bell, and John Shalf. Software design space exploration for exascale combustion co-design. In Julian Martin Kunkel, Thomas Ludwig, and Hans Werner Meuer, editors, *Supercomputing*, pages 196–212, Berlin, Heidelberg, 2013. Springer Berlin Heidelberg.

[15] A. Bhattacharyya and T. Hoefler. Pemogen: Automatic adaptive performance modeling during program runtime. In *2014 23rd International Conference on Parallel Architecture and Compilation Techniques (PACT)*, pages 393–404, Aug 2014.

[16] G. Chennupati, N. Santhi, S. Eidenbenz, and S. Thulasidasan. An analytical memory hierarchy model for performance prediction. In *2017 Winter Simulation Conference (WSC)*, pages 908–919. IEEE, 2017.

[17] R. L. Mattson, J. Gecsei, D. R. Slutz, and I. L. Traiger. Evaluation techniques for storage hierarchies. *IBM Systems Journal*, 9(2):78–117, 1970.

[18] Openacc. openacc: Directives for accelerators., January 2018.

[19] Mohammad Obaida and Jason Liu. Simulation of hpc job scheduling and large-scale parallel workloads. In *Proceedings of the 2017 Winter Simulation Conference (WSC 2017)*, 2017.

[20] Nikhil Jain, Abhinav Bhatele, Sam White, Todd Gamblin, and Laxmikant V. Kale. Evaluating hpc networks via simulation of parallel workloads. In *Proceedings of the International Conference for High Performance Computing, Networking, Storage and Analysis*, SC '16, pages 14:1–14:12, Piscataway, NJ, USA, 2016. IEEE Press.

[21] Kyle L Spafford and Jeffrey S Vetter. Aspen: a domain specific language for performance modeling. In *Proceedings of the International Conference on High Performance Computing, Networking, Storage and Analysis*, page 84, 2012.

[22] Nathan R Tallent and Adolfy Hoisie. Palm: easing the burden of analytical performance modeling. In *Proceedings of the 28th ACM international conference on Supercomputing*, pages 221–230, 2014.

[23] Christopher D. Carothers, Jeremy S. Meredith, Mark P. Blanco, Jeffrey S. Vetter, Misbah Mubarak, Justin LaPre, and Shirley Moore. Durango: Scalable synthetic workload generation for extreme-scale application performance modeling and simulation. In *Proceedings of the 2017 ACM SIGSIM Conference on Principles of Advanced Discrete Simulation*, SIGSIM-PADS '17, pages 97–108, New York, NY, USA, 2017. ACM.

[24] M. Mubarak, C. D. Carothers, R. B. Ross, and P. Carns. Enabling parallel simulation of large-scale hpc network systems. *IEEE Transactions on Parallel and Distributed Systems*, 28(1):87–100, Jan 2017.

[25] Gengbin Zheng, Gunavardhan Kakulapati, and Laxmikant V Kalé. Bigsim: A parallel simulator for performance prediction of extremely large parallel machines. In *Parallel and Distributed Processing Symposium, 2004. Proceedings. 18th International*, page 78, 2004.

[26] Christopher D Carothers, David Bauer, and Shawn Pearce. ROSS: A high-performance, low-memory, modular Time Warp system. *Journal of Parallel and Distributed Computing*, 62(11):1648–1669, 2002.

[27] Gopinath Chennupati, Nanadakishore Santhi, Stephen Eidenbenz, Robert Joseph Zerr, Massimiliano Rosa, Richard James Zamora, Eun Jung Park, Balasubramanya T. Nadiga, Jason Liu, Kishwar Ahmed, and Mohammad Abu Obaida. Performance prediction toolkit. https://github.com/lanl/PPT, 2017.

[28] Kishwar Ahmed, Mohammad Obaida, Jason Liu, Stephan Eidenbenz, Nandakishore Santhi, and Guillaume Chapuis. An integrated interconnection network model for large-scale performance prediction. In *Proceedings of the 2016 Annual ACM Conference on SIGSIM Principles of Advanced Discrete Simulation (SIGSIM-PADS)*, pages 177–187, 2016.

[29] Kishwar Ahmed, Jason Liu, Stephan Eidenbenz, and Joe Zerr. Scalable interconnection network models for rapid performance prediction of hpc applications. In *Proceedings of the 18th IEEE International Conference on High Performance Computing and Communications (HPCC)*, pages 1069–1078, 2016.

[30] G. Chennupati, N. Santhi, R. Bird, S. Thulasidasan, A. H. A. Badawy, S. Misra, and S. Eidenbenz. A scalable analytical memory model for cpu performance prediction. In Stephen Jarvis, Steven Wright, and Simon Hammond, editors, *Proceedings of the 8th International Workshop on High Performance Computing Systems. Performance Modeling, Benchmarking, and Simulation, PMBS@SC*, pages 114–135. Springer, 2017.

[31] G. Chapuis, S. Eidenbenz, and N. Santhi. Gpu performance prediction through parallel discrete event simulation and common sense. In *Proceedings of the 9th EAI International Conference on Performance Evaluation Methodologies and Tools*, 2015.

[32] Nandakishore Santhi, Stephan Eidenbenz, and Jason Liu. The simian concept: Parallel discrete event simulation with interpreted languages and just-in-time compilation. In L. Yilmaz, W. K V. Chan, I. Moon, T. M. K. Roeder, C. Macal, and M. D. Rossetti, editors, *Proceedings of the 2015 Winter Simulation Conference*, pages 3013–3024, Piscataway, New Jersey, 2015. Institute of Electrical and Electronics Engineers, Inc.

[33] Seyong Lee and Jeffrey S. Vetter. Openarc: Extensible openacc compiler framework for directive-based accelerator programming study. In *Proceedings of the First Workshop on Accelerator Programming Using Directives*, WACCPD '14, pages 1–11, Piscataway, NJ, USA, 2014. IEEE Press.

[34] Vikram S Adve, Rajive Bagrodia, Ewa Deelman, and Rizos Sakellariou. Compiler-optimized simulation of large-scale applications on high performance architectures. *Journal of Parallel and Distributed Computing*, 62(3):393 – 426, 2002.

[35] Scott Pakin and Patrick McCormick. Hardware-independent application characterization. In *International Symposium on Workload Characterization (IISWC)*, pages 111–112, Portland, Oregon, USA, 2013. IEEE.

[36] E. Berg and E. Hagersten. StatCache: a probabilistic approach to efficient and accurate data locality analysis. In *IEEE International Symposium on - ISPASS Performance Analysis of Systems and Software, 2004*, pages 20–27, 2004.

[37] Ptx: Nvidia parallel thread execution, December 2017.

[38] B. Kalla, N. Santhi, A. H. A. Badawy, G. Chennupati, and S. Eidenbenz. A probabilistic monte carlo framework for branch prediction. In *Proceedings of the 2017 IEEE International Conference on Cluster Computing (CLUSTER)*. IEEE, 2017.

Formal Abstract Modeling of Dynamic Multiplex Networks

Cristina Ruiz-Martin
Carleton University /
Universidad de Valladolid
Ottawa, ON K1S 5B6 Canada
cruiz@eii.uva.es

Gabriel Wainer
Carleton University
Ottawa, ON K1S 5B6 Canada
gwainer@sce.careleton.ca

Adolfo Lopez-Paredes
Universidad de Valladolid
Valladolid, Castilla y León 47250 Spain
aparedes@eii.uva.es

ABSTRACT

We describe an Abstract Model for Diffusion Processes to simulate diffusion processes in multiplex dynamic networks using formal modeling and simulation (M&S) methodologies (in this case, the DEVS formalism). This approach helps the users to implement diffusion processes over a network by using the network specification and the diffusion rules. The result of combining the network specifications and the diffusion rules is an Abstract Model for Diffusion Processes, which is formally defined in DEVS, and can be converted into a computerized model. Using the proposed Abstract Model for Diffusion Processes, we can study a diffusion process in multiplex networks with a formal simulation algorithm, improving the model's definition. We present a case study using the CDBoost simulation engine.

KEYWORDS

Diffusion Processes, Multiplex Networks, DEVS, Formal Modeling and Simulation

ACM Reference format:

Cristina Ruiz-Martin, Gabriel Wainer, and Adolfo Lopez-Paredes. 2018. Formal Abstract Modeling of Dynamic Multiplex Networks. In Proceedings of SIGSIM Principles of Advanced Discrete Simulation (SIGSIM-PADS' 18). ACM, New York, NY, USA, 12 pages.
https://doi.org/10.1145/3200921.3200922

1 INTRODUCTION

A diffusion process is a phenomenon where an element is spread from a place with high concentration to a place where the concentration is low. The study of such phenomena has been useful in various domains [1]: Medicine (e.g. studying of spreading of disease over a population), Management (e.g. analyzing how a new idea or change is accepted in a company), Social Science (e.g. checking the effect of an information disseminated in a Social Network in the behavior of the people), etc.

Permission to make digital or hard copies of all or part of this work for personal or classroom use is granted without fee provided that copies are not made or distributed for profit or commercial advantage and that copies bear this notice and the full citation on the first page. Copyrights for components of this work owned by others than ACM must be honored. Abstracting with credit is permitted. To copy otherwise, or republish, to post on servers or to redistribute to lists, requires prior specific permission and/or a fee. Request permissions from Permissions@acm.org.
SIGSIM-PADS '18 , May 23–25, 2018, Rome, Italy
© 2018 Association for Computing Machinery.
ACM ISBN 978-1-4503-5092-1/18/05...$15.00
https://doi.org/10.1145/3200921.3200922

Diffusion processes have been studied building a multiplex network (i.e. a set of interconnected entities with different types of relations) that defines the relations between the entities involved in the process and defining the rules the diffusion process follows [2]. Then, these specifications are translated into a computer program that is simulated to generate results. Unfortunately, most of the existing research about simulation of diffusion processes in multiplex or multiplex dynamic networks does not provide insight on the M&S methodology and platforms they use. For example, Xiong et al [3] run a numerical simulation to study the effect of the diffusion of innovation in social networks but no information on the simulation aspects is presented. Khelil et al [4] use their own simulator written in Java to implement a model to study information dissemination strategies in mobile ad hoc networks, but no information is provided about the simulation details. Numerous cases are similar to these.

Not only the simulation aspects are neglected: the model definition is normally informal, and difficult to analyze. To overcome the lack of formalization, and the details of implementation, we here propose a formal Abstract Model for Diffusion Processes (from here on, DAM, *Diffusion Abstract Model*) that allows us to define and implement diffusion processes in multiplex dynamic networks by using the definition of the network and the diffusion rules for the process. This model is an integral component of a formal architecture defined in [5] that allows defining and studying diffusion processes in multiplex networks.

Having the DAM formally defined allows one having the diffusion model and its implementation separated, therefore model verification and validation are simplified and development time reduced. One can think about the formal model prior to implementation, analyze different experiments that could be conducted on the model, and finding complex errors before spending valuable time in coding. In our case, we use Discrete Events Systems specifications (DEVS) [6] since diffusion process in multiplex networks can be modeled using a discrete event approach and DEVS is well suited. It provides a formal framework to study hierarchical modular models, which is well adapted for modeling diffusion models. Since the models, simulators, and experiments are independent, the same model can be implemented on different platforms and the verification process can be improved. As the simulation algorithms for DEVS have been formally defined, this helps in achieving separation of concerns and building complex applications that can be verified with ease, focusing only on the modeling aspects. To simulate the DEVS models, we use the CDBoost framework. CDBoost is a cross-platform DEVS simulator implemented in C++11 that allows a direct conversion of

DEVS functions into C++ code. This is the formal methodology and the simulation tools used to define the DAM, can be used to achieve repeatable simulation studies.

Some of the advantages of this new model architecture are as follows:

- the model can be defined using formal modeling and simulation (M&S) methodologies

- we can study dynamic networks, and defined a mechanism for storing the time when the change occurs

- we can update the properties at runtime.

- we defined an XML specification for the behavior of the diffusion model, which allows us to define complex rules. This allows us to remove software dependencies.

The rest of the paper is organized as follows. In section 2, we discuss related work on diffusion processes and we briefly explain DEVS and CDBoost. In section 3, we present the DAM and the architecture where it is integrated. In section 4, we explain a general implementation of the DAM using DEVS. In section 5, we present some simulation results of the application of the DAM to study an information diffusion process inside an organization. Finally, in section 6, we present the conclusions of this work.

2 BACKGROUND

Many diffusion processes have been specified using differential equations or other types of rules such as if-then rules. For example, many diffusion processes in medicine have been studied using Susceptible-Infected-Recovered (SIR) models, which are formally defined using differential equations. (e.g. [7]).

In fact, much of the research work on diffusion processes is based on the definition of new algorithms invented in the field of Medicine. There are algorithms to study preventive measures to protect the population against a disease [8], [9], to study the propagation of specific diseases such as dementia [10], etc. These algorithms, although developed for medical applications, have sometimes been applied to study problems in other fields, such as communications in mobile networks [4] or the diffusion of information and opinion adoption in social networks [11]–[13].

However, as mentioned in the introduction, the diffusion algorithms are normally converted into ad-hoc computer programs that include the network. There is no formal definition of the model. Likewise, the M&S methodology used or the simulation platform where the model is implemented are not detailed.

Generalizing diffusion processes from simplex to multiplex networks is not simple. Although there have been some advances in this area, it is still an open research field [14]. For example, several diffusion processes (e.g. linear diffusion, random walks, etc.) have already been generalized [2], [15]. In [16], the authors proposed a match between the elements of diffusion processes in social networks and the concepts used in Agent Based Modeling (ABM) techniques. They also proposed to use ABM to study the diffusion problem in social networks as a method to obtain empirical results and to connect theoretical and empirical research.

Some recent research has focused on formalizing the study of diffusion processes in multiplex networks [17], [18] using ABM,

Network Theory and DEVS. The authors presented an architecture to simulate information diffusion processes in multiplex dynamic networks. They defined a model using a server-proxy architecture where the servers represent the behavior of the nodes in the network model (i.e. the rules to transmit and assimilate the information), and the proxies define the diffusion rules for each type of link (i.e. the different types of connections between nodes) in the network model. Both servers and proxies are modeled using DEVS, and they are coupled to represent network nodes. The connections between the nodes in the networks are used to build the DEVS Top Model that represents multiplex networks. In order to be able to model dynamic networks (changes on the number of nodes or the connections between them), the authors store all possible network configurations and they use Dynamic DEVS [19], and a database to store all the network configurations and the properties that define the behavior of the nodes.

In [20], the authors adapted the above-mentioned architecture to study business processes in the healthcare sector. They modified the architecture to include Business Process Model and Notation (BPMN) in order to study the impact of dynamic allocation of patients in the healthcare pathway.

Following the research line presented in [17], [18], we introduce a new architecture where the model (DAM) is abstract and generic and can be instantiated to simulate any kind of diffusion process in multiplex networks.

We used the DEVS formalism [6] as the formal basis to develop the DAM, as DEVS provides a framework to develop hierarchical models in a modular way, allowing model reuse and thus, reducing development time and testing. There are different DEVS simulators such as JAMES [21], JDEVS [22], DEVSJava [23], CDBoost [24], etc. We used CDBoost, a fast cross-platform DEVS simulator implemented in C++11. CDBoost provides simple interfaces to the modeler, who can transform a DEVS model to a DEVS simulation. At the user level, it allows defining atomic and coupled models, and since the output format of the simulation is flexible (i.e. the user can configure it), it can be defined in such way that helps the analysis of the results. Figures 4 and 5 show the CDBoost simulator definition to implement DEVS models. Figure 1 shows a template to implement an atomic model, and figure 2 a template to define coupled models.

```
1 struct AtomicName_defs{ //Input&Output Port declaration
2     struct input_port1 : public in_port< MSGi1> {};
3     struct input_portn : public in_port< MSGin> {};
4     struct output_port1 : public out_port< MSGo1> {};
5     struct output_portn : public out_port< MSGon> {};   };
6
7 template<typename TIME>
8 class AtomicName{
9  using defs=AtomicName_defs;//port definition in context
10  public:
11  struct state_type{ //Define your state variables here   };
12  state_type state;
13  AtomicName() noexcept {//parameters/initial state values}
14
15 //DEVS functions
16 void internal_transition() {//Define internal transition
17     function           }
18 void external_transition(TIME e, typename make_message_bags
```

```
19      <input_ports>::type mbs) {
20 //Define your external function here        }
21   void    confluence_transition(TIME    e,    typename
22     make_message_bags <input_ports>::type mbs) {
23 // confluence function here            }
24 typename  make_message_bags<output_ports>::type  output()
25    const {  // Output function
26   typename make_message_bags<output_ports>::type bags;
27   //Define your output function here. Fill bags
28   return bags;                    }
29 TIME time_advance() const {
30    //Define the time advance function          }
31 };
```

Figure 1. DEVS atomic model implementation in CDBoost.

As seen in the figure, first, we declare the model ports as a structure (lines 1-5) and the atomic model as a class (lines 7-31). Each atomic model class has the set of state variables grouped together in a structure (lines 11). It also has a model constructor to instantiate the model parameters and initial values (line 13). We implement all the DEVS functions (internal, external, confluence, output and time advance, in lines 15-31) in C++. The code in bold cannot be modified (it is part of the simulator).

The coupled models are implemented using the template provided in figure 2. We instantiate all the atomic models with their parameters (lines 1-6) and then we define the coupled models (including the top model).

```
1 //*****INSTANTIATE ATOMICS *******//
2 template<typename TIME>
3 class iestream_int : public iestream_input<int,TIME> {
4 public:
5 iestream_int(): iestream_input<int,TIME>
6 ("inputs/test_filterNetworks.txt") {};   };
7 //*****DEFINE COUPLED *******//
8 struct inp_in_1 : public in_port<int>{};
9 struct outp_out_2 : public out_port<double>{};
10 using iports_C1 = std::tuple< inp_in_1 >;
11 using oports_C1 = std::tuple< outp_out_2 >;
12 using submodels_C1=models_tuple<filterNet, iestream_int> ;
13 using eics_C1=tuple<EIC
14     <inp_in_1,iestream_int, iestream_defs::in> >;
15 using eocs_C1 =tuple< EOC
16   < filterNet, filterNet _defs::out, outp_out_2> >;
17 using ics_C1=tuple<IC
18     <iestream_int,iestream_defs::out,
19         filterNet, fiterNet _defs::in> >;
20
21 using C1=coupled_model <TIME,iports_C1,oports_C1,
22         submodels_C1,eics_C1,eocs_C1,ics_C1>;
23
24 int main(){ //Call the simulator
25   runner<NameOfTimeClass, NameOfTopModel, logger_top> r{0};
26   r.runUntil(300000); }
```

Figure 2. DEVS coupled and top model implementation in CDBoost.

Figure 2 is an implementation of the coupled model shown in figure 3. We first declare the coupled model ports (lines 8-9). We then define the top model components: input ports (line 10), output ports (line 11), submodels (line 12), external input couplings (line 13-14), external output couplings (line 15-16) and

internal couplings (line 17-19). The coupled model (line 21-22) is a tuple of all these components. The last step is to call the simulator (lines 24-26). We set the name of the time class and the top model name (line 25), and simulation running time (line 26).

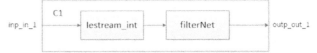

Figure 3. Example of DEVS coupled model defined in fig. 2

3 ABSTRACT MODEL FOR DIFFUSION PROCESSES DEFINITION

To model and simulate diffusion processes in multiplex dynamic networks, we proposed the architecture presented in figure 4 [5], whose main component is the diffusion abstract model.

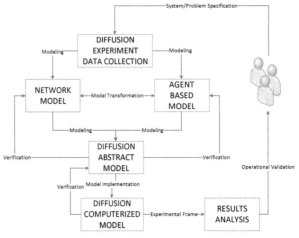

Figure 4: An architecture to simulate diffusion processes in multiplex dynamic networks

The architecture includes six components as follows:

a) Diffusion experiment data collection: we need to obtain all the requirements, specifications, and data available for the problem under study. This information can be gathered manually (e.g., through interviews or text analysis), or automatically (e.g. using different types of sensors). In general, the diffusion experiment data is provided by experts in the domain. If the information is incomplete, the domain experts should provide additional data, instructions about how to collect it, or, if not available, approve a set of assumptions.

b) Network model: it is an organized representation of the *Diffusion experiment data* using Network Theory. It provides a formal representation of the relations among the components of the system. Although this is a formal model, there are different tools like Gephi [26], Pajek [27], MuxViz [28], etc. that allows the model to be defined using a graphical interface, and it allows storing the network model in various formats (tables, graphs, XML). The model is built following the *Diffusion experiment data* document.

c) Agent-Based model: it is a representation of the behavior of those in charge of the diffusion process, the objects they use for diffusing the element, and the properties of the relationships among these objects. It is defined using ABM techniques, and it can be implemented using different methods: specific software platforms such as NetLogo, Repast [29], using an XML definition, or a formal specification like a DEVS model.

d) DAM: the DAM, the main object of this research, is an abstract and formal representation of the *Diffusion experiment data* that matches elements in both the *Network* and the *Agent-based* models. It is a formal specification (in our case, we use DEVS, but it could be defined using other formalisms, like System Dynamics, State charts, etc.). One could also define the DAM combining different formalisms, as long as there is a way to connect them (for instance, a metamodel).

e) Diffusion Computerized Model (DCM): it is a computer implementation of the *DAM*. It can be built using different simulators; in our case, we used a DEVS simulator called CDBoost [30]. Once all the components of the *DAM* are implemented, the top-level model can be defined either manually or automatically by processing the *Network* and *Agent-based* models.

f) Results Analysis: the results provided by the *DCM* can be analyzed using different methods, statistical and data visualization tools (such as R [31], PowerBI [32], etc.).

The DAM is the central part of the architecture, which we will describe in detail. It is defined a generic container that follows the structure presented in figure 5.

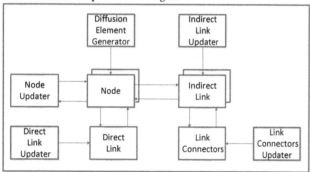

Figure 5. DAM structure

It includes nine components.

1. Node: it is a representation of a vertex in the Network model, including all its input and output connections. It also matches an Agent in the in the Agent-Based model, since the Agents are the nodes in the Network model. Here is where we define the behavior of the diffusion process on each node.

2. Indirect Link: it represents the properties of the input and output connections of a node in the Network model. It also matches the objects used by the agents to carry the diffusion process. Each of them is different. Once all the objects used by the agents to carry the diffusion process have been modeled, each *Indirect Link* will contain a different subset of them based on input and output links of the node.

3. Direct Link: it represents direct connections between *Node* models. It represents the properties of the links in the *Network* model that have a direct connection between nodes. In the *Agent-based* model, it represents the connections handled with-

out using any additional objects. It can be defined as an atomic or coupled model based on the complexity and the level of detail needed for diffusion rules on direct connections. For example, in the case of information transmission face-to-face, it can be as simple as an atomic model that transmits the message after a delay or it can be a coupled model that combines the environmental noise and the distance between the people and introduce a disturbance in the contentment of the message.

4. Link Connectors: this single model represents how the objects used by the diffusion agents are connected. It does not have a direct match to the *Network* model. In the *Agent-based* model, it represents the properties of the relations among the *Indirect Links* and how they are connected. Link Connectors are similar to Direct Links, but they represent the rules the diffusion process follows between indirect links. For instance, in a diffusion process for communication, if indirect links represent messages through Facebook or text messaging, the Link Connectors model can be defined as a coupled model with two components: *Internet* and *Mobile Network*, with a switch to direct the messages to the appropriate network.

5. Diffusion Element Generator: it generates elements to be diffused over time. It defines the initial location of the diffusion elements in the *Network* and *Agent-based* models, and the new ones introduced over time.

6. Updaters: they modify the properties of the models at runtime. They allow us to model dynamic *Networks* where not only change the connections but also the nodes and links. With the updaters, we can modify the properties of the *Indirect Link, Link Connectors, Node* and *Direct Link* models without modifying any model in the structure.

As we have already mentioned, each of these components could be modeled and implemented using different formal methods. In this paper, we will show its definition using DEVS.

The *Indirect Link Updater, Link Connectors Updater, Direct Link Updater* and *Diffusion Element Generator* are defined as four different instances of a DEVS atomic model that is parameterized to generate updates in the properties of the other components. This is done using the information in an external file. It can also include the element to be diffused in the model. In order to instantiate these models we use any C++ type (i.e. *int, pair, struct* etc.) that matches the information stored in the external file.

The *Node Updater* can be either an atomic or a coupled model (depending on the complexity of the rules to update the properties of the node). It updates the properties of the *Nodes* like the other updaters, but in this case, the properties can be updated using both information stored in an external file and data included in the model (e.g. the properties of other nodes)

Node and *Indirect Link* are DEVS coupled models that have several filters and atomic or coupled models that represent the behavior of the diffusion process. The atomic and coupled models inside *Node* and *Indirect Links* are parameterized based on the specifications provided in the Network and the Agent-based models. We broadcast the diffusion messages, and filter the ones that should be assigned to each component. The components of the model identify if the message (i.e. a diffusion element or a property update) is for them.

Figure 6 represents the structure of the *Indirect Link* Coupled. It has one filter for each input port and an atomic or coupled model for each type of link on the *Indirect Link*. It also contains a *Sink* (added for validation purposes; if a message arrives at the *Sink*, it means that the model received a message for a link not included in the model; this means there is an implementation error or a mismatch in the model definition).

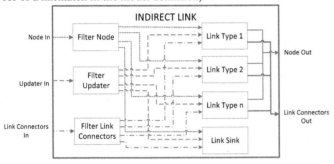

Figure 6. Indirect Link coupled model

All these models (both atomic and coupled) have been defined formally using DEVS. In Appendix I we show the formal definition of one of these DEVS atomic models: the *Switch*, used to redirect the messages that come from the *Indirect Links* to the corresponding model inside the *Node*. The implementation of this model and its behavior is explained in section 4, figure 7. Likewise, in Appendix II we show the formal definition of a DEVS coupled model: *Indirect Links* (figure 6).

All the models have been defined using the same process. As we can see, the formal definition of the model contributes to model validation. For example, in the *Switch* (see Appendix I), we may forget to passivate the model when *messagesPassing* is empty and we can find such errors by just looking at the formal definition. We can also find varied errors in the model definition; for instance, if when there is an input in *setAnswerIn* we set the state variable *state* to SEND, instead of ANSWER, we can detect that by simply checking the formal model (prior to any implementation or simulation). In the *Indirect Links* coupled model (see Appendix II), we know that the type of message in *NodeIn* port is *DiffusionElements*. When we connect *Indirect Links* to *Node* model, we know that the type of message in the port *IndirectLinksOut* of *Node* model must be *DiffusionElements*. Otherwise, the model is not valid. We can find these errors in the model formal specifications with ease, without wasting valuable time in building a computer model that is wrong, in the early phases of the model, which will save efforts in the latter phases.

4 DAM IMPLEMENTATION USING DEVS[1]

As discussed earlier, once all the models have been formally defined and its formal behavior studied, we to translate them into computerized DEVS models using the CDBoost simulator. The

parameterized DEVS atomic models, introduced in section 3, are implemented using the template provided in figure 1.

Figure 7 shows the implementation of the *switch* atomic model that is used to redirect the messages that comes from the *Indirect Links* to the corresponding model inside the *Node*. We chose this example as it allows showing some of the implementation details and the DEVS functions are simple (the rest of the atomic models are built following a similar logic: they are formally specified using DEVS, and implemented in CDBoost).

```
1  struct switch3Out_defs{    //Port definition
2  struct sendOut,answerOut,decideOut: public out_port<MSG> {};
3  struct diffusionElementIn : public in_port<MSG> {};
4  struct setAnswerIn,setDecideIn: public
5      in_port<SET_STATE_ANS> {};
6  struct setSendIn : public in_port<SET_STATE_SEND> {};
7  };
8  class switch3Out {  // DEVS atomic model definition
9  public:
10  DeviceType id; //Parameter
11  enum SwitchState{ANSWER,SEND,DECIDE};//state definition
12  state_type state;
13  struct state_type{
14     vector <MSG> outMsg;
15     SwitchState  state;  };
16 ..
17 void internal_transition() { state.outMsg.clear();}
18
19 void external_transition(TIME e, typename
20      make_message_bags<input_ports>::type mbs)
21 if(!get_messages<typename defs::setAnswerIn>(mbs).empty())
22    state.state = SwitchState::ANSWER;
23 if(!get_messages<typename defs::setSendIn>(mbs).empty())
24    state.state = SwitchState::SEND;
25 if(!get_messages<typename defs::setDecideIn>(mbs).empty())
26    state.state = SwitchState::DECIDE;
27 for (const auto &x : get_messages<typename
28      defs:: diffusionElementIn >(mbs)) {
29   if(x.to.type == id) state.outMsg.push_back(x); }        }
30
31 typename make_message_bags<output_ports>::type output()
32      const { // output function
33  typename make_message_bags<output_ports>::type bags;
34   switch(state.state){
35    case SwitchState::ANSWER:
36     for (int i = 0; i < (state.outMsg.size()); i++)
37     get_messages<typename defs::answerOut>(bags).
38       push_back(state.outMsg[i]);
39    case SwitchState::SEND:
40     for (int i = 0; i < (state.outMsg.size()); i++)
41     get_messages<typename defs::sendOut>(bags).
42       push_back(state.outMsg[i]);
43    case SwitchState::DECIDE:
44     for (int i = 0; i < (state.outMsg.size()); i++)
45     get_messages<typename defs::decideOut>(bags).
46        push_back(state.outMsg[i])
47    }
48  return bags;          }
49
50 TIME time_advance() const { // time_advance function
51  return (state.outMsg.empty() ? infinity() : TIME());
52  }
53 };
```

Figure 7. Computer Model of the Switch atomic model

---

[1] The documentation is available at:
https://github.com/SimulationEverywhere/NEP_DAM.git

The model redirects the message in the *DecideIn* port to the appropriate output port based on the model state (answer, decide, send). We use different output ports according to the model's state. The model follows the template presented in Section 2. The external transition function (lines 19-29) stores a messages received through *diffusionElementIn* port in *OutMsg* variable. It also sets the value of the *state* variable based on the inputs in the other ports *SetDecideIn*, *SetSendIn* and *SetAnswerIn*. When the time is consumed, we activate the output function (lines 31-48), which sends the messages stored in the *OutMsg* variable through the output port that the state variable determines. Then, we execute the internal transition function (line 17), which clears the *OutMsg* variable. Finally, the time advance function (lines 50-52) passivates the model if there is nothing to send, and triggers an instantaneous event (time advance 0) is there is something to send.

We store the parameters that define the behavior of each model in XML files. If the behavior of all nodes is the same, we will only have one XML with the parameters for that behavior (for example, if we study the diffusion of a virus over a population, where the individuals are infected with the same probability). If we need more complex behaviors, we can define it in different XML files (for instance, if different groups of individuals react differently to the virus, we might have different XML files to define the behavior of the nodes; for instance, the individuals that do not are infected because they are immune, the ones that are infected with low probability because they are vaccinated and the ones that are infected with high probability). An extreme example is where all the nodes have different behavior. In this case, we have as many XML files as nodes. This case is the one presented later on to study the information dissemination inside an organization.

We parse these XML files to instantiate the parameterized DEVS models in CDBoost and build the DAM automatically. The model parameters are dependent on the application, however, the process and the general implementation can be adapted easily. Here we show how to build the DAM using as a case study a diffusion process inside an organization.

Figure 8 presents an example of an XML file where we define the behavior of a person. It represents how the person behaves in terms of information transmission. In our model, some characteristics are attributes (i.e. they are fully specified in the diffusion model and therefore, they remain constant) and other are parameters (i.e. they are not completely defined in the model due to lack of information, or we want to change them to study their effect on the process). We use XML tags to define each of the parameters and attributes (and their values are defined as the content of the tags).

```
1 <?xml version="1.0" ?>
2 <AgentBehavior>
3   <Id>First Responder 20</Id>
4   <Location>55D6</Location>
5   <ReactionTime>00:00:10:000</ReactionTime>
6   <AnswerPriorityType>DEVICE_PRIORITY </AnswerPriorityType>
7   <SendPriorityType> PRIORITY_LIST </SendPriorityType>
8   <MyDevices>
9     <PriorityDevice priority="1" device="MOBILEPHONE"
```

```
10     send2Multiple="false" sendSeparateFromReceive="false"/>
11     ...
12   </MyDevices>
13   <SortedTasks>
14     <PriorityTask priority="1" task="ANSWER"/>
15     <PriorityTask priority="2" task="SEND"/>
16   ...
17   <SortedTasks>
18   <AnswerDevicePriority>
19     <PriorityDevice priority="1" device="RADIO" />
20     ...
21   </AnswerDevicePriority>
22   <AnswerPersonPriority>
23     <PriorityPerson priority="1" id="1"/>
24   ...
25     <PriorityPerson priority="3" id="97"/>
26   </AnswerPersonPriority>
27   <SendCommandPriority>
28     <PriorityCommandTo priority="1" to="1" msg="
29     Tell population to stay at home" />
30        ...
31     <PriorityCommandTo priority="3" to="97" msg="
32       Tell population to stay at home" />
33   </SendCommandPriority>
34   <ActionExecutionPriority>
35   <PriorityAction priority="1" id="Tell population to stay
36     at home"/>
37   </ActionExecutionPriority>
38   <CommunicationRelations>
39   <RelationPerson id="1">
40     <Device device="RADIO"/>
41     <Device device="MOBILEPHONE"/>
42   </RelationPerson>
43   <RelationPerson id="5">
44     <Device device="BEEPER"/>
45   </RelationPerson >
46     ...
47   </CommunicationRelations>
48   <MessageBehavior>
49   <MsgReceived from="1" content="Tell people to stay at
50     home">
51     <Msg2Send to="5" content="Tell people to stay at home
52   acknowledgement" cmpulsory="true" send2Multiple="false"/>
53     <Action2Do id=" Tell population to stay at home "/>
54   </MsgReceived>
55   </MessageBehavior >
56   <ActionBehavior>
57   <Action id="Tell population to stay at home">
58     <AverageExecutionTime time="00:10:00:000"/>
59     <Location>55D6</Location>
60     <Msg2Send to="1" content=" Tell population to stay at
61       home completed" compulsory="true" 57bsend2Multiple =
62       "false"> <Device device="BEEPER"/></Msg2Send>
63   </Action>
64   </ActionBehavior>
65 </AgentBehavior>
```

Figure 8. XML definition a person's behavior

The behavior of node (i.e. person) is defined between the tags *<AgentBehavior>*. *Id* is an attribute that identifies the person, based on the organizational structure. *Location* is a dynamic attribute that represents the location of the person. *Reaction Time* is a parameter that indicates how long it takes to react to a stimulus. *Answer Priority Type* is a parameter that identifies the priority of the person to receive a specific command (i.e. the elements that are diffused in the model), and it can be based on *who* is sending the command, on the *device* that is receiving the message, or at random. *Send Priority Type* identifies how the person chooses the commands s/they will send. Their priority can be based on a *priority list*, on *arrival time* or at random. The value inside the tags represents the value of the attribute. Here, we have First Responder 20, located in position 55D6. Their reaction time is 10s, and they prioritize the reception of commands based on the device they came from. For sending commands, they have a priority list. *MyDevices* includes all the devices the agent can use; and it has as many elements as devices. Each device is represented as a tag (*PriorityDevice*) with four attributes (*priority, device, send2Multiple, sendSeparateFromReceive*). *SortedTasks* represents how the agent sorts the tasks they should conduct under an emergency scenario. *AnswerDevicePriority* can have as many entries as devices. *AnswerPersonPriority* has as many elements as individuals the agent has relation with, with two attributes: *priority* and *id*. In this example, receiving a message from person 1 has the highest priority. Person 97 has priority 3. *SendCommandPriority* classifies the set of messages the person may send during an emergency. Every element has three attributes: *priority*, receiver (*to*) and content of a message (*msg*). In this example, transmitting "Tell population to stay home" to person 1 has a high priority. Transmitting "Tell population to stay home" to person 97 has priority 3. *ActionExecutionPriority* has two elements: *priority* and *id*. In this case, "Tell people to stay at home" has the highest priority. *CommunicationRelations* identifies the relations with different individuals. It has one element per individual the agent is connected to. *MessageBehavior* represents how the agent behaves when they receive messages. Finally, *ActionBehavior* identifies how the person should behave when doing an action.

As we mentioned, in order to implement the coupled models, we first need to instantiate the atomic models inside them. To do so, we use one function for each type of coupled. An example of this function is shown in Figure 9.

```
1 /***Instantiate atomics inside the coupled***/
2 pair<vector<string>,vector<string>> AtomicsCoupled;
3 create_atomics_text_msg_device(DeviceType, Id, delay,
4        outOfOrderAcknow){
5 create_atomic_inbox(DeviceType,Id, delay,outOfOrderAcknow);
6  string inbox = "inbox"+DeviceType+Id;
7 create_atomic_outbox(DeviceType,Id,delay, outOfOrderAcknow);
8  string outbox = "outbox"+DeviceType+Id;
9 create_atomic_msgClassifierNewReadCon(DeviceType, Id));
10
11  /****Define coupled: first the I/O ports ****/
12  "using iports_"+DeviceType+Id+"=<inp_setOutOfOrder,
13 inp_network, inp_fromKeyboard>;";    // input ports
14 "using oports_"+DeviceType+Id+
15        "=<outp_toScreen,outp_network>;";
16
17  "using submodels_"+DeviceType+Id+"= models_tuple<"+inbox+
18 ","+outbox+","+msgClassifierNewReadCom+">;"; // SUBMODELS
19
20  //External Input Couplings - eics
21  "using eics_"+DeviceType+Id+" =tuple<"EIC<
22  inp_setOutOfOrder," +inbox+",inbox_defs<SetDeviceState>
23        ::setStateIn>,";
24  "EIC<inp_setOutOfOrder,"+outbox+",outbox_defs
```

```
25        <SetDeviceState>::setStateIn>,";
26  "EIC<inp_network,"+inbox+", inbox_defs<SetDeviceState>
27        ::newIn>,";
28  "EIC<inp_fromKeyboard,")+msgClassifierNewReadCom+",
29     msgClassifierNewRead_defs<Communication>::in>>;";
30
31  //External Input Couplings - eocs
32  "using eocs_"+DeviceType+Id+" =tuple<";
33  "EOC<"+inbox+",inbox_defs<SetDeviceState>::displayOut,
34        outp_toScreen>,";
35  "EOC<"+outbox+", outbox_defs<SetDeviceState>::displayOut,
36    outp_toScreen>,";
37   "EOC<"+outbox+", outbox_defs<SetDeviceState>::networkOut,
38        outp_network>";
39  >;"
40
41  //Internal Couplings - ics
42  "using ics_"+DeviceType+Id+" =tuple<";
43  "IC<"+msgClassifierNewReadCom+",msgClassifierNewRead_defs
44     <Communication>::newOut,"+outbox+",outbox_defs
45     <SetDeviceState>::newIn>,";
46  "IC<"+msgClassifierNewReadCom+", msgClassifierNewRead_defs
47     <Communication>::readOut,"+inbox+" ,inbox_defs
48     <SetDeviceState>::readIn>>;";
49 }
```

Figure 9 Generating the DEVS computerized model of the coupled models e-mail, beeper, and fax

These functions use the XML file in figure 8, and we convert it into the syntax needed by CDBoost. The connections inside the coupled are defined using the logics explained in figure 2 for the coupled models implementation. The rules are written in a way that the output of the function (shown in figure 10) contains all the code needed. Figure 9 shows the implementation of the function used to instantiate a coupled model representing devices that send/receive text (i.e. email). Figure 10 shows the output of this function: the atomics inside the coupled are instantiated and the coupled model is defined following CDBoost definitions, so it can be simulated. We have chosen a simple example to explain the logic behind it. The rest of the functions are implemented following a similar logic taking into account more parameters of the XML file.

```
1 //Atomic models inside the instantiated coupled model
2 template<typename TIME>
3 class msgClassifierNewReadCom : public
4    msgClassifierNewRead<Communication, TIME> {
5 public:
6 msgClassifierNewReadCom(): msgClassifierNewRead<
7    Communication, TIME>(TIME("00:00:500")) {};
8 };
9 template<typename TIME>
10 class inboxFAX1 : public inbox<SetDeviceState, TIME> {
11 public:
12 inboxFAX1():inbox<SetDeviceState,TIME>(DeviceId (DeviceType
13    ::FAX,"1"),TIME("00:00:500"), TIME("00:01:000")){};
14 };
15 template<typename TIME>
16 class outboxFAX1 : public outbox<SetDeviceState, TIME> {
17 public:
18 outboxFAX1(): outbox<SetDeviceState, TIME>(DeviceId
19    (DeviceType::FAX,"1"),TIME("00:00:500"),TIME("00:01:000"))
20    {};      };
21 // instantiated coupled model
```

```
22 using iports_FAX1 = tuple<inp_setOutOfOrder,inp_network,
23        inp_fromKeyboard>;
24 using oports_FAX1 = tuple<outp_toScreen,outp_network>;
25 using submodels_FAX1=models_tuple<inboxFAX1,outboxFAX1,
26    msgClassifierNewReadCom>;
27 using eics_FAX1 =std::tuple<
28    EIC<inp_setOutOfOrder,inboxFAX1, inbox_defs
29        <SetDeviceState>::setStateIn>,
30    EIC<inp_setOutOfOrder,outboxFAX1, outbox_defs
31        <SetDeviceState>::setStateIn>,
32    EIC<inp_network, inboxFAX1, inbox_defs
33        <SetDeviceState>::newIn>,
34    EIC<inp_fromKeyboard,msgClassifierNewReadCom,
35        msgClassifierNewRead_defs<Communication>::in> >;
36
37 using eocs_FAX1 =tuple<
38    EOC<inboxFAX1,inbox_defs<SetDeviceState>::displayOut,
39      outp_toScreen>,
40    EOC<outboxFAX1, outbox_defs<SetDeviceState>::displayOut,
41      outp_toScreen>,
42    EOC<outboxFAX1, outbox_defs<SetDeviceState>::networkOut,
43        outp_network>       >;
44
45 using ics_FAX1 =std::tuple<
46    IC<msgClassifierNewReadCom, msgClassifierNewRead_defs
47      <Communication>::newOut, outboxFAX1,outbox_defs
48      <SetDeviceState>::newIn>,
49    IC<msgClassifierNewReadCom, msgClassifierNewRead_defs
50      <Communication>::readOut,inboxFAX1, inbox_defs
51      <SetDeviceState>::readIn>       >;
```

Figure 10. Output of the function explained in Figure 9

In Figure 9 (lines 1-9), we instantiate the atomic models used inside the couple as we show in Figure 10 (lines 1-20). We call a function that takes as inputs the atomic model parameters and returns the model instantiated in a format that CDBoost understands. The function takes as inputs the type of text message device (i.e. e-mail, fax or beeper), the id of the person that owns the device (i.e. the Id in the agent XML file), and two characteristics of the devices: the delay introduced in the communication and the time it takes to acknowledge that it is out of order.

The rest of the figure defines the coupled model instantiation. Lines 11-19 (Figure 9) returns the coupled model input and output ports and the submodels inside the coupled implemented as a tuple as shown in Figure 10 (lines 21-26). Lines 20-30 (Figure 9) generates the External Input Couplings (EIC) as a tuple of tuples of 3 elements: the name of the input port, the name of submodel connected to the input port, and the input port name of the submodel (lines 27-36 figure10) External Output Couplings (EOC) are defined as the EIC but with a different order: submodel name, output port name of the sub model and output port name of the coupled (see lines 31-39 in Figure 9 for the function definition and lines 37-43 in Figure 10 for the output). Finally, Internal Couplings (IC) are defined as a tuple of tuples of four elements: name of the outcoming subcomponent, sub model output port name, the name of the incoming sub, sub model input port name. In Figure 9 (lines 41-49), we show the code that generates the implementation. The output of the code is shown in Figure 10 (lines 45-51).

The top-level model is built using a program that takes the XML files where the agents are defined, it reads each XML file and transforms them into a structure to generate the parameters of all the functions explained earlier in this section. The output is a file with thousands of lines of code that CDBoost understands. This file includes all the atomic and coupled models' instantiated, which, once compiled, generates the Diffusion Computer model ready to generate results.

```
1  int main(int argc, char ** argv) {
2      int numberOfPersons = stoi(argv[1]);
3      string folder = argv[2];
4      string mainModel = string("../TOPMODEL/MainTop.cpp");
5      string content, tSUBMODELS, tIC, tEIC, tEOC, tIPORTS;
6      string tOPORTS = "outp_taskDeviceFinished,
7          outp_taskActionFinished";
8
9      myModelfile.open(mainModel);
10     TOP = open_coupled(string("TOP"));
11
12     ifstream infile("NEP_Cadmium_Headers");
13     //Define Headers and I/O ports inside MainTop.cpp
14     for(int i=0; infile.eof()!=true ; i++)
15     // get content of infile
16         content += infile.get();
17     myModelfile << content << endl;
18
19     for(int i = 1; i <= numberOfPersons; i++){
20     // DEVICES
21     in = folder+string("P")+to_string(i)+string(".xml");
22     person.load(in);
23     DEVICES = DevicesCoupledModel(person);
24        for(int j = 0; j<DEVICES.first.size(); j++)
25        myModelfile << DEVICES.first[j] << endl;
26        for(int j = 0; j<DEVICES.second.size(); j++)
27        myModelfile << DEVICES.second[j] << endl;
28     }
29 ...
```

Figure 11. Code snippet of the top model generator

Figure 11 shows a part of the program that generates the top model (i.e. an instance of the DAM to study an information diffusion process), which can be seen in Figure 12. The rest of the program is developed following the same logic. We use the number of agents (i.e. the number of XML files to be loaded) and their directory path. The number of agents is used to define the number of instances of *Devices* and *Person* models inside the coupled model, as shown in lines 2 and 19. In lines 5-7 we define all the variables needed to define the top coupled model. Then, we define our coupled model. First, we parse a file where the headers of CDBoost and of the parameterized DEVS atomic models are defined (lines 12-17). The top model ports are also defined in that file. The output of this part of the program is shown in figure 18, lines 1-8. Then, we call the functions explained earlier to generate the DEVS component in the top model. In lines 19-28 (Figure 11), we show the definition of all the *Devices* coupled models. For each agent, we define a *Devices* model by loading the proper XML and calling the function that generates the coupled model (line 23). We then generate all the atomic instantiated models and the coupled model in *MainTop.cpp* (lines 24-27). Figure 12 shows a code snippet of the output of this.

```
1 struct inp_generator : public in_port<Command>{};
2 // SET INPUT PORTS FOR COUPLED
3 struct inp_network : public in_port<Communication>{};
4 ...
5 outp_myLocation : public out_port<PeopleLocation>{};
6  // SET OUTPUT PORTS FOR COUPLED
7 outp_network : public out_port<Communication>{};
8 ...
9 template<typename TIME>
10   // Define atomic and coupled unit devices
11 class filterDevicesNetwork1: public
12       filterDevicesNetwork<TIME> {
13 public: filterDevicesNetwork1():
14       filterDevicesNetwork<TIME>("1") {};              };
15
16 template<typename TIME>
17 class filterDevicesSetOutOrder1: public
18       filterDevicesSetOutOrder<TIME> {
19 public: filterDevicesSetOutOrder1():
20       filterDevicesSetOutOrder<TIME>("1") {};          };
21
22 template<typename TIME>
23 class phoneMOBILEPHONE1 : public phone<SetDeviceState,
24            TIME> {
25 public: phoneMOBILEPHONE1(): phone<SetDeviceState,TIME>
26  (DeviceId(DeviceType::MOBILEPHONE, "1"),TIME("00:00:500"),
27   TIME("00:01:000")) {};   };
28
29 template<typename TIME>
30 class phoneLANDLINEPHONE1 : public phone<SetDeviceState,
31       TIME> {
32 public: phoneLANDLINEPHONE1(): phone<SetDeviceState,
33     TIME>(DeviceId(DeviceType::LANDLINEPHONE,"1"),
34     TIME("00:00:500"),TIME("00:01:000")) {};       };
35 //DEFINE COUPLED DEVICE
36 using iports_DEVICES1 = tuple<inp_setOutOfOrder,
37   inp_in_com,inp_network>;
38 using oports_DEVICES1 = tuple<outp_out_com, outp_network>;
39 using submodels_DEVICES1 = models_tuple<
40   filterDevicesSetOutOrder1, filterDevicesNetwork1,
41   filterDevicesMicroKeyboard, sinkDevices_atomic,
42   phoneMOBILEPHONE1, phoneLANDLINEPHONE1,>
43 using eics_DEVICES1 = tuple<
44   EIC<inp_setOutOfOrder,filterDevicesSetOutOrder1,
45     filterDevicesSetOutOrder_defs::in>,
46   EIC<inp_in_com,filterDevicesMicroKeyboard,
47     filterDevicesMicroKeyboard_defs::in>,
48   EIC<inp_network,filterDevicesNetwork1,
49     filterDevicesNetwork_defs::in>          >;
50 ...
```

Figure 12. Output of the program defined in Figure 11

5 CASE STUDY: INFORMATION DIFFUSION

In this section, we present a case study where the DAM is used to simulate an information diffusion process in an organization. Inside the organization, the people have different communication mechanism to transmit the information such as Landline Phones, Radio, E-mail, Mobile Phones, Face-to-Face communications, etc.

We used the original data from an existing Nuclear Emergency Plan (NEP) in Spain. All the requirements related to the problem are defined in a requirements document [33]–[35] that contains a comprehensive definition of the NEP organization, the

communications means to transmit the information and the rules each person follows to transmit the information. Using this data, we defined the XML files presented in Figure 8 for each person involved in the diffusion process.

To study the information diffusion process we instantiate the DAM into a NEP DAM as follows:

- Each *Node* is instantiated as *Person* (i.e. as a person working in the emergency), whose behavior is defined using a parameterized DEVS coupled model.

- Each *Indirect Link* model is instantiated as a *Devices* model. *Devices* is a coupled model that contains all the devices the specific person can use. It is instantiated using the attribute *<MyDevices>* in the XML file.

- The *Links Connector* is mapped into the *Networks* (i.e. a coupled model that contains all the networks connecting specific devices: Radio, Internet, satellite, etc.).

- The *Direct Link* is mapped to a *Face-to-Face Connector* because in our model the direct links represent people talking face to face.

- *Indirect Links Updater* and *Links Connectors Updater* are instantiated to *Devices* and *Networks Updaters* respectively since they introduce change on the state of *Devices* and *Networks* models. They model if the devices or networks break or recover dynamically.

- *Node Updater* is mapped to *People in Location*, since the only attribute of the *Person* model we want to track is the people who share location and therefore they can communicate face-to-face.

- *Direct Link Updater* is not included in this specific instantiation since we are not interested in modifying the properties that may affect face-to-face communications such as environmental noise.

- *Diffusion Element Generator* is converted into the *Command Generator* since the diffusion elements in this specific process are commands that give information to people to solve the emergency.

Based on this definition, we executed a version of the NEP DAM including 149 persons with their Devices, including the Head of the Nuclear Emergency Plan and the Radiological Group. The Computer Model is generated automatically using the XML files that represent the individual behavior of each person, as explained in section 4. If the data presented in the requirements document is stored in a structured way (e.g. tables), it can be automatically parsed to create these XML files. The data in the requirements document can also be directly stored in XML format. If the data is stored in natural language as a set of text specifications, it should be manually translated to XML format or an intermediated structured format that allows creating the XML files automatically.

We have focused on studying what happens when the command "Establish Emergency Level 0" is decreed by the NEP Director and the specific communication device inside the Radiological Group fails with different probabilities. The failure may represent that the device runs out of battery, it does not receive a signal, it breaks, etc. We have simulated different scenarios where this device fails with different probabilities (i.e. 10%, 20%, etc.).The simulations represent a 95% Confidence Interval for the mean of people that receive the command "Establish Emergency Level 0". The confidence interval is represented as notches in the plot (figure 13). This analysis provides some information to decision makers and it is useful to validate our model.

Based on the NEP specifications, we know that 63 people should receive a command from the head of the radiological group. We also know that the Radiological group only uses a *radiological group device* (RGD, a specific device with mixed radio-phone communication).

Figure 13 shows the number of people that receive the command "Establish Emergency Level 0" when we simulate different probabilities of failure of the *RGD*. We use a box plot in which the triangle represents the mean, the horizontal line the median and the circles the outliers.

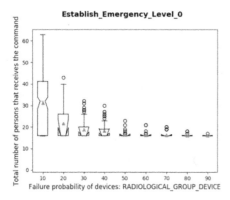

Figure 13 *RGD* failures

We can see that, regardless the failure probability, some people always receive the command. This number remains constant since they are part of the NEP leadership and they do not use the RGD to communicate. However, even with a 10% failure probability, in 75% of the cases, less than 40 people receive the command and the median is around 30. If the failure probability increases to 20%, the median is drastically reduced to less than 20 people. This value remains constant when the failure probability increases over 20%. Based on this analysis and taking into account the definitions of the NEP, we can conclude that we cannot afford a failure rate of only 10% in the RGDs because in more than 75% of the cases less than 40 people out of 63 receive the command.

Figure 14 shows how many times each device is used based on the failure probability of the RGD. We use these results to validate our model.

In figure 14 a), we can see that the beeper is not used (the mean, medium and quartiles are all zero). Although only the beeper is shown, we obtain the same results for fax, e-mail, private landline phone, two radio channels - REMAR and REMER -, satellite phone, and TrankiE - a phone-radio used by the police -. This result is correct, as the specification document says that none of these devices should be used by the radiological group.

In figure 14 (b-e), we show that the data distribution is uniform when we simulate failures in the RGD. The number of attempts to establish the communication causes variability in the different simulations. These results validate the model based on the NEP specifications, which says that the Radiological Group only use the RGD. This restriction justifies why the plots in figure 14 (a-e) are uniform for the different failure probabilities.

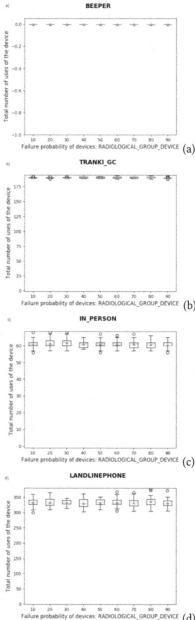

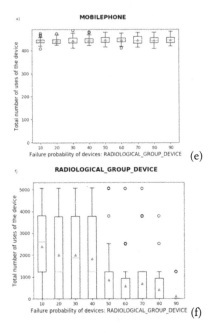

(e)

(f)

Figure 14 Number of activations of the different devices when the RGD fails with different probabilities.

Figure 14 f) shows two different trends. When the failure probability is low (less than 50%), the number of activations of the RGD is high. The variability for each failure probability is also high (i.e. wide interquartile range). When the failure probability is 50% or greater, the number of activations is significantly reduced and the variability is lower. The mean of the number of RGD activations shows a decreasing trend. When the failure probability is low, there are many devices working. If a device does not fail, the owner keeps trying to communicate (i.e. the total number of activations of the device is high). But if they see that their device is not working, they stop using it. Therefore, when a device fails and the owner has something to send the information transmission process is blocked. In those cases, the number of activations for the devices is lower. An increase in the failure probability is translated in an increase of the number of devices broken. Then, the probability to block the information transmission increases. This explains why the mean decreases. Additionally, figure 14 f) shows, that regardless the failure probability, there are cases (i.e. simulations) where the RGD is activated just one time. These results show that there is a critical person in the process, and they can block the whole information transmission if their device is broken (this has been confirmed analyzing the simulation logs and NEP specifications), which confirms that if the device of the Radiological Group head is broken, the whole process is blocked.

Based on these results, we can see we need to review the communications within the Radiological group. The simulation results allowed us to come with following questions that affect the organization: why the people within the radiological group cannot use their mobile phone or e-mail? Is there any security issue (e.g. authentication, encryption, etc.)? The discussion of these questions with decision makers will bring new scenarios to

analyze to test different solutions. Then, to simulate a new scenarios they just update the model parameters in the XML files, such as the devices for each person or the communication devices that they can use with other people. Then, they run the program that automatically instantiates the DAM and generates the computerized model and runs the simulation.

6 CONCLUSIONS

We presented an Abstract Model for diffusion processes in multiplex networks, and discussed its definition and implementation using DEVS and CDBoost. To show how we get results using the DAM, we presented an information diffusion process inside an organization (a real nuclear emergency plan from Spain), and studied the effects of failures in their communication channels, focusing on the effect of different failure probabilities.

By using the DAM to simulate diffusion process in multiplex dynamic networks, we show how a formal definition provides several advantages which were detailed along the paper. A major advantage is that it allows validating the model before implementation, which improves the model quality and cost. The case study presented this the paper has shown how the DAM can generate results for different scenarios without modifying a line of code. We have also provided information to decision makers in order to improve the communications inside one group of the NEP: the radiological group.

Future research lines will focus applying the DAM to study other diffusion processes in multiplex dynamic networks.

REFERENCES

[1] M. Newman, "The structure and function of complex networks," *SIAM Rev.*, vol. 45, no. 2, pp. 167–256, 2003.

[2] S. Gómez, A. Díaz-Guilera, J. Gómez-Gardeñes, C. J. Pérez-Vicente, Y. Moreno, and A. Arenas, "Diffusion Dynamics on Multiplex Networks," *Phys. Rev. Lett.*, vol. 110, no. 2, p. 28701, 2013.

[3] H. Xiong, W. Puqing, and G. V Bobashev, "Multiple Peer Effects in the Diffusion of Innovations on Social Networks: A Simulation Study," *SSRN Electron. J.*, 2015.

[4] A. Khelil, C. Becker, J. Tian, and K. Rothermel, "An epidemic model for information diffusion in MANETs," *Proc. 5th ACM Int. Work. Model. Anal. Simul. Wirel. Mob. Syst. - MSWiM '02*, p. 54, 2002.

[5] C. Ruiz-Martin, "An architecture to simulate diffusion processes in multiplex dynamic networks," in *2017 Winter Simulation Conference (WSC)*, 2017, pp. 4630–4631.

[6] B. P. Zeigler, H. Praehofer, and T. G. Kim, *Theory of modeling and simulation: integrating discrete event and continuous complex dynamic systems*. Academic press, 2000.

[7] V. Capasso and G. Serio, "A generalization of the Kermack-McKendrick deterministic epidemic model," *Math. Biosci.*, vol. 42, no. 1–2, pp. 43–61, 1978.

[8] W. Wang, Q.-H. Liu, S.-M. Cai, M. Tang, L. A. Braunstein, and H. E. Stanley, "Suppressing disease spreading by using information diffusion on multiplex networks," *Sci. Rep.*, vol. 6, no. 7600, p. 29259, 2016.

[9] C. Granell, S. Gomez, and A. Arenas, "Dynamical interplay between awareness and epidemic spreading in multiplex networks," *Phys. Rev. Lett.*, vol. 111, no. 12, pp. 1–10, 2013.

[10] A. Raj, A. Kuceyeski, and M. Weiner, "A Network Diffusion Model of Disease Progression in Dementia," *Neuron*, vol. 73, no. 6, pp. 1204–1215, 2012.

[11] O. Yağan and V. Gligor, "Analysis of complex contagions in random multiplex networks," *Phys. Rev. E - Stat. Nonlinear, Soft Matter Phys.*, vol. 86, no. 3, pp. 1–11, 2012.

[12] E. Cozzo, R. A. Baños, S. Meloni, and Y. Moreno, "Contact-based Social Contagion in Multiplex Networks," *Phys. Rev. E - Stat. Nonlinear, Soft Matter Phys.*, vol. 88, no. 5, pp. 1–5, Jul. 2013.

[13] E. Estrada and J. Gómez-Gardeñes, "Communicability reveals a transition to coordinated behavior in multiplex networks," *Phys. Rev. E - Stat. Nonlinear, Soft Matter Phys.*, vol. 89, no. 4, pp. 1–5, 2014.

[14] M. Kivela, A. Arenas, M. Barthelemy, J. P. Gleeson, Y. Moreno, and M. A.

Porter, "Multilayer networks," *J. Complex Networks*, vol. 2, no. 3, pp. 203–271, Sep. 2014.

[15] S. Boccaletti, G. Bianconi, R. Criado, C. I. del Genio, J. Gomez-Gardeñes, M. Romance, I. Sendiña-Nadal, Z. Wang, and M. Zanin, "The structure and dynamics of multilayer networks," *Phys. Rep.*, vol. 544, no. 1, pp. 1–122, 2014.

[16] Y. Jiang and J. C. Jiang, "Diffusion in Social Networks: A Multiagent Perspective," *IEEE Trans. Syst. Man, Cybern. Syst.*, vol. 45, no. 2, pp. 198–213, Feb. 2015.

[17] Y. Bouanan, G. Zacharewicz, B. Vallespir, J. Ribault, and S. Y. Diallo, "DEVS based Network: Modeling and Simulation of Propagation Processes in a Multi-Layers Network," in *Proceedings of the Modeling and Simulation of Complexity in Intelligent, Adaptive and Autonomous Systems 2016*, 2016.

[18] C. Ruiz-Martin, Y. Bouanan, G. Wainer, G. Zacharewicz, and A. Lopez-Paredes, "A hybrid approach to study communication in emergency plans," in *Proceedings of the 2016 Winter Simulation Conference*, 2016, pp. 1376–1387.

[19] F. J. Barros, "Modeling formalisms for dynamic structure systems," *ACM Trans. Model. Comput. Simul.*, vol. 7, no. 4, pp. 501–515, 1997.

[20] M. Sbayou, Y. Bouanan, G. Zacharewicz, J. Ribault, and J. François, "DEVS modelling and simulation for healthcare process application for hospital emergency department," *Simul. Ser.*, vol. 49, no. 1, 2017.

[21] J. Himmelspach and A. M. Uhrmacher, "A component-based simulation layer for JAMES," in *Proceedings of the eighteenth workshop on Parallel and distributed simulation - PADS '04*, 2004, p. 115.

[22] J.-B. Filippi and P. Bisgambiglia, "JDEVS: an implementation of a DEVS based formal framework for environmental modelling," *Environ. Model. Softw.*, vol. 19, no. 3, pp. 261–274, Mar. 2004.

[23] H. S. Sarjoughian and B. P. Zeigler, "DEVSJAVA: Basis for a DEVS-based Collaborative M & S Environment," in *Proceedings of SCS International Conference on Web-Based Modeling and Simulation*, 1998.

[24] D. Vicino, D. Niyonkuru, G. Wainer, and O. Dalle, "Sequential PDEVS Architecture," in *DEVS '15 Proceedings of the Symp on Theory of M&S: DEVS Integrative M&S Symposium*, 2015, pp. 165–172.

[25] C. Ruiz-Martin, G. Wainer, and A. Lopez-Paredes, "DISCRETE-EVENT SIMULATION OF DIFFUSION PROCESSES IN DYNAMIC MULTIPLEX NETWORKS," *SIMPAT*.

[26] M. Bastian, S. Heymann, and M. Jacomy, "Gephi: An open source software for exploring and manipulating networks.," *ICWSM*, vol. 8, pp. 361–362, 2009.

[27] W. De Nooy, A. Mrvar, and V. Batagelj, *Exploratory social network analysis with Pajek*. Cambridge University Press, 2005.

[28] M. De Domenico, M. A. Porter, and A. Arenas, "MuxViz: a tool for multilayer analysis and visualization of networks," *J. Complex Networks*, p. cnu038, 2014.

[29] C. Nikolai and G. Madey, "Tools of the Trade: A Survey of Various Agent Based Modeling Platforms," *J. Artif. Soc. Soc. Simul.*, vol. 12, no. 22, 2009.

[30] G. Wainer, *Discrete-Event Modeling and Simulation: A Practitioner's Approach*. CRC Press, 2009.

[31] R. Ihaka and R. Gentleman, "R: A Language for Data Analysis and Graphics," *J. Comput. Graph. Stat.*, vol. 5, no. 3, pp. 299–314, 1996.

[32] Microsoft, "Power BI," 2015. [Online]. Available: https://powerbi.microsoft.com/es-es/.

[33] C. Ruiz-Martin, "Modelo Organizacional para la Gestión de Emergencias," Universidad de Valladolid, 2014.

[34] C. Ruiz-Martin, M. Ramírez Ferrero, J. L. Gonzalez-Alvarez, and A. Lopez-Paredes, "Modelling of a Nuclear Emergency Plan: Communication Management," *Hum. Ecol. Risk Assess. An Int. J.*, vol. 21, no. 5, pp. 1152–1168, 2015.

[35] C. Ruiz-Martin, A. Lopez-Paredes, and G. Wainer, "Applying complex network theory to the assessment of organizational resilience," *IFAC-PapersOnLine*, vol. 48, no. 3, pp. 1224–1229, 2015.

APPENDIX I

The formal definition of Switch atomic model is as follows:

$$Switch(Id) = <X, Y, S, ta, \delta_{ext}, \delta_{int}, \delta_{con}, \lambda>$$

Where

$$X = \left\{ \begin{array}{c} ("diffusionElementIn", diffusionElement), \\ ("setAnswerIn", setStateAnswer), \\ ("setSendIn", setStateSend), \\ ("setDecideIn", setStateDecide) \end{array} \right\}$$

$diffusionElement \in DiffusionElements$

$DiffusionElements \in \forall structure\ with\ field\ "destinatary"$

$setStateAnswer, setStateSend, setStateDecide \in \forall structure$

$$Y = \left\{ \begin{array}{c} ("sendOut", diffusionElement \cup \emptyset)U \\ ("answerOut", diffusionElement \cup \emptyset)U \\ ("decideOut", diffusionElement \cup \emptyset)| \\ diffusionElement \in (DiffusionElements|destinatary = Id) \end{array} \right\}$$

$$S = \left\{ \begin{array}{c} messagesPassing, state\ | \\ messagesPassing = \emptyset \cup \\ messagesPassing\{diffusionElement\ |\ destinatary = Id\} \\ state \in \{ANSWER, SEND, DECIDE\} \end{array} \right\}$$

$ta(s)$
$$= \left\{ \begin{array}{c} messagesPassing = \emptyset \rightarrow \infty \\ messagesPassing = \{diffusionElement\ |\ destinatary = Id\} \rightarrow 0ms \end{array} \right\}$$

$\delta_{ext}(S, e, X)$
$$= \left\{ \begin{array}{c} (X\ in\ diffusionElementIn\ |destinatary = Id) \rightarrow messagesPassing += X \\ (X\ in\ setAnswerIn) \rightarrow state = ANSWER \\ (X\ in\ setSendIn) \rightarrow state = SEND \\ (X\ in\ setDecideIn) \rightarrow state = DECIDE \end{array} \right\}$$

$\delta_{int}(S) = \{messagesPassing = \emptyset\}$

$\delta_{con}(S, e, X) = \delta_{int}(S) + \delta_{ext}(S, e, X)$

$$\lambda(S) = \left\{ \begin{array}{c} if(state = ANSWER) \rightarrow send\ messagesPassing\ by\ answerOut \\ if(state = SEND) \rightarrow send\ messagesPassing\ by\ sendOut \\ if(state = DECIDE) \rightarrow send\ messagesPassing\ by\ decideOut \end{array} \right\}$$

APPENDIX II

The formal definition of Indirect Links coupled model is as follows:

$$Indirect\ Links = <X, Y, D, \{M_d|d \in D\}, EIC, EOC, IC>$$

Where

$$X = \left\{ \begin{array}{c} ("NodeIn", diffusionElement)U \\ ("LinkConnectorsIn", diffusionElement)U \\ ("UpdaterIn", stateUpdate) \end{array} \right\}$$

$diffusionElement \in DiffusionElements$

$stateUpdate \in StateUpdates$

$DiffusionElements \in \forall structure\ with\ field\ "Destinatary"$

$StateUpdates \in \forall structure\ with\ field\ "LinkType"$

$$Y = \left\{ \begin{array}{c} ("NodeOut", diffusionElement)U \\ ("LinkConnectorsOut", diffusionElement) \end{array} \right\}$$

$$D = \left\{ \begin{array}{c} FilterNode, FiterUpdater, FilterLinkConnectors, \\ LinkType_1, LinkType_2, \ldots, LinkType_n, \\ LinkSink \end{array} \right\}$$

$$M = \left\{ \begin{array}{c} M_{FilterNode}, M_{FiterUpdater}, \ldots, M_{FilterLinkConnectors} \\ M_{LinkType1}, M_{LinkType2}, \ldots, M_{LinkTypen}, \\ M_{LinkSink} \end{array} \right\}$$

EIC
$$= \left\{ \begin{array}{c} ((Self, Self_{NodeIn}), (FilterNode, FilterNode_{In})), \\ ((Self, Self_{UpdaterIn}), (FilterUpdater, FilterUpdater_{In})), \\ ((Self, Self_{LinkConnectorsIn}), (FilterLinkConnectors, FilterLinkConnectors_{In})) \end{array} \right\}$$

EOC
$$= \left\{ \begin{array}{c} ((LinkType1, LinkType1_{NodeOut}), (Self, Self_{NodeOut})), \\ \ldots \\ ((LinkTypen, LinkTypen_{NodeOut}), (Self, Self_{NodeOut})) \\ ((LinkType1, LinkType1_{LinkConnectorsOut}), (Self, Self_{LinkConnectorsOut})), \\ \ldots \\ ((LinkTypen, LinkTypen_{LinkConnectorsOut}), (Self, Self_{LinkConnectorsOut})) \end{array} \right\}$$

IC
$$= \left\{ \begin{array}{c} ((FilterNode, FilterNode_{LT1Out}), (LinkType1, LinkType1_{NodeIn})), \\ \ldots \\ ((FilterNode, FilterNode_{LTnOut}), (LinkTypen, LinkTypen_{NodeIn})), \\ ((FilterNode, FilterNode_{LTn+1Out}), (LinkSink, LinkSink_{NodeIn})), \\ \ldots \\ ((FilterNode, FilterNode_{LTmOut}), (LinkSink, LinkSink_{NodeIn})), \\ ((FilterUpdater, FilterUpdater_{LT1Out}), (LinkType1, LinkType1_{UpdaterIn})), \\ \ldots \\ ((FilterUpdater, FilterUpdater_{LTnOut}), (LinkTypen, LinkTypen_{UpdaterIn})), \\ ((FilterUpdater, FilterUpdater_{LTn+1Out}), (LinkSink, LinkSink_{UpdaterIn})), \\ \ldots \\ ((FilterUpdater, FilterUpdater_{LTmOut}), (LinkSink, LinkSink_{UpdaterIn})), \\ ((FilterLinkConnectors, FilterLinkConnectors_{LT1Out}), (LinkType1, LinkType1_{ConnectorsIn})), \\ \ldots \\ ((FilterLinkConnectors, FilterLinkConnectors_{LTnOut}), (LinkTypen, LinkTypen_{ConnectorsIn})), \\ ((FilterLinkConnectors, FilterLinkConnectors_{LTn+1Out}), (LinkSink, LinkSink_{ConnectorsIn})), \\ \ldots \\ ((FilterLinkConnectors, FilterLinkConnectors_{LTmOut}), (LinkSink, LinkSink_{ConnectorsIn})) \end{array} \right\}$$

$n = \#LinkTypes\ in\ Indirect\ Link$

$m = Total\ \#LinkTypes\ in\ the\ model$

The Ultimate Share-Everything PDES System

Mauro Ianni
Sapienza, University of Rome
Lockless S.r.l.
mianni@diag.uniroma1.it
ianni@lockless.it

Romolo Marotta
Sapienza, University of Rome
Lockless S.r.l.
marotta@diag.uniroma1.it
marotta@lockless.it

Davide Cingolani
Sapienza, University of Rome
Lockless S.r.l.
cingolani@diag.uniroma1.it
cingolani@lockless.it

Alessandro Pellegrini
Sapienza, University of Rome
Lockless S.r.l.
pellegrini@diag.uniroma1.it
pellegrini@lockless.it

Francesco Quaglia
University of Rome "Tor Vergata"
Lockless S.r.l.
francesco.quaglia@uniroma2.it
quaglia@lockless.it

ABSTRACT

The share-everything PDES (Parallel Discrete Event Simulation) paradigm is based on fully sharing the possibility to process any individual event across concurrent threads, rather than binding Logical Processes (LPs) and their events to threads. It allows concentrating, at any time, the computing power—the CPU-cores on board of a shared-memory machine—towards the unprocessed events that stand closest to the current commit horizon of the simulation run. This fruitfully biases the delivery of the computing power towards the hot portion of the model execution trajectory. In this article we present an innovative share-everything PDES system that provides (1) fully non-blocking coordination of the threads when accessing shared data structures and (2) fully speculative processing capabilities—Time Warp style processing—of the events. As we show via an experimental study, our proposal can cope with hard workloads where both classical Time Warp systems—based on LPs to threads binding—and previous share-everything proposals—not able to exploit fully speculative processing of the events—tend to fail in delivering adequate performance.

KEYWORDS

Discrete Event Simulation; PDES; Pending Event Set; Lock-free Synchronization; Speculative Simulation; Shared Memory; Share Everything

ACM Reference Format:
Mauro Ianni, Romolo Marotta, Davide Cingolani, Alessandro Pellegrini, and Francesco Quaglia. 2018. The Ultimate Share-Everything PDES System. In *SIGSIM-PADS '18: SIGSIM Principles of Advanced Discrete Simulation CD-ROM, May 23–25, 2018, Rome, Italy*. ACM, New York, NY, USA, 12 pages. https://doi.org/10.1145/3200921.3200931

Permission to make digital or hard copies of all or part of this work for personal or classroom use is granted without fee provided that copies are not made or distributed for profit or commercial advantage and that copies bear this notice and the full citation on the first page. Copyrights for components of this work owned by others than the author(s) must be honored. Abstracting with credit is permitted. To copy otherwise, or republish, to post on servers or to redistribute to lists, requires prior specific permission and/or a fee. Request permissions from permissions@acm.org.
SIGSIM-PADS '18 , May 23–25, 2018, Rome, Italy
© 2018 Copyright held by the owner/author(s). Publication rights licensed to the Association for Computing Machinery.
ACM ISBN 978-1-4503-5092-1/18/05...$15.00
https://doi.org/10.1145/3200921.3200931

1 INTRODUCTION

Parallel Discrete Event Simulation (PDES) [7] is a powerful methodology, which provides the support for simulating huge/large and complex discrete-event systems. PDES has been conceived in order to enable the exploitation of (massively) parallel computing systems. This is achieved by partitioning the simulation model into simulation objects (also known as Logical Processes - LPs) which are enabled to process simulation events concurrently.

Along its life, this methodology has been integrated with techniques and solutions aimed at continuously improving its capability to fruitfully exploit computing resources, with the ultimate objective of improving performance and scalability. However, until recently, the most of the literature techniques were based on recognizing an individual simulation object as the work unit within the optimization process. Consequently, optimizations of PDES have been essentially based on optimizing the run time dynamics of PDES systems under the common way of thinking that simulation events are not fully representative as individuals in the optimization process. Rather, aggregates of events have been seen as the *weight* to be assigned to a simulation object in order to determine how to manage it in the simulation run. As an example, an object targeted by sets of CPU-demanding events is typically considered as a heavy-weight object, a factor that has been considered as relevant to bind that object to a specific thread—or CPU-core—in order to enable balanced advancement of the logical time across all the objects (see, e.g., [3]).

In more recent times, the advent of multi-core shared-memory machines has generated a new way of devising optimizations of PDES. This is based on the idea that all threads—so all CPU-cores—running the PDES platform can fully share finer grain work units, namely individual events possibly bound to different simulation objects. This is the *share-everything* PDES paradigm conceived in [15]. It has the intrinsic advantage of enabling the delivery of the overall used computing power to the events that are—at any time—the closest ones to the current commit horizon of the simulation. In fact, this paradigm imposes no limitation on what simulation objects can be dispatched for execution by a thread along the simulation execution timeline—a limitation that is instead typical of common PDES systems based on partitioning the objects across worker threads. Such a new approach is simple in principle, in fact it is based on the concept of a fully-shared event pool containing the events destined to whichever simulation object, from which all the threads extract the higher priority events (those with timestamps closer to the current commit horizon) for processing, and into which the same threads put newly generated events.

On the other hand, fully sharing the workload of events across all threads poses hard problems in terms of managing the computing power in a truly scalable and effective way. In fact, a share-everything PDES engine capable of exploiting such computing power should guarantee that:

A) threads do not block each other while accessing shared data structures, namely the event pool and also the actual states of the simulation objects—otherwise thread synchronization would become a bottleneck;

B) threads do not wait for each other because of potential causality constraints between the simulation events (so the objects) they are currently running—otherwise virtual-time synchronization would become a major factor preventing hardware parallelism exploitation.

Overall, an ideal share-everything PDES platform should guarantee scalability along the following two dimensions in a combined manner: 1) wall-clock-time coordination across threads and 2) virtual-time coordination across simulation objects, ultimately managed by threads. While point 1) has recently been tackled by a few works [12, 16]—they provided non-blocking algorithms for managing the fully shared event pool and share-everything-suited event-dispatching rules that avoid collisions across threads in the access to the state of the simulation objects—a holistic design coping with both the above points in a combined manner is still lacking. Such a design is the objective of this article, where we present a share-everything PDES system that entails speculative execution capabilities of the simulation objects—guaranteeing scalability of virtual-time coordination—and fully non-blocking wall-clock-time coordination across threads.

Technically, our work provides solutions for a set of problems intrinsically related to the construction of speculative share-everything PDES systems, which were not tackled by the literature. They are:

- the definition of non-blocking algorithms for managing a fully-shared pending-event set that contains both schedule-committed events (those produced by the execution of other events that have been detected to be safe and causally consistent) and non-committed ones (those that are the result of speculative, not yet committed, processing actions), which might need to be (logically) canceled;

- the definition of non-blocking algorithms for dispatching the events to be processed across threads in such a way that threads never collide on a same simulation object and causal consistency is detected on-the-fly—also exploiting lookahead information—leading to the possibility to optimize the way events are actually processed (in terms of configuration of event-undo support). Consequently, our PDES system provides solutions for combining on a fine-grain basis (event by event), conservative and speculative processing techniques.

As a matter of fact, our share-everything PDES system can cope with hard-workload scenarios where there are (sudden) skews in the distribution of the events across simulation objects along virtual time. These skews possibly create relatively short bursts of events to be processed at a subset of the objects, while other objects have no (or few) events to be processed along that same virtual time window. In these scenarios traditional PDES-oriented load balancing approaches, based on medium-term binding between objects and threads, have scarce capability to react to the sudden unbalance that may materialize, which can lead to an increase of the likelihood of wasted computation in case of speculative processing. The share-everything paradigm that we adopt considers events as fully-shared workload units, thus being able to concentrate the computing power, say threads, on any burst of events that materializes among subsets of objects—any thread can in fact take care of processing whatever event in these bursts, thus contributing to promptly advance the currently hot portions of the simulation model. Furthermore, the speculative processing capabilities we include in our PDES system enable threads to process these bursts with no blocking phase along virtual time, as instead it occurs in previous share-everything proposals like [12].

On the downside, the price our share-everything PDES system pays stands in the impossibility to exploit large or extreme scale clusters of distributed memory resources, which can instead be exploited by traditional non-shared memory bound PDES engines [2]. However, the perspective of our design is strengthened by the always rising trend towards larger numbers CPU-cores on a same shared-memory chipset, motivated by the already reached power wall affecting the growth of the computing speed of individual CPU-cores. On the other hand, future PDES architectures could be envisaged where on each individual shared-memory machine an instance of our share-everything PDES platform could be run, and the instances could, in their turn, be clustered via additional coordination mechanisms on a distributed memory platform.

Our share-everything PDES system has been released as open source[1] and we also report experimental data for an assessment of our proposal in comparison with traditional PDES and previous share-everything solutions not entailing speculative capabilities.

The remainder of this article is structured as follows. In Section 2 related work is discussed. Section 3 presents the design of our *ultimate* share-everything PDES system. Experimental results are reported in Section 4.

2 RELATED WORK

Our proposal is along the path of building PDES systems that are optimized for execution on shared-memory machines. This topic has been addressed in the literature by several works and in compliance with various objectives. In [22, 24–26] the authors provide solutions for reorganizing traditional-style PDES systems, making them more suited for shared-memory platforms. Few solutions optimize the architecture of the communication facilities across the threads. Other solutions take advantage of the possibility for any thread to promptly access the state of any simulation object and of its event queue when a re-bind between objects and threads is needed—for load balancing—depending on the objects' current weight in the computation. In some case, interference from external workload is also considered in the re-bind. Our solution is completely different from these proposals since it is not based on traditional partitioning

---

[1]Source code available at https://github.com/HPDCS/USE
Artifact available at https://doi.org/10.5281/zenodo.1196287

of the workload (say the objects) across the threads, and on periodic re-evaluation of partitions. Rather, we consider any individual event as a work unit that can be dispatched along any thread in the PDES system.

The works in [5, 17, 18] exploit shared memory for enriching the PDES programming model in order to provide support for sharing information across simulation objects. This objective is achieved by means of transactional memory, software instrumentation or operating system facilities. However, these proposals are still bound to the traditional PDES paradigm. In fact, they have been integrated into environments that still rely on object (namely workload) partitioning across threads, rather than fine-grain sharing of individual work units—single events—like in our approach.

Clearly, the solution we provide also stands along the path of building environments where threads coordinate in the access to the fully-shared event pool—or more generally to shared data structures—in a highly scalable manner. The topic of providing event-pool data structures enabling concurrent accesses has been addressed in [1], which proposes an approach based on fine-grain locking of a sub-portion of the data structure upon performing an operation. However, the intrinsic scalability limitations of locking still lead this proposal to be not suited for large levels of parallelism, as also shown in [19]. Rather, in our ultimate share-everything PDES system we base concurrent accesses to shared data structures on non-blocking algorithms, which have been shown to be much more prone to scalability.

As for non-blocking management of sets by concurrent threads, various proposals exist, such as lock-free linked lists [10], skip-lists [20] and Calendar Queues [15, 16]. A few of these proposals, like [15, 16], have been exploited as building blocks in the share-everything PDES paradigm. However, the outcoming solutions do not fit scenarios where two or more threads pick from the shared-event pool events destined to a same simulation object. In these scenarios, threads still block each other because of a critical section implementing the processing stage of the events at the destination object, which limits scalability especially with workloads entailing event bursts at subsets of objects. This problem has been tackled in [12], where non-blocking event-pool management is combined with CPU-dispatching rules that avoid collisions of multiple threads on the state of a same simulation object. However, differently from our proposal, none of these solutions guarantees non-blocking coordination in virtual time. In fact, they are all based on a kind of *wait-until-validated* paradigm, which does not allow multiple events to be processed speculatively on a same object as in Time-Warp style [13]—in fact, just one event can be processed speculatively at each object, and is then committed (namely validated) or rolled back depending on blocking virtual-time synchronization conditions, before any other event at that same object can be CPU-dispatched. In our solution, we enable Time-Warp style speculation, while still keeping all the advantages from non-blocking thread coordination in the access to shared data structures along wall-clock time.

Non-blocking operations on event pools have also been studied in [9], which presents a variation of the Ladder Queue where the elements are at any time bound to the correct bucket, which is an unordered list. The extraction from an unordered bucket returns the first available element, which does not necessarily correspond to the one with the minimum timestamp. This proposal is intrinsically tailored for PDES systems relying on speculative processing, where unordered extractions leading to causal inconsistencies within the simulation model trajectory are reversed (in terms of their effects on the simulation model trajectory) via rollback mechanisms. In our proposal we guarantee the ordering of the events in the shared pool, which allows us to put in place the smart combination of conservative (say safe) and speculative processing at the level of each individual event—also thanks to the explicit exploitation of the lookahead in the simulation model—thus enabling the optimization of the rollback support, an aspect that is not considered in [9]. Also, in this work the non-blocking data structure is essentially used as a CPU-dispatching support allowing threads to pick the next event of some object concurrently with other threads. However, differently from our present proposal, binding mechanisms between sets of objects and sets of threads are still considered, thus making the approach not fully compliant with the share-everything paradigm.

The recent proposal in [11] explores the idea of managing concurrent accesses to a shared pool by relying on Hardware Transactional Memory (HTM) support. Insertions and extractions are performed as HTM-based transactions, hence in non-blocking mode. However, the level of scalability of this approach is limited by the level of parallelism in the underlying HTM-equipped machine, which nowadays is relatively small. Also, HTM-based transactions can abort for several reasons, not necessarily related to conflicting concurrent accesses to a same portion of the data structure. As an example, they can abort because of conflicting accesses to the same cache line by multiple CPU-cores, which might be adverse to PDES models with, e.g., very large event pools. Our proposal does not require special hardware support, thus fully eliminating the secondary effects caused by, e.g., HTM limitations on the abort rate of the operations.

3 THE PDES SYSTEM

As in classical PDES, our system supports models that are partitioned in simulation objects whose execution is carried out by Logical Processes (LPs). LPs are sequential entities and a specific LP is CPU-dispatched when a Worker Thread (WT), triggers the execution of the handler of an event destined to it. A share-everything arrangement of the PDES platform leads to a scenario where: (i) an LP can be CPU-dispatched by whichever WT at any point of the simulation execution; (ii) all the events are maintained by a unique pool fully shared across all the WTs.

In our design, the system has two main data structures:

(A) a set of *LP Control Blocks* (LPCBs), which are used to keep metadata representing the system-level view of the advancement of the LP in simulation time—this is a concept disjoint from the actual application level state of the simulation object encapsulated by the LP;

(B) a set of events—either already processed, or to be processed, or logically canceled—maintained into the aforementioned fully-shared unique pool which we refer to as *Scheduling Queue* (SQ).

At first approximation, the main execution loop carried out by all the WTs consists in: i) fetching some event to be processed from the SQ; ii) performing a rollback of the target LP, if required;

iii) executing the event; iv) updating the LPCB; v) inserting newly generated events into the SQ.

As for point i), the fetch operation is contextual to the try-lock of the target LP. Hence, no WT will ever fetch an event bound to an LP that is currently locked by some other WT. Overall, no mutual block among WTs will ever occur in the attempt to access the same LP, since the WT that will experience a failure of its try-lock operation will simply go ahead scanning the event pool in order to take an event destined to some other LP. This also guarantees isolation of WTs' accesses to a given LPCB and to the corresponding simulation object state, in both forward and rollback mode.

Concerning the other operations accessing the SQ within the main loop, as we will discuss, they are all carried out in a non-blocking fashion—including secondary updates on individual nodes' data in order to correctly represent their state (e.g. logically cancelled because of a rollback) within the speculative processing scheme, as discussed in the following.

3.1 Architectural Details

3.1.1   LP Control Blocks. Each LPCB is formed by a set of variables which hold metadata needed by the simulation engine to detect any relevant runtime condition related to the LP, including its involvement in causality errors. Noteworthy, among others, the LPCB keeps a pointer named bound to the last processed event, whose timestamp represents therefore the Local Virtual Time (LVT) of the simulation object associated with the LP. The actual buffer keeping the event pointed by bound still stands in the SQ, so that event processing leads to no actual removal from that queue. Unlinkage from this queue will occur when we detect that the event is either definitively causally consistent—it is a committed event—or it should not appear along the execution—it is an event generated by a rolled back one. Discriminating whether the event has been processed, or it is in a different state with respect to the state of the target LP and of all the other LPs, will take place via a proper state machine coded into the event-buffer metadata. The state diagram for this state machine will be discussed shortly.

The LPCB also maintains a non-negative integer named epoch which keeps track of the total number of rollback operations the LP has experienced. This information essentially tells in what incarnation the LP is currently executing along its forward path, given that a rollback leads to a new incarnation—a new LP life after the causality error.

Moreover, each LPCB keeps metadata to retrieve what we call the local_queue of the simulation object, which is used to maintain the history of processed events at that LP. Those that are rolled back are not included in this queue. Also, local_queue is built in our system as a view of event-buffers associated with the LP which are anyhow kept within the SQ. In other words, local_queue is built by relying on cross event-buffers' linkage standing aside of their linkage into the SQ. The reason for having such a view, rather than only relying on the global view of events in the SQ, stands in the management of both state reconstruction—which in our system is based on checkpointing and coasting forward—and CPU-dispatching of the next-to-be-processed event of the LP. Finally, the LPCB keeps the lock actually used to support try-lock operations when WTs try to take on the job of working on the LP.

3.1.2   Events Representation. In our PDES system, an event is a simple memory buffer—the event-buffer—exchanged between two LPs, or sent from some LP to itself. The actual exchange takes place through insertion and extraction operations to/from the SQ. Each event originates on one LP, called *sender*, and targets another LP, called *receiver*, which could be the same event's source LP.

Each event-buffer is made up by (a) metadata—used by the PDES system for treating the event—and by (b) the actual payload conveying the information to be delivered to the event-handler for application level processing. In this section we focus our attention on metadata, given that our system is application agnostic, and can support generic simulation models.

An event-buffer associated with the event *e* keeps the following metadata:

- the id of the LP which generates and sends the event, and the id of the LP which must receive and execute it, respectively hold by sender and receiver fields;
- the timestamp ts at which the event must occur along simulation time;
- a field epoch, which maintains the epoch of the receiver LP at the time when it processed the event;
- a pointer parent to the event *p*, whose execution has generated *e*;
- a field parentEpoch, which represents sender LP's epoch when *p* has been processed, namely the incarnation number of the sender LP at the generation time of *e*;
- a variable state used to represent the current state of the event within a finite-state machine, which drives the event management logic at the level of the PDES system.

Since our system entails speculative execution capabilities, possible violations of timestamp order might occur, and rollback operations are required in order to restore the correct execution trajectory of an LP (a timeline), as well as to undo the production of new events along the incorrect trajectory. In general, an event experiences several life stages. We define as *committed* the simulation trajectory of an LP that is observable at the end of a concurrent execution entailing no timestamp order violation. Every event that is visible within that simulation trajectory, is defined as *committed* or *safe*. On the contrary, events could be *retracted*, meaning that they cannot longer exist in any time-line.

In our system an event being processed flushes newly produced events to the SQ before the execution phase is over. Therefore, the unprocessed (or being-processed) event with the minimum timestamp is a safe event that corresponds to the commit horizon, namely the Global Virtual Time (GVT) of the speculative run.

Given that, thanks to the try-lock mechanism, two events destined to the same LP cannot be concurrently processed by WTs, we can exploit the lookahead (LA) of the simulation model to compute safety of whatever event to be processed (or being processed) according to the following expression:

$$is\_safe(e) \quad = \quad (e.\texttt{ts} \in [GVT, GVT + LA) \; \wedge$$
$$\nexists \, e' : e.\texttt{lp} = e'.\texttt{lp} \, \wedge \, e'.\texttt{ts} < e.\texttt{ts}) \quad (1)$$

If an event *e* is not safe—meaning that Equation 1 does not currently hold for it—and gets speculatively processed, its execution might be undone because of the arrival of a straggler destined to the same

LP. However, in such a scenario, the event *e* could be still *valid*, meaning that it is requested to appear as executed along some timeline of the destination LP. On the other hand, if the event was generated by some other event that is undone, the former becomes *invalid*. In fact, it should no way appear in the correct timeline of the destination LP—in classical Time Warp these are events canceled by their corresponding anti-events.

Such as for the safety, our system detects if a particular event *e* has become invalid at a given point in wall-clock time by exploiting event-buffer metadata. In particular, an event *e* is currently valid if and only if (i) its parent *p* is currently valid as well and (ii) the execution of *p* that generated *e* has not been undone. Exploiting event metadata, the definition of validity can be formalized by the following recursive function:

$$is\_valid(e) = \begin{cases} true, & \text{if } e.\text{type} = \text{INIT} \\ (e.\text{parentEpoch} = e.\text{parent.epoch}) \wedge \\ \quad is\_valid(e.\text{parent})], & \text{otherwise} \end{cases} \quad (2)$$

The above formalization is based on having the validity of an event always depending on the validity of its parent. The unique exception is the INIT event —used to just setup the simulation initial state, including the states of the LPs— which is safe (hence valid) by construction.

To check whether an event *e* has been re-executed or not, we harness the parentEpoch information kept by the event-buffer, which is compared to the epoch of its parent *p*. As said before, *e*.parentEpoch and *p*.epoch have been set with the epoch of the sender LP at the time the event *p* has been executed. Since the LPs' epochs are updated after a rollback takes place, if an event is re-processed, its epoch number will be updated with the new LP's epoch. As soon *p*.epoch is not equal to—more precisely greater than—*e*.epoch, it means that the parent is living within a new and different timeline, to which the child event *e* does no longer belong. Consequently, if *e*.parentEpoch = *p*.epoch we can infer that the event *p* has not been re-executed, and therefore still stands on the original timeline that generated *e*.

In our share-everything PDES system we do not immediately unlink events from the SQ when they become invalid. This is because we manage the queue via non-blocking algorithms. As a consequence, a node in the queue—namely, an event-buffer—might be required to still stand into the queue to facilitate the execution of non-blocking queue traversals by WTs. In fact, they can use that node as a link between others, even though the corresponding event appears to be as no longer relevant for the execution of any LPs' timeline. Also, temporarily keeping invalid event-buffers into the SQ is a way to asynchronously notify the other WTs currently traversing the SQ that something has changed along the timeline of some LP—since invalid event-buffers expose updated metadata—which may in its turn drive the actions by these same WTs. In other words, each single node in the SQ is associated with a state machine that helps supporting a fine grain coordination across WTs, implemented according to the non-blocking paradigm.

Figure 1 shows the actual state machine within which each event-buffer lives. How state transitions occur based in the pseudo-code executed by WTs will be discussed in Section 3.2, while in this section, we illustrate the "meaning" of each state. A newly produced

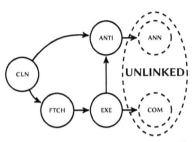

Figure 1: State diagram for the event's life-cycle.

event, just inserted into the SQ, is born with a clean state (CLN) representing that no operation has been performed yet on the event-buffer—except its insertion, clearly with the correct metadata such as the epoch of the sender LP. Note however that, starting from the wall-clock-time instant the event appears to be incorporated into the queue, any WT can be already traversing it, possibly updating its state. When a WT finds an event-buffer *e* marked with the CLN state in the SQ, it logically extracts (fetches) *e*, by marking it as FTCH—we recall that for this to occur, the WT must have observed the presence of the event-buffer, and must have successfully executed the try-lock on the target LP. In fact, two different WTs cannot take on the job of concurrently processing a same event destined to a given LP, which would require special features in the programming model (and in its runtime) that are aside of the work we are presenting. Marking an event-buffer as FTCH leads to notify that the event is currently in charge to some WT.

It is possible that, when the WT successfully try-locks the LP associated with an event-buffer in the CLN state, this event has already become invalid, since the execution of its parent might have been undone or invalidated. When a WT observes this condition while traversing the SQ, it makes the event transit to the logical ANTI state, whose name evokes the anti-event concept—meaning that it simply does no longer belong to the simulation trajectory, along any timeline. All the state transitions are implemented atomically in our software, given that they can be carried out by concurrent WTs. For potentially conflicting (mutually excluding) transitions—such as CLN→ FTCH and CLN→ ANTI—we rely on the Compare-and-Swap (CAS) machine instruction. For non-conflicting ones, we simply use atomic memory writes—such as test-and-set—abstracted by the SET statement in the pseudo-code. Therefore, the transition to ANTI excludes the possibility for a WT to successfully transit the node to FTCH. It is clear that an event still complying with the validity rules expressed by Equation 2, might really be no longer valid. It is only a matter of time for the WTs to detect that such information related to validity is reflected into the state of the parent event. On the other hand, speculative processing is already known to accept the risk of processing something that seems to be consistent, in terms of timestamp ordering, but which is actually no longer consistent given that something is happening concurrently along model execution.

An event successfully marked as FTCH is returned to the main loop of the WT, where it will be processed, as we shall describe. Here, the event transits to the "execution" state, say EXC, meaning that the event-handler actually took it for performing the corresponding LP state manipulations.

Overall, the ANTI state, still reachable from the EXC state, is used to discriminate that the PDES system knows that the event does no longer belong to any valid LP timeline, either if it has been already fetched and executed by some thread—thus it passed through EXC—or if it is found to be invalid prior being fetched. The ANTI state is reached via a transition from EXC when a rollback occurs related to the passage of the event to the invalid state. Therefore, it will not need to be re-processed after the rollback. The PDES system can detect that a rollback needs to be executed when a WT traverses the SQ comparing the metadata of the LP and those kept by the event-buffer (such as the current LVT of the LP and the event timestamp, or its parent's state). These checks are anyhow executed without the need for locking the target LP. If the event marked as ANTI is found to stand in the future—or on a new timeline after a rollback of the target LP—the event is simply transited to the ANN state, an absorbing state leading to the unlink of the event from the SQ.

Similarly, when an event ends its life-cycle and appears along the correct LP timeline, it is logically marked as COM (commit state). Clearly, an event transits to COM after being processed if it is found to be a safe one. In this case it is also unlinked from the SQ. Although unlinked from the SQ, an event-buffer in the COM state will be garbage collected (reused) successively, as we shall discuss, since some child could still refer to it for validity assessment according to Equation 2. Another motivation for retaining the event is its usefulness for state reconstruction purposes in a rollback phase, as we will also discuss.

As a final note, an event can persist in the EXC state across multiple executions, caused by rollbacks, up to the point in time when its safety is assessed, or it becomes invalid.

3.1.3 Scheduling Queue. The Scheduling Queue (SQ) used in our share-everything PDES system is a conflict-resilient lock-free priority queue that sorts event-buffers (across all the LPs) on the basis of their timestamps. In particular, it is a Calendar Queue supporting non-blocking operations. We borrow its implementation from [16], reshuffling it in order to meet the needs of our innovative share-everything PDES system. At a logical level, such a queue can be abstracted as a generic non-blocking ordered linked list like the one proposed by Harris [10]—although being much more efficient thanks to its multi-bucket organization leading to amortized constant-time access. Relying on this abstraction allows us to hide the complexity of non-blocking Calendar Queue operations, which are not the focus of this article—jointly enabling us to focus on how we exploit non-blocking capabilities of such priority queue in our PDES system.

In our reshuffle, the priority queue has an ENQUEUE API and two other primitives: GETMIN, which retrieves a pointer to the event with the smallest timestamp which is still linked to the queue, and GETNEXT, which retrieves the pointer to the event which immediately follows—along virtual time—the one identified by its input argument. Thanks to this support we can build a cross-layer optimized FETCH operation that returns in a non-blocking mode a to-be-processed event associated with some LP not currently locked by any WT (see Section 3.2.2 for the details). Further, the SQ supports an UNLINK API which is used to disconnect a generic event from the SQ—those that transit to the ANN or COM state—still in non-blocking fashion.

Before returning an event e, a WT executing a FETCH executes a try-lock operation on the target LP. If this operation fails, the WT slides to the subsequent event in the queue—the one successive to e. This is done thanks to the exploitation of the above mentioned get services in the queue API. This sliding scheme is iterated up to the point where a try-lock on the LP targeted by some event, encountered along the queue, executes successfully.

According to the event's state diagram in Figure 1, fetched (or already processed) events are not unlinked from the SQ. In fact, an event could be re-executed due to a rollback. Hence, it must be visible in future queue explorations by concurrent WTs in order to be properly handled. Moreover, our event validity definition (see Equation 2) implies that parent metadata could be accessed while assessing the state of its children. Therefore, the actual garbage collection of the event-buffer—leading to its reuse—is also determined by the relation between the GVT value and the timestamp of child events, as we shall discuss. On the other hand, the logical removal of the node in the COM state associated with the minimum timestamp value from the SQ via the UNLINK API is enough to move forward—beyond that node—the pointer to the new minimum timestamp element into the queue. As said, this is because in our PDES system the removal of that COM event, which was previously processed, already led to incorporate into the SQ all its children, if any.

3.2 Worker-Thread Algorithm

3.2.1 Main loop. The pseudocode of the main loop carried out by any WT is shown in Algorithm 1. Initially a call to the FETCH procedure is executed to retrieve from the SQ an event to be handled (processed or undone/retracted), which is destined to an LP not currently in charge of another WT—namely, locked by the caller WT. The FETCH procedure returns to the caller WT a pointer to the event to be handled, and the indication of whether the event is safe (computed according to Equation 1) or at least valid. The FETCH procedure also returns the minimum timestamp of the non-committed event standing into the SQ, namely the current GVT value. Further, according to state transitions, such procedure may lead events destined to whatever LP to transit from CLN to ANTI while traversing the SQ. This is based on validity checks as expressed by Equation 2.

Regardless the retrieved event's current state, the thread checks if its timestamp is smaller than the LP's LVT, namely the time reached by the LP executing the event pointed by its bound variable in the LPCB. In the positive case a ROLLBACK is triggered in order to bring back the LP's state to the timestamp of the last event preceding the retrieved straggler event and belonging to the current timeline. At the end of the ROLLBACK procedure the simulation state is compliant with respect to the execution of the currently retrieved event. If this event was already marked as EXC, it simply persists into this state. Otherwise, it will transit from FTCH to EXC.

Before the execution of the event, a MAKEUNDOABLE operation is called, which implements whatever policy for making the current state transition undoable (namely, rollbackable). In our implementation we opted for a traditional periodic checkpointing approach. Based on the selected policy, if the log is taken, the log-node is linked to the corresponding event (the one pointed to by bound), for correct alignment of the data structures. We note that the safety information associated with the event retrieved via FETCH can be

Algorithm 1 Simulation Loop

1: **procedure** SIMULATIONLOOP()
2:    $<evt, safe, valid, gvt> \leftarrow$ FETCH()
3:    $curLP \leftarrow evt$.receiver
4:    **if** $evt \neq$ null **then**
5:        **if** evt.ts $< curLP$.bound.ts **then**
6:            ROLLBACK($curLP, evt$.ts)
7:        **if** $\neg valid$ **then**
8:            SET(evt.state$\leftarrow$ ANTI)
9:        **else**
10:            MAKEUNDOABLE($curLP, evt, safe$)
11:            LINKTOLPQUEUE($curLP$.bound, evt)
12:            evt.epoch $\leftarrow curLP$.epoch
13:            $newEvts \leftarrow$ EXECUTE(evt)
14:            FLUSH()
15:            $curLP$.bound $\leftarrow evt$
16:            SET(evt.state, EXC)
17:        UNLOCK($curLP$.lock)
18:        **if** $safe =$ TRUE **then**
19:            UNLINK(evt)
20:    GVTOPERATIONS(gvt)

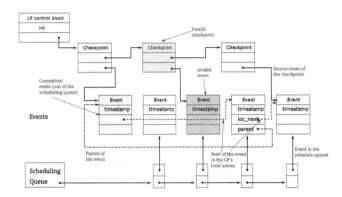

Figure 2: Data structures of LP state, SQ and events, and relative relationships.

exploited for optimizing the management of the undo support. In our case, it could lead to take a checkpoint and to rejuvenate the checkpoint period if the event will never be undone—this will enable reducing coasting forward overhead by inserting a log exactly on the currently committed event of the LP. On the other hand, if reverse computing approaches were employed (see [4, 6]), the safety information would simply tell that there will be no need to generate data/metadata for reversing the event execution. The relation among the different data structures we used to manage each individual LP is schematized in Figure 2. By the scheme we see how the event queue of the LP—namely local_queue—is incorporated into the SQ—which is global to all the LPs. Thus, the LP local queue represents a sort of view on such global queue achieved via a parallel linked list. The processed event is linked to the per-LP view of the SQ via LINKTOLPQUEUE, so as to make it immediately available for any purpose, including coasting forward if requested.

The real event-processing phase starts by updating the event epoch with the LP current one, in order to represent its current incarnation within the LP current timeline. Then, the event is executed by invoking the application-level event-handler provided by the simulation model. New events possibly produced along the event-handler execution are stored in a local buffer, in order to FLUSH them to the SQ at the end of the current event execution. At this point, to complete event processing, the event state is atomically set to EXC and the LP bound is updated in order to point to the current event.

The order of those operations is fundamental to guarantee correctness. In fact, newly produced events are flushed into the SQ before their parent's processing is finalized, otherwise we would violate the definition of GVT we rely on. So, it is important to postpone the update of the current bound and of the state of the event after the flush operation.

Clearly, once updated the event state, the WT releases the lock on the target LP, thus enabling concurrent WTs to eventually take care of whatever event destined to the same LP, as in the spirit of the share-everything paradigm. Finally, if the FETCH procedure indicates that the event is a safe one, the final logical transition to the COM state is directly executed by the in-charge WT, which unlinks the event from the SQ.

At the end of the main loop, despite what happened before, some housekeeping tasks are performed, which take place via the GVTOPERATIONS procedure. Specifically, this procedure is used to reclaim memory associated with no longer useful event-buffers, as well as checkpoints. As we will clarify while explaining the structure of the FETCH procedure, event-buffers are initially unlinked from the SQ when they will no longer need to be handled, which means they are committed or have been annihilated, transiting respectively in COM and ANN states. On the other hand, the event-buffers in the COM state still remain into the per-LP local_queue, while the event-buffers in the ANN state are inserted (upon their unlink from the SQ) into per-WT retirement queues. All these event-buffers can be actually reused (hence reclaimed by the memory system) only after the GVT value oversteps the maximum timestamp of any child possibly generated by their execution. This is because validity of an event-buffer in our system is based on referring the state of a parent event-buffer according to Equation 2. To easily keep track of such condition at runtime, each event-buffer is also filled with a timestamp field which exactly keeps such a maximum child-timestamp. While executing the GVTOPERATIONS procedure, the WT deallocates all the event-buffers from its list of ANN nodes which satisfy such condition. The same occurs for the nodes in the local_queue of the LP that the WT is currently in charge of.

3.2.2 The Fetch Procedure. The FETCH procedure, whose pseudocode is shown in Algorithm 2, has two objectives: (i) returning an event to be processed by the WT main loop; (ii) unlinking no-longer needed events from the SQ and hence from the per-LP views of this queue. This procedure uses two local variables gvt and $jmpLP$. The former keeps the timestamp of the minimum event still linked to the SQ, the latter keeps the set of LPs targeted by "skipped" events—the events that have been traversed by the WT without actually locking the target LP.

Algorithm 2 Fetch procedure

```
F1:  procedure FETCH()
F2:      evt ← GETMIN()
F3:      gvt ← evt.ts
F4:      jmpLPs ← {}
F5:      while evt ≠ null do
F6:          LP ← evt.receiver
F7:          evtState ← evt.state
F8:          safe ← is_safe(evt,gvt,jmpLP)
F9:          in_past ← evt.ts ≤ LP.bound.ts
F10:         valid ← is_valid(evt)
F11:         if TRYCLEANANDSKIP(evt,jmpLPs,
F12:                     LP,safe,in_past, valid) then
F13:             if TRYLOCK(LP.lock) then
F14:                 curr ← GETLOCALNEXTANDVALID(evt)
F15:                 if curr ≠ evt then
F16:                     valid ← true
F17:                     safe ← is_safe(curr,gvt,jmpLP)
F18:                     in_past ← evt.ts ≤ LP.bound.ts
F19:                 if ¬valid then
F20:                     if in_past then
F21:                         return ⟨evt, safe, gvt⟩
F22:                     SET(evt.state← ANTI)
F23:                 evtState ← CAS(evt.state, CLN, FTCH)
F24:                 switch(evtState)
F25:                     case CLN:
F26:                         return ⟨evt, safe, valid, gvt⟩
F27:                     case EXC:
F28:                         if ¬in_past then
F29:                             return ⟨evt, safe, valid, gvt⟩
F30:                         else if ¬safe
F31:                             jmpLPs ← jmpLPs ∪ {LP}
F32:                         break
F33:                 RELEASELOCK(LP.lock)
F34:             else
F35:                 jmpLP ← jmpLP ∪ {LP}
F36:         evt ← GETNEXT(evt)
```

Algorithm 3 TryCleanAndSkip procedure

```
C1:  procedure TRYCLEANANDSKIP(evt,jmpLPs,LP,
C2:                          safe,in_past, valid)
C3:      tryLock ← true
C4:      if valid then
C5:          if in_past then
C6:              if safe ∧ evtState = EXC then
C7:                  UNLINK(evt)
C8:              else
C9:                  jmpLPs ← jmpLPs ∪ {LP}
C10:                 tryLock ← false
C11:     else
C12:         if evtState = CLN then
C13:             evtState ← CAS(evt.state, CLN, ANTI)
C14:         if evtState = ANTI then
C15:             UNLINK(evt)
C16:         tryLock ← false
C17:     return tryLock
```

Algorithm 4 GetLocalNextAndValid procedure

```
G1:  procedure GETLOCALNEXTANDVALID(curr)
G2:      LP ← curr.receiver
G3:      lNext ← GETLOCALNEXT(LP.bound)
G4:      while lNext ≠ null ∧ ¬is_valid(lNext) do
G5:          SET(evt.state← ANTI)
G6:          UNLINK(evt)
G7:          lNext ← GETLOCALNEXT(LP.bound)
G8:      if lNext ≠ null ∧ lNext.ts < evt.ts then
G9:          return lNext
G10:     return curr
```

First, the FETCH procedure retrieves the current minimum from the SQ by invoking GETMIN and storing its timestamp into gvt. Also, it initializes $jmpLP$ as an empty set. Then, for each traversed event evt a safety check is performed—so we check if $evt.ts \in [gvt, gvt + LA)$ and $LP \notin jmpLP$, where LP is the receiver of evt (this is the implementation of the check on the safety condition expresses in Equation 1). Moreover, we check if evt is in the past of the LP timeline by comparing the timestamps associated with evt and the LP bound. Then, TRYCLEANANDSKIP is executed. This is a non-blocking procedure aimed at unlinking from the SQ events that have expired their lifetime (they are into an absorbing state, namely COM or ANTI) or telling whether the current event has to be processed by returning a boolean value set to true. The latter case is associated with any event, which is not in absorbing states, and requires the target LP to execute it and/or to rollback the LP state. All these checks are carried out by the TRYCLEANANDSKIP procedure relying on the metadata we included in our event-buffers and in the LPCBs. If TRYCLEANANDSKIP returns true, then the WT try-locks the target LP. If this fails, then the WT skips to the subsequent event into the SQ, by relying on the GETNEXT API. This

pattern is iterated up to the point where the WT successfully locks a target LP, or the tail of the SQ is reached—GETNEXT returns null. While traversing the SQ, the $jmpLP$ variable is populated, keeping track of all the LPs for which the WT observed something to be present into the SQ, until some target LP is locked. This set is used to compute the safety of an event.

When some target LP is successfully locked, evt is checked again to determine whether it is in the past of the LP. This is because in the wall-clock-time interval between the first check on evt performed by TRYCLEANANDSKIP and the current processing phase, some other WT may have changed the actual bound of the target LP.

Then WT invokes GETLOCALNEXTANDVALID (Algorithm 4), that returns an event $lNext$ which is either the first valid event following the bound of LP into its local view of the SQ—the local_queue—or the event just fetched from the SQ. We need this procedure to check whether some event that is subsequent to the bound into local_queue has a timestamp lower than the one just fetched from the SQ, which represents a critical scenario to cope with. Such a scenario is illustrated via an example shown in Figure 3. Suppose that WT A holds a lock on an LP X because it is processing an event e. If another thread B tries to acquire the lock on X for processing an event f such that e precedes f ($e \to f$), it will fail and continue to analyze the next event g. This event is such that $e \to f \to g$ and

Wall-clock time	Thread A	Thread B
1:	Check Event A on LP 1	
2:	Trylock on LP 1	
3:	Success	Check Event A on LP 1
4:	Process Event A	Trylock on LP 1
5:	.	Fail
6:	.	Check Event B on LP 1
7:	.	Trylock on LP 1
8:	.	Fail
9:	Release lock on LP 1	Check Event C on LP 1
10:		Trylock on LP 1
11:		Success
12:		Process Event C

Figure 3: The scenario tackled by GetLocalNextAndValid.

targets X, so B will try to acquire again the lock on that LP. If in the meanwhile A has released the lock on X, B takes the lock and starts processing g. Supposing that e, f and g are all valid events, B executes g moving forward the bound of LP X. If f has a CLN state, executing g is not problematic since some WT eventually retrieves f and executes it after triggering a rollback as if it were a straggler event. Conversely, if f has an EXC state, no WT will ever execute such event again since it appears to be in the past of the current trajectory. This situation is prevented to occur exactly by the presence of GetLocalNextAndValid, that searches for an event (f) with higher priority than the currently fetched one (g) from the SQ.

Then, if the GetLocalNextAndValid procedure returns a different element with respect to the one originally identified, the relative validity information is updated. Thus, the first performed check is about the event validity—note that this check is carried out outside the locking region of the target LP. Since in the TryCleanAndSkip procedure invalid and CLN events are correctly marked (as ANTI) and unlinked, here we can assume that if we met an invalid event-buffer, it is not a newly inserted one. In this case we have to perform a rollback if and only if it is in the past of the current incarnation (epoch) of LP, otherwise we atomically set its state to ANTI, in order to notify that the event no more needs to be processed.

Otherwise, if the event was observed to be valid, WT tries to atomically apply the state transition CLN→FTCH with the CAS instruction. Of course, if it has been concurrently marked as ANTI by another WT that has seen the event as invalid, the CAS will fail.

After reading the actual state value of the event as a result of the CAS instruction[2], a switch case on it is carried out, implementing the events' finite-state machine discussed in Section 3.1.2. If the state is CLN, we know that the event has never been fetched and executed, thus, it is directly returned to the main loop. As discussed, it is up to the main loop to check if it is a straggler or not and trigger a rollback if required. The second case is the one where we have an EXC state, meaning that the event has been executed at least once. It follows that, it can be re-executed if and only if it is beyond the LP bound, meaning that it is in the future of the actual incarnation of the LP trajectory, namely the LP timeline. This is an event that has been rolled back and is still valid in the current (refreshed after the rollback) timeline. If the event is committable, namely if it is

safe, we can unlink it from the global queue, otherwise we can skip the event by adding the LP to the $jmpLP$ set, releasing the lock and retrieving another event.

Once the switch case has been executed, we can release the lock on the target LP, since here the event state can only be set to ANTI or EXC. In any case, the event unlink, that transits the event to the COM or ANN state, will be performed by any WT in TryCleanAndSkip, thus completing the event life-cycle.

4 EXPERIMENTAL ASSESSMENT

In this section we present performance results for a comparison of our Ultimate Share-Everything PDES system—which we refer to as USE—and the last generation Share-Everything solution presented in [12]—which we refer to as SE. The latter does not entail Time-Warp style processing of the events since, for each LP, at most one event is executed speculatively, and is eventually committed or aborted before any other event for the same LP can be CPU-dispatched. Its unique event pool—fully shared across WTs—only keeps so called *schedule-committed* events, which all need to appear along the LP timeline, thus not requiring the non-blocking management of any state machine for determining their actual role (across multiple ones) along model execution (e.g. if they need to be retracted because of the rollback of the parent). In other words, SE is blocking in virtual-time synchronization, while USE is fully non-blocking in both wall-clock-time thread coordination, and virtual-time LP synchronization, also thanks to its more sophisticated—and still non-blocking—logic for the management of the fully-shared event-pool data structure. For completeness of the analysis, we also include another competitor, which is the ROOT-Sim last generation traditional-PDES environment [23] not based on the share-everything paradigm—it adopts partitioning of the LPs across threads, with dynamic rebind for load-balancing purposes. It anyhow entails optimizations in its internal organization suited for shared-memory machines [24].

All the tests have been run on a 32-core HP ProLiant machine equipped with four 2GHz AMD Opteron 6128 processors and 64 GB of RAM. Each processor has 8 physical cores that share a 12MB L3 cache (6 MB per each 4-cores set), and each CPU-core has a 512KB private L2 cache. The machine is equipped with 64 GB of RAM—organized in 8 NUMA nodes—and we used Linux (kernel 3.2) as operating system.

The number of WTs running within all the used PDES systems we are comparing has been varied from 1 to 32 in order to perform a scalability study. All the reported data points have been computed as the average over 10 runs, executed with different seeds for the pseudo-random generation of event timestamps.

4.1 Results with PHOLD

As first test-bed application we used the classical PHOLD benchmark [8] configured with 1024 LPs. Each LP schedules events for any other LP in the system, with an exponential timestamp increment. As usual for PHOLD, event processing leads to spending some CPU-time via a busy loop emulating a given event granularity. In our experiments we set the loop to give rise to events with granularity of the order of 60 or 120 microseconds, thus spanning between fine-to-mid values leading to a representative setting for testing

---

[2] As in most common implementations, we assume that CAS returns the original value of the targeted memory location independently of whether its update fails.

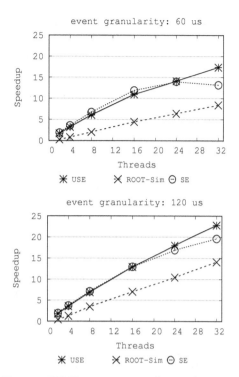

Figure 4: PHOLD speeup results - no hot-spot.

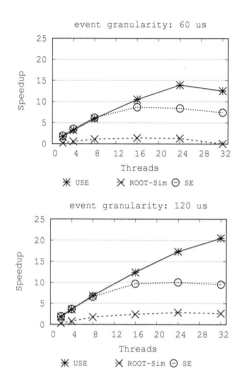

Figure 5: PHOLD speedup results - hot-spot.

parallel processing platforms—larger grain events might mask platform level costs for parallelization/coordination/rollback-support independently of the used PDES paradigm, share-everything vs traditional.

In one PHOLD configuration we included 10 hot-spot LPs, towards which 50% of the events injected by the other LPs are routed. It is known that PDES workloads with hot-spots are difficult to manage since they might provide unbalance in case of traditional PDES platforms relying in the binding between LPs and WTs—load-balancing, as in ROOT-Sim, can anyhow mitigate this problem. Also, they are difficult to manage in share-everything PDES systems where WTs can block one another because of the need to process events at a same LP (the hot-spot one) and the need for waiting the advancement of the spots before being able to advance the other LPs because of blocking (non-Time Warp style) virtual-time synchronization, as it may happen in SE. We decided to experiment with this kind of complex workload just to study how our new approach could overcome such known limitations. In any case, for fairness, we also report data with the PHOLD model configured with no hot-spots, thus naturally leading to a more balanced advancement of virtual time (per wall-clock-time unit) across the LPs, independently of the underlying execution platform among the ones we compare. Finally, in this study we focus on a zero-lookahead scenario.

In Figure 4 we report data related to the configuration with no hot-spot. By the plots we see that SE suffers from performance degradation with respect to USE. In fact, USE allows achieving a maximum speedup—over sequential execution—which is about 34% (resp 18%) better than the one provide by SE for event granularity set to 60 (resp. 120) microseconds. Such a maximum value

is achieved for 32 WTs, where USE allows for better exploitation of parallelism, via speculative processing, with respect to SE. We would to note that even if the speculation support in USE is much more lightweight than in traditional speculative PDES, simpler approaches that support a limited level of speculation (e.g., one event for SE) can be more efficient in particular scenarios with a reduced computational power (up to 16 cores) and fine-grain events (60 microseconds); this is why in Figure 4 we note a slightly overcome of SE's performance with respect to USE. In any case, both SE and USE perform better than traditional speculative PDES, namely ROOT-Sim, since they avoid a lot of operations that the traditional engine needs to carry out. As an example, in our USE proposal, the cancellation of events that are no longer valid does not require any anti-event—since it is embedded within the non-blocking event state-machine management in the form of a simple event-buffer state transition. Also, no output queues are generated and traversed for managing rollbacks, since all the work is supported at the level of the SQ where the "positive" copy of the events is posted—still thanks to event-buffers state machines.

When moving to the hot-spot case—whose speedup data are provided in Figure 5—the potential of USE becomes definitely more evident. SE shows performance worse than USE, just because of the impossibility to provide scalable virtual-time synchronization (with no speculation) when hot-spot LPs tend to slow down the advancement of the commit horizon of the simulation. For this workload, USE can provide performance up to 64% (resp. 105%) better than SE for event granularity set to 60 (resp. 120) microseconds. This is a hard-workload scenario which ROOT-Sim cannot cope with in effective manner, even though it implements load-balancing. In

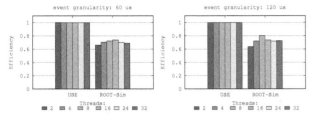

Figure 6: PHOLD efficiency - no hot-spot.

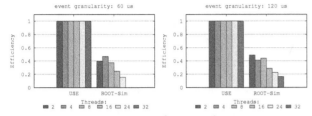

Figure 7: PHOLD efficiency - hot-spot.

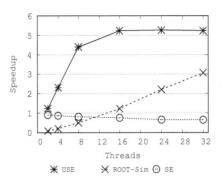

Figure 8: Speedup results for TCAR.

fact, with very few spots—10 in our case—long term planning in the distribution of the workload does not capture sudden unbalance, which becomes extremely adverse to performance especially when the number of WTs oversteps the number of hot-spot LPs. On the contrary, USE allows to concentrate the overall computing power towards all the events that are close to the current commit horizon, regardless of their distribution with respect to the hot-spots (or other LPs). As a result, the system gains much more effective parallel execution, with much less likelihood of rollback operations. This phenomenon is evidenced by the efficiency data[3] in Figure 7, where we show that even for this hard workload, USE achieves almost 100% of efficiency, as opposed to ROOT-Sim, which only achieves the order of 40% or less. In Figure 6 ROOT-Sim performs better in the configuration with no hot-spots where it reaches much higher values of efficiency around 70%, though still significantly lower than USE. This shows the effectiveness of delivering the computational power to the highest priority events.

4.2 Results with TCAR

As the second test-bed application, we used a variant of the Terrain-Covering Ant Robots (TCAR) model presented in [14]. In this model, multiple robots (say agents) are located into a region (the terrain) in order to explore it. TCAR simulations are usually exploited to determine tradeoffs between the number of employed robots, and the latency for exploring the target region, e.g., for rescue purposes. Factors such as the speed of movement (depending on, e.g., environmental conditions or obstacles) can be also considered.

In our implementation of TCAR, the terrain to be explored is represented as an undirected graph, therefore a robot is able to move from one space region to another in both directions. This mapping is created by imposing a specific grid on the space regions. The robots are then required to visit the entire space (i.e., cover the whole graph) by visiting each cell (i.e., graph node) once or

---

[3]We recall that the efficiency of a speculative PDES run is the ratio between the number of committed events, and the total number of processed events, namely committed plus rolled back.

multiple times. Differently from the original model in [14], we have used hexagonal cells—each one modeled by an LP—rather than squared ones. This allows for a better representation of the robots' mobility featuring real world scenarios since real ant robots (e.g., as physically realized in [21]) have the ability to steer to any direction.

The TCAR model relies on a node-counting algorithm, where each cell is assigned a counter that gets incremented whenever any robot visits it. So, the counter tracks the number of *pheromones* left by ants, to notify other ones of their transit. Whenever a robot reaches a cell, it increments the counter and determines its new destination. Destination choice is a very important factor to efficiently cover the whole region, and to support this choice the trail counter is used. In particular, a greedy approach is used such that, when a robot is in a particular cell, it targets the neighbor with the minimum trail count. A random choice takes place if multiple cells have the same (minimum) trail count.

The original TCAR model adopts a *pull* approach for gathering trail counters from adjacent cells. To provide an optimized implementation for PDES, achieved by reducing the volume of interactions (events) across the LPs, we adopted a *push* approach, relying on a notification event which is used to inform all neighbors of the newly updated trail counter whenever a robot enters a cell. Then, each LP modeling a cell stores in its own simulation state the neighbors' trail-counters values, making them available to compute the destination when simulating the transit of a robot. In the used TCAR configuration, we included the evaluation of a new state value for the cell whenever a robot enters it, so as to mimic the evolution of a given phenomenon within the cells. This computation has been based on a linear combination of exponential functions (like it occurs for example when evaluating fading on wireless communication systems due to environmental conditions). We configured TCAR with 1024 cells, with 15% of the cells initially set to be occupied by one robot.

In Figure 8 we show speedup results with the TCAR model. An important aspect for this application is that it shows significantly finer grain events—of the order of a few microseconds—compared to the used configurations of PHOLD. This stresses the execution of the different tested engines along another dimension, with respect to what done with PHOLD. In such a scenario, the overhead for parallelization that is paid by a traditional engine like ROOT-Sim, including its lower efficiency compared to USE, leads to very limited speedup. The same is true for SE, given its impossibility to carry out Time-Warp style speculative processing and the consequent active waiting, namely spinning behind a lock, for causality re-alignment, that increases contention on the underlying memory subsystem. Instead, USE allows achieving speedup that increases up to 16 threads. It then flattens, indicating somehow that more threads do not longer pay-off for performance reduction. We note that USE reaches its maximum speedup beyond a number of thread resources much less than ROOT-Sim indicating its superior ability to exploit actual model parallelism even when scaling up the amount of resources to more limited extents.

5 CONCLUSIONS

In this article we have presented an innovative design of a share-everything PDES system. It allows exploiting CPU-cores on board of shared-memory machines for carrying out the execution of sim-ulation models while guaranteeing: (1) non-blocking coordination of threads in the access to shared data structures and (2) fully speculative—Time Warp-style—processing of the events. No previ-ous literature proposal in the share-everything class shows these two features in combination. Compared to classical Time-Warp PDES—based on binding of LPs to threads—our proposal allows speculative processing of any individual event along whichever thread. Such a fine grain—event based—sharing scheme allows con-centrating the computing power towards unprocessed events that are at any time the closest ones to the commit horizon of the simu-lation. The advantage is the reduction of the incidence of rollbacks, that together with the high effectiveness of platform level non-blocking algorithms for sharing information across threads leads to extreme runtime effectiveness even under hard workload scenarios, as we have shown via an experimental study.

REFERENCES

[1] R. Ayani. LR-Algorithm: concurrent operations on priority queues. In *Proceedings of the 2nd IEEE Symposium on Parallel and Distributed Processing*, SPDP, pages 22–25, Dallas, TX, USA, 1990. IEEE Computer Society.

[2] P. D. Barnes, C. D. Carothers, D. R. Jefferson, and J. M. LaPre. Warp speed: executing time warp on 1,966,080 cores. In *Proceedings of the 2013 ACM SIGSIM conference on Principles of advanced discrete simulation - SIGSIM-PADS '13*, pages 327–336, 2013.

[3] C. D. Carothers and R. M. Fujimoto. Efficient execution of Time Warp programs on heterogeneous, NOW platforms. *IEEE Transactions on Parallel and Distributed Systems*, 11(3):299–317, 2000.

[4] C. D. Carothers, K. S. Perumalla, and R. M. Fujimoto. Efficient optimistic parallel simulations using reverse computation. *ACM Transactions on Modeling and Computer Simulation*, 9(3):224–253, 1999.

[5] L.-l. Chen, Y.-s. Lu, Y.-P. Yao, S.-l. Peng, and L.-d. Wu. A well-balanced Time Warp system on multi-core environments. In *Proceedings of the 2011 IEEE Workshop on Principles of Advanced and Distributed Simula-tion*, PADS, pages 1–9. IEEE Computer Society, 2011.

[6] D. Cingolani, A. Pellegrini, and F. Quaglia. Transparently mixing undo logs and software reversibility for state recovery in optimistic PDES. *ACM Trans. Model. Comput. Simul.*, 27(2):11:1–11:26, 2017.

[7] R. M. Fujimoto. Parallel discrete event simulation. *Communications of the ACM*, 33(10):30–53, 1990.

[8] R. M. Fujimoto. Performance of Time Warp under synthetic workloads. In *Proceedings of the Multiconf. on Distributed Simulation*, pages 23–28. 1990.

[9] S. Gupta and P. A. Wilsey. Lock-free pending event set management in time warp. In *Proceedings of the 2014 ACM SIGSIM Conference on Principles of advanced discrete simulation*, PADS, pages 15–26. 2014.

[10] T. L. Harris. A pragmatic implementation of non-blocking linked-lists. In *Proceedings of the 15th International Conference on Dis-tributed Computing*, volume 2180 of *DISC*, pages 300–314. Springer Berlin/Heidelberg, 2001.

[11] J. Hay and P. A. Wilsey. Experiments with hardware-based trans-actional memory in parallel simulation. In *Proceedings of the 2015 ACM/SIGSIM Conference on Principles of Advanced Discrete Simulation*, pages 75–86, 2015.

[12] M. Ianni, R. Marotta, A. Pellegrini, and F. Quaglia. Towards a fully non-blocking share-everything PDES platform. In *Proceedings of the 21st IEEE Internat Symp. on Distributed Simulation and Real Time Appli-cations*, pages 25–32, 2017.

[13] D. R. Jefferson. Virtual time. *ACM Trans. on Programming Languages and Systems*, 7(3):404–425, 1985.

[14] S. Koenig and Y. Liu. Terrain coverage with ant robots: a simulation study. In *Proceedings of the fifth international Conference on Autonomous agents*, AGENTS, pages 600–607. ACM, 2001.

[15] R. Marotta, M. Ianni, A. Pellegrini, and F. Quaglia. A lock-free o(1) event pool and its application to share-everything PDES platforms. In *Proceedings of the 20th IEEE/ACM International Symposium on Dis-tributed Simulation and Real Time Applications*. 2016.

[16] R. Marotta, M. Ianni, A. Pellegrini, and F. Quaglia. A conflict-resilient lock-free calendar queue for scalable share-everything PDES platforms. In *Proceedings of the 2017 ACM SIGSIM Conference on Principles of Advanced Discrete Simulation*, pages 15–26, 2017.

[17] A. Pellegrini, S. Peluso, F. Quaglia, and R. Vitali. Transparent spec-ulative parallelization of discrete event simulation applications us-ing global variables. *International Journal of Parallel Programming*, 44(6):1200–1247, 2016.

[18] A. Pellegrini and F. Quaglia. Transparent multi-core speculative par-allelization of DES models with event and cross-state dependencies. In *Proceedings of the 2014 ACM/SIGSIM Conference on Principles of Ad-vanced Discrete Simulation*, pages 105–116. 2014.

[19] R. Rönngren and R. Ayani. A comparative study of parallel and se-quential priority queue algorithms. *ACM Transactions on Modeling and Computer Simulation*, 7(2):157–209, 1997.

[20] H. Sundell and P. Tsigas. Fast and lock-free concurrent priority queues for multi-thread systems. *J. Parallel Distrib. Comput.*, 65(5):609–627, 2005.

[21] J. Svennebring and S. Koenig. Building Terrain-Covering Ant Robots: A Feasibility Study. *Autonomous Robots*, 16(3):313–332, 2004.

[22] B. P. Swenson and G. F. Riley. A New Approach to Zero-Copy Message Passing with Reversible Memory Allocation in Multi-core Architec-tures. In *Proceedings of the 2012 ACM/IEEE/SCS 26th Workshop on Principles of Advanced and Distributed Simulation*, pages 44–52, 2012.

[23] The High Performance and Dependable Computing Systems Re-search Group (HPDCS). ROOT-Sim: The ROme OpTimistic Simulator. https://github.com/HPDCS/ROOT-Sim, 2012.

[24] R. Vitali, A. Pellegrini, and F. Quaglia. Towards symmetric multi-threaded optimistic simulation kernels. In *Proceedings of the 26th Workshop on Principles of Advanced and Distributed Simulation*, PADS, pages 211–220. IEEE Computer Society, jul 2012.

[25] J. Wang, N. B. Abu-Ghazaleh, and D. V. Ponomarev. AIR: application-level interference resilience for PDES on multicore systems. *ACM Trans. Model. Comput. Simul.*, 25(3):19:1–19:25, 2015.

[26] J. Wang, D. Jagtap, N. B. Abu-Ghazaleh, and D. Ponomarev. Parallel discrete event simulation for multi-core systems: Analysis and optimization. *IEEE Trans. Parallel Distrib. Syst.*, 25(6):1574–1584, 2014.

Zero Energy Synchronization of Distributed Simulations

Aradhya Biswas and Richard Fujimoto
School of Computational Science and Engineering,
Georgia Institute of Technology
Atlanta, Georgia, USA 30332
aradhya.biswas@gatech.edu, fujimoto@cc.gatech.edu

ABSTRACT

The question of the energy consumed by synchronization algorithms for distributed simulation programs is addressed. The concept of zero energy synchronization is introduced wherein a distributed simulation program incurs no additional energy cost for synchronization. A theoretical approach to achieving zero energy synchronization using an oracle is described. An energy efficient implementation of the YAWNS algorithm, termed Low Energy YAWNS (LEY) is presented. It is shown that LEY can yield, in principle, zero energy synchronization for many classes of applications. Preliminary experimental results are presented showing that LEY achieves significantly less energy consumption compared to a conventional implementation of YAWNS that does not consider energy use as a design goal. Further, these experimental results indicate that LEY achieves energy consumption only modestly greater than that of an execution of the same application using an oracle for the test cases that were examined. These results suggest that it may be feasible to develop practical distributed simulation synchronization algorithms that approach zero energy synchronization.

CCS CONCEPTS

• Computing methodologies~Discrete-event simulation • Computing methodologies~Distributed simulation

KEYWORDS

Distributed Simulation Programs; Energy; Synchronization

ACM Reference format:

Aradhya Biswas, Richard Fujimoto. 2018. Zero Energy Synchronization of Distributed Simulations. In *Proceedings of ACM SIGSIM Conference on Principles of Advanced Discrete Simulation*, Rome, Italy, *May 2018 (PADS'18)*, 12 pages. https://doi.org/10.1145/3200921.3200938

Permission to make digital or hard copies of all or part of this work for personal or classroom use is granted without fee provided that copies are not made or distributed for profit or commercial advantage and that copies bear this notice and the full citation on the first page. Copyrights for components of this work owned by others than the author(s) must be honored. Abstracting with credit is permitted. To copy otherwise, or republish, to post on servers or to redistribute to lists, requires prior specific permission and/or a fee. Request permissions from Permissions@acm.org.
SIGSIM-PADS'18, May 23–25, 2018, Rome, Italy
© 2018 Copyright held by the owner/author(s).
ACM ISBN 978-1-4503-5092-1/18/05…$15.00
https://doi.org/10.1145/3200921.3200938

1 INTRODUCTION

Concerns of the energy and power consumed by computing applications are increasing in importance. In mobile and embedded computing applications energy consumption has long been a major concern because reductions of energy consumption can lead to longer times between recharging batteries or enable the use of smaller, lighter batteries.

Trends such as ubiquitous computing, edge computing and the Internet of Things highlight that an area of increasing interest concerns the execution of distributed simulation programs on mobile and embedded computing platforms. For example, dynamic data-driven application systems (DDDAS) [1] involve incorporating live data to improve simulation model predictions for online decision making. Placing simulations in close physical proximity to sensors can provide faster response times or the use of disaggregated data compared to centralized approaches, and can circumvent privacy concerns associated with transmitting data to a centralized facility as well as reduce reliance on wide-area communication networks. Examples of data-driven distributed simulation applications using mobile computing platforms are presented in [2-4].

At the same time, interest in energy and power consumption for high performance and cloud computing applications is increasing. Power consumption has been cited as a key challenge to achieving exascale performance in supercomputers and the U.S. Department of Energy has specified 20 megawatts as the goal for the maximum power consumption for such a machine. Power is a major expense in data centers used for cloud computing. Data centers were estimated to consume approximately 70 billion kW-hours or 1.8% of the total electricity consumption in the U.S. in 2014 [5].

Despite these trends, relatively little work has been completed to date concerning the energy and power requirements of parallel and distributed simulation codes. Relatively little is known concerning the power and energy consumption properties of key algorithms, or ways to reduce or manage these concerns. This is the primary focus here.

Distributed simulation programs commonly assume the computation consists of a collection of logical processes (LPs) that exchange timestamped events, or messages. A synchronization algorithm is required to ensure that the parallel execution produces the same results a sequential execution where all events are processed in timestamp order. Synchronization algorithms are commonly classified as conservative and optimistic methods. Conservative approaches block LPs to ensure no LP ever processes events out of timestamp order. Well known examples include the

Chandy/Misra/Bryant [6] and YAWNS [7] algorithms, among others. Optimistic algorithms use a detection and recovery approach where synchronization errors, i.e., out of order event executions are detected during the execution, and their effects are erased through a rollback mechanism. Time Warp is the most well-known optimistic synchronization algorithm [8].

In the following we first review related work in power and energy consumption for parallel and distributed simulation codes. The minimum energy requirements for a distributed simulation program are defined. A property called *zero energy synchronization* is introduced for synchronization algorithms, and a theoretical approach to achieving zero energy synchronization is discussed. An energy optimized implementation of YAWNS, termed Low Energy YAWNS (LEY) is described as a practical approach to reducing the energy consumed for conservative synchronization. It is shown that LEY can, in principle, achieve zero energy synchronization for a large class of distributed simulation applications. This is followed by the results of an experimental study. This study measures the energy consumed by LEY for a set of benchmark applications. To empirically portray the advantages of LEY, the energy consumption of LEY is then compared with the energy consumption of YAWNS and a zero energy synchronization algorithm for a set of benchmark application. This is followed by a discussion of future work and conclusions.

2 RELATED WORK

There is an extensive literature in power and energy consumption and optimization techniques in the mobile and embedded computing literature, and a growing body of work considering such issues in high performance computing. However, as discussed below, there is only a limited amount of work on power and energy consumption of distributed simulation programs.

The bulk of the work examining energy and power consumption in areas such as mobile computing and embedded systems focuses on low-level elements such as hardware, operating systems, and compilers. For example, much work in operating systems considers implementation techniques to reduce power consumption while meeting performance requirements and deadlines [9-11]. Many ad hoc communication protocols have been designed for low power operation. Power mode management techniques exploit low-power modes of operation for processors, memory, storage, and communication circuits [12-14], e.g., disabling components or switched them to power saving states. A substantial body of work focuses on utilization of dynamic voltage and frequency scaling (DVFS) where voltage and clock frequency can be reduced to trade off power consumption with execution time [15-17].

Work in energy and power consumption for parallel and distributed simulation is surveyed in [18]. Empirical studies comparing the power consumed by conservative synchronization algorithms are presented in [19-21]. Measurements of energy consumption in a Time Warp system are described in [22]. Use of dynamic voltage and frequency scaling to optimize Time Warp programs is described in [23]. A study comparing the power consumed for cellular automata and queueing network models for vehicle traffic in distributed simulations is presented in [24].

3 MINIMUM ENERGY

We begin this discussion by defining the minimum amount of energy that must be consumed to execute a distributed simulation program. We assume the program consists of a collections of N logical processes LP_1, LP_2, ... LP_N and the computation performed by each LP is a sequence of event computations, where $E_{i,j}$ denotes the jth event executed by LP_i. Let $C_{i,j}$ denote the energy consumed in processing event $E_{i,j}$, exclusive of the energy required to schedule new events, discussed next. The simulation is initialized with some number of scheduled events; the energy required to initialize the simulation is not considered here. Each new event created during the simulation comes about through an event scheduling operation. Let $S_{i,j}$ denote the energy required to schedule $E_{i,j}$. If the new event is scheduled on a different processor from the LP scheduling the event, $S_{i,j}$ is defined as the energy required to send and receive the message containing the event; we implicitly consider such communications as part of the distributed simulation computation itself. If the sender and receiver reside on the same processor, we define $S_{i,j}$ to be zero. This is a simplification because some energy must be expended to allocate storage and place the event into data structures such as the local event list, however we ignore this energy to keep the model simple; inclusion of this energy, e.g., as a fixed energy cost, is a relatively straightforward extension to the model. We assume the program continues to run until there are no more scheduled events to process. We define the minimum energy required to execute the distributed simulation program as simply the energy required to process and schedule the events that it processes:

$$MinEnergy = \sum_{i,j} C_{i,j} + S_{i,j}$$

We note that this formulation does not include the energy required for the distributed simulation synchronization algorithm. For example, it does not consider energy consumption for null messages or global synchronizations in conservative algorithms, and considers only committed events for optimistic synchronization algorithms. We characterize such operations as overhead, with the goal that developers of distributed simulation systems will strive to minimize this overhead, subject to other performance goals such as minimizing execution time. We note that this formulation does depend on the application configuration[1], i.e. mapping of LPs to processors and the resulting communication pattern. This formulation also excludes energy for I/O operations. However, such can be easily added if

---

[1] Much like speed up of a parallel (or distributed) algorithm is dependent on the performance of the baseline sequential algorithm, the choice of implementation details of the baseline system while computing MinEnergy will affect any comparison made. We implicitly imply that the best possible setup is used, and leave out such implementation details for the simplicity of the model and its discussion.

significant or important for a particular simulation. Finally, it is assumed no energy is expended when a processor is idle, i.e., it only considers dynamic power consumption.

4 ZERO ENERGY SYNCHRONIZATION

The above definition for *MinEnergy* is intended to separate the energy required for distributed simulation computations, e.g., producing new computational results and distributing information to other LPs, and that required for synchronization. The expenditure of energy to produce such results seems reasonable. However, the need to expend energy to synchronize computations is less clear. In a distributed simulation program the synchronization algorithm does not perform computations that directly contribute to computational results. Rather, the purpose of the synchronization algorithm is to ensure that event computations are performed in a proper sequence to produce the same results as the corresponding sequential execution. As such, we exclude the energy required for synchronization from the definition of the minimum energy required to complete the distributed simulation computation in order to provide a basis for minimizing the energy needed for synchronization.

The above discussion raises the question of whether one must expend energy to synchronize a distributed simulation. Is it possible to synchronize a distributed simulation without any expenditure of energy beyond that required for event computations and communications? Are there fundamental requirements to consume energy for synchronization that cannot be avoided? In practice, can one hope to achieve zero energy synchronization, or close to zero energy synchronization? These are some of the questions we begin to explore here.

We define a *zero energy synchronization algorithm* as one that results in executions of a distributed simulation that requires no more than *MinEnergy* energy to complete. We next describe a simple, albeit theoretical, approach to achieving zero-energy synchronization.

Is it possible to achieve zero energy synchronization? Consider a distributed simulation program that does *not* utilize any synchronization algorithm. Each LP simply processes any unprocessed events it has in its future event list (FEL) in timestamp order, and blocks if the FEL is empty. This is equivalent to the execution of a Time Warp program that does not include operations for state saving, rollback, GVT computations, or other Time Warp specific operations. Consider an execution of this program where it happens that during the execution, the time stamp of each message received by an LP is larger than the timestamp of the last message the LP had processed. It is apparent that the energy required for this execution will be *MinEnergy*. Thus, this execution would require no energy for synchronization, satisfying our requirement for zero-energy synchronization.

Of course, the above approach does not *guarantee* correct synchronization for all executions of the code, only for one

particular execution. However, it is suggestive of an approach to achieving zero energy synchronization for arbitrary distributed simulation codes for any execution. If each LP had an oracle to tell it the next event that it should process at any instant in time, then the LP would know whether to wait for this event, or to go ahead and process the next event residing in its local FEL. More precisely, the oracle function is defined as:

$$E_{i,j} = OF(i,j) \tag{1}$$

OF returns a unique identifier for the *jth* event to be executed by LP_i. We assume the *OF* function requires no energy to execute. If LP_i has processed j events, then it simply calls *OF* $(i,j+1)$ to obtain the identifier for the next event it is to process. If the event resides in its local queue, LP_i processes the event. If not, some other LP must generate the event, so LP_i blocks until this event is received. There are several ways to implement such an oracle. For example, an oracle that returns the minimum time stamp among events the LP will later receive will also similarly allow for zero energy synchronization.

In practice, an implementation of the oracle could be achieved by first obtaining a log of an execution of the distributed simulation code. Alternatively, if one has apriori knowledge of the application, it may be possible to realize *OF* using knowledge of what events are scheduled by each LP rather than using a log. For example, if one knows that communications among LPs follow a ring topology and one can deduce the timestamp of messages it will receive from its neighbors, an implementation of the log using a minimal amount of energy can be achieved. This approach is utilized in the experiments described later.

5 OPTIMIZING ENERGY IN YAWNS

We now present an energy optimized implementation of the YAWNS synchronization protocol called Low Energy YAWNS, or simply LEY.

5.1 YAWNS

We first review the YAWNS algorithm discussed in [7]. The terminology used here is adopted from that work. Specifically, a simulation is composed of a set of the logical processes. Each simulation LP (or simply LP) simulates a logical collection of entities (or servers[2]). For this initial discussion of YAWNS we assume each LP consists of a single unit capacity server. A simulation event, defined as the atomic unit of work for the simulation, with a timestamp TS denotes a job arrival, and the server can begin serving/handling the job any time on or after simulation time TS. A unit capacity server is one that can only handle one job at a given simulation time. This implies that simultaneous simulation events corresponding to simultaneous job arrivals will result in the jobs being handled sequentially. An infinite capacity server can be viewed as a dynamic collection of

---

[2] Note that this server is a logical simulated entity, which is different from the server in the client-server implementation discussed later.

unit capacity servers, which can elastically scale depending on the number of jobs being processed concurrently. This implies that an infinite capacity server can serve any number of jobs at the same simulation time instant.

Define t as the minimum timestamp of any event in the entire simulation at one instant during the execution. Define $d_i(t)$ as the lower bound on the earliest completion time of any pending event with timestamps t, on LP_i.

With the assumption of each LP simulating a single unit-capacity server, given t, any LP_i, has a unique value for $d_i(t)$. With these assumptions and definitions, $d_i(t)$ is computed as

1. If the event list of LP_i is empty then, $d_i(t) = \infty$.
2. If LP_i has pending events in its event list, assuming no further events will be inserted into the event list, $d_i(t)$ is set as the completion time of the next event. This is equivalent to the timestamp of the next event the LP may send to another LP if it does not receive any new job arrival events in the future.

The assumption that each LP simulates a single unit capacity server can be relaxed, by computing $d_i(t)$ for an infinite capacity server as the minimum $d_i(t)$ of all individual servers that make up the infinite capacity server. The same can be extended to a multi-server site.

Next we define the lower bound on time stamp or LBTS as

$$LBTS = \min_{\text{for all sites } S_i} \{d_i(t)\} \qquad (2)$$

LBTS provides a lower bound on the timestamp of any event that can be created in the simulation given t. Along similar lines, $d_i(t)$ can be seen as a local lower bound on time stamp of any event that can be created by LP_i. Hence we denote $d_i(t)$ as $LBTS_i(t)$. Assuming each LP is composed of a single server, Eq.(2) reduces to:

$$LBTS = \min_{\text{for all LP } LP_i} \{LBTS_i(t)\} \qquad (3)$$

Finally we define the term epoch or window. As will be demonstrated shortly, each LBTS computation serves as a global barrier for synchronization. Hence we define, each update of LBTS as the end of an epoch and start of a new epoch. For simplicity, we define the LBTS value of the nth epoch as $LBTS_n$. Hence the nth epoch is marked by window $(LBTS_{n-1}, LBTS_n]$.

```
LBTS = 0
WHILE termination criteria not met
  IF (FEL not empty
      && timestamp of FEL.top <= LBTS) THEN
    process and remove top event
    communicate generated events to their
      destination
  ELSE
    compute LBTSi(LBTS)
    cooperatively compute LBTS
  END IF
END WHILE
```

Algorithm 1: YAWNS

With these in place, we now describe the algorithms. We assume each LP consists of a future event list (FEL) implemented as a priority queue, where the priority of the event is the timestamp associated with the event. Processing an event may create new events. Each event specifies a destination LP, which can be the generating LP (local event) or a remote LP (remote event). Any received event is enqueued in the FEL of the destination LP.

Algorithm 1 describes the YAWNS algorithm based on the assumptions and definitions presented above.

5.2 Low Energy YAWNS

In our prior work [25] empirical evidence suggested that communication can be a major component of the energy consumed by a distributed simulation, hence providing an avenue for optimization. Further empirical studies [26] on the effect of communication patterns on energy consumed by distributed simulations indicated that message aggregation allows for a large reduction in energy consumption. Finally, we observe that when implemented on a client server machine architecture, additional opportunities for message aggregation could be exploited. Clients can bundle all messages that need to be sent to any other client and send it to the server, and the server takes care of the message delivery to individual clients where the messages can be re-bundled based on destination. We observe that timestamp information necessary to compute LBTS values can be piggybacked onto other messages to reduce the energy consumed for global reduction computations. These observations motivated the development of LEY.

In the following we assume that increasing the number of messages that are aggregated reduces the energy consumed per bit of the total data being communicated. We relax this assumption after describing LEY.

Using similar terminology that was used to describe YAWNS, LP_i of a simulation synchronized with LEY implemented with a client-server architecture (where each LP is a client) proceeds as presented in algorithm 2.

Algorithm 3 presents the pseudo code for the LEY server. It should be noted here that a special case might arise if all LPs exhaust all their respective events in an epoch. The LBTS computed by the server would be infinity. In such a case the server can use its omniscience to compute the LBTS. For a unit-capacity LP, this would be the minimum time stamp of any event that would be sent to another LP in the next epoch. This lower bound can be further improved by considering application properties, e.g., exploiting lookahead.

As pointed out earlier, a major source of improvement in the performance of LEY is the grouping of communications by delaying the communication until the end of the epoch. The piggybacking of the LBTS value for each epoch, further reduces the energy cost for synchronization.

```
LBTS = 0
WHILE termination criteria not met
  message_buffer = []
  IF (FEL not empty
       && timestamp of FEL.top <= LBTS) THEN
    process and remove top event
    push (generated event, destination) in
      message_buffer
  ELSE
    compute LBTSi(LBTS)
    //piggyback LBTSi(LBTS) on messages
    push (LBTSi(LBTS), server) in message
      buffer
    send message_buffer to server
    receive message from server
    update FEL and LBTS
  END IF
END WHILE
```

Algorithm 2: LEY: Client side

```
FOR each LP i
    // buffer with messages destined for
    // client i in current epoch
    server_message_buffer[i] = []
END FOR

WHILE termination criteria not met
  FOR each LP i
    receive message_buffer
    FOR message in message_buffer
      update server_message_buffer[
        message.destination]
    END FOR
    update LBTS[i]
  END FOR

  compute LBTS = min_{for all i} (LBTS[i])

  FOR each LP i
    //piggyback LBTS on messages
    append LBTS in the
      server_message_buffer[i]
    send server_message_buffer[i] to LP i
    server_message_buffer[i] = []
  END FOR
END WHILE
```

Algorithm 3: LEY: Server side

Assume that after a message size of m, the energy consumed per bit increases. Then the first assumption can be relaxed by introducing a forced synchronization in a client if the aggregated message size or size of the message_buffer in algorithm 2, reaches m. This would still keep the synchronization protocol conservative, as this essentially reduces the size of the epoch and might shift the starting time of the following epoch.

5.3 Energy Consumption of LEY

We now analyze the energy consumed by LEY relative to the zero energy synchronization algorithm. With certain assumptions regarding energy consumption we show that LEY achieves zero energy synchronization for a certain class of distributed simulation applications.

Theorem 1: LEY in conjunction with the following assumptions yields the zero energy synchronization property:

   a) *Each LP generates at least one remote event in each epoch.*
   b) *Each LP receives at least one remote event in each epoch.*
   c) *A constant increase in message size causes negligible increase in energy required for communication.*

Proof:. To prove that LEY is a zero energy synchronization scheme, it would suffice to show that LEY with the given assumptions consumes no more than *MinEnergy* energy to complete the application simulation. Hence the problem reduces to comparing the energy required by a distributed simulation program simulated with LEY to that of the *MinEnergy* value corresponding to the distributed simulation application.

We prove this by reducing LEY to an oracle-based implementation of the distributed simulation application, or simply O-DS. O-DS has the zero energy synchronization property. Hence it consumes *MinEnergy* energy, with the assumption[3] that the oracle does not consume any energy.

We can prove the claim if we can construct LEY from an O-DS, such that following conditions are met.

   1. The construction does not consume any energy, in other words any changes made to O-DS do not consume any additional energy.
   2. The reduction relaxes the assumption that the oracle does not consume any extra energy.

Construction 1: Maintain a local variable, which stores the value last returned by oracle. Any available event is safe to process if it is smaller than this variable.

Construction 2: Constrain the sending and receiving of messages only when the LP blocks.

This constraint does not consume any additional energy because aggregation of messages as presented earlier can be assumed not to increase the energy consumed by the LP.

Construction 3: The oracle is consulted only when the LP blocks.

Construction 4: The oracle is implemented as in algorithm 4.

---

[3] Another implicit assumption here is that energy is not required for waiting. This follows from the definition of Minimum PDES energy.

```
DEFINE oracle()
  compute LBTS_i(LBTS)
  append (LBTS_i(LBTS), server) in
    message buffer
  send message_buffer to server
  receive message from server
  RETURN LBTS
END DEFINE
```

Algorithm 4: Oracle

As noted earlier, from the definition of MinEnergy, synchronization messages are overhead whereas an event message is not. It must also be noted that, by *construction 2* and *assumptions (a)* and *(b)* the synchronization messages are always piggybacked on event messages. Hence by the implication of *assumption (c)*, synchronization messages do not consume additional energy. Thus reducing the effective energy consumption of the oracle to sending and receiving messages to and from server, which by *construction 2* forms the part of the simulation or in other words are not overhead.

Hence we construct LEY with O-DS without consuming any more energy and relaxing the assumption of oracle with no extra energy. In other words, the constructions satisfy conditions 1 and 2. Hence LEY is zero energy given assumption a-c. This concludes the proof.

The main constraints needed to achieve zero energy synchronization are that the simulation application in each LP, or equivalently each processor, sends and receives at least one message in each epoch. For large simulations each processor will include many LPs. It is therefore reasonable to assume that there will be at least one message sent and received each epoch. Because there will typically be many messages that are aggregated together, this also implies that piggybacking timestamp information necessary to compute LBTS on such message exchanges would have negligible effect on the amount of energy consumed. In this sense, we view the constraints described above as mild constraints that will be applicable to many distributed simulation applications that arise in practice, especially large simulations with many LPs executing on each processor.

6 IMPLEMENTATION

Implementations of YAWNS, LEY, and an oracle-based synchronization mechanism were developed and used to evaluate the energy consumed by each approach for a sample application. Rather than implementing a general oracle mechanism applicable to any distributed simulation code, knowledge of the distributed simulation application was exploited in order to minimize the amount of energy required to complete oracle operations. This section describes these implementations as well as the sample application. The principal goals of this study were to determine:

a) The performance and energy consumed by the proposed synchronization scheme, LEY, relative to an implementation of YAWNS.

b) Assess the energy consumed by LEY relative to an oracle-based implementation approximating a zero energy synchronization algorithm.

We begin by describing the applications that are simulated to compare the synchronization schemes. Then follow this with a description of each of the implementations used for the study.

6.1 Applications

Two applications were used for this study. The first is the well-known PHOLD benchmark. The second is a simulation of a token-ring communications network. The applications were selected, in part, because highly efficient implementations of the oracle-based approach could be realized without resorting to the creation of a complete message log.

Phold is a widely used synthetic benchmark application by the distributed simulation community [27]. We implement a Phold application with an infinite capacity server at each LP. The Phold application can be defined as follows. When processed, each event generates one new event, and the event so generated is sent to a randomly chosen remote LP at lookahead time in future.

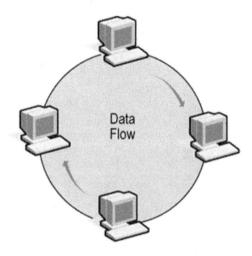

Figure 1: Token ring network topology [28]

A ring network (also called as Token-ring network [29]) is a unidirectional, Local Area Network. A ring network is formed by computing nodes connected to exactly two other nodes in the network with unidirectional links. Figure 1 shows a sample ring network with 4 nodes. Computing nodes on the network communicate with each other using tokens circulating in the network in one direction.

Assume the nodes are identified as node 0 to node 3. For a node with ID i, the ID of the next node in the ring is given $(i + 1)$ mod 4. Although each node can directly send messages to only one node in ring network, a token is used to send messages to other nodes. Suppose node 0 sends a message to node 2. To send data to a specific node, the sender must first wait for the token to arrive. When received, the token is checked if it is free. If it is free the sender marks the token as being used and writes the data for the message along with the destination ID and its own ID as the source ID into the token. The sender then forwards the token to next node in the ring. The token is then passed on from one node to next in the ring, until it arrives at the destination node, in this case node 2. The recipient node reads the data and marks the token as an acknowledgement, swaps the sender and destination ID, and sends the modified token to the next node in the ring. Eventually the token is received by the sender, which sees the acknowledged token and modifies its status to indicate it is a free token, and transmits the token back into the ring.

6.1.1 Implementation Details for Ring Network.

We simulate a multi-token ring network, similar to one presented in [30], with each LP simulating a node in the network. We make some assumptions to simulate the ring network. First, we assume that the nodes can process only one token at a time. This is consistent with our earlier note concerning single unit-capacity server LPs. This implies that if multiple tokens arrive simultaneously they would be processed sequentially, in contrast to a less pragmatic infinite capacity LP. Second, the nodes take a constant amount of time to processes a token. This assumption can be rationalized by the fact that the frequency of network hardware is much slower than that of the processors. Third, we assume uniform links and nodes. Fourth, we assume constant size tokens, consistent with previous assumption of a constant propagation delay for all links.

Suppose that at time t a token is processed in an LP. A remote event is generated for the LP simulating the next node in the ring, with a timestamp of $t + processing\_time + transmission\_time$ and the simulation time of the LP advances to $t + processing\_time$. If the token arrives while the node is busy, it is queued and is processed sequentially in time stamp order.

Each node is initialized with a constant number of tokens at simulation time $t = 0$. Given the application, the total number of tokens in circulation remains constant throughout the execution of the simulation. The LPs terminate if they reach the pre-specified maximum simulation time or the simulation as a whole has exhausted all the events that can be processed before the maximum simulation time.

The empirical evaluation focused on the effect of varying the number of nodes in the simulation or more specifically a weak scaling of the application. Table 1, summarizes the constants used for the study.

Table 1: Simulation Application Constants

Name	Value
Maximum simulation time (T)	10^6 units
Token processing time (p)	1 unit
Transmission time (t)	10 units
Num initial tokens per node (I)	10

6.1.2 Analysis of Ring Network Application.

Given the multi-token ring network application, described in previous section, total number of events processed by a LP, E, for a given max simulation time, T, is given by:

$$E = \begin{cases} \left\lceil T \times \dfrac{I}{t+p} \right\rceil, & \text{if } t + p > I \times p \\ \left\lceil T \times \dfrac{1}{p} \right\rceil, & \text{if } t + p \leq I \times p \end{cases} \qquad (4)$$

Where, I is the number of initial tokens per node, p is the token processing time and t is the transmission time. With the constants as mentioned in table 1, E should be 909091. All the implementations were verified against this value of E.

6.2 LEY and YAWNS Implementations

Implementations of LEY and YAWNS were created for this study. These are described next.

6.2.1 LEY.

We use the client server based LEY implementation presented earlier in Algorithms 2 and 3. For the specific application of the ring network simulation and the assumptions as stated in the previous section, further optimizations were considered. For example, the destination of any generated event is always the ID of the next node in the ring. Hence the destination tag was removed from the message, as the server can identify the destination based on the sender ID.

```
LBTS = 0
WHILE termination criteria not met
  IF (FEL not empty
       && timestamp of FEL.top <= LBTS) THEN
    process and remove top event
    communicate generated event to server as
       an event_message
    receive any waiting events from server
    push the received events in FEL
  ELSE
    compute LBTSᵢ(LBTS)
    send LBTSᵢ(LBTS) as a
       synchronization_message
    receive LBTS from server
    update LBTS
    receive any waiting events from server
    push the received events in FEL
  END IF
END WHILE
```

Algorithm 5: YAWNS: Client side

6.2.2 YAWNS.

To be consistent across all variations of the synchronization protocols being studied, algorithm 1 was adapted in a client server implementation of YAWNS. Algorithm 5 and 6 present the adapted version of YAWNS for the ring network simulation.

Each LP in the simulation is a client, which executes Algorithm 5. As is common in client server infrastructures clients communicate with each other through the server. Again application specific optimizations, such as skipping the destination field in the event message, were implemented.

```
Initialize server_message_buffer for each LP
LBTS = ∞
WHILE termination criteria not met
  LBTS[i] = ∞, FOR each LP i
  receive message from any client
      (say, LP i)

  IF event_message THEN
    push the message to the buffer for
      destination LP
    send any message in
      server_message_buffer[i] to LP i
    free server_message_buffer[i]
  END IF

  IF synchronization_message THEN
    update LBTS
    IF all clients have sent synchronization
      messages for this epoch THEN
      send LBTS values to all clients
      reset LBTS to infinity
    END IF
  END IF
END WHILE
```

Algorithm 6: YAWNS: Server side

It should be noted here that although the synchronization part of the implementation is generic and can apply to any distributed simulation application, the communication pattern is specific to the applications described earlier.

6.3 OLEY: Synchronization with Oracle

In terms of LEY, whenever an LP blocks, i.e., needs to synchronize, an oracle is consulted to determine the LBTS value for the next epoch. In relation to the definition of the oracle presented earlier (see equation 1), consider the definition of the LBTS presented in section 5.1 and equation 3. LBTS provides the lower bound for any event that can be created by any LP in the next epoch. Hence LBTS is also a lower bound for each individual LP. Therefore the LBTS value at any time can be treated as a valid oracle output.

There are several approaches to implementing the oracle. A general approach is to log every message sent in the simulation in a pre-simulation run and then refer to this log while simulating. However, there is an inherent, potentially significant energy cost of this oracle related to the maintenance and access of the log. A more efficient way to implement oracle is to exploit any application properties to determine the LBTS value for each epoch.

For our Phold application, the LBTS value for each epoch increments exactly by the lookahead amount. This results from the infinite capacity of the server.

For our ring network implementation we use the maximum of timestamps of the event received for an epoch as the LBTS value for the epoch. As can be inferred, this value holds due to the communication pattern and the symmetric nature of the application.

As was pointed out earlier in section 3, the setup of the baseline implementation (in this case synchronization with the oracle) is important. Hence rather than YAWNS, we modify the LEY algorithm to yield OLEY, the implementation of LEY using the oracle. In terms of implementation, an OLEY client would replace the $LBTS_i$ (LBTS) computation and piggybacking steps in LEY client (Algorithm 2) with a request to oracle. Similarly an OLEY server would skip the steps to compute and piggyback LBTS in LEY server (Algorithm 3).

7 SYSTEM CONFIGURATIONS

All simulations were developed in C++ with all communications using MPI. As was mentioned earlier, all simulations were developed with a client server architecture, where each LP was mapped to a client. In terms of implementation, each client and the server were mapped to individual MPI processes. MPI processes were assigned in a round robin fashion among the available cores.

The experiments were performed on a micro-cluster platform designed for mobile, high performance computing. The micro-cluster is comprised of NVIDIA's Jetson TK1 development boards. Each development board consists of a Tegra TK1 SOC including NVIDIA's 4-Plus-1™ Quad-Core ARM® Cortex™-A15 32-bit CPU with 4 cores operating at 2.3 GHz and 2 GB memory. Each of these boards runs Ubuntu 14.04.5 LTS. The boards communicated over an Ethernet LAN. Two such development boards were used for the study. Energy and power measurements were performed using a PowerMon2 power measurement system [31].

Power and energy values were measured for one of the two boards, called the board of interest. The server was always assigned to a process in a different development board from the board of interest. This ensures that energy values include only LPs. This is consistent with an implementation where simulations reside on edge nodes e.g. smartphones. In this client-server architecture all LPs assigned to the board of interest communicate exclusively using inter-board communications.

8 RESULTS

In this section we present the results of the empirical study using the implementations of the applications discussed earlier. The experiments were designed to provide insight into the energy consumption behavior of LEY, YAWNS and OLEY. The applications were weakly scaled to study the effect of increase in number of LPs on the metrics of interest.

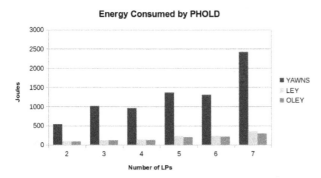

Figure 2: Energy consumed by Phold application.

8.1 Principle metrics

For these experiments YAWNS, LEY, and OLEY were compared using two principal metrics, energy consumption and execution time:

1. **Energy consumption:** The instantaneous power consumed by one of the development boards (called, the board of interest) was aggregated over the duration of the simulation execution and used to determine the average power consumption. This value is multiplied by the execution time to determine the total amount of energy consumed.
2. **Execution time:** Execution time indicates the time required for the application to complete its execution. This metric was reported using the C++ class, std::chrono::high_resolution_clock.

We restrict our experiments to a maximum of 7 LPs (8 processes). This is due to the limited number of available cores on the platform used for these experiments.

Figure 2 shows the results from energy consumption measurements for the Phold application. The amount of energy consumed largely increases with the number of LPs as one might expect, as noted below. More importantly, these measurements indicate that LEY consumes much less energy than the unoptimized version of YAWNS. This is also corroborated by energy consumption measurements of the ring network application. Further, it can be seen that LEY's energy performance approaches that of the oracle-based scheme suggesting energy performance approaching optimal.

Figure 3 shows the energy consumption of the ring network simulation. Again, LEY consumes much less energy than the original YAWNS implementation, and approaches that of the oracle-based implementation. Here we see the energy consumption does not increase uniformly as the number of LPs increases. This behavior is seen to a lesser degree in the PHOLD measurements. Upon closer inspection one observes that the trend of increasing energy occurs when only an odd or even number of LPs is considered separately. This difference in the odd and even number of LPs can be bolstered by the round robin assignment of

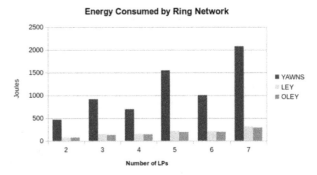

Figure 3: Energy consumed by ring network application.

LPs to processes (also, cores). With two boards, an even number of LPs are distributed evenly among the boards but an odd number of LPs causes an imbalance. This in conjunction with the uniform nature of the application leads to the observed trend.

An important observation, common to both the applications, is that the optimized synchronization scheme leads to a reduction in execution time proportional to the reduction in energy. This follows from the fact that the difference in average power consumption of the three synchronization schemes is relatively small.

Another important observation is that for both applications, LEY achieves energy consumption that is only slightly greater than that of OLEY, suggesting that practical realization of zero energy synchronization of distributed simulation codes may be feasible.

8.2 Second order metrics

The large difference in the energy consumed by YAWNS and LEY highlights the fact that the optimizations introduced in LEY provide both execution time and energy consumption benefits, relative to an energy-oblivious implementation of YAWNS. However these differences are difficult to quantify.

We characterize the performance advantage in terms of energy as *energy improvement*. *Energy improvement* is defined as the percent decrease in the amount of energy consumed by LEY when compared to that of YAWNS. Similarly, we define the synchronization overhead of a synchronization algorithm with respect to energy as the percent increase in energy required by a simulation when compared to that of the simulation with an oracle.

More precisely, the energy overhead for LEY and improvement of LEY over YAWNS is given by equations 5 and 6.

$$Energy\ Overhead = \frac{E_{LEY} - E_{oracle}}{E_{oracle}} \times 100 \qquad (5)$$

$$Energy\ Improvement = \frac{E_{YAWNS} - E_{LEY}}{E_{YAWNS}} \times 100 \qquad (6)$$

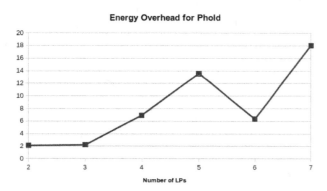

Figure 4: Overhead of LEY with Phold increases as the number of LPs increase.

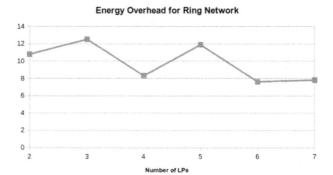

Figure 5: Overhead of LEY with Ring network is minimal and the overhead decreases as the number of LPs increase.

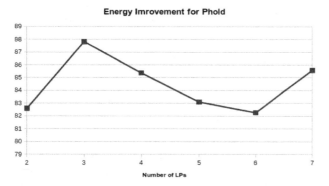

Figure 6: LEY has an average 84% energy improvement for Phold.

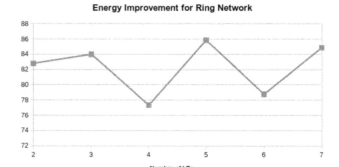

Figure 7: Ring network with LEY has an average energy improvement of 82%.

Where, E_{LEY} and E_{YAWNS} is the energy required for simulating the application with LEY and YAWNS, respectively. E_{oracle} is the energy required for simulating the application with an oracle, or in this case OLEY.

8.2.1. Energy Overhead.

Figure 4 and 5 show the *energy overhead* of LEY, as defined above, with respect to OLEY. It can be seen that the overhead is modest.

For the Phold application the increase in energy with the increase in the number of LPs is due in part to the random event distribution. In particular, assumptions (*a*) and (*b*) of theorem 1 do not hold for this application. As there might be epochs in which LPs do not receive or send any event. This causes extra message communications for synchronization which otherwise would not have been required when compared to the *MinEnergy* energy needed by the oracle based simulation. For the ring network application, the LPs have messages to send and receive in each epoch resulting in the LEY measurements to be closer to the energy consumption of OLEY. The small energy overhead is a result due to the real world implications of assumptions such as the processor does not consume energy in idle state. The interesting irregular nature of the plots can be explained as a culmination of the idle energy and the imbalance due to the round robin distribution of the LPs.

The main conclusion of the results presented for this metric is that the energy overhead of LEY is very close to that of OLEY and that the deviation from the assumptions of theorem 1 may cause a minor increase in the overhead.

8.2.2. Energy Improvement.

Figure 6 and 7 presents the energy improvement of LEY. We see about an 84% energy improvement for Phold and an average of 82% energy improvement for the ring network. In both cases the energy improvement is modestly affected by the increase in the number of LPs. The nature of energy improvements using LEY with the ring network can again be attributed to the assignment of LPs. The increase in the energy consumption of YAWNS is in proportion with that of LEY for an even number of LPs but the increase is relatively higher for odd number of LPs, as the board of interest in the latter case has more LPs than the other board.

The conclusion for this metric is that LEY outperforms YAWNS by a large magnitude, which outweighs the possible small increase in the overhead of LEY. Also, the improvement can have minor dependence on the application being simulated.

9 CONCLUSIONS AND FUTURE WORK

In this work we highlight the importance of energy consumption in distributed simulation as an important challenge facing the community. Observing that synchronization does not directly contribute to computational results produced by the simulation, we propose zero energy synchronization as a goal that distributed simulation algorithms and implementations might strive to achieve. We propose the use of an oracle both as a theoretical construct that can be used to analyze the energy required for synchronization as well as a practical method that can be used to measure energy costs associated with synchronization. To explore the feasibility of achieving zero energy synchronization, Low Energy YAWNS (LEY) is proposed. We prove that with some mild assumptions LEY can achieve zero energy synchronization for many distributed simulation codes.

To provide tangible evidence of the practicality of this work, an experimental study was completed. Empirical measurements of LEY, an implementation of YAWNS not optimized to minimize energy consumption, and an oracle based implementation designed to measure the amount of energy required to complete a simulation with a zero energy synchronization algorithm with two applications we found that LEY improves the energy consumption of the un-optimized YAWNS implementation by about 84% and incurs only a small, approximately 10% additional energy cost compared to an oracle-based approach. Execution time results showed similar improvements.

The experimental results presented here suggest that zero energy synchronization is a reasonable goal in realizing energy efficient distributed simulation codes that may be achievable in practice. We caution, however, that these results correspond to only preliminary experimentation with the synchronization algorithm, and a more thorough and comprehensive analysis and experimental study is required to draw definitive conclusions.

The zero energy synchronization concepts discussed in this work, along with the methodology utilized, suggest an approach to measure and evaluate the energy consumption of distributed simulation synchronization algorithms. We believe this approach could be useful for further research in the development of energy efficient parallel and distributed simulations.

The zero energy characterization of LEY required the assumption that each LP send and receive at least one message in each epoch. One open question concerns evaluation of the energy overhead in LEY for applications where this assumption does not hold. More broadly, the development of other zero-energy synchronization algorithms that do not require this assumption represents another area of future research.

The assumptions for zero energy synchronization point towards avenues for further improvement of the synchronization schemes to approach zero energy synchronization in real life application scenarios. For example, the assumption that energy is expended in only active state might not be possible in real world systems due to say, switching overheads, but the schemes that can optimize these pockets of energy use can further reduce the overhead. We are planning to follow up this work with characterization of more real-world applications and quantify the advantage and overheads.

ACKNOWLEDGEMENTS

Funding for this research was provided by Air Force Office of Scientific Research Award FA9550-17-1-022 and Air Force Office of Scientific Research/National Science Foundation Award 1462503.

REFERENCES

1. Darema, F., *Dynamic Data Driven Applications Systems: A New Paradigm for Application Simulations and Measurements*, in *International Conference on Computational Science*. 2004, Springer: Kraków, Poland. p. 662-669.
2. Fujimoto, R., et al., *Ad Hoc Distributed Simulations*, in *Principles of Advanced and Distributed Simulation*. 2007, IEEE: San Diego, CA. p. 15-24.
3. Kamrani, F. and R. Ayani. *Using On-Line Simulation for Adaptive Path Planning of UAVs.* in *Proceedings of the 11th IEEE International Symposium on Distributed Simulation and Real-Time Applications*. 2007.
4. Madey, G.R., et al. *Applying DDDAS Principles to Command, Control and Mission Planning for UAV Swarms.* in *Proceedings of the International Conference on Compuational Science*. 2012.
5. Shehabi, A., et al., *United States Data Center Energy Usage Report*. 2016, Lawrence Berkeley National Laboratory.
6. Chandy, K. and J. Misra, *Asynchronous distributed simulation via a sequence of parallel computations*, in *Communications of the ACM*. 1981.
7. Nicol, D.M., *The Cost of Conservative Synchronization in Parallel Discrete Event Simulations.* Journal of the Association for Computing Machinery, 1993. **40**(2): p. 304-333.
8. Jefferson, D., *Virtual Time*. ACM Transactions on Programming Languages and Systems, 1985. **7**(3): p. 404-425.
9. Saewong, S. and R. Rajkumar, *Practical voltage- scaling for fixed-priority rt-systems*, in *IEEE Real- Time and Embedded Technology and Applications Symposium*. 2003. p. 106–114.
10. Quan, G. and X. Hu, *Energy efficient fixed- priority scheduling for real-time systems on variable voltage processors*, in *Design Automation Conference*. 2001. p. 828–833.
11. Cho, K.-M., et al., *Design and implementation of a general purpose power-saving scheduling algorithm for embedded systems*, in *IEEE International Conference on Signal Processing, Communications and Computing*. 2011, IEEE: Xi'an, China. p. 1–5.
12. Hoeller, A., L. Wanner, and A. Fröhlich, *A hierarchical approach for power management on mobile embedded systems*, in *From Model-Driven Design to Resource Management for Distributed Embedded Systems*. 2006. p. 265–274.
13. Bhatti, K., C. Belleudy, and M. Auguin, *Power management in real time embedded systems through online and adaptive interplay of DPM and DVFS policies*, in *International Conference on Embedded and Ubiquitous Computing*. 2010, IEEE: Hong Kong, China. p. 184–191.
14. Niu, L. and G. Quan, *Reducing both dynamic and leakage energy consumption for hard real- time systems*, in

international conference on Compilers, architecture, and synthesis for embedded systems. 2004. p. 140–148.

15. Ge, R., X. Feng, and K.W. Cameron, *Performance-constrained Distributed DVS Scheduling for Scientific Applications on Power-aware Clusters*, in *Proceedings of the 2005 ACM/IEEE conference on Supercomputing*. 2005, IEEE Computer Society: Washington, DC, USA. p. 34--.

16. Freeh, V.W., et al., *Analyzing the Energy-Time Trade-Off in High-Performance Computing Applications.* IEEE Trans. Parallel Distrib. Syst., 2007. **18**(6): p. 835--848.

17. Hua, S. and G. Qu, *Approaching the Maximum Energy Saving on Embedded Systems with Multiple Voltages*, in *IEEE/ACM International Conference on Computer-Aided Design*. 2003. p. 26.

18. Fujimoto, R.M., *Power Consumption in Parallel and Distributed Simulations*, in *Winter Simulation Conference*. 2017.

19. Fujimoto, R.M. and A. Biswas, *An Empirical Study of Energy Consumption in Distributed Simulations*, in *IEEE/ACM International Symposium on Distributed Simulation and Real-Time Applications*. 2015.

20. Biswas, A. and R.M. Fujimoto, *Energy Consumption of Synchronization Algorithms in Distributed Simulations.* Journal of Simulation, 2017. **11**(3): p. 242-252.

21. Biswas, A. and R.M. Fujimoto, *Profiling Energy Consumption in Distributed Simulation*, in *Principles of Advanced Discrete Simulation*. 2016.

22. Maqbool, F., S.M.R. Naqvi, and A.W. Malik, *Why to Redesign PDES Framework for Smart Devices: An Empirical Study*, in

23. Child, R. and P. Wilsey, *Using DVFS to Optimize Time Warp Simulations*, in *Winter Simulation Conference*. 2012. p. 3275-3286.

24. Neal, S., R.M. Fujimoto, and M. Hunter, *Energy Consumption of Data Driven Traffic Simulations*, in *Winter Simulation Conference*. 2016.

25. Biswas, A. and R. Fujimoto. *Profiling Energy Consumption in Distributed Simulations.* in *ACM SIGSIM Conference on Principles of Advanced Discrete Simulation (PADS)*. 2016. Banff, Alberta, Canada: ACM.

26. Fujimoto, R.M., et al. *Power Efficient Distributed Simulation.* in *ACM SIGSIM Conference on Principles of Advanced Discrete Simulation*. 2017. Singapore, Republic of Singapore: ACM.

27. Fujimoto, R.M., *Performance Measurements of Distributed Simulation Strategies.* Transactions of the Society for Computer Simulation, 1989. **6**(2): p. 89-132.

28. *Network Topologies.* [cited 2018 Jan]; Available from: http://www.techiwarehouse.com/engine/3c274b63/Network-Topologies.

29. *Token-ring networks.* [cited 2018 Jan]; Available from: https://www.ibm.com/support/knowledgecenter/en/ssw_ibm_i_61/rzajt/rzajttrncon.htm.

30. Kamal, A.E., *On the Use of Multiple Tokens on Ring Networks* in *INFOCOM'90, Ninth Annual Joint Conference of the IEEE Computer and Communication Societies. The Multiple Facets of Integration*. 1990, IEEE. p. 15-22.

31. Bedard, D., et al., *PowerMon 2: Fine-grained, Integrated Power Measurement* in *RENCI Technical Report TR-09-04*. 2009.

A Power Cap Oriented Time Warp Architecture

Stefano Conoci*
Sapienza, University of Rome
conoci@diag.uniroma1.it
conoci@lockless.it

Davide Cingolani*
Sapienza, University of Rome
cingolani@diag.uniroma1.it
cingolani@lockless.it

Pierangelo Di Sanzo*
Sapienza, University of Rome
disanzo@diag.uniroma1.it
disanzo@lockless.it

Bruno Ciciani*
Sapienza, University of Rome
ciciani@diag.uniroma1.it
ciciani@lockless.it

Alessandro Pellegrini*
Sapienza, University of Rome
pellegrini@diag.uniroma1.it
pellegrini@lockless.it

Francesco Quaglia*
University of Rome "Tor Vergata"
francesco.quaglia@uniroma2.it
quaglia@lockless.it

ABSTRACT

Controlling power usage has become a core objective in modern computing platforms. In this article we present an innovative Time Warp architecture oriented to efficiently run parallel simulations under a power cap. Our architectural organization considers power usage as a foundational design principle, as opposed to classical power-unaware Time Warp design. We provide early experimental results showing the potential of our proposal.

CCS CONCEPTS

• **Computing methodologies** → **Discrete-event simulation**; • **Computer systems organization** → *Multicore architectures*; • **Software and its engineering** → *Power management*;

ACM Reference Format:
Stefano Conoci, Davide Cingolani[1], Pierangelo Di Sanzo[1], Bruno Ciciani[1], Alessandro Pellegrini[1], and Francesco Quaglia[1]. 2018. A Power Cap Oriented Time Warp Architecture. In *SIGSIM-PADS '18 : SIGSIM-PADS '18: SIGSIM Principles of Advanced Discrete Simulation CD-ROM, May 23–25, 2018, Rome, Italy*. ACM, New York, NY, USA, 4 pages. https://doi.org/10.1145/3200921.3200930

1　INTRODUCTION

Power usage has become a major concern in software applications. In this context, the objectives of power oriented design of simulation systems can be disparate. They range from the elongation of the lifetime of mobile devices involved in the simulation—as for on-line simulations or volunteer computing on mobile devices [2]—to the usage of power governors to optimize the execution of the simulation model—as for the case of Time Warp parallel simulations [4] where the CPU-core frequency is dynamically controlled in order to throttle the execution of simulation objects out of the critical path [8]. Within this panorama, we target the orthogonal

---

*Also with Lockless s.r.l.

Permission to make digital or hard copies of all or part of this work for personal or classroom use is granted without fee provided that copies are not made or distributed for profit or commercial advantage and that copies bear this notice and the full citation on the first page. Copyrights for components of this work owned by others than the author(s) must be honored. Abstracting with credit is permitted. To copy otherwise, or republish, to post on servers or to redistribute to lists, requires prior specific permission and/or a fee. Request permissions from permissions@acm.org.
SIGSIM-PADS '18 , May 23–25, 2018, Rome, Italy
© 2018 Copyright held by the owner/author(s). Publication rights licensed to the Association for Computing Machinery.
ACM ISBN 978-1-4503-5092-1/18/05...$15.00
https://doi.org/10.1145/3200921.3200930

objective of efficiently running Time Warp simulations under a power budget constraint. This problem is generally known in the literature as *power capping*, and is essentially related to the fact that infrastructure/system owners may decide to limit the power consumption of the employed machines for various reasons, including data-center cooling costs

A trivial way of imposing a power cap to Time Warp simulations would consists in running the Time Warp platform on top of a group of CPU-cores with properly tuned down performance states (i.e. operating frequency and voltage). This approach would deliver a scaled down computing power, resembling a scenario where the Time Warp application is executed on less performing hardware. However, we do not consider such an approach satisfactory, since it does not consider power efficiency as a core aspect in the design of the Time Warp architecture.

In this paper we take the different perspective of devising a new Time Warp architectural organization which is by design oriented to power capping. It allows us to control the power usage—hence the speed—of operations performed by the threads *selectively* exploiting different software paths for different classes of threads.

Typical Time Warp architectures are generally based on a unique control flow graph, which characterizes the execution of all the involved threads. Along this graph each thread typically executes both housekeeping operations and event processing. In our new design, by imposing different control flow graphs to the different threads, we propose an asymmetric scenario where a few threads run tasks that are more time critical, while other threads run less critical ones. Separating the tasks in such different classes leads to the possibility of lowering down the power state and/or the frequency of operations of a given CPU-core (running a specific thread)—which allows meeting the power cap—while still enabling more critical Time Warp tasks to be executed timely.

Our power cap oriented Time Warp architecture has been implemented as a variation of the architectural organization of the open source ROOT-Sim package [10]. In the concluding part of this paper we report early experimental results that show the potential of our proposal.

2　RELATED WORK

Common power capping techniques in the literature (e.g. [9]) are application-agnostic—they enforce power budgets at the level of server machines, without accounting for workload features of the hosted applications. Contrariwise, we explicitly optimize the execution of Time Warp-based application under a power budget.

Regarding studies in the area of parallel simulation, the works in [1, 3] provide evidence of how using different algorithms to run specific simulation models can impact power and energy overheads. One main outcome is that parallel and distributed simulations suffer from power and energy overhead more intensely than sequential simulation. This demands for innovative designs making parallel simulation systems more prone to energy and power efficiency. Our work is exactly in this direction since our objective is to devise a Time Warp architecture specifically designed to deliver optimized performance under a power cap.

The proposal in [8] controls the processor speed—via DVFS (Dynamic Voltage and Frequency Scaling)—for optimizing Time Warp performance. Lowering down the power usage can lead to emulate a throttling scheme where excessively optimistic simulation objects are slowed down by slowing down the speed of the CPU-core/thread they are bound to. Our work is orthogonal to [8] since we do not tune the performance state of threads based on their degree of speculation, but based on the different type of tasks they execute. Moreover, [8] does not address performance optimization under a power budget, as instead we do via our Time Warp architecture.

Asymmetry—in the form of the master/worker paradigm—has been exploited in [5] to process distributed simulations on public resources and desktop grid infrastructures. This work does not cope with power budgets, thus our proposal is fully orthogonal to it, although we share some baseline system design concepts such as the idea of pipelined interactions across the asymmetric threads.

3 THE ARCHITECTURE

Our power-cap oriented Time Warp architecture is based on the idea of exploiting asymmetric thread operations to carry out different tasks. In particular, we discriminate two classes of tasks, and hence of threads:

Class-1 Forward mode processing of simulation events;

Class-2 All other tasks, namely GVT (Global Virtual Time) computation, fossil collection, state saving, rollback (including coasting forward), scheduling events to be processed in forward mode, message exchange, and so on.

Threads running **Class-2** tasks are referred to as Controller Threads (CTs). Threads executing simulation events in forward mode, namely **Class-1** tasks, are instead referred to as Processing Threads (PTs). In our architecture, threads are pinned to different CPU-cores, so that we can control the performance states of the CPU-cores—with the aim of matching the power budget—which reflects into the speed of operations performed by the different threads. In this scenario, PTs play a core role in controlling how to spend the overall power budget assigned to the Time Warp system. More in detail, running PTs on top of CPU-cores configured with lower performance states generates the scenario where the execution of the overall application workload (the actual simulation events to be processed while moving forward along the simulation time) is slowed down. However, slowing down those threads does not lead to slowing down CTs, which can be hosted on other CPU-cores, which can then be run at a relatively higher power state. This enables all

Class-2 tasks to be carried in a timely manner, which is crucial to the goodness of the runtime dynamics. In fact, literature studies have shown that fast completion of housekeeping tasks, such as rollback (including state reconstruction via, e.g., coasting forward) or GVT computation (see, e.g., [7]), is fundamental in order not to impair synchronization dynamics, and not to incur the risk of higher incidence of wasted speculative computation.

In this paper we focus on shared-memory multi-core machines, so that a CT and the PTs bound to it always have access to the same data related to the simulation execution. In any case, our approach could be generalized by adopting it on top of each individual machine within a distributed memory system and making a CT and its controlled PTs reside on the same machine. On the other hand CTs residing on remote machines may interact just like traditional threads running a non-power cap oriented Time Warp platform—as an example, they might exploit message passing in case of event-communication between simulation objects managed by two PTs, each of which associated with remote CTs.

Indicating with N_{cores} the number of available CPU-cores for running the Time Warp system, and with N_{CT} and N_{PT} the number of used CTs and PTs, respectively, we have $N_{cores} = N_{CT} + N_{PT}$.

A CT controls at least one PT, thus in our architecture the inequality $N_{CT} \le N_{PT}$ holds. This is perfectly aligned with the idea of having fewer threads running more critical tasks in a timely manner, via higher power demand, and more threads running the normal forward workload, via lower power demand.

Each CT_j is in charge of managing the execution of a subset of all the simulation objects. It manages their event queues, by taking care of incorporating into the proper queues any new event destined to these objects, or canceling a previously inserted event in case of an incoming anti-event. CT_j also manages the state queues of the simulation objects, by taking checkpoints of their states and logging them into the state queue of the corresponding object.

CT_j associates the managed objects with its bound PTs according to a partitioning scheme. More in detail, a partition p_i of all the objects managed by CT_j is bound to an individual PT_i, meaning that the object belonging to the partition p_i can only be scheduled for forward execution on PT_i. This leads to the scenario where no two different PTs can work simultaneously on the state of a same object, thus preventing data conflicts. On the other hand, CT_j and its controlled PT_i might need to work on the state of a same simulation object, given that they carry out disjoint classes of tasks that may anyhow lead to operate on the same object memory image. More in detail, PT_i is in charge of manipulating the state of the object when an event is being processed in forward mode, while CT_j, beyond taking checkpoints, may also access the object state for reloading a previous checkpoint and reprocessing coasting forward events in case of a rollback. We recall that both CT_j and PT_i live on a same shared-memory machine so that they can both directly access the state image of a same object by relying on address space sharing. Given such a sharing of the accesses to the object state, a CT and all its controlled PTs need to put in place a scheduling mechanism to determine which of them can operate on the object state at any time, guaranteeing isolated access to prevent inconsistencies.

The scheduling of the actions on the objects' states is put in place in our architecture via the notion of *port* between CT_j and PT_i. A port is a bidirectional communication structure—still exploiting

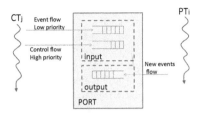

Figure 1: Structure of the port between CT and PT.

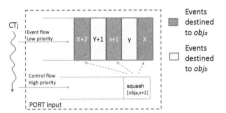

Figure 2: Example flow of event and control records.

shared memory support—based on the multiplexing of different data flows. Data that flows from CT_j to PT_i are multiplexed along two channels of the port, having different priorities. We refer to this flow-direction as *input*. Conversely, data that flows from PT_i to CT_j travels along a single channel, and we refer to this flow-direction as *output*. Figure 1 shows the port scheme.

The low priority input channel is used by CT_j to post to PT_i the events to be processed in forward mode, which are destined to the objects belonging to the p_i partition. CT_j extracts unprocessed events from the objects' event queues following the Lowest-Timestamp-First (LTF) rule, and posts them to the input channel of the port. Hence it creates into the port a pipeline of events that PT_i can extract and process, accessing the state of the corresponding objects. We note that LTF guarantees that, for each individual simulation object, the extracted events from the pipeline respect timestamp-ordering, unless (1) causal inconsistencies are revealed due to the arrival of some straggler event at that object—possibly injected by another PT_k—or (2) the cancellation of some event that passed through the pipeline, or (3) the objects produces for itself some new event with timestamp lower than another one already filled into the pipeline, which gets eventually processed. Once an event is extracted and then processed, newly produced events (if any) are posted by PT_i to the output flow of the port. These are in their turn extracted by CT_i and are incorporated into the event queues of the destination objects, if they belong to the p_i partition. Otherwise these events are sent towards the CT instance to which the corresponding objects are bound.

The accesses by CT_j and PT_i to the port are asynchronous, meaning that there is no blocking synchronization between the two threads. This allows CT_j to switch to a different PT_k it is managing whenever a port of some other PT_i—previously filled with event records—does not yet provide in output new events to handle.

Clearly, we need to include the possibility to squash portions of the current pipeline at low cost as soon as some inconsistency is detected along the flow of event records that were previously inserted, and to manage state restoration if requested because of erroneous speculation involving already processed events at some simulation object. This is the case of the arrival of a straggler event for some object, leading to the need to retract event records destined to that object which still stand into the pipeline, and to the need to rollback the object state if out-of-order processing already happened at that object. The same is true for the arrival of an anti-event annihilating some previously processed event, or one that currently stands into the pipeline. To manage these scenarios, we exploit the high priority input channel of the port, together with a mechanism that tags event records. Each event record that is inserted into the

pipeline is tagged with a unique per-object identifier, which in our case is a monotonically increasing counter value. In the example shown in Figure 2, tags for events of the simulation object obj_a range from x to $x + 2$, while those destined to the object obj_b range from y to $y + 1$. If the pipelined events destined to obj_a need to be undone then CT_j inserts into the high priority input channel a squash control record bound to obj_a, and carrying the same counter value of the last event record that was inserted into the pipeline. For the example in Figure 2, the control record is structured as squash[$obj_a, x + 2$]. PT_i extracts such a control records as soon as it finishes processing its last event record—given the higher priority of the control flow information in input to the port—and switches to a state where, upon extracting from the pipeline event records destined to obj_a and tagged with counter value up to the one of the squash control record, it simply discards them, thus avoiding to carry out processing tasks touching the state of the destination object. Essentially, squash tells to PT_i to ignore events destined to obj_a that still stand into the pipeline, which are no longer consistent in terms of timestamp ordering at the destination object. Note that event timestamps are uncorrelated from the counter value used to tag event records.

To indicate to CT_j that the squash message has been processed, and that the target object will be not accessed by PT_i till any new valid event record—tagged with a larger counter value with respect to the squash tag—will be posted, PT_i simply routes the squash control record to the output flow of the port. Upon detecting the presence of this control record, CT_j can safely act on the state of the target object in order to possibly restore a correct state snapshot, if requested. We note that when the squash control record is inserted by CT_j it is possible that the out-of-timestamp-order events for the destination object were only those standing into the pipeline. This is the scenario where the last event processed by PT_i for that object had a timestamp still compliant with causality—and CT_j does not need to perform any state restore action for the simulation object. To detect this condition, CT_j accesses a meta-data table, with one entry for each managed object, which is updated by PT_i with the timestamp of the last event it processed on any object. If the table-value associated with the object indicates that the last processed event had timestamp lower that the one associated with the causality violation that generated the squash, then no state restore operation is carried out by CT_j, which simply resumes filling the pipeline with event records destined to that object in renewed correct timestamp order.

Another important aspect in the separation of the tasks performed by CTs and PTs is the one related to checkpointing for

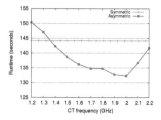

Figure 3: Performance with power cap = 30 Watt.

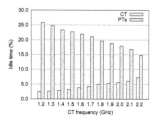

Figure 4: Percentage of idle time for CT and PTs.

creating correct snapshots for state restoration. As hinted, in our power capping oriented Time Warp architecture checkpointing is a **Class-2** task, namely one to be carried out by CTs. In order for CT_j to detect that it can safely access the state of some object to perform checkpointing, with no interference caused by forward event processing carried out by PT_i, we rely on the concept of "bubbles", similar to those used in conventional pipelined CPUs. More in detail, when CT_j determines that time has come to take a checkpoint for a given object, it inserts into the pipeline a bubble event-record, tagged with the object identifier. Upon extracting this bubble, PT_i does not carry out any processing action, rather it simply forwards the bubble towards the output flow of the port. When CT_j detects that the bubble has been posted on the port output flow it gains information that any other event that was posted before the bubble to the pipeline, which was destined to the same object, has been already processed by PT_i. Hence, CT_j can safely access in isolation the state of the object in order to take a checkpoint. Clearly, any existing policy that selects when (and of which LPs) the checkpoints should be taken can be adopted in our scheme to determine when to introduce the bubble event. The assumption for the correctness of this approach is that, once the bubble is posted to the port, no other event is posted to the port input flow for the same object till the time the bubble is observed along the output flow, and the checkpoint of the object state is taken. To achieve this, we devise a management of the objects—inspired by [6]—such that some objects can be temporarily "unschedulable' thus being not considered by the LTF scheduler.

4 EARLY EXPERIMENTAL RESULTS

To asses our proposal we have ran the widespread PHOLD benchmark, configured with 1024 objects in a bi-dimensional mesh, interacting with each other with probability set to 0.8. We set the event granularity to the coarse grain value of about 1 msec, so as to not be adverse to classical Time Warp. In fact in such a scenario most of the computation resides in forward event processing, so that

housekeeping operations, which are the most critical ones when all the threads are slowed down at the same manner to meet the power cap, represent a reduced percentage of the overall computational cost of the simulation. All runs have been executed on a 10 CPU-core machine equipped with an Intel Xeon E5-2630 v4, 256 GB of ECC memory running Debian 9 with kernel release 4.9.0. The CPU frequency ranges from 1.2 GHz at P-state 11 to 2.2 GHz at P-state 1. We do not consider turbo boosting (P-state 0) in this evaluation since it cannot be easily controlled from software and it is generally power inefficient. In Figure 3 we show the variation of the execution time with power cap set to 30 Watt for classical Time Warp[1] (named Symmetric) with all CPU-cores slowed uniformly for meeting the power budget, and our architecture with differentiated slow-down of CT and PTs (named Asymmetric). In the latter case we plot the curve as a function of the power assigned to the CT, which determines the residual power budget to be assigned to the PTs. By the plot we see that our architecture allows reducing the completion time, with increased gain when we fine tune the respective power budgets to be assigned to the asymmetric threads operating within the platform. On the other hand, the Asymmetric architecture pays the cost of leading both CT and PTs to remain sometimes idle—when no work to be carried out is posted to the opposite side of the port—as shown in Figure 4 [2]. Future work will focus on the runtime optimization of the pipelined interaction across threads and on the dynamic reallocation of the power budget based on the evolution of the simulation.

REFERENCES

[1] Aradhya Biswas and Richard Fujimoto. 2017. Energy Consumption of Synchronization Algorithms in Distributed Simulations. *J. Simulation* 11, 3 (2017), 242–252.
[2] Richard M. Fujimoto and Aradhya Biswas. 2015. On Energy Consumption in Distributed Simulations. In *Proceedings of the 3rd ACM Conference on SIGSIM-Principles of Advanced Discrete Simulation, London, United Kingdom, June 10 - 12, 2015.* 99–100.
[3] Richard M. Fujimoto, Michael Hunter, Aradhya Biswas, Mark Jackson, and Sabra Neal. 2017. Power Efficient Distributed Simulation. In *Proceedings of the 2017 ACM SIGSIM Conference on Principles of Advanced Discrete Simulation, SIGSIM-PADS 2017, Singapore, May 24-26, 2017.* 77–88.
[4] David R. Jefferson. 1985. Virtual Time. *ACM Transactions on Programming Languages and Systems* 7, 3 (jul 1985), 404–425. http://portal.acm.org/citation.cfm?doid=3916.3988
[5] Alfred J. Park and Richard M. Fujimoto. 2012. Efficient Master/Worker Parallel Discrete Event Simulation on Metacomputing Systems. *IEEE Trans. Parallel Distrib. Syst.* 23, 5 (2012), 873–880.
[6] Alessandro Pellegrini and Francesco Quaglia. 2014. Transparent Multi-core Speculative Parallelization of DES Models with Event and Cross-state Dependencies. In *Proceedings of the 2014 ACM/SIGSIM Conference on Principles of Advanced Discrete Simulation (PADS)*. ACM Press, 105–116. https://doi.org/10.1145/2601381.2601398
[7] Bruno R. Preiss, Wayne M. Loucks, and Ian D. MacIntyre. 1994. Effects of the Checkpoint Interval on Time and Space in Time Warp. *ACM Trans. Model. Comput. Simul.* 4, 3 (1994), 223–253. https://doi.org/10.1145/189443.189444
[8] Patrick Putnam, Philip A. Wilsey, and Karthik Vadambacheri Manian. 2012. Core Frequency Adjustment to Optimize Time Warp on Many-core Processors. *Simulation Modelling Practice and Theory* 28 (2012), 55–64.
[9] Sherief Reda, Ryan Cochran, and Ayse Coskun. 2012. Adaptive Power Capping for Servers with Multithreaded Workloads. *IEEE Micro* 32, 5 (Sept. 2012), 64–75. https://doi.org/10.1109/MM.2012.59
[10] The High Performance and Dependable Computing Systems Research Group (HPDCS). 2012. ROOT-Sim: The ROme OpTimistic Simulator. https://github.com/HPDCS/ROOT-Sim. (2012). https://github.com/HPDCS/ROOT-Sim

---

[1] This is the native ROOT-Sim implementation.

[2] In our experimental setup the CT posts to the port a batch of up to 128 events at a time towards each PT.

Adaptive Ladder Queue: Achieving $O(1)$ Amortized Access Time in Practice

Angelo Furfaro
DIMES – University of Calabria
Rende, CS – Italy
a.furfaro@dimes.unical.it

Ludovica Sacco
DIMES – University of Calabria
Rende, CS – Italy
l.sacco@dimes.unical.it

ABSTRACT

The data structure that handles the pending event set of a discrete event simulator is a critical component in that its performances have a direct impact on those of the overall simulation engine. Many data structures have been proposed in the literature. Among them, the Ladder Queue (LadderQ) claims $O(1)$ amortized access time. However, empirical results show that the practical achievement of such performances is highly dependent on the distribution of event timestamps and that in many cases are similar or even worse than those of heap-based priority queues. This paper proposes an adaptive extension of the LadderQ which overcomes most of its weaknesses and allows to achieve $O(1)$ amortized access time in practice.

CCS CONCEPTS

• **Theory of computation** → **Data structures design and analysis**; • **Computing methodologies** → **Discrete-event simulation**;

KEYWORDS

Discrete Event Simulation, Pending Event Set, Priority Queue, Calendar Queue, Ladder Queue

ACM Reference Format:
Angelo Furfaro and Ludovica Sacco. 2018. Adaptive Ladder Queue: Achieving $O(1)$ Amortized Access Time in Practice. In *SIGSIM-PADS '18 : SIGSIM-PADS '18: SIGSIM Principles of Advanced Discrete Simulation CD-ROM, May 23–25, 2018, Rome, Italy*. ACM, New York, NY, USA, 4 pages. https://doi.org/10.1145/3200921.3200925

1 INTRODUCTION

Discrete event simulation (DES) is a powerful modelling tool in widespread use for the study and analysis of complex systems of many fields. A very important aspect, which affects simulation performance, is the Pending Event Set (PES), management of the events that have to be handled in the future. The data structure employed to implement the PES contains all the events that have been created by the simulation but not yet processed. The main

Permission to make digital or hard copies of all or part of this work for personal or classroom use is granted without fee provided that copies are not made or distributed for profit or commercial advantage and that copies bear this notice and the full citation on the first page. Copyrights for components of this work owned by others than ACM must be honored. Abstracting with credit is permitted. To copy otherwise, or republish, to post on servers or to redistribute to lists, requires prior specific permission and/or a fee. Request permissions from permissions@acm.org.
SIGSIM-PADS '18 , May 23–25, 2018, Rome, Italy
© 2018 Association for Computing Machinery.
ACM ISBN 978-1-4503-5092-1/18/05...$15.00
https://doi.org/10.1145/3200921.3200925

loop of the simulator accesses the PES at least once per each iteration. Hence, it is critical to employ an implementation with fast access times. The Ladder Queue (LadderQ) [1] is one of the most promising one, achieving a theoretical $O(1)$ *amortized* access time complexity [2]. In this paper, we introduce the *Adaptive Ladder Queue (ALQ)* which is an improved version of the LadderQ. We demonstrated, through some implementation solutions, that ALQ overcomes the problem of the access time complexity, succeeding to achieve $O(1)$ theoretical complexity in a real word performance under various workloads. The rest of the paper is organized as follows: Section 2 discusses the related work, Section 3 describes the LadderQ; Section 4 presents our Adaptive Ladder Queue and discuss issues presented in Section 3; Section 5 shows experimental results. Finally, Section 6 draws the conclusions.

2 RELATED WORK

In the 80s, Jones [3] found out that no single implementation is the best for all applications. Similarly to the LadderQ, the *Lazy Queue* [4] is a data structure organized in three tiers, *near future*, *far future*, *very far future*, but the middle tier is simpler. A more recent study [5], in the context of sequential DEVs [6] simulations, analysed the Calendar Queue [7], the Lazy Queue [4] and the LadderQ [1], concluding that the latter outperforms all the priority queues based on event lists. In [8] priority queues are revisited to evaluate their performances in image analysis applications, applying floating-point representation to *implicit heaps*. A simple modification of the hierarchical queue is provided [8] that makes it more efficient than the implicit heaps for large queues. A multi-tier data structure for PES, based on the LadderQ, both for sequential and optimistic parallel simulations on distributed memory platforms is presented in [9]. Considering the results of the aforementioned studies, this paper adds knowledge on how managing the PES. It offers a more efficient data structure created starting from the LadderQ, that allows to achieve amortized constant time complexity both in theory and in practice thanks to the introduced improvements.

3 LADDER QUEUE

The LadderQ belongs to the *Unsorted Calendar Queue (UCQ)*, a class of *Calendar Queues* [7] where sub lists are sorted only when strictly necessary, presenting a theoretical $O(1)$ cost in both type of operations. It works deferring sorting of events only when some high priority events are close to be dequeued and arriving events are simply appended into buckets without sorting. It is divided in three tiers: *Top, Ladder, Bottom*

Top is a simple unsorted linked list where all the events are initially enqueued. *Ladder* consists of several rungs of buckets where each bucket may contain an unsorted linked list. *Bottom* contains ordered elements, ready for dequeuing. It is made up of a data structure that allows sorting the events inside it.

3.1 Queuing strategy

The event processing loop can be resumed in two main operations: dequeue and enqueue.

3.1.1 Enqueue Operation. Enqueue in LadderQ determines in which of the three tiers insert new events in input. Given an event E, with timestamp TS: if $TS \geq TopStart$ (where $TopStart$ is a temporal separation between a range of events, called epochs, specifically between the actual epoch in Ladder tier and the future epoch in Top), the event is appended to *Top*. Otherwise, TS is compared with thresholds $RCur[1], RCur[2], \ldots, RCur[NRung]$ (where $RCur[x]$ stores the timestamp of the first valid bucket in Rung[x] from which starting dequeue operations) and if $TS \geq RCur[x]$, the event is inserted into $Rung[x]$. If neither a condition is met, the event is directly inserted into *Bottom*. Considering the computational complexity of the *enqueue* operation, the latter case is to be considered as the worst one, because an insertion to the *Bottom* requires a sequential search through the list to assess the exact place where to put the element; while in the second case the operation takes constant time. Furthermore, it is not necessary to sort the events stored in the same bucket of a given *Rung*. Only one restriction has to be satisfied: *given two buckets of indexes x and y, if x < y then all the elements in bucket[x] are less than the ones in bucket[y] and vice versa.* After each insertion into *Bottom*, the algorithm checks the size of the latter to be less than a threshold, called *THRES*, otherwise a process starts to redistribute elements of this list into a new *Rung* and it is called *spawning process*. The latter is essential for performances, because reorganizing *Bottom* in a new *Rung* avoids to sort a big set of elements, so not to incur in undue computational costs.

3.1.2 Dequeue Operation. The goal of dequeuing is to take the most priority event. The operation starts from the *Bottom*, where if not empty the event can be removed. Otherwise, the event to be removed is searched in the *Ladder*. If this tier is not empty, used buckets of the last *Rung* are scrolled starting from *RCur*, until the first not empty bucket is found. At this point, its content is sorted, moved to the *Bottom* and the event with the highest priority is removed. If the *Ladder* is found empty, attention would shift on the *Top*, where the algorithm, therefore, deals with scheduling elements in the first rung to create a new *epoch*. Once events in the *Top* are scheduled, the algorithm selects the highest priority bucket, transfers it into the *Bottom* and returns the element with the highest priority. When the content of a bucket is moved into the *Bottom*, the number of the shifted events has not to be equal to *THRES*. When it is verified, a *spawning* process starts that rearranges the bucket in a new *Rung*. Now, the dequeue algorithm can initiate.

3.2 Issues

The implementation of LadderQ presents some issues, especially in its practical use, where the $O(1)$ cost is not achieved in practice.

3.2.1 Infinite rung spawning. When the cardinality of the set of events is major or equal to *THRES*, the spawning process is invoked infinite times. A solution consists in limiting the number of rungs to

use, avoiding to move en entire set of events from a bucket in a *Rung* to a bucket in the next *Rung*. The use of a threshold is substantial to avoid the process to be infinite. An issue is than introduced, once reached the fixed maximum number of rungs, the bucket that should spawn is directly transferred to the *Bottom*.

3.2.2 Reusing Ladder Structure. A common issue in the LadderQ is the excessive employment and fragmentation of the memory. So it is possible to equip the LadderQ with a pre-initialized and reusable structure, in which rungs, buckets, etc. are not destroyed, but reused to contain events of future epochs. When the available structures have not more capacity to handle future events, then new structures are created with double size of what needed, so to decrease the chance that the same problem may recur in future epochs.

3.3 Performance Analysis

The LadderQ relies on three different principles. Firstly, it postpones sorting the list only when strictly necessary that is, when some high priority events are close to being removed from the queue. Secondly, during the *enqueue* and *dequeue* operations, when the data structure gets too populated, the spawning process affects its lower part. Thereby, it is guaranteed that the *Bottom* size is always small and that good performances are achieved. Finally, during dequeue operations, the bucketwidth, unique in the Calendar Queue for the entire structure, is redefined for each Rung to reduce non-uniform distribution phenomena within them. Furthermore, it is significant to tune the *THRES* and *MaxRungs* parameters to improve performances. Despite these adjustments, LadderQ performances are halved by submitting specific datasets: non-uniformly distributed, with presence of subsets of events having the same timestamp and of cardinality greater than *THRES*.

4 ADAPTIVE LADDER QUEUE

The LadderQ does not guarantee to reach the $O(1)$ computational cost in its practical use. ALQ addresses the issue, becoming one of the most performing data structure in event simulation.

4.1 Event grouping

Handling sets with non-uniform time increment distribution and with a consistent number of events with equal timestamp, emerged as one of the main issues in LadderQ. To address events scheduled at the same time, a possibility consists of grouping them together into a single macro-event. They are treated as single element until one of them has to be dequeued, in compliance to the principle of the design pattern *Composite* [10], which allows to ignore difference between composition of elements and individual elements. Thereby, two different types of events are identified: atomic and composite (organized in lists). The event grouping operation is suitable if and only if a new element is inserted in it; elements, subject to event grouping, are the event to be inserted in the list and the event in its tail; no other events, a part from the ones just described, can be grouped, since their research would have too high computational costs. When an event is added into a list, whatever it is, *Top*, *single bucket* or *Bottom*, timestamp of the event to be inserted and the one in the tail are compared, if they match, a new composite event will be created in which to include the two. The new event is then appended in the list. Obviously, if there is already a composite event in the tail with equal timestamp, it will included it.

Finally, in case of *dequeue*, removing a composite element from the *Bottom* means removing the event with the highest priority. The list forming the composite events is emptied element by element and, when empty, it is removed from the *Bottom*.

4.2 UpGrowing

One of the main features of the *LadderQ* is to split events in *epochs*, because switching from an *epoch* to another reduce performances. A common phenomenon concerns the accumulation of future events in *Top*, while others of the current epoch are in scheduling phase. Scheduling of the future epoch starts only after the structure has used up all the events in *Bottom* and in *Rungs*. Unfortunately, in many cases, the *Top* size takes on such high values that scheduling its elements, negatively affects complexity. A solution is to demand the scheduling not only after elements in *Bottom* and *Rungs* are run out, but also when the cardinality of *Top* reaches a certain size. This operations is called *UpGrowing* and it can be executed only if the first *Rung* of the *Ladder* is empty. This constraint makes the entire operation ineffective, so the structure has been modified to let the *UpGrowing* always possible. The new structure has a doubled size. Assuming to have n *Rungs*, the original *LadderQ* structure is located from index $n/2$ to n, while *Rungs* with index lower than $n/2$ are assigned to scheduling of events subjected to *UpGrowing*.

Considering *MaxRungs* to be the maximum number of rungs, an *offset* variable is used to indicate from which index the spawning begins. *Rungs* with an index greater than or equal to *offset* are involved in spawning, while the ones with index less than *offset*, are involved in *UpGrowing*. The *offset* is dynamic: it is decreased by one each time the *UpGrowing* process occupies a *Rung*; it is increased by one each time the *Rung* (intended for spawning) with lower index is completely emptied. The minimum value of the *offset* is 0, then the *UpGrowing* cannot be performed. Obviously, the temporal order of the structure is fulfilled, because future events in a *Rung* with an index lower than the ones used so far, have been scheduled.

4.3 Substituting Linear Sort with Natural Merge Sort in Bottom

Dequeue complexity is strongly influenced by sorting in *Bottom*. The idea consists of letting two techniques coexist and choosing the most suitable depending on the context. If a single event has to be inserted into *Bottom*, a linear research will be used; instead of *Natural Merge Sort* (NMS), used when an entire bucket has to be added, specifically the content will be copied to *Bottom* and ordered with the introduced algorithm. The NMS reduces sorting times and allows to transfer all the content of the *bucket* in a single iteration.

4.4 SmartSpawning

Scheduling sets of events non-uniformly distributed leads to a consequential non-uniform distribution of the events in *buckets* of a *Rung*, to concentrate the whole set of events in few *buckets*, leaving empty the remaining ones. This scenario negatively affects all the possible operations, increasing computational costs. To avoid similar situations, the *dequeue* algorithm has been amended. After a *dequeue*, when it is necessary to reschedule events from *Top* into

rungs, only a subset of these elements is effectively removed by ruling out the *outliers*, i.e. those events having timestamps in the upper tail of the timestamp distribution among those in *Top*.

In order to determine the outliers the *mean μ* and the *standard deviation σ* of the event timestamps in *Top* are kept up to date after each insertion or removal. Only the events with a timestamp lower than $\mu + \lambda \cdot \sigma$ are removed from *Top* and rescheduled. The parameter λ can assume values between 0 and 2. For the experiments reported in Section 5.2 the value $\lambda = 1.5$ has been used.

5 EXPERIMENTAL RESULTS

The ALQ has been compared with a Java implementation of the LadderQ, the heap-based priority Queue (the `PriorityQueue` class from the `java.util` package) and a crafted version of it with event grouping. Analogously to [1], we measured the average access time to enqueue or dequeue an event under various load conditions. The *Classic Hold* (CH) model [3] has been used as a benchmark, the same distributions employed in [1] were experimented with the addition of a certain amount of events having the same timestamp.

5.1 Setup

The reported experiments were carried out on the following platform: openSUSE Leap 42.2 operating system with Linux kernel 4.4.74-x86_64, 12G RAM, Intel ® Core™ i7-3770K CPU @ 3.50GHz. The version of the Java runtime environment employed is 1.8.0_151.

The initial queue state is established by creating ten sets of events each having the same cardinality (one-tenth of the whole queue size). Let S_i the i-th set, for i ranging from 1 to 10, the timestamp of the events in S_i is a random variable $TS_i = i \cdot E[X] + X$, where X is the random variable governing the timestamp increment. Accordingly to the CH model a number $2 \cdot N$ of queue accesses are made: N dequeue operations each one followed by an enqueue. Let ts_d the timestamp of the dequeued event, the timestamp of the following enqueued event is a random variable $TS_e = ts_d + X$. The probability of having events with the same timestamp increases with the queue size because each of the initial ten sets is created by sampling the same random variable for a higher number of times. For a given queue size, the set of events is first generated accordingly to CH, then each data structure is benchmarked with the same sequence of accesses. The mean access time is computed by averaging the results of the last 40 executions out of 50. The first 10 runs are thrown away to let the Java just in time compiler to reach a steady state. An exponential distribution with mean of 1 has been used because it is defined on an open interval $[0, \infty[$. The Pareto(x_m, α) is a heavy tailed distribution, where $x_m > 0$ represents the scale parameter, that is the minimum possible value of a random variable X, and α is the shape parameter, that is a Pareto index. We fixed x_m to 1 and let α assuming the two different values $(1, 1.5)$ in order to verify how it affects mean and variance. The Change(A, B, n) is a combination of priority distributions and n is a constant value used to switch every n times from the distribution A to the distribution B. We adopted the Exponential(1) as A and the Triangular(90000,100000). The Triangular(a, b) is a continuous distribution where the random variable X is defined in the range $[a, b]$.

5.2 Experiments

Effects of the event grouping, described in Section 4, are significant and demonstrated by a purposely crafted version of the Priority Queue which supports event grouping. The performances of this data structure (PQG) are compared with those of the standard Priority Queue (PQ) and of the LadderQ (LQ). Different distributions have been tested and two are shown, all underlining the importance of composite events. Performances speeds up and theory finds

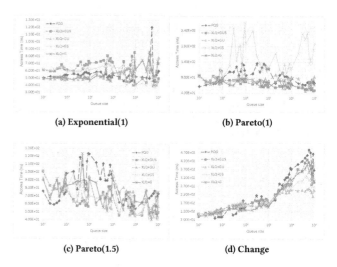

(a) Exponential(1)   **(b) Pareto(1)**

(c) Pareto(1.5)   **(d) Change**

Figure 2: Mean access time under different distributions.

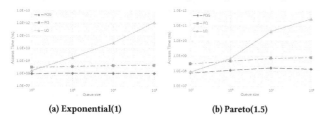

(a) Exponential(1)   **(b) Pareto(1.5)**

Figure 1: Impact of grouping and comparison.

an evidence in Figure 1, where the PQG outperforms the other two data structures. To stand out is PQ working better of the LQ, because of the generation of the queue with many contemporary events, a central weakness for the LQ. Then, in Pareto(1,1.5) and in Exponential(1), the gap performance is visible starting from a small queue size, where the LQ suffers a strong deterioration and therefore a sharp increase of the access time.

Figure 2 has four sub-figures, from *a* to *d*, in which, each one of the adopted distributions is shown: Exponential(1), Pareto(1,1), Pareto(1,1.5), Change. Now, we want to see how the addition of *SmartSpawning* and *UpGrowing* affects the performances. The java priority queue becomes more efficient when the grouping is applied, but despite the gain, it does not work fine as ALQ. This presents an outstanding behaviour in the four combinations of the three improvement measures introduced in Section 4, but the use of Grouping (*G*), UpGrowing (*U*) and SmartSpawning (*S*), all together (*GUS*), underlines a coherent and efficient pace in the whole set of distributions. Actually, the *ALQ + GUS*, for a queue size less than 10^6, is not always the best case, but overall it represents the best solution when the distribution of incoming data is not known. SmartSpawning results particularly efficient when applied to the Pareto distribution, where it marks good average values for small queue sizes and excellent values for sizes considerably large. The UpGrowing operation helps out in skewed distributions (Change), where it lets the queue to perform similarly as the size of the queue increases. Analysing individually the ALQ with event grouping we noticed it to be sensitive to Pareto(1), both being non-uniform and characterized by high variance. A high level of stability of the ALQ is evident under all distributions, instead of PQG, which has very variable performances as the queue size increases. The version with all the improvements introduced is able to react better to the various conditions as, it does not present peaks that would demonstrate a performance drop in the structure under certain conditions. Usually, a steady state of the structure emerges from the simulation performed under the Change distribution; although it represents an alternation of two different event distributions, the ALQ is able to react, while keeping execution times very low compared to all the others.

6 CONCLUSIONS

We decided to add some improvements to LadderQ to make it achieving a $O(1)$ amortized access time in practice. In order to reach our goal, four different improvements have been added: Event Grouping, UpGrowing, SmartSpawning and we introduced in *Bottom* tier the natural merge sort.

The experiments have firstly demonstrated the significant change the event grouping provides Secondly, when combined to the other improvements, it helps to further lower the computational cost. Moreover, the goodness of a solution, according to another, depends on the distribution of incoming data. Generally, the priority increment distribution that easily adapted to any conformation of incoming data, without being too influenced by the computational cost, is the GUS combination (with all the three improvements).

REFERENCES
[1] Wai Teng Tang, Rick Siow Mong Goh, and Ian Li-Jin Thng. Ladder Queue: An $O(1)$ priority queue structure for large-scale discrete event simulation. *ACM Trans. Model. Comput. Simul.*, 15(3):175–204, July 2005.
[2] R. E. Tarjan. Amortized computational complexity. *SIAM Journal on Algebraic Discrete Methods*, 6(2):306–318, 1985.
[3] Douglas W. Jones. An empirical comparison of priority-queue and event-set implementations. *Communications of the ACM*, 29(4):300–311, mar 1986.
[4] R. Ronngren, J. Riboe, and R. Ayani. Lazy queue: an efficient implementation of the pending-event set. In *[1991] Proceedings of the 24th Annual Simulation Symposium*. IEEE, 1991.
[5] Romain Franceschini, Paul-Antoine Bisgambiglia, and Paul Bisgambiglia. A comparative study of pending event set implementations for pdevs simulation. In *Proceedings of the Symposium on Theory of Modeling & Simulation: DEVS Integrative M&S Symposium*, DEVS '15, pages 77–84, San Diego, CA, USA, 2015. Society for Computer Simulation International.
[6] Bernard P. Zeigler, Herbert Praehofer, and Tag Gon Kim. *Theory of Modeling and Simulation*. Academic Press, 2000.
[7] R. Brown. Calendar queues: a fast 0(1) priority queue implementation for the simulation event set problem. *Communications of the ACM*, 31(10):1220–1227, oct 1988.
[8] Cris L. Luengo Hendriks. Revisiting priority queues for image analysis. *Pattern Recogn.*, 43(9):3003–3012, September 2010.
[9] Julius Higiro, Meseret Gebre, and Dhananjai M. Rao. Multi-tier priority queues and 2-tier ladder queue for managing pending events in sequential and optimistic parallel simulations. In *Proceedings of the 2017 ACM SIGSIM Conference on Principles of Advanced Discrete Simulation - SIGSIM-PADS'17*. ACM Press, 2017.
[10] Erich Gamma, Richard Helm, Ralph E. Johnson, and John Vlissides. *Design Patterns*. Prentice Hall, 1995.

Comparing Dead Reckoning Algorithms for Distributed Car Simulations

Youfu Chen
Multi-plAtform Game Innovation Centre
Interdisciplinary Graduate School
Nanyang Technological University
Singapore
ch0002fu@ntu.edu.sg

Elvis S. Liu*
Southern University of Science and Technology
Shenzhen, China
esyliu@sustc.edu.cn

ABSTRACT

Dead reckoning is an important technique used in distributed virtual environments (DVEs) to mitigate the bandwidth consumption of frequent state updates and the negative effects of network latency. This paper proposes a novel dead reckoning approach for common DVE applications such as multiplayer online games. Unlike traditional dead reckoning approaches that estimate the movements of remote entities with pure kinematic models, the new approach performs extrapolations with the considerations of environmental factors and human behaviours. We have performed experiments, based on a distributed car simulator, to compare the the new approach with representative existing dead reckoning approaches. The results show that the new approach gives more accurate predictions with an acceptable overhead.

CCS CONCEPTS

• **Information systems → Massively multiplayer online games**;
• **Computing methodologies → Distributed simulation**;

KEYWORDS

Dead Reckoning, Distributed Virtual Environments, Multiplayer Online Games, Distributed Simulation

ACM Reference Format:
Youfu Chen and Elvis S. Liu. 2018. Comparing Dead Reckoning Algorithms for Distributed Car Simulations. In *SIGSIM-PADS -18 : 2018 SIGSIM Principles of Advanced Discrete Simulation, May 23–25, 2018, Rome, Italy*. ACM, New York, NY, USA, 7 pages. https://doi.org/10.1145/3200921.3200939

1 INTRODUCTION

A distributed virtual environment (DVE) is a virtual reality simulation that allows users to interact in real-time even though they are at geographically different locations. DVE has been studied extensively for more than three decades. Historically, it can be traced back to the SIMNET project [4] developed by the US Department of Defense and the Multi-User Dungeon (MUD) game [1] developed by two students of the University of Essex. In recent years, large-scale DVEs have become a major trend in entertainment applications, mainly due to the enormous popularity of multiplayer online games (MOGs) [12]. These applications aim to support thousands of participants, which imposes a high load on the DVE networks.

Much of the research effort in DVE has been focused on addressing the requirement of scalability. As DVEs become more data intensive and more latency sensitive, providing scalable data distribution services is crucial for their successful deployment. A simple approach for DVE data distribution would be to have each participant (or host) regularly broadcast the entity states that it maintains. Apparently, as the scale of DVE grows, this approach would consume significant network resources. To address this problem, two techniques have been developed to reduce the bandwidth consumption. One is referred to as interest management [6], which filters irrelevant data transmissions on the DVE network. The other is referred to as dead reckoning (DR), which was introduced by SIMNET and its successor Distributed Interactive Simulation (DIS) [8] to reduce the frequency of state updates.

The basic idea of DR is simple: instead of receiving entity updates at every time step, the participants use a kinematic model (referred to as dead reckoning model (DRM)) to predict the movement of remote entities based on their last known kinematic states. In this way, the participants are able to simulate the entities' movement for a period of time without receiving any state update, and thus the bandwidth consumption can be greatly reduced. In addition, the participants also maintain DRMs for their own entities and constantly monitor the deviation between the DRMs and their corresponding actual models. When the deviation exceeds a predefined threshold, the participant would broadcast the actual state of the corresponding entity to all participants, a process commonly referred to as 'rollback', in order to correct their DRMs. Obviously, the efficiency of DR depends strongly on the prediction accuracy of the DRM. If corrections are broadcast frequently, a significant bandwidth consumption would be induced on the network. In addition, frequent corrections would also cause a large number of 'lag' effects on the participants' screen. Even with the use of smoothing algorithms [5], the illusion of presence would be seriously affected. Therefore, designing an accurate prediction model is an important requirement for DR based DVEs.

In this paper, we focus on improving the prediction accuracy of the DRM. We propose a path-assisted DR (PADR) approach, which performs extrapolations with the considerations of environmental

---

*Corresponding author

Permission to make digital or hard copies of all or part of this work for personal or classroom use is granted without fee provided that copies are not made or distributed for profit or commercial advantage and that copies bear this notice and the full citation on the first page. Copyrights for components of this work owned by others than ACM must be honored. Abstracting with credit is permitted. To copy otherwise, or republish, to post on servers or to redistribute to lists, requires prior specific permission and/or a fee. Request permissions from permissions@acm.org.
SIGSIM-PADS '18, May 23–25, 2018, Rome, Italy
© 2018 Association for Computing Machinery.
ACM ISBN 978-1-4503-5092-1/18/05...$15.00
https://doi.org/10.1145/3200921.3200939

factors and human behaviours. Our approach is designed specifically for DVEs that contain predefined paths. We also present a quantitative study to compare the prediction accuracy of the proposed approach with representative existing DR approaches. Simulation results, based on The Open Racing Car Simulator (TORCS) [2], show that the proposed approach gives more accurate extrapolations than the existing approaches with an acceptable overhead.

2 BACKGROUND AND RELATED WORK

The traditional DRM is basically of two types—first-order and second-order, which indicate the order of kinematic equations used for movement prediction. Let s denote the predicted position of an entity, s_0 denote its position in the last update, v denote the velocity, a denote the acceleration, and Δt denote the elapsed time since the last update, the kinematic equations are defined as:

$$s = s_0 + v\Delta t \tag{1}$$

$$s = s_0 + vt + \frac{1}{2}a\Delta t \tag{2}$$

Apart from the traditional DIS-based DR approach [5, 8], many improved DR algorithms have been proposed in the literature. Generally, these improved approaches focus on a major design requirement—performance, which is measured by the reduction of network bandwidth consumption. In addition, computational efficiency is also an important requirement to consider when designing an efficient DR algorithm.

Position History-Based Dead Reckoning (PHBDR) [11] is one of the early variants of the traditional DR algorithm. It predicts the future movement of an entity based on a typical curve-fitting approach. This method uses three latest reported positions sent by the remote host as the basis of extrapolation. In other words, its prediction is independent of the entity's velocity and acceleration. As a result, its correction packet size is smaller than other DR approaches since it contains only the position information.

Another approach, the auto-adaptive DR [3], adjusts the threshold value based on the user interaction with remote entities. Drawing on the concept of interest management [6], area of interest (AOI) of entities are used to determine the threshold dynamically. The algorithm assigns different thresholds to remote entities at different ranges. Therefore, entities of less interest are updated less frequently, which reduces the number of packets.

To avoid extra network consumption yielded by unpredictable movements, the pre-reckoning approach [15] issues an update packet immediately when unpredictable inputs are detected. It introduces a new threshold—angle of embrace—to indicate whether a movement is unpredictable (sharp turn) or not. By utilising this threshold, the number of rollbacks caused by unpredictable movements can be reduced.

To exploit the advantages of various DR algorithms, adaptive classifier system-based dead reckoning [14] relies on a set of rules (such as sensor ranges) to determine which DR algorithm to be adopted at run time. Once these rules are defined by the system designer, they can be discovered automatically by the DVE system.

Some prior work focuses on amelioration of the threshold value used in DR algorithms. [7] defines a metric called 'physics-consistency-cost', which takes into account the consequences caused by rollbacks. Moreover, [10] proposes a time-space threshold and a hybrid scheme in place of the traditional spatial threshold that does not consider time delay.

The approaches reviewed so far can be classified as *mechanical* DR algorithms, since their DRMs are developed based on mechanics. In this paper, we propose a novel DR algorithm called PADR, which improves prediction accuracy by considering human behaviours. Our approach can achieve a great reduction of bandwidth consumption at the cost of a small computational overhead. We have also performed a number of experiments to compare the performance of the proposed approach and the representative DR approaches reviewed in this section, based on a distributed car simulation.

3 PATH-ASSISTED DEAD RECKONING ALGORITHM

Paths are common elements in the DVEs. A Path is usually a road or track laid down by the DVE developers, which allows participants to travel from one meaningful location to another. The participants, particularly those new to the DVE, tend to make their journey along some common paths. This phenomenon can be frequently observed in motorways, narrow areas, and unfamiliar areas.

The key component of the PADR algorithm is a heuristic movement prediction model. Its basic idea is simple: participants do not move randomly in the virtual space. If they move on a path, their next position will very likely be on the same path. Therefore, instead of predicting their next position with a pure kinematic model, PADR directly places them on a predetermined position along a path or an interpolated point between two predetermined positions along a path. On the other hand, if they are not on the path, then the traditional DR prediction model will be applied. In this way, even if the assumption (that the participants tend to follow common paths) is wrong, large prediction deviation can be avoided and the prediction accuracy of the algorithm will be equivalent to the traditional DR algorithm.

The PADR algorithm is comprised of three components, namely path structure, path mapping, and state prediction. They are described in details in the following three subsections.

3.1 Path Structure

In most of the DVE implementations, paths are explicitly modelled by distinctive colours, textures, or functions. For example, on the outskirts of a town, paths are coloured in brown distinguishing from the grassland nearby; or in a race track, driving on asphalt surfaces is much faster than on the sandy ones. Moreover, some natural or artificial facilities are deemed to be part of a path, such as tunnels, bridges, or streets. To model these paths in a simulation, we use a sequence of predefined points to represent them. A path P_i (for $i = 1, 2, \ldots, M$, where M is the number of paths) is defined as a sequence of sampled points along an actual path. The element of the sampling sequence is denoted by

$$\alpha_{ik} = (x_{ik}, y_{ik}, z_{ik}), \quad k = 1, 2, \ldots, N_i \tag{3}$$

where N_i is the number of sampling points on P_i.

3.2 Path Mapping

Path mapping is a process to determine if an entity moves on a path. This process is executed when a prediction violates the entity's actual path (i.e. the deviation between the actual and predicted positions is larger than a predefined threshold). If the mapping process determines that the entity is on-path, the path-assisted model will be used as the prediction model. Otherwise, traditional DRM will be used. The prediction model will remain unchanged until another violation occurs.

However, comparing the entity's position with all sampling points in a regular manner is a computationally intensive process, which can be referred to as the brute-force approach. The time complexity of this approach is $O(\sum_{i=1}^{M} N_i)$, and the space complexity is $O(\sum_{i=1}^{M} N_i)$. Obviously, a more efficient approach should be employed.

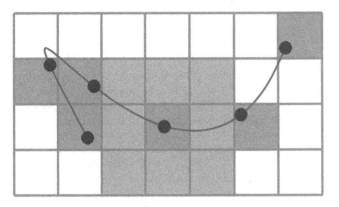

Figure 1: Path mapping

The PADR algorithm employs a spatial hashing method to speed up this process, which is illustrated by the example shown in Figure 1. In the figure, the virtual space is partitioned into uniform grids. The red curve represents an entity's trajectory and the blue dots on the trajectory are sampling points. The grid that a sampling point resides in is coloured in blue to indicates its rough location. All neighbour grids of a blue grid are coloured in red. A blue grid and its neighbouring red grids form a *detection zone* of the corresponding sampling point. If an entity moves into a detection zone and its distance to the sampling point is smaller than a predefined threshold, the entity is considered near the sampling point.

In the initialisation stage of the algorithm, every grid in a detection zone is stored in a hash map H as a key k, and its corresponding value v is the sampling point. In a certain case, a grid may become a neighbour of two sampling points, such that a key k' that belongs to a sampling point v' is identical to a key k that belongs to sampling point v, where $k' = k$. If this is the case, we need to map the grid to its nearest sampling point. Specifically, if the distance between the centre of k and v' is smaller than the distance between the centre of k and v, then the old key-value pair (k, v) will be replaced with the new pair (k, v') in the hash map.

During runtime, the mapping process is very efficient. For any entity, the algorithm first determines which grid it resides in and uses the grid as a key k to retrieve its nearest sampled point, such

that $v = H(k)$. The entity is considered off-path if the value v is not found in the hash map. If v exists and the distance between the entity and v is smaller than the threshold, the entity is considered on-path (i.e. near the sampling point v). The general case time complexity of the mapping process for each entity is $O(1)$, which is scalable for large-scale DVEs. The experimental evaluation of the mapping process is presented in Section 5.

3.3 State Prediction

State prediction is an important component of the PADR algorithm since its strength is dependent on the accuracy of its predictions. As discussed previously, if the new heuristic model can indeed increase the prediction accuracy, the number of rollbacks and the bandwidth consumption can be reduced.

The prediction process is described as follows. If the PADR algorithm determines that a participant-controlled entity is on a path and locates its nearest sampling point, in the next time step, PADR will estimate its new position based on its kinematic states as well as the path information. Both the first and second order kinematic models can be incorporated into the PADR algorithm. The algorithm first calculates the distance the entity could travel between two successive time steps. Since it is on a path, the algorithm would assume that it always moves along the path and towards the next sampling point. As discussed previously, this assumption may not be always true. The algorithm needs to regularly monitor the deviation between the entity's actual and predicted positions. Once the deviation exceeds a threshold, the algorithm would issue a rollback, which essentially *resets* the entity's position to the actual one.

It is worth to note that the size of update packet of PADR is smaller than that of the traditional DR approach. Assume that position, velocity, and acceleration, are of the same size of $3u$ in the three-dimensional space. Assume further that the sampling point index has a size of u. When an entity is on a path, the PADR algorithm may issue an $5u$ *on-path* update packet, which consists of two sampling point indices and the entity's velocity. On the other hand, when the entity is not on a path, traditional DRM would be employed. The *off-path* packet contains the entity's position and velocity for the first order model, and the position, velocity, and acceleration for the second order model, which has a size of $6u$ and $9u$, respectively. In summary, the packet size of traditional DR is 1.2 times (first order) or 1.8 times (second order) of the size of the on-path packet.

Given an on-path probability $\mathbb{P}$, the expected packet size of PADR can be calculated by

$$\bar{S}_{PADR1} = \left[5\mathbb{P}(I) + 6\mathbb{P}(I') \right] u \qquad (4)$$

for the first order model, and by

$$\bar{S}_{PADR2} = \left[5\mathbb{P}(I) + 9\mathbb{P}(I') \right] u \qquad (5)$$

for the second order model, where I is the event that the participants move along the paths and I' is the event that the participants do not move along the paths.

Figure 2 illustrates two example trajectories of the PADR and traditional DR algorithms. In the figure, the paths, the actual trajectories of the entity, and the displayed trajectories of the entity are indicated by red dashed curves, black dotted curves, and black solid

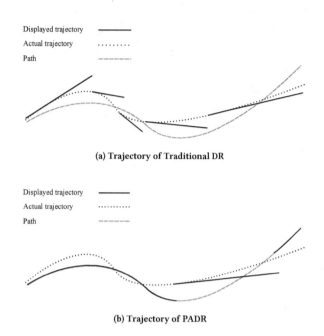

(a) Trajectory of Traditional DR

(b) Trajectory of PADR

Figure 2: Trajectories of two DR algorithms

Figure 3: A screenshot of TORCS

curves, respectively. Moreover, no convergence is applied, which implies that once the entity violates the threshold, it would be directly placed on the actual position. We can see from this example that, since the actual trajectory approximates the path, the PADR algorithm violates the threshold less frequently than the traditional DR algorithm, and therefore it issues fewer rollbacks. Consequently, the displayed trajectory of the traditional DR algorithm appears to be more intermittent, where the displayed trajectory of the PADR algorithm appears to be more continuous.

Quantitative evaluations of the two algorithms and other representative DR algorithms are presented in the Section 5.

4 IMPLEMENTATION AND SIMULATION

We have implemented and performed our experiments in TORCS, which is an open source simulator under GNU General Public License (GPL) [13]. TORCS is widely used for realistic 3D car simulations. Its screenshot is shown in Figure 3. In our experiments, each experimenter chose a vehicle to 'drive' in the simulator and compete with other non-human-controlled vehicles. Each simulation consists of three laps but the experimenter were not required to finish them. In order to compare the performance of different DR approaches in a complex and realistic environment, the road track map 'CG Track 3' provided by TORCS was chosen to be the test scenario. This map contains various road surfaces that the vehicles may be 'driven' on. For example, in a grass surface the drivers are difficult to steer and brake, while in a sand surface they are difficult to steer and accelerate. The movements of each of the experimenters (referred to as 'trace') were recorded and were analysed at the end of the simulations.

We implemented seven DR algorithms in TORCS, namely PHBDR, the first and second order of pre-reckoning, the first and second order of traditional DR, and the first and second order of the proposed PADR algorithm. The subjects of comparison are the representative DR algorithms reviewed in Section 2. All simulations were performed using the same hardware configurations. Furthermore, the unit of time in TORCS is 0.002 seconds, which implies that the kinematic states of the human-controlled vehicles were updated every 0.002 seconds in the simulations.

5 EXPERIMENTAL RESULTS AND EVALUATION

Three metrics were adopted to evaluate the DR algorithms. The first metric is the prediction accuracy of the DRM, which is measured in terms of the number of rollbacks. As discussed previously in Section 1, the performance of DR depends strongly on the prediction accuracy of the DRM. If rollbacks are issued frequently, a significant bandwidth consumption would be induced and the participants might experience serious lag effects on the client side.

The second and most important metric is bandwidth consumption, which refers to the term $M \times B$ in the resource equation described in Section 2. It reflects how well a DR algorithm can alleviate the network bandwidth consumption in a DVE. We calculated the packet size by using the method described in Section 3.3 and measured the number of packets sent during the simulations. For PHBDR, the rollback packets contain only the position of an entity; therefore its packet size is $3u$. The rollback packets of pre-reckoning and traditional DR contain a typical kinematic state of an entity, which has a size of $6u$ and $9u$ for the first and second order models, respectively.

The third metric is computational efficiency, which is an important consideration when employing DR algorithms. Due to the fact that DVEs are often used for real-time applications, using a fast DR algorithm is crucial for maintaining responsiveness as well as enhancing system scalability. The computational efficiency is measured by the elapsed CPU clock ticks to run the DR algorithms.

5.1 Simulation Map

Although the map shown on the top-right corner of Figure 3 is two-dimensional, the actual map used for the simulations is three-dimensional. Figure 4 illustrates the shape of the actual map in 3D. Compared to the 2D map, the actual track goes up and down on the z-axis, which is a typical scenario in a 3D car simulation. Figure 5 illustrates one of the trajectories generated by a participant-controlled vehicle (for three laps). We can see that the trajectories closely approximate the actual track, except in some turns. This is normal as human participants were not familiar with the track and therefore could not always turn the vehicle smoothly.

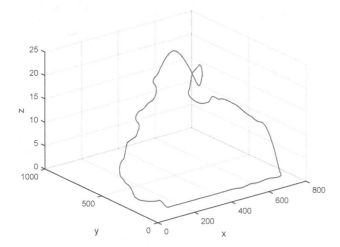

Figure 4: Path shape

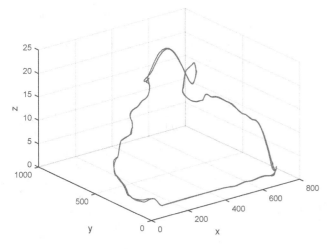

Figure 5: A collected actual trajectory

5.2 Prediction Accuracy

Figure 6 compares the seven algorithms in terms of the number of rollbacks. The first observation is that, conforming to the study in [9], all second order algorithms incurred less rollbacks than their corresponding first order versions. This suggests that the second order DRMs are always more accurate than the first order models.

Secondly, we can see that the PHBDR approach issued the most rollback packets in the experiment. Although its DRM adopts the angle of embrace concept to avoid sharp turns, it still could not keep up with the actual path. Therefore, it can be concluded that using curve fitting based on position history is insufficient to accurately predict the future path of participant-controlled vehicles.

Another noticeable information is that the prediction accuracy of pre-reckoning algorithms is almost the same as the traditional DR algorithms in both the first and second order models. In fact, the lines representing the results of the two models are overlapped on the line graph. One reason for this finding might be due to the small number of sharp turns in the simulation scenario (see Figure 4), which in turn could not demonstrate the strength of the pre-reckoning approach.

The most important finding in this experiment is the performance of the proposed PADR approach. We can see from Figure 6 that when threshold value is small, pre-reckoning and traditional DR issue slightly fewer rollbacks than PADR; however when the threshold value increases, PADR would issue fewer rollbacks than them. This is due to the fact that although the track looks like a line in Figure 5, it actually has a certain minimum width. The PADR model is able to put the extrapolated vehicle on the right track, but the prediction may not follow the exact path of the participant-controlled vehicles. When the threshold is small, the DR system would become very strict on the prediction results. It would determine that many of the PADR predictions are incorrect even though they actually follow the track. On the other hand, when the threshold increases (note that: to approximately the half-width of the track), most of the PADR predictions that follow the track would be determined as correct predictions, which leads to significantly fewer rollbacks than all other DR algorithms. According to our simulation results, the second order PADR algorithm issued at least 26% fewer rollbacks than the second best approach—the second order pre-reckoning algorithm. This suggests that the proposed PADR approach has the best prediction accuracy when the threshold approximates or is larger than the half-width of the path.

5.3 Bandwidth Consumption

Figure 7 shows the results of the second set of experiments, which compare the bandwidth consumption (in terms of total packet size) of the seven DR algorithms. The packet sizes are calculated based on the assumptions described in Section 3.3 and their unit is u. The results clearly show that the proposed PADR approach consumes less bandwidth than all other approaches.

Among the subjects of comparison, PHBDR has the best performance. Since it sent the most rollbacks in the previous set of experiments, this finding is somewhat unexpected. However, consider the fact that PHBDR's rollback packet contains only the position of the entity, which is half or one-third of the size of other approaches, its bandwidth consumption should certainly be much lower than other approaches.

Similarly, although the second order DRMs have better prediction precision (see Figure 6), they are more bandwidth-consuming than their corresponding first order version. This suggests that the

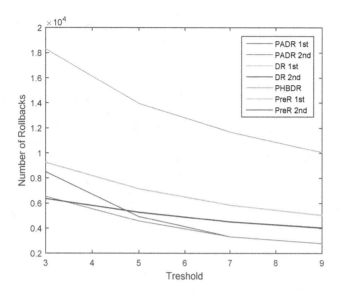

Figure 6: Prediction accuracy

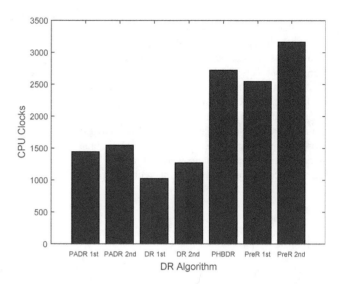

Figure 8: Computational cost

number of rollbacks is not the only consideration for minimising the bandwidth consumption, but the packet size is also an important factor.

It should also be noted that the bandwidth consumption of the pre-reckoning algorithms is almost the same as the traditional DR algorithms in both the first and second order models. Similar to the previous set of experiments, the lines representing the two algorithms are overlapped on the line graph. This confirms our expectation since they have the same packet size and issued approximately the same number of rollbacks.

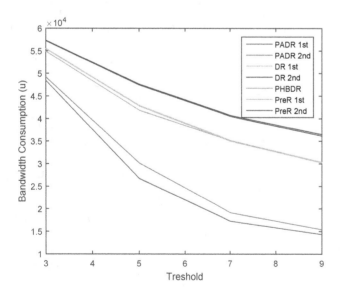

Figure 7: Bandwidth consumption

5.4 Computational Efficiency

Figure 8 shows the computational cost of the seven DR algorithms with a constant threshold value of 10. The cost is measured by the number of clock ticks the CPU spends running these algorithms. We found that PHBDR and pre-reckoning algorithms have a very high computational cost. According to our algorithm profiling, this is caused by the computation of the angle of embrace.

Furthermore, the results show that the two traditional DR algorithms are the fastest among the tested approaches. This is due to the fact that their calculations are much simpler than the others. The PADR algorithms are only slightly slower than the traditional DR algorithms. If we take the previous observations into account, it can be concluded that the PADR approaches significantly reduce the number of rollbacks and bandwidth consumption at the cost of a small computational overhead.

6 CONCLUSIONS

DR in DVE is a movement prediction technique, which is designed to reduce bandwidth consumption and alleviate the lag effects caused by network latency. Most of the existing DR approaches in the literature perform prediction based on kinematic models. This paper proposes a new DR approach called PADR, which performs extrapolations with the considerations of environmental factors and human behaviours. The new approach is particularly suitable for DVEs that contains paths such as distributed car simulations. We have implemented and evaluated seven DR algorithms on a widely used 3D car simulator—TORCS. Experimental results have demonstrated that the proposed PADR approach significantly reduces the number of rollbacks and bandwidth consumption at the cost of a small computational overhead.

Our future work concerns two main directions. First, we will evaluate PADR and other DR algorithms based on the movement data obtained from a real-life massively multiplayer online role-playing game (MMORPG). User behaviours in a MMORPG are much different from that of a car simulation. The participants usually spread out in the virtual space and do not follow a single path. Therefore, the DR algorithms are expected to perform incorrect predictions more often in a MMORPG than in a car simulation. Second, we will develop a dynamic prediction model, which generates path structures during runtime. Instead of using a predefined path, the new model will create and remove paths according to the participants' movement patterns and performs prediction based on the commonness of the trajectories.

ACKNOWLEDGMENTS

The research reported in this paper is financially supported by the Tier 1 Academic Research Fund (AcRF) under project Number RG136/14.

REFERENCES

[1] Richard Allan Bartle. 2003. *Designing Virtual Worlds*. New Riders Games.
[2] Wymann Bernhard. 2001. torcs News. http://torcs.sourceforge.net/. (2001).
[3] Wentong Cai, Francis Lee, and Lian Chen. 1999. An auto-adaptive dead reckoning algorithm for distributed interactive simulation. In *Proceedings of the thirteenth workshop on Parallel and distributed simulation*. IEEE Computer Society, 82–89.
[4] J. Calvin, A. Dickens, R. Gaines, P. Metzger, D. Miller, and D. Owen. 1993. The SIMNET Virtual World Architecture. In *Proceedings of the IEEE Virtual Reality Annual International Symposium*. 450–455.
[5] R.M. Fujimoto. 2000. *Parallel and distributed simulation systems*. Wiley.
[6] Elvis S Liu and Georgios K Theodoropoulos. 2014. Interest management for distributed virtual environments: A survey. *ACM Computing Surveys (CSUR)* 46, 4 (2014), 51.
[7] Seamus C McLoone, Patrick J Walsh, and Tomas E Ward. 2012. An enhanced dead reckoning model for physics-aware multiplayer computer games. In *Distributed Simulation and Real Time Applications (DS-RT), 2012 IEEE/ACM 16th International Symposium on*. IEEE, 111–117.
[8] David L. Neyland. 1997. *Virtual Combat: A Guide to Distributed Interactive Simulation*. Stackpole Books.
[9] Lothar Pantel and Lars C Wolf. 2002. On the suitability of dead reckoning schemes for games. In *Proceedings of the 1st workshop on Network and system support for games*. ACM, 79–84.
[10] Dave Roberts, Rob Aspin, Damien Marshall, Seamus Mcloone, Declan Delaney, and Tomas Ward. 2008. Bounding Inconsistency Using a Novel Threshold Metric for Dead Reckoning Update Packet Generation. *Simulation* 84, 5 (May 2008), 239–256.
[11] Sandeep K Singhal and David R Cheriton. 1994. *Using a position history-based protocol for distributed object visualization*. Technical Report. DTIC Document.
[12] Jouni Smed, Timo Kaukoranta, and Harri Hakonen. 2002. *A Review on Networking and Multiplayer Computer Games*. Technical Report 454. Turku Centre for Computer Science.
[13] Richard Stallman et al. 1991. Gnu general public license. *Free Software Foundation, Inc., Tech. Rep* (1991).
[14] Samir Torki, Patrice Torguet, and Cédric Sanza. 2007. Adaptive Classifier System-Based Dead Reckoning.. In *Proceedings of the 10th Immersive Projection Technology Workshop at the 13th Eurographics Symposium on Virtual Environments (IPT/EGVE 2007)*. 101–108.
[15] Xiaoyu Zhang, Denis Gračanin, and Thomas P Duncan. 2004. Evaluation of a pre-reckoning algorithm for distributed virtual environments. In *Parallel and Distributed Systems, 2004. ICPADS 2004. Proceedings. Tenth International Conference on*. IEEE, 445–452.

Fast-Forwarding Agent States to Accelerate Microscopic Traffic Simulations

Philipp Andelfinger
TUMCREATE Ltd and
Nanyang Technological University
Singapore
pandelfinger@ntu.edu.sg

Yadong Xu
TUMCREATE Ltd
Singapore
yadong.xu@tum-create.edu.sg

Wentong Cai
Nanyang Technological University
Singapore
aswtcai@ntu.edu.sg

David Eckhoff
TUMCREATE Ltd and
Technische Universität München
david.eckhoff@tum-create.edu.sg

Alois Knoll
Technische Universität München
Germany
knoll@in.tum.de

ABSTRACT

Traditionally, the model time in agent-based simulations is advanced in fixed time steps. However, a purely time-stepped execution is inefficient in situations where the states of individual agents are independent of other agents and thus easily predictable far into the simulated future. In this work, we propose a method to accelerate microscopic traffic simulations based on identifying independence among agent state updates. Instead of iteratively updating an agent's state throughout a sequence of time steps, a computationally inexpensive "fast-forward" function advances the agent's state to the time of its earliest possible interaction with other agents. To demonstrate the approach in practice, we present an algorithm to efficiently determine intervals of independence in microscopic traffic simulations and derive a fast-forward function for the popular Intelligent Driver Model (IDM). In contrast to existing acceleration approaches based on reducing the level of model detail, our approach retains the microscopic nature of the simulation. A performance evaluation is performed in a synthetic scenario and on the road network of the city of Singapore. At low traffic densities, we achieved a speedup of up to 2.8, whereas at the highest considered densities, only few opportunities for fast-forwarding could be identified. The algorithm parameters can be tuned to control the overhead of the approach.

ACM Reference Format:
Philipp Andelfinger, Yadong Xu, Wentong Cai, David Eckhoff, and Alois Knoll. 2018. Fast-Forwarding Agent States to Accelerate Microscopic Traffic Simulations. In *SIGSIM-PADS '18 : SIGSIM-PADS '18: SIGSIM Principles of Advanced Discrete Simulation CD-ROM, May 23–25, 2018, Rome, Italy*. ACM, New York, NY, USA, 12 pages. https://doi.org/10.1145/3200921.3200923

Permission to make digital or hard copies of all or part of this work for personal or classroom use is granted without fee provided that copies are not made or distributed for profit or commercial advantage and that copies bear this notice and the full citation on the first page. Copyrights for components of this work owned by others than the author(s) must be honored. Abstracting with credit is permitted. To copy otherwise, or republish, to post on servers or to redistribute to lists, requires prior specific permission and/or a fee. Request permissions from permissions@acm.org.
SIGSIM-PADS '18 , May 23–25, 2018, Rome, Italy
© 2018 Copyright held by the owner/author(s). Publication rights licensed to the Association for Computing Machinery.
ACM ISBN 978-1-4503-5092-1/18/05...$15.00
https://doi.org/10.1145/3200921.3200923

1 INTRODUCTION

Microscopic traffic simulation models represent the traffic in a road network on the level of individual vehicles that update their acceleration, velocity and position according to properties of their environment and nearby vehicles [16]. Typically, the vehicle updates occur at fixed time steps in model time. When considering scenarios spanning the road traffic of an entire city, this detailed simulation approach incurs substantial computational demands and long runtimes. Efforts to accelerate microscopic traffic simulations can be classified into two categories: hybrid modeling approaches, and parallel and distributed simulation. In hybrid modeling [1], areas in the road network are selected for which exact results on the vehicle level are not required. For such areas, vehicle movement is simulated in terms of tasks in a queueing network or as traffic flows. While hybrid modeling can achieve substantial runtime reductions, the microscopic nature of the simulation is partially surrendered. A second approach to reducing the runtime is parallel and distributed simulation, in which the simulation workload is distributed to multiple interconnected processing elements. Since fixed time steps for vehicle updates provide natural points for synchronization across processing elements, microscopic traffic simulators are well-suited for parallelization. However, when synchronizing at every time step, the achieved acceleration tends to scale far from linearly with the number of processing elements [32].

Hence, instead of the commonly applied time advancement using fixed time steps, some previous works have considered *asynchronous* state updates for agent-based simulations [2, 17, 22, 29]. Typically, the neighboring agents considered in an update are limited spatially by an agent's *sensing range*. If an agent is isolated from other agents for multiple time steps into the simulated future, the corresponding state updates can be performed without considering other agents' states. In parallel simulations, it has been shown that asynchronous state updates can reduce processor idle times by prioritizing updates that allow blocked processors to proceed. In the sequential case, the runtime can be reduced by limiting agent updates to those required to reach the simulation's termination criterion, e.g., performing only state updates that affect the state of a particular agent under consideration [29]. However, the applicability of the latter method is limited since satisfying the simulation's termination criterion commonly requires all agents to be at the same time step.

In this paper, we propose an approach for accelerating independent agent state updates using a computationally inexpensive *fast-forward function*, which updates the agent state to the first possible point in model time where an interaction can occur, skipping the intermediate updates. The approach retains the microscopic nature of the simulation. To apply the fast-forward function without violating the correctness of the simulation results, intervals in model time are identified for which agent interactions can be ruled out. A reduction in simulation execution time is achieved if the time spent on identifying such *independence intervals* is smaller than the time saved through the reduction in time steps.

Thus, we propose an algorithm that predicts independence intervals efficiently for microscopic traffic simulations on road networks represented by graphs. Further, we derive a fast-forward function for the well-known Intelligent Driver Model (IDM) [30], which governs the acceleration behavior of the simulated vehicles. The benefits of the proposed approach are evaluated in the city-scale microscopic traffic simulator CityMoS [33], both on a synthetic road network and on a representation of the road network of the city of Singapore. Since the benefit of the approach hinges on the availability and size of independence intervals, the largest performance gains are seen in areas of the road network where traffic is sparse. In cases where independence intervals are small or the overhead for identifying them is large, our approach has limited or even no benefit. The overhead can be balanced with the opportunities for fast-forwarding by adapting the frequency of identifying independence intervals and the maximum interval size.

The contributions of this paper are as follows:

(1) We propose asynchronous state updates using a fast-forward function for microscopic traffic simulation.
(2) We propose an algorithm to determine independence intervals to support asynchronous state updates.
(3) We derive a fast-forward function for the Intelligent Driver Model.
(4) We evaluate the performance benefits of the approach in simulations using two different road networks.

The remainder of this paper is organized as follows: Section 2 sketches the technical background of our work. Section 3 describes the proposed fast-forwarding approach. Section 4 provides validation and performance evaluation results. Section 5 describes remaining limitations and potential enhancements of the approach. Section 6 discusses related work. Section 7 provides a summary of our results and concludes the paper.

2 PRELIMINARIES

2.1 Agent-based modeling and simulation

In agent-based simulation, entities called agents are situated in an environment within the simulation space. An agent's environment is composed of static elements and nearby agents. At each point in model time, each agent has a *state* defined by a set of state variables. During a *state update*, an agent applies *update functions* to update the state variables according to the sensed environment. A *sensing range* limits the distance up to which the environment is considered.

We refer to a state update that reads the state variables of nearby agents as an *interaction*.

Execution mechanisms for agent-based models can be classified into two categories: in a *synchronous* execution, the simulation proceeds in cycles. In each cycle, all agents perform a state update to advance their states by one time step, which is a fixed delta in model time. In an *asynchronous* execution, some agents may advance their time further into the simulated future than other agents [29]. The fast-forwarding approach proposed in the present paper is asynchronous. In contrast to existing approaches, instead of using iterative time steps, agent states are advanced into the simulated future through a single invocation of a fast-forward function.

2.2 Microscopic traffic simulation

In microscopic traffic simulations, agents called driver-vehicle-units (DVUs) move through the simulation space according to models of the state and behavior of a human driver as well as of the vehicle operated by the driver. Typically, the simulation space is a road network modeled as a directed graph $G = (V, E)$, where edges represent roads with one or more lanes and vertices represent intersections. At each point in model time, each DVU is situated at a specific position on a lane within an edge.

DVUs perform state updates according to a car-following model (e.g., [10, 30]) and a lane change model (e.g., [11, 15]). Car-following models determine the acceleration of a vehicle according to the characteristics of the driver, the vehicle, and the surrounding traffic conditions. Commonly, the acceleration is chosen according to a desired safety gap to the vehicle ahead. Lane change models decide whether a DVU should change lanes, e.g., based on the current velocity and vehicles on other lanes. The distance up to which nearby DVUs are considered is limited by the sensing range. For simplicity, we refer to DVUs as agents or vehicles throughout the remainder of the paper.

3 PROPOSED FAST-FORWARDING APPROACH

As introduced in the previous section, in an agent-based simulation, agents update their states according to their current environment and the states of neighboring agents within their sensing range. When an agent is spatially isolated from others, the current state update depends only on the environment, which may be static or highly predictable. The proposed approach is based on the observation that if it can be guaranteed that the agent remains isolated up to a certain point in model time, the agent's state can be updated to this point immediately. By computing such updates using a fast-forward function that is less computationally expensive than a sequence of regular state updates, the overall execution time of the simulation can be reduced.

3.1 Problem definition

In this section, we formally describe state updates in agent-based simulations using traditional time-stepped updates and the proposed fast-forward function. We loosely follow the formalization by Scheutz et al. [29], who studied asynchronous state updates either to limit state updates to those required for reaching the simulation's termination criterion or to decrease communication costs in distributed simulations. In contrast to their approach, which still relies on conventional time-stepped agent updates, fast-forwarding accelerates the simulation by avoiding state updates that are guaranteed to be independent of any other agents' states.

Let τ be the time step size of the simulation. An agent state update from t to $t + \tau$ can be represented as applying a *state update function* f_τ:

$$S_a^{t+\tau} = f_\tau(S_a^t, E_a^t, N_a^t)$$

where S_a^t is the state of agent a at simulation time t. We differentiate between the environment E_a^t surrounding agent a at t, and the set of neighboring agents N_a^t that are sensed by a at t. Let f_τ^k denote applying the state update function k times:

$$f_\tau^k(S_a^t, E_a^t, N_a^t) =$$
$$f_\tau(f_\tau(\ldots(f_\tau(S_a^t, E_a^t, N_a^t), E_a^{t+\tau}, N_a^{t+\tau}), \ldots),$$
$$E_a^{t+(k-1)\tau}, N_a^{t+(k-1)\tau})$$

We introduce a *fast-forward function* g, which approximates the result of iteratively applying f_τ given $N_a^{t+i\tau} = \emptyset$, $i \in \{0, \ldots, k-1\}$:

$$|g(k\tau, S_a^t, E_a^t) - f_\tau^k(S_a^t, E_a^t, \emptyset)| = \epsilon$$

where ϵ is the approximation error. If agent a does not sense any other agent within the next k time steps, the fast-forward function g successfully approximates the final state for agent a as if iteratively applying the state update function f_τ. However, since the sensing relation may not be symmetric and g does not yield the intermediate states in $(t, t+k\tau)$ required for sensing a, other agents' state updates may deviate when applying g for a. Thus, avoiding deviations across all agents' states requires mutual independence:

$$\forall i \in \{0, \ldots, k-1\} : ((N_a^{t+i\tau} = \emptyset) \wedge (\forall a' \in A \setminus \{a\} : a \notin N_{a'}^{t+i\tau}))$$

where A is the set of agents in the simulation, and $\wedge$ denotes logical conjunction. We refer to any interval $[t, t + k\tau]$ for which the above holds as an *independence interval*.

3.2 Identifying independence intervals

To allow for the identification of independence intervals, Scheutz et al. define a *translation function*, which "determines for a given location the maximum distance an agent can travel within one update" [28]. By determining the area that agents may travel to within the next k updates, independence intervals can be identified. In contrast to the translation function, the proposed fast-forward function determines the *full* agent state after k updates in case of independence from other agents' states. Thus, in contrast to the iterative time steps used by Scheutz et al., the fast-forward function allows for agent state updates across multiple time steps through a single function evaluation. We assume that the fast-forward function is accompanied by a *scanning* function, which additionally yields the time at which an agent first arrives at a given target distance if independence from other agents' states is given.

In this section, we propose methods for identifying opportunities for fast-forwarding. For efficiency, the methods are applied on the spatial granularity of edges of a graph representing the simulation space. First, we formulate conditions under which agents can be fast-forwarded across individual graph edges. Subsequently, we propose an algorithm to identify fast-forwarding opportunities across sequences of edges.

We assume that the simulation space, i.e., the road network, is represented by a graph $G = (V, E)$ comprised of a set of directed edges E representing roads, and a set of vertices V representing intersections. During an agent's lifetime, the agent traverses a predefined sequence of connected edges. Each edge traversal may require multiple state updates. Interactions with other agents can increase the number of updates required to traverse an edge. Each edge has an assigned weight l representing its length, l being at least the sensing range. For simplicity, in our description we disregard the spatial extent of the agents themselves, which we do however consider in our implementation of the approach.

3.2.1 Single-link scanning.
If an agent a has achieved the highest possible velocity on an edge and is located sufficiently far ahead of all other agents so that it is guaranteed that a will remain outside any other agent's sensing range, a may be eligible for fast-forwarding. To limit our consideration to the agent's current edge, we ensure that a cannot yet sense the next edge on its route and cannot be sensed from the previous edge. More formally, an independence interval for agent a covers the time interval for which the following conditions hold:

$$v(a) = v_{\max} \wedge$$
$$d(a) > r \wedge$$
$$d(a) < l - r \wedge$$
$$\forall a' \in \bar{A} \setminus \{a\} : d(a') < d(a) - r$$

where $v(a)$ and $d(a)$ are agent a's current velocity and position on the current edge, $\bar{A}$ is the set of agents on the same edge as a, r is the sensing range, l is the length of the current edge, and $v_{\max}$ is the speed limit on the edge.

3.2.2 Multi-link scanning.
We now extend the identification of independence intervals to sequences of graph edges (cf. Figure 1). Our goal is to determine for each agent an interval during which the agent never shares an edge with another agent. In the following, we describe Algorithm 1, which determines such intervals.

The algorithm proceeds in two stages: in the first stage, each agent registers its occupancy intervals at the edges that may be traversed within a configurable *scanning horizon*. The scanning horizon limits the scanning overheads. Each edge stores the earliest time it is sensed by any agent (*occupiedFrom*), with an initial value of ∞. If a registering agent exits the edge earlier than the current value of *occupiedFrom*, we store the agent as a candidate for fast-forwarding (*earliestAgent*), together with its sensing time and exit time. Otherwise, the registering agent may interact with a previously registered agent; thus, we set *earliestAgent* to *nil*.

In the second stage, each agent once again iterates over the edges reachable within the scanning horizon. Starting at an agent a's current edge, agent a can be fast-forwarded across the longest sequence of edges for which *earliestAgent* = a and for which the exit time is within the scanning horizon.

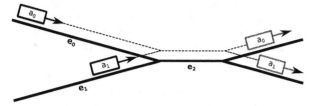

(a) Two agents a_0, a_1 passing the same edge e_2.

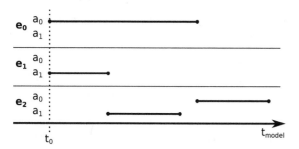

(b) Occupancy intervals for edges e_0, e_1, e_2. Since a_0 and a_1 never share their starting edges with other agents, they can be fast-forwarded across e_0 and e_1, respectively. Further, since a_0 and a_1 never occupy e_2 at the same time, both can be fast-forwarded across e_2. Thus, at minimum, the independence intervals of both a_0 and a_1 extend to the time at which the successor edge to e_2 is sensed.

Figure 1: Example of identifying independence intervals across multiple graph edges.

By limiting fast-forwarding to the agent who first occupies an edge, some opportunities are not exploited. An example is given in Figure 1: although agent a_0 never occupies edge e_2 at the same time as a_1, a_0 will not be fast-forwarded across edge e_2. To limit the costs of the scanning process, we do not consider such situations.

The size of the independence intervals depends on the scanning horizon as well as the period in model time after which single-link and multi-link scanning are repeated, which must be balanced with the incurred scanning overhead. Our implementation evaluated in Section 4 applies single-link and multi-link scanning with a configurable period length in model time. The effects of varying the scanning parameters are evaluated in Section 4.2.

3.3 Fast-forward function for the Intelligent Driver Model

In this section, we derive a fast-forward function and a scanning function for the Intelligent Driver Model (IDM). Instead of determining a vehicle's future states iteratively throughout multiple time steps, given independence from other vehicles, the functions will directly yield the vehicle state or the time. At a point $t_{initial}$ in model time, we have a vehicle's current state given by its velocity $v_{initial}$ and position $d_{initial}$. To be able to fast-forward vehicles, our goal is to calculate the vehicle state after t additional units of time. The state is comprised of the velocity v_{final} and the position d_{final}. We refer to the function that yields these two values as the *fast-forward function*. Further, for identifying independence intervals, we require the velocity $v_{projected}$ and time $t_{projected}$ at which a vehicle

---

Algorithm 1 Identifying independence intervals across multiple graph edges.

```
1:  procedure STAGEONE
2:      for each a ∈ A do
3:          e ← a.currentEdge
4:          sensingTime ← currentTime
5:          exitTime ← currentTime + travelTime(a, e, e.length − a.position)
6:          register(e, a, sensingTime, exitTime)
7:          sensingTime ← currentTime +
8:                  travelTime(a, e, e.length − a.position − sensingRange)
9:          e ← a.getSuccessorEdgeOnRoute(e)
10:         while e ≠ nil and exitTime ≤ scanningHorizon do
11:             nextSensingTime ← exitTime +
12:                     travelTime(a, e, e.length − sensingRange)
13:             exitTime ← exitTime + travelTime(a, e, e.length)
14:             register(e, a, sensingTime, exitTime)
15:             sensingTime ← nextSensingTime
16:             e ← a.getSuccessorEdgeOnRoute(e)
17: procedure STAGETWO
18:     for each a ∈ A do
19:         upperBoundTime ← −1
20:         e ← a.currentEdge
21:         while e ≠ nil do
22:             if e.earliestAgent ≠ a then
23:                 break
24:             e ← a.getSuccessorEdgeOnRoute(e)
25:             upperBoundTime ← e.occupiedFrom
26:         if upperBoundTime ≠ −1 then
27:             a.setIndependenceInterval(currentTime, upperBoundTime)
28: procedure REGISTER(e, a, sensingTime, exitTime)
29:     if exitTime >= currentTime + scanningHorizon then
30:         exitTime ← ∞
31:     if exitTime < e.occupiedFrom then
32:         e.earliestAgent ← a
33:         e.earliestAgentExitTime ← exitTime
34:     else if sensingTime ≤ e.earliestAgentExitTime then
35:         e.earliestAgent ← nil
36:     e.occupiedFrom ← min(e.occupiedFrom, sensingTime)
```

has traveled an additional distance d. We refer to the function that yields these two values as the *scanning function*.

In IDM, vehicles accelerate according to the following differential equation [30]:

$$\frac{dv}{dt} = a_0 \left(1 - \left(\frac{v}{v_0} \right)^\delta - \left(\frac{s_0 + vT + (v\Delta v)/(2\sqrt{a_0 b_0})}{s} \right)^2 \right)$$

Here, a_0 is the maximum acceleration, v is the current velocity, v_0 is the target velocity, s_0 is the minimum desired distance to the vehicle ahead, b_0 is the comfortable braking deceleration, and s and Δv are the position and velocity differences to the vehicle ahead. δ is a parameter typically set to 4 [30]. We perform our computations for this value.

When IDM is employed in time-stepped microscopic traffic simulations, the above equation is evaluated at each time step for each vehicle to calculate the vehicle's acceleration and to update its velocity and position accordingly.

Typically, a sensing range r is applied that limits the distance up to which vehicles adapt their acceleration to other nearby vehicles.

For $s > r$, the acceleration is determined solely by the *free road term*:

$$\frac{dv}{dt} = a_0 \left(1 - (\frac{v}{v_0})^\delta\right)$$

For $\delta = 4$, integration after separation of variables yields the time required to accelerate from 0m/s to v:

$$t(v) = \frac{v_0}{4a_0} \left(-\log(v_0 - v) + \log(v_0 + v) + 2\arctan(\frac{v}{v_0})\right)$$

When accelerating from initial velocity $v_\text{initial} > 0$m/s, the time elapsed when velocity v is reached is given by:

$$t_{v_\text{initial}}(v) = t(v) - t(v_\text{initial})$$

The distance that the vehicle has traveled when reaching velocity v can be obtained as follows:

$$d(v) = \int \frac{v}{a(v)} dv = \frac{v_0^2}{2a_0 \operatorname{arctanh}\left((\frac{v}{v_0})^2\right)}$$

Solving for v:

$$v(d) = v_0 \sqrt{-\tanh\left(-\frac{2a_0 d}{v_0^2}\right)}$$

Now we have the components of the *scanning function*:

$$v_\text{projected} = v\left(d + d(v_\text{initial})\right)$$

$$t_\text{projected} = t_\text{initial} + t\left(v_\text{projected}\right) - t(v_\text{initial})$$

After skipping state updates, we must allow the simulation to resume regular time-stepped agent state updates. Thus, we round to the nearest smaller timestep t_final and calculate the components of the *fast-forward function*:

$$v_\text{final} = v\left(t_\text{final}\right)$$

$$d_\text{final} = d_\text{initial} + d\left(v_\text{final}\right)$$

We do not have a closed form for $v(t)$. However, since $t(v)$ is twice differentiable, we can postulate $t(v) - t = 0$ and apply Halley's root-finding method [9] to compute v numerically at cubical convergence speed. We terminate once the change in values is below 10^{-10}.

Due to varying speed limits among the roads in a traffic simulation, vehicles may exceed the speed limit if the limit decreases among subsequent roads. An extension to IDM has been proposed to apply decelerations to vehicles using the following differential equation [16]:

$$\frac{dv}{dt} = -a_0 \left(1 - (\frac{v_0}{v})^\delta\right)$$

We derive fast-forward and scanning functions for this situation as well. For $\delta = 4$, integration after separation of variables yields:

$$t(v) = -\frac{1}{2a_0} \left(v_0(\arctan(\frac{v_0}{v}) - \operatorname{arctanh}(\frac{v_0}{v})) + 2v\right)$$

We can obtain the distance at velocity v as follows:

$$d(v) = \int \frac{v}{a(v)} dv = -\frac{1}{2a_0} \left((v^2 - v_0^2)\operatorname{arctanh}((\frac{v_0}{v})^2)\right)$$

Here, we apply Halley's method to obtain $v(d)$ and $v(t)$ and proceed as above.

Now we have fast-forward and scanning functions covering both acceleration and deceleration based on the continuous formulation of IDM. Since the time-stepped state updates in a simulation only approximate the acceleration behavior prescribed by the model, a deviation occurs between the fast-forward function and iterative time steps. The magnitude of the deviation depends on the time step size τ and vanishes for $\tau \to 0$. The effects of the deviation are discussed in the following section. We quantify the deviation in Section 4.1.

3.4 Discussion

IDM is defined by a time-continuous differential equation specifying a vehicle's acceleration behavior. Time-stepped microscopic traffic simulations approximate the specified behavior by calculating new acceleration values at each time step and updating the vehicles' velocities and positions accordingly. Smaller time step sizes increase the quality of the approximation, but are associated with higher computational cost. In contrast, the fast-forward function produces a "smooth" acceleration behavior without discretization to intermediate time steps. As such, updates performed using the fast-forward function can in fact be considered more in line with the intended acceleration behavior of IDM than iterative time-stepped updates. Still, when applying fast-forwarding, the simulation results will deviate from a purely time-stepped execution. A further potential source of deviations is given by the fact that occupancy intervals are determined using the scanning function, and are therefore affected by deviations as well. When a vehicle does not approach a road segment using the fast-forward function but using iterative time steps, the predicted occupancy interval may slightly deviate from the observed interval during which the vehicle occupies the road segment. Thus, it is possible that a vehicle is fast-forwarded based on the incorrect assumption that it will be isolated on the road segment. However, if the edges of the considered graph are substantially longer than the sensing range, it is unlikely that that such a deviation will lead to a vehicle entering another vehicle's sensing range. We did not observe this latter type of deviation in our experiments.

4 EVALUATION

In this section, we aim to answer the following questions:

- *How large is the deviation in the simulation results between a purely time-stepped execution and the proposed fast-forwarding approach?*
- *In which scenarios and to what degree can fast-forwarding accelerate microscopic road traffic simulations?*

Our evaluation is performed using the city-scale microscopic traffic simulator CityMoS [33]. Two road networks are considered: a synthetic grid-shaped road network (cf. Figure 2a), and a representation of the road network of Singapore (cf. Figure 2b). The grid network is comprised of 64×32 rectangles, each edge being 200m in length. There are two edges between two adjacent vertices with opposite traffic directions, resulting in a total length of 1600km. In the Singapore network, the average and total length of the edges is around 36.2m and 8700km, respectively. In both scenarios, origin and destination pairs are chosen uniformly at random on the road network. Route planning is based on Dijkstra's algorithm, using the edges' lengths and speed limits as their weights. Agents start their trips uniformly at random in model time. In the grid scenario, we started the measurements after a warm-up phase of 1800s to achieve

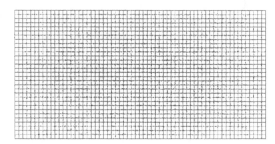

(a) Grid road network with around 10 000 vehicles.

(b) Singapore road network with around 19 500 vehicles.

Figure 2: Considered road networks with traffic, blue dots denoting vehicles.

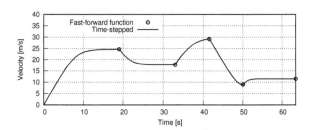

Figure 3: Example of the velocity calculated using time-stepped updates and fast-forwarding on a sequence of road segments with randomized lengths and speed limits, for a time step size of 0.5s.

roughly constant agent populations of 500, 2 000, and 10 000. After the warm-up phase, each measurement continued for 1h of model time. In the Singapore scenario, we used a warm-up phase of 1800s and subsequently measured the performance for 1h of model time while the agent population is ramping up to about 6 000 and 19 500 agents, respectively. Vehicles accelerate according to IDM[30] and perform lane changes according to the rules described in [32]. We configured a sensing range of 40m facing forward.

We varied the following algorithm parameters:

- **Single-link and multi-link scanning period**: the identification of independence intervals and the fast-forwarding are performed periodically. Since the scanning overhead depends on whether individual graph edges or sequences of graph edges are considered, the period length for each variant is varied separately.

- **Scanning horizon**: the overhead of scanning and the size of independence intervals depend on the maximum delta in model time that agents may be fast-forwarded.

For the grid scenario, we performed a parameter sweep to study the effect of different parameter combinations on the simulation performance. The levels in seconds of model time were $\{0.5, 2, 8, 32\}$ and $\{0.5, 2, 8, 32, 128\}$ for the single-link and multi-link scanning period, and $\{16, 64, 256\}$ for the scanning horizon. In the Singapore scenario, we applied a simple auto-tuning approach to select and vary parameter combinations at runtime: a set of preconfigured parameter combinations is set one after the other, measuring the simulation progress per unit wall-clock time for each combination. The simulation then proceeds with the best-performing parameter combination. The auto-tuning process is repeated once either

1200s of model time have passed or the simulation performance has changed by more than a factor of 2. We configured the following parameter combinations for the single-link scanning period, multi-link scanning period, and the scanning horizon: (2, 32, 64), (2, 128, 64), (4, 32, 64), (4, 128, 64), and (2, ∞, 64). In the grid scenario, each simulation run was repeated at least 3 times. Each run of the Singapore scenario was repeated 20 times. All performance measurements were performed on a single core of an Intel i5-7400 CPU running at 3.00GHz with 16GiB of RAM.

4.1 Validation

To evaluate the deviation between the simulation results of a purely time-stepped execution and our fast-forwarding approach, we first consider a single vehicle and compare the distance after a certain amount of model time when traversing a sequence of road segments with varying speed limits. We then compare aggregated statistics over all vehicles across entire simulation runs.

4.1.1 Individual fast-forwarding operations. The relationship between time-stepped and fast-forwarding updates is illustrated in Figure 3. We plot the velocities computed using time-stepped updates on a sequence of road segments of randomized lengths and speed limits, and compare the results with those of evaluating the fast-forward function at the end of each road segment. Visually, the deviation between the two methods is marginal.

To quantify the deviation, we recorded the relative deviation between a vehicle's position calculated using fixed time steps and fast-forwarding after 60s of traveling time across a sequence of roads with lengths uniformly distributed between 50m and 500m and speed limits uniformly distributed between 10m/s and 30m/s. We performed 10 000 runs each for step sizes of 0.1s and 0.5s. The overall distance traveled was between about 625m and 1630m. The result is shown in Figure 4. Most deviations are lower than 0.3% for time step size 0.1s, and lower than 1.5% for time step size 0.5s. The largest observed deviations were 0.85% and 3.29%, respectively. The slight bias towards negative deviations is likely due to the use of different equations for acceleration and deceleration behaviors (cf. Section 3.3). However, as discussed in Section 3.4, we note that since the fast-forward function is based directly on the time-continuous formulation of IDM, the results after fast-forwarding may in fact be considered closer to the desired acceleration behavior than the results after a sequence of time-stepped updates.

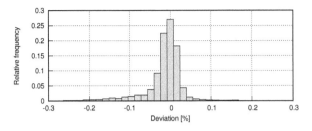

(a) Time step size 0.1s.

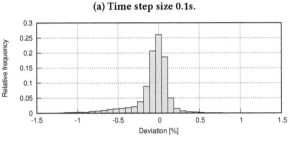

(b) Time step size 0.5s.

Figure 4: Relative deviation between positions calculated using iterative time steps and fast-forwarding after 60s of traveling time across a sequence of road segments with randomized lengths and speed limits.

Table 1: Average trip durations [s] in time-stepped and fast-forwarding runs with 95% confidence intervals.

Scenario	Grid		
Agent count	500	2 000	10 000
Time-stepped	371.4 ± 0.6	371.0 ± 0.6	377.4 ± 0.1
Fast-forwarding	371.4 ± 1.6	371.0 ± 2.6	377.3 ± 0.3

Scenario	Singapore	
Peak agent count	6 000	19 500
Time-stepped	859.2 ± 4.0	1096.5 ± 5.3
Fast-forwarding	860.0 ± 3.8	1099.7 ± 5.9

4.1.2 Grid and Singapore scenarios. For the grid and Singapore scenarios, we conduct the validation with respect to the average trip duration, which is a commonly studied metric in transportation engineering. The comparison results are shown in Table 1. We performed a parameter sweep across the scanning parameters for the grid scenario. The validation results are given for the parameter combinations resulting in the lowest execution times. For the Singapore scenario, the parameters were configured at runtime using auto-tuning. The time step size was 0.1s. We observe that in both scenarios, there is no significant deviation in the overall simulation results between the time-stepped execution and fast-forwarding.

4.2 Performance measurements

4.2.1 Fast-forward function. To understand the potential for performance gains using the proposed approach, we first compare the computational cost of iterative time-stepped agent updates and updates using the proposed fast-forward function. We simulate

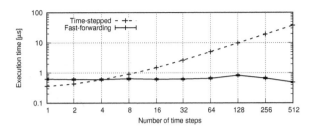

Figure 5: Wall-clock computation time required for a certain number of steps using time-stepped execution and fast-forwarding for a time step size of 0.1s.

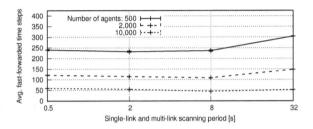

Figure 6: Average number of time steps skipped per fast-forwarding operation in the grid scenario with a fixed scanning horizon of 64s and identical single-link and multi-link scanning periods. Although larger scanning periods provide fewer fast-forwarding opportunities, the number of time steps per individual fast-forwarding operation increases.

a single vehicle on a road segment of 10km length. Initially, the velocity is 0km/h. The vehicle accelerates to the speed limit of 100km/h. In Figure 5, we compare the wall-clock time required to execute a certain number of time steps to the time required to advance a vehicle by the same distance using fast-forwarding. Due to the fine-grained nature of agent updates, each measurement was repeated 10^7 times in the time-stepped case, and 100 000 times for fast-forwarding. The figure shows averages over the repetitions. 95% confidence intervals are plotted but are too small to be visible.

Figure 5 shows that the execution time of the fast-forward function is roughly constant, whereas the execution time of time-stepped updates depends approximately linearly on the number of steps. Although the fast-forward function is associated with higher computational cost than an individual time-stepped state update, fast-forwarding outperforms time-stepped updates beyond 4 consecutive steps. Thus, assuming no additional overheads, fast-forwarding is beneficial when the average number of fast-forwarded time steps is larger than 4. Generally, reducing the time step size of the simulation will allow for a larger number of skipped time steps per fast-forwarding operation. However, due to the overall increase in time steps, the proportion of skipped time steps across the simulation run will remain roughly the same.

4.2.2 Grid scenarios. Figure 6 shows the average number of time steps skipped per fast-forwarding operation in the grid scenario with a time step size of 0.1s, varying the single-link and multi-link scanning periods. Even in the most congested scenario with 10 000

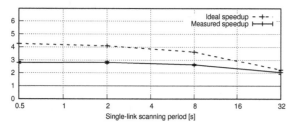

(a) Multi-link scanning period 8s, scanning horizon 64s.

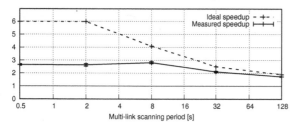

(b) Single-link scanning period 2s, scanning horizon 64s.

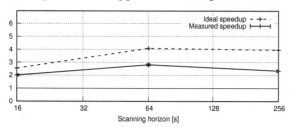

(c) Single-link scanning period 2s, multi-link period 8s.

Figure 7: Ideal and measured speedup with 500 agents in the grid scenario.

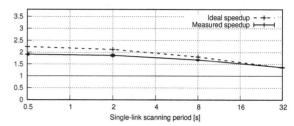

(a) Multi-link scanning period 8s, scanning horizon 64s.

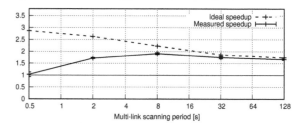

(b) Single-link scanning period 0.5s, scanning horizon 64s.

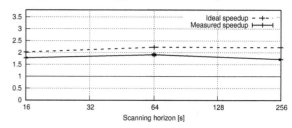

(c) Single-link scanning period 0.5s, multi-link period 8s.

Figure 8: Ideal and measured speedup with 2 000 agents in the grid scenario.

agents, around 50 time steps were skipped per fast-forwarding operation, far beyond the break-even point of 4 time steps shown in Figure 5.

Figures 7 to 9 show the overall speedup achieved using the fast-forwarding approach compared with a purely time-stepped execution for the grid scenario for 500, 2 000, and 10 000 agents, respectively. In addition, we plot the relative reduction in state updates, which indicates the ideal speedup through the fast-forwarding approach when disregarding the overhead for identifying independence intervals and the evaluation of the fast-forward function. For instance, if the number of time steps is reduced by 50%, the ideal speedup is 2.

We can observe in Figure 7 that due to substantial opportunities for fast-forwarding with only 500 agents, frequent single-link and multi-link scanning and a large scanning horizon are beneficial. In Figure 7b, when the multi-link scanning period is increased, the ideal speedup decreases substantially from multi-link scanning periods of 2s to 8s. However, the measured speedup is virtually unchanged due to the trade-off between the scanning overhead and the benefit of skipping updates. The largest speedup achieved with 500 agents is 2.82 with single-link and multi-link scanning periods of 2s and 8s, and a scanning horizon of 64s. With 2 000 agents (cf. Fig. 8), the trade-off between identifying opportunities for fast-forwarding and the associated overhead becomes more pronounced: a speedup

of 1.91 is achieved with single-link and multi-link scanning periods of 0.5s and 8s, respectively, and a scanning horizon of 64s, whereas no speedup is achieved when decreasing the multi-link scanning period of 0.5s (cf. Fig. 8b). Compared to the above two cases, the most congested scenario with 10 000 agents (cf. Fig. 9) provides fewer opportunities for fast-forwarding. Additionally, since the costs of identifying independence intervals increases with the number of agents, frequent multi-link scanning is not beneficial. A maximum speedup of 1.12 is achieved with single-link and multi-link scanning periods of 0.5s and 128s, and a scanning horizon of 16s.

Overall, the measurements show that controlling the overhead for identifying independence intervals is critical when applying our approach in practice. Further, the opportunities for fast-forwarding decrease with denser traffic.

4.2.3 Singapore scenario. The performance results for the Singapore road network are shown in Table 2. We observe that 22.1% and 10.3% of time steps were skipped using auto-tuning for peak agent counts of 6 000 and 19 500, respectively. The average number of time steps per fast-forwarding operation for both cases is much larger than the break-even point of 4 steps (cf. Figure 5). With 6, 000 agents, a speedup of 1.22 is achieved. With 19 500 agents, only few opportunities for fast-forwarding could be identified, allowing for a speedup of 1.05.

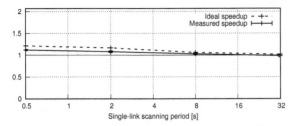

(a) Multi-link scanning period 0.5s, scanning horizon 16s.

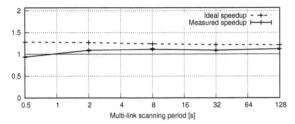

(b) Single-link scanning period 0.5s, scanning horizon 16s.

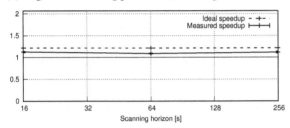

(c) Single-link scanning period 0.5s, multi-link period 128s.

Figure 9: Ideal and measured speedup with 10 000 agents in the grid scenario.

Table 2: Performance in the Singapore scenario with scanning parameters configured using auto-tuning.

Peak agent count	6 000	19 500
Time-stepped execution time [s]	214.3 ± 3.4	789.1 ± 5.9
Steps skipped [%]	22.1 ± 0.1	10.3 ± 0.1
Steps skipped per fast-forwarding	85.45 ± 0.16	81.4 ± 0.15
Scanning overhead [s]	2.5 ± 0.0	7.4 ± 0.1
Fast-forwarding overhead [s]	2.0 ± 0.0	4.9 ± 0.0
Speedup	1.22 ± 0.03	1.05 ± 0.01

5 DISCUSSION

In this section, we discuss limitations and potential enhancements of the proposed fast-forwarding approach.

Applicability to more complex models and other domains: in the present paper, we assume that the fast-forward and scanning functions return a single agent state and time, implying that the routes of the agents (i.e., the sequences of edges) will not change after scanning has been performed. Depending on the considered simulation model, agents may change their routes on interaction with other agents or even spontaneously. For instance, an agent may re-route when it detects traffic congestion. To consider such models,

we could either terminate the scanning process at the first point in time when a change is possible, or determine occupancy intervals for all possible branches. Both approaches may substantially reduce the opportunities for fast-forwarding compared to what has been shown in the simulation scenarios of the present paper. If routing decisions are made stochastically, pre-sampling from the pseudo-random number stream may still enable prediction of the agents' routes. In the extreme case of entirely unpredictable routes, fast-forwarding would be limited to disjoint areas reachable by agents according to their maximum velocity.

From the problem analysis in Section 3.1, we can infer that the applicability of our approach to other types of time-stepped agent-based simulations depends on the specific models used. The approach is applicable to models that allow for the prediction of future agent states and to scenarios where independent agent updates occur. For instance, in crowd simulations using predefined routes on a two-dimensional simulation space, the path taken by isolated agents may be fully predictable. The performance benefits of the approach depend on the computational cost of the fast-forward function relative to time-stepped updates as well as the costs for determining independence intervals.

Deviations compared to time-stepped execution: As discussed in Section 3 and evaluated in Section 4.1, state updates performed using the fast-forward function deviate slightly from those performed using iterative time steps. Although the fast-forward function can be argued to be closer to the behavior specified in IDM and the deviations are low, two undesirable properties emerge: first, as with any state alteration in an agent-based simulation, deviations may propagate through the road network. Second, the deviations depend on the parametrization of the fast-forwarding approach, i.e., on the frequency of scanning and on the scanning horizon. Thus, the approach interlinks the *execution* of the simulation and the observed *behavior* of the simulation. Ideally, to allow modelers to clearly identify cause-and-effect relationships when modifying the model or scenario, these two aspects should be decoupled.

Influence on statistics collection and visualization: Typically, in an agent-based simulation, statistics are gathered by periodically aggregating over the states of the agents in the simulation, e.g., over the velocities of the vehicles on a road network. Usually, the period of aggregation is a multiple of the time step size. If updates are performed asynchronously according to the proposed approach, agents may be fast-forwarded beyond the point when statistics are to be collected. A simple solution is to limit the scanning horizon to the next statistics gathering time. Visualization tools could apply interpolation to approximate agent states at time steps that have been skipped through fast-forwarding.

Further opportunities for fast-forwarding: the proposed multi-link scanning approach operates on the granularity of edges in a road network. Thus, if the modeled road network has a high percentage of edges that are substantially longer than the sensing range of vehicles, many opportunities for fast-forwarding are not exploited. By identifying independence intervals on a finer granularity, additional fast-forwarding opportunities could be unlocked. However, more complex scanning may incur an increase in overhead. Further, for efficiency, we limited fast-forwarding to the first agent that senses a graph edge. Fast-forwarding of multiple agents occupying the same edge at disjoint time intervals within the scanning horizon may enable further speedup in some scenarios. Further, in road traffic simulations that consider traffic lights, trivial opportunities for fast-forwarding may be given for vehicles stopped in front of traffic lights. Such vehicles can be fast-forwarded to the next state change of the traffic lights. Finally, we only consider skipping opportunities for individual agents. An increase in fast-forwarding opportunities may be possible if the fast-forward function can be extended to clusters of agents.

Controlling overhead: a number of ways present themselves to control the scanning overhead and thus to enable more complex scanning procedures: first, the proposed algorithm is parametrized with the scanning periods and scanning horizon. Our evaluation showed that the optimal values for the parameters depend strongly on the considered scenario. Thus, we applied a simple auto-tuning scheme to adapt the scanning parameters according to the traffic conditions of the Singapore scenario.

Second, in addition to the variation of congestion across model time, congestion also typically shows variations across the simulated space. For instance, during peak hours a highly congested speedway will provide few opportunities for fast-forwarding, in contrast to sparsely populated roads in residential areas. In such situations, to avoid unnecessary computations, scanning could be restricted to areas outside congested areas. However, further considerations are then required to maintain correctness. Since vehicles may enter or exit congested areas within the considered scanning horizon, excluding agent interactions would require a safety margin around these areas, which could be defined based on static information such as speed limits.

Finally, the scanning operation may be offloaded to a separate processor. Within the accuracy allowed by the time step size, previously identified occupancy intervals may be outpaced by the simulation's progress, but not invalidated. Thus, after scanning, fast-forwarding could be applied to all agents that have not yet progressed beyond the target time. Further, during scanning, the scanning function is evaluated a number of times for each relevant vehicles independently, providing ample opportunities for parallelization, e.g., on graphics processing units.

6 RELATED WORK

In this section, we give an overview of previous work focusing on identifying and exploiting independence between state updates for parallelization of discrete-event simulations and for accelerating sequential and parallel time-stepped agent-based simulations. Further, we discuss hybrid modeling and simulation approaches that execute parts of a simulation microscopically, while applying less detailed and therefore less computationally intensive models for parts of the simulation where full accuracy is not required.

6.1 Exploiting independent state updates

The approach proposed in the present paper bears some similarities with methods from the field of parallel and distributed simulation, which is concerned with the execution of individual simulation runs on a set of inter-connected processing elements [8]. To reduce the cost of synchronization between processing elements, methods have been proposed to exploit *lookahead*, i.e., the difference in

model time between an event's creation and execution time [7]. If a lower bound on the lookahead can be determined either prior to the simulation or at runtime [18, 24], intervals in model time can be identified during which processing elements can compute independently. Some previous works consider the minimum model time required for a sequence of events to propagate to a remote processing element [3, 4, 19, 20, 23, 27, 31]. Similarly to our approach, intervals of independence are derived according to the topology of the modeled system. However, instead of exploiting the identified independence for parallel execution, in our work, we accelerate sequential simulations by performing independent agent state updates using a computationally inexpensive fast-forward function. A further similarity exists to optimistically synchronized parallel and distributed simulations [6, 26], where some computations are performed speculatively and rolled back when a violation of the simulation correctness is detected. In our approach, the identification of occupancy intervals can be seen as speculative state updates under the assumption of independence among agents. When independence between the agent updates cannot be guaranteed, the results are discarded.

Some previous works have considered ways of accelerating time-stepped agent-based simulations by identifying independent state updates among agents: Scheutz et al. [13, 28, 29] apply a *translation function* that reflects the furthest possible amount of movement of an agent to determine an *event horizon* in model time. By identifying non-overlapping areas among multiple agents' event horizons, time intervals of mutually independent updates can be identified. Now, in the context of sequential agent-based simulations, agent updates can be prioritized to achieve the simulation's termination criterion with the minimum number of state updates. For instance, if the focus of the simulation study is on a particular agent, only the state updates directly or indirectly affecting this agent must be performed. In distributed agent-based simulations, idle times due to data dependencies can be reduced by prioritizing agent updates according to the data dependencies across processing elements. In contrast to our work, runtime reductions are achieved through changes in the ordering of agent updates, not through accelerating the state updates themselves. Since road traffic simulations are typically executed until all agents have reached a certain point in model time, the approach by Scheutz et al. would not accelerate such simulations.

Buss et al. [2] proposed a discrete-event modeling approach for scenarios involving movement and sensing. Instead of explicitly updating an entity's location over a sequence of time steps, events are scheduled at points in model time where changes in movement occur. However, determining suitable event scheduling times for sets of interacting vehicles may incur substantial overhead. Thus, in contrast to the purely discrete-event approach proposed by Buss et al., our proposed fast-forwarding approach maintains a time-stepped execution for all agents currently involved in an interaction. Further, while the work by Buss et al. and another work with a similar focus by Meyer [22] share with ours the general idea of avoiding explicit intermediate state changes, the main challenge lies in determining the points in model time when interactions between entities may occur and in determining the new agent state. In the present paper, we address these challenges in the context of microscopic road traffic simulations.

Less closely related to our approach is the concept of simulation cloning [14]. In this approach, the total execution time of a set of simulation runs is reduced by computing only the divergent state updates across multiple runs. For instance, if the behavior of only a single agent is modified across multiple runs, state changes of other agents that are unaffected by this agent are not recomputed [25]. Similarly, in updatable and exact-differential simulation [5, 12], intermediate events of an initial full simulation run are stored. Subsequent simulation runs branch off from this initial simulation run, reusing stored events that are unaffected by the branching. As in these approaches, fast-forwarding exploits the independence between state updates to accelerate simulations. However, instead of avoiding recomputation, the fast-forwarding approach proposed in the present paper avoids computation of some updates entirely.

Finally, the term "fast-forwarding" was used previously in other contexts where existing information is exploited to advance a simulated entity in model time. In the updatable simulations proposed by Ferenci et al. [5], some repeated event executions can be avoided, thus "fast-forwarding" the corresponding simulated entity. Mauve et al. [21] use the term "fast forward" to describe the re-execution of events after a rollback in the context of optimistic synchronization for distributed virtual environments.

6.2 Hybrid traffic simulation

In hybrid traffic simulation [1], microscopic models are combined with mesoscopic or macroscopic models to balance simulation fidelity and performance. Spatial or temporal segments of the simulation are selected in which a reduction in modeling detail and accuracy is acceptable. In these segments, vehicles are considered in aggregate, e.g., as sets of tasks in a queuing network or in terms of fluid dynamics. As a consequence, it is not always possible to study an individual vehicle across its entire route. The fast-forwarding approach proposed in the present paper bears a superficial similarity with hybrid traffic simulation in its reliance on an analytical solution for some of the state updates instead of a purely time-stepped execution. However, fast-forwarding is applied only if it is ensured that within the accuracy allowed by the simulation's time step size, the simulation results are unaffected. Since fast-forwarding does not consider agents in aggregate, each vehicle's progress on its route can still be studied individually.

7 CONCLUSIONS AND OUTLOOK

We propose an approach to accelerate microscopic traffic simulation by identifying intervals of independent state updates and performing such independent updates using a computationally inexpensive fast-forward function. The approach maintains the microscopic nature of the simulation. We derived a fast-forward function for the well-known Intelligent Driver Model. We evaluated the approach for a synthetic scenario and the road network of the city of Singapore. Our validation shows that the deviation from a purely time-stepped execution is marginal. The performance benefit of the approach depends strongly on the level of agent density in the scenarios. For scenarios with sparse traffic, a speedup of up to 2.8 was achieved, whereas with dense traffic, the reduced amount of opportunities for fast-forwarding allowed for only limited performance gains. One avenue for future work lies in identifying further opportunities for fast-forwarding, e.g., by increasing the spatial resolution

of the approach, or by considering clusters of cars jointly. Further, methods to control the overhead of the approach could improve performance. For instance, avoiding attempts for fast-forwarding in congested areas of the road network could reduce unnecessary computations, while requiring further considerations to maintain correctness. Offloading the computational overhead to a separate processing element could hide some of the overhead. Finally, the fast-forwarding approach could be extended to models with more complex agent movement behaviors such as crowd models.

8 ACKNOWLEDGMENTS

This work was financially supported by the Singapore National Research Foundation under its Campus for Research Excellence And Technological Enterprise (CREATE) programme.

REFERENCES

[1] Wilco Burghout, Haris Koutsopoulos, and Ingmar Andreasson. 2005. Hybrid Mesoscopic-Microscopic Traffic Simulation. *Transportation Research Record: Journal of the Transportation Research Board* 1934 (2005), 218–255.

[2] Arnold H Buss and Paul J Sánchez. 2005. Simple Movement and Detection in Discrete Event Simulation. In *Proceedings of the Winter Simulation Conference*. Winter Simulation Conference, 992–1000.

[3] Moo-Kyoung Chung and Chong-Min Kyung. 2006. Improving Lookahead in Parallel Multiprocessor Simulation Using Dynamic Execution Path Prediction. In *Proceedings of the Workshop on Principles of Advanced and Distributed Simulation*. IEEE, 11–18.

[4] Ewa Deelman, Rajive Bagrodia, Rizos Sakellariou, and Vikram Adve. 2001. Improving Lookahead in Parallel Discrete Event Simulations of Large-scale Applications Using Compiler Analysis. In *Proceedings of the Workshop on Parallel and Distributed Simulation*. IEEE Computer Society, Washington, DC, USA, 5–13. http://dl.acm.org/citation.cfm?id=375658.375659

[5] Steve L Ferenci, Richard M Fujimoto, Mostafa H Ammar, Kalyan Perumalla, and George F Riley. 2002. Updateable Simulation of Communication Networks. In *Proceedings of the Workshop on Parallel and Distributed Simulation*. IEEE Computer Society, 107–114.

[6] Richard Fujimoto. 2015. Parallel and Distributed Simulation. In *Proceedings of the Winter Simulation Conference*. IEEE Press, 45–59.

[7] R. M. Fujimoto. 1988. Lookahead in Parallel Discrete Event Simulation. *Proceedings of the International Conference on Parallel Processing, Vol. 3* (1988), 34–41.

[8] Richard M Fujimoto. 2000. *Parallel and Distributed Simulation Systems*. Wiley New York.

[9] Walter Gander. 1985. On Halley's Iteration Method. *The American Mathematical Monthly* 92, 2 (1985), 131–134.

[10] Peter G Gipps. 1981. A Behavioural Car-following Model for Computer Simulation. *Transportation Research Part B: Methodological* 15, 2 (1981), 105–111.

[11] Peter G Gipps. 1986. A Model for the Structure of Lane-changing Decisions. *Transportation Research Part B: Methodological* 20, 5 (1986), 403–414.

[12] Masatoshi Hanai, Toyotaro Suzumura, Georgios Theodoropoulos, and Kalyan S Perumalla. 2015. Exact-differential Large-scale Traffic Simulation. In *Proceedings of the Conference on Principles of Advanced Discrete Simulation*. ACM, 271–280.

[13] Jack Harris and Matthias Scheutz. 2012. New Advances in Asynchronous Agent-based Scheduling. In *Proceedings of the International Conference on Parallel and Distributed Processing Techniques and Applications*. WorldComp, 1.

[14] Maria Hybinette and Richard M Fujimoto. 2001. Cloning Parallel Simulations. *ACM Transactions on Modeling and Computer Simulation* 11, 4 (2001), 378–407.

[15] Arne Kesting, Martin Treiber, and Dirk Helbing. 2007. General Lane-changing Model MOBIL for Car-following Models. *Transportation Research Record: Journal of the Transportation Research Board* 1999 (2007), 86–94.

[16] Arne Kesting, Martin Treiber, and Dirk Helbing. 2008. Agents for Traffic Simulation. In *Multi-Agent Systems Simulation and Applications*, Adelinde M. Uhrmacher and Danny Weyns (Eds.). CRC Press, Chapter 11, 325–356. http://arxiv.org/abs/0805.0300

[17] Michael Lees, Brian Logan, and Rob Minson. 2005. Modelling environments for distributed simulation. In *Environments for Multi-Agent Systems*. 150–167. http://www.springerlink.com/index/81g6x6elxhx9tbnq.pdf

[18] Y.-B. Lin and E.D. Lazowska. 1990. Exploiting Lookahead in Parallel Simulation. *IEEE Transactions on Parallel and Distributed Systems* 1, 4 (1990), 457–469. https://doi.org/10.1109/71.80174

[19] Jason Liu and David M Nicol. 2002. Lookahead Revisited in Wireless Network Simulations. In *Proceedings of the Workshop on Parallel and Distributed Simulation*. IEEE Computer Society, 79–88.

[20] Boris D. Lubachevsky. 1989. Efficient Distributed Event-Driven Simulations of Multiple-Loop Networks. *Commun. ACM* 32, 1 (1989), 111–123.

[21] Martin Mauve, Jürgen Vogel, Volker Hilt, and Wolfgang Effelsberg. 2004. Local-lag and Timewarp: Providing Consistency for Replicated Continuous Applications. *IEEE Transactions on Multimedia* 6, 1 (2004), 47–57.

[22] Ruth Meyer. 2014. Event-Driven Multi-Agent Simulation. In *International Workshop on Multi-Agent Systems and Agent-Based Simulation*. Springer, 3–16.

[23] Richard A Meyer and Rajive L Bagrodia. 1999. Path Lookahead: a Data Flow View of PDES Models. In *Proceedings of the Workshop on Parallel and Distributed Simulation*. IEEE, 12–19.

[24] D.M. Nicol and J.H. Saltz. 1988. Dynamic Remapping of Parallel Computations with Varying Resource Demands. *IEEE Trans. Comput.* 37, 9 (1988), 1073–1087. https://doi.org/10.1109/12.2258

[25] Philip Pecher, Michael Hunter, and Richard Fujimoto. 2015. Efficient Execution of Replicated Transportation Simulations with Uncertain Vehicle Trajectories. *Procedia Computer Science* 51 (2015), 2638–2647.

[26] Kalyan S Perumalla, Mohammed M Olama, and Srikanth B Yoginath. 2016. Model-Based Dynamic Control of Speculative Forays in Parallel Computation. *Electronic Notes in Theoretical Computer Science* 327 (2016), 93–107.

[27] Patrick Peschlow, Andreas Voss, and Peter Martini. 2009. Good News for Parallel Wireless Network Simulations. In *Proceedings of the International Conference on Modeling, Analysis and Simulation of Wireless and Mobile Systems*. ACM, 134–142.

[28] Matthias Scheutz and Jack Harris. 2010. Adaptive Scheduling Algorithms for the Dynamic Distribution and Parallel Execution of Spatial Agent-based Models. *Parallel and Distributed Computational Intelligence* 269 (2010), 207–233.

[29] Matthias Scheutz and Paul Schermerhorn. 2006. Adaptive Algorithms for The Dynamic Distribution and Parallel Execution of Agent-based Models. *J. Parallel and Distrib. Comput.* 66, 8 (2006), 1037–1051. https://doi.org/10.1016/j.jpdc.2005.09.004

[30] Martin Treiber, Ansgar Hennecke, and Dirk Helbing. 2000. Congested Traffic States in Empirical Observations and Microscopic Simulations. *Physical Review E* 62, 2 (February 2000), 1805–1824.

[31] Jun Wang, Zhenjiang Dong, Sudhakar Yalamanchili, and George Riley. 2013. Optimizing Parallel Simulation of Multicore Systems Using Domain-Specific Knowledge. In *Proceedings of the Conference on Principles of Advanced Discrete Simulation*. ACM, 127–136.

[32] Yadong Xu, Wentong Cai, Heiko Aydt, Michael Lees, and Daniel Zehe. 2017. Relaxing Synchronization in Parallel Agent-based Road Traffic Simulation. *ACM Transactions on Modeling and Computer Simulation - Special Issue on PADS 2015* 27, 2 (2017), 14:1–24.

[33] Daniel Zehe, Suraj Nair, Alois Knoll, and David Eckhoff. 2017. Towards City-MoS: A Coupled City-Scale Mobility Simulation Framework. In *5th GI/ITG KuVS Fachgespräch Inter-Vehicle Communication*. FAU Erlangen-Nuremberg.

A Binary Search Enhanced Sort-based Interest Matching Algorithm

Tianlin Li, Wenjie Tang*, Yiping Yao and Feng Zhu
College of System Engineering
National University of Defense Technology, Changsha, Hunan, CHINA
ltl@mail.ustc.edu.cn, {tangwenjie, ypyao, zhufeng}@nudt.edu.cn

ABSTRACT

In distributed simulation, communication based on publish/subscribe will generate large amount of irrelevant data transmissions, and thereby degrading the performance. To solve the problem, HLA standard defines data distribution management to filter unnecessary communication. Among several famous interest matching algorithms, the sort-based algorithm has been proven to be the most efficient method in most scenarios. However, the potential of existing sort-based algorithm has not been fully exploited, due to the overhead of sorting the bounds can be further reduced and a portion of unnecessary bit operations can be eliminated. In this paper, we propose a binary search enhanced sort-based interest matching algorithm (BSSIM). Based on a different sufficient and necessary condition to judge interval overlapping, the size of list to be sorted can be remarkably reduced. Moreover, unnecessary bit operations can be eliminated by binary searches. Experimental results show that BSSIM algorithm outperforms the sort-based algorithm, and approximately 64%-159% performance improvement can be achieved at different scenarios.

KEYWORDS

Interest matching, sort-based algorithm, binary search

1 INTRODUCTION

In distributed simulation, federates exchange information based on the publish/subscribe method. The method provides significant flexibility than explicitly sending messages, but it would also generate large amount of irrelevant data transmissions. HLA standard provides data distribution management (DDM) services [1] to filter unnecessary data transmissions and therefore reduce communication overhead among federates. Producers of data utilized DDM services to assert properties of their data (update region), while consumers of data may utilize DDM services to specify their data requirements (subscription region). Then, RTI distributes data from producers to consumers based on interest matching between these regions. Hence, interest matching plays a key role in data distribution management.

Currently, interest matching algorithms mainly include brute force algorithm (also called region-based algorithm), grid-based approach, hybrid approach and sort-based approach. They have their own strong points and weak points. Among them, the sort-based algorithm is the most promising and efficient. However, the sort-based algorithm still has several major drawbacks [6]. In such algorithms, sorting the bounds of regions and large number of bit operations will generate a lot of additional overhead, which means that there is still some potential to improve the sort-based interest matching algorithm.

In this paper, we propose a binary search enhanced sort-based interest matching algorithm, aiming at reducing the sorting overhead and avoiding unnecessary bit operation. Based on a novel sufficient and necessary condition to judge interval overlapping, the size of the list to be sorted can be remarkably reduced. Moreover, by means of binary searches, additional bit operation can be eliminated.

The rest of the paper is organized as follows. Section 2 introduces several existing interest matching algorithms. Section 3 describes our proposed interest matching algorithm in detail. Section 4 describes the experiments and analysis of the results. Section 5 concludes the whole paper and overviews the future work.

2 RELATED WORKS

This section mainly introduces existing interest matching algorithms, brute force, grid-based, hybrid and sort-based algorithm, and analyzes their advantages and disadvantages.

Brute force, also known as region based, compares update region with subscription region one by one to obtain the overlap information. This approach can achieve exact matching results, while the computation complexity is $O(N^2)$.

In Grid-based [2] algorithm, the interest space is divided into grids, so all update regions and subscription regions are mapped to one or several grids. This algorithm considers the regions in the same grid intersect. This algorithm is efficient, while the matching result is not exact.

Hybrid algorithm [3] is the combination of brute force and grid-based algorithm. On the basis of grid-based algorithm, brute force approach is applied for each grid to obtain the exact

Permission to make digital or hard copies of all or part of this work for personal or classroom use is granted without fee provided that copies are not made or distributed for profit or commercial advantage and that copies bear this notice and the full citation on the first page. Copyrights for components of this work owned by others than ACM must be honored. Abstracting with credit is permitted. To copy otherwise, or republish, to post on servers or to redistribute to lists, requires prior specific permission and/or a fee. Request permissions from Permissions@acm.org.
SIGSIM-PADS '18 , May 23–25, 2018, Rome, Italy
© 2018 Association for Computing Machinery.
ACM ISBN 978-1-4503-5092-1/18/05...$15.00
https://doi.org/10.1145/3200921.3200941

matching results. When the number of grids is G, the cost of the algorithm is $O(N^2/G)$. However, G value is difficult to choose in real simulation, because the number of regions and the size of interest space are uncertain.

Sort-based algorithm proposed by Gary et al [4] uses the idea of sorting bounds of regions to obtain overlap information. For each dimension, all the upper and lower bounds of update and subscription regions are put into list L and sort L in ascending order. The length of L is 4*N. When N is large, the sorting overhead cannot be ignored. Traverse L and remove a value from the queue each time. When the value is the lower bound of update region Ui, then put the id of Ui into set UpdateSet. If the value is the lower bound of subscription region Si, then put the id of Si into SubscribeSet. When the value is the upper bound of update region Ui, then remove the id from UpdateSet, and Ui intersect with all the subscription regions in SubscribeSet. It is same for the upper bounds of subscription regions. In this way, overlap information can be obtained.

Raczy et al [5] also proposed a sort-based matching algorithm, which is similar to the sort-based algorithm described above. The difference is an N * N bit matrix M is used to maintain and store the overlap information. Through operating the sorted queue and changing the values in M, the final overlapping information can be obtained.

Ke Pan et al [6] proposed an efficient sort-based algorithm with $O(maxRS/D_{UB}*N^2)$ computation complexity and $O((maxRS/D_{UB})^2 * N^2)$ storage complexity. maxRS is the maximum range size of all intervals, and D_{UB} is the size of the interest space. Thus the performance of this algorithm depends on the ratio of $maxRS/D_{UB}$. When the ratio is small, the algorithm is more efficient, however, when the ratio becomes larger, the performance becomes worse. In this algorithm, binary search is scheduled when mapping U_{UB} and U_{LB} onto the S_{LB} and S_{UB} sorted list. Then the maximum update region range size maxURRS and the maximum subscription region range size maxSRRS are used as judging conditions to obtain overlapping information. But in our proposed algorithm, binary search is directly used to obtain overlapping information.

3 BSSIM ALGORITHM

This section will describe BSSIM algorithm in detail, and provide theoretical analysis of computation complexity. For simplicity, we only focus on how the algorithm works in one dimension.

3.1 Sufficient and Necessary condition for interval overlapping

The common way to judge the overlap relationship of two regions is to compare their upper and lower bounds. There are two kinds of regions, update region U and subscription region S. The range of region U is $[U_{LB}, U_{UB})$, and S is $[S_{LB}, S_{UB})$. As shown in Figure 1, there are total four cases when U overlaps with S. In fact, they can be further categorized into two cases, one is the lower bound of U locates in S, the other is the lower bound of S locates in U. According to this observation, we provide two

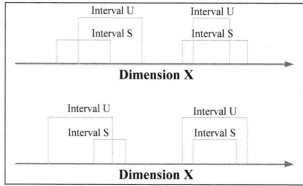

Figure 1: total overlapping cases of two regions

necessary and sufficient conditions to determine region overlapping.

$$U_{LB} \in [S_{LB}, S_{UB}) \tag{1}$$

OR

$$S_{LB} \in [U_{LB}, U_{UB}) \tag{2}$$

These necessary and sufficient conditions built the foundation of the BSSIM algorithm. Comparing to the sufficient and necessary conditions proposed in [6], the proposed necessary and sufficient conditions have more operations, but it can bring benefits to sorting.

3.2 Algorithm Description

Based on the sufficient and necessary conditions for calculating overlap information, the core work of BSSIM algorithm is to acquire the overlap information between all lower bounds of update (subscription) regions and subscription (update) regions for each dimension. That is to say, for each update region we should determine which lower bounds of subscription regions locate in this update region, satisfying condition (2). And for each subscription region we should determine which lower bounds of update regions locate in this subscription region, satisfying condition (1).

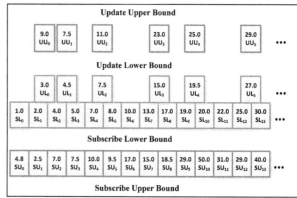

Figure 2: four lists, SL, SU, UL and UU

Firstly, all lower bounds of update regions and subscription regions are sorted independently in ascending order. So we can obtain 4 lists, as shown in Figure 2, they are SL, SU, UL, UU. SL stores all the lower bounds of subscription regions in ascending order, and SU list stores the corresponding upper bounds. Similarly, UL and UU are used to store the bounds of all update regions. Sorting lower bounds of regions can accelerate the efficiency of acquisition on overlapping information. Besides, two auxiliary lists are used to store corresponding update region id and subscription id respectively.

How to take advantage of the ordered list SL and UL to obtain the overlap information more efficiently is the key question. Here we introduce two parameters, namely comparison index upper limit (CIU) and comparison index lower limit (CIL). Every interval has a pair of CIU and CIL in each dimension. As shown in Figure 3, CIL and CIU of region $[UL_0, UU_0]$ are 2 and 5, similarly, CIL and CIU of interval $[SL_0, SU_0]$ are 0 and 1. For a update region U, CIL denotes the minimum index of the lower bounds that overlap with U, while CIU denotes the maximum index of the lower bounds that overlap with U. Therefore, region $[SL_2, SU_2]$, $[SL_3, SU_3]$, $[SL_4, SU_4]$ and $[SL_5, SU_5]$ overlap with $[UL_0, UU_0]$, while $[UL_0, UU_0]$ and $[UL_1, UU_1]$ overlap with $[SL_0, SU_0]$. When all CIL and CIU values for all update and subscription regions are obtained, the overlap information in one dimension can be obtained.

Hence, the second step is to calculate CIL and CIU values for each update and subscription region for each dimension. In view of list SL and UL have been sorted, CIL value can be easily obtained by comparing values in SL with values in UL. When calculating CIU value for a region, if comparing the region's upper bound with values in SL or UL one by one, calculating CIU values for N regions will generate $O(N^2)$ computational complexity in the worst case. Therefore, we introduce the binary search method to find CIU values efficiently. Binary search method can help locating CIU value quickly, eliminating unnecessary comparison. Considering that the CIL value for a region has been determined, so the searching range for binary search is [CIL, N]. Then the computational complexity of calculating a CIU value is $O(logN)$ in the worst case.

The last step of our proposed algorithm is to assign the value of bit arrays. Each update and subscription region corresponds to a bit array, all values are initialized as 0, used to store the overlap information. In the last step, CIL and CIU values have been determined, so the values in bit arrays can be assigned as 1 based on CIL and CIU values.

In summary, the procedure of BSSIM algorithm can be summarized as three phases. As shown in Figure 4, the first phase is sorting lower bounds of all update and subscription regions independently (step 3-4). The second phase is to calculate CIL and CIU values for update and subscription regions (step 5-8). Last phase is the assignment of bit arrays to generate overlap information based on CIL and CIU values (step 9).

To analyze the computation complexity, for simplicity, we suppose there are N update regions and N subscription regions. Sorting N update regions and N subscription regions with quick sort method requires about $O(2NlogN)$. While in the original

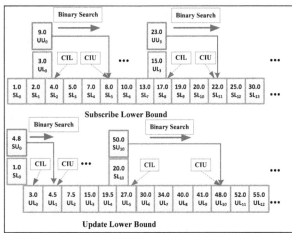

Figure 3: calculate CIU values with binary search method

sort-based algorithm, sorting the bounds requires about $O(4Nlog(4N))$. Calculating CIL values for N update regions and N subscription regions requires $O(N)$. While calculating CIU values using binary search requires $O(NlogN)$. Generating overlap information will be quadratic in the worst case when the length of every [CIL,CIU] interval is proportional to N. Finally, the total computation complexity will be quadratic in the worst case.

```
BSSIM(Update, Subscribe, N){
    // store CIU and CIL values for update regions
    1 UpdateCIL[N]={0}, UpdateCIU[N]={0};
    // store CIU and CIL values for subscription regions
    2 SubscribeCIL[N]={0}, SubscribeCIU[N]={0};
    //sorting lower bounds of update regions
    3 {UL, UU} = sort(Update);
    //sorting lower bounds of subscription regions
    4 {SL, SU} = sort(Subscribe);
    // calculating CIL values for all update regions
    5 UpdateCIL = ComputeCIL(UL , SL);
    // calculating CIL values for all subscription regions
    6 SubscribeCIL = ComputeCIL(SL , UL);
    // calculate the CIU value for each update region
    7 UpdateCIU = ComputeCIU(UU, SL, UpdateCIL);
    // calculate the CIU value for each subscription region
    8 SubscribeCIU=ComputeCIU(SU,UL,SubscribeCIL);
    9 AssignmentofBitArrays();
}
```

Figure 4: Procedure of BSSIM algorithm

4 EXPERIMENT RESULTS

In this section, several experiments are constructed to compare our proposed algorithm with the sort-based proposed in [4]. Gary Tan et al introduced the concept of overlap rate to verify algorithm efficiency, which represents the ratio of total update and subscription regions to the routing space. Therefore overlap rate is also used as an experimental parameter. At this time, overlap rate is the ratio of the total length of update and subscription regions to the length of interest space. In the below formula, I is the region length, L stands for the length of the interest space. The length of all regions is same and fixed, but the lower bounds of all regions are distributed in the interest space uniformly. When the overlap rate and number of regions are determined, the length of interest space can be determined.

$$overlap\ rate = \frac{\sum_{i=1}^{N} l_i}{L}$$

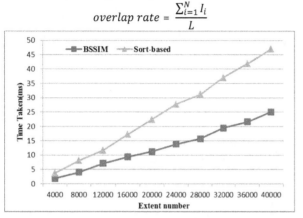

(a): overlap rate is 0.01

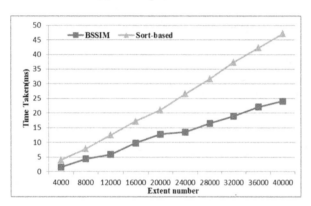

(b): overlap rate is 1

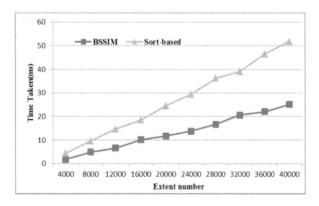

(c): overlap rate is 100

Figure 5: performance comparison

Different overlap rates are utilized to construct more comprehensive experiments, in order to fully verify the efficiency of the algorithm. There are 3 overlap rates, namely 0.01, 1 and 100, represent low overlap rate, medium overlap rate and high overlap rate respectively. The number of update and subscription regions extends from 4000 to 40000 in incremental steps of 4000. In each experiment, the experiment program uses original sort-based proposed in [4] and the BSSIM algorithm to calculate the overlap information between update and subscription regions using same data set independently. Then modify the data set and repeat the program for 100 iterations and calculates the average performance for the 100 iterations. As shown in Figure 5, our proposed algorithm is not affected by the overlap rate. In fact, according to analysis in previous section, the time complexity is not affected by the overlap rate. In different overlap rates, our algorithm always performs much better than original sort-based algorithm when the number of update and subscription regions changes from 4000 to 40000, and about 64%-159% performance improvement can be achieved at different overlap rates. There are two main reasons why our proposed algorithm can take such a big superiority. One reason is that the length of bounds list is 4*N in original sort-based algorithm, in the BSSIM algorithm, though there are two list SL and UL to sort, the length of each list is N, so our proposed algorithm have advantages in sorting, especially when the sorting occupies a large proportion of computational overhead in practice. The other reason is that when generating overlap information, the original sort-based algorithm introduces a large number of bit operations. However, the length of the bit array is N and large proportion of bit operations are unnecessary.

5 CONCLUSION AND FUTURE WORK

In this paper, we proposed a binary search enhanced sort-based interest matching algorithm (BSSIM). There are two major improvement compared to sort-based algorithm. One is shortening the length of bounds list to be sorted. The other improvement is eliminating a portion of unnecessary bit operations. Experimental results show that BSSIM algorithm outperforms the sort-based algorithm at different overlap rates. Next, more experiments should be done to compare BSSIM with other interest matching algorithms.

REFERENCES

[1] Daniel J. Van Hook and James O. Calvin, "Data distribution management in RTI 1.3". In Proceedings of the Simulation Interoperability Workshop, Spring 1998.
[2] Gary Tan, Rassul Ayani, YuSong Zhang and Farshad Moradi, "Grid-based Data Management in Distributed Simulation". Proceedings of 33rd Annual Simulation Symposium, Washington, U.S.A., April 2000.
[3] G. Tan, Y. Zhang and R. Ayani, "A Hybrid Approach to Data Distribution Management". Proceedings of the 4th IEEE International Workshop on Distributed Simulation and Real-Time Applications, Aug. 2000, pp. 55-61.
[4] Yu Jun, Come Raczy and Gary Tan, "Evaluation of Sort-based Matching Algorithm for the DDM". Proceedings of the 16th Workshop on Parallel and Distributed Simulation, Washington, USA, May 2002.
[5] Raczy C, Tan G and Yu J, "A Sort-Based DDM Matching Algorithm for HLA". ACM Transactions on Modeling and Computer Simulation, 2005, 15(1):14-38.
[6] Ke Pan, Stephen John Turner, Wentong Cai and Zengxiang Li, "An Efficient Sort-Based DDM Matching Algorithm for HLA Applications with a Large Spatial Environment". 21st International Workshop on Principles of Advanced and Distributed Simulation (PADS'07). San Diego, California, USA, 2007.

Evaluation of Conflict Resolution Methods for Agent-Based Simulations on the GPU

Mingyu Yang
TUMCREATE Ltd and
Nanyang Technological University, Singapore
yangmy@ntu.edu.sg

Philipp Andelfinger
TUMCREATE Ltd and
Nanyang Technological University, Singapore
pandelfinger@ntu.edu.sg

Wentong Cai
Nanyang Technological University, Singapore
aswtcai@ntu.edu.sg

Alois Knoll
Technische Universität München, Germany
knoll@in.tum.de

ABSTRACT

Graphics processing units (GPUs) have been shown to be well-suited to accelerate agent-based simulations. A fundamental challenge in agent-based simulations is the resolution of conflicts arising when agents compete for simulated resources, which may introduce substantial overhead. A variety of conflict resolution methods on the GPU have been proposed in the literature. In this paper, we systematize and compare these methods and propose two simple new variants. We present performance measurements on the example of the well-known segregation model. We show that the choice of conflict resolution method can substantially affect the simulation performance. Further, although methods in which agents actively indicate their interest in a resource require the use of costly atomic operations, these methods generally outperform the alternatives.

ACM Reference Format:
Mingyu Yang, Philipp Andelfinger, Wentong Cai, and Alois Knoll. 2018. Evaluation of Conflict Resolution Methods for Agent-Based Simulations on the GPU. In *Proceedings of SIGSIM-PADS '18: SIGSIM Principles of Advanced Discrete Simulation CD-ROM (SIGSIM-PADS '18)*. ACM, New York, NY, USA, 4 pages. https://doi.org/10.1145/3200921.3200940

1 INTRODUCTION

Agent-based simulation is widely applied to evaluate systems in domains such as traffic engineering and biology. In contrast to macroscopic simulations, agent-based simulation considers the interactions between the participating entities in detail, incurring substantial computational load. Since most agent-based simulations exhibit a certain degree of locality w.r.t. the simulation space and involve state updates for all agents at the same logical time, graphics processing units (GPUs) have proven to be well-suited for parallelization of agent-based simulations.

If at a given point in logical time, all agent states are updated concurrently, multiple agents may request the same resource, e.g.,

a location in the simulation space. If the simulation model does not specify how such conflicts are to be resolved, a generic method is required. We suggest that to generate meaningful simulation results, such a method should exhibit three properties: exactly one agent should acquire the resource, the outcome should be deterministic, and no bias should be introduced.

Sequential simulators perform agent state updates one after the other. If considering the actions taken by each agent's predecessors, conflicts are avoided entirely. While some models specify such a one-by-one update of agents (e.g., [11]), the opportunities for parallel processing are severely limited [6]. In the GPU context, conflict resolution is complicated by the indeterminism in the progress of the processing elements. The key challenge is to produce deterministic and unbiased results while still achieving high performance.

In this paper, we make the following contributions: **1.** We systematize the GPU-based conflict resolution approaches from the literature and discuss how bias can be avoided. **2.** We propose two new conflict resolution variants. **3.** We present a performance evaluation of the existing and proposed conflict resolution approaches[1].

2 FUNDAMENTALS

In agent-based simulation, the agent state is represented by a set of variables associated with each agent. In the following, we assume that the simulation proceeds in *cycles*. During each cycle, all agents update their states, accessing only the previous state of other agents.

We define a **conflict** as a situation in which an agent requests a resource that has already been requested by another agent at the same logical time. An example is given by the Sugarscape model [1], in which agents compete for pieces of sugar. In the case of discrete spatial simulations, multiple agents may request the same unoccupied cell on a grid, yet only one of the agents (the "winner") can occupy that cell. The goal of a conflict resolution method is to determine exactly one winner for each conflict. Roughly, conflict resolution involves two steps: first, each agent indicates its interest in a resource. Second, a tie-breaking mechanism determines the winner. All remaining agents then select another resource. A simulation is **deterministic** iff the same result is obtained from repeated simulation runs using the same pseudo-random number generator seed [8]. Determinism is considered important for analyzing simulation results and for debugging [3].

Permission to make digital or hard copies of all or part of this work for personal or classroom use is granted without fee provided that copies are not made or distributed for profit or commercial advantage and that copies bear this notice and the full citation on the first page. Copyrights for components of this work owned by others than the author(s) must be honored. Abstracting with credit is permitted. To copy otherwise, or republish, to post on servers or to redistribute to lists, requires prior specific permission and/or a fee. Request permissions from permissions@acm.org.

SIGSIM-PADS '18 , May 23–25, 2018, Rome, Italy

© 2018 Copyright held by the owner/author(s). Publication rights licensed to the Association for Computing Machinery.
ACM ISBN 978-1-4503-5092-1/18/05...$15.00
https://doi.org/10.1145/3200921.3200940

---

[1]https://github.com/GPUCR

A model may specify rules for breaking ties. However, we consider the case where the model does not specify a tie-breaking policy. Thus, we postulate that all agents interested in the same resource should have the same probability of acquiring the resource, i.e., given n conflicts with m involved agents on average, the expectation for the number of conflicts won should be n/m for each agent. This requirement implies that the tie-breaking mechanism should not systematically favor certain agents or states, which we refer to as **bias**. As an example, a biased tie-breaking mechanism in a traffic simulation may favor vehicles entering a road from a certain direction, which could introduce behaviors not specified in the model. The required considerations are similar to the handling of simultaneous events in discrete-event simulations [8].

To illustrate the principles of conflict resolution on a simple example, we consider the **segregation model** by Schelling [11], in which agents compete for locations in a two-dimensional cellular simulation space. However, the considered conflict resolution methods are also applicable to more complex models, e.g., when agents move on a graph or compete for resources other than locations.

In the segregation model, agents are assigned one of two types. The "happiness" of each agent is calculated based on the number of agents of the same type in the eight adjacent cells. In each simulation cycle, each unhappy (*moveable*) agent moves to a random position in a configurable neighborhood. Conflicts occur whenever multiple agents attempt to move to the same position. We consider cells containing moveable agents as unoccupied. Thus, there are at least as many unoccupied cells as moveable agents.

3 CONFLICT RESOLUTION METHODS

A simple way of resolving conflicts is used in the MatSim traffic simulator [12]: agents attempt to obtain a resource by atomically writing to a variable associated with each resource. The earliest agent successfully obtains the resource, whereas the other agents fail. The atomic write operation ensures that exactly one agent obtains the resource. However, determinism is not among the design goals of MatSim [5]. Although the method identifies a winner for each conflict, if no additional action is taken, the results depend on the execution order among the processing elements. In the following, we only consider deterministic approaches.

We propose a classification of the existing approaches into two categories, *push* and *pull*, which are differentiated by the manner in which potential assignments between agents and resources are written to memory. In push approaches, agents actively try to obtain the resources by writing to a variable associated with the desired resource. Generally, push approaches require the use of atomic operations to control concurrent accesses to the resources. In pull approaches, possible assignments are stored locally by the active entities. For instance, if agents take the active part, each agent stores the determined assignment in a per-agent variable. Thus, no atomic operations are required. Subsequently, scanning is performed by the resources to determine the interested agents.

We further differentiate among tie-breaking methods: with *incremental tie-breaking*, predefined priorities are applied as the agents register their interest, so that a winner has been identified once the last agent has registered. With *postponed tie-breaking*, the interested agents are explicitly stored in a list. Subsequently, the list is sorted and a pseudo-random number is drawn to determine the winner.

Algorithm 1 Iterative Push

```
1: while A ≠ ∅ do
2:    for each a ∈ A in parallel do
3:       a.r ← SelectResource(R)
4:       AtomicMax(registry[a.r], a.priority)
5:    Synchronize()
6:    for each r ∈ R in parallel do:
7:       priority ← registry[r]
8:       if priority ≠ nil then
9:          a ← GetAgent(priority); Assign(a, r)
10:         A ← A \ {a}; R ← R \ {a.r}
11:   Synchronize()
```

For brevity, we describe all methods using incremental tie-breaking, however, our performance evaluation covers both approaches.

3.1 Push

In push approaches, agents actively indicate their interest in a resource by writing to a variable associated with the resource.

Iterative Push: Lysenko et al. [2] proposed a conflict resolution method based on atomic operations. In the first stage, each agent attempts to atomically write a unique priority to a per-resource variable. The assignment of suitable priorities will be discussed in Section 4. An atomic maximum operation ensures that the final result holds the value written by the agent with the highest priority. After performing a global synchronization to guarantee that all results of the first stage have been written to memory, in the second stage, each resource checks whether it has been selected by an agent. If that is the case, the agent is assigned the resource. The two stages are repeated for a number of *iterations* until all agents have acquired a resource. Iteration here is defined as a series of kernel calls that complete the assign and acquire stages. Pseudo-code is provided in Alg. 1 where A is the set of agents intending to obtain a resource, and R is the set of resources.

Non-Iterative Push: We propose a variant of Alg. 1 that requires only one iteration per simulation cycle: each agent attempts to store its priority in a per-resource variable using an atomic maximum operation. In contrast to Alg. 1, each agent considers the previously stored priority returned by the atomic operation to determine whether its priority is the current maximum. If another agent already registered a higher priority, the current agent immediately attempts to obtain another resource. Otherwise, if the agent has displaced a previously registered agent, the current GPU thread takes control of the displaced agent and repeats the procedure until it has registered the highest priority for a resource. Since displaced agents are moved immediately, a simulation cycle concludes in one iteration. With non-iterative push, the overall number of conflicts is larger than with iterative push, where agents that have already obtained a resource do not take part in subsequent iterations. However, due to a reduction in memory accesses and synchronization points, our approach still outperforms iterative push (cf. Section 5).

3.2 Pull

In pull approaches, write accesses by agents and resource are limited to local variables. Thus, atomic operations are avoided. In an early work on GPUs, a pull approach was proposed by Perumalla et al. [6]: first each resource selects a random neighboring agent and stores its identifier locally. Each agent then scans for resources that have selected the respective agent. If the number of resources is

Algorithm 2 Iterative Pull

```
1: while A ≠ ∅ do
2:    for each a ∈ A in parallel do
3:        a.targetResource ← SelectResource(R)
4:    Synchronize()
5:    for each r ∈ R in parallel do
6:        A_r ← ∅
7:        for each a in the neighborhood of r do
8:            if a.targetResource = r then
9:                A_r ← A_r ∪ {a}
10:       if |A_r| ≥ 1 then
11:           a_r ← MaxPriority(A_r); Assign(a_r, r)
12:           A ← A \ {a_r}; R ← R \ {r}
13:   Synchronize()
```

exactly one, there is no conflict and the agent can obtain the target resource. Otherwise, the resource is not obtained by any agent. Since this approach does not resolve conflicts competing for the same resource, it is not included in our evaluation.

An iterative pull approach is used in FLAME GPU [7]. First, each agent selects a resource and stores a resource identifier in a per-agent variable. Then, each resource scans for interested agents. The winner of a conflict is determined based on the agents' priorities. This process is repeated until all agents have obtained resources. The approach avoids atomic operations. However, scanning for interested agents incurs substantial overhead if a large neighborhood is considered. The iterative pull approach is shown in Alg. 2.

3.3 Sampling and Permutation

We propose a simple conflict resolution approach targeting models where agents compete for resources selected uniformly at random from a global set. With unrestricted agent movement, Schelling's segregation model is an instance of this model class. The approach is based on the observation made previously by Perumalla et al. [6] that the desired result of a simulation cycle is a random injective mapping between agents and resources. We directly determine such a mapping by a two-step approach. First, a random sample is drawn from the resources. Second, a random permutation of the agents is computed to determine the mapping to the resources (cf. Fig. 1). Pseudo-code is provided in Alg. 3. For random sampling and permutation, we rely on parallel algorithms by Sanders et al. [9, 10]. For random sampling, we ported existing CPU code[2], whereas random permutation was implemented from scratch. For Schelling's segregation model with limited neighborhoods, the approach is not applicable: since agents compete for overlapping sets of resources, the probability of selecting a given resource varies among agents.

4 AVOIDING BIAS

Clearly, the requirement of unbiased conflict resolution (cf. Sec. 2) is satisfied by *postponed* tie-breaking: once the set of interested agents has been identified, the agents are sorted and a random number is drawn to select the winner of the conflict. However, with *incremental* tie-breaking, care must be taken not to introduce undesired bias into the simulation. We illustrate the issue using Schelling's segregation model: it may seem natural to use the agents' current position as their priorities. However, if the neighborhood considered for movement is limited, this choice of priorities introduces a bias into the movement directions of agents. Consider the situation

[2]https://github.com/sebalamm/DistributedSampling

Algorithm 3 Sampling and Permutation

```
1: R_S ← RandomSample(R, |A|)
2: A_P ← RandomPermute(A)
3: Synchronize()
4: for each a_i ∈ A_P in parallel do
5:    Assign(a_i, R_S[i])
```

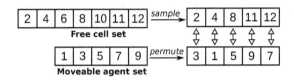

Figure 1: Sampling and Permutation.

0	1	2	3	4		0	1	2	3	4
5	6	7	8	9		5	6	7	8	9
10	11	12	13	14		10	11	12	13	14
15	16	17	18	19		15	16	17	18	19
20	21	22	23	24		20	21	22	23	24

Figure 2: Illustration of bias caused by fixed priorities.

in Figure 2, where agent priorities are chosen by their current positions. Agents may move to locations in a 3×3 neighborhood. We show two possible target positions chosen by the agent at position 12. The gray rectangles denote the source position of agents that may compete for the same position. If the agent intends to move to position 6, any competing agent will have a lower priority, i.e., the agent will always win the conflict and be able to move. In contrast, if the agent intends to move to position 18, any competing agent will have a higher priority, i.e., the agent will lose the conflict and will have to select a new target position. Since this type of asymmetry affects the other reachable target positions as well, the general tendency for agents is to move to the top left of the simulation space. The bias is more pronounced at small neighborhood sizes.

Independence between winning probabilities and agent states can be achieved by choosing random priorities for each simulation cycle. We extended the push approach by generating a random permutation and assigning the results as the agents' priorities, which is similar to shuffling the agents' movement order in sequential agent-based simulations. It is necessary to generate a new permutation at the beginning of each cycle to avoid introducing a randomized but consistent bias pattern. When permuting the priorities at each cycle, the relative priorities of the competing agents are chosen without favoring certain agents or agent states systematically. Thus, as with postponed tie-breaking, the results are unbiased.

5 PERFORMANCE EVALUATION

We measured the performance of the different conflict resolution approaches using the segregation model on a system equipped with a NVIDIA Tesla K20Xm with CUDA 7.5. 99% confidence intervals are plotted but are too small to be visible.

Figure 3 compares the execution times of simulations using iterative push, non-iterative push and sampling and permutation when agents move without spatial restrictions. Since in the pull approach, resources scan the entire grid for interested agents, it is about 2000 times slower than the other approaches and thus excluded from the

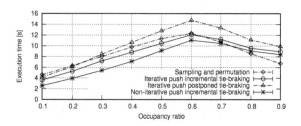

Figure 3: Simulation runtime with global movement.

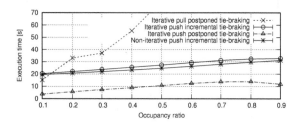

Figure 4: Simulation runtime with limited neighborhood.

figure. As the non-iterative approaches depend on incremental tie-breaking, combinations with postponed tie-breaking are excluded as well. We varied the occupancy ratio, i.e., the ratio of populated cells, from 0.1 to 0.9. The simulation space was a grid of about 16 million (4096 × 4096) cells. The agents' happiness threshold was set to 5. The simulation was terminated after 100 simulation cycles. The results show a minor runtime reduction of non-iterative push over iterative push. The sampling and permutation approach performs worse under low occupancy ratios. However, for occupancy ratios above 0.7, sampling and permutation outperforms the push approaches. The reason is that at high occupancy ratios, with the push approaches, agents will perform many retries until an open cell is found and potential conflicts are won. Sampling and permutation avoids these situations by directly mapping agents to the open cell set. At a smaller grid size of 1024 × 1024 cells, the relative performance of the push approaches remained roughly the same. However, sampling and permutation was outperformed by a factor of about 2.9 to 5.2. Generally, the performance is affected by the number of moveable agents and conflicts. The largest number of conflicts was generated at an occupancy ratio of 0.6, coinciding with the longest observed execution times.

The performance of iterative push is affected by the number of iterations required to resolve all conflicts, which can be computed by iteratively determining the number n of agents that lose a conflict according to the birthday paradox [4]: $n = |A| - |C| + |C|(1 - \frac{1}{|C|})^{|A|}$, where $|A|$ is the number of agents and $|C|$ is the number of cells.

Figure 4 shows the execution times of the various approaches when the agent movement is limited to a 3 × 3 neighborhood on a grid of 4096 × 4096 cells. For incremental tie-breaking, the approach described in Section 4 to avoid bias is used. As discussed in Section 3.3, sampling and permutation cannot be apply to restricted neighborhoods. In contrast to the unrestricted movement, the incremental tie-breaking approaches require the computation of random permutations in order to avoid bias. If an agent cannot find an unoccupied cell, its neighborhood is enlarged in steps of 3

cells after 10 trials each. We observed neighborhoods up to 63 × 63 cells at occupancy ratio 0.9. Since in the pull approach, the cells scan for interested agents, they have to consider the largest neighborhood used by any agent in the current iteration. Accordingly, iterative pull was substantially slower than the push approaches, requiring up to 1127 seconds at an occupancy ratio of 0.9. Given these results, we did not implement iterative pull with incremental tie-breaking. Iterative and Non-iterative push with incremental tie-breaking requires the computation of a random permutation for each simulation cycle. Since postponed tie-breaking does not require this step, it consistently achieved the lowest execution times.

6   CONCLUSIONS AND OUTLOOK

We systematized and evaluated conflict resolution approaches for agent-based simulation on GPUs from the literature and proposed two new variants. Our measurements indicate that if agents compete for resources globally without restriction to a certain neighborhood, a non-iterative approach achieves best performance. If the numbers of agents and conflicts are both large, a direct computation of a random mapping between agents and resources performed the best. If agents consider resources within a limited neighborhood, a postponed tie-breaking between competing agents substantially outperformed the alternatives. We further discussed ways to avoid bias in the conflict resolution. Our current observations were made only based on the classic segregation model, which is simple but often used to illustrate the power of agent-based modeling. Future work could extend our observations to more practical applications such as traffic simulation.

7   ACKNOWLEDGMENTS

This work was financially supported by the Singapore National Research Foundation under its Campus for Research Excellence And Technological Enterprise (CREATE) programme.

REFERENCES

[1] Joshua M Epstein and Robert Axtell. 1996. *Growing Artificial Societies: Social Science from the Bottom up.* Brookings Institution Press.
[2] Mikola Lysenko and Roshan M. D'Souza. 2008. A Framework for Megascale Agent Based Model Simulations on Graphics Processing Units. *Journal of Artificial Societies and Social Simulation* 11, 4 (2008), 10.
[3] Thom McLean and Richard Fujimoto. 2000. Repeatability in Real-Time Distributed Simulation Executions. In *Proceedings of the Workshop on Parallel and Distributed simulation.* IEEE, 23–32.
[4] Michael Mitzenmacher and Eli Upfal. 2005. *Probability and Computing: Randomized Algorithms and Probabilistic Analysis.* Cambridge University Press.
[5] Kai Nagel, Dominik Grether, Ulrike Beuck, Yu Chen, Marcel Rieser, and Kay W Axhausen. 2008. Multi-Agent Transport Simulations and Economic Evaluation. *Jahrbücher für Nationalökonomie und Statistik* 228, 2-3 (2008), 173–194.
[6] Kalyan S Perumalla and Brandon G Aaby. 2008. Data Parallel Execution Challenges and Runtime Performance of Agent Simulations on GPUs. In *Proceedings of the Spring Simulation Multiconference.* SCS, 116–123.
[7] Paul Richmond. 2014. Resolving Conflicts Between Multiple Competing Agents in Parallel Simulations. In *European Conf. on Parallel Processing.* Springer, 383–394.
[8] Robert Rönngren and Michael Liljenstam. 1999. On Event Ordering in Parallel Discrete Event Simulation. In *Proceedings of the Workshop on Parallel and Distributed Simulation.* IEEE, 38–45.
[9] Peter Sanders. 1998. Random Permutations on Distributed, External and Hierarchical Memory. *Inform. Process. Lett.* 67, 6 (1998), 305–309.
[10] Peter Sanders, Sebastian Lamm, Lorenz Hübschle-Schneider, Emanuel Schrade, and Carsten Dachsbacher. 2018. Efficient Parallel Random Sampling – Vectorized, Cache-Efficient, and Online. *ACM Trans. Math. Softw.* 44, 3 (2018), 29:1–29:14.
[11] Thomas C Schelling. 1971. Dynamic Models of Segregation. *Journal of Mathematical Sociology* 1, 2 (1971), 143–186.
[12] David Strippgen and Kai Nagel. 2009. Using Common Graphics Hardware for Multi-Agent Traffic Simulation with CUDA. In *Proceedings of the 2nd International Conference on Simulation Tools and Techniques.* ICST, 62.

Hybrid Simulation of Dynamic Reaction Networks in Multi-Level Models

Tobias Helms
University of Rostock
Rostock, Germany
tobias.helms@uni-rostock.de

Pia Wilsdorf
University of Rostock
Rostock, Germany
pia.wilsdorf@uni-rostock.de

Adelinde M. Uhrmacher
University of Rostock
Rostock, Germany
adelinde.uhrmacher@uni-rostock.de

ABSTRACT

Methods combining deterministic and stochastic concepts present an efficient alternative to a purely stochastic treatment of biochemical models. Traditionally, those methods split biochemical reaction networks into one set of slow reactions that is computed stochastically and one set of fast reactions that is computed deterministically. Applying those methods to multi-level models with dynamic nestings requires coping with dynamic reaction networks changing over time. In addition, in case of large populations of nested entities, stochastic events can still decrease the runtime performance significantly, as reactions of dynamically nested entities are inherently stochastic. In this paper, we apply a hybrid simulation algorithm combining deterministic and stochastic concepts to multi-level models including an approximation control. Further, we present an extension of this simulation algorithm applying an additional approximation by executing multiple independent stochastic events simultaneously in one simulation step. The algorithm has been implemented in the rule-based multi-level modeling language ML-Rules. Its impact on speed and accuracy is evaluated based on simulations performed with a model of Dictyostelium discoideum amoebas.

CCS CONCEPTS

• **Computing methodologies** → **Modeling and simulation**; *Multiscale systems*; • **Applied computing** → **Computational biology**;

KEYWORDS

Multi-level Modeling, Biochemical Reaction Networks, Hybrid Simulation

ACM Reference Format:
Tobias Helms, Pia Wilsdorf, and Adelinde M. Uhrmacher. 2018. Hybrid Simulation of Dynamic Reaction Networks in Multi-Level Models. In *SIGSIM-PADS '18 : SIGSIM-PADS '18: SIGSIM Principles of Advanced Discrete Simulation CD-ROM, May 23–25, 2018, Rome, Italy*. ACM, New York, NY, USA, 12 pages. https://doi.org/10.1145/3200921.3200926

Permission to make digital or hard copies of all or part of this work for personal or classroom use is granted without fee provided that copies are not made or distributed for profit or commercial advantage and that copies bear this notice and the full citation on the first page. Copyrights for components of this work owned by others than the author(s) must be honored. Abstracting with credit is permitted. To copy otherwise, or republish, to post on servers or to redistribute to lists, requires prior specific permission and/or a fee. Request permissions from permissions@acm.org.
SIGSIM-PADS '18 , May 23–25, 2018, Rome, Italy
© 2018 Copyright held by the owner/author(s). Publication rights licensed to the Association for Computing Machinery.
ACM ISBN 978-1-4503-5092-1/18/05...$15.00
https://doi.org/10.1145/3200921.3200926

1 INTRODUCTION

Proteins, vesicles, individual cells, and cell populations denote different levels of an organizational hierarchy. The dynamics at one level influence the dynamics at other levels — from the lower levels to the upper levels (upward causation) and from the upper levels to the lower levels (downward causation) [4]. To understand central cellular processes such as cell proliferation and differentiation, the careful orchestration of intra- and intercellular dynamics needs to be explored. Therefore, modeling and simulation tools that a) support a compact description of such models, b) are firmly rooted in a sound semantics, and c) provide an efficient execution [16] are needed. The latter implies serious challenges, as operating at multiple organization levels is often accompanied by multi-scale dynamics.

Many cell biological systems under study are characterized by a combination of reactions acting at different time scales. Simulating those models stochastically with methods based on the stochastic simulation algorithm [14] is often prohibitively slow, since each reaction firing is executed individually and therefore, most of the computation time is spent to execute many *fast* reactions. Nevertheless, simulating those models deterministically by integration methods is also often not suitable, since they ignore important stochasticity resulting from small numbers of reactants. Methods combining deterministic and stochastic algorithms are a suitable approach to solve this conflict. These *hybrid* methods partition the set of reactions typically based on their time scales into *slow* and *fast* reactions. Instead of executing the entire model stochastically or deterministically, these methods execute the fast reactions by deterministic algorithms and only the slow reactions by stochastic algorithms. Consequently, they form piecewise deterministic Markov processes [9], i.e., between stochastically scheduled events the system progresses by numerical integration deterministically.

Altogether, a plethora of hybrid approaches for biochemical reaction networks have been developed within the last two decades [24]. The application of these methods to multi-level models with static structures and a fixed reaction set is rather straightforward. However, many multi-level models are characterized by dynamic nesting, e.g., due to the fusion and fission of vesicles or the proliferation of cells. The reaction network of such models changes over time, i.e., reactions are removed and added to the network during a simulation. This has to be considered in the design of the modeling language and the simulation algorithms.

Various modeling languages exist to implement biochemical reaction networks, e.g., SBML [17], BioNetGen [2], Kappa [8], and ML-Rules [21], each with its own focus on features and usability. SBML has been developed as an exchange format of biochemical reaction networks between concrete modeling languages. Graphical user interfaces have moved it to an applicable modeling language. BioNetGen and Kappa focus on models with complex bounding structures between entities. In contrast, the design of ML-Rules has been driven to support dynamically nested biochemical reaction networks. Although its pure stochastic simulation algorithm is able to simulate dynamic reaction networks, it is not suitable for many complex models, because different time scales are a central property of such models, e.g., intracellular reactions in a cell population model are typically much faster than intercellular reactions.

In [16], among other algorithms, we also sketched a first draft of a hybrid simulator for models with dynamic reaction sets identifying specific challenges of the endeavor. The usual strategy to partition reactions solely based on their propensities does not work, since reactions changing the reaction network cannot be calculated deterministically. Further, nested entities are treated as discrete objects uniquely characterized by their attributes and their content in ML-Rules. A treatment of these nested entities as concentrations in the deterministic regime does not appear to be a viable approach. Consequently, reactions updating these dynamically nested entities are natural candidates for stochastic events.

Besides, the nesting of cell biological models typically forms a rather flat yet broad tree structure. The performance of a hybrid simulator can be degraded by those models due to many stochastic events fragmenting the integration steps. This increases the interaction overhead of the stochastic simulator with the integration method and reduces the effectiveness of an adaptive step-size control of the integration method. However, these stochastic events typically do not immediately depend on each other, e.g., in case a mitochondrion is created in a cell, the creation of a mitochondrion in another cell is not affected directly. If these multiple independent stochastic reactions can be executed in one simulation step, assuming an acceptable loss of accuracy, the step size of the continuous, deterministic execution regime will be increased, the interaction overhead reduced, and the effectiveness of the adaptive step-size control of the integration method improved.

In the following, first we demonstrate how to apply a hybrid simulation algorithm to dynamically nested biochemical models with dynamic reaction sets including a rejection mechanism and an approximation control. Afterward, we present an extension of the present algorithm with an additional approximation mechanism that targets the independent stochastic reactions taking place at higher organizational levels. Therefore, we first introduce the theoretical background of biochemical reaction networks and multi-level models in Section 2 and Section 3. Afterward, we present the developed hybrid simulation algorithm in Section 4, to finally evaluate the methods based on a model of spatial aggregation processes of the Dictyostelium discoideum amoebas in Section 5.

2 BIOCHEMICAL REACTION NETWORKS

The state of a biochemical reaction network is represented by a vector $X = (x_1, x_2, \ldots, x_n) \in \mathbb{N}^n$, x_i denotes the amount of a specific species such as a protein. The dynamics of a model are defined by a set of reactions $R = \{R_1, R_2, \ldots, R_m\}$. A reaction R_i is described by a change vector $\mathbf{v}_i = (v_1, v_2, \ldots, v_n) \in \mathbb{Z}^n$ defining the changes of the state when firing R_i and a propensity function $a_i : \mathbb{N}^n \rightarrow \mathbb{R}^+$ defining the rate of a reaction. For example, a

---

Algorithm 1 Calculation of a stochastic simulation step with the *Direct Method* [14]).

t: current simulation time,
$X = (x_1, x_2, \ldots, x_n) \in \mathbb{N}^n$: the state vector.
$R = \{R_1, R_2, \ldots, R_m\}$: the set of reactions.
$\mathbf{v_i} \in \mathbb{Z}^n$: state change vector of reaction R_i.
$a_1(X) \ldots a_m(X)$: propensities of the reactions $R_1, \ldots R_m$.
$a_0(X)$: sum of all reaction propensities.

```
1   // Calculate propensity sum of all reactions
2   a₀(X) := ∑ᵢ₌₁ᵐ aᵢ(X)
3
4   // Select a reaction to be executed
5   x := U(0, a₀(X))
6   i := min{j|j ∈ {1...m} ∧ ∑ᵢ₌₁ʲ aᵢ(X) > x}
7
8   // Advance simulation time by sampling from an
9   // exponential distribution with rate λ = a₀(X)
10  t := t + Exp(a₀(X))
11
12  // Execute selected reaction
13  X := X + vᵢ
```

reaction network given the state vector $X = (A, B, C)$ could be described as follows:

$$
\begin{array}{llll}
R_1: & B \rightarrow A & \mathbf{v}_1 = (1, -1, 0) & a_1(X) = k_1 \cdot B \\
R_2: & C \rightarrow & \mathbf{v}_2 = (0, 0, -1) & a_2(X) = k_2 \cdot C \\
R_3: & A + C \rightarrow B & \mathbf{v}_3 = (-1, 1, -1) & a_3(X) = k_3 \cdot A \cdot C.
\end{array}
$$

Typically, biochemical reaction networks are simulated deterministically or stochastically. A deterministic simulation can be achieved by converting a reaction network to a set of ordinary differential equations (ODEs) and applying numerical integration methods to calculate the ODEs [20]. In this case, species populations are interpreted as continuous concentrations, i.e., $X \in (\mathbb{R}^+)^n$. For example, converting the exemplary reactions to ODEs would result in

$$
\begin{aligned}
\frac{dx_1}{dt} &= k_1 \cdot B - k_3 \cdot A \cdot C \\
\frac{dx_2}{dt} &= k_3 \cdot A \cdot C - k_1 \cdot B \\
\frac{dx_3}{dt} &= -k_2 \cdot C - k_3 \cdot A \cdot C.
\end{aligned}
$$

However, stochastic effects are important in case of small entity numbers. Therefore, simulating a biochemical reaction network stochastically can be required by interpreting it as a continuous-time Markov chain (CTMC) and applying a stochastic simulation algorithm (SSA) [14]. Following this interpretation, one state of a biochemical reaction network model corresponds to a well mixed solution encoded as a multiset of chemical species represented by X, i.e., all entities are treated in a "population-based" manner and reactions act on species amounts. Algorithm 1 describes the calculation of a simulation step with the *Direct Method* – a basic variant of the SSA. Initially, the sum $a_0(X)$ of all reaction propensities is calculated (line 2), which is needed to select a concrete reaction to be fired (lines 5-6) and to calculate the time advance of a simulation step (line 10). The probability $P(R_i)$ to select reaction R_i is its relation of its propensity to the propensity sum: $P(R_i) = \frac{a_i(X)}{a_0(X)}$. The time advance is calculated by sampling a value from the exponential distribution with rate $a_0(X)$. Finally, the state vector is updated by adding the change vector of the selected reaction to it (line 13).

Due to the individual calculation of each reaction firing, the stochastic simulation of a biochemical reaction network is often computationally costly and motivated the development of many variants and improvements, e.g., [6, 13, 22, 27]. To overcome the computational costs of a pure stochastic simulation, a common strategy is to split a set of reactions into two sets — one set is calculated deterministically and the other set is calculated stochastically. This strategy is especially efficient if a model contains reactions with propensities differing by several orders of magnitude, since a stochastic simulator would spend most of the runtime to execute firings of the "fast" reactions. For example, Haseltine and Rawlings present a simulator that initially partitions the set of reactions into *fast* and *slow* reactions (R^f and R^s) depending on heuristics, e.g., considering reactants, products, rate constants, and the initial species amounts [15]. Algorithm 2 describes the calculation of a simulation step with this hybrid simulator. Basically, the *Direct Method* is applied to the slow reactions, but the fast reactions are additionally integrated before a slow reaction is fired (line 14). Since the time advance as well as the selected slow reaction are not adapted after integrating the fast reactions, an error is induced by this simulator and it is therefore approximate. To reduce the induced error of the simulator, Haseltine and Rawlings propose a *probability of no slow reaction* to decrease the step size τ if necessary [15]. Generally speaking, an artificial slow reaction with no effect would be added to the reaction set with a manually chosen propensity thereby also increasing the computational effort of the simulation by additional simulation steps.

Further similar hybrid simulators for biochemical reaction networks exist. They typically differ in the used partition criteria. For example, species amounts are often considered while partitioning the reactions, i.e., a fast reaction should not change a species with a small amount that should be simulated stochastically [26]. Another approach is to separate reactions based on the meaning of species, as using only propensities and amounts do "not always provide a convenient description of the hybrid stochastic process" [7].

Another class of hybrid simulators for biochemical networks is also adapting the partition of slow and fast reactions during a simulation, since it is possible that fast reactions become slow over time and vice versa. The simulator presented in [19] dynamically splits species into discrete and continuous species depending on their amount, i.e., if the amount drops below a threshold t_{low}, a species is classified as discrete and if the amount exceeds a second higher threshold t_{high}, a species is classified as continuous. A reaction is only treated deterministically, if all reactant and product species are classified as continuous species. Two thresholds t_{low} and t_{high} are used to avoid rapid changes of species classifications. In [26], an additional approximation is added to the hybrid simulator by executing multiple stochastic reactions during one simulation step. A time leap value Δt is used to execute the integration step from t to $t + \Delta t$ with all fast reactions and the SSA is applied to the slow

---

Algorithm 2 Calculation of a hybrid simulation step with the simulator presented in [15].
t: current simulation time,
$R^s = \{R_1^s, \ldots R_{m_s}^s\}$: slow reaction set,
$R^f = \{R_1^f, \ldots R_{m_f}^f\}$: fast reaction set
$a_1^s(X) \ldots a_{m_s}^s(X)$: propensities of slow reactions,
$a_0^s(X)$: sum of all slow reaction propensities.
$\tilde{X}$: intermediate state after integrating the fast reactions and before executing a slow reaction.

```
1   // Calculate propensity sum of slow reactions
2   a₀ˢ(X) := Σᵢ₌₁ᵐˢ aᵢˢ(X)
3
4   // Select a slow reaction to be executed based on the slow
5   // reaction set Rˢ
6   x := U(0, a₀ˢ(X))
7   i := min{j|j ∈ {1...m} ∧ Σᵢ₌₁ʲ aᵢˢ(X) > x}
8
9   // Calculate a simulation time advance by sampling from an
10  // exponential distribution with rate λ = a₀ˢ(X)
11  τ := Exp(a₀ˢ(X))
12
13  // Integrate fast reactions until t+τ
14  X̃ := integrate(X, Rᶠ, t, t+τ)
15
16  // Advance simulation time
17  t := t + τ
18
19  // Execute selected slow reaction
20  X := X̃ + vᵢˢ
```

reactions repeatedly until the execution time of a slow reaction is greater than $t + \Delta t$.

Finally, some hybrid simulators do not integrate fast reactions directly [5, 11]. Instead, they assume that stationary distributions exist for all species involved in fast reactions that can either be computed analytically ([5]) or empirically ([11]). These distributions are used to update the propensities of slow reactions, which are simulated as usual using the SSA. Although this approach avoids integrating the fast reactions, it can only be applied if 1) fast reactions result in stationary distributions for all involved species of the fast reactions and 2) these distributions are reached fast, i.e., much faster than the next firing time of a slow reaction.

3 MULTI-LEVEL BIOCHEMICAL REACTION NETWORKS

Multi-level biochemical reaction networks describing dynamics of proteins, vesicles, cells and cell populations work on different organization levels. The dynamics of such networks are characterized by upward and downward causation, i.e., lower levels influence upper levels and vice versa — these are essential concepts for many cell-biological systems [23]. Further, these networks are characterized by a dynamic nesting of entities, e.g., caused by movements, cell division or elimination. Typically, entities that are able to contain other entities are distinguished from "atomic" entities that cannot contain other entities. In the following, the former are called *compartments*, the latter are called *leaves*. All entities contained by a compartment are called its *sub entities*. The compartment that

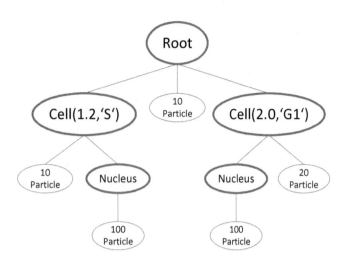

Figure 1: The state of an ML-Rules model forms a tree. Compartments are marked with bold lines.

contains sub entities is referred to as their *context*. Leaves are often treated in a "population-based" manner, i.e., identical leaves in the same context are merged and extended by an amount value representing the copy number of the leave representative. In contrast to leaves, compartments are typically treated individually, i.e., identical compartments are not merged and compartments do not have an amount value — basically, an agent metaphor is applied to describe compartments. Compartments and often also leaves can be equipped with attributes to describe complex states and behavior. The rule-based modeling language ML-Rules is used to describe multi-level biochemical reaction networks and supports the mentioned features, i.e., entities can be attributed and dynamically nested [21].

Altogether, a state of a multi-level biochemical reaction network model is a nested multiset and always forms a tree of entities. For example, Figure 1 shows a tree of an exemplary model state. The Root compartment is used as the top-level compartment. In this example, the Root compartment contains two compartments of species Cell with different attribute values and ten identical leaves of species Particle. The first attribute of a Cell species could represent its volume. The second attribute could represent the current phase of the Cell entity. Both Cell compartments contain one Nucleus compartment and a number of Particle leaves. Finally, both Nucleus compartments again contain Particle leaves.

The dynamics of multi-level reaction networks have to be defined by nested rule schemes consisting of reactant pattern, products and a kinetic reaction rate:

```
Reactant + ... -> Product + ... @ Rate
```

A reactant pattern describes an entity by its species type and its attributes; in case of compartments also by its sub entities. For example, the rule scheme

```
R1: Particle:p -> @ #p * k1
```

in ML-Rules syntax describes the elimination of a Particle entity with mass action kinetics, i.e., the elimination rate of Particle entities is proportional to their amount (#p). Nested reactants can be used to add context information to a rule scheme. For example, the rule scheme

```
R2: Cell(vol,'S')[Particle:p + s?]
    -> Cell(vol+norm(1,0.1),'S')[s?]
    @ #p * k1 / vol
```

in ML-Rules syntax also describes Particle elimination, but only considers Particle entities that are in Cell compartments in the phase 'S'. The volume of the Cell is represented by the variable vol, i.e., any volume is accepted and in addition, it is also used to influence the reaction rate. Further, the volume of the Cell compartment is increased by a sample of a Normal distribution with mean 1 and variance 0.1. In general, multi-level reaction networks shall allow the application of arithmetic and self-defined functions to calculate attribute values of products and even to calculate complex products, e.g., to filter a compartment or to split a compartment. The variable s? is a specific variable used in ML-Rules to represent all sub entities of a context without matched reactants. Therefore, only one Particle entity is removed from a matched Cell compartment when executing a reaction based on this rule scheme.

Multi-level models can be interpreted as CTMCs and therefore be simulated stochastically by the SSA [28]. During a simulation, the reaction set R of a multi-level model is calculated by matching the current state X of the system against all rule schemes of the model. For example, the rule scheme R1: Particle:p -> @ #p * k1 applied to the model state given in Figure 1, results in five reactions being instantiated, one in the Root compartment, two in both Cell compartments and two in both Nucleus compartments. In the case of ML-Rules, following its semantics [28], the execution of a reaction is processed by removing all matched reactants from the current state and adding all products to the current state. In case of leaves, this strategy can be realized simply by changing their amount values. Nevertheless, in case of compartments, more effort is needed by the simulator, as they have to be removed completely from the current state including their content and they have to be created again if they are part of the products.

The reaction set in multi-level models is typically not fixed, but it can change over time and has therefore to be maintained during a simulation. Firstly, reaction set changes can either be caused by structural changes induced by a reaction, i.e., compartments are removed or created. For example, in case the entity Cell(1.2,'S') shown in Figure 1 would be split into two Cell entities

```
Cell(1.2,'S')[5 Particle + Nucleus[50 Particle]],
```

the exemplary rule schema R1: Particle:p -> @ #p * k1 applied to the new model state would then result in seven concrete reactions. Secondly, numerical attributes of leaves can lead to reaction set changes, since the domain of numerical attributes is infinite ($\mathbb{R}$). Therefore, in case numerical attributes are used, it might not be possible to enumerate all instances of attribute values at the beginning of a simulation and thus it is not possible to create one species type for each instance of a leave.

Two important classes of rules and reactions can be distinguished in multi-level models: *basic* and *complex* rules and reactions. *Basic* rules only lead to *basic* reactions; these are not allowed to change, remove or create compartments, and they are not allowed to apply functions to calculate attribute values of leaves. For example, the rule R1 is a basic rule, since no compartments are influenced by executing a reaction based on this rule — only the amount of a `Particle` entity in a specific context has to be updated. Due to these restrictions, the set of basic reactions is closed under reaction execution, i.e., executing *basic* reactions does not cause the removal or addition of reactions to the reaction set, but only propensity updates. In contrast, *complex* rules lead to *complex* reactions; these can change, remove and add compartments, use *functions on solutions* to calculate products and *functions on attributes* to calculate attribute values of products.

In case a multi-level model only consists of *basic* rules, it has a fixed compartmental structure and it is possible to enumerate all attribute values of leaves. Therefore, the nested multiset structure of such a model can be flattened to a vector, its reaction set be calculated initially, and the standard SSA is applicable as described in Algorithm 1, resulting in significant speedups [16].

4 HYBRID SIMULATION OF MULTI-LEVEL MODELS

Distinguishing *basic* and *complex* rules and reactions is the starting point for developing a hybrid simulator for multi-level reaction networks with dynamic reaction sets. Based on Algorithm 2 and our initial draft of a hybrid simulator presented in [16], we developed a simulator applying concepts of hybrid simulators for reaction networks to multi-level models including an approximation control and a rejection mechanism. Algorithm 3 illustrates the execution of one simulation step of the developed simulator.

Initially, the propensity sum $a_0^c(X)$ of all complex reactions is calculated and used to calculate the execution time τ of the next complex reaction to occur (lines 2-4). Analogously to the probability of no slow reaction discussed by Haseltine and Rawlings in [15], we introduce an explicit probability $r \in [r_{min}, 1]$ to fire one complex reaction to reduce potential approximation errors. The r-quantile $Q(r)$ of $Exp(a_0^c(X))$ is calculated and used as a threshold execution time for the next complex reaction (line 6). If an execution time $\tau \geq Q(r)$ is sampled, the simulator advances to $t + Q(r)$ (line 31), integrates the basic reactions until $t + Q(r)$ (line 8) and does not execute any complex reaction (line 28). For example, assuming $r = 0.1$, the probability to sample an execution time $\tau < Q(r)$ is 10%, i.e., with a probability of 90%, no complex reaction is executed. If an execution time $\tau < Q(r)$ is sampled, the simulator advances to $t + \tau$ (line 31), integrates the basic reactions until $t + \tau$ (line 8), and executes one complex reaction (lines 23-26). The `execute` method (line 26) updates the reaction sets after firing the complex reactions.

The relative propensity change Δ of the system caused by the integration step (line 10) is used in combination with the variables ϵ_{min}, ϵ_{max}, and ϵ_{reject} ($\epsilon_{min} < \epsilon_{max} < \epsilon_{reject}$) to decide whether a) to reject the current step and set r to a minimum value r_{min} if $\Delta > \epsilon_{reject}$ (lines 11-13), b) to decrease r if $\Delta > \epsilon_{max}$ (lines 16-17), i.e., getting more accurate, or c) to increase r if $\Delta < \epsilon_{min}$ (lines 18-19), i.e., getting less accurate. Consequently, Δ is used

---

Algorithm 3 The execution of one simulation step of a hybrid simulator for dynamic reaction networks.

$r \in [r_{min}, 1]$: probability to fire one complex reaction,
R^b: set of basic reactions,
R^c set of complex reactions,
$a_1^c, \ldots, a_{|R^c|}^c$: propensities of complex reactions,
X: current state of the system,
$\tilde{X}$: intermediate state after integrating the basic reactions and before executing a complex reaction.

```
1    // Calculate propensity sum of all complex reactions
2    a₀ᶜ(X) := ∑ᵢ₌₁^|Rᶜ| aᵢᶜ(X)
3    // Calculate execution time of next complex reaction
4    τ := Exp(a₀ᶜ(X))
5    // Compute time threshold for the next complex reaction
6    Q(r) := -ln(1-r) / a₀ᶜ(X)
7    // Integrate basic reactions until t + min (τ, Q(r))
8    X̃ := integrate(X, Rᵇ, t, t + min(τ, Q(r)))
9    // Calculate relative propensity change of X and X̃
10   Δ := |1 - ∑ᵢ₌₁^|Rᶜ| aᵢᶜ(X̃)/a₀ᶜ(X)|
11   if (Δ > ε_reject) {
12       // Reject step, i.e., do not update X and t
13       r := r_min
14   } else {
15       // Depending on Δ, adapt r
16       if (Δ > ε_max) {
17           r := max(r_min, r/2)
18       } else if (Δ < ε_min) {
19           r := min(1, r·2)
20       }
21       if (τ < Q(r)) {
22           // Select a complex reaction to be executed
23           x := U(0, a₀ᶜ(X))
24           i := min{j|j ∈ {1...m} ∧ ∑ᵢ₌₁^j aᵢᶜ(X) > x}
25           // Execute the selected complex reaction
26           X := execute(X̃, Rᵢᶜ)
27       } else {
28           X := X̃
29       }
30       // Advance simulation time
31       t := t + min(τ, Q(r))
32   }
```

---

to estimate the approximation error of a simulation step and the variables ϵ_{max}, ϵ_{min}, and ϵ_{reject} are used to control the adaptation of r. The initial value of r for a simulation has to be manually set by the user. The variable ϵ_{min} is a threshold to allow decreasing the accuracy by increasing r — if the relative propensity change of the complex reactions due to the integration of the basic reactions is smaller than ϵ_{min}, r is doubled. Analogously, ϵ_{max} is a threshold to increase the accuracy by decreasing r — if the relative propensity change of the complex reactions due to the integration of the basic reactions is larger than ϵ_{min}, r is halved. The variable ϵ_{reject} is introduced to avoid large errors induced by abrupt propensity changes for example caused by complex rate equations. After executing a reject, the variable r is set to a minimum value to avoid repetitive rejects. Altogether, this presented approximation control does not base on a direct error prediction and can therefore not guarantee a specific accuracy. However, adding a more predictive error estimation is challenging, since rate equations of reactions of multi-level models can be arbitrary complex resulting in unpredictable and discontinuous behavior.

Introducing the presented probability to fire one complex reaction is valid and does not change the reaction time distribution of the complex reactions since exponentially distributed reaction times are assumed which therefore are memoryless:

(1) The probability that a reaction time X is sampled in $[0, x]$ from $Exp(\lambda)$ can be calculated by: $P(X \leq x) = 1 - e^{-\lambda \cdot x}$.

(2) The r-quantile of $Exp(\lambda)$ is $Q(r) = \frac{-ln(1-r)}{\lambda}$.

(3) Assuming $x < Q(r)$, the probability to fire one complex reaction does not affect $P(X \leq x)$.

(4) Assuming $x > Q(r)$, one has to show that if $X > Q(r)$, advancing the simulation time to $Q(r)$ and sampling a new firing time Y from $Exp(\lambda)$ is equal to $P(X \leq x)$:

   (a) Based on the definition of quantiles, $P(X \leq Q(r)) = r$; therefore $P(X > Q(r)) = 1 - r$.

   (b) Consequently, to show that the probability to fire one complex reaction is equal to $P(X \leq x)$, the following expression must hold:

$$P(X \leq x) = P(X \leq Q(r))$$
$$+ P(X > Q(r)) \cdot P(Y \leq x - Q(r))$$
$$\text{replace } P(X \leq Q(r)) \text{ and } P(X > Q(r)):$$
$$= r + (1 - r) \cdot P(Y \leq x - Q(r))$$
$$\text{insert definition of } P(Y \leq x - Q(r)):$$
$$= r + (1 - r) \cdot (1 - e^{-\lambda(x - Q(r))})$$
$$\text{replace } Q(r) \text{ with } \frac{-ln(1 - r)}{\lambda}:$$
$$= r + (1 - r) \cdot (1 - e^{-\lambda(x - \frac{-ln(1-r)}{\lambda})})$$
$$= 1 - e^{-\lambda \cdot x}.$$

Basically, the hybrid simulator shown in Algorithm 3 follows the common structure of hybrid simulators for biochemical reaction networks: the set of reactions is partitioned into two sets, whereas one set is treated deterministically and the other set is treated stochastically and either zero or exactly one reaction of the stochastic set is executed during one simulation step. However, cell biological models are increasingly characterized by many compartments not interacting directly with each other, e.g., models that need to consider intra- as well as intercellular dynamics on the same time scale in heterogeneous cell populations (or even tissues). Complex reactions often influence only few other complex reactions, e.g., the creation of a mitochondrion in one cell does probably not affect the creation of a mitochondrion in another cell immediately, similarly interactions between cells and the impact of individual cells that proliferate are locally constrained. Consequently, inspired by the hybrid simulator presented by Salis and Kaznessis in [26], we extend the hybrid simulator in Algorithm 3 by an additional approximation process executing multiple independent complex reactions in one simulation step. This allows for larger integration intervals and less computational overhead (updating ODEs for the integration method, adapt state vector for the integration method etc.). Further, this additional approximation should be applicable

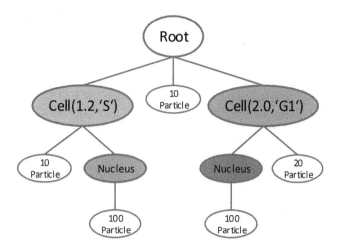

Figure 2: Illustration of the blocking mechanism from Algorithm 4.

with an acceptable loss of accuracy in case of models with broad tree structures consisting of many compartments acting on the same time scale.

Applying the approach of Salis and Kaznessis directly to models that rely on a dynamic set of reactions is not suitable. By following their approach, the hybrid simulator would execute multiple complex reactions successively within a time interval Δt while integrating the basic reactions only once from t to $t + \Delta t$. Since complex reactions can change the reaction set, the set of ODEs could be changed – possibly resulting in inconsistencies. For example, if a cell proliferates, the two newly created cells (which form the product of the complex reaction) would not be influenced by any basic reaction until $t + \Delta t$. In case a cell dies due to a complex reaction, all contained entities would have still been influenced by non-existing basic reactions until $t + \Delta t$.

Therefore, we follow another strategy for dynamic reaction networks and solve these problems by firing multiple complex reactions simultaneously in one step sampling one execution time with an Erlang distribution — a distribution used to sample the execution time of n independent exponentially distributed events with rate λ. To apply this strategy, all executed complex reactions are not allowed to influence each other, i.e., they must be independent. Otherwise, inconsistencies could occur, e.g., a cell splits and dies at the same time. Two reactions R_1 and R_2 influence each other if the intersection of the sets of compartments changed by R_1 (R_2) is not empty. This especially means that each complex reaction is only allowed to fire at most once. Figure 2 illustrates this blocking approach of reactions. Two reactions shall be executed in parallel, each changing one of the blue compartments. Therefore, since the `Nucleus` compartment of the `Cell(1.2,'S')` (orange) compartment is changed, the `Cell(1.2,'S')` compartment is not allowed to be changed by any other executed reaction. However, reactions executed *inside* this compartment could still be selected, e.g., the elimination of a `Particle`. The second reaction changing the compartment `Cell(2.0,'G1')` (red) blocks all of its sub compartments, i.e., its `Nucleus` compartment is not allowed to be changed by any other selected reaction, because it could also be changed by this reaction by functions on solutions.

Altogether, this approach might block more compartments than necessary, e.g., if the reaction changing the Cell(2.0,'G1') compartment is based on the exemplary rule scheme R2 (see Section 3), i.e., the volume is increased by eliminating one Particle, the Nucleus compartment would not have to be blocked. Nevertheless, improving the precision of the blocking mechanism is challenging due to functions on solutions changing sub entities of a compartment by applying functions like filter. An additional categorization of complex rule schemes could tackle this issue by distinguishing rule schemes differing in their complexity. However, in case of ML-Rules, it is also challenging to improve the precision of the blocking mechanism due to the execution semantics of ML-Rules reactions [28]: reactants are removed from the state and products are added to the state when executing a reaction. Generally speaking, there is no relation between reactant compartments and product compartments, i.e., the Cell reactant in rule scheme R2 is not the same entity as the Cell product of this rule scheme. Therefore, the simulation algorithm does remove a compartment with its content and creates a new compartment with content when executing such a reaction resulting in a reaction set change. This issue could be solved by applying a different execution semantics considering the relation of reactant and product compartments.

Algorithm 4 illustrates the hybrid simulator with multiple complex reaction firings per leap. It uses two auxiliary methods during its calculation:

- changedCompartments(R_i^c): return all compartments including their sub compartments that are changed by the complex reaction R_i^c. For example, if a complex reaction would split the entity Cell(1.2,'S') shown in Figure 1, not only the Cell entity is changed, but also the Nucleus compartment enclosed by the Cell.
- contextHierarchy(R_i^c): return all context compartments up to the Root compartment of the complex reaction R_i^c. For example, if a complex reaction would add a new compartment into one of the Nucleus compartments in Figure 1, this Nucleus compartment and its context Cell compartment are part of the context hierarchy of the reaction. The Root compartment is not part of the context hierarchy.

Since this simulator allows each complex reaction in R^c to fire at most once in one step, the maximum number of fired complex reactions in one step is $|R^c|$ (in that case all complex reactions are independent from each other). However, to control the accuracy of the simulator, this maximum number is reduced by the parameter $r \in [r_{min}, 1]$, i.e., only $\lfloor |R^c| \cdot r \rfloor$ complex reactions are allowed to fire at most in one step. If $|R^c| \cdot r < 1$, the algorithms falls back to Algorithm 3, using r as the probability to fire one complex reaction (lines 2-3).

The set C of complex reactions to be fired is determined by repeating the SSA reaction selection process $\lfloor |R^c| \cdot r \rfloor$ times (lines 10-18). A candidate reaction R_i^c is only added to C if it has not already been added and if the compartments changed by this reaction are not blocked. Applying the SSA reaction selection process successively guarantees that at least one reaction is selected and it considers the distribution of the reaction rates, i.e., the probability to select

---

Algorithm 4 Pseudo-Code of the hybrid simulator with multiple complex reaction firings per leap.

R^b: set of basic reactions,
R^c: set of complex reactions
C: set of selected complex reactions to be executed,
$a_1^c \ldots a_{m_c}^c$: propensities of complex reactions,
X: current state of the system,
$\tilde{X}$: intermediate state after integrating the basic reactions and before executing complex reactions.

```
1    // Fallback to Algorithm 3
2    if (|R^c| · r < 1) {
3        execute simulation step with Algorithm 3
4    } else {
5        // Calculate the propensity sum of complex reactions
6        a_0^c(X) := Σ_{i=1}^{|R^c|} a_i^c(X)
7        // C_blocked contains all blocked compartments
8        C_blocked := ∅
9        // Select set of complex reactions to be executed
10       for l ∈ {1, ... ⌊|R^c| · r⌋} {
11           x := U(0, a_0^c(X))
12           i := min{j|j ∈ {1...m} ∧ Σ_{i=1}^{j} a_i^c(X) > x}
13           C_changed := changedCompartments(R_i^c)
14           if (R_i^c ∉ C && C_blocked ∩ C_changed = ∅) {
15               C := C ∪ {R_i^c}
16               C_blocked := C_blocked ∪ C_changed ∪ contextHierarchy(R_i^c)
17           }
18       }
19       // Sample the execution time τ
20       τ := Erlang(a_0^c(X), |C|)
21       // Integrate basic reactions until t + τ
22       X̃ := integrate(X, R^b, t, t+τ);
23       Δ := |1 - Σ_{i=1}^{|R^c|} a_i^c(X̃)/a_0^c(X)|
24       if (Δ > ε_reject) {
25           // reject step, i.e., do not update X and t
26           r := max(r_min, r/2)
27       } else {
28           // Depending on Δ, adapt r
29           if (Δ > ε_max) {
30               r := max(r_min, r/2)
31           } else if (Δ < ε_min) {
32               r := min(1, r · 2)
33           }
34           // Execute the selected complex reactions
35           for (R_i^c ∈ C) {
36               X̃ := execute(X̃, R_i^c)
37           }
38           X := X̃
39           t_{j+1} := t_j + τ
40       }
41   }
```

---

complex reactions with high rates is larger than to select complex reactions with low rates. Due to the blocking mechanism of the selection, an additional error is induced that essentially depends on the model structure and has to be considered when applying this method for each model individually. However, since Algorithm 4 shall be applied to models with a broad tree structure with many compartments acting on the same time scale, we assume this error to be small since many complex reactions are independent from each other in this case.

After determining the set C of complex reactions to be executed, the time advance τ is sampled from an Erlang distribution with rate $\lambda = a_0^c(X)$ and shape $n = |C|$ (line 20). By using the Erlang distribution, all selected complex reactions are fired at the same simulation time. Next, the basic reactions are integrated until $t + \tau$ (line 22). Analogously to Algorithm 2, the relative propensity change Δ caused by the integration step is used to reject the current step, increase or decrease the parameter r (lines 23-33). Finally, in case the step is not rejected, all selected complex reactions are executed (lines 35-37), the state X is updated (line 38) and the time is advanced (line 39). The execution order of the complex reactions is not important since they are independent from each other. Therefore, they could naturally also be executed in parallel.

5 EVALUATION

To evaluate the performance and accuracy of the presented hybrid simulator, we executed simulations with a model of Dictyostelium discoideum amoebas illustrating the aggregation process of those amoebas in space [1]. Dictyostelium discoideum amoebas are unicellular eukaryotic cells communicating with each other via the diffusible second messenger molecule cAMP, which is regulated by intracellular signaling mechanisms in each amoeba [18]. Besides the intracellular mechanisms, the amoebas and the cAMP molecule move in space, whereby multicellular slugs are formed by the amoebas over time. Based on the work of Calovi et al. [3], a regular grid-based n × n structure is used in this model to represent the space, i.e., each amoeba is located in a grid-cell. For the initial state of the model, one amoeba is placed in each grid-cell. Rules are defined to enable amoebas and cAMP molecules to move from a grid-cell to all eight surrounding grid-cells defined by the Moore-neighborhood. The signaling components influenced by the intracellular signaling mechanisms and the cAMP molecule are represented by *leaves*. In contrast, the amoebas and the grid cells are represented by *compartments*. Figure 3 sketches a possible state of the model. The Grid compartments are placed in the Root compartment of the model. These compartments use two numerical attributes to represent their coordinates, and they contain a variable number of Amoeba compartments and one leave of species cAMP. The amoeba compartments themselves contain various signaling components like ACA.

All intracellular dynamics are described by *basic* rules changing the signaling components, but not the amoebas or the grid-cells. Further, the movement of the cAMP molecules within the grid-cells is represented by basic rules, since no compartments are changed. However, the movement of amoebas is represented by a *complex* rule, since the amoeba compartment is removed in its current grid-cell and added to a surrounding grid-cell — thereby invaliding all related reactions within the old grid-cell and enabling reactions in the new grid-cell.

Besides their classification, the basic and complex reactions also differ in their time scales, i.e., the intracellular dynamics and the cAMP movement are much faster than the amoeba movement. Therefore, simulating this model purely stochastically is impracticable — the simulation of one amoeba already takes many hours for a suitable amount of simulation time (e.g., 1000 minutes). Altogether, this model is a suitable benchmark for a hybrid

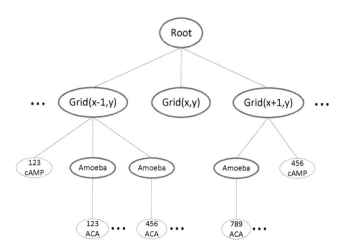

Figure 3: Sketch of a possible state tree of the Dictyostelium discoideum model.

simulator for dynamic reaction networks in multi-level models, as it represents a broad tree structure with fast basic rules and slow complex rules. The complete ML-Rules implementation of the model is available at the paper-related repository at https://git.informatik.uni-rostock.de/mosi/pads2018/hybrid-simulation.

We use three configurations with different variable values of Algorithm 3 (Configurations 1-3) and one configuration of Algorithm 4 (Configuration 4) for the experiments:

(1) Algorithm 3 with $r_{min} = 0.01$, $\epsilon_{min} = -\infty$, $\epsilon_{max} = \infty$, $\epsilon_{reject} = \infty$, r is initially set to 0.01
(2) Algorithm 3 with $r_{min} = 0.1$, $\epsilon_{min} = -\infty$, $\epsilon_{max} = \infty$, $\epsilon_{reject} = \infty$, r is initially set to 0.1
(3) Algorithm 3 with $r_{min} = 0.001$, $\epsilon_{min} = 0.01$, $\epsilon_{max} = 0.05$, $\epsilon_{reject} = 0.1$, r is initially set to 0.01
(4) Algorithm 4 with $r_{min} = 0.001$, $\epsilon_{min} = 0.01$, $\epsilon_{max} = 0.05$, $\epsilon_{reject} = 0.1$, r is initially set to 0.01

Further, all configurations apply the DormandPrince853 [10] integration method. We use the implementation available in the Apache Commons Math library[1] with the following parameters:

- minStep = 1.0e-8
- maxStep = 10.0
- scaleAbsoluteTolerance = 1.0e-8
- scaleRelativeTolerance = 1.0e-8.

Altogether, the configurations (1) and (2) have a fixed r and do not perform rejects due to ϵ_{max}, ϵ_{min}, and ϵ_{reject}. In contrast, the configurations (3) and (4) adapt r during runtime and perform rejects; r is increased if an integration step changes the propensity of the complex reactions less than 1%. Further, r is decreased if the propensity changes more than 5%. A reject is performed if the propensity change exceeds 10%.

To consider different complexities of the model, we use $n \in \{5, 7, 10\}$ for the regular grid-based n × n structure forming the space of the model. Since one amoeba is placed within each grid-cell

---

[1]http://commons.apache.org/proper/commons-math/ (Version 3.6.1)

for the initial state of the system, the number of amoebas is also influenced by the three grid size values. All simulation runs have been executed until simulation time 5000 (in minutes) and 40 replications have been executed to produce reliable results. For the experiment specification and execution, we use the simulation experiment specification language SESSL [12] and its recently published updated ML-Rules binding [29]. The complete SESSL specification of the experiments is available at the paper-related repository at https://git.informatik.uni-rostock.de/mosi/pads2018/hybrid-simulation.

To measure the accuracy of the simulation runs, we focus on the aggregation of the amoebas. Therefore, in Figure 4, we illustrate the average amoeba aggregation α of amoeba amounts a_{xy} per grid-cell at position (x, y) during the simulation runs based on the calculation of the standard deviation:

$$\alpha = \sqrt{\frac{1}{n^2 - 1} \sum_{x \in \{1, ..., n\}} \sum_{y \in \{1, ..., n\}} (a_{xy} - 1)^2}.$$

Therefore, $\alpha = 0$ initially at simulation time $t = 0$, since one amoeba is placed in each grid-cell. While aggregating to larger cluster, α is increasing and in case all amoebas are in the same grid-cell, $\alpha = n$. The amoeba aggregation shown in Figure 4 of all four simulator configuration is similar and does not differ significantly. Besides, the aggregation is similar for the three grid sizes, because with $n = 7$ and $n = 10$, the amoeba form several small cluster until simulation time $t = 5000$. For these grid sizes, the amoeba need more simulation time to form large clusters increasing the aggregation α. In addition to these results, Figure 5 illustrates the detailed aggregation of amoebas at simulation time $t = 5000$ by counting the grid-cells with specific numbers of amoebas. Again, the simulation results do not differ significantly supporting the observation that the accuracy of the four considered simulator configurations is similar.

Figure 6 shows the runtime results of the four simulator configurations. Further, the average runtime and the standard deviation are given in Table 1 and the executed simulation steps are illustrated in Figure 7. As expected, for all three grid sizes, the simulator configuration (1) performs worst, as the probability to perform one complex reaction r is 0.01 and many simulation steps are executed without firing one stochastic reaction. Increasing r to 0.1 in simulator configuration (2) results in larger step sizes and one tenth executed simulation steps compared to simulator configuration (1), decreasing the runtime significantly for all grid sizes (ca. 60% for $n = 5$ and $n = 7$, and ca. 72% for $n = 10$). Using an adaptive r further decreases the number of required simulation steps and the runtime. The reduction of simulation steps is achieved by using larger values for r: on average, the simulator configuration (3) sets $r \approx 0.43$ for $n = 5$, $r \approx 0.8$ for $n = 7$, and $r \approx 0.9$ for $n = 10$. Since the impact of one amoeba on the whole system decreases with an increasing number of amoeba, the propensity differences Δ calculated by Algorithm 3 decrease and therefore, larger values for r are reached by the simulator.

Finally, enabling the simulator to execute multiple complex reactions in one simulation step (simulator configuration (4)) further decreases the runtime (ca. 90% for $n = 5$, $n = 7$, and $n = 10$ compared to simulator configuration (1)). Interestingly, the number of

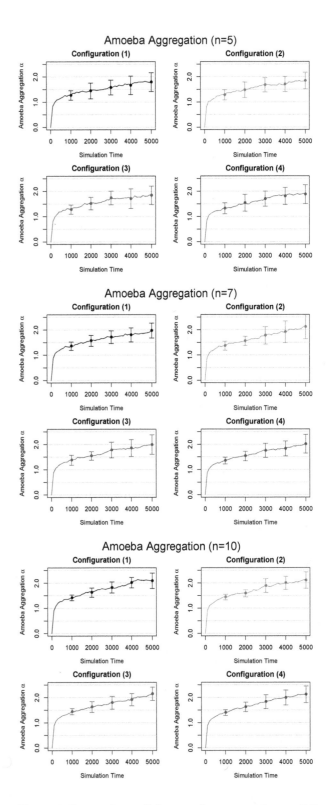

Figure 4: Comparison of the amoeba aggregation α of the three different grid sizes and the four simulator configurations.

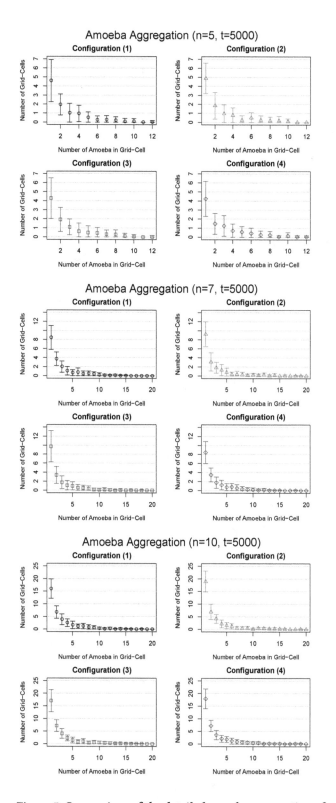

Figure 5: Comparison of the detailed amoeba aggregation of the three different grid sizes and the four simulator configurations.

Table 1: Rounded average runtime in seconds (standard deviation in brackets) of the four simulator configurations for the three grid sizes.

n	(1)	(2)	(3)	(4)
5	1668 (519)	699 (136)	232 (72)	136 (24)
7	7657 (1730)	2744 (442)	2375 (534)	573 (222)
10	39081 (3227)	10760 (1232)	8528 (1074)	4277 (1675)

required simulation steps even decreases with this simulator configuration when increasing the grid size (ca. 910 steps on average for $n = 5$, ca. 610 steps on average for $n = 7$, ca. 470 steps on average for $n = 10$). The number of potential stochastic reactions essentially depends on the grid size and the existing amoebas. Therefore, the more potential reactions are available, the less likely it is for Algorithm 4 to fall back to Algorithm 3 and consequently, the proportion of simulation steps without executing a complex reaction reduces with an increasing grid size (ca. 67% for $n = 5$, ca. 50% for $n = 7$ and ca. 28% for $n = 10$). At the same time, the number of simulation steps executing complex reactions is not increasing significantly, since more reactions are executed simultaneously (2 reactions on average with $n = 5$, 3 reactions on average with $n = 7$, and 7 reactions on average with $n = 10$). The benefit of configuration (4) compared to configuration (3) is largest with $n = 7$ — increasing the step size due to multiple stochastic events seems to have the biggest impact on the integration method with this grid size for this particular model. Although there is also a benefit with $n = 10$, it is smaller indicating that performance improvements by executing multiple stochastic reactions are exhausted at some point. However, since complex reactions executed stochastically in one simulation step are independent from each other, they naturally could also be executed in parallel further improving the effectiveness of this additional approximation.

6 CONCLUSION

An increasing number of cell biological models rely on dynamic reaction networks with a reaction set changing at runtime, e.g., due to the creation or elimination of cells. In this paper, we apply concepts of hybrid simulator for biochemical reaction networks to multi-level models with dynamic reaction sets. The presented algorithm relies on a categorization of reactions into *basic* and *complex* reactions depending on their impact on the reaction set. Whereas basic reactions are not allowed to cause the reaction set to change, complex reactions can change the reaction set and therefore require an update mechanism to be applied. Based on both reaction types, a hybrid simulator can be realized by simulating the set of basic reactions deterministically and the set of complex reactions stochastically. Nevertheless, due to the possibility of complex propensity functions, e.g., arbitrary functions that relate expressive dynamics at multiple levels in these models, minor changes caused by basic reactions can have a significant impact on complex reactions. Therefore, we included a dynamic approximation control and a rejection mechanism to the simulator. Besides, since cell biological models are often characterized by nestings forming a broad tree structure, we extend the hybrid simulator by an additional approximation process executing multiple independent complex reactions in one

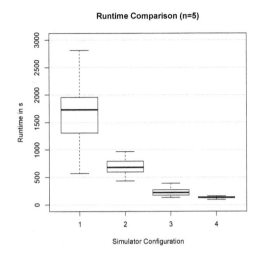

Runtime Comparison (n=5)

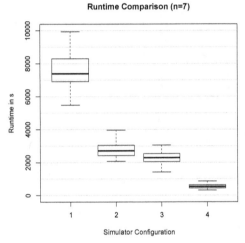

Runtime Comparison (n=7)

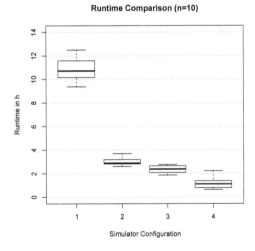

Runtime Comparison (n=10)

Figure 6: Runtime comparison of hybrid simulator with the four considered simulator configurations and three different grid sizes ($n = 5 \rightarrow$ Top, $n = 7 \rightarrow$ Middle, $n = 10 \rightarrow$ Bottom).

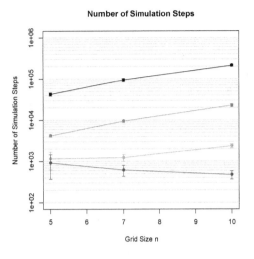

Number of Simulation Steps

Figure 7: Number of simulation steps with a logarithmic scale of the four simulator configurations: (1) $\rightarrow$ black, (2) $\rightarrow$ red, (3) $\rightarrow$ green, and (4) $\rightarrow$ blue.

simulation step, see Algorithm 4. For suitable models, this allows for larger integration intervals and less computational overhead (updating ODEs for the integration method, adapt the state vector for the integration method etc.) with an acceptable loss of accuracy.

Our evaluation with a Dictyostelium discoideum model [1] shows the benefit of an adaptive probability r to fire one complex reaction. Moreover, extending the hybrid simulator to approximate the execution of complex reactions further improves the performance without a noticeable loss of accuracy. This observation underlines our assumption that complex reactions can be simulated simultaneously in systems with large populations of nested entities, where complex reactions within different compartments do not affect each other directly.

Since the integration method consumes most of the computational time with the extended hybrid simulator, our further research focuses on the evaluation of different integration methods and parameter values. However, our further research also includes sensitivity analyses of the simulator parameter referring to their impact on performance and accuracy. To improve the blocking mechanism of the extended hybrid simulator, we will introduce a relation between reactant and product compartments within the execution semantics of ML-Rules. Further, we will apply the hybrid simulator to complex models of ongoing simulation studies, e.g., an extended cod population model based on the cod model presented in [25].

The code of ML-Rules is open source and publicly available at https://git.informatik.uni-rostock.de/mosi/mlrules. Further, all experiment descriptions in SESSL and instructions to reproduce the experiments of this paper can be found in the paper-related repository at https://git.informatik.uni-rostock.de/mosi/pads2018/hybrid-simulation.

ACKNOWLEDGMENTS

This research is supported by the German Research Foundation (DFG) via research grants ESCeMMo (UH-66/14) and ELAINE (SFB 1270).

REFERENCES

[1] Marco Beccuti, Mary Ann Blätke, Martin Falk, Simon Hardy, Monika Heiner, Carsten Maus, Sebastian Nähring, and Christian Rohr. 2015. Dictyostelium discoideum: Aggregation and Synchronisation of Amoebas in Time and Space. *Dagstuhl Reports: Multiscale Spatial Computational Systems Biology (Dagstuhl Seminar 14481)* 4, 11 (2015), 195–214.

[2] Michael L. Blinov, James R. Faeder, Byron Goldstein, and William S. Hlavacek. 2004. BioNetGen: Software for Rule-based Modeling of Signal Transduction Based on the Interactions of Molecular Domains. *Bioinformatics* 20, 17 (2004), 3289–3291.

[3] Daniel S. Calovi, Leonardo G. Brunnet, and Rita M. C. de Almeida. 2010. cAMP diffusion in *Dictyostelium discoideum*: A Green's function method. *Physical Review E* 82 (2010), 011909. Issue 1. https://doi.org/10.1103/PhysRevE.82.011909

[4] Donald T. Campbell. 1974. "'Downward Causation' in Hierarchically Organised Biological Systems. In *Studies in the Philosophy of Biology: Reduction and Related Problems*. Macmillan Education UK, 179–186. https://doi.org/10.1007/978-1-349-01892-5_11

[5] Yang Cao, Daniel T. Gillespie, and Linda Petzold. 2005. The slow-scale stochastic simulation algorithm. *The Journal of Chemical Physics* 122, 1 (2005). https://doi.org/10.1063/1.1824902

[6] Yang Cao, Hong Li, and Linda Petzold. 2004. Efficient formulation of the stochastic simulation algorithm for chemically reacting systems. *The Journal of Chemical Physics* 121, 9 (Sept. 2004), 4059–4067. https://doi.org/10.1063/1.1778376

[7] Alina Crudu, Arnaud Debussche, and Ovidiu Radulescu. 2009. Hybrid stochastic simplifications for multiscale gene networks. *BMC Systems Biology* 3, 89 (2009). https://doi.org/10.1186/1752-0509-3-89

[8] Vincent Danos and Cosimo Laneve. 2004. Formal molecular biology. *Theoretical Computer Science* 325, 1 (2004), 69–110.

[9] M. H. A. Davis. 1984. Piecewise-Deterministic Markov Processes: A General Class of Non-Diffusion Stochastic Models. *Journal of the Royal Statistical Society. Series B (Methodological)* 46, 3 (1984), 353–388.

[10] J.R. Dormand and P.J. Prince. 1980. A family of embedded Runge-Kutta formulae. *J. Comput. Appl. Math.* 6, 1 (1980), 19–26. https://doi.org/10.1016/0771-050X(80)90013-3

[11] Weinan E, Di Liu, and Eric Vanden-Eijnden. 2005. Nested stochastic simulation algorithm for chemical kinetic systems with disparate rates. *The Journal of Chemical Physics* 123, 19 (2005). https://doi.org/10.1063/1.2109987

[12] Roland Ewald and Adelinde M. Uhrmacher. 2014. SESSL: A Domain-specific Language for Simulation Experiments. *ACM Transactions on Modeling and Computer Simulation (TOMACS)* 24, 2 (2014), 11:1–11:25. https://doi.org/10.1145/2567895

[13] Michael A. Gibson and Jehoshua Bruck. 2000. Efficient Exact Stochastic Simulation of Chemical Systems with Many Species and Many Channels. *The Journal of Chemical Physics* 104, 9 (Feb. 2000), 1876–1889. https://doi.org/10.1021/jp993732q

[14] Daniel T Gillespie. 1977. Exact Stochastic Simulation of Coupled Chemical Reactions. *The Journal of Physical Chemistry* 81, 25 (1977), 2340–2361. https:

//doi.org/10.1021/j100540a008

[15] Eric L. Haseltine and James B. Rawlings. 2002. Approximate simulation of coupled fast and slow reactions for stochastic chemical kinetics. *The Journal of Chemical Physics* 117, 15 (2002), 6959–6969. https://doi.org/10.1063/1.1505860

[16] Tobias Helms, Tom Warnke, Carsten Maus, and Adelinde M. Uhrmacher. 2017. Semantics and Efficient Simulation Algorithms of an Expressive Multi-Level Modeling Language. *ACM Transactions on Modeling and Computer Simulation (TOMACS)* 27, 2, Article 8 (2017), 8:1–8:25 pages. https://doi.org/10.1145/2998499

[17] Michael Hucka, Lucian P. Smith, Darren J. Wilkinson, Frank T. Bergmann, Stefan Hoops, Sarah M. Keating, Sven Sahle, and James C. Schaff. 2010. The Systems Biology Markup Language (SBML): Language Specification for Level 3 Version 1 Core. *Nature Precedings* (2010). https://doi.org/10.1038/npre.2010.4959

[18] Jongrae Kim, Pat Heslop-Harrison, Ian Postlethwaite, and Declan G. Bates. 2007. Stochastic Noise and Synchronisation during *Dictyostelium* Aggregation Make cAMP Oscillations Robust. *PLoS Computational Biology* 3, 11 (2007), e218. https://doi.org/10.1371/journal.pcbi.0030218

[19] Thilo Krüger and Verena Wolf. 2016. Hybrid Stochastic Simulation of Rule-Based Polymerization Models. In *Proceedings of the 5th International Workshop on Hybrid Systems Biology*. 39–53. https://doi.org/10.1007/978-3-319-47151-8_3

[20] Tomas G. Kurtz. 1981. *Approximation of Population Processes*. SIAM.

[21] Carsten Maus, Stefan Rybacki, and Adelinde M. Uhrmacher. 2011. Rule-based multi-level modeling of cell biological systems. *BMC Systems Biology* 5, 166 (2011). https://doi.org/10.1186/1752-0509-5-166

[22] James M. McCollum, Gregory D. Peterson, Chris D. Cox, Michael L. Simpson, and Nagiza F. Samatova. 2006. The sorting direct method for stochastic simulation of biochemical systems with varying reaction execution behavior. *Computational Biology and Chemistry* 30, 1 (2006), 39–49. https://doi.org/10.1016/j.compbiolchem.2005.10.007

[23] Denis Noble. 2006. *The Music of Life: Biology Beyond Genes*. Oxford University Press.

[24] Jürgen Pahle. 2009. Biochemical simulations: stochastic, approximate stochastic and hybrid approaches. *Briefings in Bioinformatics* 10, 1 (2009), 53–64. https://doi.org/10.1093/bib/bbn050

[25] Maria E. Pierce, Tom Warnke, Uwe Krumme, Tobias Helms, Cornelius Hammer, and Adelinde M. Uhrmacher. 2017. Developing and validating a multi-level ecological model of eastern Baltic cod (Gadus morhua) in the Bornholm Basin - A case for domain-specific languages. *Ecological Modelling* 361 (2017), 49–65. https://doi.org/10.1016/j.ecolmodel.2017.07.012

[26] Howard Salis and Yiannis Kaznessis. 2005. Accurate hybrid stochastic simulation of a system of coupled chemical or biochemical reactions. *The Journal of Chemical Physics* 122, 5 (2005). https://doi.org/10.1063/1.1835951

[27] Thanh, Vo Hong and Priami, Corrado and Zunino, Roberto. 2014. Efficient rejection-based simulation of biochemical reactions with stochastic noise and delays. *The Journal of Chemical Physics* 141, 13 (2014). https://doi.org/10.1063/1.4896985

[28] Tom Warnke, Tobias Helms, and Adelinde M. Uhrmacher. 2015. Syntax and Semantics of a Multi-Level Modeling Language. In *Proceedings of the 3rd ACM SIGSIM Conference on Principles of Advanced Discrete Simulation*. 133–144. https://doi.org/10.1145/2769458.2769467

[29] Tom Warnke, Tobias Helms, and Adelinde M. Uhrmacher. 2017. Reproducible and flexible simulation experiments with ML-Rules and SESSL. *Bioinformatics* (2017). https://doi.org/10.1093/bioinformatics/btx741

Co-simulation of FMUs and Distributed Applications with SimGrid

Benjamin Camus
Univ. Rennes, Inria, CNRS, IRISA
F-35000 Rennes
benjamin.camus@inria.fr

Anne-Cécile Orgerie
Univ. Rennes, Inria, CNRS, IRISA
F-35000 Rennes
anne-cecile.orgerie@irisa.fr

Martin Quinson
Univ. Rennes, Inria, CNRS, IRISA
F-35000 Rennes
martin.quinson@irisa.fr

ABSTRACT

The Functional Mock-up Interface (FMI) standard is becoming an essential solution for co-simulation. In this paper, we address a specific issue which arises in the context of Distributed Cyber-Physical System (DCPS) co-simulation where Functional Mock-up Units (FMU) need to interact with distributed application models. The core of the problem is that, in general, complex distributed application behaviors cannot be easily and accurately captured by a modeling formalism but are instead directly specified using a standard programming language. As a consequence, the model of a distributed application is often a concurrent program. The challenge is then to bridge the gap between this programmatic description and the equation-based framework of FMI in order to make FMUs interact with concurrent programs. In this article, we show how we use the unique model of execution of the SimGrid simulation platform to tackle this issue. The platform manages the co-evolution and the interaction between IT models and the different concurrent processes which compose a distributed application code. Thus, SimGrid offers a framework to mix models and concurrent programs. We show then how we specify an FMU as a SimGrid model to solve the DCPS co-simulation issues. Compared to other works of the literature, our solution is not limited to a specific use case and benefits from the versatility and scalability of SimGrid.

CCS CONCEPTS

• **Computing methodologies** → **Discrete-event simulation**; **Simulation tools**; *Continuous simulation*; *Distributed programming languages*; • **Computer systems organization** → *Embedded and cyber-physical systems*;

KEYWORDS

co-simulation, FMI, distributed system, cyber-physical system

ACM acknowledges that this contribution was authored or co-authored by an employee, contractor or affiliate of a national government. As such, the Government retains a nonexclusive, royalty-free right to publish or reproduce this article, or to allow others to do so, for Government purposes only.

SIGSIM-PADS '18 , May 23–25, 2018, Rome, Italy
© 2018 Association for Computing Machinery.
ACM ISBN 978-1-4503-5092-1/18/05. . . $15.00
https://doi.org/10.1145/3200921.3200932

ACM Reference Format:
Benjamin Camus, Anne-Cécile Orgerie, and Martin Quinson. 2018. Co-simulation of FMUs and Distributed Applications with SimGrid. In *SIGSIM-PADS '18 : 2018 SIGSIM Principles of Advanced Discrete Simulation, May 23–25, 2018, Rome, Italy*. ACM, New York, NY, USA, Article 4, 12 pages. https://doi.org/10.1145/3200921.3200932

1 INTRODUCTION

Cyber-Physical Systems (CPS) can be defined as *"physical and engineered systems whose operations are monitored, coordinated, controlled and integrated by a computing and communication core"* [27]. In this article, we focus on a specific (although common) class of CPS called Distributed-CPS (DCPS) that are CPS equipped with a geographically distributed computing application –i.e. an application that consists of several concurrent processes, possibly remotely located, and interacting through message exchanges. Such systems include notably smart-grid [21], smart-home [16], cloud infrastructure [12] and smart-city [32].

In most cases, a Modeling and Simulation (M&S) process is required to design and study DCPS systems. However, several expert skills belonging to different scientific fields may be required. In this multidisciplinary approach, each domain comes with its own try and tested models and tools. The challenge is then to have a unified approach with a set of heterogeneous M&S tools (i.e. models and simulation pieces of software). A growing strategy to tackle this challenge is co-simulation [17] which consists in coupling different stand-alone M&S tools, so that they simulate the whole system together. The advantages of co-simulation include that (1) it enables to study the global behavior of the system, (2) it enforces a clear separation of concerns in the M&S process and (3) it enables to reuse and factorize efforts put into the development and validation of M&S tools. Yet, co-simulation raises two main challenges. First, managing interoperability [14] consists in ensuring that simulation software codes – that may have different API and be written in different programming languages – can exchange usable data during the simulation. Then, the multi-paradigm challenge [29] requires to bridge he different modeling formalisms that are used by the M&S tools. In the case of CPS, this often implies managing a hybrid simulation that combines discrete dynamics (for the computing systems) and continuous dynamics (for the physical systems) [10].

Since 2010, the Functional Mock-up Interface (FMI) standard [4] of the Modelica Association is becoming an essential solution toward co-simulation. It offers a unified framework and an API to control equation-based models of multiphysical systems (e.g. electrical, mechanical, thermal systems). The strength of the standard is that it is supported by over 100 M&S tools[1]. These tools enable (1) to design a model and export it as an FMU (Functional Mock-up Unit) –i.e. a simulation unit compliant with FMI– (2) and/or to import and use an FMU as a component in their modeling environment. Several frameworks have been proposed to perform co-simulation of FMUs [3, 11, 15], and to integrate continuous FMUs into discrete event formalism environments [7, 13, 24].

In this paper, we address another issue which arises in the context of DCPS co-simulation where FMU components need to interact with distributed application models. The core of the problem is that, in general, complex distributed application behaviors cannot be easily and accurately captured by a modeling formalism (e.g. finite automata) [9]. Instead, the most common approach consists in directly specifying a distributed application using a standard programming language. As a consequence, the model of a distributed application corresponds often a concurrent program which runs on a single computer. The challenge is then to bridge the gap between this programmatic description and the equation-based framework of FMI in order to make FMUs interact with concurrent programs. Considering the diversity of DCPS previously cited, an ad-hoc solution should be avoided in favor of a more versatile approach.

In this article, we show how we use the unique execution model of the SimGrid M&S platform [9] –and more precisely its concept of separated entities' virtualization– to tackle this issue. SimGrid is a versatile platform for the simulation of distributed systems which embeds a set of rigorously validated IT models (e.g. CPU, IP network, disk, energy consumption). The platform manages the co-evolution and the interaction between these models and the different concurrent processes which compose a distributed application code. Thus, SimGrid offers a framework to mix models and concurrent programs. Our contribution is then to specify an FMU as a SimGrid model to ease the simulation of DCPS. Compared to other works in the literature [6, 16, 21, 32], our solution is not limited to a specific use case and benefits from the versatility of SimGrid and its validated IT models.

The rest of the article is organized as follow. In Section 2, we describe for illustration purpose the simple yet representative use-case of a chiller failure in a data-center. This use-case illustrates all along the article the challenges of DCPS simulation and our contributions. Section 3 presents the FMI standard and the SimGrid platform. Section 4 details how we integrate FMU into the SimGrid framework. Finally, Section 5 shows how we validate our proposition with the co-simulation of our use-case.

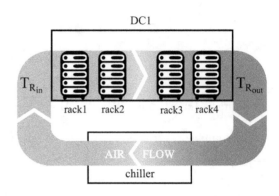

Figure 1: Physical model of the data-center.

2 REPRESENTATIVE USE CASE

For illustration purpose, we consider the simulation of a failure in the chiller of a data-center (DC) called DC1. We consider that the failure occurs when the chiller demand (which depends on the heat dissipation induced by computations) becomes too high. After the failure occurrence, a safety mechanism shuts down the power supply if the temperature becomes too high to preserve machines. We want to simulate the computing processes which cause and handle the failure. This requires to model both the distributed application deployed in the DC, and the physical processes of heat transfers.

This use case is representative because it implies:

(1) coupling different M&S tools (OpenModelica and SimGrid),
(2) which use different modeling paradigms (algebraic/differential/discrete equations and concurrent programs),
(3) with discrete (distributed application execution) and continuous (the temperature evolution) dynamics in interaction (the distributed application changes the computers' heat dissipation, and the room temperature triggers power shutdown that kills the running programs).

In the following we describe the different models, their co-simulation and the faced challenges.

2.1 Physical system of the DC

To describe the nominal behavior of the physical systems, shown in Figure 1, we use a simplified version of the model of [12]. We consider a Computer Room Air Handler (CRAH) that sends an airflow through the computing units (called Physical Machines – PM) racks to cool the DC. Thanks to the chiller, the inlet air temperature is always equal to the same temperature $T_{R_{in}}(t)$. As the air passes through the rack, its temperature increases because of the heat dissipation of the DC $Q_{DC}(t)$. This quantity is defined as follows:

$$Q_{DC}(t) = P_{load_{DC}}(t) + Q_{others_{DC}}(t) \qquad (1)$$

$P_{load_{DC}}(t)$ is an input of the model which corresponds to the power consumption and heat dissipation of the PMs. $Q_{others_{DC}}(t)$ corresponds to the heat dissipation of the other

[1]according to http://fmi-standard.org

devices of the DC (e.g. lighting, Power Distribution Unit) and is equal to:

$$Q_{others_{DC}}(t) = \alpha \times P_{load_{DC}}(t) \qquad (2)$$

Considering the mass of the air in the room m_{air} and its specific heat C_p, the outlet air temperature $T_{R_{out}}(t)$ corresponds to:

$$T_{R_{out}}(t) = T_{R_{in}} + \frac{Q_{DC}(t)}{m_{air} \times C_p} \qquad (3)$$

The cooling demand of the chiller $Q_{cooling}(t)$ is defined as follows:

$$Q_{cooling}(t) = Q_{DC}(t)/\eta_{cc} \qquad (4)$$

With η_{cc}, the inefficiency in the coil of the CRAH.

When the chiller stops working, the inlet and outlet air temperatures become equal and they start increasing according to the following equation:

$$\frac{dT_{R_{out}}}{dt} = \frac{Q_{DC}(t)}{m_{air} \times C_p} \qquad (5)$$

A boolean discrete variable *power* determines the status of the power supply in DC1. It is initially set to 1 meaning that power supply is working. When the temperature reaches a critical threshold *tempThreshold*, the power supply is shut down –i.e. *power* = 0. The following discrete equation models the behavior of the safety mechanism:

when $T_{R_{out}}(t) >= tempThreshold$ **then** $power = 0$ (6)

The status of the chiller is modeled by a boolean variable *chiller*. The chiller is initially in state 1, meaning that it is working. When the load of the chiller reaches a critical threshold *criticalLoad*, the failure occurs and the status of the chiller switches to 0, meaning that it stops working. This is modeled by the following discrete equation:

when $Q_{cooling}(t) >= criticalLoad$ **then** $chiller = 0$ (7)

The expected behavior of the system is that when the chiller is working, the inlet temperature remains constant and the load of the chiller varies with the power consumption of the computing units. When that computing load is too high, the chiller load will eventually reach the critical threshold, inducing a chiller failure. The room temperature will then increase with a rate proportional to the PMs' power consumption. Once the temperature reaches the critical threshold, the power supply is shut down, stopping all computing units.

2.2 Distributed application of the DC

We consider a scheduling algorithm which sequentially deploys Virtual Machines (VM) on the PM of the data center DC1, while another data center DC2 is used as a backup solution. The whole IT system is shown in Figure 2.

Each VM is a computer system emulation which requires a given amount of the computing resources (i.e. CPU and memory) of its PM to execute. When creating a VM, the

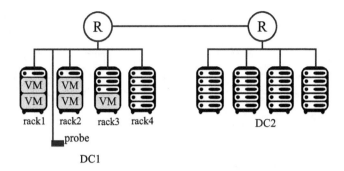

Figure 2: IT model of the data-centers.

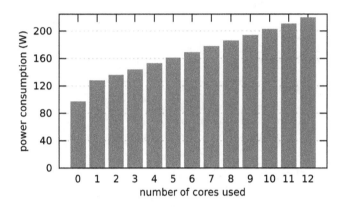

Figure 3: Consumption model of the PM.

user specifies its size –i.e the maximum amount of computing resources it can use on the PM. Thus, several VMs can run on a single PM with sufficient resources. We consider for the sake of simplicity that a VM always runs at full capacity when deployed –i.e. 100% of the PM resources required by the VM are used.

The scheduler behavior corresponds to a simple first-fit algorithm (described by Algorithm 1). We consider that it takes 10 seconds to deploy a VM on a PM. PMs consume 0W when turned off. When turned on, we use the power consumption model of [20] which is based on real watt-meter measurements and consider a PM to consumes 97W when idle, 128W when using 1 core, and 220W when working at full capacity. As shown in Figure 3, the power consumption of a PM depends linearly on its CPU usage between 1 core used and max [18]. As a consequence, with Algorithm 1 the power consumption of DC1 will increase with the number of deployed VMs.

A probe monitors the chiller status. When a failure is detected, the probe sends a message through an IP network to an emergency manager deployed in another DC called DC2. Upon reception, the emergency manager kills the scheduling algorithm to stop the deployment of VMs in DC1. It also immediately shuts down unused PMs to limit the room temperature. Then, the emergency manager relocate the VMs to DC2, to save as many as possible of them before the power supply shutdown. We perform live migrations of VM

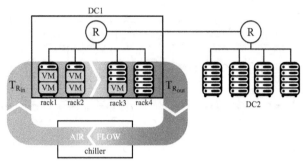

(a) Global system studied.

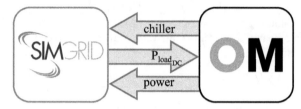

(b) Data exchanges between SimGrid and OpenModelica (OM)

Figure 4: Co-simulation of the chiller failure.

Algorithm 1: Scheduling algorithm to deploy VM in DC1

---

while DC1 is not full **do**
  Let pmList be the list of PM of DC1.
  for pm in pmList **do**
    if pm as enough cores available to run a VM **then**
      deploy VM on pm
      break
    end if
  end for
end while

Algorithm 2: Emergency algorithm managing chiller failure in DC1

---

wait for emergency message
shut down unused PM in DC1
Let deployedVM be the list of all VMs deployed on DC1.
for vm in deployedVM **do**
  Let pm0 be the PM hosting vm.
  Let pmList2 be the list of PMs of DC2.
  for pm1 in pmList2 **do**
    if pm1 as enough cores available to run vm **then**
      migrate vm on pm1
      if pm0 is empty **then**
        shut down pm0
      end if
      break
    end if
  end for
end for

---

to ensure a continuity of service. With a live migration, the memory of a VM is progressively sent to the destination PM while the VM is running on the source PM. Once the transfer is done, the VM is shut down on the source PM and restarted on the destination PM. The time to migrate a VM strongly depends on the memory transfer time [1]. The manager shuts

down the PM once all its VMs are migrated. The behavior of the emergency manager is described by Algorithm 2.

The distributed application is then composed of several processes, namely the scheduling algorithm, the emergency manager processes, all the VM deployed on the PM, and the probe monitoring the chiller. We implement this application in SimGrid, and rely on its IT models of IP network, CPU usage and energy consumption for the simulation.

2.3 Co-simulation challenges

To study the considered use-case, we employ dedicated simulation tools: OpenModelica for the equation-based chiller failure model, and SimGrid for the distributed application and its power consumption over the DC. We need to couple our OpenModelica and SimGrid models as shown in Figure 4. The PM power consumption computed by SimGrid is used as input (i.e. $P_{load_{DC}}(t)$) of the physical models of OpenModelica. On the other side, any change to the model's discrete variables (i.e. *chiller* and *power*) triggers events in the distributed application.

This coupling rises the following issues:

- How to manage interoperability between OpenModelica and SimGrid ?
- How to make the distributed application processes co-evolve with the physical system models ?
- How to manage interactions between the computing processes and the physical models ?
- How to detect discrete state changes in the continuous system evolution, and trigger the induced discrete events in the distributed application ?

In the following, we detail the FMI standard and the SimGrid platform that we want to combine to address these issues.

3 CONTEXT
3.1 The FMI standard

FMI [4] aims at proposing a generic way to export, import and control equation-based models and their solvers. Using FMI, a model which may be composed of a mixture of differential,

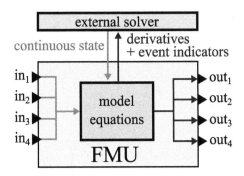

Figure 5: FMI for model-exchange.

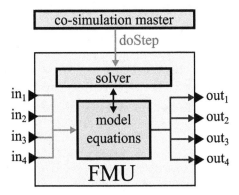

Figure 6: FMI for co-simulation.

algebraic and discrete-time equations, can be exported under a standard format as an FMU. This FMU is a black-box (thus protecting the intellectual property of the model) with input and output ports which correspond to the input and output variables of the model. Each FMU can then be controlled using a standardized API, regardless the M&S tool used to generate it. In this way, FMI addresses the interoperability issue between different M&S tools.

FMI provides two ways of exporting and importing a model: FMI for co-simulation (FMI-CS) and FMI for model-exchange (FMI-ME). With **FMI-ME** (depicted in Figure 5), only the model (i.e. the equations) is exported. Thus an FMU-ME requires a numerical solver in order to be simulated. As a consequence, this export mode is mainly interesting in the context of model exchanges between equation-based tools, which is out of the scope of this article.

With **FMI-CS** (depicted in Figure 6), a model is exported with a passive solver that can be controlled by any M&S environment importing this FMU-CS. Because they do not require any external solver, FMU-CS can be integrated into a discrete M&S environments. This fits particularly well into our context of DCPS simulation. In the following, we detail this FMI-CS standard and its limits to make our proposition fully understandable for non-specialist.

The co-evolution of an FMU-CS with its environment is based on the concept of communication points. These communication points, which have to be set by the environment of the FMU, correspond to points in the simulated time where (1) the FMU simulation must be stopped, and (2) exchanges of data can be performed between the FMUs and its environment. Between two communication points, an FMU evolves independently of its environment.

From a software perspective, the FMU interface is composed of a set of C functions, and an XML file. The C functions control the FMU, whereas the XML file describes the FMU capacities and interface. More precisely, the XML file describes names, types (i.e. Real/Integer/Boolean/String), variability (constant/discrete/continuous) and causality (input/output/parameter) of the variables. The C interface enables to control an FMU-CS with the following operations [22]:

- a `doStep` integrates the FMU until a given communication point. Note that, an FMU may enforce fixed communication step-size. This limitation is then specified in the FMU description file. In this case, if the step-size required by `doStep` is not compatible with the fixed step-size, the method will fail to execute.
- a `getOutput` gets the current outputs of the FMU.
- a `setInput` sets the inputs of the FMU. In case of instantaneous dependencies between inputs and outputs, this method may change the outputs of the FMU. Depending on the FMU, a `doStep` of duration 0 may also be required to update outputs.
- `getState` and `setState` are optional operations used to export/import the model state. They enable to perform a rollback during the simulation of the model.

In its current state, FMI-CS is not yet fully compliant with hybrid simulation requirements [5, 11, 28]. In particular, an FMU only supports continuous and piecewise continuous input/output time signals. As a consequence, an FMU-CS cannot produce discrete event signals which are essential to communicate with event-based models. Also, the date of the next discrete event cannot be obtained from a FMU-CS. Although the scheduled 2.1 extension of the standard might solve this issue[2], we need to adapt to this constraint in the meantime.

In the model of our use-case, we use FMI-CS to export our thermal system model as an FMU using the dedicated features of OpenModelica. Thus, we obtain a simulation unit (shown in Figure 7) which is ready to interact and co-evolve with other models in different M&S environments. However, due to the limitation of the standard, the exact dates of the power supply shutdown and the chiller failure cannot be known in advance from the FMU. Also, the FMU is not able to trigger an event at these moments to notify the distributed application.

3.2 The SimGrid Platform

SimGrid [9] is a versatile platform dedicated to the scalable simulation of distributed applications and platforms. It can notably be used to study cluster, grid, peer-to-peer, Cloud, wide/local-area networks. It is grounded on sound simulation

---

[2]according to http://fmi-standard.org/downloads/ as of 24. Jan 2018.

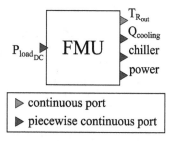

Figure 7: Block diagram view of the thermal system model of our use-case, exported as an FMU.

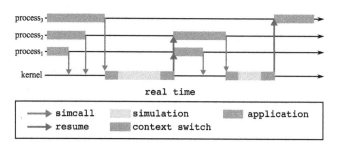

Figure 8: Example of simulation execution in SimGrid (according to the real time).

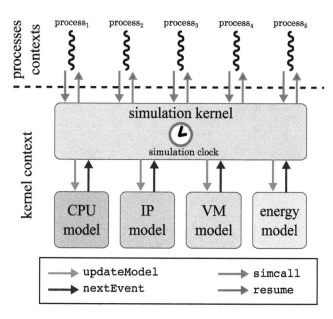

Figure 9: Simulation architecture of SimGrid.

models of CPUs [30], TCP/IP networks [31], VMs [19], and energy consumption [18] which are theoretically sound and experimentally assessed. Using these models, SimGrid accurately simulates the resources usage (i.e. CPU and bandwidth sharing), the execution time and the energy consumption of a distributed application code. Thus, platform enables to simulate the behavior of a distributed system on a single-computer. SimGrid has grounded over 200 scientific works. SimGrid is implemented in C/C++ and available in open source at http://simgrid.org.

The SimGrid models are used to determine:

(1) how much computing resources are allocated to each action of the distributed application, e.g. how much bandwidth is used by each data transfer.

(2) when each action ends, e.g. when do the data transfers end.

The SimGrid models are based on the discrete event paradigm, where an internal event corresponds to the completion of an action. Each model can be controlled using two operations:

- `updateModel()` updates the model to the current simulated time.
- `nextEvent()` get the date of the next internal event of the model.

SimGrid compartmentalizes the execution of the distributed processes to strictly manage their co-evolution and interactions with the models. This design, where each interaction of the processes with their environment is strictly mediated by a kernel is highly inspired from the classical design of an

Operating System. To that extend, SimGrid gives a dedicated execution context to each process of the distributed application. These execution contexts can be implemented either with classical threads or with lighter *continuations* [2] mechanisms.

This architecture, depicted in Figures 8 and 9, was first introduced to enable the parallel execution of the user processes [26] without relying of fine-grain locking of the simulator internals. It also enables the formal verification of legacy distributed applications, since their interactions with their environment are strictly controlled by the framework when they run within the simulator [25].

During a typical SimGrid simulation, all user processes are conceptually executed in parallel (in practice, parallelism can be disabled on user request). A **simulation kernel**, which has its own execution context, is in charge of:

(1) managing the simulation state (e.g. the simulation clock),

(2) coordinating the processes and models' executions, and

(3) mediating interactions between user code and models.

Some process actions can modify the state of a model. In our use case, examples of such actions include: starting a VM, sending data through the network, using CPU, migrating a VM and turning off a PM. When a process wants to perform an action that modifies the state of a model, it needs to use the *simcall* mechanism of the kernel. This mechanism is the equivalent of a system call in a classical OS. It causes the process to be blocked until the requested action ends in the simulation. As a consequence (1) the simulation clock may change between the time when a process is blocked and resumed by a simcall, and (2) every process computation that occurs between two simcalls are considered to be instantaneous in the simulated time.

When all processes are blocked at given simulation time, a context switch is performed to the kernel in order to move forward simulation time. The kernel first sequentially (and in a deterministic order) changes the models' states according to the requests made by the processes. Then, following a discrete event logic, it synchronizes the models and processes executions by:

(1) calling the `nextEvent` method of each model in order to determine the time of the earliest internal event;

(2) updating the simulation clock and sequentially calling the `updateModel` method of all the models in order to move forward the simulation to the earliest internal event time;

(3) eventually resuming the processes whose simcalls ends. This step cause a context switch to the processes.

The Figure 8 summarizes this simulation behavior. Thanks to this unique model of execution, SimGrid can mix simulation models with distributed application code in order to perform scalable and deterministic simulation. We propose to take advantage of this feature in our context of DCPS simulation, by embedding each FMU-CS into a dedicated SimGrid model. In the following, we detail this proposition.

4 CONTRIBUTION

As shown in Figure 10, our approach is to import FMU-CS into a dedicated model which is added in the SimGrid simulation kernel. The kernel can then control the FMU like any other model. Note that with this mechanism, several FMUs can be imported in SimGrid, each of them being associated with a dedicated model. All the FMUs can then interact separately with the distributed application processes.

In traditional discrete event and multi-physical equation-based tools, such as an FMU co-simulation master, or Open-Modelica, the input/output connections between an FMU and its environment are determined a priori at the model design time. Moreover, these links are in general hardwired and cannot be changed at run-time. In order to integrate FMU-CS in the SimGrid environment, we use a more flexible interaction mechanism which can handle the complexity of concurrent program behavior. Indeed, any of the computing processes is likely to interact with an FMU. Moreover, some of these processes may be created or killed during the simulation. As a consequence, with some complex concurrent code, it is very difficult –if not impossible– to determine a priori the interactions between each process and an FMU.

In the following, we detail how the FMU execution is coordinated with the distributed application (Section 4.1), how FMUs and distributed programs interact (Section 4.2), and how we overcome the FMI-CS limitation in terms of hybrid simulation (Section 4.3).

We rely on FMI++ [33] to implement our solution. This library provides high-level functionalities to load and manipulate FMUs in order to ease their integration in discrete simulation tools.

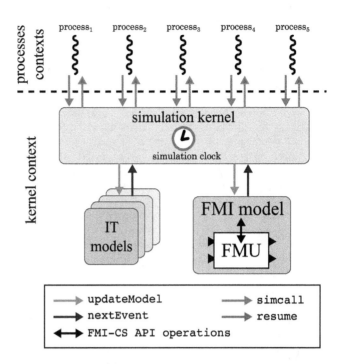

Figure 10: Integration of FMU into the simulation architecture of SimGrid.

4.1 Coordination of FMU and distributed application

When the `updateModel` method of this SimGrid model is called by the kernel, it performs a `doStep` in order to move forward the FMU to the desired simulation time. This mechanism enables then to coordinate the simulations of the FMU and the distributed application.

In order to simulate our use-case, we can then import the FMU of our thermal system model in SimGrid. The thermal system will then co-evolve with the distributed application running in the data-centers.

Note that, as the SimGrid kernel performs discrete event simulations, our synchronization mechanism requires the FMU to support variable communication step-sizes. To handle an FMU that does not comply with this constraint, we can use the dedicated `FixedStepSizeFMU` wrapper of FMI++. This wrapper, implements a fixed step-size simulation algorithm that positions the FMU as close as possible to the required communication point. This may induce inaccurate results as the model synchronization is not perfectly done. However, this inaccuracy is inherent to fixed-step size simulation models.

4.2 Continuous input and output interactions

To enable flexible interactions between the FMUs and the distributed applications, we make all the input and output ports of all the FMUs imported in SimGrid accessible to all the running processes. We extend the SimGrid API with two methods that can be used by the processes in order to interact with the FMUs:

- getReal/Integer/Boolean/String(string name) returns the current value of the variable name.
- setReal/Integer/Boolean/String(string name, double/int/bool/string value, bool doStep) sets the value of the variable name to value. If needed, the doStep parameter can be set to true in order to perform a doStep of duration 0 to update the FMU outputs. As it modifies the state of the FMU –which is now considered as a SimGrid model– this function triggers a SimGrid simcall. The inputs of the FMU is then set within the kernel context of SimGrid in order to maintain a deterministic simulation execution. This simcall ends at the same simulation time, making the set operations instantaneous from the simulation point of view.

In our use-case, we use these methods to update the PM power consumption in the FMU with the value computed by SimGrid. The Algorithms 3 and 4 show how we easily extends the Algorithms 1 and 2 for this purpose. We also design a simple sampling process behavior (shown in Algorithm 5) to observe the continuous state trajectory of the FMU (i.e. the evolution of the temperature in DC1) during the simulation.

Algorithm 3: Extension (in red) of the scheduling algorithm in order to interact with the FMU.

> **while** DC1 is not full **do**
>   Let pmList be the list of PM of DC1.
>   **for** pm in pmList **do**
>   **if** pm as enough cores available to run a VM **then**
>   deploy VM on pm
>   Let p be the current power consumption of DC1.
>   setReal("$P_{load_{DC}}$",p)
>   break
>   **end if**
>   **end for**
> **end while**

4.3 discrete event interaction

In order to comply with the requirements of hybrid modeling, we have to overcome the limitations of FMI-CS in terms of discrete event behavior (introduced in Section 3.1). We design an event triggering mechanism which emulates discrete event output signals from the continuous output of the FMU. Thanks to this mechanism, discrete changes in the FMU (e.g. the chiller failure and power supply shutdown in our use case) can then be notified to the distributed application.

We extend the SimGrid API with the following method:

```
registerEvent(bool (*condition)(vector<string>),
              void (*callback)(vector<string>),
              vector<std::string> parameters)
```

Algorithm 4: Extension (in red) of the emergency algorithm to interact with the FMU.

> wait for emergency message
> shutdown unused PM in DC1
> Let p be the current power consumption of DC1.
> setReal("$P_{load_{DC}}$",p)
> Let deployedVM be the list of all VM deployed on DC1.
> **for** vm in deployedVM **do**
>   Let pm0 be the PM of vm.
>   Let pmList be the list of PM of DC2.
>   **for** pm1 in pmList2 **do**
>   **if** pm1 as enough cores available to run vm **then**
>   migrate vm on pm1
>   **if** pm0 is empty **then**
>   shutdown pm0
>   **end if**
>   Update p.
>   setReal("$P_{load_{DC}}$",p)
>   break
>   **end if**
>   **end for**
> **end for**

Algorithm 5: sampling algorithm which monitors the temperature evolution.

> **while** true **do**
>   double temp = getReal("$T_{R_{out}}$")
>   save the value of temp in output log
>   wait x seconds
> **end while**

This method registers an event notification request to the SimGrid model that embeds the FMU. This mechanism enables flexible interactions between the FMU and the distributed application since any process of the distributed application can use it at any simulated time. Moreover, each process is free to specify in which conditions the event occurs by specifying the condition function. Each process also sets what is its impact on the distributed application by specifying the callback method. For instance, this effect can range from simple logging activity to process kill, creation, resuming or suspending. When executed, both condition and callback receive parameters as input.

Each time registerEvent is called by a process, an instantaneous simcall, in terms of simulated time, is triggered to ensure a deterministic simulation, and the event notification request is stored in the SimGrid model which contains the FMU. The event conditions are evaluated immediately and after each modification of the FMU state –i.e. after each call to setReal/Integer/Boolean/String and updateModel. When the condition is satisfied, the associated callback function is executed to propagate the event effect in the distributed application. The event notification request is then deleted

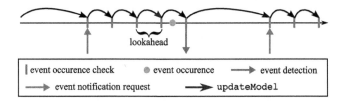

Figure 11: Example of event detection with the lookahead strategy.

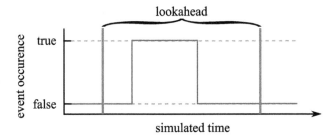

Figure 12: Example of undetected event occurrence with the lookahead strategy.

(but note that the callback function is free to register another similar request).

When at least one event notification request is pending, we use a classical lookahead exploration strategy in order to accurately determine the occurrence time of events. This strategy, shown in Figure 11, consists in scheduling internal events at regular intervals (using the `nextEvent` method of the SimGrid model) in order to frequently check if an event has occur in the FMU. The fixed delay between these intervals corresponds to the lookahead of the model. It is determined by the user at the FMU import time. Setting the lookahead is about finding a trade-off between accuracy and performance, as both determine the event detection precision, and the frequency of event checks. A known limitation of this strategy is that it may miss some event occurrences if the lookahead is too large (as shown in Figure 12). We could have used other event detection algorithms that may be more accurate and efficient (like bisectional search, regular falsi or the Illinois algorithm [23]). However, these strategies are less generic as they are only compliant with FMUs which implement the optional rollback features [8]. As soon as there are no pending event notification requests, the SimGrid model containing the FMU stops scheduling internal events.

Getting back to our use-case, we can use this mechanism to handle the events related to the chiller failure and the power supply shutdown. The behavior of the probe that waits for the chiller failure and sends a message to the emergency manager is formalized by the Algorithm 6. This algorithm uses a `zeroValue` condition function that returns true when the *chiller* output variable of the FMU is equal to 0, and a `wakeMeUp` callback function that simply resumes the probe process execution. In order to manage the power supply shutdown, we register an event notification at the beginning

of the simulation with a condition function that detects when *power* = 0, and a callback function that creates the PM shutdown process.

Algorithm 6: algorithm of the probe detecting chiller failure.

`registerEvent(zeroValue,wakeMeUp,nullptr)`
suspend the execution of this process
send the message to the emergency manager

---

5 EVALUATION

To evaluate our solution, we perform the co-simulation of our use-case and study the simulation results. In the following, we detail how we validate our solution. We first describes our experimental scenario in Table 1. Then, we detail and interpret the simulation results in Section 5.1. Finally, we detail our validation process in Section 5.2.

5.1 Results interpretation

Figure 13 shows the simulation results of our co-simulation with SimGrid: the power consumption of the system, the temperature of DC1, the status of the chiller, and the power supply over time. We can see that from simulation time 0 to time 260, the power consumption of DC1 (computed by SimGrid) and the chiller load (computed by the FMU-CS) increase progressively. This is due to the scheduling algorithm (Algorithm 1) that is deploying VM every 10 seconds.

At time 260, the chiller load exceeds the critical load of 23,000 W and the chiller stops functioning. As a consequence, the chiller load falls immediately down to 0, the temperature starts increasing, and the probe sends a message to notify this issue. After a transmission delay simulated by the TCP model of SimGrid, this message is received at time 260.263 by the emergency manager (Algorithm 2) which immediately shutdowns the unused PM in DC1. As a consequence, the power consumption of DC1 decreases suddenly from 17,310 W to 9,668.8 W.

Then, from time 260.263 to time 846.614, the emergency manager migrates VMs from DC1 to DC2. This causes an increase of the power consumption of DC2 and a decrease of the power consumption of DC1. Note that the power consumption of DC1 changes at a faster rate than the power consumption of DC2. This is due to the PM shutdowns performed by the emergency manager in DC1. We can see that, by transferring the computation load from DC1 to DC2, the emergency manager progressively limits the temperature increase in DC1. However this is not sufficient and, at time 846.614, the temperature reaches the critical threshold of 40°C and the power supply of DC1 is shut down. This event is successfully propagated to SimGrid as all the PMs are immediately turned off and the total power consumption rapidly reaches 0. These results are in complete accordance with the expected behavior.

Domain	Parameters	Value
	inlet air temperature $T_{R_{in}}$	24 °C
	mass of the air in the room m_{air}	294 kg
	specific heat	1.006 kJ/kg
Physical system model	cooling inefficiency	0.9
	chiller critical load $criticalLoad$	23 kW
	temperature threshold $tempThreshold$	40 °C
	ratio of the other devices in the total DC heat dissipation	0.2
	number of PM in each DC	129
	PM core size	12
	PM maximum power consumption	220 W
	PM power consumption when using 1 core	128 W
IT model	PM idle power consumption	97 W
	PM off power consumption	0 W
	VM RAM size	3 Go
	VM core size	6
	VM deployment time (i.e. delay between two deployments)	10 sec
Co-simulation	lookahead value (i.e. event detection precision)	0.01 sec

Table 1: Experimental conditions.

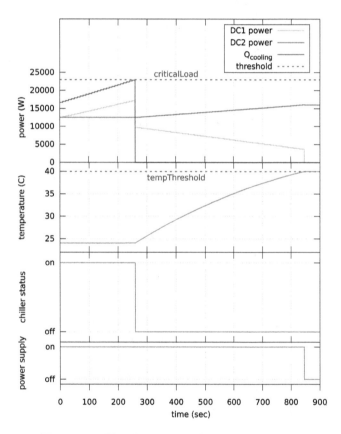

Figure 13: Simulation results of the use-case.

5.2 Validation

As shown in Figure 14, to validate this co-simulation, we compare these results with the trajectory generated by a monolithic simulation performed with OpenModelica. As

it is not possible to model and simulate our IT system in Modelica, we use the power consumption traces generated by SimGrid as input of OpenModelica. We found similar simulation results. Because it immediately depends on the PM power consumption, the chiller failure occurs at the exact same simulation time. The power shutdown occurs less than 0.001 second earlier in the OpenModelica simulation. This is in accordance with our expectations because it corresponds to the event detection precision (i.e. the lookahead) that we set in our co-simulation.

In order to test our capacity to handle several FMUs, we split our physical model into two FMUs. The first FMU embeds the equation 7 and corresponds to the chiller failure model. The second FMU contains the other equations of the physical model. We modify the Algorithm 3 and 4 to update the two FMU inputs. The event notification request related to the chiller failure (resp. power supply shutdown) is now registered in the first (resp. second) FMU. The co-simulation results obtained are again similar to the monolithic simulation. Therefore, these experiments demonstrates the validity of our solution.

6 CONCLUSION

In this article, we detailed how FMU-CS are integrated into the SimGrid platform in order to manage the co-simulation of multi-physical models and concurrent programs. Our contribution consists in embedding FMUs into a dedicated SimGrid model. We proposed an extension of the SimGrid API that enables flexible interactions between FMU and concurrent program. In particular, we defined a dynamic generation mechanism of discrete event signals that overcomes the limitations of FMU in terms of hybrid simulation. We experimentally validated our solution by demonstrating that our co-simulation of a chiller failure in a data-center gives similar results when compared to a monolithic simulation.

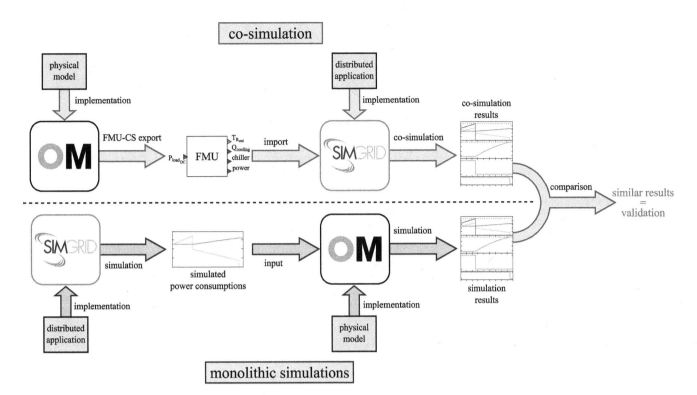

Figure 14: Validation process.

From a software perspective, it is important to note that our solution does not require any extension of the SimGrid simulation kernel. It corresponds then to a SimGrid plug-in. All our code is open-source and it will be soon integrated in the SimGrid distribution.

Our solution has several advantages:

- **versatility:** we can import models from the numerous multi-physical M&S tools that support the FMI-CS standard. Also, we benefit from the validated IT models of SimGrid and its diversity of application contexts. Thus, FMU-CS can now interact with Grids, Clouds, High Performance Computing infrastructures or Peer-to-Peer systems.

- **reproducibility:** we benefit from the OS-based simulation architecture of SimGrid that ensures deterministic co-simulation between FMUs and concurrent programs.

- **scalability:** thanks to the optimized model of execution of SimGrid, FMU-CS can simultaneously interact with a very large amount a concurrent processes.

A limit of our approach is that we rely on a lookahead algorithm to detect event occurrences in the FMU. This strategy may be less efficient and accurate than other algorithms of the literature but it is more generic in term of FMU integration. Also, we are able to import simultaneously several FMUs into SimGrid and make them interact with concurrent processes. However, the potential interactions between these FMU have to be handled in an ad-hoc way. Considering the complexity of FMU interactions which often require numerical methods (e.g. algebraic loop resolution, numerical error estimation) a more generic and automatic solution is required.

In future work, we plan to extend our proposition in order to integrate tools that support the FMU-ME standard. We also plan to implement other event-detection algorithms to increase the accuracy and performance of our co-simulations. As soon as they will be available, we want to take advantage of the new FMI 2.1 extensions for hybrid simulation. Finally, we plan to use this work in order to simulate green computing systems where Smart-Grid models interact with distributed cloud infrastructures.

REFERENCES

[1] S. Akoush, R. Sohan, A. Rice, A. W. Moore, and A. Hopper. 2010. Predicting the Performance of Virtual Machine Migration. In *2010 IEEE International Symposium on Modeling, Analysis and Simulation of Computer and Telecommunication Systems*. IEEE, Miami Beach, FL, USA, 37–46. https://doi.org/10.1109/MASCOTS.2010.13

[2] A. W. Appel and T. Jim. 1989. Continuation-passing, Closure-passing Style. In *Proceedings of the 16th ACM SIGPLAN-SIGACT Symposium on Principles of Programming Languages (POPL '89)*. ACM, New York, NY, USA, 293–302. https://doi.org/10.1145/75277.75303

[3] Jens Bastian, Christop Clauß, Susann Wolf, and Peter Schneider. 2011. Master for Co-Simulation Using FMI. In *Proceedings of the 8th International Modelica Conference*. Linköping University Electronic Press; Linköpings universitet, Dresden, Germany, 115–120.

[4] Torsten Blochwitz, Martin Otter, Johan Åkesson, et al. 2012. Functional mockup interface 2.0: The standard for tool independent exchange of simulation models. In *Proc. 9th International*

Modelica Conference. The Modelica Association, Munich, Germany, 173–184.

[5] David Broman, Christopher Brooks, Lev Greenberg, Edward A. Lee, Michael Masin, Stavros Tripakis, and Michael Wetter. 2013. Determinate Composition of FMUs for Co-simulation. In *Proceedings of the Eleventh ACM International Conference on Embedded Software*. IEEE Press, Piscataway, NJ, USA.

[6] Benjamin Camus, Fanny Dufossé, and Anne-Cécile Orgerie. 2017. A Stochastic Approach for Optimizing Green Energy Consumption in Distributed Clouds. In *SMARTGREENS 2017 - Proceedings of the 6th International Conference on Smart Cities and Green ICT Systems*. SciTePress, Porto, Portugal, 47–59. https://doi.org/10.5220/0006306500470059

[7] Benjamin Camus, Virginie Galtier, Mathieu Caujolle, Vincent Chevrier, Julien Vaubourg, Laurent Ciarletta, and Christine Bourjot. 2016. Hybrid Co-simulation of FMUs using DEV&DESS in MECSYCO. In *Proceedings of the Symposium on Theory of Modeling & Simulation - DEVS Integrative M&S Symposium*. Society for Modeling & Simulation International (SCS), Pasadena, CA, USA.

[8] Benjamin Camus, Thomas Paris, Julien Vaubourg, Yannick Presse, Christine Bourjot, Laurent Ciarletta, and Vincent Chevrier. 2018. Co-simulation of cyber-physical systems using a DEVS wrapping strategy in the MECSYCO middleware. *SIMULATION* 0, 0 (2018), 0037549717749014. https://doi.org/10.1177/0037549717749014

[9] Henri Casanova, Arnaud Giersch, Arnaud Legrand, Martin Quinson, and Frédéric Suter. 2014. Versatile, Scalable, and Accurate Simulation of Distributed Applications and Platforms. *J. Parallel and Distrib. Comput.* 74, 10 (June 2014), 2899–2917. http://hal.inria.fr/hal-01017319

[10] Francois E Cellier. 1979. Combined continuous/discrete system simulation languages–usefulness, experiences and future development. *Methodology in systems modelling and simulation* 9, 1 (1979), 201–220.

[11] Fabio Cremona, Marten Lohstroh, Stavros Tipakis, Christopher Brooks, and Edward A. Lee. 2016. FIDE – An FMI Integrated Development Environment. In *SAC'16*, ACM (Ed.). ACM, Pisa, Italy.

[12] Leandro Fontoura Cupertino, Georges Da Costa, Ariel Oleksiak, Wojciech Piatek, Jean-Marc Pierson, Jaume Salom, Laura Siso, Patricia Stolf, Hongyang Sun, and Thomas Zilio. 2015. Energy-Efficient, Thermal-Aware Modeling and Simulation of Datacenters: The CoolEmAll Approach and Evaluation Results. *Ad Hoc Networks* vol. 25 (February 2015), pp. 535–553. http://oatao.univ-toulouse.fr/15206/ Thanks to Elsevier editor. The definitive version is available at http://www.sciencedirect.com The original PDF of the article can be found at Ad Hoc Networks website : www.sciencedirect.com/science/journal/15708705.

[13] Joachim Denil, Bart Meyers, Paul De Meulenaere, and Hans Vangheluwe. 2015. Explicit Semantic Adaptation of Hybrid Formalisms for FMI Co-simulation. In *Proceedings of the Symposium on Theory of Modeling & Simulation: DEVS Integrative M&S Symposium (DEVS '15)*. Society for Computer Simulation International, San Diego, CA, USA, 99–106. http://dl.acm.org/citation.cfm?id=2872965.2872979

[14] Saikou Y. Diallo, Heber Herencia-Zapana, Jose J. Padilla, and Andreas Tolk. 2011. Understanding interoperability. In *Proceedings of the 2011 Emerging M&S Applications in Industry and Academia Symposium*. SCS, San Diego, CA, USA, 84–91.

[15] Virginie Galtier, Stephane Vialle, Cherifa Dad, et al. 2015. FMI-Based Distributed Multi-Simulation with DACCOSIM. In *DEVS '15 Proceedings of the Symposium on Theory of Modeling & Simulation: DEVS Integrative M&S Symposium*. Society for Computer Simulation International, Munich, Germany, 39–46.

[16] Leilani Gilpin, Laurent Ciarletta, Yannick Presse, Vincent Chevrier, and Virginie Galtier. 2014. Co-simulation Solution using AA4MM-FMI applied to Smart Space Heating Models. In *7th International ICST Conference on Simulation Tools and Techniques*. ICST (Institute for Computer Sciences, Social-Informatics and Telecommunications Engineering), Lisbon, Portugal, 153–159.

[17] Cláudio Gomes, Casper Thule, David Broman, Peter Gorm Larsen, and Hans Vangheluwe. 2017. Co-simulation: State of the art.

CoRR abs/1702.00686 (2017), 157. arXiv:1702.00686 http://arxiv.org/abs/1702.00686

[18] Franz C. Heinrich, Tom Cornebize, Augustin Degomme, Arnaud Legrand, Alexandra Carpen-Amarie, Sascha Hunold, Anne-Cécile Orgerie, and Martin Quinson. 2017. Predicting the Energy Consumption of MPI Applications at Scale Using a Single Node. In *IEEE Cluster*. IEEE, Honolulu, HI, USA, 92–102.

[19] T. Hirofuchi, A. Lebre, and L. Pouilloux. 2015. SimGrid VM: Virtual Machine Support for a Simulation Framework of Distributed Systems. *IEEE Transactions on Cloud Computing* PP, 99 (Sept. 2015), 1–14.

[20] Yunbo Li, Anne-Cécile Orgerie, and Jean-Marc Menaud. 2015. Opportunistic Scheduling in Clouds Partially Powered by Green Energy. In *IEEE International Conference on Green Computing and Communications (GreenCom)*. IEEE, Sydney, Australia, 448–455.

[21] Saurabh Mittal, Mark Ruth, Annabelle Pratt, et al. 2015. A System-of-systems Approach for Integrated Energy Systems Modeling and Simulation. In *Proceedings of the Conference on Summer Computer Simulation*. SCS/ACM, Chicago, Illinois, USA, 1–10.

[22] MODELISAR Consortium and Modelica Association. 2014. Functional Mock-up Interface for Model Exchange and Co-Simulation – Version 2.0, July 25, 2014. Retrieved from https://www.fmi-standard.org. (2014).

[23] Cleve Moler. 1997. Are We There Yet? Zero Crossing and Event Handling for Differential Equations. *Matlab News & Notes Simulink 2, special edition* (1997), 16–17.

[24] W. Muller and E. Widl. 2013. Linking FMI-based components with discrete event systems. In *Proc. SysCon*. IEEE, Orlando, FL, USA, 676–680. https://doi.org/10.1109/SysCon.2013.6549955

[25] Anh Pham, Thierry Jéron, and Martin Quinson. 2017. Verifying MPI Applications with SimGridMC. In *Proceedings of the First International Workshop on Software Correctness for HPC Applications (Correctness'17)*. ACM, New York, NY, USA, 28–33. https://doi.org/10.1145/3145344.3145345

[26] Martin Quinson, Cristian Rosa, and Christophe Thiery. 2012. Parallel Simulation of Peer-to-Peer Systems. In *Proceedings of the 2012 12th IEEE/ACM International Symposium on Cluster, Cloud and Grid Computing (Ccgrid 2012) (CCGRID '12)*. IEEE Computer Society, Washington, DC, USA, 668–675. https://doi.org/10.1109/CCGrid.2012.115

[27] Ragunathan (Raj) Rajkumar, Insup Lee, Lui Sha, and John Stankovic. 2010. Cyber-physical Systems: The Next Computing Revolution. In *Proceedings of the 47th Design Automation Conference*. ACM, New York, NY, USA, 731–736.

[28] Jean-Philippe Tavella, Mathieu Caujolle, Charles Tan, Gilles Plessis, Mathieu Schumann, Stéphane Vialle, Cherifa Dad, Arnaud Cuccuru, and Sébastien Revol. 2016. Toward an Hybrid Co-simulation with the FMI-CS Standard. (April 2016). Research Report.

[29] Hans Vangheluwe, Juan De Lara, and Pieter J Mosterman. 2002. An introduction to multi-paradigm modelling and simulation. In *Proceedings of the AIS'2002 Conference (AI, Simulation and Planning in High Autonomy Systems)*. SCS, Lisboa, Portugal, 9–20.

[30] Pedro Velho. 2011. *Accurate and Fast Simulations of Large-Scale Distributed Computing Systems*. Theses. Université Grenoble Alpes.

[31] Pedro Velho, Lucas Schnorr, Henri Casanova, and Arnaud Legrand. 2013. On the Validity of Flow-level TCP Network Models for Grid and Cloud Simulations. *ACM Transactions on Modeling and Computer Simulation* 23, 4 (Oct. 2013), 23:1–23:26.

[32] Kunpeng Wang, Peer-Olaf Siebers, and Darren Robinson. 2017. Towards Generalized Co-simulation of Urban Energy Systems. *Procedia Engineering* 198 (2017), 366 – 374. https://doi.org/10.1016/j.proeng.2017.07.092 Urban Transitions Conference, Shanghai, September 2016.

[33] E. Widl, W. Müller, A. Elsheikh, M. Hörtenhuber, and P. Palensky. 2013. The FMI++ library: A high-level utility package for FMI for model exchange. In *2013 Workshop on Modeling and Simulation of Cyber-Physical Energy Systems (MSCPES)*. IEEE, Berkeley, CA, USA, 1–6. https://doi.org/10.1109/MSCPES.2013.6623316

Calling Sequence Calculation for Sequential Co-simulation Master

Slaven Glumac
AVL-AST d.o.o.
Zagreb, Croatia
slaven.glumac@avl.com

Zdenko Kovačić
University of Zagreb
Zagreb, Croatia
zdenko.kovacic@fer.hr

ABSTRACT

This paper explores the improvement of non-iterative co-simulation master. A simple hybrid system is depicted and analyzed. Based on this analysis guidelines for calculating the calling sequence are introduced. Guidelines allow the implementation of a new constraint programming algorithm. This algorithm allows better calling sequence selection based solely on information about connecting the co-simulation network. The algorithm is confirmed by the example of co-simulation of a hybrid electric vehicle. In this example, the constraint programming algorithm found a subjectively good calling sequence without any involvement of the model developer.

CCS CONCEPTS

• **Mathematics of computing → Permutations and combinations**; **Discretization**; *Mathematical software*;

KEYWORDS

non-iterative co-simulation, FMI, sequential master, calling sequence, hybrid system, constraint programming

ACM Reference Format:
Slaven Glumac and Zdenko Kovačić. 2018. Calling Sequence Calculation for Sequential Co-simulation Master. In *Proceedings of SIGSIM-PADS '18: SIGSIM Principles of Advanced Discrete Simulation CD-ROM (SIGSIM-PADS '18)*. ACM, New York, NY, USA, 4 pages. https://doi.org/10.1145/3200921.3200924

1 INTRODUCTION

The design of complex systems includes simultaneous and distributed development in different engineering domains. Co-simulation facilitates this process by enabling distributed modeling and early detection of problems [14]. The standardization of co-simulation interface is presented with Functional Mock-up Interface [7].

In practice co-simulation has a limit in the number of co-simulation slaves [14]. One of the reasons may be prevalent use of non-iterative (explicit) co-simulation [5]. With a non-iterative co-simulation master it is possible to configure scheduling, extrapolation techniques and step-size [4]. There has already been work done on extrapolation methods and step-size selection [3–6, 11]. However, the

Permission to make digital or hard copies of all or part of this work for personal or classroom use is granted without fee provided that copies are not made or distributed for profit or commercial advantage and that copies bear this notice and the full citation on the first page. Copyrights for components of this work owned by others than the author(s) must be honored. Abstracting with credit is permitted. To copy otherwise, or republish, to post on servers or to redistribute to lists, requires prior specific permission and/or a fee. Request permissions from permissions@acm.org.

SIGSIM-PADS '18 , May 23–25, 2018, Rome, Italy

© 2018 Copyright held by the owner/author(s). Publication rights licensed to the Association for Computing Machinery.
ACM ISBN 978-1-4503-5092-1/18/05...$15.00
https://doi.org/10.1145/3200921.3200924

scheduling, and in particular, the calling sequence calculation is less covered topic. In [2] a contractivity condition is presented which can determine the calling sequence of continuous white box systems in sequential modular time integration. There is a report on order reduction of the simulation error when changing the calling sequence [10]. Furthermore, practical complex systems introduce events that require an extension of analysis for continuous systems [9]. The effects of an instantaneous event can not be fully compensated with non-iterative co-simulation, and there is very little work on this topic.

This paper tries to focus on the question of how to improve a hybrid co-simulation given only mandatory information and a simple sequential co-simulation master. The information is limited to black box co-simulation slaves and connections between their ports. To the best of authors knowledge, the presented algorithm for the calling sequence calculation is a new contribution for the configuration of sequential non-iterative co-simulation. In the following section, definitions of co-simulation slave, co-simulation network and co-simulation master are formally given. The following section presents a set of guidelines for calculating the calling sequence of co-simulation slaves. A constraint algorithm is formulated which implements the guidelines. The verification of the algorithm follows in the next section. A hybrid electrical vehicle co-simulation is used to verify the algorithm.

2 CO-SIMULATION MODEL

A co-simulation slave according to the FMI 2.0 standard is a tuple:

$$F_i = (S_i, U_i, Y_i, D_i, s_i, set_i, get_i, doStep_i) \quad (1)$$

where S_i is a set of internal states of F_i, U_i is a set of input variables, Y_i is a set of output variables, $D_i \subset U_i \times Y_i$ is a set of output-input dependencies[1] s_i is an initial state of the FMU, set_i is a function which sets the value to an input variable, get_i is a function which returns the value of an output variable, and

$$doStep_i : (S_i, \mathcal{R}^+) \to S_i \quad (2)$$

is a function which implements a simulation step. This model of a co-simulation slave has been adopted and adapted from [8]. The $doStep_i$ has been modified to disable will the ability to reject a step size given by the master. This implies that a slave does not provide the master any event information. A network of co-simulation slaves is a tuple:

$$N = (F, P) \quad (3)$$

where $F = \{F_1, F_2, \ldots F_n\}$ is a set of co-simulation slaves, U is a set of input variables of all co-simulation slaves, and Y is a set of output

---

[1] Output-input dependency information is an optional part of the FMI 2.0 standard.

Algorithm 1 Sequential co-simulation master

Require: $N, \sigma, \Delta t, t_0, t_{end}$
  $t = t_0$ ▷ Initialization phase
  for $r \in I$ **do**
    for $i \in I$ **do**
      $y_j = P(u_i);$ $v = get_j(s_j, y_j);$ $s_i = set_i(s_i, u_i, v)$
  while $t < t_{end}$ **do**   ▷ Computation phase
    for $r \in I$ **do**
      $i = \sigma(r)$
      for $u_i \in U_i$ **do**
        $y_j = P(u_i);$ $v = get_j(s_j, y_j);$ $s_i = set_i(s_i, u_i, v)$
      $s_i = doStep_i(s_i, \Delta t)$
    $t = t + \Delta t$
---

variables of all co-simulation slaves, $P : U \rightarrow Y$ is a mapping of output-input connections.

A co-simulation master is a function which takes a network of co-simulation slaves N, a start time t_0, an end time t_{end} and produces the timed sequence output of all co-simulation slaves. A co-simulation master studied in this paper is a sequential master presented in the Algorithm 1. That master is determined by the communication step size Δt and the calling sequence of slaves:

$$\sigma : I \rightarrow I \qquad (4)$$

where $I = \{1, 2, \cdots, n\}$ is a set of indices of co-simulation slaves. The calling sequence σ is a permutation of slave indices and introduces a master parameter required to tune each co-simulation network. There are $n!$ possible sequences which make a choice of a calling sequence very difficult in the case of a large number of co-simulation slaves. The implementation in the Python programming language of the Algorithm 1 can be found at [13].

3   SEQUENCE CALCULATION

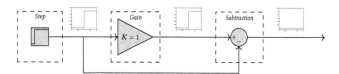

Figure 1: A co-simulation network simulates a *Step* signal and its propagation through co-simulation slaves; *Gain* and *Subtraction*.

The example *Step Subtraction* (Figure 1) has been created based on simultaneous event example in [9]. The event monitored in the example is a step jump of a signal value and its propagation through the co-simulation network. It is used to highlight some of the phenomena which arise with the modification of a calling sequence applied to a hybrid co-simulation. The implementation of co-simulation slaves used in the example *Step Subtraction* can be found at [12]. The example presents a network of three ($n = 3$) co-simulation slaves; the *Step*, the *Gain* and the *Subtraction* (Figure 1). The first co-simulation slave *Step* simulates a unit step signal:

$$y_1(t) = \mu(t - t_{step}) \qquad (5)$$

The second co-simulation slave *Gain* simulates a gain of an input signal:

$$y_2(t) = Ku_2(t) \qquad (6)$$

The third co-simulation slave *Subtraction* simulates a subtraction of input signals:

$$y_3(t) = u_{31}(t) - u_{32}(t) \qquad (7)$$

This network has $n! = 3! = 6$ possible calling sequences. Each of them has been assigned to the Algorithm 1 and executed. The influence of a calling sequence is visible in Figure 2. The plot can be reproduced using the Python implementation found at [13]. The event propagated through the co-simulation network (Figure 1) is a jump of a signal value. The results in Figure 2 show that this event is delayed with respect to the reference if the calling sequence is inappropriate. The two sequences that give results matching to analytic ones are (1,2,3) and (3,1,2).

The output-input dependency of the *Gain* can explain away some of the non-matching results. It is the reason the event observed at the input of the *Gain* is immediately propagated to its output. This is the reason calling sequences (1, 2, 3), (1, 3, 2), (3, 1, 2) give correct results for output of *Gain*. In these sequences the *Gain* follows the

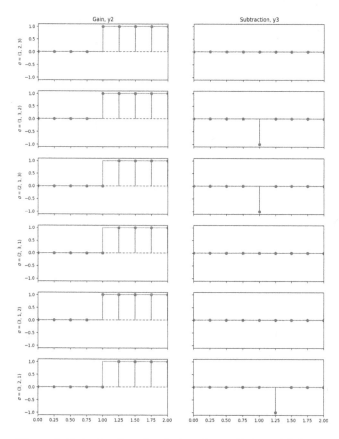

Figure 2: Outputs of co-simulation slaves *Gain* and *Subtraction* is monitored for different calling sequences (blue)and compared with their analytic reference plotted red. The indices of co-simulation slaves *Step*, *Gain* and *Subtraction*, respectively 1, 2 and 3 are used to denote calling sequences.

Step in the sequence and there is no time delay between the two slaves.

OBSERVATION 1 (OUTPUT-INPUT DEPENDENCIES). *Let there exist a connection $y_j = P(u_i)$ between slave i and slave j and the input variable of slave i is in its list of output-input dependencies $(u_i, y_i) \in D_i$. The slave j should follow slave i in the calling sequence, i.e.:*

$$\sigma(j) < \sigma(i)$$

Non-simultaneous input of the *Subtract* can explain away the remaining incorrect sequence. The sequence (1, 3, 2) gives different results for the output of the *Subtract* compared to the analytic solution. The sequence causes the *Step* to be executed before the *Subtract* and the *Gain* after the *Subtract*. A jump event should be observed simultaneously at both inputs of the *Subtract* and this is not the case for this particular sequence. The sequence (3, 1, 2) introduces a delay on both inputs of the *Subtract* and, perhaps counterintuitive, results in the correct output of the slave.

GUIDELINE 1 (SIMULTANEOUS INPUTS). *Let*

$$J_i = \left\{ j \ : \ \forall u_i \in U_i. \ y_j = P(u_i) \right\}$$

denote the set of slave indices connected to inputs of a slave i. Either all slaves in J_i should lead i in a calling sequence or follow i in a calling sequence, i.e.:

$$(\forall j \in J_i. \ \sigma(j) < \sigma(i)) \wedge (\forall j \in J_i. \ \sigma(j) > \sigma(i))$$

This guideline does not require any additional information for the implementation other than connection information P. It implies that the introduction of delays is not as important as their coordination.

The sequence (3, 1, 2) yields results equal to the analytic solution, although it introduces a delay in the co-simulation network. This particular sequence would fail if the *Gain* introduces a change in the magnitude of the signal. It would leave the sequence (1, 2, 3) as the only sequence matching the analytic results. These observations give the following guideline:

GUIDELINE 2 (COMMUNICATION DELAY MINIMIZATION). *Let d be the function counting the number of delays in the calling sequence:*

$$d(\sigma) = \sum_{i=1}^{n} \forall j \in J_i. \ \sigma(i) < \sigma(j)$$

The number of communication delays in a co-simulation should be minimized.

An additional argument for the previous guideline comes from the control theory. It can be safely assumed that co-simulation slaves are connected in closed loops[2]. Phase margin is a well established relative stability measure in the control theory [15]. It measures the amount of lag introduced to a closed loop system needed to bring it to the verge of instability. A co-simulation network is a discrete system which introduces additional lags with communication delays. With a delayed output-input connection $u[k] = y[k - 1]$, a phase lag introduced is equal to $\omega\Delta t$ for each delay.

---

[2] In an open loop, each slave can be executed separately without the need for synchronization. Timed sequences can be stored and read from a database.

Algorithm 2 Sequence calculation algorithm

Require: F, P

$S = \{\sigma : \sigma \in S_n \ \wedge \ g(\sigma)\}$

$S_{min} = \left\{ \sigma_{min} : \sigma_{min} = \arg \min_{\sigma \in S} d(\sigma) \right\}$

return S_{min}

The implementation of the Algorithm 2 is done in the Python programming language, and is available at [13]. It implements the Guidelines 1 and 2 using constraint programming. The predicate function g implements Guideline 1. Since output-input dependency information is optional part of the FMI 2.0 standard, g did not implement the Observation 1 (Output-Input Dependencies) as a guideline.

The Algorithm 2 calculates a set of calling sequences. This set can contain zero or more sequences depending on the co-simulation network. It is the topic of the future work how to modify the presented algorithm to produce a single calling sequence.

4 HYBRID ELECTRICAL VEHICLE EXAMPLE

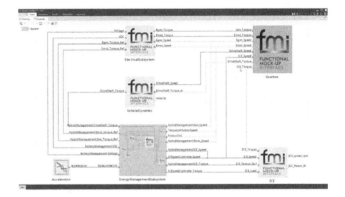

Figure 3: A co-simulation network used to model a hybrid electrical vehicle.

The example in this section is a co-simulation of a hybrid electrical vehicle (Figure 3). The co-simulation network presented is used as an installation example in AVL Model.CONNECT R2017f [1]. It contains 10 co-simulation slaves compliant to the FMI 2.0 standard; *ElectricalSubsystem, Gearbox, VehicleDynamics, ICE, RateLimiter, BatteryManagement, TorqueLimitation, Product, HybridManagement,* and *ICESpeedController*. This network simulates the behavior of a hybrid electrical vehicle during a stepwise signal *Acceleration* reference. It exhibits a number of events due to switching between the electrical motor, the internal combustion engine and the electrical generator.

In order to observe the effect of selecting a calling sequence, the torque on the drive shaft of the hybrid electrical vehicle is monitored. The co-simulation is run with the sequential co-simulation master and different calling sequences; manually adjusted one, one calculated automatically with the Algorithm 2, and a poorly chosen one. The comparison of these three calling sequences is presented in Figure 4. The calling sequence manually adjusted by the engineer

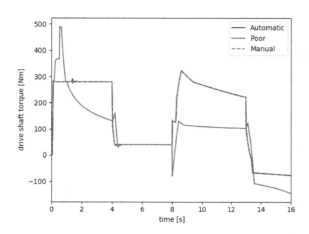

Figure 4: The drive shaft torque signal after a co-simulation with the fixed co-simulation step size of $T = 1$ ms. The plot compares the automatically calculated sequence (blue) and a poor calling sequence (green) to the manually adjusted reference one (dashed red).

is considered correct due to engineer's knowledge of the system. The poor calling sequence can exhibit quite a different behavior as seen in the figure.

Due to the number of possible calling sequences ($10! = 3628800$), a good choice can take quite a lot of trial and error attempts by an engineer. This increases the time before reaching the first successful co-simulation run. The automated calculation of the calling sequence gives an important advantage. The calling sequences obtained by the Algorithm 2 do not require a simulation run or any additional evaluation criteria. For the particular co-simulation network Algorithm 2 produces a set with a single calling sequence. Even though the manually adjusted calling sequence slightly outperforms the automated one, the decrease in configuration time can highly outweigh this imperfection.

5 CONCLUSION

This paper proposes a constraint programming algorithm for calculating the calling sequence for a non-iterative sequential co-simulation master. Constraints used in the algorithm are based on the guidelines introduced in the paper. To the best of authors knowledge both guidelines and the constraint programming algorithm are new contributions to the field of research. The algorithm is implemented in the Python programming language, and available at [13].

The proposed algorithm produces a set of candidate calling sequences that satisfy the guidelines. Since a set of sequences is produced, a sequential co-simulation may not be completely determined by the algorithm. Even worse, the produced set may be an empty set, i.e. the algorithm may not find a solution at all. These shortcomings will be addressed in the authors' future work.

Despite some drawbacks, the algorithm has an appealing property that it allows calculating a calling sequence only with information about connecting the co-simulation network. This advantage

has been demonstrated on the example of hybrid electrical vehicle co-simulation network. The configuration of this network is such that the algorithm produces a set of sequences containing a single calling sequence. The calculated sequence was slightly worse in accuracy than the one manually adjusted by a model developer. However, the calling sequence obtained by the model developer was obtained by repeated trial and error attempts. The trial and error approach requires multiple co-simulation runs while the proposed constraint programming algorithm requires only connection information. The cause of slightly worse behavior of the automatically calculated calling sequence and how it can be mitigated needs to be further explored. One obvious extension to the algorithm should be to add all available, but yet missing output-input dependency information in the exemplary co-simulation network. This topic is planned to be a part of authors' future work.

REFERENCES

[1] 2017. Model.CONNECT™ - IODP Portfolio - avl.com. (15 Dec. 2017). https://www.avl.com/-/model-connect-

[2] Martin Arnold. 2010. Stability of Sequential Modular Time Integration Methods for Coupled Multibody System Models. *Journal of Computational and Nonlinear Dynamics* 5, 3 (May 2010), 031003–031003–9. https://doi.org/10.1115/1.4001389

[3] Martin Arnold, Christoph Clauß, and Tom Schierz. 2014. Error Analysis and Error Estimates for Co-simulation in FMI for Model Exchange and Co-Simulation v2.0. In *Progress in Differential-Algebraic Equations*. Springer, Berlin, Heidelberg, 107–125. https://tinyurl.com/ycdng83s DOI: 10.1007/978-3-662-44926-4_6.

[4] M. Benedikt and F. R. Holzinger. 2016. Automated configuration for non-iterative co-simulation. In *2016 17th International Conference on Thermal, Mechanical and Multi-Physics Simulation and Experiments in Microelectronics and Microsystems (EuroSimE)*. 1–7. https://doi.org/10.1109/EuroSimE.2016.7463355

[5] Martin Benedikt, Daniel Watzenig, and Anton Hofer. 2013. Modelling and analysis of the non-iterative coupling process for co-simulation. *Mathematical and Computer Modelling of Dynamical Systems* 19, 5 (Oct. 2013), 451–470. https://doi.org/10.1080/13873954.2013.784340

[6] M Benedikt, D Watzenig, J Zehetner, and A Hofer. 2013. Nepce—a nearly energy preserving coupling element for weak-coupled problems and co-simulation. In *IV International Conference on Computational Methods for Coupled Problems in Science and Engineering, Coupled Problems*.

[7] Torsten Blochwitz, Martin Otter, Johan Åkesson, Martin Arnold, Christoph Clauss, Hilding Elmqvist, Markus Friedrich, Andreas Junghanns, Jakob Mauss, Dietmar Neumerkel, Hans Olsson, and Antoine Viel. 2012. Functional Mockup Interface 2.0: The Standard for Tool independent Exchange of Simulation Models. In *Proceedings of the 9th International Modelica Conference*. The Modelica Association, 173–184. https://doi.org/10.3384/ecp12076173

[8] David Broman, Christopher Brooks, Lev Greenberg, Edward A. Lee, Michael Masin, Stavros Tripakis, and Michael Wetter. 2013. Determinate Composition of FMUs for Co-simulation. In *Proceedings of the Eleventh ACM International Conference on Embedded Software (EMSOFT '13)*. IEEE Press, Piscataway, NJ, USA, 2:1–2:12. http://dl.acm.org/citation.cfm?id=2555754.2555756

[9] David Broman, Lev Greenberg, Edward A. Lee, Michael Masin, Stavros Tripakis, and Michael Wetter. 2015. Requirements for Hybrid Cosimulation Standards. In *Proceedings of the 18th International Conference on Hybrid Systems: Computation and Control (HSCC '15)*. ACM, New York, NY, USA, 179–188. https://doi.org/10.1145/2728606.2728629

[10] Martin Busch. 2012. *Zur effizienten Kopplung von Simulationsprogrammen*. kassel university press GmbH.

[11] M. Busch and Bernhard Schweizer. 2011. An explicit approach for controlling the macro-step size of co-simulation methods. In *Proceedings of the 7th European Nonlinear Dynamics Conference (ENOC 2011): July 24 - 29, 2011, Rome, Italy*, D. Bernadini (Ed.). 1–6. http://tubiblio.ulb.tu-darmstadt.de/77923/

[12] Slaven Glumac. 2017. BenchmarkFMUs: Configurations of components compliant to FMI 2.0 specification. (May 2017). https://github.com/sglumac/BenchmarkFMUs original-date: 2017-05-15T17:00:23Z.

[13] Slaven Glumac. 2018. Sequential Co-simulation. (Jan. 2018). https://github.com/sglumac/sequential_co_simulation original-date: 2018-01-07T12:31:45Z.

[14] Cláudio Gomes, Casper Thule, David Broman, Peter Gorm Larsen, and Hans Vangheluwe. 2017. Co-simulation: State of the art. *arXiv:1702.00686 [cs]* (Feb. 2017). http://arxiv.org/abs/1702.00686 arXiv: 1702.00686.

[15] Katsuhiko Ogata. 2009. *Modern Control Engineering* (5 edition ed.). Pearson, Boston.

Handling Dynamic Sets of Reactions
in Stochastic Simulation Algorithms

Till Köster
University of Rostock
Albert-Einstein-Straße 22
18059 Rostock, Germany
till.koester@uni-rostock.de

Adelinde M. Uhrmacher
University of Rostock
Albert-Einstein-Straße 22
18059 Rostock, Germany
adelinde.uhrmacher@uni-rostock.de

ABSTRACT

Reaction selection is a major and time consuming step of stochastic simulation algorithms. Current approaches focus on constant sets of reactions. However, in the case of multiple agents whose behaviors are governed by diverse reactions at multiple levels, where the number and structure of agents and the number of reactions varies during simulation. Therefore, we equip different variants of stochastic simulation algorithms with strategies to handle dynamic sets of reactions. We implement the next reaction method with a heap and the direct reaction method with two tree-based selection strategies, compare their performance, and discuss open questions for future research.

CCS CONCEPTS

• **General and reference** → **Performance**; • **Computing methodologies** → **Modeling and simulation**; **Discrete-event simulation**; • **Mathematics of computing** → **Trees**;

ACM Reference Format:
Till Köster and Adelinde M. Uhrmacher. 2018. Handling Dynamic Sets of Reactions in Stochastic Simulation Algorithms. In *SIGSIM-PADS '18 : SIGSIM-PADS '18: SIGSIM Principles of Advanced Discrete Simulation CD-ROM, May 23–25, 2018, Rome, Italy*. ACM, New York, NY, USA, 4 pages. https://doi.org/10.1145/3200921.3200943

1 MOTIVATION AND INTRODUCTION

In many scientific areas, such as epidemiology [8], demography [13], or computational biology [9], *stochastic simulation algorithms* that are based on a continuous-time Markov chain semantics are well established methods. Due to the advances in expressive domain-specific languages, simulation models become more and more complex, often integrating different modeling paradigms and structuring mechanisms [7]. The efficient simulation of these models is quite challenging, particularly if the dynamics of models are changing as well. In these models the internal behavior of multiple agents, their nesting, their interactions, and their creation and removal are governed by multiple reactions. The structure of agents in turn

Permission to make digital or hard copies of all or part of this work for personal or classroom use is granted without fee provided that copies are not made or distributed for profit or commercial advantage and that copies bear this notice and the full citation on the first page. Copyrights for components of this work owned by others than the author(s) must be honored. Abstracting with credit is permitted. To copy otherwise, or republish, to post on servers or to redistribute to lists, requires prior specific permission and/or a fee. Request permissions from permissions@acm.org.
SIGSIM-PADS '18 , May 23–25, 2018, Rome, Italy
© 2018 Copyright held by the owner/author(s). Publication rights licensed to the Association for Computing Machinery.
ACM ISBN 978-1-4503-5092-1/18/05. . . $15.00
https://doi.org/10.1145/3200921.3200943

changes the number of reactions during the simulation frequently. Handling reactions is a major and time consuming step of stochastic simulation algorithms in general, and, as such, has been subject to extensive research.

1.1 Reaction selection in stochastic simulation algorithms

In the context of stochastic simulation algorithms, models are typically formed by N integer variables $S_1, \ldots, S_N$, with $S_i \geq 0$, which interact via M reactions $R_1, \ldots, R_M$. These reactions might refer to biochemical reactions, but also to infections or marriage proposals, depending on the application domain. The probability function $p(\tau, i|x, t)d\tau$ determines the probability that given the current state $X(t) = x$, the next reaction in the system will occur in the infinitesimal time interval $[t + \tau, t + \tau + d\tau]$ and will be the reaction R_i [2]. Each possible reaction R_i is associated with a *propensity* $a_i(x)$ which presents the rate with which a reaction occurs, and determines the likelihood of a reaction to occur in the next infinitesimally small time-interval. $a_0(x)$ denotes the sum $a_0(x) = \sum_{i=1}^{M} a_i(x)$ over all reactions' propensities. τ is an exponential random variable with mean $1/a_0(x)$. The i-th reaction will be executed next with a probability of $a_i(x)/a_0(x)$. The key performance aspect of SSA that we are going to investigate is the selection of the next reaction R_i.

Various methods exist for making this decision. Those can be broadly categorized into two classes: *Direct Methods* and *First-reaction*-style methods.

Direct Methods. The direct method [2] calculates the time increment at which reaction R_i shall be executed by generating a random number that is exponentially distributed with rate $a_0(x)$ $(\tau = 1/a_0(x) \ln\left(1/U(0, 1)\right))$. $U(0, 1)$ denotes a uniformly distributed number between zero and one. To select the reaction to be executed, i.e., R_i, it performs a prefix-sum (accumulated sum) over all $a_i(x)$ to determine the smallest i for which $\sum_{i'=1}^{i} a_{i'}(x) > U(0, 1) \cdot a_0(x)$ is reached. Improvement in this selection (at least for the average, but not the worst case), have been made by moving reactions with higher propensity closer to the beginning [10].

Logarithmic selection via trees. Various methods exist that use tree data structures and caching techniques to move from $O(M)$ to logarithmic complexity [1, 4]. An overview and discussion of the various aspects can be found in [6]. The general idea among these different methods is similar. All reactions are structured in some tree data structure (or equivalently a matrix with column sums) that iteratively stores sub sums of reaction propensities. Now selecting a reaction corresponds to traversing the tree from the root. The path length to any reaction, independent of whether they are stored at the leaves only or at all nodes, is then of logarithmic complexity. One interesting expansion of that is to use Huffmann-trees, that provide an optimal average path length [10].

Rejection based methods. The latest generation of selection methods revolves around the idea that propensity changes mostly tend to be small [11]. By introducing acceptance/rejection regions around the exact values one can achieve performance improvements up to constant complexity for applicable models [12].

First Reaction Methods and Variants. Many improvements of the stochastic simulation algorithms are based on the first reaction method. The first reaction method draws for every reaction $R_{i'}$ a uniformly distributed random number $U(0, 1)$, and calculates for all reactions $R_{i'}$ the values $\tau_{i'} = 1/a_{i'}(x) \ln(1/U(0, 1))$ and then selects the smallest τ_i of the $\tau_{i'}$ and the reaction R_i to be executed. Similar to the direct method, the first reaction method disregards all other calculations once τ and the reaction are selected.

A significant performance improvement came to this by means of the *next reaction method* (NRM) [1]. As in the first reaction method, all $\tau_{i'}$ are calculated. However, now they are used as traditional events scheduled to occur at a specific time point.

After the selected reaction R_i is executed, only those reactions $R_{i'}$ need to be rescheduled whose propensities are affected due to executing R_i. This moves the complexity of reaction selection in NRM from linear ($O(M)$ for the first reaction method) to an effort that depends on the used priority queue [3], thus usually, of log-type.

1.2 Changing number of potential reactions

In the above approaches, typically the set of reactions $R_1, ... R_M$ is considered to be constant, i.e., $M = |R_{i'}|$. We have to adapt this notion as being dependent on the state, to $M(x)$. Since the internal behavior of agents and their interaction is governed by multiple reactions, with the number of agents, the number of reactions changes that need to be considered to select R_i and to calculate the overall sum a_0, the set of individual propensities $a_{i'}$, and the time advance τ. In addition, the expressiveness of the language can further increase the effort in calculating and maintaining the set of propensities and reactions, e.g., by allowing arbitrary functions and dynamic nestings.

2 METHODOLOGY

To test the impact of adding and removing reactions on the performance of the simulator, we implemented several variants of the SSA and tested the performance of their reaction selection:

- next reaction method with heap
- basic direct reaction method (not shown, as not relevant in application)
- direct reaction method with an n-ary
  - sparse tree
  - dense tree

2.1 General Interface

For investigating the performance of reaction selection only a small interface to the rest of the simulator is needed. The **handle object** is a lightweight abstraction used to reference individual reactions

in the container. It may contain means for the container to identify any particular object, e.g. a pointer or an index. Also the following function interfaces for the **reaction container object** need to be defined:

- `handle container::add( reaction )`
- `void container::remove( handle )`
- `void container::modify( handle, old_propensity, new_propensity )`
- `<handle, timestep> container::select()`
- `reaction container::get( handle )`

The **add** function adds an object to the reaction store. It returns a handle so the object can later be referenced if for example the entity that has added the reaction is removed and thus the reaction is no longer valid. Based on the handle, any reaction can be **removed** from the container. Whenever the actual propensity of any reaction is changed, the **modify** function needs to be called to notify the container to make changes (if needed) to its internal accounting. To simplify this process, the old as well as the new propensities are included into the interface. The **selection** function then returns the handle to the reaction that is being selected as well as the time step forward. Finally, the **getter** provides the means to access the underlying reaction from its handle.

2.2 Next reaction method

An established way to implement priority-queues, as needed for the Next Reaction Method (NRM), are heaps. For the actual implementation of our NRM, we have a few specific requirements, in addition to being efficient: (1) ability to remove and to add elements (2) ability to modify priority of an element (could be implemented by removing and adding an element).

The well established *boost.heap*[1] library fulfills all of these requirements. Boost is readily available on all platforms. *boost.heap* also provides various different heap/queue variants. Our initial tests have shown the Fibbonacci heap to be the best performing one for our use case.

2.3 Tree based direct reaction method

The key data structure we are investigating in this paper is that of the tree based selection. We are using the array representation of d-ary trees (fan-out d), where based on the index i of any element, we can compute the memory location of the parents, siblings and children in constant time. We are using 1 and not 0 based indexing. Each tree node holds

- the reaction R_i as payload
- the accumulated rate σ_i of itself (local propensity a_i) and all child nodes. Thus this condition should always hold:

$$\sigma_i = a_i + \sum_{\substack{k=0,\ k<M}}^{d-1} \sigma_{i \cdot d + k}$$

- an id y_i that is different from the index i.

The id y_i is used to identify the node, even if its position in the tree has changed. The handle only needs to hold that id. The container also houses a lookup array l of indices. The i-th entry of the lookup array corresponds to the tree index of the node with that

[1]available at: http://www.boost.org/doc/libs/release/libs/heap/

id, meaning $l_{y_i} = i$. This allows for constant time object retrieval. We investigate two strategies for handling dynamic sets of reactions. The *dense* and the *sparse* method.

Selection of a reaction in the tree is a simple recursive process. We accumulate propensities a_i, as we traverse the tree, until we have reached the random threshold $u = U(0, 1) \cdot a_0$. Starting at the root, we can check if the local reaction's propensity a_i is enough to cross the threshold u. If not, we look at the accumulated propensities σ_i of the children. We don't need to look at the grand children since their a_i are already included in the children. This leads to logarithmic complexity.

2.3.1   Sparse tree approach. In the sparse tree approach, whenever a reaction is removed, only that individual node is set empty. This includes (recursively) informing the parent nodes to update their accumulated propensities. Furthermore, the index of this particular node is stored in the list F of available indices. Whenever a reaction is added to the system, it is first checked if any nodes are free ($|F| > 0$). Once an index is used again, it is removed from F. If no nodes are free, the node is added at the end of the tree-array. $M(x)$ is increased and the parents are informed to update their propensities. Notably, the size of the tree is $\geq M(x)$, leading to suboptimal average path length in node selection.

2.3.2   Dense tree approach. In the dense approach, we keep the tree as dense as possible. Whenever a reaction is removed, the pertaining node is swapped with the last node in the tree (rightmost node at the bottom level). Then that last node is removed. This requires a recursive update for the accumulated propensities from two points in the tree (the place where the to-be-removed node was and the very last node). On the other hand, the tree does not have any empty nodes, minimizing traversal time needed for selection or other tree updates.

2.4   Random number generation

There are two kinds of floating point random numbers needed for the reaction selection. Uniform random numbers in the zero to one interval and those following the exponential distribution. We use the `<random>`-library of the C++11 standard. The underlying random bits are generated using Mersenne-Twister [5]. We measured the generation of the expensive exponential random numbers to be in the 100ns range on our system. However, in application, this number is expected to be worse as there is overhead in generating only a single random number compared to generating many and taking the average.

3   BENCHMARKS

A configurable benchmark model was created in order to supply varying workloads for the different tree implementations. The implementation of the simulator was instrumented with timers at the interface to the reaction container. The time for each call as well as the number of calls were measured. We deliberately chose to focus on those numbers as they provide a more meaningful value in terms of general applicability of the data-structures. The overall execution time depends very much on the model in question, in particular on the interdependence of the different reactions. All measurements were taken after a significant warm up time.

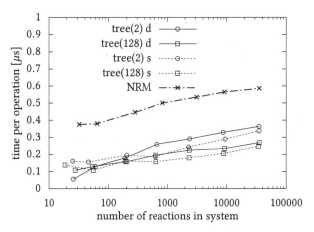

Figure 1: Time to add one reaction to the system

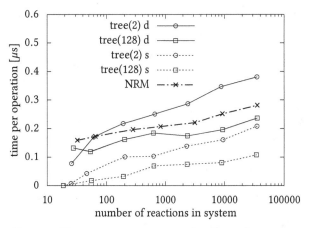

Figure 2: Time to remove one reaction from the system

Environment and Software. The benchmarks were run on a current generation linux workstation with an Intel Xeon E5-1630 v4 CPU at 3.70GHz. Boost was used (for NRM) in Version 1.64. The code was compiled with gcc version 7.3.1. on a machine running Fedora Ninux 27. The C++ implementation for each of the reaction store and selectors are made available in our GIT repository[2]. They are implemented as single header files and, aside from NRM requiring boost, do not need any other dependency than the standard library. All containers are templatized and, as such, should be very easy to integrate into other simulators.

4   RESULTS AND CONCLUSIONS

The results for the time of operations for differently sized systems can be found in the figures. Broader trees (plotted with a fan-out of 128 with a square marker) are more useful, for adding (fig. 1), removing (fig. 2) and modifying (fig. 4) a reaction. This can be attributed to the lower number of jumps beeing necessary in the tree. There is no overhead since those operations never need to iterate through the children. For the selection (fig. 3), a broader tree

---

[2]https://git.informatik.uni-rostock.de/mosi/dynamic_reaction_container

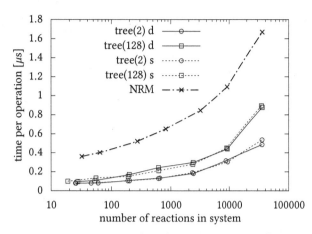

Figure 3: Time to select the next reaction to fire

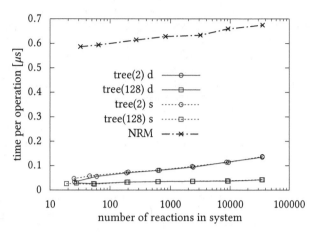

Figure 4: Time to modify the rate of one reaction

is unfavorable, as one needs to iterate through the children of each node. As expected, when looking at removing a reaction (fig. 2), the sparse variant is faster than the dense one since there is only one branch of the tree that needs to be updated, instead of two. Interestingly, we also see a minor advantage for the sparse variant when considering the time for an add operation (fig. 1). This can be attributed to the shorter average path to the root of the tree from the position of insertion. In the dense variant, we always need to iterate through all levels of the tree. In the sparse version, this is not the case. The larger the tree gets the smaller this difference gets because the ratio of path length to node number decreases. The Next Reaction Method (NRM) generally scales similar to the tree methods. However, when looking at selection, modification, and addition of reactions, we see a similar constant offset. This can be attributed to the rescheduling effort needed for this method. Whenever the rate of a reaction is modified, the reaction needs to be assigned a new time to execute. This involves the relatively costly calculation of an exponential random number. In conclusion, we can say that the sparse method with a large fan-out has proven to be the best among the compared variants. This is especially true when considering that in regular models there are usually multiple add/remove/modifications for every select operation.

This paper presents an initial investigation into the possibilities of integrating dynamic reaction sets into efficient stochastic simulation algorithms. Numerous possibilities for future work exist. We are currently investigating rejection based methods [11] for their applicability. It would also be interesting to improve the dense tree method by finding a common ancestor when updating to avoid double access to nodes. Other approaches exploit differences in the reactions' propensities (i.e. test more likely reactions first). This should be rather straightforward to integrate into our tree-based direct reaction method. Currently, the benchmark model is configured to have a reasonably steady number of reactions when performing the measurements. It would be interesting to explore the possibilities of restructuring the tree if (too) many nodes are left empty. Finally, the overhead of many children for selection has been addressed by using a different tree for child selection [6]. We intend to explore this option as well.

ACKNOWLEDGMENTS

This research is supported by the German Research Foundation (DFG) via research grant ESCeMMo (UH-66/14)

REFERENCES

[1] Michael A. Gibson and Jehoshua Bruck. 2000. Efficient Exact Stochastic Simulation of Chemical Systems with Many Species and Many Channels. *The Journal of Physical Chemistry A* 104, 9 (March 2000), 1876–1889. https://doi.org/10.1021/jp993732q
[2] Daniel T. Gillespie. 2007. Stochastic simulation of chemical kinetics. *Annual Review of Physical Chemistry* 58 (2007), 35–55. https://doi.org/10.1146/annurev.physchem.58.032806.104637
[3] Matthias Jeschke and Roland Ewald. 2008. Large-Scale Design Space Exploration of SSA. In *Computational Methods in Systems Biology (Lecture Notes in Computer Science)*. Springer, Berlin, Heidelberg, 211–230. https://doi.org/10.1007/978-3-540-88562-7_17
[4] Hong Li et al. 2006. Logarithmic direct method for discrete stochastic simulation of chemically reacting systems. *Journal of Chemical Physics* 16 (2006).
[5] Makoto Matsumoto and Takuji Nishimura. 1998. Mersenne Twister: A 623-dimensionally Equidistributed Uniform Pseudo-random Number Generator. *ACM Trans. Model. Comput. Simul.* 8, 1 (Jan. 1998), 3–30. https://doi.org/10.1145/272991.272995
[6] Sean Mauch and Mark Stalzer. 2011. Efficient Formulations for Exact Stochastic Simulation of Chemical Systems. *IEEE/ACM Transactions on Computational Biology and Bioinformatics* 8, 1 (Jan. 2011), 27–35. https://doi.org/10.1109/TCBB.2009.47
[7] Carsten Maus, Stefan Rybacki, and Adelinde M. Uhrmacher. 2011. Rule-based multi-level modeling of cell biological systems. *BMC Systems Biology* 5, 1 (2011), 166. https://bmcsystbiol.biomedcentral.com/articles/10.1186/1752-0509-5-166
[8] Steven Riley et al. 2003. Transmission dynamics of the etiological agent of SARS in Hong Kong: impact of public health interventions. *Science (New York, N.Y.)* 300, 5627 (June 2003), 1961–1966. https://doi.org/10.1126/science.1086478
[9] Tamás Székely and Kevin Burrage. 2014. Stochastic simulation in systems biology. *Computational and Structural Biotechnology Journal* 12, 20 (Nov. 2014), 14–25. https://doi.org/10.1016/j.csbj.2014.10.003
[10] Vo Hong Thanh and Roberto Zunino. 2014. Adaptive tree-based search for stochastic simulation algorithm. *International journal of computational biology and drug design* 7, 4 (2014), 341–357.
[11] Vo Hong Thanh, Roberto Zunino, and Corrado Priami. 2015. On the rejection-based algorithm for simulation and analysis of large-scale reaction networks. *The Journal of Chemical Physics* 142, 24 (June 2015), 244106. https://doi.org/10.1063/1.4922923
[12] Vo Hong Thanh, Roberto Zunino, and Corrado Priami. 2017. Efficient Constant-Time Complexity Algorithm for Stochastic Simulation of Large Reaction Networks. *IEEE/ACM Transactions on Computational Biology and Bioinformatics* 14, 3 (May 2017), 657–667. https://doi.org/10.1109/TCBB.2016.2530066
[13] Tom Warnke, Oliver Reinhardt, Anna Klabunde, Frans Willekens, and Adelinde M. Uhrmacher. 2017. Modelling and simulating decision processes of linked lives: An approach based on concurrent processes and stochastic race. *Population Studies* 71, sup1 (Oct. 2017), 69–83. https://doi.org/10.1080/00324728.2017.1380960

Granular Cloning: Intra-Object Parallelism in Ensemble Studies

Philip Pecher[1], John Crittenden[2], Zhongming Lu[3], Richard Fujimoto[1]

[1]School of Computational Science and Engineering
[2]School of Civil and Environmental Engineering
Georgia Institute of Technology
Atlanta, GA 30332, USA
[3]Beijing Normal University, Beijing Shi, 100875, China
philip161@gmail.com, john.crittenden@ce.gatech.edu, zhongming.lu@bnu.edu.cn, fujimoto@cc.gatech.edu

ABSTRACT

Many runs of a computer simulation are needed to model uncertainty and evaluate alternate design choices. Such an ensemble of runs often contains many commonalities among the different individual runs. Simulation cloning is a technique that capitalizes on this fact to reduce the amount of computation required by the ensemble. Granular cloning is proposed that allows the sharing of state and computations at the scale of simulation objects as small as individual variables, offering savings in computation and memory, increased parallelism and improved tractability of sample path patterns across multiple runs. The ensemble produces results that are identical to separately executed runs. Whenever simulation objects interact, granular cloning will resolve their association to subsets of runs though binary operations on tags. Algorithms and computational techniques required to efficiently implement granular cloning are presented. Results from an experimental study using a cellular automata-based transportation simulation model and a coupled transportation and land use model are presented providing evidence the approach can yield significant speed ups relative to brute force replicated runs.

KEYWORDS

Cloning; multiprocessors; parallel algorithms; parallel simulation; algorithms; performance; scale; speedup; acceleration; experimentation; scenario; design; shared computation; incremental simulation

ACM Reference Format:

Philip Pecher, John Crittenden, Zhongming Lu, and Richard Fujimoto. 2018. Granular Cloning: Intra-Object Parallelism in Ensemble Studies. In Proceedings of SIGSIM Principles of Advanced Discrete Simulation (SIGSIMPADS' 18). ACM, New York, NY, USA, 12 pages. https://doi.org/10.1145/3200921.3200927

Permission to make digital or hard copies of all or part of this work for personal or classroom use is granted without fee provided that copies are not made or distributed for profit or commercial advantage and that copies bear this notice and the full citation on the first page. Copyrights for components of this work owned by others than the author(s) must be honored. Abstracting with credit is permitted. To copy otherwise, or republish, to post on servers or to redistribute to lists, requires prior specific permission and/or a fee. Request permissions from Permissions@acm.org.

SIGSIM-PADS '18 , May 23–25, 2018, Rome, Italy
© 2018 Copyright is held by the owner/author(s). Publication rights licensed to ACM. ACM ISBN 978-1-4503-5092-1/18/05...$15.00
https://doi.org/10.1145/3200921.3200927

1. INTRODUCTION

Computer simulation shows its strength by its flexibility to model a vast set of domains. However, its power is limited by the accuracy of the underlying model and the computational performance of the simulations. This paper focuses on alleviating the latter constraint. State changes are either driven by event-scheduling or by time-stepping though simulated time. The method described in this paper, termed granular cloning, can be utilized in both time-traversal modes, in both serial and parallel computer architectures, and – for parallel systems – in both optimistic and conservative synchronization protocols. Granular cloning exploits redundant computations across multiple runs of a model at the scale of individual simulation objects. Since it only affects common computations the results are equivalent to explicitly enumerating these runs. The runs are differentiated by random inputs and/or variations in the model scenarios.

In stochastic simulation, randomness is injected in input variables to model uncertainty of the system under investigation (SUI). The performance of granular cloning is improved with the use of common random numbers because the pseudorandom number steams can be shared by all the logical runs. If one wishes to introduce variability, granular cloning can be further improved by altering individual elements of the stream or augmenting the stream with more elements.

In many simulation studies, the objective is to find a feasible policy that leads to desirable output statistics. The number of feasible configurations often grows exponentially with the number of controllable discrete factors one is considering. Consider a network with ten nodes where one wishes to place one of three different router models at each node. The number of possible configurations is 3^{10}. While there are methods for efficiently searching the often nonconvex configuration space, many runs will still be required. For each scenario, it is also desirable to complete many runs to obtain a point estimate of the output statistic with low bias and spread.

When variation is introduced into a set of runs of a certain model, the collective is referred to as an ensemble. An ensemble study may have a set of objectives, including characterizing (e.g., for validation) or optimizing certain model parameters [15]. Whatever the way variation is introduced, random input or scenario variation, granular cloning superimposes all runs of an ensemble into one run and only explicitly stores the actual and most granular state differences across these runs, rather than larger supersets of state. Ensembles may be batched together based on a partitioning that is favorable for granular cloning. These conditions are discussed later. For example, suppose we model a particle p in a neighborhood of other particles and some gaps of "empty" space. We wish to investigate the evolution of the neighborhood for two different polarity values of p (two different *versions*). If most of the simulation state remains the same for both versions, it would be inefficient to explicitly store two sets of the entire state. We only allocate memory for neighboring particles if they are affected differently for a version compared to the other version. The number of objects with state differences for a given version in this example tends to grow monotonically with simulated time. Explicit enumeration of all runs would be wasteful because of the common states and behaviors across the runs. The technique is generally applicable for Monte-Carlo simulation, although one could construct adversarial models where the runs are completely different at model initialization, in which case the approach collapses into explicit enumeration of runs. At the same time, the technique incurs a small overhead whenever different simulation objects interact with each other. However, there are heuristics that can be used to reduce the overhead cost, which depend on the object interactions of the underlying application.

The next section describes related work. In Section 3, we define the notation and terminology from the simulation cloning literature [1] along with cloning concepts. Section 4 describes how cloning can be extended to state objects within LP's. Section 5 brings attention to the quantitative conditions under which computational performance can be harvested without loss in output accuracy; this is expressed in a simple mathematical inequality that is intuitive from a geometric view. Experimental results of use cases are given in Section 6, varying key parameters that affect the computational performance.

2. RELATED WORK

The concept of cloning memory segments has been used extensively since Von Neumann introduced it for fault tolerance in 1956 [3]. Since then, it has influenced modern relational database systems, distributed memory management, and other areas of computer systems. In addition to describing this historical context in detail, [1] contains a survey of domain-specific simulation models where cloning has been used previously. Common themes in the relevant literature include computation sharing (reuse of common state or events) and incremental simulation.

Reducing the execution time and memory requirements of replicated simulation instances without affecting the accuracy of output statistics has been investigated in both domain specific and general (yet, typically, simulation-engine-specific) settings. Domain-specific use cases generally allow more state to be logically shared by grouping together similar replications at suitable times during the execution, and/or otherwise exploit the underlying application's specific characteristics for space/time efficiency. Relevant examples include the following.

In [4], Pecher, Hunter, and Fujimoto present a lazy evaluation and speculative execution scheme for physical cloning of vehicle objects in microscopic traffic simulation. Vehicle objects that are independent of output statistics propagate tags containing the replication numbers they "touch." Their numbers are compared to vehicle objects that have a dependency on output statistics. If there is a version match between the vehicle types,

a physical clone must be launched via a rollback to a relevant saved state for explicit computation. Lentz et al. [5] apply incremental cloning to test different signature paths in a digital logic simulation for potential faults. The "offspring" (clone) of a "parent" is limited to four logical output values. Vakili [6] uses a so-called *standard clock* scheme (an implementation of *single-clock multiple systems*, or *SCMS*) approach to execute – on a SIMD computer system - the same events simultaneously across multiple synchronized replications, which are parametrized differently (e.g., different service disciplines in a queue). The injected positive correlation makes this approach especially useful in simulation-based optimization (ranking & selection), albeit for a restricted class of applications.

Unlike these prior efforts, the granular cloning approach described here does not rely on domain-specific properties. Although domain-specific methods can exploit knowledge of the given application, general techniques are by definition more flexible. As discussed next, more general techniques have been developed. It is possible that combinations of these techniques complement each other if they exploit different aspects of the underlying application.

An example of a more general technique is the parallel cloning scheme introduced by Hybinette and Fujimoto in [1] that applies to the distributed LP event-scheduling paradigm. It is summarized in Section 3 because our granular cloning scheme will be described with similar terminology and notation. Just as with parallel cloning, granular cloning also makes heavy use of set-manipulation algorithms. Furthermore, the underlying mechanism for both algorithms consists of sharing state logically, while incrementally allocating physical memory. However, granular cloning offers a much finer grained mechanism that focuses on cloning individual objects rather than entire logical processes, and is agnostic to the underlying simulation executive paradigm. Chen, Turner, Cai et al. have extended the distributed cloning algorithms for the High Level Architecture (HLA) in [16] along with HLA's data distribution management (DDM) in [17].

Ferenci et al. [7] presents an incremental scheme termed *updatable simulation*, where one first logs the events and sample path of a baseline run and hopes to reuse the state modifications from it for subsequent runs. Subsequent runs then determine what horizon of logged events can be reused at a given timestep where an event is to be processed. In the ideal case, a sequence of $r \gg 1$ events can be composed together, rather than separately, to act on the current state. If the runs are sufficiently different, the event horizon r will be zero at each event-processing timestep and nothing can be reused. The *staged simulation* technique discussed in Walsh and Sirer [8] caches previous event invocations, decomposes them, reuses previously computed and/or similar results, and reorders restructured events for their efficient scheduling. Stoffers et al. [12] extends automatic memoization to impure functions where side effects are permitted (subject to a few constraints). Granular cloning differs from these approaches in that it does not rely on reusing previously computed results.

Granular cloning is perhaps most closely related to recent work by Li, Cai, and Turner [18] which focuses on tree-based cloning algorithms for agent-based models. A cloning tree contains nodes that map to simulation instances (versions) that have a different parameter than their parents. Each such instance is associated with two data structures: *AgentPool* and *Context*. The former contains agents whose characteristics are unique to that instance, while the latter contains references to shared agents in ancestor nodes. During the execution of an instance, the relevant agents from a child's ancestors are copied. A child instance performs clone condition checking as follows. If a *Context* agent (shared with an ancestor node) senses a parameter variation or an agent in the respective *AgentPool*, a clone is generated and moved to the *AgentPool*. Execution of simulation instances within the clone tree occur level-by-level in a breadth-first manner. In contrast to this simulation instance-hierarchical scheme, granular cloning does not use a tree hierarchy; rather, it associates tags with object realizations and clone condition checking occurs by comparing the tags of interacting objects. Granular cloning accesses relevant objects in arrays rather than by tree traversal. A bit masking scheme is used to efficiently implement version management. Superficially, granular cloning applies to granular subsets of state, while [18] applies to agent objects, though potentially one could adapt the algorithm from [18] to encompass the same scale. Furthermore, at any given timestep, the parallelism in [18] is limited by the available nodes at any level of the clone tree (batch-by-batch); in granular cloning, all objects may be executed concurrently at any timestep.

Granular cloning utilizes a kind of data dependency detection for interacting objects (or state variables thereof). Granular cloning compares properties of versions associated with these objects. Detecting various properties of data dependencies with the end goal of accelerating simulation execution has been studied in other works as well. Quaglia and Baldoni [19] investigate data dependencies associated with a simulation object *over several events*. The scheme can be used to accelerate certain optimistic simulations by increasing event-level parallelism. The definition of "intra-object parallelism" in [19] differs from the usage in this paper and in [10]. In [19], the parallelism refers to the state transitions (i.e., events) that an object is exposed to, while here (and in [10]) it refers to the variations in the object's state. Marziale et al. [20] measure the *amount of* data dependencies across processes in order to create suitable groups of these processes ("granular LPs") dynamically in a Time Warp-based environment. The grouping that is derived from dependencies in [20] applies to subsets of state (logical processes), while they apply to subsets of runs in this paper. Furthermore, the grouping sequence for granular cloning is unique.

3. CLONING PARALLEL SIMULATIONS

Hybinette and Fujimoto [1] introduce the concept of simulation cloning in the context of distributed and interactive simulations where the analyst can intervene and dynamically evaluate alternative futures (*clones*, identified by a *version* number that is incremented chronologically: i = 1, 2, 3, ...) at *decision points* and find a policy that offers advantages over others. A decision point must specify how a given clone differs in its state from a given reference version and at which timestep it occurs. However, different courses of action may also be defined a priori to evaluate different scenarios and inject uncertainty into certain input variables; they can also be triggered by certain conditions at runtime. Clones are generated by specifying them at decision points or through certain interactions between logical processes (LPs). The underlying system architecture used in [1] is based

on distributed LPs and the executive operates with the event-scheduling paradigm. The physical system is mapped into a model in the computer and the state of this model is partitioned into LPs (identified with j = A, B, C, ...). During runtime, LPs exchange time-stamped messages to change their state and schedule new events; an LP only changes its state after processing an event (scheduled by itself or with a message received from another LP). Consider a simulation that evaluates two scenarios where, at some timestep $t_b > 0$, some partial component of the state differs among them.

Simulation cloning makes use of *computation sharing* because:

- the sample path up to the decision point is only computed once. The set of *virtual logical processes* (*VLP*) being mapped to by each clone are shared by a shared memory region in the computer system, namely the corresponding *physical logical processes* (*PLP*), and
- only the VLP's that differ in their state after the decision point are explicitly duplicated (as a *PLP*) in memory and processed separately and in parallel; the VLP's that are identical continue to be shared within a corresponding PLP. As the given clone starts affecting state in other VLP's, further PLP's will be incrementally spawned. An important point with respect to one key contribution of this paper is that the algorithm in [1] clones an entire VLP, even if there is just a small difference in a state object within the VLP.

VLP's exchange virtual messages among each other, but each virtual message maps to a single physical message and each VLP maps to a single PLP. Whenever several virtual instances are mapped to a particular physical instance (that is, if they have the same state), computations are essentially shared. A given VLP is identified by (i) the *LP identifier* and (ii) the *version* of the clone it refers to. A given version is associated with a set of VLP's for every LP in the model.

It is useful to define some notation prior to delving into the actual cloning algorithm. As mentioned before, the entire state of a model is partitioned into LP's (identified by j= A, B, C,...) and each version (identified by i = 1, 2, 3, ...) maps to a set of VLP's. Subsequently, we will refer to a particular VLP as $V(i,j)$. If, for fixed j, several VLP's map to the same PLP (only if they share the same state), the corresponding PLP is denoted $P(i,j)$ and i is the minimum version number of the VLP's pointing to $P(i, j)$.

To implement simulation cloning, one must alter the simulation executive to incorporate (i) *message cloning* and (ii) *process cloning*. Message cloning simply refers to a simple mechanism whereby a message sent from a PLP (sharing several versions in a set called *VSendSet*) and received by a PLP (sharing several versions in a set called *VRcvSet*) must be forwarded to other PLP's mapped to from versions contained in *VSendSet* that are not in *VRcvSet*. Process cloning occurs when a PLP is mapped to by versions not contained in a receiving message. The respective message may cause a modification in the state of all versions that the PLP represents, which would clearly be invalid for the states that are not in the message's *VSendSet*. The full process cloning algorithm from [1] is (S^C denotes the complement of set S with respect to the universe of versions):

(1)　　　　Get VSendSet from message
(2)　　　　Get VRcvSet from local state
(3)　　　　VPsUnaffected = $VSendSet^C \cap VRcvSet$
(4)　　　　VPsMoveToClone = VPsUnaffected
(5)　　　　VPsRequested = $VSendSet \cap VRcvSet$
(6)　　　　If (!(PhysicalReceiver $\cap$ VPsRequested)) then
　　　　　　　　　　VPsMoveToClone = VPsRequested
(7)　　　　If (VPsMoveToClone $\neq$ {}) then
　　　　　　　　　　Cloned PLP = min(VPsMoveToClone)

4. GRANULAR CLONING

4.1 Intuition

A straightforward extension to simulation cloning approach from [1] is to replace the process cloning step with one that only clones state differences. An associative map is maintained for each PLP that maps a given version i to a record that contains information regarding *where* and *how* a PLP differs from shared state. In Figure 1, an LP modeling an airport initially shares the state for versions 1 and 2 and receives an airliner arrival event that only occurs in version 1. To maintain correctness for version 2, simulation cloning now copies the entire LP state prior to handling of the arrival. Granular cloning instead only duplicates the state that the arrival event handler would modify. These duplicated state variables are now valid for version 2 (airliner absent), while the variables they were copied from may now be safely overridden for the version 1 arrival event.

Relative to the parallel cloning scheme from Section 3 granular cloning should perform well if a given LP owns

1. a sufficiently large partition of the entire state space,

2. event handlers where state changes tend to be fragmented over the state variables, rather than over its entire state,

3. event handlers where unmodified state variables are insensitive to the changes to the state variables that are modified.

One could, of course, simply take the parallel cloning scheme and redefine each LP to encompass only a single state object. In doing so, however, one potentially increases the communication between the LP's which can significantly degrade performance.

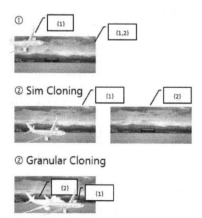

Figure 1: Rather than duplicate the entire LP, granular cloning only duplicates the state that changes. ©Free-Photos, Creative Commons 0

If - instead of the event-scheduling based approach - the simulation executive uses a timestepped agent-based model (ABM), which may be part of a federation, one can associate each agent, and any state object in general, with a set of versions (a *version set*). This not only comes with all the benefits discussed before (i.e., savings in space and time because of shared computations), but also through increasing the parallelism in a shared memory machine (under certain circumstances), especially if the number of replications is a soft constraint. For a given version v (out of V total runs), an ABM typically executes, over several iterations (depending on the input model), for each timestep $< T$, the behavior of $e < E$ agents. Within a fixed version, timestep, and entity, a kernel (or, transition function) is typically executed that reads from various state objects of the previous timestep, and writes to the given agent's state objects for the current timestep.

Figure 2 shows a so-called *time-space diagram* (see [11]) for a concrete example.

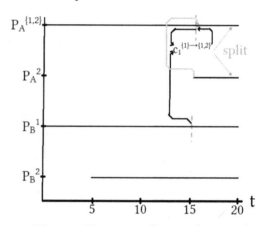

Figure 2: Time-space diagram for granular cloning split.

The horizontal axis measures simulated time and the vertical axis contains discrete state space objects (in memory). The lines within the quadrants represent sample paths, here denoting simply the presence of a given physical state object. The state objects use a similar notation as that used for PLP's in Section 3. Here, the superscript refers to the versions mapping to the state object and the subscript denotes the identifier for the state object. At $t=15$, the *kernel* of A for its sole version set {1, 2} is executed, depicted as c_1. A kernel is a sequence of instructions computed for a version set of a single agent (called the *kernel object*) and is not permitted to write to any other object. If any write operation in the kernel depends on a read operation of other objects, the intersection of the read sources' version sets is compared to the version set of the kernel object. If the kernel object contains members not present in the intersection of the read sources, the kernel object splits. If one were to not split the kernel object, the state of the kernel object would be overwritten for the versions that are contained in it, but not in the read sources, potentially leading to errors.

4.2 Formulation

As summarized before, a timestepped ABM - from a high-level view - typically has the following operational scheme:

```
for s in scenarios
    initialize_model(s)
    for t in timesteps
        for a in agents
            a.kernel /*also called transition
                or step */
```

Algorithm 1: Agent-based model - operational outline (traditional)

When granular cloning is applied to these kind of models, it obviates the need to explicitly enumerate the scenarios (since all of them are superimposed). However, at runtime, granular cloning needs to perform some bookkeeping, in order to trace dependencies between objects that are now associated with versions (*versioned objects*). As the simulation progresses, versioned objects that originally shared state across all versions start to diverge from the shared state to a version-specific state. From a high-level view, the operational scheme for granular cloning applied to a timestepped ABM looks like:

```
initialize_model(scenarios)
for t in timesteps
    for a in agents
        for vo in a.versionedobjects
            a.GC_interaction /*kernel with
                granular cloning */
```

Algorithm 2: Agent-based model - operational outline (granular cloning)

In some sense, the outermost loop in Algorithm 1 has been logically replaced with the innermost loop in Algorithm 2. However, we hope to iterate over fewer than scenarios.number (the total number or runs, or versions) in the innermost loop of Algorithm 2 by exploiting common state across the versionedobjects. The degree of reduction (or state-sharing) needs to be sufficiently high to offset the additional overhead that occurs in a.GC_interaction (in Algorithm 2) relative to a.kernel (in Algorithm 1). Most of what follows in this subsection is concerned with the details of the last line (a.GC_interaction) in Algorithm 2. In fact, a.GC_interaction is presented as Algorithm 3 and represents the high-level granular cloning kernel management by ensuring that versioned objects that diverge from any shared state have the kernel applied to them as well. In order to (i) report potential diverging splits in versioned objects and to (ii) dispatch the actual kernel function on versioned objects, Algorithm 3 calls Algorithm 4 (GC_transition()). (i) is computed in Algorithm 5 (handle_conflicts()). The diagram in Figure 3 summarizes this granular cloning mechanism.

Granular cloning for agent-based models is differentiated from conventional execution in that it needs to preserve the integrity of the superimposed sample path. Before executing any transition function, granular cloning first ensures that no version-specific state of the kernel object is being wrongly overwritten for a dependency that does not match that version (this check is done in a function called handle_conflicts()). If there is a version conflict, the current kernel object needs to be split. The split object is handled after the current kernel object.

At a high level, the kernel management algorithm for a set of kernel objects – here, versionedobjects, is as follows:

```
VersionObj[] split_versionedobjects
for VersionObj versioned_obj in versionedobjects
    GC_transition(versioned_obj,
        split_versionedobjects)
while split_versionedobjects.has_elements
    GC_transition(split_versionedobjects.pop,
        split_versionedobjects)
```

Algorithm 3: High-level granular cloning kernel management

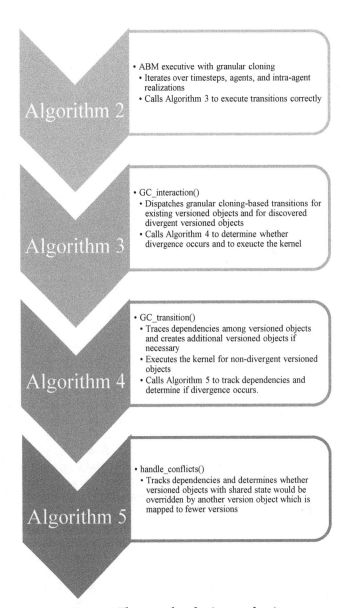

Figure 3: The granular cloning mechanism

split_versionedobjects maintains potential split kernel objects that fragment from the currently considered kernel object and still need to be handled by the kernel. For example, suppose a given kernel object, versioned_obj, is associated with versions 1 and 3, and the granular cloning transition manager GC_transition() determines that versioned_obj needs to be split from the version set {1,3} into {1} and {3}. In this case, GC_transition() will only override the kernel object corresponding to the intersection of the versions sets of all read sources. Suppose, in our example, the intersection is {1}. Now, the kernel object for {3} is still unhandled and still needs to be processed. In the while-block of the granular cloning kernel manager, we simply execute the kernel for all these split objects until they are all handled.

A given object's version set is encoded in unsigned integers where bits are set for corresponding version indices; granular cloning makes heavy use of bit manipulation. For example, the following binary value encodes a mapping to versions 1 and 3 (1-based indexing) among 32 total versions:

0000 0000 0000 0000 0000 0000 0000 0101

The granular cloning-wrapped kernel function GC_transition() performs the following steps:

```
GC_transition()(VersionObj vo, VersionObj[]
  splits)
  VersionObj[] potential_splits =
    vo.handle_conflicts()
  Versions unaffected_versions
  if potential_splits.has_splits
    splits.emplace_back(potential_splits)
    unaffected_versions =
      potential_splits.get_versions()
  vo.skernel(unaffected_versions)
```

Algorithm 4: Low-level granular cloning kernel wrapping

As previously mentioned, splits is an output argument that will store unhandled versioned objects in case we need to split the current kernel object vo. Whether splitting will occur depends on the comparison of the version set of vo and the versions of all objects we read in the kernel (i.e., all dependencies of the kernel object vo). The handle_conflicts() method determines if the version set intersection of all objects that are being read in the kernel (all dependencies) are a strict subset of the kernel object vo's version set. If they represent a strict subset, the unhandled split version objects need to be stored in splits. The version set of the unhandled split version objects are maintained in the unaffected_versions variable. Finally, we execute the superimposed kernel, skernel(), for the kernel object vo, but only for the versions that are not included in the unhandled splits – that is, the logical complement of unaffected_versions. For the complement of unaffected_versions we can be sure that we can read the corresponding version sets from all the read sources because handle_conflicts() already filtered out the maximal version set we can manage (by the definition of set intersection).

In handle_conflicts(), a tie breaker rule will determine what version number serves as the foundation of integrity checking. An arbitrary selector, like the filtering for the minimum version, will denoted with SEL. Once that version is determined, one must filter neighboring objects for corresponding sets. Consider the following example:

$$\{2\}\text{-Read}\rightarrow\{1,2\}\leftarrow\text{Read-}\{1\}$$
$$\uparrow$$
$$\text{Read}$$
$$|$$
$$\{1,2\}$$

In this case, the min-selector uses version 1. The intersection of {1,2} and {1} is {1} and so we split {1,2} into {1} and {2}. We update {1} with the kernel and leave the state mapped to version set {2} unaffected; {2} will be handled in the while-loop of Algorithm 3 later. The state of the kernel object (after the split, only associated with {1}) does not only depend on the state of the versioned object to the right, but also on one on the bottom. The while-loop of Algorithm 3 ensures that any fragment of the current kernel object will be handled by the read sources that are omitted (those fragments will potentially be split further).

Without an automated runtime that can inspect all object identifiers of a kernel invocation, it is necessary for the user to specify what objects the kernel accesses. In many ABM's the read sources consist of some neighborhood – in a given coordinate system - around the kernel object. For example, in Conway's Game of Life [14], a given kernel object (a cell that can assume a state of 1 or 0), which is located in a 2D grid, reads from its eight neighbors. In the general handle_conflicts() method (listed in Algorithm 5), it is assumed that one can access the entire state of the previous timestep (OLD) as well as the read sources relative to the kernel object (NBR) by some defined addressing scheme (i.e., coordinate system for most ABM's). There are more general variants for handle_conflicts()and some of them may be more efficient for a particular application. One can also engineer optimized versions for specific application where certain characteristics are exploited. For example, one fairly common characteristic among cellular automata is that all the versions are present (with mutual exclusivity) for each element of NBR.

```
VersionObj handle_conflicts()
  Version ref_version = SEL(this.versions)
  VersionObj[] read_sources =
    get_sources(this, OLD, NBR)
  VersionObj[] ref_vo = filter(read_sources,
    ref_version)
  Version working =
    intrsct(getversions(ref_vo),this.versions)
  For Version v in
    working.get_onehots_except(ref_version)
      working = intrsct(working,
        getversions(filter(read_sources, v)))
  if working != this.versions
    VersionObj res(this.state, working)
    res.set_splits(true)
    return res
  else
    VersionObj res(WILDCARD_S, WILDCARD_V)
    res.set_splits(false)
    return res
```

Algorithm 5: One possible general variant of handle_conflicts()

Algorithm 5 first arbitrarily picks a reference version from the kernel object's version set with the selector function SEL. It then proceeds to collect all the kernel dependencies and filters those objects with the reference version that was just selected. A working version set is then used to determine whether there is version-consistency between the dependencies' (ref_vo) and the kernel object's respective version sets. The intersection ensures that we enter skernel() with the maximal version set that is still common among all dependencies (and the kernel object itself) and preservers correctness. The for-loop ensures that transitive dependencies of non-reference versions are captured. To crystalize this in a small example:

$$\{2,4\}\text{-Read}\rightarrow\{1,2,3\}\leftarrow\text{Read-}\{1,2\}$$

Using a min-selector, we would have a reference version of 1. working would capture $\{1,2\}\cap\{1,2,3\}=\{1,2\}$ before entering the for-loop. If we did not have the for-loop intersections, the skernel() would later only read the dependency on the right (associated with version set $\{1,2\}$). However, the kernel object is also associated with version 2. Version 2 depends on the left-versioned object that is associated with $\{2,4\}$. Therefore, to preserve correctness, one must include transitively linked versions as well. The for-loop grabs all non-reference versions from working and then tries to find these transitive dependencies. The conditional branch at the end simply reports back to the caller whether a split needs to occur. If there are elements in the kernel object that are not present in the relevant read sources, a split occurs. Otherwise, the version sets are synchronized which is indicated by a flag in the returned object. The skernel() method behaves exactly like the traditional kernel with the exception that we have to filter for the version set of the kernel object among the read sources, namely for vo.get_versions() \ unaffected_versions (where \ is the set minus operator) and separate out the split version set from the kernel object. Read sources that are associated with version sets that represent a strict superset of the kernel object version set are treated exactly like those that are associated with vo.get_versions() \ unaffected_versions. The additional versions in the superset simply refer to state being shared with other versions. Since we do not write to the read objects, the presence of the additional versions is irrelevant.

For event-scheduled simulation executives, granular cloning is compatible with both optimistic and conservative synchronization protocols. For the latter, each LP will proceed to execute local events up to the synchronization point without violating local causality. The only difference compared to the traditional approach is that messages and objects are associated with versions and, whenever events are processed, the comparison of "version set"-tags occurs (via the granular cloning algorithms described). For situations in which the lookahead value is state-dependent, local causality is guaranteed if the lookahead values are derived *across all versions of a given LP* (there may exist further optimizations whereby correctness can be ensured if this is relaxed). For optimistic synchronization protocols, the same granular cloning algorithms are used during normal execution. However, during rollbacks one needs to ensure that anti-messages annihilate messages with the same version set and that state saving captures the version sets associated with simulation objects (message acknowledgements are also version set specific). A straggler message may trigger a "global" rollback (i.e., for all versions) even if it only affects a few versions. Although forward progress is guaranteed with a global rollback (as in traditional Time Warp), it may cause rollback thrashing. To counteract this, it may be possible to modify the granular cloning rollback mechanism to preemptively query a rollback's version dependencies across LPs and only affect an isolated subset of the versions, while the execution of unaffected versions can proceed in parallel (since the rollback does not apply to them). These extensions are beyond the scope of this paper.

4.3 Optimizations and Heuristics

As previously mentioned, it is possible to optimize the general approach for handle_conflicts() for a specific kernel. For example, sometimes a particular state value of the kernel object determines that few other objects need to be read than if the state of the current kernel object is assumed to be unknown. However, it should be emphasized that this is not necessary for granular cloning - unlike some other methods for computation sharing. Algorithm 6 shows a simplified version of an optimized handle_conflicts(). It exploits the application-specific fact that the kernel reads from at most one object and that we can "look ahead" which object will be read based on the current state of the kernel object.

```
VersionedObj handle_conflicts()
  if this.state == STATE0
    VersionedCell[] neighbor =
      OLD[get_index()+NBR[0]]
    for VersionedObj lvn in neighbor
      /*assume neighbor is sorted by min
      Version*/
      if versions.has_a_match(
        lvn.get_versions()) and
        !versions.is_contained_in(
        lvn.versions)
          return VersionedCell(
            this.state,
            this.versions.diff(
              this.versions.intersection(
                lvn.versions
                )
              )
            )
  else if this.state == STATE1 /* remaining cases */
  return VersionedCell() //no conflict
```

Algorithm 6: An application-specific variant of the handle_conflicts() method (applied on the kernel object) that exploits the property that there is at most one object dependency by peeking at the kernel object's state and then filtering the read sources.

Algorithm 6 first decides where in the old state of the model environment, OLD, it needs to look for the relevant object. As mentioned, the correct location depends on the state of the kernel object. In order to avoid displaying redundant code, only one of the conditional branches is shown completely (the one for STATE0). The algorithm then iterates over the versioned instances of the object and tries to discern whether the relevant instance is in (version-)conflict with the kernel object's version set. If so, it returns the split object. If not, the end of the function will return an empty object. The caller will then be able to discern whether the returned object is split or not.

This is just a small sample of possible optimizations. There are many properties that can be exploited, ranging from (i) dense and globally-sensitive version sets to (ii) sparse, localized, and clustered version sets. In applications that fall under the former category (i), it may be the case that explicitly enumerating sample paths corresponding to single versions after the branching point outperforms the general handle_conflicts() scheme; in this case, the computations are only shared up to the branching point. For applications in the latter category (ii), where one wishes to simulate many versions, it may prove fruitful to abandon the unsigned integer representation and instead adopt a compressed representation of version sets. Indices could be used to map to particular version sets in aggregate data structures.

5. EXPECTED PERFORMANCE FOR AGENT-BASED GRANULAR CLONING

Intuitively, one expects better performance (more shared computation) if the state variation is introduced late and if there is a slow spread of version-differentiated sample path relative to the entire state space. Better performance is also expected if the overhead from granular cloning is much smaller than the transition function.

Consider an agent based simulation (*ABS*) that simulates E agents over T (>0) timesteps (t is a particular timestep) over R runs (r is a particular run). At a given run, timestep, and for a given agent, a kernel (or, transition function) with work W_{kernel} is executed. Although the W_{kernel} for granular cloning is slightly more complex than the one for traditional execution, the same factor will be used for both: The only additional granular cloning overhead is a potential split of the kernel object (which is a constant-time operation). Both the traditional and the granular cloning kernels access interacting objects in constant time. The key for the former is the object id, while for the latter it consists of both the object id and relevant version set. After p % of these timesteps, decision points are injected whereby the state $S(t)$ differs from the baseline sample path (which is identified with version id, $r = 1$). At each timestep after $\lceil p*T \rceil$, each agent reads the state of E_{read} $(\leq E)$ agents. $1 \leq \varrho(t) \leq R$ is a function that – for granular cloning - returns the average number of version sets at timestep t across all agents E. $\kappa_{conflicts}$ (> 1) scales W_{kernel} by the additional overhead from handle_conflicts().

The speedup of granular cloning vs. traditional replicated execution is approximated by:

$$\frac{E \times W_{kernel} \times T \times R}{E \times \kappa_{conflicts} \times W_{kernel} \times \Sigma_{t=0}^{T} \varrho(t)} = \frac{T \times R}{\kappa_{conflicts} \times \Sigma_{t=0}^{T} \varrho(t)}$$

Without a mechanism for re-merging split objects, $\varrho(t)$ is monotonically increasing. Furthermore, $\varrho(t)$ cannot exceed R for any t because a version number is the most atomic element of an object and, by assumption, no more than R runs are simulated. Therefore, $T \times R \geq \Sigma_{t=0}^{T} \varrho(t)$. Figure 4 shows three example growth rates of $\varrho(t)$ with overlaid trendlines. The fastest-rising curve $\varrho'(t)$ would not be expected to yield a significant speedup and, depending upon the implementation of handle_conflicts(), the scaling with $\kappa_{conflicts}$ may even dominate the payoff expression above the curve $T \times R - \Sigma_{t=0}^{T} \varrho(t)$. The growth rates primarily depend on the percentage of the total state space that is being read in an object's kernel at a point in time. A constant number (without any noticeable bias for detecting certain types of state variables) would likely yield the linear $\varrho''(t)$ divergence pattern in Figure 4.

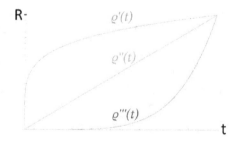

Figure 4: Lower growth rates yield better performance for granular cloning.

6. EMPIRICAL EVALUATION

The performance of granular cloning is evaluated with two models, both of which are described in more detail later. In brief, they consist of:

(i)   a cellular automaton- (CA-) based traffic simulation on a 1D grid, which is a boundary case of the Nagel-Schreckenberg traffic model [13].

(ii)   a distributed setting that simulates a basic integrated transportation and land use model (ITLUM), where one process executes (i) and another process executes a land use model from Lu et al. [2]. The execution of both processes occurs in a synchronous fashion per timestep.

The ITLUM benchmark is a useful test case because in many usage scenarios replicated runs will often only modify one model, e.g., the land use or the transportation model, but not both. As such, this is an interesting test case to explore the benefits of cloning in general, and granular cloning in particular. Further, ITLUM represents a class of simulations of practical interest to communities concerned with urban planning and the sustainable growth of cities.

For both models, the number of runs is limited to 32; the version tags assigned to objects are 32-bit unsigned integers. In settings with more runs, one could assign wider tags for even greater speedups. The machine that generated these results uses an Intel Core i7 6700 ™ (4 physical cores, 8 logical) and 32GB DDR4 memory. All programs were compiled from C++ and the distributed implementation uses MSMPI. Unit tests were successfully completed to ensure that states of the granular cloning match the explicit execution of the same runs.

The next three subsections discuss the conceptual models, and the two subsections thereafter report the performance results. Opportunities for attractive applications as well as limitations in adversarial problems due to tradeoffs are highlighted.

6.1 Conceptual Model: CA Traffic Simulation

A 1D CA models one road in a neighborhood. Each cell of the array is either set or cleared, the former representing a cell by a vehicle and the latter the absence of a vehicle. At discrete timesteps every vehicle will move forward (towards the right) by one cell if the cell ahead is clear. Vehicles "wrap around" when they reach the rightmost cell. The initial array state is populated randomly. This ruleset is referred to as Wolfram Rule 184 which is also used to model several other systems. However, there is a slight modification relative to this behavior that is described by Wolfram Rule 184. A vehicle will sample random cells in front of it and not move forward if the perceived traffic intensity is deemed too high, namely with probability $p = 1-[0.9+0.1*ESTIMATED\_TRAFFIC\_INTENSITY]$,   where $ESTIMATED\_TRAFFIC\_INTENSITY$ is determined by the ratio [number of sampled cells that are occupied]/[number of sampled cells]. In the experimental design, the number of sampled cells is varied with powers of two to illuminate its impact on the speedup. The length of the 1D array and the number of timesteps are also varied in the performance section.

6.2 Conceptual Model: Land Use Model

The land use model used is a translation from the Netlogo model of Lu et al. [2] into C++. A detailed description of the model is beyond the scope of this paper, but can be found in the reference guide of [2]. At a high level, the ABM maintains a 24x24 grid that represents 9 square miles of greenfield, which is developed with single-family dwellings over a 30-year period. It also contains on the order of 100 input, output and state variables. The agents in the model include homebuyers and developers, which interact with the local government (taxation and infrastructure improvements) and the grid. In each of the 30 time steps:

1.   1000 homebuyers bid on up to 10 properties,

2.   property transactions are settled,

3.   new properties are constructed, and

4.   local taxes are collected to improve the infrastructure.

The model was developed to compare two stormwater development policies against each other to find out how many apartment homebuyers they would incentivize.

6.3 Conceptual Model: ITLUM

The two models from the previous subsections were coupled into an ITLUM. During the 4th phase of the land use model of [2], namely the tax collection and infrastructure improvement phase, the transportation cost savings of a neighborhood are derived from the degradation of the road infrastructure and depreciation of public transit. However, these variables were fixed in the original model. Using an actual transportation simulation to determine these variables dynamically may improve the credibility and validity of the results. The traffic intensity of the neighborhood roads is understood to be proportional to the population density of the neighborhood. These communication ideas inspire the federation sequencing pipeline for the ITLUM shown in Figure 5.

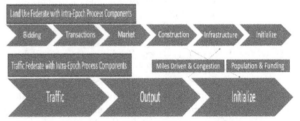

Figure 5: ITLUM Federation Sequencing Pipeline

As the ratio between (i) the execution time of one epoch of the land use node and (ii) the execution time of one epoch of the transportation node approaches 0, the speedup of the ABS dominates the overall speedup.

6.4 Evaluation: CA Traffic Simulation on a Single Process

Figure 6 shows the speedup of the granular cloning approach executing 32 versions in one single replication, compared to the traditional approach of executing a single version for each of 32 replications. Each of the 32 replications alters the state at a uniformly drawn timestep at a uniformly drawn cell. The speedups were determined using measured CPU times for a single process executing the transport model only.

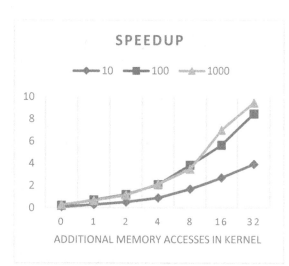

Figure 6: Speedup of the transport model of three different cell-to-timestep ratios

The three lines refer to three different scenarios differentiated by the space-to-time ratio (the cell-count divided by the time-step count). The speedup is less impressive if there are only a few timesteps relative to the numbers of cells because a given version has less time available to propagate its specific behavior into the global state. The speedup increases with the computational load in the transition function as the relative overhead of the granular cloning algorithm diminishes. The computational load is injected by enhancing the traffic intensity sampling resolution of the given driver (see the description of the transportation conceptual model above). It should be noted that merging versions that share the same state together at certain intervals in the granular cloning mode did not improve the performance significantly.

Figure 7 shows, for the 10 space-to-time ratio, the speedup if one realizes the differences among the replications late. As mentioned above, the differences among the 32 replications are uniformly drawn in the 1D grid space and across all timesteps. However, if one restricts the realized timesteps to only be drawn in the last 20% or 50% of timesteps, the version-specific local state perturbations have fewer opportunities to propagate through the global state space. This directly translates into computational savings in memory and execution time. As can be seen in the figure, the jump from the 50% scenario to the 20% scenario is less dramatic. Early branches pose a significant computational burden on granular cloning. In an adversarial scenario, the speedup is less than 1 because the physical sample path is equivalent to that in the traditional approach and one cannot reap the benefits of shared computations up to the decision point. The shared computations after the decision point are out-shadowed by the granular cloning overhead. With regard to the performance model from Section 5, $\varrho(t)$ for this particular model would exhibit a linear growth trend based on the kernel which attempts to detect collisions.

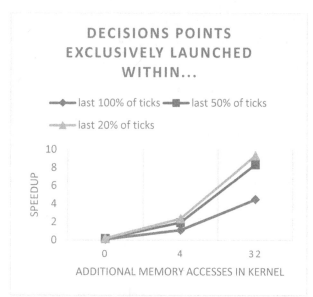

Figure 7: Speedup of the transport model if uniform scenario alterations are drawn in restricted time intervals

6.5 Evaluation: ITLUM on Two Processes

The following tables show the speedup results of the combined ITLUM model described above for 30 simulated years each. The speedup quantities are not measured relative to sequential execution of the two processes separately; rather, they are relative to the parallel execution of the two processes where only the transport model uses the traditional approach of explicitly enumerating all the replications: $S = T_{parallel,traditional} / T_{parallel,granular}$. A column headed by the expression $S_{TI=IC}$ denotes speedup figures that were obtained from models where IC instructions in the transition function for each object's update in the next timestep were computed. The data exchanged between the two simulators in a synchronized/blocking fashion. This is also why the speedup quantities in the following tables are derived from wall-clock intervals. If they were based on CPU time, they could be misleading as a result of the platform context-switching from a blocking process. However, the drawback is that platform-specific factors may pollute the times. Nevertheless, a second set of replications confirmed that the numbers were close to those in the first set.

Table 1: Speedup for cellcount/timesteps = 100 and start of decision points commences at timestep=0

Cell count	$S_{TI=4}$	$S_{TI=32}$
1,000	0.93	1.03
10,000	1.04	3.39

Table 2: Speedup for cellcount/timesteps = 100 and start of decision points commences halfway through

Cell count	$S_{TI=4}$	$S_{TI=32}$
1,000	1.01	1.07
10,000	1.13	3.29

Table 3: Speedup for cellcount/timesteps = 10 and start of decision points commences at timestep=0

Cell count	$S_{TI=4}$	$S_{TI=32}$
1,000	0.99	1.35
10,000	0.92	3.07

Table 4: Speedup for cellcount/timesteps = 10 and start of decision points commences halfway through

Cell count	$S_{TI=4}$	$S_{TI=32}$
1,000	1.00	1.66
10,000	1.11	4.11*

In the entry marked with * was also evaluated with a transition function count of 64 and 128, which resulted in speedups of 4.89 and 5.96, respectively. Since the only speedups that can be reaped in take place in the transport simulator, it determines the overall speedup provided it takes longer per epoch than the land use simulator. Because of reasons discussed before, the instruction count of the driver's transition function has a significant impact on the overall speedup. In general, especially high performance is expected when there is a large number of runs, the variation is introduced late, the behavior (transition function or event handler) is complex in relation to the overhead, and/or when individual objects do not have the opportunity to quickly affect the entire state space in a unique fashion.

6.6 Evaluation: 2x4 XOR-HOLD (Event-Scheduling on Eight Processes)

In addition to these agent-based and timestepped models, granular cloning was also compared against traditional simulation cloning in a distributed event-scheduling setting (with 8 processes). The benchmark used here is *2x4 XOR-HOLD* (2 LPs, 4 versions each) using a conservative barrier synchronization based approach. In addition to simply processing and scheduling events (*HOLD*), LPs in XOR-HOLD also own state variables (represented as an integer array) and modify them in their (sole) event handler. More specifically, they access their array at an index randomly sampled by the sender and apply logical exclusive OR of the sender's corresponding value to their own value at that index. Versions are realized as random variations in individual state variables (integers) at the start of the simulation. When the array sizes are set to 100,000 and the number of total events processed per LP set to 300,000, the obtained average speedup is 1.68 (standard error = 0.08). The

speedup was again based on wallclock time until the simulation terminates using each method.

7. CONCLUSION AND FUTURE WORK

The granular cloning framework offers performance improvements without loss in accuracy for a broad range of simulation applications where one wishes to execute several runs that share similar sample paths. Instead of being restricted to the scale of extended partitions of the state space, the explicit state representation occurs at the exact minimal scale where state differs. Our experimental results show order-of-magnitude speedup in some cases and illustrate that performance is increased when:

- the number of replications is large,
- the transition functions (in timestepped models) or the event handlers (in event-scheduling models) are relatively complex, and
- the state among runs is similar, especially at the beginning of the run, so that the framework may reuse more shared computations, rather than duplicate redundant work. In many applications, the replication-specific variation tends to explode throughout the state space as simulated time increases.

There are interesting further research questions related to granular cloning. For example, how should one batch together runs of various scenarios to apply simulation-based optimization methods (scenarios vs. random input)? Another research topic lies in approximate computing: one could reduce the overhead of granular cloning interactions selectively, which relaxes correctness; in this fashion, bias is traded off for variance. It is also an open question of whether there are more efficient algorithms to keep track of the state-version associations, especially for common applications. Another open research area is how different simulation acceleration techniques contribute to speedup when they are used in groups across a broad range of benchmarks.

We plan to release a general-purpose library that allows users to encapsulate their simulation objects into granular cloning objects as well as the interactions among these objects into granular cloning interactions. As in the simulation cloning library of [1], the granular cloning runtime will manage the bookkeeping of the varying state of a given object to the replication number (version) internally.

ACKNOWLEDGMENTS

Support for this research was provided by NSF Grants 3676778 and 1745580.

REFERENCES

[1]　Maria Hybinette and Richard Fujimoto. 2001. Cloning parallel simulations. Commun. ACM Transactions on Modeling and Computer Simulation (TOMACS), 11(4), 378-407.

[2]   Z Lu, D. Noonan, J. Crittenden, H. Jeong, and D. Wang. 2013. Use of impact fees to incentivize low-impact development and promote compact growth. Environmental science & technology, 47(19), 10744-10752.

[3]   John von Neumann. 1956. Probabilistic logics and the synthesis of reliable organism from unreliable components. Princeton University Press.

[4]   Philip Pecher, Michael Hunter, and Richard Fujimoto. 2015. Efficient Execution of Replicated Transportation Simulations with Uncertain Vehicle Trajectories. Procedia Computer Science 51 (2015): 2638-2647.

[5]   Karen Panetta Lentz, Elias S. Manolakos, Edward Czeck, and Jamie Heller. 1997. Multiple experiment environments for testing. Journal of Electronic Testing 11, no. 3 (1997): 247-262.

[6]   Pirooz Vakili. 1992. Massively parallel and distributed simulation of a class of discrete event systems: A different perspective. ACM Transactions on Modeling and Computer Simulation (TOMACS), 2(3), 214-238.

[7]   Steve Ferenci, Richard Fujimoto, Mostafa Ammar, Kalyan Perumalla, and George Riley. Updateable simulation of communication networks. 2002. Proceedings of the sixteenth workshop on Parallel and distributed simulation pp. 107-114. IEEE Computer Society.

[8]   Kevin Walsh and Emin Gün Sirer. Simulation of large scale networks I: staged simulation for improving scale and performance of wireless network simulations. 2003. Proceedings of the 35th conference on Winter simulation: driving innovation. pp. 667-675.

[9]   SLX   FAQs. http://www.wolverinesoftware.com/SLXFAQs.htm. Accessed: 2018-01-04

[10] James Henriksen. An introduction to SLX [simulation software]. 1995. Simulation Conference Proceedings, 1995. Winter. IEEE.

[11] Richard M. Fujimoto. 1989. The virtual time machine. Proceedings of the first annual ACM symposium on Parallel algorithms and architectures. ACM.

[12] Mirko Stoffers, Daniel Schemmel, Oscar Soria Dustmann, and Klaus Wehrle. 2016. Automated Memoization for Parameter Studies Implemented in Impure Languages. Proceedings of the 2016 annual ACM Conference on SIGSIM Principles of Advanced Discrete Simulation. pp. 221-232. ACM.

[13] Kai Nagel and Michael Schreckenberg. A cellular automaton model for freeway traffic. 1992. Journal de physique I 2, no. 12 2221-2229.

[14] John Conway. The game of life. 1970. Scientific American 223, no. 4

[15] Richard Fujimoto, Conrad Bock, Wei Chen, Ernest Page, and J. Panchal. Research Challenges in Modeling and Simulation for Engineering Complex Systems. 2016. NSF Report

[16] Dan Chen, Stephen J. Turner, Wentong Cai, Boon Ping Gan, and Malcolm Yoke Hean Low. Algorithms for HLA-based distributed simulation cloning. 2005. ACM Transactions on Modeling and Computer Simulation (TOMACS). 15, no. 4. 316-345.

[17] Dan Chen, Stephen J. Turner, Wentong Cai, Georgios K. Theodoropoulos, Muzhou Xiong, and Michael Lees. Synchronization in federation community networks. 2010. Journal of parallel and distributed Computing 70, no. 2. 144-159.

[18] Xiaosong Li, Wentong Cai, and Stephen J. Turner. Cloning Agent-Based Simulation. 2017. ACM Transactions on Modeling and Computer Simulation (TOMACS). 27, no. 2. 15.

[19] Francesco Quaglia and Roberto Baldoni. Exploiting intra-object dependencies in parallel simulation. 1999. Information Processing Letters 70 (3), 119-125.

[20] Nazzareno Marziale, Francesco Nobilia, Alessandro Pellegrini, and Francesco Quaglia. Granular time warp objects. 2016. Proceedings of the 2016 ACM SIGSIM Conference on Principles of Advanced and Discrete Simulation

Porting Event & Cross-State Synchronization to the Cloud

Matteo Principe
Sapienza, University of Rome
Lockless S.r.l.
matteo.principe92@gmail.com
principe@lockless.it

Tommaso Tocci
Barcelona Supercomputing Center
tommaso.tocci@bsc.es

Alessandro Pellegrini
Sapienza, University of Rome
Lockless S.r.l.
pellegrini@diag.uniroma1.it
pellegrini@lockless.it

Francesco Quaglia
University of Rome "Tor Vergata"
Lockless S.r.l.
francesco.quaglia@uniroma2.it
quaglia@lockless.it

ABSTRACT

Along the years, Parallel Discrete Event Simulation (PDES) has been enriched with programming facilities to bypass state disjointness across the concurrent Logical Processes (LPs). New supports have been proposed, offering the programmer approaches alternative to message passing to code complex LPs' relations. Along this path we find *Event & Cross-State* (ECS), which allows writing event handlers which can perform in-place accesses to the state of any LP, by simply relying on pointers. This programming model has been shipped with a runtime support enabling concurrent speculative execution of LPs limited to shared-memory machines. In this paper, we present the design of a middleware layer that allows ECS to be ported to distributed-memory clusters of machines. A core application of our middleware is to let ECS-coded models be hosted on top of (low-cost) resources from the Cloud. Overall, ECS-coded models no longer demand for powerful shared-memory machines to execute in reasonable time. Thanks to our solution, we retain indeed the possibility to rely on the enriched ECS programming model while still enabling deployments of PDES models on convenient (Cloud-based) infrastructures. An experimental assessment of our proposal is also provided.

CCS CONCEPTS

• **Computing methodologies** → **Discrete-event simulation**; • **Theory of computation** → *Shared memory algorithms*; • **Software and its engineering** → *Distributed memory*;

ACM Reference Format:
Matteo Principe, Tommaso Tocci, Alessandro Pellegrini, and Francesco Quaglia. 2018. Porting Event & Cross-State Synchronization to the Cloud. In *SIGSIM-PADS '18: SIGSIM Principles of Advanced Discrete Simulation CD-ROM, May 23–25, 2018, Rome, Italy*. ACM, New York, NY, USA, 12 pages. https://doi.org/10.1145/3200921.3200929

Permission to make digital or hard copies of all or part of this work for personal or classroom use is granted without fee provided that copies are not made or distributed for profit or commercial advantage and that copies bear this notice and the full citation on the first page. Copyrights for components of this work owned by others than the author(s) must be honored. Abstracting with credit is permitted. To copy otherwise, or republish, to post on servers or to redistribute to lists, requires prior specific permission and/or a fee. Request permissions from permissions@acm.org.
SIGSIM-PADS '18 , May 23–25, 2018, Rome, Italy
© 2018 Copyright held by the owner/author(s). Publication rights licensed to the Association for Computing Machinery.
ACM ISBN 978-1-4503-5092-1/18/05...$15.00
https://doi.org/10.1145/3200921.3200929

1 INTRODUCTION

For a long time, the literature on Parallel Discrete Event Simulation (PDES) has been focused on improving the runtime behavior of PDES systems under its traditional programming model [12], where interactions between concurrent simulation objects—also known as Logical Processes (LPs)—were expressed only via event exchange. Along this path, we can find solutions oriented to load balancing [2, 4, 8, 14], to the optimization of rollback management in case of speculative processing [5, 9], and to the effectiveness of platform-level data structures and algorithms [15].

More recently, also thanks to significant changes in hardware platforms occurred since the time PDES was born, new trends of research emerged. Specifically, the possibility to rely on multi-core machines offering shared-memory support has given rise to new programming approaches for PDES, together with their transparent runtime support. These new programming approaches improve, on the one hand, the expressiveness and flexibility of model implementation while, on the other hand, they improve the execution performance when compared to explicit event scheduling to implement interactions among LPs.

Along this research path we find solutions enabling the sharing of subset of LP attributes [7], making them accessible while processing any event, or solutions oriented to let the concurrent execution of events share global data across multiple cores [17]. These proposals enable the programmer to store data produced/updated by the execution of some event in such a way that these same data can be directly accessed when later (or concurrently) processing another event—with no need for any explicit data passing at the application software level. Lines of code can be therefore reduced, together with the volume of messages that need to be exchanged at the level of the PDES platform.

A highly-flexible programming approach still based on the exploitation of shared-memory support is referred to as *Event & Cross-State* (ECS) [18]. It allows the programmer to write event handlers that can access any memory location belonging to the state of any LP via pointers. Accesses are supported in both read and write mode, thus providing a very expressive way to implement the event logic. Indeed, any event can observe the current state of the overall model or can update any of part of it. This is possible even though the runtime system manages the LPs concurrently, thus enabling the concurrent execution of multiple event handlers at the same time.

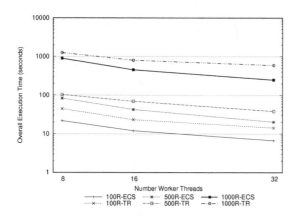

Figure 1: Traditional PDES vs Parallel ECS-based Execution Times (Log Scale on y-axis).

Correctness of read/write operations—namely causal consistency of the operations on the basis of data/timestamp dependencies—are transparently supported via the integration of both operating-system and user-space facilities. Also, ECS is conceived to work with speculative-processing runtime environments, thus enabling the exploitation of parallelism while processing independent event execution paths on multi-core systems.

To illustrate the power of ECS, we report in Figure 1 the execution time of a traditionally-coded robot exploration model (based on explicit event exchange), and of the same model coded and run on top of ECS. Both implementations have been run on the same PDES speculative platform, namely ROOT-Sim [23], with or without ECS support. The core parameter that has been varied between 100 and 1000 is the number of robots (marked as 'R'), each modeled by a different LP. The number of cells forming the region of interest, still modeled by different LPs, is set to 4096. The plot shows the execution time while varying the number of threads used to run the model between 8 and 32. All experiments are carried out on an HP ProLiant G7 machine with 32 physical cores and 64 GB of RAM. The results show that, independently of the number of robots and the number active worker threads, ECS-based runs provide a performance increase with respect to traditional PDES, which ranges from 19% to 58%. Also, event handlers in the ECS case require 25% less lines of C code[1]. However, one limitation of ECS is related to the fact that its runtime support targets a single shared-memory machine. Therefore, if some scale up of the computing power is required to run more demanding models in reasonable time, the user is forced to resort to a single higher-end multi-core machine.

In this paper we tackle the following question: "*can we run ECS-based models on top of clusters of low-cost resources (i.e., with limited parallelism) like spot instances from the Cloud?*". Enabling this kind of deploy would allow programmers to still access via pointers any LP state in read/write mode, and would allow end users to run large models without the need for a costly shared-memory machine. A distributed memory cluster made up by low cost (virtual) machines would in fact suffice.

---

[1] Models source code is available at https://github.com/HPDCS/ROOT-Sim/ on the models branch.

We respond positively to such a question by providing innovative operating-system and platform-level capabilities, which make ECS a distributed middleware enabling such a seamless execution on top of distributed-memory systems. Essentially, we provide an innovative memory-management support for Linux on x86_64 systems based on new kernel-level facilities, which virtualizes a unique address space on top of a distributed memory system. At the same time, the innovative middleware facilities transparently track per-thread read/write accesses onto this address space in order to trigger the execution of middleware-level tasks. They (re)-materialize memory pages associated with the state of a simulation object at the correct simulation time on the (remote) node were the event performing the access is running. In other words, our memory-management system implements a *lease-based mechanism* where some operating system pages—and its content related to a given virtual-time instant along model execution—is granted for use to (and materialized on) a given node for a while, depending on model execution's trajectory and overall state accesses.

It is important to note that our ultimate goal is not to improve performance when running ECS-based models in the Cloud, compared to traditional PDES models run on the same Cloud platforms. Rather, our aim is to enable ECS-based programming in the Cloud, with direct benefits in terms of simplification of the programmer's job, while still guaranteeing adequate runtime performance.

Our innovative middleware has been integrated within the ROOT-Sim PDES environment [23], and is available for download. In this paper we also report experimental results showing the feasibility of our approach with real-world simulation models.

The remainder of this paper is structured as follows. In Section 2 we discuss related work. Section 3 introduces our reference PDES system organization. The facilities offered by the ECS distributed middleware are presented in Section 4. Experimental results showing the viability of our solution are provided in Section 5.

2 RELATED WORK

In the recent years, a lot of research effort has been spent to enable PDES systems to fruitfully exploit (low-cost) resources from the Cloud (or virtualized environments in general) to run large models. Some works have been targeted at studying the effects of hypervisor configurations on the runtime dynamics of PDES systems [25, 26], particularly on the side of virtual machine (VM) scheduling and cross-VM communication. These studies have targeted both conservative and optimistic PDES, as the basis to determine whether the Cloud can represent a fruitful infrastructure for complex and large scale PDES simulations. The exploitation of distributed resources, such as Cloud (spot) resources, is a central target also for our work. However the main difference between what we propose and the previous literature studies is that the latter are still bound to the traditional PEDS programming model. In particular, the considered PDES platforms adhere to the paradigm in which the model developer is forced to reason about LP data separation and cannot implement rely to in-place cross-LP state access. Rather, we target more innovative programming paradigms, such as ECS. We therefore target an orthogonal goal, which nonetheless is of similar relevance.

Full state partitioning as in traditional PDES—with event handlers only accessing the state of a single LP—is a programming model leading to deployment of PDES systems which have been shown to be capable of exploiting extreme-scale distributed infrastructures and supercomputing-oriented facilities [1]. Such platforms are not the central target of our proposal. However, enabling ECS to run on distributed-memory systems opens the way to exploiting differentiated classes of computing clusters (including higher-end ones) in conjunction with the innovation in the offered programming model—which breaks disjointness in the accesses to the LP states by event handlers.

As for the enrichment of the programming facilities in PDES systems, the literature shows solutions oriented to enabling data sharing across LPs. The approach in [3] discusses how LP state sharing might be emulated by using a separate LP hosting the shared data and acting as a centralized server. There, also the notion of *version records* is introduced, where multi versioning is used to maintain shared data in order to cope with read/write operations occurring at different logical times while avoiding unneeded rollbacks. This is an approach similar to the one proposed in [16], where a theoretical presentation of algorithms to implement a Distributed Shared Memory mechanism is provided, and one of the provided algorithms proposes to implement variables as multi-version lists where write operations install new version nodes and read operations find the most suitable version. The above approaches are different from what we propose given that instead of mapping accesses to message-passing, we support in-place access to LP state buffers. Retrieving actual operating system pages is fully transparent to the application and is demanded to the innovative distributed ECS middleware we present. Also, we do not limit sharing to a particular memory portion (such as the state image of the centralized server), since any memory buffer representing a portion of the whole simulation model state can be accessed. Contextually, we provide the support for application-transparent distributed deploy of the PDES system entailing such sharing facilities, thus not limiting the support for state sharing to shared memory machines. This overcomes the limitation of the original ECS runtime support [18], which was bound to a single shared-memory machine.

In [10], the notion of *state query* is introduced, according to which any LP needing the value of a portion of the state that belongs to a different LP can issue a query message to it and then waits for a reply containing the suitable value. If this value is later detected to be no longer valid, an anti-message is sent so as to invalidate the query. Again, this approach relies on message passing, and is not transparent to the application programmer, who needs to embed the usage of query messages within the application code.

The work in [13] proposes to integrate the support for shared state in terms of global variables, by basing the architecture on [6]. Although this proposal supports in-place read/write operations as we do (i.e., LPs directly access the only copy of the data, avoiding a commit phase at the end of the execution of an event), it provides no transparency, as the application-level code must explicitly register LPs as readers/writers on shared variables. Also, it does not scale to distributed memory clusters of machines—like Cloud based clusters. Our proposal avoids all these limitations, by also allowing the sharing of dynamically-allocated buffers within the LP state, for which pre-declaration of the potential need to access cannot

be raised at startup—hence intrinsically leading actual access to be determined as a function of the specific execution trajectory while running the application.

The issue of transparency has been tackled in [17], where shared data are allowed to be accessed by concurrent LPs without the need for pre-declaring the intention to access. This has been achieved via user transparent software instrumentation, in combination with a multi-version scheme, either allowing the redirection of read operations to the correct version of the data (on the basis of the timestamp) or forcing rollbacks of causally inconsistent reads. This solution is targeted at the management of global variables. Instead, our proposal is suited for data sharing of dynamically allocated memory chunks logically incorporated within the state of each individual LP, while still providing parallelism and synchronization transparency. Further, that proposal is limited to shared memory machines, while our primary focus in this paper is to port the ECS enriched programming model onto distributed memory clusters.

The work in [7] proposes a framework targeted at multi-core machines and based on Time Warp, where so called Extended Logical Processes (Ex-LPs), defined as a collection of LPs, have public attributes that are associated with variables which can be accessed by LPs in other Ex-LPs. The work proposes to handle the accesses to shared attributes by relying on a specifically targeted Transactional Memory (TM) implementation, where events are mapped to transactions and the actual implementation of the TM is based on [13]. One core difference between our proposal and the one in [7] is that the latter requires a-priori knowledge of the attributes to be shared, which need to be a-priori mapped to TM managed memory locations. Rather, our proposal allows for sharing any memory area within the heap, without the need for a-priori knowledge of whether some sharing on a specific area can occur. This increases the level of transparency. In fact, the programmer is allowed to let any LP that takes control touch any valid memory location within the global simulation state without the need for any particular care, just like it occurs in sequential-style programming and related sequential execution scenarios. Overall, we "transactify" the access to memory chunks across different concurrent LPs without the need to mark data portions subject to transactional management by the programmer. Further, as a second core difference, the work in [7] does not support cross-LP accesses on distributed-memory systems, which is the primary target of our work to enable exploiting clusters from the Cloud.

Finally, our proposal has relations with approaches that bridge shared and distributed memory programming in general contexts. Among them, we mention PGAS (Partitioned Global Address Space) [22]. However, these solutions do not cope with virtual time-based speculative synchronization, thus not enabling the local materialization of remote data versions complying with timestamp-ordered accesses. In other words, our solution is already specialized to speculative PDES, while the others would require additional modules to be designed in order to accomplish the same objective. As for PGAS, another difference stands in that it relies on compiler-based instrumentation to intercept memory accesses, and to detect whether they refer to remote data. On the contrary, we rely on kernel level facilities operating at the granularity of individual operating system pages, which avoids paying the cost of running instrumented software at all the accesses.

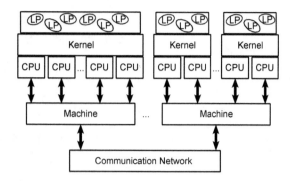

Figure 2: Reference System Organization

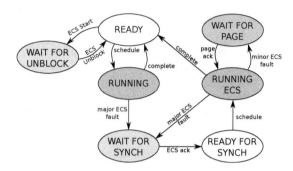

Figure 3: LP State Machine

3 REFERENCE SYSTEM

A high-level schematization of our reference PDES system is depicted in Figure 2. Simulations are supported by a set of (possibly non-homogeneous) processing units, scattered across any number of machines (i.e., computing nodes). On each computing node, any number of *simulation kernel instances* can be running. These instances are developed according to the symmetric multi-threaded paradigm [24], where shared memory is used to support intra-kernel synchronization. Distributed communication is supported by some network interconnection.

According to this organization, a symmetric simulation kernel instance spawns, at simulation startup, a number of concurrent worker threads which is the same as the number of processing units assigned to the kernel instance. Each of these worker threads is stuck to a single processing unit for the whole lifetime of the simulation run. The simulation model's LPs are then assigned to the worker threads according to some *binding rule*. This LP binding ensures that, for a certain interval of wall-clock time, only one worker thread can schedule events destined to one LP. The binding can be recomputed either periodically or depending on runtime parameters, in order to evenly distribute the workload of the simulation on the available computing power.

Therefore, in the most general setting, our reference system model is made up of the following elements:

- A number K of simulation kernel instances (forming up the *KernelSet*), which are scattered across the available computing nodes.
- Each simulation kernel instance $k \in KernelSet$ runs a set of concurrent worker threads, denoted as $TSet_k$. These worker threads rely on shared memory for their internal communication and synchronization tasks.
- At any wall-clock time instant, a worker thread $t \in TSet_k$ is in charge of CPU-dispatching events for a set of bound LPs, denoted as $LPSet_t$. As mentioned before, at any time instant, one LP is managed only by one worker thread. Therefore, $LPSet_i \cap LPSet_j = \emptyset \quad \forall i,j \quad i \neq j$.

Given the distributed nature of the simulation system, at any time an LP_i discriminates between a set of *local LPs*, namely all the LPs bound to any worker thread $w \in TSet_k$ such that $LP_i \in LPSet_t$ and $t, w \in TSet_k$, and a set of *remote LPs*, in any other case.

4 DISTRIBUTED-MEMORY ECS

4.1 Basics

Similarly to the original proposal in [18], our distributed ECS architecture is based on two orthogonal facilities which are transparently offered by the simulation platform. On the one hand, while simulation events are being executed, the platform is able to *detect* that the running LP is accessing the state of another LP, possibly hosted by a remote simulation kernel instance. At the same time, the platform is able to enforce a (distributed) protocol to *synchronize* the Local Clocks of the LPs involved in an ECS synchronization, so as to allow them to observe a consistent view on the simulation state.

In our organization, *cross-state access detection* is provided by innovative kernel-level facilities, which let different worker threads of the platform share the same logical pages although with different access privileges. Therefore, a page fault upon accessing the simulation state of a different LP is the initiation of an ECS synchronization, as it will be later discussed. At the same time, *LP synchronization* is enforced by relying on a (distributed) communication protocol, based on the notion of *control messages*. A control message is a message exchanged across two different LPs, in a way completely similar to event transfer. Nevertheless, with one single exception, control messages are not incorporated into the receiver's event queue, as they are associated with ephemeral state transitions which must not be replayed upon a rollback operation, and must be purely handled at the level of the PDES platform.

Correctness of the whole simulation is guaranteed by two facts: i) the execution of an event by a LP can be *suspended*; ii) every LP is always in an execution state according to the state machine depicted in Figure 3, which allows the PDES platform to correctly interpret the system events and control messages which target every LP.

As for point i) above, we rely on User-Level Threads (ULT), namely CPU contexts which can be saved and restored at any time instant by a worker thread $t \in TSet_k$. In particular, to give control to a LP, the worker thread in charge of it changes its CPU context, allowing the execution of the event to take place in an isolated environment, which has also its own stack. In this way, whenever the simulation platform takes back control, it might determine that the event's execution has to be temporarily suspended, and it de-schedules the running LP (i.e., it restores the CPU context related to the worker thread running in *platform mode*). Later, the worker thread can decide to resume the execution of the suspended event,

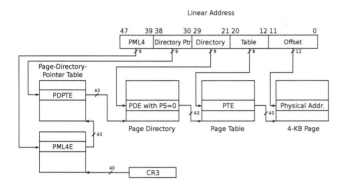

Figure 4: The Paging Scheme in x86_64 Processors.

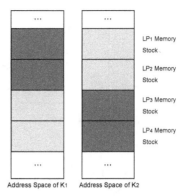

Figure 5: LP Memory Map Organization

and this is done by simply restoring the LP's CPU state. Having a separate stack for every LP within a single worker thread (which has its own system stack) ensures the correctness of the preemptive event execution. For a thorough technical description of the approach used to realize this facility in an application-transparent manner, we refer the reader to [19].

With respect to point ii) above, the state machine reported in Figure 3 has three different types of states: *blocked states* (gray-shaded) are associated with a LP which has been descheduled while executing an event, thanks to the ULT facility; *ready states* (white-colored) are associated with LPs which can be activated, either to start processing a new event, or to resume the execution of a preempted event; *running states*, which are associated with LPs currently executing an event. This organization allows to implement the *smallest-timestamp first* scheduling strategy [12] of each worker thread quite easily, given that only LPs in a ready state can be activated. The transitions across the different states are related to two main kind of events: some are associated with the aforementioned *cross-state access detection*, others with the actual *LP synchronization*. We will thoroughly describe these transitions later.

4.2 Memory Management

In order to support cross-state access detection, the runtime environment must enforce a memory management policy which allows in a simple way to map the memory chunks destined for usage by a LP—via the invocations to the traditional malloc library—to a given memory addresses range. This is particularly important given that we must discriminate between memory accesses which target the simulation states of different LPs, which can be either local or remote.

Indeed, the goal is to detect at runtime what LP's state is being targeted by a memory access by relying on pure address-space mapping. When the simulation is started up according to the distributed system model described in Section 3, there are multiple (distributed) processes living in separate virtual address spaces. We therefore need an agreement across the different kernel instances to map LPs states to the same virtual address ranges. Given that we target full transparency towards the application-level programmer, who is allowed to rely as well on dynamic memory allocation, such an agreement could be impossible or over-costly at runtime.

We have therefore resorted, in a way similar to what has been proposed in [21], to a *deterministic memory map manager*. In particular, according to the original shared-memory tailored ECS proposal in [18], each LP is associated with a 1 GB *memory stock*, or a multiple of this memory unit. As illustrated in Figure 5, the base address of this stock is deterministically computed by every simulation kernel instance. In this way, all simulation kernel instances map LP stocks to a same contiguous region of the virtual address space, where the stocks are uniquely associated with an address range which does not overlap.

Given that a simulation-kernel instance manages a pre-defined set of LPs, thanks to its worker threads, at simulation startup these memory stocks are delivered to a fine-grained memory manager, such as the one presented in [20], which ensures that the simulation model's memory requests can be served thanks to traditional APIs, such as malloc or new.

Overall, this organization delivers memory buffers in a *non-anonymous* way—although transparently with respect to the application—where the buffers destined to serve memory requests by a LP are guaranteed to fall within a memory stock located in a contiguous virtual address region reserved to host the state of that specific LP. In the case of remote LPs, the virtual addresses are initialized and never used to serve memory requests, by all kernels which do not host such LPs (these are the grey regions in Figure 5).

4.3 Kernel-Level Support

Cross-state access detection is ultimately supported by a close interaction with ad-hoc operating system's facilities offered by a custom Loadable Kernel Module (LKM). This module offers two different levels of interaction: *explicit* interaction is supported by a set of ioctl commands, to let worker threads notify the kernel when a given LP is starting to process an event; *implicit* interaction allows the kernel to notify the userspace runtime environment whenever a LP is accessing the state of a different LP.

4.3.1 Explicit Interaction. When the module is loaded, it creates the single-access device file /dev/ecs. Upon simulation startup, the simulation kernel opens this file to let the module know that its threads must be managed according to the below-described logic, and relies on the SET_VM_RANGE ioctl command to tell the module what is the range of virtual addresses associated with the LPs.

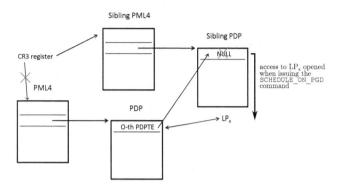

Figure 6: ECS Schedule Example

For the sake of clarity, we report in Figure 4 how a virtual address is mapped to a physical address on x86_64 systems. The CR3 control register keeps a pointer to a first-level paging table. From this table, it is possible to traverse four different levels of indirection, until a physical page is located in memory. The (virtual) linear address is decomposed into five different fields, which determine the offset at each level of the chain where the pointer to the next level is found. The last displacement is the offset within the physical page, into which the memory access is falling.

The memory map depicted in Figure 5 is allocated so that the page table respects an important invariant. We allocate LPs' memory stocks so that the whole GB (or the set of GBs) of memory is aligned to one single entry in the Page Directory Pointer (PDP) table. In this way, any access to any physical page related to the simulation state of a LP can be immediately mapped to the actual LP thanks to the PDP entry used in the virtual-to-physical address resolution. Therefore, thanks to the enforced deterministic memory allocation scheme, the payload of the SET_VM_RANGE ioctl command is simply the initial address of the first memory stock reserved for LP_0, and the total number of bytes reserved for the states of all the LPs.

To actually determine when a LP is accessing the state of a different LP, worker threads inform the kernel module what is the LP which will be activated for event execution via another ioctl command named SCHEDULE_ON_PGD. This command activates a kernel-level logic implemented in the module which installs a *sibling page table* on the CR3 register of the CPU core running the worker thread. In particular, the invocation of the SCHEDULE_ON_PGD command puts in place the policy illustrated in Figure 6. The sibling page table is constructed by relying on a cloned PML4 table associated with the virtual memory of the whole process—this can be easily retrieved by the module from current->mm->pgd—and by a clone of the PDP tables which point to the simulation state of any LP, be it local or remote. These cloned PDP tables are zeroed in the entries reserved for the LP states, except for the entry associated with the currently-scheduled LP (notified via the ioctl call) so that whenever an access is made towards a different LP's simulation state, it generates a memory fault.

Having different sibling PML4 tables associated with the different concurrent worker threads leads to the possibility to concurrently dispatch and execute different LPs—this is done by having each worker thread opening the access to the stocks associated with the

---

Algorithm 1 ECS Page Fault Kernel Handler

1: **procedure** FAULTHANDLER(pt_regs* *regs*)	
2: **if** *current* → *mm* = NULL **then**	▷ F1
3: DOPAGEFAULT( )	
4: **return**	
5: **if** *current* → *pid* is not registered **then**	▷ F2
6: DOPAGEFAULT( )	
7: **return**	
8: *target* ← READCR2( )	
9: **if** PML4(*target*) not in LP range **then**	▷ F3
10: DOPAGEFAULT( )	
11: **return**	
12: **else**	
13: **if** PDP(*target*) = NULL **then**	▷ F4
14: *fault_type* ← *Major*	
15: **else**	
16: **if** GETPTESTICKYBIT(*target*) **then**	▷ F5
17: *fault_type* ← *Minor*	
18: SETPRESENCEBIT(*target*)	
19: **else**	
20: **if** ¬GETPRESENCEBIT(*target*) **then**	▷ F6
21: DOPAGEFAULT( )	
22: **if** GETPDESTICKYBIT(*target*) **then**	
23: *fault_type* ← *Minor*	▷ F7
24: SETPAGESTICKYFLAG(*target*)	
25: **else**	
26: **return**	
27: **else**	▷ F8
28: *fault_type* ← *AccessChange*	
29: SETPAGEPRIVILEGE(*target*, WRITE)	
30: Switch to the original Page Table	▷ F9
31: Copy to userspace fault information	
32: Push on userspace stack *regs* → *ip*	
33: *regs* → *ip* ← ECSHANDLER	▷ F10

LP it is currently dispatching—while still having the possibility to determine whether any of the dispatched LPs is confining its memory references within its own stocks. The assumption underlying this type of organization is that, when there is the need for opening access to a given stock, the corresponding memory management information is already present in the associated PDP entry of the original page tables. This is not guaranteed by simply validating virtual memory addresses via mmap, which leaves memory into the empty-zero state. To overcome this problem, when we initialize the memory map depicted in Figure 5, beyond calling mmap, we also explicitly write a null byte into one single virtual page of the stock. In this way, the Linux kernel traps the access to empty-zero memory and allocates the whole chain of page tables for managing the pages within the stock (although a single one of these pages is really allocated). This guarantees the existence of the PDP entry associated with the stock, to be filled into the corresponding sibling PDP entry upon dispatching the LP owning the stock. We note that relying on more traditional facilities, such as mprotect would not be viable. Indeed, this would setup policies which are enforced for the whole process, while our approach allows different threads within the same process (the simulation kernel) to observe different memory access privileges, at a negligible cost.

4.3.2 Implicit Interaction.

4.3.2 Implicit Interaction. In order to let the userspace runtime environment know when a LP is accessing a different LP's simulation state, we have to intercept the artificial memory faults which are generated by the sibling page table installed in the CR3 register of every CPU core. To this end, when the LKM is loaded, it changes the IDT table (directly accessible via the IDT register) in order to make the pointer to the page-fault handler point to an ad-hoc ECS fault handler (rather than the original do_page_fault function within the Linux kernel) implemented within the module. This ad-hoc ECS fault handler is the core of the detection of a cross-state access, and its pseudocode is reported in Algorithm 1.

Once the ECS fault handler is activated, it first checks whether the handler is activated to resolve a minor page fault (**F1**) or if the fault is associated with the thread of a non-registered process (**F2**), i.e., a process which did not open the /dev/ecs device file. In both cases, it calls the traditional kernel's fault handler and then returns, as the fault has been resolved elsewhere. If the thread is registered with the LKM—it is a thread running within the PDES system—we retrieve from the CR2 control register the *target* address of the memory fault. We first check whether this address belongs to a PML4 entry which keeps LPs memory stocks (**F3**) because, in the negative case, this is a memory fault at the level of the simulation platform which must be resolved via the traditional DoPageFault kernel facility.

We then discriminate what kind of access the LP is making to other LPs. In particular, if the PDP entry associated with the target address is zeroed (**F4**), this means that we are accessing the simulation state of a different LP for the first time. This is the case thanks to the fact that upon scheduling a LP, the SCHEDULE_ON_PGD ioctl command explicitly clears all PDP entries pointing to the memory stocks reserved for different LPs. We refer to this situation as an *ECS Major Fault*. In this case, we give back control to the simulation platform by modifying the instruction pointer's value to make it point to the EcsHandler platform function (**F10**), which will be later described. Before doing this (**F9**), we copy to userspace (in a per-thread buffer) all the information related to the fault (namely the fault type, the faulting memory target, and the address of the faulting instruction), we switch to the original page table by reinstalling into CR3 the original PML4 address found at current->mm->pgd, and we push on userspace stack the original value of the instruction pointer, to let the execution flow be eventually resumed.

The userspace ECS handler, discussed in details in Section 4.5, starts a (distributed) synchronization protocol across the involved LPs, to let them observe a consistent snapshot. When synchronizing towards a remote LP, the LKM has to determine what are the memory pages accessed both in read and write mode, to fetch this content from the remote process hosting the LP. To this end, the userspace handler eventually invokes a LKM facility via the SET_PAGE_PROTECTION ioctl command. The logic associated with this command is similar in spirit to what an invocation of mprotect would do on the stock. As said, we cannot rely on it as it would modify the memory view for all threads.

Conversely, we exploit the organization of a Page-Table Entry (PTE), which is depicted in Figure 7, in the original memory view. In particular, we scan all PTE entries which can be reached starting from the PDE entry associated with the given remote LP towards which the scheduled one is synchronizing. All non-null PTE entries,

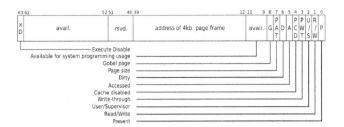

Figure 7: Page-Table Entry (4KB Page)

which are thus associated with an actual materialized page, have the *presence bit* (bit 0) set to 1, to indicate that the Page Base Address is a valid (physical) base pointer for the page. We explicitly force the presence bit to zero, thus generating an additional artificial memory fault whenever such a page (installed by the userspace handler) is accessed. To discriminate whether a fault is artificial or not, due to the above-described scheme, before clearing the presence bit we set bit 9 in the same PTE entry. This is a *programmer's available bit* that we use as a sticky bit—a bit which can be exploited by the LKM to implement additional facilities not supported by the processor firmware. While performing this action, we similarly set one available bit in the PDE entry, to mark the whole memory stock as associated with a remote LP.

Eventually, the LP which initiated the ECS synchronization is re-scheduled, the sibling page table is loaded into the CR3 register of the core where the worker thread is currently running on, and the cleared presence bit will generate a memory fault. This condition is reflected in Algorithm 1 at points **F5**, **F6**, and **F7**. The fault handler first determines whether the page is already materialized, possibly due to a previous execution of an ECS synchronization, by checking if the sticky flag in the associated PTE is set (**F5**). In this case, the presence bit is set back to 1, and an ECS Minor Fault is delivered to the userspace handler, to start the retrieval of the remote pages actually involved in the memory access. Conversely, if the sticky bit is not set, we have to materialize the page if and only if the presence bit in the PTE is not set (**F6**). In this case, we call the original do_page_fault kernel handler. We now discriminate again whether this is a memory fault related to the access to non-materialized pages of local vs remote LPs, by checking the sticky bit in the PDE entry which was previously set. In this case (**F7**), we activate the userspace handler notifying an ECS Minor Fault to retrieve the remote pages, only after having set as well the sticky bit in the PTE entry, to realign the page table to a consistent state according to the logic of the fault handler.

The check at **F6** is important, as it covers as well an additional case. When a LP accesses a remote page in read mode, we explicitly prevent the possibility to access the local copy of the page installed by the userspace handler in write mode by setting bit 1 of the associated PTE to zero. This bit (see Figure 7) is the *read/write bit* which, when set to zero, generates a memory fault when the page is accessed in write mode. In this case (**F8**) we explicitly set back this bit to 1, enabling the possibility to write the page, and deliver an ECS Access Change Fault to the userspace handler. This is an important aspect, as we will later show how this can optimize the finalization of the ECS protocol, in terms of write back actions of

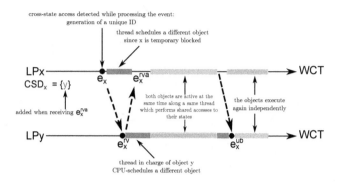

Figure 8: LP Synchronization along Wall-Clock-Time (WCT)

dirty pages towards the node that hosts the master copy of the LP state involved in ECS accesses.

As an additional note, if the target LP involved in ECS is hosted by the the same machine where the source LP resides, the target LP has its operating system pages already locally mapped in the address space. Hence no write-back policy of dirty pages toward the original node needs to be put in place. I this case the sibling page tables setup unleashes full read/write access to the target LP state—based on the SCHEDULE_ON_PGD ioctl command issue at the PEDS platforms level—thus saving the costs for managing read vs write faults.

Further, our solution is able to handle both 4KB page size (which exactly relies on all the 4 levels of paging we described above) and large pages, namely 2MB pages. In the latter case, the sibling chain that maps a 2MB page will only entail 3 levels of page-tables, namely PML4/PDP/PDE. In fact, our custom fault handler, while traversing the original chain of page-tables, is able to determine whether the target page is a large one or not, and to setup the sibling page-tables' chain accordingly. We exploited swapoff/swapon services natively offered by Linux in order to temporarily avoid asynchronous modifications of the original page-tables' chain due to page swapping by the kswapd daemon, which would otherwise interfere with our management of the page-table entries.

4.4　The LP Synchronization Protocol

Before entering in the details of the userspace ECS handler, we discuss the (distributed) protocol to synchronize two LPs whenever a cross-state access is detected. Synchronization is supported by control-message passing among the involved nodes. The basic scheme is depicted in Figure 8.

Cross-state accesses must be supported in such a way to ensure that the state snapshot observed by the event-handler is consistent, although generated by a speculative execution. Hence, the LPs whose states are accessed while processing an individual event all need to figure as aligned (in logical time) to the timestamp of the event. This is achieved by encapsulating the cross-state access within an atomic action that is, in its turn, based on an ad-hoc synchronization protocol triggered on demand, if and only if a cross-state access is detected.

The synchronization starts by having LP_x at which the cross-state access is detected send a *rendezvous start* control message

e_x^{rv} tagged with a system-wide unique mark[2] towards the destination LP_y. LP_x's execution is then suspended, thanks to the above-mentioned ULT facilities, and it enters the *Wait For Synch* state described in Section 4.1. Once this control message is received and incorporated into the destination LP's event queue, LP_y will eventually reach this event either thanks to forward execution of events in the queue, or due to a rollback operation if e_x^{rv} is a straggler message. The logic associated with the processing of e_x^{rv} is that LP_y is put in the *Wait for Unblock* state and sends back to LP_x a *rendezvous ack* control message e_x^{rva}. Once e_x^{rva} is delivered at LP_x, it moves LP_x to the *Ready for Synch* state, which eventually leads LP_x to be reactivated. The id of LP_y is added to the *Cross-State Dependency* table of LP_x (CSD_x), which is passed as an argument of the SCHEDULE_ON_PGD ioctl command to determine what PDP entries should be opened for access in the sibling page table temporarily installed in the CR3 register of the core running the worker thread.

At this point, LP_x and LP_y are aligned to the same logical time instant, and LP_x can access the state of LP_y. In case LP_y is remote, these accesses will generate additional page faults. These will be associated with additional control messages, as discussed later in Section 4.5. This scheme can be iterated multiple times, so that within the execution of a single event, LP_x can synchronize with any number of LPs. The same rendezvous mark is used to track the synchronization, so that in case any of the LPs undergoes a rollback operation, all synchronized LPs can be rolled back as well[3]. The ECS synchronization terminates when LP_x completes the execution of the currently-scheduled event. At this time, it sends to all synchronized LPs a *rendezvous unblock* message e_x^{ub}, so that all LPs can now start again executing independently.

By the above description, the materialization of a cross-state access leads to a non-persistent relation between two or more LPs. In fact, given that cross-state synchronization is operated on a per-event basis, after the finalization of the event that led to cross-state accesses, the involved LPs start again executing alone along their own simulation trajectories. However, in general contexts, a cross-state access by the application code could be the evidence that two (or more) LPs are actually starting to execute in a synergistic way, in terms of overall simulation model execution trajectory.

4.5　Userspace ECS Management

When the LKM notifies the runtime environment that two LPs have to be ECS-synchronized, the handler depicted in Algorithm 2 is activated. This handler performs different actions depending on the type of ECS fault which is notified by the LKM.

The ECS Major Fault case (**H1**) is associated with the initiation of the (distributed) protocol described in Section 4.4. First, a system-wide unique mark is generated, and a rendezvous start message is sent to the LP keeping the portion of the simulation state which is being accessed by the currently-scheduled event. The id of the target LP is delivered by the LKM, as it is uniquely associated with the PDP entry related to the faulting memory address. The running LP then enters the *Wait for Synch* state, and the target LP

---

[2]These marks are fastly generated by relying on the Cantor Pairing Function using the global id of the LP and a local monotonic counter.
[3]For a thorough description of the rollback strategy and all its implications on liveliness and correctness of the approach, we refer the reader to [20].

Algorithm 2 Userspace ECS Handler

```
 1: procedure ECSHANDLER(type, info)
 2:     if type = Major then                                    ▷ H1
 3:         ECS_mark ← GENERATE_MARK( )
 4:         SEND(RENDEZVOUS, info.targetLP, currentLVT)
 5:         LP_state ← WAIT_FOR_SYNCH
 6:         CSD ← CSD ∪ {info.targetLP}
 7:         DESCHEDULE( )
 8:     else if type = Minor then                               ▷ H2
 9:         disasm ← DISASSEMBLE(info.rip)
10:         write_mode ← disasm.write
11:         page_addr ← BASEADDR(info.target)
12:         pages ← PGCOUNT(info.target, disasm.span)
13:         if write_mode then
14:             ADDTOWRITELIST(page_addr, pages)
15:         else
16:             ADDTOREADLIST(page_addr, pages)
17:         SEND(PAGE_LEASE, info.targetLP, currentLVT)
18:         LP_state ← WAIT_FOR_PAGE
19:         DESCHEDULE( )
20:     else if type = AccessChange then                        ▷ H3
21:         page_addr ← BASEADDR(info.target)
22:         ADDTOWRITELIST(page_addr, 1)
```

is added to the CSD of the running LP. Finally, the running LP is descheduled thanks to the ULT facilities described before. In this way, the running LP will never be activated until the rendezvous ack is received, as previously described.

The ECS Minor Fault case (**H2**), which is associated only with the access to the simulation state of a remote LP, has to first identify what kind of operation is being executed on the shared state, namely a read or a write operation. This information is only kept in the low-level assembly instruction which has triggered the ECS synchronization. Therefore, we rely on in-place dynamic disassembly of such an instruction, which can be immediately found in the model's address space by looking at the address which caused the memory fault. Again, this information is delivered to the userspace handler by the LKM, together with a snapshot of the relevant CPU registers as observed by the faulting instruction.

The disassembler[4] provides several relevant pieces of information regarding the faulting instruction. Among these, we can determine whether the instruction is accessing in read or write mode, and the size of the memory access. The latter information is used in conjunction with the target memory address where the instruction has faulted, as notified by the LKM, to determine the base address of the first (remote) page which has to be transferred to the local node, and the number of pages. This information is sent to the destination LP as an additional control message, named PAGE_LEASE, before putting the LP in the blocked *Wait for Page* state. Once this control message is received at the target LP. Since the target LP is already in a blocked state, we are actually acquiring a *lease* on the pages, having the LP which originated the ECS synchronization keep a temporary master copy of the content of that portion of the state. These pages can be safely installed into the local address space,

[4]In our implementation, we have used the x86 disassembler provided by hijacker, which is available at https://github.com/HPDCS/hijacker.

Figure 9: Page Touch Lists

thanks to the non-overlapping organization of the memory map manager depicted in Figure 5.

To keep track of what pages have been leased by a LP, we maintain two *page-touch lists*. One list is associated with pages accessed in read mode, which we refer to as *read list*, while the other (the *write list*) is associated with pages accessed in write mode. The two lists keep as well the id of the LP the original page belongs to, as depicted in Figure 9. This is due to the fact that during the execution of an event, a LP is allowed to synchronize with any number of LPs, thus we must keep track of the ownership of each page. To reduce the complexity of this management, each node in the list is associated with a PTE entry, where a bitmap of 512 bits (one for each page) is used to determine whether the corresponding page has been locally acquired or not.

When accessing a page in read mode, the LP has already acquired a lease on it and a copy of the page content is already installed in the local address space. Since the underlying operating system has granted access in read mode only, once the event handler accesses the same page in write mode, a new fault is detected. Nevertheless, this latter fault can be resolved locally. When activating the userspace handler for an ECS Access Change Fault (**H3**), the LKM has already upgraded the access privilege to write mode. The userspace has only to move the page from the read list to the write list, in the corresponding PTE node.

The two lists are used as well upon the finalization of an event involved in an ECS synchronization. Once the event's execution is completed, the runtime environment has to send a rendezvous unblock control message, in order to notify the synchronized LPs that they can resume their normal execution. The semantic of this event is augmented by adding to it a payload which is composed of all the pages for which a lease in write mode has been acquired during the execution of the event. This allows the destination kernel instances to update the content of the simulation state of the involved LPs according to a write-back scheme, just before giving back control to them. In this way, the states are reconciled, and every LP in the system can observe a simulation state snapshot which is consistent with the logic of the event handler just executed at the ECS originating LP.

4.6 Memory Reclaim

Due to our organization, the amount of pages materialized on a local node for remote LPs is always increasing. We have devised a simple memory reclaim policy which entails to periodically reset the memory map organization described in Section 4.2.

This operation is supported by having one single worker thread at each node invoke a sequence of munmap/mmap for every memory stock associated to remote LPs. In this way, we instruct the underlying operating system to release all memory pages which have been materialized during the execution of remote cross-state synchronizations. It is fundamental to execute this operation in isolation, i.e. when no other thread has any operation related to a remote ECS still pending. In our implementation, we have resorted to a periodic check, with a period of around 30 seconds, where all threads notify through shared variables whether they have pending remote synchronization, and an additional shared variable is used to delay the initiation of a remote ECS if a memory reclaim phase is in progress.

5 EXPERIMENTAL ASSESSMENT

5.1 Testbed Platform

Our ECS distributed middleware has been integrated in the ROOT-SIM open source PDES platform [23], which is used as the testbed PDES system in our experimental study. This platform offers to the users the possibility to run on a fully shared memory machine, or on a cluster of distributed memory machines. In the latter case communication between remote nodes exploits MPI. This same layer has been exploited in the ECS distributed middleware in order to implement both the message exchange protocol that makes threads running on different nodes coordinate with each other, and the actual transfer of virtual pages associated with the LPs' state from one node to another.

We have run experiments on a cluster of virtualized nodes, composed of Virtual Machines equipped with AMD Opteron 2.6 GHz vCPUs, that have been deployed on a private Cloud infrastructure. The VMs are hosted by the VMware Workstation hypervisor (version 10.0.4 build-2249910) hosted on top of a HP ProLiant server equipped with 100 GB of RAM and 8 AMD Opteron 6376 CPUs running at 2.6 GHz. Each one has four cores (for a total of 32 physical cores). We have installed Debian 6.0.7 with Linux kernel 3.2. Each VM has 8 GB of memory, and we run experiments with single-vCPU and dual-vCPU configurations of the VMs, thus overall mimicking different configurations of a cluster of mid-range computing nodes. All the available vCPUs are used by ROOT-Sim to carry out the simulation.

5.2 Benchmark Applications

To assess the viability of our proposal we provide data related to two different simulation models, each of which is presented in this section.

5.2.1 Multi-robot Exploration. As first benchmark application, we use the same multi-robot exploration and mapping simulation model that has been used for the experiments whose outcomes have been presented in Figure 1. This model has been developed according to the results in [11], and is based on a group of robots set out into an unknown space, with the goal of exploring it. The map of the explored space is constructed by relying on the notion of *exploration frontier*. By keeping a representation of the explored world, the robot is able to detect which is the closest unexplored area it can reach, computes the fastest way to reach it and continues the exploration. The overall space to be explored is bi-dimensional, and is partitioned into adjacent hexagonal regions, where obstacles are setup in order to limit the freedom of robot move. Each region is such that the evolution of a specific phenomenon, such as wind or a fire event, is modeled via proper simulation events occurring at the LP modeling the region. This kind of model is useful for mimicking a scenario where an open space is modified by, e.g., an accident and the robots are used to explore it for, e.g., rescue activities.

The robots explore independently of each other until one coincidentally detects another robot in its proximity. Whenever two robots enter a proximity region they verify the goodness of their position hypothesis by creating a rendez-vous point, and trying to meet again there. If the hypothesis is verified, they exchange the data acquired during the exploration, thus reducing the exploration time and allowing for a more accurate decision of the actions to be taken. Additionally, if the robots actually meet in the rendez-vous point, it means that the estimation of their respective position is correct. Therefore, they can form a *cluster* and start exploring the environment in a collaborative way.

In an implementation of this model based on the traditional PDES paradigm—relying on disjointness of the accesses to the LPs' states by the event-handler—the discovery of the presence of a nearby robot requires that LPs modeling the robots communicate to each other their current position, or they have to notify their individual positions to specific LPs (i.e., the regions). In either case, explicit cross-LP exchange of simulation events is requested. The same is true for the exchange of knowledge on the exploration process across robots.

On the other hand, the ECS programming model allows for a completely transparent synchronization of the LPs involved in any mutual state update, which therefore simplifies the development process of the simulation model. In fact, as already hinted in Section 1, ECS-based coding of this model saves up to 25% of C-based code lines in event handlers. More in detail, each LP modeling a region instantiates in its private simulation state—by relying on a standard call to malloc()—a *presence bitmap*. Each bit is associated with a specific robot, and its value is associated with the robot being in the region or not. By relying on a fast bitmap scan, each robot is able to discover which robots are present in the region. This is done by relying on a code block where the modeler is not required to rely on any platform-specific API—rather he simply exploits pointer-based access to whatever region's state when processing an event at a robot, namely the region entrance event. The event-handler can access the region bitmap to detect other robots and to indicate it is currently standing into that region. Also, the robot can acquire information about the environment by directly reading this information from the region state, still thanks to ECS support. If one robot is found to already be in the cell, then the newly entering robot simply "merges" its view of the environment. This can be easily done by still relying on direct access to the other robot's state.

In our simulations the model was configured to have 484 LPs modeling individual regions, and their evolution along simulation time, and 4 LPs modeling the robots exploring the overall space.

5.2.2 Data-Grid. As second benchmark application, we rely on a data-grid simulation. It is based on distributed/replicated cache servers, each keeping a subset of the whole set of keys in the entire data-set. Particularly, we consider a model where atomicity of the distributed updates is ensured by running the 2-Phase-Commit (2PC) protocol across the nodes keeping keys that belong to the write set of the transactional operations. In this model, the simulated

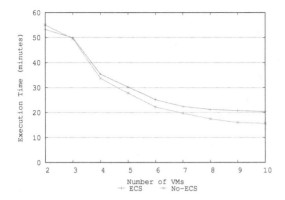

Figure 10: Execution Time - Multi-robot Model

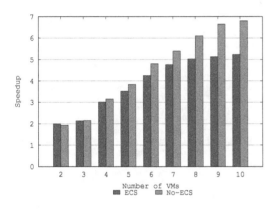

Figure 11: Speedup with respect to Sequential Simulation - Multi-robot Model

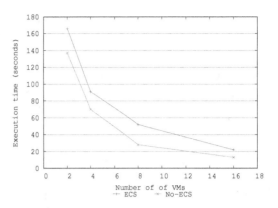

Figure 12: Execution Time Results for the Data-Grid Model with Single-vCPU VMs

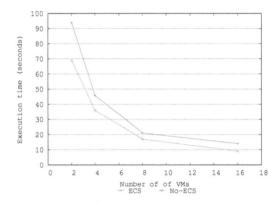

Figure 13: Execution Time Results for the Data-Grid Model with Dual-vCPU VMs

transaction coordinator needs to schedule the arrival of a *prepare request* event to the involved sites—those keeping the replicas of the data it locally handles—which needs to carry information about the write set. These sets may entail hundreds of data-item keys—numerical IDs in our implementation—and are populated at the coordinator while simulating the execution of the transactional task. They are therefore instantiated by the transaction-coordinator LP within its local state. For this model we consider two different implementations, one not relying on ECS, which transmits the write set as the payload of the *prepare request*—for this configuration the programmer is in charge of explicitly coding the pack/unpack of the write set—and another one based on ECS, where the write sets are directly accessed via pointers by the involved simulated nodes (hence the *prepare request* event only needs to carry the pointer indicating where to find the information related to the simulated 2PC phase).

We simulated a data-grid system with 256 nodes (with degree of replication 2 of each ⟨*key, value*⟩ pair in the data-grid), with closed-system configuration in terms of number of clients (and hence number of transactions) running within the system. Particularly, we set the number of active concurrent clients continuously issuing transactions to 256—embedded into the simulation logic of each cache server. This configuration resembles scenarios where the 256

clients operate as front end servers (co-located with the simulated data-platform nodes) with respect to end-client applications. Also, we set the amount of keys touched in write mode by transactional tasks to the order of 1000, while each cache server keeps 100000 items.

5.3 Results

In Figure 10 we report the variation of the execution time (average over 10 runs) for the multi-robot model while varying the number of VMs up to 10—in the single-vCPU configuration. The data show that, with this model, the distributed ECS version has a good scalability up to 7/8 VMs, which tends to diminish for larger VM counts. In fact, up to 8 VMs the execution time with ECS is no more than 15% worse than the one without ECS, and the speedup over the sequential execution, shown in Figure 11, is essentially linear up to 7 VMs. On the other hand, with larger VM counts the non-ECS version scales slightly better, as expected. However, this improved scalability comes at the cost of more code lines, motivated by the need for coding the model in pure data separation across the LPs.

In Figure 12 we show the execution time results for the data-grid model, with variation of the number of VMs up to 16—in single-vCPU configuration. The data are essentially aligned with those observed with the multi-robot model with the only difference that ECS allows scaling down the execution time also with larger VM counts. In fact, although showing overhead with respect to the non-ECS version, its reduction in the execution time does not flatten. One motivation stands in the fact that the data-grid model has less frequent LP interactions, with respect to the robot-explore model, which occur only upon the simulated 2PC phase involving multiple data accesses by a transactional task—the individual accesses are in fact simulated locally by each individual LP. Further, while in the multi-robot model cross-LP accesses under ECS have a read/write profile—involving page write-back—in the data-grid model they are mostly read accesses that only inspect the write-set involved in the 2PC kept by the LP simulating the transaction coordinator.

In Figure 13 we show the variation of the execution time for the data-grid model when using VMs equipped with dual-VCPS. In this case each simulation kernel instance has two threads and the interaction across LPs based on cross-LP state accesses are sometimes served by an individual machine within the same address space—rather than from a remote one via page transfers. In such a deployment the distance between the ECS and the non-ECS version is reduced, meaning that with our distributed ECS middleware, infrastructure-level investments related to clusters of more powerful VMs pay-off in terms of improved reduction of the execution time. Overall, competitive tradeoff between infrastructure costs and performance can be achieved while still getting the benefits from the more expressive programming model offered by ECS, as compared to the traditional one relying on disjoint LP state accesses. On the other hand, as discussed in the introduction section, moving to significantly more powerful shared-memory machines—possibly hosted in the Cloud—can even lead ECS to provide, together with a more expressive programming support, improvements in the actual performance of the PDES system.

6　CONCLUSIONS

We have presented a middleware-level architecture that allows the expressive ECS programming model for PDES—originally conceived only for shared-memory machines—to be deployed on distributed-memory clusters. The core target of this work is to enable models coded according to ECS to be efficiently ran on top of (low-cost) Cloud resources. Experimental results with two different real-world simulation models, deployed on a cluster of up to 16 VMs hosted on a private Cloud, show the viability of our proposal, and its effectiveness in fruitfully exploiting increasingly powerful virtual resources. Overall, our proposal allows to improve the actual tradeoffs between the achievable runtime performance, the infrastructure-level investments, and the simplification of code development—the latter thanks to an expressive PDES programming support.

REFERENCES

[1] Peter D. Barnes, Christopher D. Carothers, David R. Jefferson, and Justin M. LaPre. 2013. Warp speed: executing time warp on 1,966,080 cores. In *Proceedings of the 2013 ACM SIGSIM conference on Principles of advanced discrete simulation - SIGSIM-PADS '13*. 327. https://doi.org/10.1145/2486092.2486134

[2] Azzedine Boukerche and Sajal K Das. 1997. Dynamic load balancing strategies for conservative parallel simulations. In *Proceedings of the 11th Workshop on Parallel and Distributed Simulation (PADS)*. 20–28.

[3] David Bruce. 1995. The treatment of state in optimistic systems. *SIGSIM Simul. Dig.* 25, 1 (July 1995), 40–49. https://doi.org/10.1145/214283.214297

[4] Christopher D. Carothers and Richard M Fujimoto. 2000. Efficient execution of Time Warp programs on heterogeneous, NOW platforms. *IEEE Transactions on Parallel and Distributed Systems* 11, 3 (2000), 299–317.

[5] Christopher D. Carothers, Kalyan S Perumalla, and Richard M. Fujimoto. 1999. Efficient optimistic parallel simulations using reverse computation. *ACM Transactions on Modeling and Computer Simulation* 9, 3 (1999), 224–253.

[6] K. Mani Chandy and Rivi Sherman. 1989. Space-time and simulation. *Proceedings of the SCS Multiconference on Distributed Simulation* (1989), 53–57.

[7] Li-li Chen, Ya-shuai Lu, Yi-Ping Yao, Shao-liang Peng, and Ling-da Wu. 2011. A Well-balanced Time Warp system on multi-core environments. In *Proceedings of the 2011 IEEE Workshop on Principles of Advanced and Distributed Simulation (PADS)*. IEEE Computer Society, 1–9. https://doi.org/10.1109/PADS.2011.5936752

[8] Myongsu Choe and Carl Tropper. 2001. Flow control and dynamic load balancing in Time Warp. *Transactions Soc. Comput. Simul. Int.* 18, 1 (2001), 9–23.

[9] Davide Cingolani, Alessandro Pellegrini, and Francesco Quaglia. 2017. Transparently mixing undo logs and software reversibility for state recovery in optimistic PDES. *ACM Trans. Model. Comput. Simul.* 27, 2 (2017), 11:1–11:26.

[10] Alessandro Fabbri and Lorenzo Donatiello. 1997. SQTW: a mechanism for state-dependent parallel simulation. Description and experimental study. In *Proceedings of the Workshop on Parallel and Distributed Simulation*. 82–89. https://doi.org/10.1109/PADS.1997.594590

[11] Dieter Fox, Jonathan Ko, Kurt Konolige, Benson Limketkai, Dirk Schulz, and Benjamin Stewart. 2006. Distributed Multirobot Exploration and Mapping. *Proc. IEEE* 94, 7 (2006), 1325–1339. https://doi.org/10.1109/JPROC.2006.876927

[12] Richard M. Fujimoto. 1990. Parallel discrete event simulation. *Commun. ACM* 33, 10 (1990), 30–53.

[13] Kaushik Ghosh and Richard M. Fujimoto. 1991. Parallel Discrete Event Simulation Using Space-Time Memory.. In *Proceedings of the International Conference on Parallel Processing*. CRC Press, 201–208.

[14] David W. Glazer and Carl Tropper. 1993. On process migration and load balancing in Time Warp. *IEEE Transactions on Parallel and Distributed Systems* 4, 3 (1993), 318–327. https://doi.org/10.1109/71.210814

[15] Julius Higiro, Meseret Gebre, and Dhananjai M. Rao. 2017. Multi-tier priority queues and 2-tier ladder queue for managing pending events in sequential and optimistic parallel simulations. In *Proceedings of the 2017 ACM SIGSIM Conference on Principles of Advanced Discrete Simulation, SIGSIM-PADS 2017, Singapore, May 24-26, 2017*. 3–14.

[16] Horst Mehl and Stefan Hammes. 1995. How to integrate shared variables in distributed simulation. *SIGSIM Simulation Digest* 25, 2 (1995), 14–41. https://doi.org/10.1145/233498.233499

[17] Alessandro Pellegrini, Sebastiano Peluso, Francesco Quaglia, and Roberto Vitali. 2016. Transparent speculative parallelization of discrete event simulation applications using global variables. *International Journal of Parallel Programming* (apr 2016). https://doi.org/10.1007/s10766-016-0429-2

[18] Alessandro Pellegrini and Francesco Quaglia. 2014. Transparent multi-core speculative parallelization of DES models with event and cross-state dependencies. In *Proceedings of the 2014 ACM/SIGSIM Conference on Principles of Advanced Discrete Simulation (PADS)*. ACM Press, 105–116. https://doi.org/10.1145/2601381.2601398

[19] Alessandro Pellegrini and Francesco Quaglia. 2017. A fine-grain time-sharing Time Warp system. *ACM Transactions on Modeling and Computer Simulation* 27, 2 (May 2017). https://doi.org/10.1145/3013528

[20] Alessandro Pellegrini, Roberto Vitali, Francesco Quaglia, Alessandro Pellegrini, and Francesco Quaglia. 2015. Autonomic state management for optimistic simulation platforms. *IEEE Transactions on Parallel and Distributed Systems* 26, 6 (2015), 1560–1569.

[21] Sebastiano Peluso, Diego Didona, and Francesco Quaglia. 2011. Application transparent migration of simulation objects with generic memory layout. In *Proceedings of the 25th Workshop on Principles of Advanced and Distributed Simulation*. IEEE Computer Society, 169–177. https://doi.org/10.1109/PADS.2011.5936755

[22] Tim Stitt. 2010. An introduction to the partitioned global address space (PGAS) programming model. (2010).

[23] The High Performance and Dependable Computing Systems Research Group (HPDCS). 2012. ROOT-Sim: The ROme OpTimistic Simulator. https://github.com/HPDCS/ROOT-Sim. (2012). https://github.com/HPDCS/ROOT-Sim

[24] Roberto Vitali, Alessandro Pellegrini, and Francesco Quaglia. 2012. Towards symmetric multi-threaded optimistic simulation kernels. In *Proceedings of the 26th Workshop on Principles of Advanced and Distributed Simulation (PADS)*. IEEE Computer Society, 211–220. https://doi.org/10.1109/PADS.2012.46

[25] Srikanth B. Yoginath and Kalyan S. Perumalla. 2013. Optimized hypervisor scheduler for parallel discrete event simulations on virtual machine platforms. In *6th International ICST Conference on Simulation Tools and Techniques, SimuTools '13, Cannes, France, March 6-8, 2013*. 1–9.

[26] Srikanth B. Yoginath and Kalyan S. Perumalla. 2015. Efficient parallel discrete event simulation on cloud/virtual machine platforms. *ACM Trans. Model. Comput. Simul.* 26, 1 (2015), 5:1–5:26.

Adaptive Methods for Irregular Parallel Discrete Event Simulation Workloads

Eric Mikida
University of Illinois at Urbana-Champaign
mikida2@illinois.edu

Laxmikant Kale
University of Illinois at Urbana-Champaign
kale@illinois.edu

ABSTRACT

Parallel Discrete Event Simulations (PDES) running at large scales involve the coordination of billions of veryfi ne grain events distributed across a large number of processes. At such large scales optimistic synchronization protocols, such as TimeWarp, allow for a high degree of parallelism between processes, but with the additional complexity of managing event rollback and cancellation. This can become especially problematic in models that exhibit imbalance resulting in low event efficiency, which increases the total amount of work required to run a simulation to completion. Managing this complexity becomes key to achieving a high degree of performance across a wide range of models. In this paper, we address this issue by analyzing the relationship between synchronization cost and event efficiency. Wefi rst look at how these two characteristics are coupled via the computation of Global Virtual Time (GVT). We then introduce dynamic load balancing, and show how, when combined with low overhead GVT computation, we can achieve higher efficiency with less synchronization cost. In doing so, we achieve up to 2× better performance on a variety of benchmarks and models of practical importance.

ACM Reference format:
Eric Mikida and Laxmikant Kale. 2018. Adaptive Methods for Irregular Parallel Discrete Event Simulation Workloads. In *Proceedings of SIGSIM Principles of Advanced Discrete Simulation, Rome, Italy, May 23–25, 2018 (SIGSIM-PADS'18)*, 12 pages.
https://doi.org/10.1145/3200921.3200936

1 INTRODUCTION

Discrete Event Simulation (DES) is a powerful tool for studying interactions in complex systems. These simulations differ from traditional time-stepped simulations in that the events being simulated occur at discrete points in time, which may not be uniformly distributed throughout the time-window being simulated. This makes DES ideal for modeling systems such as trafficfl ow, supercomputer networks, and integrated circuits [10, 16, 30]. Each of these modeling systems create events which a DES simulator executes in timestamp order. As these systems being simulated grow in size and complexity, the capability of sequential DES becomes insufficient, and the need for a more powerful simulation engine presents itself.

Parallel Discrete Event Simulations (PDES) can potentially increase the capability of sequential simulations, both by decreasing time to solution and by enabling larger and more detailed models to be simulated. However, this shift to a distributed execution environment raises the question of how to maintain timestamp order across multiple independent processes. Various synchronization protocols for PDES have been proposed and well studied to address this concern. In this paper, we focus on the Time Warp protocol originally proposed by Jefferson et al. [17]. In the Time Warp protocol, events are executed speculatively, and when a causality error between events is detected, previously executed events are rolled back until a point in time is reached where it is safe to resume forward execution.

The Time Warp protocol has been shown to achieve high performance and scalability at large scales in numerous instances [4, 21], however it is often the case that the models used in these studies naturally result in a uniform and balanced execution. In realistic models where the execution has a more irregular distribution, there is the possibility of cascading rollbacks as described in [12]. In this paper we aim to improve the performance and robustness of the Time Warp protocol by developing techniques that adaptively deal with irregularity and imbalance present in more realistic models operating at large scales. In order to do so we focus on two related characteristics that factor into a simulations performance: efficiency and synchronization cost, where efficiency is the ratio of committed events to total number of events executed.

The work and results presented in this paper utilize the CHARM++ Adaptive Discrete Event Simulator (Charades). Charades was originally implemented as a CHARM++ version of the Rensselaer Optimistic Simulation System (ROSS) [7]. ROSS has repeatedly demonstrated high performance at large scales, especially for network topology models [4, 23, 29]. In [21], Mikida et al. demonstrates the effectiveness of building ROSS on top of the CHARM++ adaptive runtime system, where performance of the models tested was improved by 1.4 − 5× due to a more effective management offi ne-grained communication. Charades is based on this CHARM++ version of ROSS, but with major changes to the underlying infrastructure to exploit more of the features of CHARM++.

In Section 4, we study different configurations of the GVT computation and their effects on synchronization cost and event efficiency. We show a coupling between event efficiency and synchronization cost, which creates a tradeoff between the two quantities. In Section 5 we study load balancing as an additional way to control event efficiency, and show evidence that load balancing can be used to improve efficiency in GVT algorithms which sacrifice event efficiency for lower synchronization costs.

Permission to make digital or hard copies of all or part of this work for personal or classroom use is granted without fee provided that copies are not made or distributed for profit or commercial advantage and that copies bear this notice and the full citation on thefi rst page. Copyrights for components of this work owned by others than ACM must be honored. Abstracting with credit is permitted. To copy otherwise, or republish, to post on servers or to redistribute to lists, requires prior specific permission and/or a fee. Request permissions from permissions@acm.org.
SIGSIM-PADS'18, May 23–25, 2018, Rome, Italy
© 2018 Association for Computing Machinery.
ACM ISBN 978-1-4503-5092-1/18/05...$15.00
https://doi.org/10.1145/3200921.3200936

The main contributions we make in this paper are:

- Analysis of the tradeoff between synchronization cost and event efficiency present in blocking GVT algorithms
- Development of a scalable version of a non-blocking GVT algorithm for distributed systems
- Improvements to an existing distributed load balancing strategy for PDES use cases
- Analysis of load balancing as an additional efficiency control in concert with the non-blocking GVT algorithm

2 BACKGROUND AND RELATED WORK

In this section, we describe CHARM++ and Charades, the software infrastructure used throughout the rest of this paper, as well as ROSS which the work was originally based upon. We also discuss related work in the area of GVT algorithms and load balancing in PDES.

2.1 CHARM++

CHARM++ is a parallel programming framework built upon the notion of parallel asynchronous objects, called chares [1, 3]. Instead of decomposing applications in terms of cores or processes, CHARM++ applications are decomposed into collections of chares. The CHARM++ runtime system manages the placement of these chares and coordinates the communication between them.

Forward progress of an application is based on message-driven execution. Chares communicate via asynchronous one-sided messages, and only chares with incoming messages are scheduled for execution. This allows the runtime to adaptively schedule chares for execution based on the availability of work, and also leads to an adaptive overlap of communication and computation. This overlap relies on the fact that CHARM++ applications are generally over-decomposed: there are many more chares in the application than there are cores.

Over-decomposition also gives the runtime system flexibility in location management of chares, and enables another important feature of CHARM++: migration. Since the location and scheduling of chares is managed entirely by the runtime system, it has the freedom to migrate chares between different hardware resources as it sees fit. This enables features such as automated checkpoint/restart, fault-tolerance, and dynamic load balancing.

CHARM++ has a robust dynamic load balancing framework, enabled by migratable chares, which allows applications to dynamically balance load across processes during execution. The load balancing framework monitors execution of chares as the application runs, and migrates chares based on the measurements it takes and the chosen load balancing strategy. There are many built-in load balancing strategies distributed with CHARM++, as described in Section 5. These strategies vary widely in factors such as overhead incurred, whether or not communication is taken into account, and how the load information is aggregated across processes.

2.2 ROSS

ROSS is a massively parallel PDES implementation developed at RPI [6]. It utilizes the Time Warp protocol to synchronize optimistic simulations, where the specific mechanism for recovering from causality violations is based on reverse execution. Each LP has a

forward event handler and a reverse event handler. When a causality violation occurs, the affected LPs execute reverse event handlers for events in the reverse order until they reach a safe point in virtual time to resume forward execution. ROSS is implemented on top of MPI, and demonstrates high performance and scalability on a number of models. Barnes et al. obtained 97× speedup on 120 racks (1.6 million cores) of Sequoia, a Blue Gene/Q system at Lawrence Livermore National Laboratory, when compared to a base run on 2 racks [4], and they have a number of publications showing highly scalable network models [23, 29].

In [21], ROSS is reimplemented on top of CHARM++ in order to take advantage of the adaptive and asynchronous nature of the CHARM++ runtime system. The primary difference between the MPI and CHARM++ implementations is the encapsulation of LPs as chares in the CHARM++ implementation, which enables the runtime system to adaptively schedule and migrate LPs during simulation execution. Suitability of the CHARM++ programming model for PDES applications is evidenced by a decrease in the size of the code base by 50%, and by the increased performance and scalability for the PHOLD benchmark and the Dragonfly model simulating uniform traffic patterns. PHOLD event rates were increased by up to 40%, while the event rate for the Dragonfly model were reported to be up to 5× higher.

2.3 Charades

Charades is the simulation engine used for the experiments in this paper, and is an evolution of the CHARM++ version of ROSS. The underlying infrastructure has been redesigned so that the GVT computation and the Scheduler are separated into two distinct and independent sets of chares. This allows for a modular class hierarchy for the GVT manager chares, which aids in the development of different GVT algorithms that can be selected from and instantiated at runtime. Furthermore, the separation of the Scheduler and GVT manager into independent sets of chares allows the runtime to more effectively overlap work between GVT computation and event execution. This is particularly important for the work in Section 4, where the work of the GVT computation is overlapped with event execution to decrease synchronization costs.

In addition to the redesigned infrastructure, Charades LPs are also migratable by virtue of being written as chares with routines for serialization and DE-serialization. This allows them to work within the CHARM++ load balancing infrastructure. Furthermore, the LPs monitor various metrics that can be fed into the load balancing framework as a substitute for CPU time when determining the load of an LP.

2.4 GVT Computation

A significant amount of work has been devoted to the study of the GVT computation in optimistic simulations. The frequency at which it needs to occur, and the fact that it requires global information can cause it to become a major bottleneck if not synchronized properly. Non-blocking GVT algorithms have been shown to be successful on shared-memory systems by both Gomes et al. [15] and Fujimoto et al. [13]. On distributed systems, non-blocking algorithms which rely on atomic operations and machine clocks were studied by Chen et al. [9] and as part of the ROSS simulation system in [5].

Srinivasan's implementation in [27] relies on hardware support, specifically optimized for communicating global synchronization information. The SPEEDES simulation system also implemented an algorithm for computing the GVT without blocking event execution, however it did so by preventing the communication of new events until after the GVT computation [28].

For this work we have implemented a GVT algorithm targeted at high performance distributed computing environments based on the distributed snapshot algorithms proposed by Mattern and Perumalla [18, 25]. The GVT algorithm work is dynamically overlapped with other simulation tasks by the runtime system, including scheduling, event reception and execution, fossil collection, and rollbacks. We specifically look at the GVTs effects on event efficiency and synchronization cost. A more detailed description is given in Section 5 as well as results on 2048 processes.

2.5 Load Balancing

In [8], load balancing was shown to be effective for PDES applications running in a network of multi-user workstations. Similarly, [14] demonstrates dynamic load balancing on shared-memory processors by utilizing active process migration. Meraji et al. [20] shows benefits of load balancing for gate-level circuit simulations, and Deelman et al. utilizes load balancing for explicitly spatial models [11]. Here, we propose a more generalized load balancing framework, and one that is focused on HPC environments. We specifically look at load balancing as a tool to improve efficiency in conjunction with the GVT methods described in Section 4.

3 MODELS

To develop a better understanding of the impact of the techniques explored in this paper, we focus on variations of three diverse models with wide applicability: PHOLD, Dragonfly [22], and Traffic [2].

3.1 PHOLD

PHOLD is arguably the most commonly used micro-benchmark in the PDES community [4, 12, 31]. A basic PHOLD configuration is specified by 6 parameters: number of LPs (N), number of starting events (E), end time (T), lookahead (L), mean delay (M), and percentage of remote events (P). At the beginning of the simulation, N LPs are created, each with with an initial set of E events to be executed. During the execution of an event, a PHOLD LP creates and sends a new event to be executed in the future, and thus the simulation progresses. The execution of events is performed until the simulation reaches virtual time T.

For sending a new event, an event executed at time t creates an event that should be executed at time $t + d$, where d is the delay. Delay is calculated as the sum of the lookahead, L, and a number chosen randomly from an exponential distribution with mean M. With probability P, the destination of the new event is chosen randomly from a uniform distribution; otherwise, a self-send is done.

By default, PHOLD leads to a highly uniform simulation with each LP executing roughly the same number of events distributed evenly throughout virtual time. Hence, it is not a good representative of irregular and unbalanced models. We extend the base PHOLD with a number of parameters which control event and

work distribution in order to make it a suitable representative of more complex simulation workloads. First, each LP is parameterized by the amount of time it takes to execute an event, which is controlled via a loop inside of forward execution that checks wall time until the set amount has elapsed. Secondly, the percentage of remote events, P, is now also set at the LP level rather than at the global level for the whole simulation, which means certain LPs can be set to do self-sends more frequently than others. By adjusting the distributions of these two parameters, an imbalance can be created both in the amount of work done by each LP as well as the number of events executed by each LP.

For the experiments in this paper we use four specific configurations for PHOLD. The baseline configuration (PHOLD Base) is a balanced configuration that has 64 LPs per process with $E = 16$, $L = 0.1$, $M = 0.9$ (for an expected delay of 1.0 per event), and $T = 1,024$. For the runs in this paper, this equates to $N = 131,072$ total LPs and $2,097,152$ initial events. For the base case, all LPs use $P = 50\%$ and each event is set to take approximately 1 nanosecond to process. The following unbalanced configurations modify the last two parameters for subsets of LPs to create different types of imbalance.

The work imbalance configuration (PHOLD Work) designates 10% of LPs as heavy LPs that take 10 nanoseconds to process each event instead of the baseline of 1 nanosecond. This results in a configuration with approximately twice the total work as PHOLD Base. The heavy LPs occur in a contiguous block starting at an arbitrarily chosen LP ID 2, 165. This offset was chosen so that the block of heavy LPs does not align evenly with the 64 LPs per process, creating more variation in processor loads that contain heavy LPs.

The event imbalance configuration (PHOLD Event) designates 10% of LPs as greedy LPs that have a remote percentage of 25% instead of 50%, meaning they are twice as likely to do a self-send than the remaining LPs. These greedy LPs are again set in a contiguous block starting at 2, 165.

The final configuration (PHOLD Combo) is a combination of the previous two configurations. 10% of the LPs starting at LP ID 2, 165 are both heavy and greedy, i.e. they perform ten times the work to process each event in comparison to other LPs, and are also twice as likely to do a self-send when compared to normal LPs.

3.2 Dragonfly

The Dragonfly model performs a packet-level simulation of the dragonfly network topology used for building supercomputer interconnects. We use a model similar to the one described in [21] and [22]. The Dragonfly model consists of three different types of LPs: routers, terminals, and MPI processes. The MPI process LPs send messages to one another based on the communication pattern being simulated. These messages are sent as packets through the network by the terminal and router LPs.

In this paper we experiment with four different communication patterns: Uniform Random (DFly UR) where each message sent goes to a randomly selected MPI process, Worst Case (DFly WC) where all traffic is directed to the neighboring group in the dragonfly topology, Transpose (DFly Trans) where message is sent to diagonally opposite MPI process, and Nearest Neighbor (DFly NN) where each message is sent to an MPI process on the same router.

The particular network configuration used in this paper has 24 routers per group and 12 terminals per model, which results in 6,936 routers connected to 83,232 terminals and MPI processes. Note that all these traffic patterns simulate balanced workloads with roughly the same number of MPI messages received by each simulated MPI process. Furthermore, only the network traffic is simulated, and compute time of each MPI process is ignored.

3.3 Traffic

The traffic model used in this paper is an extension of a traffic model available in the production version of ROSS [2], with added configuration parameters to create realistic scenarios. This model simulates a grid of intersections, where each intersection is represented as an LP. Each intersection is a four-way intersection with multiple lanes. Cars traveling through this grid of intersections are transported from one grid point to another through events. Different events in this simulation represent cars arriving at an intersection, departing from an intersection, or changing lanes.

Our baseline traffic configuration (Traffic Base) simulates 1,048,576 cars in a 256 × 256 grid of intersections for a total of 65,536 total LPs. Each car chooses a source and a destination uniformly at random from the set of intersections and travels from source to destination. From this base configuration we derive three unbalanced configurations by modifying the distribution of sources and destinations of the cars. This results in a different initial distribution of events per LP, as well as a distribution which changes over time as cars move throughout the grid.

The first configuration (Traffic Dest) represents what traffic may look like before a large sporting event, where a higher proportion of cars are traveling to a similar destination. In this particular configuration, 25% of the cars choose destinations in a 16 × 16 block area at the bottom right corner of the grid, and the rest of the cars choose their destination randomly.

The second configuration (Traffic Src) represents what traffic may look like after the sporting event, where a higher proportion of cars have a similar source. In this case, 10% of the cars start from a 16 × 16 block area at the top left corner of the grid and the rest of the cars are evenly distributed.

The final configuration (Traffic Route) is a combination of the previous two scenarios, where 10% of cars originate from the top left 16×16 area, and 25% of cars choose the bottom right 16×16 grid as their destination. This leads to similar patterns as the previous two distributions, but with the added effect of more cars following similar routes between their sources and destinations.

4 GLOBAL VIRTUAL TIME COMPUTATION

The calculation of the Global Virtual Time (GVT) is a critical part of an optimistic PDES simulation. The GVT is the latest virtual time that has been reached by every LP in the simulation, and therefore events prior to the GVT can be committed and their memory reclaimed via *fossil collection*. In order to prevent the simulator from running out of memory, the GVT must be computed frequently in order for fossil collection to keep up with the high rate of event creation. This, combined with the fact that the GVT computation requires global information, means that the GVT computation can quickly become a very costly bottleneck if not handled properly.

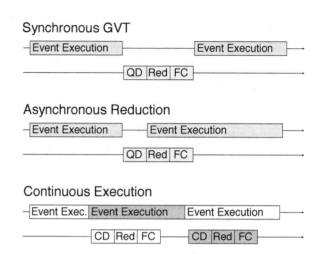

Figure 1: A depiction of three different algorithms for the GVT computation.

Furthermore, the synchronization required for the GVT computation can have additional side effects on event execution within the simulation.

In this section, we study two key components of a GVT calculation: trigger and algorithm. The trigger determines when and how often GVT is computed. The algorithm describes the actual process of computing the GVT, including how the computation is synchronized with the execution of LPs. The original implementation of Charades uses a count-based trigger and a fully synchronous GVT algorithm. This scheme is similar to the one implemented within ROSS and has achieved high performance and scalability as stated in Section 2. We will take this configuration as a baseline for comparing a virtual time-based trigger, and two GVT algorithms with varying degrees of asynchrony.

4.1 GVT Trigger

The trigger determines when to compute the GVT, and by extension, the state of the simulation when the GVT computation begins. The existing trigger is one based on event count. Specifically, each processor stops executing events and signals it is ready to take part in the GVT computation after executing N events, where N is a runtime parameter. This means that, in simulations where events take roughly the same amount of time to process, each processor will have roughly equal amounts of work during each GVT interval.

The second trigger we will be looking at is one based on a virtual time leash. With the leash-based trigger, each processor stops executing events and signals it is ready to take part in the GVT computation after progressing T units of virtual time from the previous GVT. The aim of this trigger is to keep each processor progressing at roughly the same rate, while placing less importance on keeping the amount of work done by each processor balanced.

4.2 GVT Algorithm

The GVT trigger controls when the scheduler signals it is ready to compute a GVT, however the behavior of the simulator during the computation, including when event execution resumes, is controlled by the GVT algorithm itself. In the baseline synchronous algorithm event execution is blocked until the entire GVT computation is completed. It utilizes the Quiescence Detection library in CHARM++ [26] to wait for all sent events to be received before computing the GVT. The algorithm consists of three parts, as shown in Figure 1 (top): Quiescence Detection (QD), an All-Reduce (Red), and Fossil Collection (FC). Since LPs are suspended for the entire GVT computation, this scheme theoretically has the highest overhead. However, since all LPs are suspended, this scheme also computes the maximal GVT since it knows the exact time reached by each LP. Computing the maximal GVT also results in freeing of maximal memory during fossil collection.

The following two algorithms preserve this basic structure, but attempt to exploit the asynchrony in CHARM++ in various ways to decrease the time that LPs must block.

4.2.1 Asynchronous Reduction.
The first technique we utilize to decrease the GVT synchronization cost exploits asynchronous reductions for the All-Reduce component of the computation. After quiescence is reached in the synchronous scheme, LPs are still blocked until after the reduction and the fossil collection occurs (Figure 1 (top)). This leaves many processors idle while the All-Reduce is being performed, even though the result of the All-Reduce is not required to execute more events. To address this shortcoming, we can restart event execution as soon as quiescence is reached and each processors local minimum is known, as shown in Figure 1 (mid). This allows the runtime system to adaptively overlap event execution with the All-Reduce and fossil collection, which reduces idle time by allowing processors to do meaningful work when they are not actively involved in the GVT computation.

4.2.2 Continuous Execution.
The asynchronous reduction scheme described above still requires event execution to completely stop during quiescence detection, which, as we'll see in our experimental results, is the more costly part of the GVT synchronization. The second technique we explore aims at completely eliminating the need for LPs to block, allowing for continuous event execution throughout the simulation. In order to accomplish this, we use the concept of phase based completion detection to implement a scheme similar to the those described by Mattern and Perumalla [18, 24, 25].

In this algorithm, we use the completion detection library (CD) in CHARM++ [1] as a replacement for the QD phase of the previous two algorithms. Unlike QD, completion detection monitors only a subset of messages, and is triggered once all of those messages have been received. By carefully tagging subsets of events and running multiple CD instances independently, we enable continuous execution of events overlapped with the GVT computation.

The execution of the continuous scheme is split into two recurring phases, which we refer to as the red phase and the white phase, as shown in Figure 1 (bot). Each phase is managed by a single instance of the CD library. When an event is sent in the white phase, it is tagged as a white event and the white CD instance is informed so it can increment its count of sent events. Similarly, events sent during the red phase are tagged as red. When an event is received, the corresponding CD instance is informed based on the event's tag so it can increment its count of received events. When it is

Model	Synchronous		Continuous	
	Count	Leash	Count	Leash
PHOLD Base	97%	98%	95%	95%
PHOLD Work	75%	76%	52%	52%
PHOLD Event	54%	84%	60%	60%
PHOLD Combo	54%	93%	31%	31%
DFly Uniform	74%	62%	36%	36%
DFly Worst	39%	91%	2%	2%
DFly Trans	31%	85%	27%	27%
DFly NN	68%	93%	67%	67%
Traffic Base	46%	96%	54%	55%
Traffic Src	12%	97%	16%	16%
Traffic Dest	51%	96%	52%	52%
Traffic Route	11%	97%	15%	15%

Table 1: Table comparing event efficiencies between the two different triggers. The leash trigger results in higher efficiency for almost all model configurations.

time to switch from one phase to the next, the CD instance for the current phase is informed that no more events will be sent, which triggers a series of reductions for that CD instance to determine the total number of events sent and received. Once the CD instance detects that the number of sent events equals the number of received events, the GVT can be computed with an All-Reduce of the local minima followed by fossil collection. Throughout the entire process, events are still being executed in the next phase, and the work from event execution is overlapped with work for the CD library, GVT computation, and fossil collection.

One additional difference in this new scheme is how the GVT is computed from local minima. In the previous two schemes, since total quiescence is reached, all events have been received and the GVT is simply the minimum of all received events. However, the continuous scheme never requires full quiescence so there may be events inflight that could affect the GVT. In particular, when switching from one phase to another, for example from white to red, the simulator is waiting on all white events to arrive but also sending outgoing red events. Once all white events have been received the simulator can guarantee the minimum timestamp of red events sent in the future, however it must also take into account red events that have already been sent. Since it has no guarantee that any of the previously sent red events have been received it must track these events from the sender side. Specifically, between the time that the phases are switched and events for the previous phase have all been received, each processor must track the minimum timestamp of outgoing events and take that into account when contributing to the minimum All-Reduce.

4.3 Experimental Results
The following experiments were done on all models and configurations described in Section 3, using each combination of GVT trigger and algorithm. Runs were done on 64 nodes (2,048 cores) of the Blue Waters system at NCSA. The parameters for each trigger were tuned to achieve the best performance. Multiple runs of each

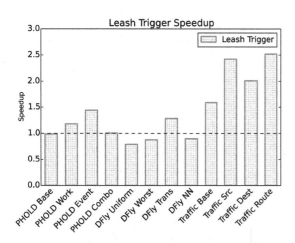

Figure 2: Speedup of the leash-based trigger over the count-based trigger, both using the synchronous GVT algorithm.

Model	Sync	Async Reduction	
PHOLD Base	2.75s	2.32s	(16%)
PHOLD Work	9.23s	8.73s	(5%)
PHOLD Event	5.96s	5.50s	(8%)
PHOLD Combo	25.14s	24.56s	(2%)
DFly Uniform	3.42s	3.79s	(-11%)
DFly Worst	4.73s	3.07s	(35%)
DFly Trans	7.51s	5.51s	(27%)
DFly NN	0.59s	0.28s	(53%)
Traffic Base	5.27s	4.16s	(21%)
Traffic Src	22.20s	20.80s	(6%)
Traffic Dest	8.30s	7.15s	(14%)
Traffic Route	26.35s	24.66s	(6%)

Table 2: Table comparing the amount of time LPs spend blocking (in seconds) under the synchronous and asynchronous GVT reduction algorithms, as well as the percent improvement when using the asynchronous reduction.

configuration were performed, but in all cases variance between runs was negligible.

4.3.1 Leash-Based Trigger. In analyzing the effects of the different GVT configurations, we look both at synchronization cost and event efficiency and how each one impacts event rate. First, analyzing each GVT trigger under the baseline synchronous scheme demonstrates the impact that the GVT trigger has on overall performance. After tuning the count-based trigger for the highest event rate, the virtual time leash for the leash-based trigger was initially chosen so that the total number of GVT computations for the simulation would be similar to what was required by the count metric. Then the leash was increased or decreased accordingly to find optimum performance. In almost all cases, the best performance came by decreasing the leash, which resulted in more GVT computations and a higher synchronization cost, but a higher event efficiency.

Table 1 shows the event efficiency for the two triggers, with the leash-based trigger achieving higher efficiency for all but one model configuration. In many cases the improvement in efficiency is significant, especially in the Traffic model where the leash-based trigger achieves at least 96% efficiency in all configurations. The models that see less benefit from the leash-based trigger are those where the distribution of events across LPs is roughly uniform: PHOLD Base, PHOLD Work, and DFly Uniform. The increased efficiency means fewer rollbacks, and so each model has to execute fewer events when running to completion under the leash-based trigger. Figure 2 shows the speedup of the leash-based trigger when compared to the count-based trigger, where we see significant speedups for most of the model configurations. In particular, the Traffic model sees over 2x speedup for its unbalanced configurations due to the drastic improvements to efficiency. For model configurations where the efficiency between the two triggers was comparable, the event rates are similar for both and may even slightly favor the count-based trigger. In these cases, the leash-based trigger often spent more time where LPs were blocked waiting for the GVT, either due to the leash trigger computing GVT more often, or due to an imbalance

in the amount of time spent blocking on the GVT since the number of events computed on each PE varies per GVT in the leash-based trigger.

4.3.2 Asynchronous Algorithms. Where the trigger had a more profound effect on event efficiency, the primary impact of the different GVT algorithms is in reducing the synchronization cost. Due to the fact that the leash-based trigger provided comparable or better performance in most cases, we will first look at the effects of each GVT algorithm when using the leash trigger. Table 2 shows the amount of time LPs spent blocking on the GVT computation for the synchronous algorithm and the asynchronous reduction algorithm. Time spent blocking when using the continuous algorithm is zero in all cases, so is not shown in the table. The table also shows the percent change, and we see a reduction in time blocking by over 20% in most of the Dragonfly models, and over 10% in PHOLD Base, Traffic Base, and Traffic Dest. However this also highlights the fact that the majority of the time spent blocking on the GVT comes from Quiescence Detection. In Figure 3 (right), which plots the speedup of the two GVT algorithms when compared to the synchronous algorithm, we see that in most cases the speedup from the asynchronous reduction scheme is comparable to the reduction in blocking time. The results are especially pronounced in the Dragonfly and Traffic models, which have a lower ratio of event work to GVT work, whereas the PHOLD models generate more events and a smaller fraction of them are able to be executed during the time freed up by the asynchronous reduction.

Figure 3 shows the effects of the continuous algorithm which eliminates all LP blocking during the GVT. In cases where the asynchronous reduction was able to improve event rate by reducing synchronization cost, we see that the continuous scheme was able to be even more effective, achieving up to 1.5× speedup for DFly Uniform and Traffic Base, and 3× speedup for DFly NN. For DFly Worst, PHOLD Event, and PHOLD Combo, the efficiency is significantly worse, which outweighs the benefits of the reduced synchronization cost.

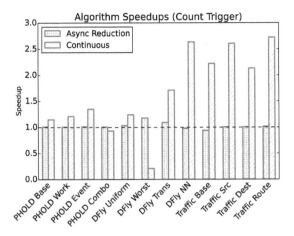
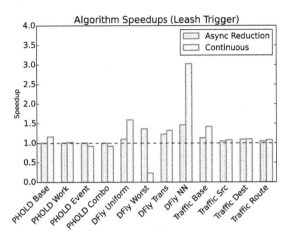

Figure 3: The relative speedup of each GVT algorithm when compared to the synchronous version.

When looking at how the different algorithms affect the count-based trigger in Figure 3 (left), we see largely the same patterns but with much larger speedups for the continuous algorithm. Figure 4 plots the actual event rates of the continuous algorithm for both triggers, and shows the the performance is nearly identical regardless of the trigger used. This is further backed up by nearly identical efficiencies under each trigger as shown in Table 1. This reveals an important side-effect of the other two GVT algorithms, which is that by blocking the LPs during at least part of the GVT computation, the amount of optimistic execution allowed by the simulator is bounded by the GVT computation. LPs can not get too far ahead due to the fact that either after N events, or T units of virtual time depending on the trigger, they must block while other LPs are allowed to catch up. The effects of this already showed up when comparing the two triggers under the synchronous algorithm. LPs in the count trigger can still get arbitrarily far ahead in virtual time depending on the distribution of events, but under the leash trigger LPs cannot, which keeps LPs closer together in virtual time reducing the likelihood of causality violations. Once that artificial bounding is removed from the GVT computation, the rate at which LPs progress through virtual time is completely unbounded and solely up to the characteristics of the models themselves. This results in lower efficiencies when compared to the synchronous scheme, which limits the benefits from the reduced synchronization costs. This limit is less detrimental under the count-based trigger due to the fact that it already has relatively lower efficiencies when compared to the leash-based trigger.

4.4 Summary

Analysis of the above GVT techniques shows a clear coupling between event efficiency and synchronization costs. The algorithms that block event execution while waiting for quiescence achieve a higher event efficiency by bounding the amount of execution. Tighter leashes further improve efficiency while simultaneously causing more frequent GVT computations, creating a tradeoff between efficiency and synchronization. The continuous algorithm

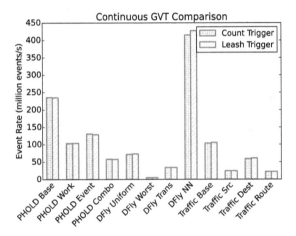

Figure 4: Comparison of the event rates for the continuous GVT algorithm under both triggers.

attempts to completely remove the synchronization cost, which in turn results in lower efficiency from the now unbounded optimism. In the next section we look at a method for improving efficiency independent of the GVT computation in order to decouple efficiency and synchronization.

5   LOAD BALANCING

In the previous section, we explored a tradeoff between synchronization cost and event efficiency. In many cases, enforcing more synchronization was able to increase the event efficiency, and resulted in a higher event rate. However, after a certain point, the synchronization cost outweighs the benefits gained from higher efficiency. Furthermore, as shown with the continuous GVT scheme, completely removing the synchronization cost of the global barrier may result in even higher performance despite large decreases in efficiency. In this section, we explore another method for affecting the efficiency of simulations: dynamic load balancing. When the distribution of events across processors is unbalanced, processors with little work can run far ahead of the rest, and be forced to rollback frequently as a result. Improving efficiency with load balancing will allow us to lower the synchronization cost of the GVT computation, while still maintaining a certain degree of efficiency.

LPs in Charades are implemented as chares in CHARM++. This allows the runtime system to manage the location of LPs as well as migrate them for purposes such as dynamic load balancing. During simulation execution, the load of each LP can be measured as CPU time automatically by the runtime system, or by metrics specific to Charades. Once the simulator is ready to perform load balancing, the load statistics are collected and LPs redistributed according to the particular load balancing strategy being used. For the experiments in this section we will be working with two different strategies: GreedyLB and DistributedLB.

GreedyLB is a centralized strategy that collects profiling information about all LPs on a single processor before redistributing them using a greedy algorithm. It iteratively assigns the most heavy unassigned LP to the least loaded processor until LPs have been assigned. As this can result in almost every LP being migrated, we also test a variation of GreedyLB that attempts to limit the number of migrations when reassigning the LPs.

DistributedLB is a fully distributed strategy that utilizes probabilistic migration and a gossip protocol as described in [19] to minimize the overhead of load balancing. First, a global reduction is done to determine the average load of all processors. Information about which processors are under-loaded is then propagated throughout the system via "gossip" messages. Once gossip is complete, the overloaded processors asynchronously attempt to shift some of their load to the under-loaded ones in a probabilistic fashion. In initial experiments, this did little to affect the performance of our simulations due to very few objects successfully migrating. For this work, we have modified the DistributedLB algorithm by breaking up the load transferring step into multiple phases. In earlier phases, only the most overloaded processors have the opportunity to shift their load, which makes it less likely that their attempts will fail due to other processors transferring load fi rst. In subsequent phases, the threshold for which processors can shift load is relaxed. This prioritizes reducing the ratio of max to average load more aggressively than the original implementation.

In addition to the two different strategies, we examine two different load metrics for determining the load of an LP. The fi rst is CPU time, which is automatically measured by the runtime system. The second is the number of committed events. Using committed events as a measure of load aims to ignore incorrect speculation when balancing load by only focusing on meaningful work done by each LP.

5.1 Experimental Results

The following experiments were run using the six unbalanced configurations of PHOLD and Traffic, on 64 nodes (2,048 cores) of Blue Waters. Due to the fact that the communication patterns in Dragonfly were uniformly balanced in the amount of work for each MPI process, load balancing had little effect on performance and is therefore omitted from this section. In each case, load balancing

was triggered after the completion of a GVT computation and fossil collection had occurred. This allowed for the most memory within the LPs to be freed before migrating them to minimize the migration footprint. The particular GVT which triggered load balancing was determined via some manual tuning, and was always somewhere within the fi rst 10% of a simulation in order to allow enough time for load statistics to be gathered. In all the results presented, statistics shown are for the entire simulation run, which includes execution both before and during the load balancing phase. Initially we focus our analysis on the isolated effects of load balancing under the synchronous GVT algorithm. Furthermore, we focus on the best load balancing strategy for each model only, allowing more space to analyze the effects of load balancing and the different load balancing metrics. For PHOLD, DistributedLB performed the best, where as GreedyLB was the best load balancer for the traffic model. As stated in the previous section, variation between multiple runs was negligible.

Figure 5 shows speedup of each model configuration with each load measure, compared to results without load balancing. With the exception of Traffic Dest with the count-based trigger, there is an increase in performance in each model configuration with at least one of the load metrics. The two primary causes for the increased event rate are improved balance of work across processors, and increased event efficiency. The magnitude of each effect depends heavily on the trigger used, where load balancing serves to improve on the shortcomings of that particular metric.

5.1.1 Synchronization Cost and Balance. In the case of Charades, the work we are interested in balancing is the execution of events in between GVT computations. Between two GVT computations, each processor has a set amount of work which, based on the trigger, is either a specified number of events to execute, or an amount of virtual time to traverse. Processors that fi nish their work early due to an imbalance in the number of events, weight of events, or a higher efficiency resulting in less rollbacks and re-execution will therefore reach the next GVT computation quicker and begin blocking before other processors. Figure 6 plots the min, max, and mean time spent blocking on the GVT across all processors. In the cases with no load balancing, many models exhibit a wide range of times indicative of imbalance across processors.

For the leash-based trigger, load balancing is able to decrease the range of times, as well as lowering the max and average, meaning less overall time spent waiting on the GVT. For configurations with work imbalance, namely PHOLD Work and PHOLD Combo, we see that the CPU load metric is particularly effective at decreasing wait times. For other models where the imbalance is primarily due to different distributions of events, both metrics are effective at both lowering the amount of time waiting as well as shrinking the range of times. These effects are prominent with the leash-based trigger due to the fact that the amount of work per GVT interval that is enforced by the trigger is not necessarily equal across all processes and depends on the distribution of events. Load balancing attempts to balance the amount of work required for each processor to traverse each interval, where the leash-based trigger still plays the role of keeping each processors rate of progress through virtual time balanced. This results in less variation in how long it takes each processor to get from one GVT computation to the next.

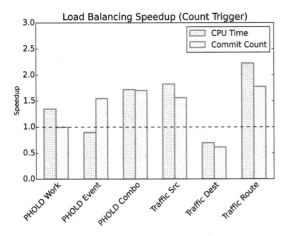
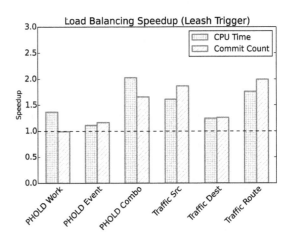

Figure 5: Speedup of each model configuration with each load balancing metric, compared to configurations with no load balancing.

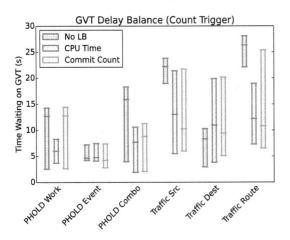
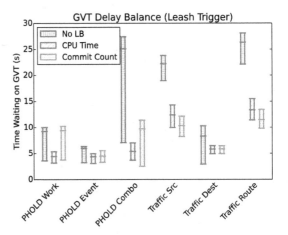

Figure 6: Min, max, and mean time across all processors spent blocking on the GVT computation. Processors with very little work in a given interval will block longer waiting for others to catch up.

The left-hand side of figure 6 shows the GVT wait time for the count-based metric. Load balancing is not nearly as effective at shrinking the range of times, and in the traffic models we actually see a wider range. The count-based metric inherently enforces balanced GVT intervals for models like Traffic where all events take roughly the same amount of time. However, load balancing still manages to decrease the overall amount of time waiting on the GVT in almost every case. This is due to a net gain in efficiency when using load balancing as shown on the left-hand side of figure 7. The improved efficiency results in less overall work to complete the simulation and therefore fewer GVT calculations.

5.1.2 Efficiency. When comparing the efficiency for the two different triggers in figure 7, we see that the effectiveness of load balancing is the opposite of what we saw when looking at the GVT

wait time. In this case, since the count-based trigger does little to enforce high efficiencies, load balancing is far more successful at increasing efficiency for these configurations. Every model but Traffic Dest saw an increase in efficiency, with the results being particularly good for PHOLD Event with the commit metric, and PHOLD Combo with both. The effects are less pronounced for the Traffic models where we only see modest gains in efficiency. While PHOLD has no communication locality, as every LP is sending to every other LP with the same probability, migrating LPs did not effect communication costs. For Traffic however, there is high degree of communication locality, so while migrating objects may provide a better balance of the number of events executed and committed across processors, it also causes higher communication costs between heavily communicating LPs. For the leash-based trigger, which enforced very high efficiency in the Traffic model, we see

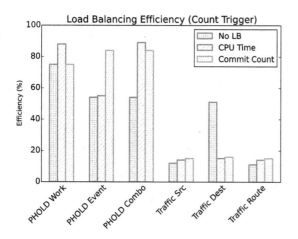
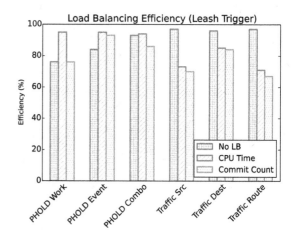

Figure 7: Efficiency of each model with and without load balancing.

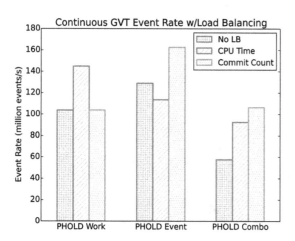
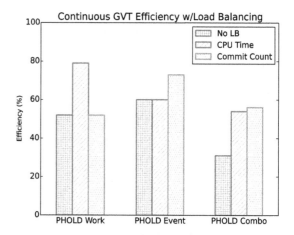

Figure 8: Comparison of the continuous GVT algorithm with and without load balancing.

that load balancing actually lowers the efficiency due to more roll-backs and event cancellations between the heavily communicating LPs.

5.1.3 Combining Load Balancing and Continuous GVT.

The fact that load balancing is able to improve efficiency is especially important when considering the fact that the limiting factor in performance of the continuous GVT algorithm from Section 4 was a decrease in event efficiency. Figure 8 shows the event rates for the continuous GVT algorithm when load balancing is introduced. We see event rate improved in all cases by up to 2×. All three have at least 1.6× speedup over the original baseline configurations, and PHOLD Work and PHOLD Event achieve their highest event rates for any configuration studied in this paper. The efficiency plot in figure 8 further reinforces the impact of the different load metrics. When all other synchronization from the GVT is removed, it becomes clear that when addressing different types of imbalance the

correct load metric must be chosen in order to achieve the best efficiency. For PHOLD Work, where the primary cause of imbalance is the amount of work per event, the CPU load metric improved efficiency by a factor of around 1.6× but the commit count metric had no effect at all. The opposite is true for PHOLD Event where the primary cause of imbalance is an uneven distribution of events. For PHOLD Combo, both metrics do well but it is conceivable that a combination of the two metrics may be even more effective.

Unfortunately, in the case of the Traffic model, the efficiency becomes much too low in the continuous case. Combining that with the communication locality issue described earlier means that the continuous scheme with load balancing is ineffective, and the rollbacks and especially cancellation events cascade out of control. This points to a need for a communication aware load balancing strategy, which would keep tightly coupled LPs in close proximity in an attempt to minimize the number of rollbacks and event cancellations between them.

5.2 Summary

By introducing automated load balancing into Charades, we are able to increase the event rate of unbalanced models by improving both balance and efficiency. Depending on the type of imbalance in the model, different metrics for defining the load of an LP will improve the capability of the load balancing framework, as each metric addresses different aspect of a simulation. Furthermore, the effect of load balancing on event efficiency comes without additional synchronization cost, so it becomes particularly effective when combined with the continuous GVT from Section 4. However, load balancing was not effective at addressing efficiency in models with balanced workloads such as Dragonfly. Furthermore, for the Traffic model, load balancing was less effective due to high communication locality and much lower efficiencies. We leave it as future work to further explore how careful use of different load metrics and balancing strategies can detect and deal with event efficiency independent from load balance. We also plan to develop light-weight distributed strategies for better handling models with high communication locality in order to handle negative side effects such as an increase in cancellation events.

6 CONCLUSION

Software that enables scalable execution of discrete event simulation is desirable in several domains. However the irregular, dynamic andfi ne-grained nature of many PDES models makes it difficult to scale. In particular, the event efficiency in such models can be difficult to manage and often requires the need for high synchronization costs. In this paper, we evaluated several techniques for managing the tradeoff between synchronization cost and event efficiency. We also provide a scalable implementation of a non-blocking GVT algorithm to remove the synchronization cost entirely. Up to 2× better performance is shown for a variety of models running on 2048 processors.

Furthermore, we explore dynamic load balancing as a technique to manage event efficiency, without requiring explicit synchronization from the GVT computation. In unbalanced model configurations, load balancing is shown to increase both event rate and event efficiency. By combining load balancing with the continuous GVT algorithm, even higher performance is achieved for our unbalanced version of the PHOLD benchmark than with any of the other techniques in this paper, and shows that load balancing can mitigate efficiency loss independently of the GVT algorithm used.

REFERENCES

[1] The charm++ parallel programming system manual. http://charm.cs.illinois.edu/manuals/html/charm++/manual.html.

[2] Ross source code on github. https://github.com/carothersc/ROSS, visited 2016-03-20.

[3] B. Acun, A. Gupta, N. Jain, A. Langer, H. Menon, E. Mikida, X. Ni, M. Robson, Y. Sun, E. Totoni, L. Wesolowski, and L. Kale. Parallel Programming with Migratable Objects: Charm++ in Practice. SC, 2014.

[4] P. D. Barnes, Jr., C. D. Carothers, and D. R. e. a. Jefferson. Warp speed: Executing time warp on 1,966,080 cores. In Conference on Principles of Advanced Discrete Simulation, SIGSIM-PADS, pages 327–336, New York, NY, USA, 2013.

[5] D. Bauer, G. Yaun, C. D. Carothers, M. Yuksel, and S. Kalyanaraman. Seven-o'clock: A new distributed gvt algorithm using network atomic operations. In Proceedings of the 19th Workshop on Principles of Advanced and Distributed Simulation, PADS '05, pages 39–48, Washington, DC, USA, 2005. IEEE Computer Society.

[6] D. W. Bauer Jr., C. D. Carothers, and A. Holder. Scalable time warp on blue gene supercomputers. In Proceedings of the 2009 ACM/IEEE/SCS 23rd Workshop on Principles of Advanced and Distributed Simulation, PADS '09, pages 35–44, Washington, DC, USA, 2009. IEEE Computer Society.

[7] C. D. Carothers, D. Bauer, and S. Pearce. ROSS: A high-performance, low-memory, modular Time Warp system. Journal of Parallel and Distributed Computing, 62(11):1648–1669, 2002.

[8] C. D. Carothers and R. M. Fujimoto. Efficient execution of time warp programs on heterogeneous, now platforms. IEEE Trans. Parallel Distrib. Syst., 11(3):299–317, Mar. 2000.

[9] G. G. Chen, Boleslaw, and K. Szymanski. Time quantum gvt: A scalable computation of the global virtual time in parallel discrete event simulations.

[10] N. Choudhury, Y. Mehta, T. L. Wilmarth, E. J. Bohm, and L. V. . Kalé. Scaling an optimistic parallel simulation of large-scale interconnection networks. In Proceedings of the Winter Simulation Conference, 2005.

[11] E. Deelman and B. K. Szymanski. Dynamic load balancing in parallel discrete event simulation for spatially explicit problems. In Parallel and Distributed Simulation, 1998. PADS 98. Proceedings. Twelfth Workshop on, pages 46–53, May 1998.

[12] R. M. Fujimoto. Performance of time warp under synthetic workloads. Distributed Simulation Conference, 1990.

[13] R. M. Fujimoto and M. Hybinette. Computing global virtual time in shared-memory multiprocessors. ACM Trans. Model. Comput. Simul., 7(4):425–446, Oct. 1997.

[14] D. W. Glazer and C. Tropper. On process migration and load balancing in time warp. IEEE Transactions on Parallel and Distributed Systems, 4(3):318–327, Mar 1993.

[15] Z. X. F. Gomes, B. Unger, and J. Cleary. A fast asynchronous gvt algorithm for shared memory multiprocessor architectures. SIGSIM Simul. Dig., 25(1):203–208, July 1995.

[16] E. J. Gonsiorowski, J. M. LaPre, and C. D. Carothers. Improving accuracy and performance through automatic model generation for gate-level circuit pdes with reverse computation. In Proceedings of the 3rd ACM SIGSIM Conference on Principles of Advanced Discrete Simulation, SIGSIM PADS '15, pages 87–96, New York, NY, USA, 2015. ACM.

[17] D. Jefferson and H. Sowizral. Fast Concurrent Simulation Using the Time Warp Mechanism. In Proceedings of the Conference on Distributed Simulation, pages 63–69, July 1985.

[18] F. Mattern. Efficient algorithms for distributed snapshots and global virtual time approximation. Journal of Parallel and Distributed Computing, 18:423–434, 1993.

[19] H. Menon and L. Kalé. A distributed dynamic load balancer for iterative applications. In Proceedings of SC13: International Conference for High Performance Computing, Networking, Storage and Analysis, SC '13, pages 15:1–15:11, New York, NY, USA, 2013. ACM.

[20] S. Meraji, W. Zhang, and C. Tropper. On the scalability and dynamic load-balancing of optimistic gate level simulation. Trans. Comp.-Aided Des. Integ. Cir. Sys., 29(9):1368–1380, Sept. 2010.

[21] E. Mikida, N. Jain, E. Gonsiorowski, P. D. Barnes, Jr., D. Jefferson, C. Carothers, and L. V. Kale. Towards pdes in a message-driven paradigm: A preliminary case study using charm++. In Proceedings of the 2016 ACM SIGSIM Conference on Principles of Advanced Discrete Simulation, SIGSIM PADS '16. ACM, May 2016.

[22] M. Mubarak, C. D. Carothers, R. Ross, and P. Carns. Modeling a million-node dragonfly network using massively parallel discrete-event simulation. In High Performance Computing, Networking, Storage and Analysis (SCC), 2012 SC Companion:, pages 366–376, Nov 2012.

[23] M. Mubarak, C. D. Carothers, R. B. Ross, and P. Carns. Using massively parallel simulation for mpi collective communication modeling in extreme-scale networks. In Proceedings of the 2014 Winter Simulation Conference, WSC '14, pages 3107–3118, Piscataway, NJ, USA, 2014. IEEE Press.

[24] K. S. Perumalla, A. J. Park, and V. Tipparaju. Gvt algorithms and discrete event dynamics on 129k+ processor cores. In *High Performance Computing (HiPC), 2011 18th International Conference on*, pages 1–11, Dec 2011.

[25] K. S. Perumalla, A. J. Park, and V. Tipparaju. Discrete event execution with one-sided and two-sided gvt algorithms on 216,000 processor cores. *ACM Trans. Model. Comput. Simul.*, 24(3):16:1–16:25, June 2014.

[26] A. B. Sinha, L. V. Kale, and B. Ramkumar. A dynamic and adaptive quiescence detection algorithm. Technical Report 93-11, Parallel Programming Laboratory, Department of Computer Science , University of Illinois, Urbana-Champaign, 1993.

[27] S. Srinivasan and P. F. Reynolds, Jr. Non-interfering gvt computation via asynchronous global reductions. In *Proceedings of the 25th Conference on Winter Simulation*, WSC '93, pages 740–749, New York, NY, USA, 1993. ACM.

[28] J. S. Steinman, C. A. Lee, L. F. Wilson, and D. M. Nicol. Global virtual time and distributed synchronization. In *Proceedings of the Ninth Workshop on Parallel and Distributed Simulation*, PADS '95, pages 139–148, Washington, DC, USA, 1995. IEEE Computer Society.

[29] N. Wolfe, C. D. Carothers, M. Mubarak, R. Ross, and P. Carns. Modeling a million-node slimfl y network using parallel discrete-event simulation. In *Proceedings of the 2016 ACM SIGSIM Conference on Principles of Advanced Discrete Simulation*, SIGSIM-PADS '16, pages 189–199, New York, NY, USA, 2016. ACM.

[30] Y. Xu, W. Cai, H. Aydt, M. Lees, and D. Zehe. An asynchronous synchronization strategy for parallel large-scale agent-based traffic simulations. In *Proceedings of the 3rd ACM SIGSIM Conference on Principles of Advanced Discrete Simulation*, SIGSIM PADS '15, pages 259–269, New York, NY, USA, 2015. ACM.

[31] S. B. Yoginath and K. S. Perumalla. Optimized hypervisor scheduler for parallel discrete event simulations on virtual machine platforms. In *Proceedings of the 6th International ICST Conference on Simulation Tools and Techniques*, SimuTools '13, pages 1–9, ICST, Brussels, Belgium, Belgium, 2013. ICST (Institute for Computer Sciences, Social-Informatics and Telecommunications Engineering).

Fine-Grained Local Dynamic Load Balancing in PDES

Jonatan Lindén
Dept. of Information Technology
Uppsala University, Sweden
jonatan.linden@it.uu.se

Pavol Bauer
Dept. of Information Technology
Uppsala University, Sweden
pavol.bauer@it.uu.se

Stefan Engblom
Dept. of Information Technology
Uppsala University, Sweden
stefane@it.uu.se

Bengt Jonsson
Dept. of Information Technology
Uppsala University, Sweden
bengt@it.uu.se

ABSTRACT

We present a fine-grained load migration protocol intended for parallel discrete event simulation (PDES) of spatially extended models. Typical models have domains that are fine-grained discretizations of some volume, e.g., a cell, using an irregular three-dimensional mesh, where most events span several voxels. Phenomena of interest in, e.g., cellular biology, are often non-homogeneous and migrate over the simulated domain, making load balancing a crucial part of a successful PDES. Our load migration protocol is local in the sense that it involves only those processors that exchange workload, and does not affect the running parallel simulation. We present a detailed description of the protocol and a thorough proof for its correctness. We combine our protocol with a strategy for deciding when and what load to migrate, which optimizes both for load balancing and inter-processor communication using tunable parameters. Our evaluation shows that the overhead of the load migration protocol is negligible, and that it significantly reduces the number of rollbacks caused by load imbalance. On the other hand, the implementation mechanisms that we added to support fine-grained load balancing incur a significant cost.

KEYWORDS

Parallel Discrete-Event Simulation; PDES; Load Balancing; Load Migration; Load Metric

ACM Reference Format:
Jonatan Lindén, Pavol Bauer, Stefan Engblom, and Bengt Jonsson. 2018. Fine-Grained Local Dynamic Load Balancing in PDES. In *Proceedings of SIGSIM Principles of Advanced Discrete Simulation (SIGSIM-PADS'18)*. ACM, New York, NY, USA, 12 pages. https://doi.org/10.1145/3200921.3200928

1 INTRODUCTION

Discrete Event Simulation (DES) is an important tool in a wide-ranging area of applications, such as integrated circuit design,

systems biology, epidemics, etc. To improve performance and accommodate for large scale models, a vast repertoire of techniques have been developed for Parallel DES (PDES) during the last 30 years [15, 20, 25]. New synchronization techniques have been triggered by the advent of multicore processors (e.g., [6, 26, 31]). Still, achieving good performance and speedup for larger numbers of processing elements has proven to be very difficult in the general case.

In PDES, the simulation model is partitioned onto logical processes (LPs), each of which processes timestamped events to evolve its partition along a local simulation time axis. Events that affect the state of neighboring LPs are exchanged to incorporate inter-LP dependencies. A number of synchronization techniques have been developed in order to guarantee that causally dependent events are processed in the right order, ranging from conservative [25] to optimistic [20] approaches, with many intermediate design choices (see, e.g., the surveys [8, 19]). Such intermediate protocols can reduce the performance loss caused by temporary variations in relative speed of different LPs. However, perhaps the most important prerequisite for high efficiency in PDES is that the simulation load is evenly partitioned over LPs This follows from the observation that the total simulation speed can never exceed that of the slowest LP (assuming a one-to-one correspondence between LPs and processors). For simulation models where the distribution of work does not vary over time, this can be achieved by a good static partitioning of the model before simulation starts. However, in many simulation models, the distribution of work varies with time. For instance, in systems biology, the phenomena of interest are often non-homogeneous and migrate over the simulation domain; examples include nerve signals, and the oscillation of proteins involved in the cell division of bacteria [14]. For such models, good parallel performance requires a dynamic load balancing mechanism, which detects when load imbalances arise and corrects them by migrating load between LPs.

Most existing approaches perform dynamic load balancing as a globally coordinated operation, at specified (often regular) time intervals [3–5, 12, 18, 23, 27–29, 32]. For models, where the load migrates continuously over the domain of the simulation model, load imbalances arise locally, and it seems more natural to let rebalancing be a local operation, which involves only those LPs that are affected by the migrating load, and is performed on-line. Such a mechanism must be designed carefully to preserve correctness of the underlying simulation.

Permission to make digital or hard copies of all or part of this work for personal or classroom use is granted without fee provided that copies are not made or distributed for profit or commercial advantage and that copies bear this notice and the full citation on the first page. Copyrights for components of this work owned by others than ACM must be honored. Abstracting with credit is permitted. To copy otherwise, or republish, to post on servers or to redistribute to lists, requires prior specific permission and/or a fee. Request permissions from permissions@acm.org.
SIGSIM-PADS'18, May 23–25, 2018, Rome, Italy
© 2018 Association for Computing Machinery.
ACM ISBN 978-1-4503-5092-1/18/05...$15.00
https://doi.org/10.1145/3200921.3200928

In this paper, we present an online fine-grained dynamic load migration protocol, which is local in the sense that it concerns only those LPs that are affected by the migrated load. Our protocol is defined for simulation of spatial models that are discretized into *subvolumes* (also known as voxels) which are partitioned onto LPs. An example model is a bacterial cell, where the state of each voxel is represented by a number of entities of different proteins. Each LP is mapped to a core in a multicore processor. Our protocol migrates individual voxels between LPs, with low overhead for the underlying simulation algorithm. It assumes no restrictions on the topology of the simulation domain, nor on the number of LPs adjacent to a migrated element.

Our underlying implementation uses the time-warp protocol [20], with some optimizations. One of these is the use of *aggregated anti-messages*, each representing a set of inter-core anti-messages, that reduce inter-core communication to improve performance. These require extra care in the migration protocol, since their semantics may change as a result of voxel migration. We have therefore developed a proof of correctness of our time-warp protocol with voxel migration. The proof is inspired by that of [22], but adapted to our version of time-warp with aggregated anti-messages, and thereafter extended to cover the migration protocol.

A load balancing mechanism must also include a load metric which represents the amount of load on an LP, and a mechanism for deciding which voxels to migrate where. Defining a good load metric in optimistic PDES is challenging, since natural metrics such as the average CPU load, are no good indicators of the actual simulation progress, since CPUs may be busy processing rollbacks. Many existing approaches [1, 10, 12, 27] to load balancing in PDES base their load migration choices on an LPs load metric related to some global computation including all LPs' load metrics. As our load migration protocol is local, there is a need for a local load metric. Here, our starting point is that observed synchronization costs, such as rollback processing, are very likely caused by load imbalance. In the ideal case, when the load is perfectly balanced, (almost) no messages arrive too late, and thus there should be no need for rollbacks. We therefore use the number of locally incurred rollbacks as a load metric. Even though it is not realistic to completely avoid rollbacks, it is reasonable to assume that by continuous dynamic rebalancing of the load, their incurred overhead should be substantially lower than the overhead of adding an optimism control protocol: our simulator therefore does not employ any additional optimism control.

We show the correctness of the load balancing protocol, and evaluate the performance of our approach, together with two simple metrics for when and where load balancing is needed, on realistic benchmarks from computational cellular biology. Our evaluation shows that the overhead of the load migration protocol is negligible and that it significantly reduces the number of rollbacks caused by load imbalance. On the other hand, the implementation mechanisms that we added to support fine-grained load balancing incur a significant cost.

The paper is organized as follows. In the next section, we give an overview of related work. In Section 3, some necessary background and the main ideas of our load migration protocol is presented. In Section 4, a detailed description of the load migration protocol is given. In Section 5, we provide a correctness argument for the

migration protocol. In Section 6, we give a short outline of the load metric and load balancing algorithm that we've used for the evaluation of the migration protocol, in Section 7.

2 RELATED WORK

We review related work that addresses three aspects of the load balancing problem: protocols for load migration, load metrics, and finally how load balancing is initiated.

Load Migration Protocols. Different works have considered different granularity of the transferred load of a migration. Deelman and Szymanski [10] consider a dynamic load balancing mechanism on a two-dimensional circular model. The model is partitioned into segments, each assigned to an LP. Thus, this is a rather simple topology, where each LP only has two neighbors. The load balancing mechanism moves entire columns of the simulated domain between adjacent processing elements. Similarly Schlagenhaft et al. [30] move clusters of basic elements between processing elements. However, they discard the option of moving single elements between partition, which we have opted for in this paper. They argue that no significant change in load balance is achieved when moving small basic elements between processors, but do not further investigate how the granularity of the migrations affects performance. We argue that load imbalance is a local phenomenon, thus accordingly migrations have to be fine-grained.

Load balancing through process migration is studied in Glazer and Tropper [18], Reiher and Jefferson [28] (and in [29], but there process migration was only mimicked). It requires operating system support, and with large numbers of migration units the overhead becomes substantial.

Load balancing for conservative simulation in a shared-memory environment is addressed by Gan et al. [16]. In their dynamic partitioning scheme, LPs are shared through a central pool. To use their method, it has to be decided when an LP should be put back into the pool and simulation should continue at another LP, e.g., when an LP is blocked in conservative simulation. The same decision is non-trivial in optimistic PDES.

A few works outline their load migration protocol, albeit very concisely [1, 4]. We give a detailed description of the load migration protocol and a correctness proof.

Load Metrics. Many proposed load metrics relate to either the local virtual time of each LP in relation to wall-clock time [12, 18, 27, 29, 30] or in relation to the GVT [23], in some cases also related to the number of processed or committed (i.e., with timestamp smaller than GVT) events [23, 27]. Deelman and Szymanski [10] use the number of future scheduled events, weighted by imminence. Instead, we look at the number of incurred rollbacks, which to the best of our knowledge has not been evaluated before.

In comparison to load balancing procedures of other aggregated LP approaches such as [1, 10, 30] (and to some extent [27]), our load metric is local to each basic element of computation, and not aggregated per cluster/LP (depending on notation used).

Some works have taken the communication cost between LPs in account [1, 10, 27]. In [27], a load metric and a communication metric is used alternately during migration. In [10], the communication cost of a migration is handled implicitly by only allowing whole columns of the 2-dimensional simulation state to be migrated. In [1], the migration candidate (with high load metric) with the smallest communication metric is selected. Our method is similar to that in [1], but it is local (i.e., the migration candidates come from a small region).

Initiation of Load Balancing. Many papers on load balancing in PDES prescribe that the load balancing should be initiated at regular time periods, ranging from less than 5 seconds of wall-clock time to 10 minutes of simulation time [3, 5, 18, 23, 27–29, 32, 33], sometimes also expressed in multiples of GVT computations [4, 12]. The optimal period depends on the model and the speed of the computer on which the simulator is running. In our method, load balancing is initiated by a high rollback rate, thus it is independent of the computer speed and dependent on the model to a lower degree.

Some papers have looked into a more dynamic approach to initiation of load balancing. In [1], a non-static interval is used, based on measurements taken every 3 seconds. In [7], a non-static interval is used, based on data updated every 500 events received. In [30] and [1], the authors try to account for the temporary performance decrease a load migration incur. In [1], a migration is initiated first when the integral of the actual throughput of the simulator, using migrations, is superior to the integral of a projected estimated throughput, had no load balancing taken place.

3 FRAMEWORK

Our load balancing protocol is developed in the context of spatial stochastic simulation. Since this context has influenced some of our design decisions, we describe it here briefly.

3.1 Spatial Stochastic Simulation

The reaction-diffusion master equation (RDME) [17] describes systems where entities diffuse in some volume and may undergo transitions, or reactions, when in proximity to each other. The RDME is a popular tool for modeling biological systems where the population of entities is low and discrete effects therefore play an important role for the behavior of the systems.

In the context of RDME, simulation models are defined over a spatial domain, which is discretized into *subvolumes*, also known as *voxels*. Each voxel contains a discrete *copy number* of entities of some set of species (e.g., proteins). The dynamics of the model is described by a spatially extended Markov process, in which two types of transitions are possible: (i) in a *reaction* a combination of species residing in a voxel reacts and produces a new combination within the same voxel, (ii) in a *diffusion* a single entity of a species moves to a neighboring voxel. In general, each voxel can host several types of reactions with different combinations of entities. The inter-event times between reactions and diffusions are stochastic, highly variable and without a lower bound. An important feature of typical models is that diffusions are significantly more common than reactions (by at least a factor of 10), and that the local state of each voxel is relatively simple (consisting of the copy numbers of all participating species).

Practically, the RDME is simulated using sampling methods that produce single trajectories from the relevant probability space. The most commonly used such method is the Next Subvolume Method

(NSM) [13]. The NSM algorithm takes the form of DES, whose event queue contains the next occurrence time of the next event within each voxel. The execution of that voxel event first decides (by a random draw) which particular reaction or diffusion will occur, and then performs it: the the states of concerned voxels are updated, and the voxel's next occurrence time is inserted into the event queue.

3.2 Parallelization using Standard Time Warp

Since the number of voxels is typically large, the natural approach to parallelization is to partition the set of voxels into subdomains, each of which is assigned to an LP, which is then mapped to a processing element. Each LP simulates the dynamics of its subdomain, using the NSM algorithm. We use the Time Warp synchronization mechanism [20] without optimism control. In order to support migration of voxels between LPs, voxel-specific information is stored in a self-contained structure, which for each voxel v maintains

- v.state, the local state of v,
- v.next, the time of its next event occurrence,
- v.history, the history of its processed events,
- v.routing, a routing table maps each voxel neighbor in the simulation model to the index of the LP on it is located.

We let LVT(v) be the time of the most recent event in v.history; intuitively, this is the local simulation time of voxel v. Each LP LP_i itself maintains LP-global information, viz.

- $LP_i.EventQueue$, a time-sorted event queue, containing the occurrence time of the next event of each voxel in its subdomain,
- $LP_i.bnd$, which maps each neighboring LP LP_j of LP_i to the set of voxels of LP_i that have some neighbor on LP_j. This is used to define the meaning of aggregated anti-messages (defined below), i.e., voxels in $LP_i.bnd(LP_j)$ will be rolled back when an aggregated anti-message is received from LP_j.

Each pair of neighboring LPs exchange messages via unidirectional channels. We let $chan_{i \to j}$ denote the channel from LP_i to LP_j (there is then also a channel $chan_{j \to i}$ in the opposite direction). Each diffusion to a voxel residing on a different LP induces a message to that LP. We use $v \xrightarrow{t} v'$ to represent a message denoting that a diffusion from voxel v to voxel v' has occurred at time t (the message also contains the diffused species, which we ignore here). Channels also carry other types of messages: anti-messages, and control messages associated with the migration protocol, which are described later.

Each LP advances the simulation by finding the next event to process, either from the top of its event queue or from a message that is at the front of an incoming channel. Thereafter, the event is processed by (1) updating the states of affected voxels, (2) adding the event to the histories of affected voxels, and (3) if the event was taken from the event queue, determining a new next event time for the initiating voxel. If the event is a diffusion to another LP, a diffusion message is transmitted to the neighbor.

Selective Rollback. Whenever the next event to process is an incoming diffusion message of form $v \xrightarrow{t} v'$ such that $t \leq$ LVT(v') (also called a *straggler*), a rollback is initiated. To do so, events are processed "backwards" until such a previous time is reached. A simple approach would be to roll back all events performed by the LP of v' with a time stamp higher than t. However, it is typically less costly to perform a *selective rollback*, which only rolls back events that may be causally dependent on rolled back events involving v' [2, 9]. In addition, rollback of causally dependent events performed on other LPs must be initiated by sending anti-messages to concerned LPs. In our algorithm, anti-messages are aggregated per LP, i.e., in each rollback, at most one anti-message is sent per neighboring LP. An aggregated anti-message from LP_i to LP_j only carries a single timestamp, which is the minimum timestamp of a rolled back inter-LP diffusion at LP_i which also involves LP_j. Since the anti-message is only a single timestamp, it will initiate rollback of all inter-LP diffusions involving both LP_i and LP_j, even those that are not causally dependent on the initiating straggler.

More precisely, the rollback procedure on an LP_i can be described by specifying for each voxel v of LP_i a rollback time $RBT(v)$, and for each neighbor LP_j of LP_i, a time $AMT(LP_j)$ for its anti-message. These times are the largest ones (including ∞) that satisfy the following constraints:

(1) if a straggler $v \xrightarrow{t} v'$ arrives to LP_i, then $RBT(v') < t$,
(2) if voxels v and v' of LP_i have performed a joint diffusion at time t with $RBT(v) \le t$, then $RBT(v') \le t$,
(3) if voxel v of LP_i has performed a diffusion $v \xrightarrow{t} v'$ such that $v' \in LP_j$ and $RBT(v) \le t$, then $AMT(LP_j) \le t$,
(4) if voxel v of LP_i has performed a diffusion $v \xrightarrow{t} v'$ such that $v' \in LP_j$ and $AMT(LP_j) \le t$, then $RBT(v) \le t$.

Intuitively, Conditions 1 and 2 describe the causality constraints for rolling back voxels on LP_i, Condition 3 specifies the timestamp of the aggregated anti-message to LP_j, and Condition 4 specifies the additional rollback that is caused by assuming that the anti-message represents all diffusions between LP_i and LP_j that are not earlier than $AMT(LP_j)$.

When an aggregated anti-message from LP_j with time t arrives to LP_i, then a rollback is initiated with the same constraints as above, except that condition 1 is replaced by

(1') if voxel v of LP_i has received a diffusion $v' \xrightarrow{t'} v$, with $v' \in LP_j$ and $t \le t'$, then $RBT(v) < t'$.

4 MIGRATION ALGORITHM

In this section, we describe in detail the essential algorithms involved in the migration protocol. We start by describing the data structures being used, thereafter we describe the rollback and anti-message routines, and finally we describe the processing of messages and the core migration protocol.

4.1 Migration of a Voxel

A voxel v is migrated between two LPs by sending a control message $\vec{v}$ containing v. In the implementation, what is actually sent is a pointer to the structure representing v, which includes v.history, v.routing and v.next. Both the sending and the receiving LP will update relevant status information concerning v upon sending and receiving this message. The main challenge is that any messages being in flight to the migrated voxel v have to be rerouted, and must be guaranteed to arrive in the correct order. That is, to ensure correctness, it must be guaranteed that for any pair of voxels v_0, v_1, messages sent from v_0 to v_1, including anti-messages, are received in the same order as they are sent. A particular challenge is that anti-messages are aggregated, and that their meaning changes as a

result of the migration. The protocol must therefore be carefully designed to consider also this complication.

In Algorithm 1 the procedure for sending a voxel v from LP_{src} to LP_{dst} is described. At line 2, the LOCK function ensures that no voxel neighbor to v is migrated simultaneously with v, details are described in Algorithm 3. Essentially, it atomically sets a *migration flag* on the channel to each neighboring LP that maintains a voxel neighbor to v. If one such flag already is set, i.e., the migration of some voxel neighbor v' to v has already been initiated, then the migration of v is aborted. At lines 3 and 4, v is removed from the local state. At line 6 internal routing information of v's neighboring voxels are updated to locate v on LP_{dst}. At line 7 the boundary list of voxels bordering LP_{dst} is updated to contain all neighboring voxels of v. The function returns a set of neighbors Neigh on which v had neighbors. Since the neighbors in Neigh has voxels who are neighbors to v, these neighbors have to be informed about the migration, by means of message sent at line 10. The actual voxel is sent to LP_{dst} at line 11.

Algorithm 1 Sending a voxel v from LP_{src} to some LP_{dst}.

1　**function** SENDVOXEL(v)
2　　**if** LOCK(v) **then return**
3　　$EventQueue \leftarrow \{\langle v_k, t \rangle \mid \langle v_k, t \rangle \in EventQueue \land v_k \ne v\}$
4　　State $\leftarrow$ State $\setminus v$
5　　**for each** $v_{nbr} \in LP_{src}$ that is a neighbor to v **do**
6　　　$v_{nbr}.\text{routing}[v] \leftarrow LP_{dst}$
7　　　$bnd(LP_{dst}) \leftarrow bnd(LP_{dst}) \cup v_{nbr}$
8　　**for each** $LP_k \ne LP_{src}$ with a neighbor to v **do**
9　　　remove v from $bnd(LP_k)$
10　　　SEND($mv_v(LP_{dst}), LP_k$)
11　　SEND($\vec{v}, LP_{dst}$)

Our protocol for migrating a voxel v_m from LP_{src} to LP_{dst} makes use of the following control messages.

$\overrightarrow{v_m}$ is a control message, which transfers the migrated voxel v_m,

$mv_{v_m}(LP_{dst})$ is sent by LP_{src} to each LP (except LP_{dst}) whose domain contains neighbors of v_m, announcing that the voxel v_m has just been sent to LP_{dst},

$recv_{v_m}$ is sent by LP_{dst} to each LP (except LP_{src}) whose domain contains neighbors of v_m, announcing that the voxel v_m has just been received at LP_{dst},

$forw_{v_m}$ is sent to LP_{dst} by each LP (except LP_{src}) whose domain contains neighbors of v_m, announcing that they has received $recv_{v_m}$ and is about to send normal messages (containing diffusion events) to v_m.

An overall description of the message protocol for migrating a voxel v_m follows.

- LP_{src} initiates the migration by sending $\overrightarrow{v_m}$ to LP_{dst}. At the same time, LP_{src} also sends the message mv_{v_m} to each neighbor LP_k (except LP_{dst}) whose domain contains some voxel neighbor of v_m, announcing that the voxel v_m has just been sent to LP_{dst}. For each such neighbor LP_k, and also for LP_{dst}, LP_{src} creates a temporary data structure, denoted $log_{k \to src}(v_m)$, in which it stores all received messages and anti-messages to v_m; these messages will thereafter be retrieved by LP_k in order to forward them to LP_{dst}.

- upon receipt of mv_{v_m}, each LP_k (except LP_{src} and LP_{dst}) which formerly sent messages to v_m via $chan_{k \to src}$, will first send the message $forw_{v_m}$ to LP_{dst}, announcing that it will start to send messages to v_m over $chan_{k \to dst}$. Thereafter, it retrieves all such messages sent, but not yet received, from $log_{k \to src}(v_m)$ and $chan_{k \to src}$, and thereafter forwards them (in order) to LP_{dst} (over $chan_{k \to dst}$).
- Upon receipt of $\overrightarrow{v_m}$, LP_{dst} sends a message $recv_{v_m}$ to LPs (except LP_{src}) whose domain contains neighbors of v_m, announcing that the voxel v_m has been received at LP_{dst}. Thereafter, it will (in the same manner as LP_k in the previous step) retrieve all messages to v_m sent, but not yet received, from $log_{dst \to src}(v_m)$ and $chan_{dst \to src}$. The events in these messages are then rolled back.

The control messages $recv_{v_m}$ and $forw_{v_m}$ block, i.e., prevent any message from being received, from the channels from which they were retrieved, unless $mv_{v_m} < recv_{v_m}$ and $\overrightarrow{v_m} < forw_{v_m}$, respectively (where $<$ denotes order of reception).

In Algorithm 2, the detailed protocol logic for how an LP handles the different types of incoming messages is described. For each message type, the description refers to lines in Algorithm 2, unless stated otherwise. In the algorithm, the LP where a message is received is denoted LP_i, and the sending LP is denoted LP_k.

$\overrightarrow{v}$ The message $\overrightarrow{v}$ carries a migrating voxel v. Upon receipt of $\overrightarrow{v}$, LP_i first updates its bookkeeping information: v is added to the local state (lines 3 and 4), the routing tables of v's neighboring voxels are updated (lines 5 to 8), v is marked as located on LP_i in each neighbouring voxel's internal routing table (line 6), and v's local neighbors are also removed from the list of voxels bordering LP_k, if they no longer have any neighbours on LP_k (line 8). Thereafter, a message $recv_v$ is sent to each LP (other than LP_k) with a neighbor voxel of v, informing that the migration has completed (line 11). If any incoming channel is closed due to the migration of v (i.e., a message $forw_v$ has been received from some LP_j), it can now be reopened (line 12). Thereafter, LP_i retrieves all pending messages sent from LP_i to v, from the temporary structure $log_{i \to k}(v)$ stored at LP_k and from $chan_{i \to k}$; this retrieval also transforms aggregated anti-messages (with only a time t) into voxel-specific anti-messages (denoted $-t_v$). The retrieval from the channel is performed in the function Project, described by (1) below. The sequence of retrieved messages are collected into the ordered list M_v (line 13). The projected diffusions are simultaneously removed from the corresponding channel, and the migration flag for v in $chan_{i \to k}$ is unset, indicating that no more messages should be added to the backlog $log_{i \to k}(v)$ when messages are received from $chan_{i \to k}$ (lines 15 and 16). Finally, the state of v and the messages in M_v are rolled back (lines 17 to 20), to avoid any ordering conflicts of future and already sent messages.

$mv_v(LP_j)$ This type of message is sent to LPs that have voxel neighbors to some migrating voxel $\overrightarrow{v}$ destined for LP_j, but which are not the recipient of $\overrightarrow{v}$ (at line 10 in Algorithm 1). Upon the receipt of the message at some LP_i, retrieves into M_v all pending messages sent from LP_i to v, from the temporary structure $logik(v)$ stored at LP_k and from $chan_{i \to k}$ in

the same way as described for messages of type $\overrightarrow{v}$ (using the function Project). The messages in M_v are forwarded to LP_j, the new LP of v, in the same order they previously were sent to LP_k, prefixed by a message of type $forw_v$ (lines 26 and 27). Thereafter, for each voxel-neighbor v_n to v residing on LP_i, the LPs boundary information is updated as follows: If v_n has no other voxel neighbors on LP_k, then v_n is removed from the list of voxels representing the boundary to LP_k (line 31). The set of v's voxel neighbors is then stored in $mvbnd$, tagged with v (line 32). The voxels will later be added to the boundary of LP_k facing LP_j. If the channel from LP_j to LP_i is marked as closed, then it is reopened, and each voxel-neighbor v_n are immediately added to the list of voxels bordering to LP_j (lines 33 to 36).

$recv_v$ This type of message is sent by the LP receiving a message $\overrightarrow{v}$ to LPs that are not the sender of the message $\overrightarrow{v}$, but have voxels neighboring v. Upon receipt of a message $recv_v$ at LP_i, a check is done whether a corresponding message mv_v has been received, by checking if tag v exists in the set $mvbnd$ (line 38). If not, the channel to LP_i is closed to enforce that a message mv_v is received first for each migration of a voxel. Otherwise, the set of v's neighboring voxels on LP_k, previously bordering LP_i, are now included in the boundary towards LP_j (line 41).

$forw_v$ This type of message is sent by an LP that has voxels neighboring some recently migrated voxel v, but was neither the sender nor the recipient of the corresponding migration message $\overrightarrow{v}$. It is sent to the LP to which v has been migrated. The message indicates that after the transmission of $forw_v$ from LP_k to LP_j, LP_k starts forwarding messages destined for v to LP_j. Upon receipt of $forw_w$, LP_j checks if $\overrightarrow{v}$ has already been received. If not, the channel $chan_{k \to j}$ is closed (line 50). This enforces that $\overrightarrow{v}$ is received before any messages destined for v.

$-t$ When receiving an anti-message $-t$ from LP_k at time t, the history of each voxel v that may have received a diffusion from LP_k is scanned (line 43). If there is such a diffusion $w \xrightarrow{t'} v, w \in LP_k$ which happened after t, rollback v_i to t' (line 44). Then, for all voxels that have been migrated to some other LP, say LP_j, and who previously were on the boundary to LP_k (and thus have an entry in $chan_{k \to i}$.flags), a copy of the anti-message is put in the corresponding backlog (line 45).

$w \xrightarrow{t} v$ When receiving a diffusion, if the receiving voxel v has migrated, the diffusion is added to the backlog of messages for v, located on $chan_{k \to i}$ (line 53). If the diffusion is a straggler, a rollback is performed (line 55), before processing the diffusion (line 56).

The Project function (1) extracts all messages in a channel $chan$ destined for a voxel v. It should be noted, that the channel is protected by a lock, thus the effect of Project is observed to take place instantaneously for any LP. The projection is done as follows: The messages in $chan$ are recursively traversed. Diffusions destined for v are returned, and anti-messages $-t$ are converted to local anti-messages $-t_v$, only affecting v. Other messages are

Algorithm 2 Receipt of message from LP_k at LP_i.

1 **function** HANDLEMESSAGE(m)
2   **if** $m = \vec{v}$ **then**
3     $EventQueue \leftarrow$ insert $(EventQueue, \langle v.\text{next}, v \rangle)$
4     $State \leftarrow State \cup v$
5   **for each** $v_{\text{nbr}} \in LP_i$ that is a neighbor to v **do**
6       $v_{\text{nbr}}.\text{routing}[v] \leftarrow LP_i$
7   **if** v_{nbr} has no more neighbors on LP_k **then**
8   remove v_{nbr} from $bnd(LP_k)$
9   add v to $bnd(LP_k)$
10   **for each** $LP_j \neq LP_k$ with a neighbor to v **do**
11   SEND(recv_v, LP_j)
12   **if** $chan_{j \to i}$ closed by migration of v **then** open $chan_{j \to i}$
13    $M_v \leftarrow log_{i \to k}(v) + \text{PROJECT}(chan_{i \to k}, v)$
14    $log_{i \to k}(v) \leftarrow \emptyset$
15   remove all diffusions destined for v from $chan_{i \to k}$
16   remove $\langle v, LP_k \rangle$ from $chan_{i \to k}.\text{flags}$
17    $t_{\min} \leftarrow \min\{ t \mid w \xrightarrow{t} v \in M_v \vee -t \in M_v \vee -t_v \in M_v \}$
18   ROLLBACK($v, t_{\min}$)
19   **for each** $w \xrightarrow{t} v \in M_v$ **do**
20   ROLLBACK(w, t)
21   **if** $m = \text{mv}_v(LP_j)$ **then**
22    $M_v \leftarrow log_{i \to k}(v) + \text{PROJECT}(chan_{i \to k}, v)$
23    $log_{i \to k}(v) \leftarrow \emptyset$
24   remove all diffusions destined for v from $chan_{i \to k}$
25   remove $\langle v, LP_k \rangle$ from $chan_{i \to k}.\text{flags}$
26   SEND(forw_v, LP_j)
27   SEND(M_v, LP_j)
28    $V_{\text{bnd}} \leftarrow \{v_{\text{nbr}} \mid v_{\text{nbr}} \in LP_i \wedge v_{\text{nbr}} \text{ neighbor to } v\}$
29   **for each** $v_{\text{nbr}} \in V_{\text{bnd}}$ **do**
30   **if** v_{nbr} has no more neighbors on LP_k **then**
31   remove v_{nbr} from $bnd(LP_k)$
32      $mvbnd \leftarrow mvbnd \cup \langle v, V_{\text{bnd}} \rangle$
33   **if** $chan_{j \to i}.\text{closed}$ **then**
34      $bnd(LP_j) \leftarrow bnd(LP_j) \cup V_{\text{bnd}}$ s.t. $\langle v, V_{\text{bnd}} \rangle \in mvbnd$
35   **if** $chan_{j \to i}$ closed by migration of v **then**
36   open $chan_{j \to i}$
37   **if** $m = \text{recv}_v$ **then**
38   **if** $\nexists V_{\text{bnd}}.\langle v, V_{\text{bnd}} \rangle \in mvbnd$ **then**
39   close channel $chan_{k \to i}$
40   **else**
41      $bnd(LP_k) \leftarrow bnd(LP_k) \cup V_{\text{bnd}}$s.t.$\langle v, V_{\text{bnd}} \rangle \in mvbnd$
42   **if** $m = -t$ **then**   ▷ *Aggregated anti-message*
43   **for each** $v \in bnd(LP_k)$ **do**
44   ROLLBACK(v, t)   ▷ *According to (1'), Section 3*
45   **for each** $\langle v, LP_j \rangle \in chan_{k \to i}.\text{flags}$ **do**
46      $log_{j \to i}(v) \leftarrow log_{j \to i}(v) \cdot -t_v$
47   **if** $m = -t_v$ **then**   ▷ *Local anti-message*
48   ROLLBACK(v, t)   ▷ *According to (1'), Section 3*
49   **if** type $= \text{forw}_v$ **then**
50   **if** $v \notin State$ **then** close $chan_{k \to i}$
51   **if** $m = w \xrightarrow{t} v$ **then**   ▷ *Regular diffusion to v*
52   **if** $v \notin State$ **then**   ▷ *v is migrated to some other LP*
53      $log_{k \to i}(v) \leftarrow log_{k \to i}(v) \cdot m$
54   **if** $t \leq LVT(v)$ **then**   ▷ *Handle straggler*
55   ROLLBACK(v, t)
56   process $w \xrightarrow{t} v$

filtered out.

$$\text{PROJECT}(chan, v) = \begin{cases} m \cdot \text{PROJECT}(chan, v) & \text{if } m = w \xrightarrow{t} v \\ -t_v \cdot \text{PROJECT}(chan, v) & \text{if } m = -t \\ \text{PROJECT}(chan, v) & \text{otherwise} \end{cases} \quad (1)$$

In Algorithm 3, we see the mechanism for preventing simultaneous migrations of neighboring voxels. For all channels coming from LPs where v has a neighbor, a migration flag is set marking that an attempt migrating v is undertaken (line 5). If, after having set the flag, a flag of the corresponding neighbor is seen on the outgoing channel, all flags already set on the channels are unset, and the lock procedure returns false (line 8). If the procedure manages to set all flags without seeing a flag set on a corresponding outgoing channel, it has succeeded the migration may take place, and returns true.

Algorithm 3 Prevent simultaneous migration of a voxel v from LP_i and any of its neighbors v_n.

1 **function** LOCK(v)
2   $V_n \leftarrow \{v_n \mid v_n \notin LP_i \wedge v_n \text{ neighbor to } v\}$
3   **for each** $v_n \in V_n$ **do**
4     $m \leftarrow v.\text{routing}[v_n]$
5     $chan_{m \to i}.\text{flags} \leftarrow chan_{m \to i}.\text{flags} \cup v$
6   **if** $v_n \in chan_{i \to m}.\text{flags}$ **then**
7   unset all set flags and **abort**
8   **return false**
9   **return true**

p

5 CORRECTNESS

In this section, we give a proof for the correctness of our migration protocol. It is inspired by that of [22], but adapted to cover our version of time-warp with aggregated anti-messages and voxel migration. We will focus on the property of safety: that any parallel execution produces the same simulation run as the corresponding sequential simulation algorithm. The notion of "produced simulation run" is well-defined if the simulation model is deterministic, so that a simulation run is uniquely determined by the initial state and the transition rules, which in our case are fixed (we make the assumption that no two events in a voxel have exactly the same time-stamp). In the presence of random events, the simulation is made deterministic by using deterministic pseudorandom number generators, whose states are included in the local states of the corresponding voxels, and which are reverted together with the voxel state when performing rollbacks.

As described in Section 3, our simulation models consist of voxels, which evolve the state of the model by performing reactions, which are local, and diffusions that also affect the state of a neighbouring voxel. Within a voxel v, the simulation run is defined by the ordered sequence $v.\text{history}$ of its processed time-stamped events. We define $\text{In}^{v'}(v)$ as the sequence of processed incoming diffusion from v' in $v.\text{history}$, and let $\text{Out}^{v'}(v)$ be the sequence of sent diffusions to voxel v' in $v.\text{history}$. A sequential simulation run satisfies the following two properties.

(i) The history $v.\text{history}$ in a sequential simulation is the one that is uniquely determined by following the simulation rules from the initial voxel state and the sequences $\mathrm{In}^{v'}(v)$ of processed incoming diffusion messages from each neighbour v' in the simulation model.

(ii) For each pair v, v' of neigbour voxels in the simulation model, $\mathrm{In}^v(v') = \mathrm{Out}^{v'}(v)$, i.e., the sequence of incoming diffusions to v' from v is the same as the sequence of outgoing diffusions from v to v'.

Property (i) uses the assumption that no two events in v.history have exactly the same timestamp. Property (ii) follows by noting that in a sequential simulation, a diffusion from v to v' is simultaneously added both to v.history and to v'.history.

Conversely, any completed simulation run, which is constructed from voxel histories that satisfy (i) and (ii) is the same as the uniquely defined simulation run. We can then establish safety of the parallel simulation by proving that it satisfies properties (i) and (ii).

Property (i) for the parallel simulation algorithm can be established by checking that each step (both forward simulation steps and rollbacks) in the simulation algorithm respect the rules of the simulated model. This is not difficult, an we omit the details.

Property (ii) is less straightforward: in general it does not hold during the simulation run, since diffusion messages and anti-messages may be in transit between v and v' when they reside on different LPs. We will therefore replace property (ii) by a set of invariants that hold during the simulation, and which imply property (ii) when the simulation is completed and channels are empty. In the remainder of this section, we will formulate and prove this set of invariants. In Subsection 5.1 we formulate and prove them for our version of the underlying Time Warp algorithm. Then, in Subsection 5.2, we will extend them to our migration protocol.

Notation. We say a message is of the form $v \rightarrow v'$ if it is sent from v and destined for v'. We write a timestamp ordered sequence of messages $m_0 \cdot m_1 \cdots m_n$, where we let m_0 be the oldest message in the sequence, and m_n the most recent. We use $+\!\!\!+$ to denote concatenation of sequences. We let $\mathrm{In}^v(v')$ be the sequence of processed diffusion messages of form $v \rightarrow v'$ in v'.history, and let $\mathrm{Out}^{v'}(v)$ be the sequence of sent diffusion messages of form $v \rightarrow v'$ in v.history. In particular, no anti-messages occur in the histories. The time of the earliest anti-message affecting a voxel v (aggregated or local), in a channel $chan$, is denoted $chan.\mathrm{min}(v)$. If there is no such anti-message, $chan.\mathrm{min}(v)$ is ∞.

5.1 Correctness for Time Warp

Intra-LP Consistency. For all pairs v, v' of voxel, that reside on the same LP, the incoming and outgoing diffusion histories are always consistent.

$$\mathrm{In}^v(v') = \mathrm{Out}^{v'}(v). \tag{IV1}$$

PROOF SKETCH OF (IV1). Since each LP processes messages in timestamp order, all diffusions from v to v' are added in timestamp order. At each processing of some event with a timestamp t, both $\mathrm{In}^v(v')$ and $\mathrm{Out}^{v'}(v)$ will be extended with the same diffusion. A local rollback caused by a straggler or received anti-message will, by rule (2) of the rollback operation, remove all diffusions from both $\mathrm{In}^v(v')$ and $\mathrm{Out}^{v'}(v)$ whose timestamps are greater than some common time t, thereby preserving (IV1). □

Inter-LP Consistency. In the case where the two voxels reside on different LPs, messages reside in a channel $chan$ connecting the two LPs, before being received. Thus we must characterize the relationship between in- and out-histories at voxels and the messages in the corresponding channels. To this end, we define the *effect* with respect to voxels v and v' of the messages in a sequence $chan$, denoted $\mathrm{effect}_{v \rightarrow v'}(chan)$, as follows.

$$\underset{v \rightarrow v'}{\mathrm{effect}}(chan \cdot m) = \begin{cases} \underset{v \rightarrow v'}{\mathrm{effect}}(chan) \cdot m & \text{if } m = v \xrightarrow{t} v' \\ \underset{v \rightarrow v'}{\mathrm{rm}_t(\mathrm{effect}}(chan)) & \text{if } m = -t \text{ or } m = -t_{v'} \\ \underset{v \rightarrow v'}{\mathrm{effect}}(chan) & \text{otherwise} \end{cases} \tag{2}$$

where $\mathrm{rm}_t(chan)$ is obtained by removing all messages with timestamp $\geq t$ from $chan$. Intuitively, $\mathrm{effect}_{v \rightarrow v'}(chan)$ is the subsequence of diffusions from v to v' in $chan$ that will not be reverted by a later anti-message in $chan$. This property can be derived from (2) and expressed as the following property of $\mathrm{effect}_{v \rightarrow v'}(chan)$.

$$\underset{v \rightarrow v'}{\mathrm{effect}}(m \cdot chan) = \begin{cases} m \cdot \underset{v \rightarrow v'}{\mathrm{effect}}(chan) & \text{if } m = v \xrightarrow{t} v' \text{ and} \\ & (\nexists m' \in chan.\exists t' \geq t. \\ & (m' = -t' \text{ or } m' = -t'_{v'})) \\ \underset{v \rightarrow v'}{\mathrm{effect}}(chan) & \text{otherwise} \end{cases} \tag{3}$$

Let v and v' be two neighboring voxels on two different LPs, communicating through a channel $chan$, and let $t = chan.\mathrm{min}(v')$. Then the sequences of diffusions from v to v' in the two voxel histories are related by the following invariant.

$$\mathrm{rm}_t(\mathrm{In}^v(v')) +\!\!\!+ \underset{v \rightarrow v'}{\mathrm{effect}}(chan) = \mathrm{Out}^{v'}(v) \tag{IV2}$$

PROOF SKETCH OF (IV2). We establish the invariant by induction over the length of a simulation run. Initially, $\mathrm{In}^v(v')$ and $\mathrm{Out}^{v'}(v)$ and the channel are empty, and the invariant holds trivially. Assume non-empty $\mathrm{In}^v(v')$ and $\mathrm{Out}^{v'}(v)$, and a state of the channel $chan$ such that Invariant (IV2) holds. We will let $\mathrm{In}'^v(v')$, $\mathrm{Out}'^{v'}(v)$, and $chan'$ be their states after the performed action. Let $t = chan.\mathrm{min}(v')$. Line numbers refer to Algorithm 2. We get the following cases depending on the performed action.

- v's LP sends a diffusion m of form $v \xrightarrow{t} v'$ to v''s LP. Then $\mathrm{In}'^v(v') = \mathrm{In}^v(v')$, and $\mathrm{Out}'^{v'}(v) = \mathrm{Out}^{v'}(v) \cdot m$, and $chan' = chan \cdot m$. We get
  $\mathrm{Out}'^{v'}(v) = \mathrm{Out}^{v'}(v) \cdot m = $ (by (IV2))
  $\mathrm{rm}_t(\mathrm{In}^v(v')) +\!\!\!+ \mathrm{effect}_{v \rightarrow v'}(chan) \cdot m = $ (by (2))
  $\mathrm{rm}_t(\mathrm{In}^v(v')) +\!\!\!+ \mathrm{effect}_{v \rightarrow v'}(chan \cdot m) = $
  $\mathrm{rm}_t(\mathrm{In}'^v(v')) +\!\!\!+ \mathrm{effect}_{v \rightarrow v'}(chan \cdot m)$.

- v's LP sends an aggregated anti-message $-\hat{t}$ to v''s LP, while reverting diffusions in $\mathrm{Out}^{v'}(v)$ with a timestamp $\geq \hat{t}$, since $v \in \mathrm{LP}_{\mathrm{dst}}.bnd(\mathrm{LP}_{\mathrm{src}})$ (Condition 4 in the the calculation of RBT in the rollback operation in Section 3). Let $t' = \mathrm{min}(t, \hat{t})$. Then $t' = chan'.\mathrm{min}(v')$.
  We have $\mathrm{Out}'^{v'}(v) = \mathrm{rm}_{\hat{t}}(\mathrm{Out}^{v'}(v)) = $ (by (IV2))
  $\mathrm{rm}_{\hat{t}}(\mathrm{rm}_t(\mathrm{In}^v(v'))) +\!\!\!+ \mathrm{rm}_{\hat{t}}(\mathrm{effect}_{v \rightarrow v'}(chan)) = $ (by (2))
  $\mathrm{rm}_{t'}(\mathrm{In}^v(v')) +\!\!\!+ \mathrm{effect}_{v \rightarrow v'}(chan \cdot -\hat{t}) = $
  $\mathrm{rm}_{t'}(\mathrm{In}'^v(v')) +\!\!\!+ \mathrm{effect}_{v \rightarrow v'}(chan')$.

- v''s LP receives a diffusion m of form $v \xrightarrow{t} v'$ from v's LP (line 51). Details are analogous and omitted.

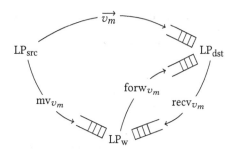

Figure 1: Schematic of LPs involved in the migration of voxel v_m, and the types of messages, $\overrightarrow{v_m}, \mathrm{mv}_{v_m}, \mathrm{recv}_{v_m}$ and forw_{v_m}, being involved in the migration.

- v''s LP receives an anti-message of form $-\hat{t}$ or $-\hat{t}_{v'}$ from v's LP, reverting diffusions in $\mathrm{In}^v(v')$ with a timestamp $\geq \hat{t}$ (lines 42 and 47). Again, details are analogous.

$\square$

5.2 Correctness for the Migration Protocol

In this section, we show that the algorithm maintains consistency when extended with migrations of voxels between two LPs. The migration protocol introduces several types of control messages, viz., $\overrightarrow{v_m}, \mathrm{mv}_{v_m}, \mathrm{recv}_{v_m}$ and forw_m. Since the migration protocol does not modify the histories of voxels directly, effect is defined to ignore such control messages c, i.e., $\mathrm{effect}_{v \to v'}(chan \cdot c) = \mathrm{effect}_{v \to v'}(chan)$.

An aggregated anti-message $-t$ changes in meaning when a voxel v_m is migrated from $\mathrm{LP}_{\mathrm{src}}$ to $\mathrm{LP}_{\mathrm{dst}}$. If $-t$ is sent from $\mathrm{LP}_{\mathrm{src}}$, after $\overrightarrow{v_m}$, then it does not affect messages sent from v_m to v on $\mathrm{LP}_{\mathrm{dst}}$, which is achieved by the removal of v_m from bnd in the algorithms (line 9 in Algorithm 1 and line 8 in Algorithm 2). To capture this, we define an operator $\mathrm{cut}_{m'}$, which simply truncates a sequence after the first occurrence of m', by

$$\mathrm{cut}_{m'}(m \cdot chan) = \begin{cases} m & \text{if } m = m' \\ m \cdot \mathrm{cut}_{m'}(chan) & \text{otherwise} \end{cases}$$

5.2.1 Consistency between sender and receiver of migrated voxel. Now, we are ready to define the invariants. Let v_m and v be two neighboring voxels, where v_m, previously located on $\mathrm{LP}_{\mathrm{src}}$, is being migrated to the same LP as v, $\mathrm{LP}_{\mathrm{dst}}$. We have to show the consistency of messages in both directions relative the migration direction. After the transmission of $\overrightarrow{v_m}$, and before $\overrightarrow{v_m}$ has been received, we have the following two invariants.

- For diffusions from v_m to v:
  Let $t = (\mathrm{cut}_{\overrightarrow{v_m}}(chan_{\mathrm{src} \to \mathrm{dst}})).\min(v)$. Then we have

  $$\mathrm{rm}_t(\mathrm{In}^{v_m}(v)) + \underset{v_m \to v}{\mathrm{effect}}(\mathrm{cut}_{\overrightarrow{v_m}}(chan_{\mathrm{src} \to \mathrm{dst}})) \\ = \mathrm{Out}^v(v_m). \tag{IV3}$$

  This invariant is analogous to (IV2), but considers only the part of $chan_{\mathrm{src} \to \mathrm{dst}}$ that precedes $\overrightarrow{v_m}$.

- For diffusions from v to v_m:
  Let $t = (log_{\mathrm{dst} \to \mathrm{src}}(v_m) + chan_{\mathrm{dst} \to \mathrm{src}}).\min(v_m)$. Then

  $$\mathrm{rm}_t(\mathrm{In}^v(v_m)) + \underset{v \to v_m}{\mathrm{effect}}(log_{\mathrm{dst} \to \mathrm{src}}(v_m) + chan_{\mathrm{dst} \to \mathrm{src}}) \\ = \mathrm{Out}^{v_m}(v). \tag{IV4}$$

  This invariant extends (IV2) by considering that diffusions from v to $\overrightarrow{v_m}$ are collected in $log_{\mathrm{dst} \to \mathrm{src}}(v_m)$.

We note that v_m neither can send nor receive any messages while in transit, thus the proof of Equation (3) is only concerned with v receiving a message, and the proof of Equation (4) is only concerned with v sending a message.

5.2.2 Correctness of receipt of migrated voxel. During migration of a voxel v_m, consistency is defined by Equations (3) and (4). When the migrated voxel v_m has been received and processed by $\mathrm{LP}_{\mathrm{dst}}$, these invariants are replaced by Invariant (IV1), stating that v_m is locally consistent with all its neighbors $v \in \mathrm{LP}_{\mathrm{dst}}$. Again, we omit the details.

5.2.3 Consistency between voxel being migrated and neighboring voxels on other domains. Let v_m, v be two neighboring voxels, where v_m is being migrated from $\mathrm{LP}_{\mathrm{src}}$ to $\mathrm{LP}_{\mathrm{dst}}$ and v is located on a third LP, LP_{w}, as depicted in Figure 1. At the transmission of $\overrightarrow{v_m}$, a message mv_{v_m} is sent to all neighboring LPs except the receiver of $\overrightarrow{v_m}$ (line 10 in Algorithm 1). At the receipt of $\overrightarrow{v_m}$, a message recv_{v_m} is sent to all neighbors, except the sender of $\overrightarrow{v_m}$ (line 11 in Algorithm 2). Thus, in the following, we have to take into account if the control messages mv_{v_m} and recv_{v_m} have been received or not, since they affect the protocol. We split the argument into the two possible directions in which messages may be sent, viz. $v_m \to v$ and $v \to v_m$.

Case $v_m \to v$: We let $-t$ be the earliest anti-message preceding the message mv_{v_m} in $chan_{\mathrm{src} \to \mathrm{w}}$ or succeeding the message recv_{v_m} in $chan_{\mathrm{dst} \to \mathrm{w}}$. The cut operator reflects that anti-messages change in meaning upon receipt of mv_{v_m} (line 31 in algorithm 2). After the transmission of $\overrightarrow{v_m}$, but before mv_{v_m} has been received by LP_{w}, we have

$$\mathrm{rm}_t(\mathrm{In}^{v_m}(v)) + \underset{v_m \to v}{\mathrm{effect}}(\mathrm{cut}_{\mathrm{mv}_{v_m}}(chan_{\mathrm{src} \to \mathrm{w}}) + chan_{\mathrm{dst} \to \mathrm{w}}) \\ = \mathrm{Out}^v(v_m). \tag{IV5}$$

Intuitively, this invariant extends (IV2) by considering that diffusions from v_m to v are found preceding mv_{v_m} in $chan_{\mathrm{src} \to \mathrm{w}}$. After the reception of v_m by $\mathrm{LP}_{\mathrm{dst}}$, they are then transmitted over $chan_{\mathrm{dst} \to \mathrm{w}}$. We also note, that after the reception of mv_{v_m} by LP_{w}, any outstanding diffusions from v_m to v are in $chan_{\mathrm{dst} \to \mathrm{w}}$, obeying the corresponding instance of (IV2).

Case $v \to v_m$: In this direction, we have two cases, depending on whether LP_{w} has yet observed the migration or not:

- mv_{v_m} has been received by LP_{w}.
  We let t be the time of the earliest anti-message in $chan_{\mathrm{w} \to \mathrm{dst}}$ following forw_{v_m}; if forw_{v_m} is not in $chan_{\mathrm{w} \to \mathrm{dst}}$, let t be the time of the earliest anti-message in $chan_{\mathrm{w} \to \mathrm{dst}}$. Then

  $$\mathrm{rm}_t(\mathrm{In}^v(v_m)) + \underset{v \to v_m}{\mathrm{effect}}(chan_{\mathrm{w} \to \mathrm{dst}}) = \mathrm{Out}^v(v_m) \tag{IV6}$$

  This invariant is essentially the same as (IV2).

- mv_{v_m} has not been received by LP_w.
  We let t be the time of the earliest anti-message in $log_{w \to src}(v_m)$ and $chan_{w \to src}$.

$$rm_t(In^v(v_m)) + \underset{v \to v_m}{\text{effect}}(log_{w \to src}(v_m) + chan_{w \to src}) \\ = Out^v(v_m) \tag{IV7}$$

This invariant reflects that messages from v to v_m are stored in $log_{w \to src}(v_m)$ until mv_{v_m} is received by LP_w.

Invariants (IV6) and (7) are also established by induction over the steps of the algorithm. Details are omitted for space reasons.

6 LOAD BALANCING

In this section, we describe the load metric, the communication metric, and the load balancing algorithm that we use for the evaluation of the load migration protocol in the next section.

Load balancing can be seen as an online local rebalancing technique for data partitioning. In our case, the simulator is given an initial partition of the model, generated offline by the METIS library [21]. Due to factors not available to the offline partitioning, such as a dynamic or variable load, the partitions may need continuous rebalancing locally to ensure that the load remains balanced. Data partitioning and rebalancing algorithms typically try to optimize for a balanced workload and minimize communication.

For the evaluation of the migration protocol we selected a load balancing that takes two metrics into account: a load metric based on the number of rollbacks caused by stragglers received at a particular voxel, which is used to initiate a load balancing locally, and a communication minimizing step that selects some voxel in the vicinity whose migration minimizes communication. Below, we first define the metrics, and then the load balancing algorithm.

The load metric is defined per voxel. We define the *inverse voxel load* for a period of wall-clock time Δt and voxel v as

$$L_v = \frac{\Delta t}{\Delta r_v},$$

where Δr_v is the total number of rollbacks during time Δt, including secondary, that are incurred due to stragglers received at v. The measure could be seen as the mean distance, in wall clock time, between two consecutive rollbacks. The *inverse rate of rollbacks* is then defined as the limit of L_v as Δt goes to 0.

We define the communication metric, or the *gain*, of a voxel v on LP LP_i relative a neighboring LP LP_j as

$$g_{ij}(v) = \frac{||\{E(v, v') \mid v' \in LP_j\}||}{||\{E(v, v') \mid v' \in LP_i\}||},$$

where $E(v, v')$ denotes an edge, i.e., a communication channel, between v and v'. Thus, the gain is defined as the *external degree* towards LP_j over the *internal degree*. The gain as defined above describes how well connected a voxel is to its domain.

The load balancing algorithm is defined in terms of the load metric and the gain of a voxel. If the inverse rate of rollbacks surpasses a threshold, R, then a request for load balancing is sent to the LP LP_{src} that sent the last straggler to v (a simplification, which nevertheless should result in a correct destination of the request most of the time). Upon receipt of the request at LP_{src}, the voxel neighbor to v with the highest gain is selected for migration. To limit bad migrations that do not improve the load or communication balance,

we introduce a *gain threshold*, G, so that only voxels with a gain superior to G may be migrated.

The successful migration of one or more of the neighboring voxels to v, based on the load and communication metrics defined above, would serve two purposes. First, migrating voxels balances the amount of work between two LPs, and potentially reduces the number of future rollbacks. Second, a high rate of rollbacks at the boundary also means a high rate of local communication between two or more voxels located on different LPs. The migration thus also reduces inter-LP communication, if the voxels to migrate are chosen wisely, e.g., by selecting to migrate the voxel that minimizes the communication.

7 EVALUATION

In this section, we evaluate the performance of the migration protocol coupled with the load balancing algorithm and the load and communication metrics defined in Section 6. We try to specifically understand the performance of the migration protocol and its shortcomings, as it can be used together with many different load balancing algorithms and load and communication metrics.

We look at the following questions:

- What is the overhead of the migration protocol? (Section 7.4)
- How to tune the threshold for the load measure? (Section 7.5)
- How well does the protocol, together with a load balancing algorithm, adapt to a changing load? (Section 7.6)
- How does load balancing perform compared to optimism control? (Section 7.7)

7.1 Algorithms Evaluated

For the evaluation of the load balancing algorithm, we use three algorithms:

NSM An efficient sequential NSM implementation, taken from the URDME framework[11].

R-PNSM The so-called Refined PNSM algorithm of [24], that uses optimism control.

PNSM-LB The load balancing parallel NSM algorithm described in this paper, derived from the R-PNSM algorithm.

We compare the results of the PNSM-LB algorithm with and without load balancing activated to the sequential NSM algorithm and the parallel R-PNSM algorithm. Of particular interest is that the R-PNSM algorithm include optimizations that are possible when statically assigning the partitions to LPs. One such optimization is that there is only a single rollback history per LP. In contrast, the load balancing parallel NSM algorithm of this paper has arranged the data so that each voxel easily can be moved from one LP to another; in particular, each voxel has its own rollback history. We can estimate the cost of the compromises that we have taken when restructuring the parallel NSM algorithm to enable load migration, by comparing the performance of the PNSM-LB algorithm without load balancing to the performance of the R-PNSM algorithm.

7.2 Benchmarks

To evaluate the algorithm, we use two types of benchmarks:

- Simulation of the Min-protein system in a three-dimensional unstructured (i.e., an irregular mesh) model of the *E. coli* bacterium [14]. The Min-protein has a central role in the cell division of the bacterium, where the oscillation of the min-proteins help determine the position of the septum, the new cell wall. The model consists of 5 species, and the dynamics are described by 5 reactions. It is complicated by some reactions only taking place on the membrane of the cell. We present data for two different stages of cell division, short and long, comprising 1500 and 2700 voxels, respectively. The two models are denoted mincde[s] and mincde[L], respectively. Due to the oscillation of the proteins, the load is highly dynamic. Since the number of voxels is small, the amount of available parallelism is limited.

- Simulation of a reversible isomerization process, where two species are randomly transformed into each other, and may diffuse freely with equal diffusion rates within a spherical domain. The domain is represented as a 3-dimensional unstructured mesh, and comprises ∼ 13000 voxels. The load is well balanced, and the number of reaction events stand in a 1:10 proportion to the number of diffusions events. The model is denoted sphere.

7.3 Experimental Setup

The experiments are run on a 4 socket Intel Sandy Bridge E5–4650 machine. Each processor has 8 cores and 20 MB L3-cache. Hyper-threading was turned off, and threads were pinned to cores. The operating system of the machine is Linux 4.9.0, and the binaries were compiled using GCC version 6.3.0. The models were initially partitioned using the multilevel k-way partitioning method from the METIS library [21].

7.4 Overhead of Migration Protocol

We would like to understand how much overhead the migration protocol incurs during a simulation. The migration of a voxel may cause rollbacks, which in turn may cause anti-messages. Therefore, we have traced the time spent sending and receiving all types of control messages involved in a migration, including time spent on processing rollbacks and anti-messages generated by the migration of a voxel. In none of the benchmark runs presented here did the total cost of the migration protocol exceed 0.5%.

7.5 Tuning of the Rate and Gain Parameters

In this section, we tune the inverse rollback rate parameter R for locally initiating a migration of a voxel and the gain threshold parameter G, as described in Section 6.

In Figures 2 and 3, results for tuning of the inverse rollback rate parameter R and the gain threshold parameter G of the migration mechanisms is presented. In the figures, each line represents one value of the gain threshold. R is varied from 0 (no migration) to 80, and the gain threshold is varied from 0.5 to 0.7. The left hand sub-figure within each figure shows the speedup relative to not using migration, and the right hand sub-figure shows the total number of rollbacks occurring during the simulation. In Figure 2 the tuning is done on the mincde[s] benchmark for 3 threads. The maximum speedup, of about 15% over when no migration is used, is reached with a rollback rate threshold R of 40, and a gain threshold G of 0.6–0.7. In Figure 3, the tuning is done on the same benchmark, run

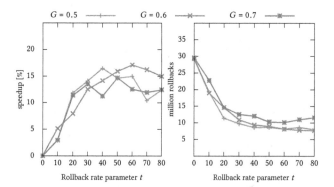

Figure 2: Inverse rollback rate parameter R impact on the number of rollbacks and speedup. Evaluated on the mincde[s] benchmark, 3 threads. Speedup relative $R = 0$.

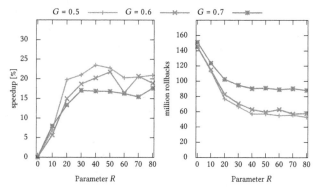

Figure 3: Inverse rollback rate parameter R impact on the number of rollbacks and speedup. Evaluated on the mincde[s] benchmark, 16 threads. Speedup relative $R = 0$.

with 16 threads. Here, the maximum speedup, with an improvement of 25% over when no migration is used, is reached at a rollback rate threshold R of 10–20, for a gain threshold G of 0.6–0.7. Beyond $R = 20$, the results tend to become noisier, not resulting in significantly better speedup than for a low rollback rate threshold.

In general, the run time improvement of using load migration over not using migration peaks at about 25%, with greater improvement being achieved for more threads. With a few number of threads, each thread has more work to do, and thus leaving less room for improvement by load balancing. The number of rollbacks is greatly reduced, by a factor of 2–4. The decrease in rollbacks is in line with the performance improvement, given the amount of time spent on rollbacks relative the total execution time.

7.6 Effective Utilization

In this section, we look at the effect load balancing has on the amount of time individual LPs spend on rollback overhead, i.e., processing rollbacks and redoing the rolled back time interval (roughly estimated to take the same amount of time as the rollbacks themselves) and anti-messages, denoted *non-useful* work. In Figure 4, we visualize a simulation run of the mincde[s] benchmark on 16 threads. Each bar represents the time allocation of one individual

LP, divided into useful and non-useful work. The variance of the amount of time spent on non-useful work is more than halved when using migration. However, as can be seen by the amount of non-useful work even with load balancing activated, we can conclude that the load imbalance is still momentarily high during the simulation.

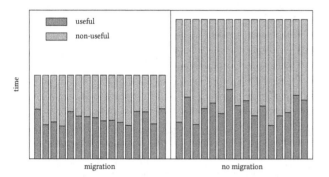

Figure 4: Instrumentation data for each thread of the R-PNSM and PNSM-LB algorithms on the mincde[s] benchmark, 16 threads.

To illustrate in more detail, we try to visualize the rollbacks and the behavior of the load balancing mechanism during a simulation. In Figures 5 and 6, a timeline of the simulation of the mincde[s] benchmark with the PNSM-LB algorithm on 3 threads is depicted. For each thread, one individual timeline is depicted, horizontally. In each timeline, the total population, the number of voxels, and the number of rollbacks is shown. In Figure 5, no migration is used. We see how the population varies with time, and how the number of rollbacks increases when the population difference between LPs is big. We also see how the middle LP always has more work to do than its two neighbors, and suffers from practically no rollbacks. In Figure 6, migration is used. We see that during the entire simulation, there are much fewer rollbacks, and the rollbacks are more evenly distributed over the LPs. The population still varies, but the middle LP has in general a lower population than in Figure 5, i.e., the load is better balanced.

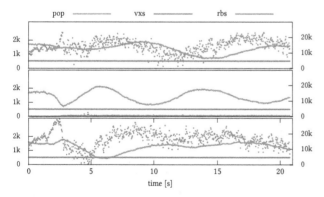

Figure 5: Time series of the population, number of voxels and rollbacks per LP in the mincde[s] benchmark run with the PNSM-LB algorithm without load balancing for 3 threads.

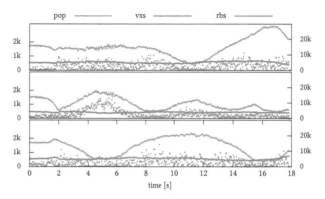

Figure 6: Time series of the population, number of voxels and rollbacks per LP in the mincde[s] benchmark run with the PNSM-LB algorithm with load balancing for 3 threads.

7.7 Performance

In this section, we compare the scaling of the PNSM-LB algorithm with and without load migration, and also compare it to the R-PNSM algorithm, from which it is derived.

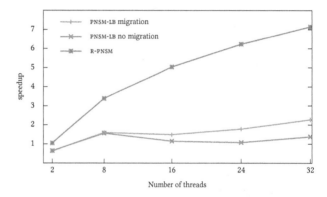

Figure 7: scaling over NSM on the sphere[s] benchmark.

First, in Figure 7, we see the speedup over the sequential NSM for the parallel algorithms, evaluated on the sphere[s] benchmark. The benchmark is uniform in load, and we see as expected that the R-PNSM algorithm, which does not have any control logic to handle migrations, perform much better. However, for the PNSM-LB algorithm, that has been restructured to handle migrations, using load balancing is better than not using load balancing, with up to a 65% better speedup on 32 threads. The fact that there actually is an improvement indicates that the initial partitioning provided by the METIS library is not perfect. In Figures 8a and 8b, we see the speedup over NSM for the parallel algorithms, evaluated on the mincde[s] and the mincde[L] benchmarks, respectively. We see that for up to 8 threads, the parallel algorithms show approximately the same performance. For 16 threads, the R-PNSM algorithm clearly has better performance. The difference between the PNSM-LB algorithm with and without load balancing is minimal for less than 16 threads. We believe this to be due to a suboptimal load balancing algorithm, that does not make the best decision on where to move and when to move the voxels. For 16 threads, using load balancing results in approx. 25% better speedup than when not using load balancing, in both benchmarks.

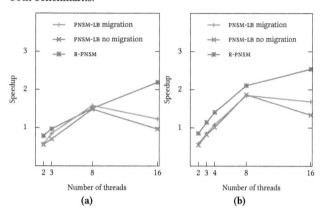

Figure 8: Scaling over NSM on the mincde[s] **(a) and the** mincde[L] **(b) benchmarks.**

In general, we see that the R-PNSM algorithm scales better than the PNSM-LB algorithm, particularly for the benchmark with the well-balanced model (Figure 7). We note again that the PNSM-LB algorithm is derived from the R-PNSM algorithm. Hence, the difference in scalability between the R-PNSM algorithm and the PNSM-LB algorithm without load balancing represents the performance cost of modifying the algorithm so that load balancing can be applied. E.g., intra-LP diffusions, which make up the majority of the events, affect two voxels, and require updating one event history per affected voxel in the PNSM-LB algorithm, instead of a single event history as in the R-PNSM algorithm.

8 CONCLUSIONS

We have described a load migration protocol aimed at fine-grained dynamic load balancing. The protocol works across aggregated anti-messages, a technique used to reduce inter-LP communication. The protocol has been evaluated together with a local load metric and load balancing algorithm. The load balancing is shown to reduce the number of incurred rollbacks by a factor of 2–4, and the speedup is improved by up to 25%, due to a reduced number of rollbacks.

We observe that the main challenge is the performance penalty incurred by restructuring the existing PDES algorithm in such a way that it is suitable for load balancing. We hypothesize that the R-PNSM algorithm benefits from having better data locality and more efficiently uses shared data structures, such as the event history and the model state.

ACKNOWLEDGMENTS

This work was supported in part by the Swedish Research Council within the UPMARC Linnaeus centre of Excellence.

We would like to thank the reviewers for their observant and helpful comments.

REFERENCES

[1] H. Avril and C. Tropper. 1996. The Dynamic Load Balancing of Clustered Time Warp for Logic Simulation. *SIGSIM Simul. Dig.* 26, 1 (July 1996), 20–27.

[2] P. Bauer, J. Lindén, S. Engblom, and B. Jonsson. 2015. Efficient Inter-Process Synchronization for Parallel Discrete Event Simulation on Multicores. In *Proc. SIGSIM PADS.* ACM, 183–194.

[3] A. Boukerche and S. K. Das. 1997. Dynamic load balancing strategies for conservative parallel simulations. *SIGSIM Simul. Dig.* 27, 1 (June 1997), 20–28.

[4] C. Burdorf and J. Marti. 1993. Load Balancing Strategies for Time Warp on Multi-User Workstations. *Comput. J.* 36, 2 (1993), 168–176.

[5] C. D. Carothers and R. M. Fujimoto. 1996. Background Execution of Time Warp Programs. *SIGSIM Simul. Dig.* 26, 1 (July 1996), 12–19.

[6] L. Chen, Y. Lu, Y. Yao, S. Peng, and L. Wu. 2011. A Well-Balanced Time Warp System on Multi-Core Environments. In *Proc. PADS.* IEEE, 1–9.

[7] M. Choe and C. Tropper. 1999. On learning algorithms and balancing loads in Time Warp. *Proc. PADS*, 101–108.

[8] S. R. Das. 2000. Adaptive Protocols for Parallel Discrete Event Simulation. *J. Oper. Res. Soc.* 51, 4 (2000), 385–394.

[9] E. Deelman and B. K. Szymanski. 1997. Breadth-First Rollback in Spatially Explicit Simulations. In *Proc. PADS.* IEEE, 124–131.

[10] E. Deelman and B. K. Szymanski. 1998. Dynamic Load Balancing in Parallel Discrete Event Simulation for Spatially Explicit Problems. *SIGSIM Simul. Dig.* 28, 1 (July 1998), 46–53.

[11] B. Drawert, S. Engblom, and A. Hellander. 2012. URDME: a modular framework for stochastic simulation of reaction-transport processes in complex geometries. *BMC Syst. Biol.* 6, 76 (2012).

[12] K. El-Khatib and C. Tropper. 1999. On Metrics for the Dynamic Load Balancing of Optimistic Simulations. In *Proc. Hawaii Int'l Conf. on System Sciences.* IEEE.

[13] J. Elf and M. Ehrenberg. 2004. Spontaneous separation of bi-stable biochemical systems into spatial domains of opposite phases. *Syst. Biol.* 1, 2 (2004), 230–236.

[14] D. Fange and J. Elf. 2006. Noise-Induced Min Phenotypes in E. coli. *PLOS Comput. Biol.* 2, 6 (June 2006), e80.

[15] R. M. Fujimoto. 1990. Parallel Discrete Event Simulation. *Commun. ACM.* 33, 10 (1990), 30–53.

[16] B. P. Gan, Y. H. Low, S. Jain, S. J. Turner, W. Cai, W. J. Hsu, and S. Y. Huang. 2000. Load Balancing for Conservative Simulation on Shared Memory Multiprocessor Systems. In *Proc. PADS.* IEEE, 139–146.

[17] C. W. Gardiner. 2007. *Handbook of stochastic methods.* Springer.

[18] D. W. Glazer and C. Tropper. 1993. On Process Migration and Load Balancing in Time Warp. *IEEE Trans. Parallel Distrib. Syst.* 4, 3 (1993), 318–327.

[19] S. Jafer, Q. Liu, and G.A. Wainer. 2013. Synchronization methods in parallel and distributed discrete-event simulation. *Simul. Model. Pract. Th.* 30 (2013), 54–73.

[20] D. R. Jefferson. 1985. Virtual Time. *ACM Trans. Program. Lang. Syst.* 7, 3 (1985), 404–425.

[21] G. Karypis and V. Kumar. 1998. A Fast and High Quality Multilevel Scheme for Partitioning Irregular Graphs. *SIAM J. Sci. Comput.* 20, 1 (Jan. 1998), 359–392.

[22] J. I. Leivent and R. J. Watro. 1993. Mathematical Foundations of Time Warp Systems. *ACM Trans. Program. Lang. Syst.* 15, 5 (1993), 771–794.

[23] Z. Lin and Y. Yao. 2015. Load Balancing for Parallel Discrete Event Simulation of Stochastic Reaction and Diffusion. In *Int'l Conference on Smart City/SocialCom/SustainCom.* IEEE, 609–614.

[24] J. Lindén, P. Bauer, S. Engblom, and B. Jonsson. 2017. Exposing Inter-Process Information for Efficient Parallel Discrete Event Simulation of Spatial Stochastic Systems. In *Proc. SIGSIM PADS.* ACM, 53–64.

[25] J. Misra. 1986. Distributed Discrete-Event Simulation. *ACM Comput. Surv.* 18, 1 (1986), 39–65.

[26] A. Pellegrini, R. Vitali, S. Peluso, and F. Quaglia. 2012. Transparent and Efficient Shared-State Management for Optimistic Simulations on Multi-core Machines. In *Proc. MASCOTS.* IEEE, 134–141.

[27] P. Peschlow, T. Honecker, and P. Martini. 2007. A Flexible Dynamic Partitioning Algorithm for Optimistic Distributed Simulation. In *Proc. PADS.* IEEE, 219–228.

[28] P. L. Reiher and D. R. Jefferson. 1990. Virtual Time Based Dynamic Load Management in the Time Warp Operating System. *Trans. Soc. Comput. Simul. Int.* 7, 9 (1990), 103–111.

[29] F. Sarkar and S. K. Das. 1997. Design and implementation of dynamic load balancing algorithms for rollback reduction in optimistic PDES. In *Proc. MASCOTS.* IEEE, 26–31.

[30] R. Schlagenhaft, M. Ruhwandl, C. Sporrer, and H. Bauer. 1995. Dynamic Load Balancing of a Multi-cluster Simulator on a Network of Workstations. *SIGSIM Simul. Dig.* 25, 1 (July 1995), 175–180.

[31] J. Wang, D. Jagtap, N. B. Abu-Ghazaleh, and D. Ponomarev. 2014. Parallel Discrete Event Simulation for Multi-Core Systems: Analysis and Optimization. *IEEE Trans. Par. Distr. Syst.* 25, 6 (2014), 1574–1584.

[32] L. F. Wilson and W. Shen. 1998. Experiments in Load Migration and Dynamic Load Balancing in SPEEDES. In *Proc. 30th Winter Simulation Conf.* IEEE, 483–490.

[33] Y. Xu, W. Cai, D. Eckhoff, S. Nair, and A. Knoll. 2017. A Graph Partitioning Algorithm for Parallel Agent-Based Road Traffic Simulation. In *Proc. SIGSIM PADS.* ACM, 209–219.

Author Index

NOTES